Edition **3**

Your Introduction to Education
Explorations in Teaching

Sara Davis Powell
Belmont Abbey College

PEARSON

Boston   Columbus   Indianapolis   New York   San Francisco   Upper Saddle River
Amsterdam   Cape Town   Dubai   London   Madrid   Milan   Munich   Paris   Montreal   Toronto
Delhi   Mexico City   São Paulo   Sydney   Hong Kong   Seoul   Singapore   Taipei   Tokyo

Vice President and Editorial Director:
  Jeffery W. Johnston
Executive Editor: Ann Castel Davis
Development Editor: Bryce Bell
Editorial Assistant: Janelle Criner
Vice President, Director of Marketing: Margaret
  Waples
Marketing Manager: Darcy Betts-Prybella
Project Manager: Kerry Rubadue
Operations Manager: Michelle Klein
Senior Art Director: Diane Lorenzo
Cover and Text Designer: Wee Design Group

Cover Images: Mitch Diamond/Getty
  Images; Quavondo/Getty Images; Monkey
  Business/Fotolia; Andy Dean/Fotolia
Media Project Manager: Noelle Chun
Full-Service Project Management: S4Carlisle
  Publishing Services
Composition: S4Carlisle Publishing Services
Printer/Binder: Courier Kendallville
Cover Printer: Courier Kendallville
Text Font: ITC Garamond Std

Credits and acknowledgments for materials borrowed from other sources and reproduced, with permission, in this textbook appear on the appropriate page within the text.

Every effort has been made to provide accurate and current Internet information in this book. However, the Internet and information posted on it are constantly changing, so it is inevitable that some of the Internet addresses listed in this textbook will change.

Library of Congress Control Number: 2013956206

10 9 8 7 6 5 4 3 2 1

ISBN-10:   0-13-356328-6
ISBN-13: 978-0-13-356328-3

Dedication

Jesse White teaches in an innovative charter school system that serves students who live in low-income homes, with families that do not speak English as their primary language. He represents dedicated teachers everywhere who make critical differences in the lives of their students. To these teachers, and to Jesse, my son, I dedicate this third edition.

Preface

Your Introduction to Education: Explorations in Teaching

Using an approach that is unique among introduction to education college texts, the third edition of *Your Introduction to Education: Explorations in Teaching* takes you on a journey into authentic classrooms and guides you through issues and dilemmas as they affect real teachers and students in real schools to help you determine whether teaching is for you and, if so, what your teaching identity may be.

The most distinctive feature of this text is how it weaves the real-life experiences of 10 teachers and 12 students from 4 schools across the country into its content. These people and places are drawn from urban, suburban, and rural settings, allowing us to examine teaching and learning from a variety of perspectives.

The teachers and students are from Summit Station, Ohio; Spanish Fork, Utah; Mt. Pleasant, South Carolina; and Fresno, California. Classroom scenarios, person-to-person features, and nearly every photo in this book—along with hours of video—are the direct result of time the author spent at each school with every one of the teachers, principals, students, and family members we meet.

Current and relevant issues in education are discussed in engaging ways through two new features: **The Opinion Page** and **SocialMEdia**. **The Opinion Page** feature presents real opinion editorials published in recent newspapers from across the country to explore today's dilemmas and controversies. You are asked to think about your own opinions and respond to prompts that require reflection and critical thinking. In each **SocialMEdia** feature, a social media tool is presented through a teaching and learning lens to ignite your imagination and sense of innovation concerning possibilities for your own future classrooms.

The **art** and **service** of teaching are emphasized right alongside the science of teaching. Just as we know that effective teachers teach the *whole* child, we also know that teachers are most effective when they use both their minds and hearts, as well as their gifts and talents, to interact with students in growth-promoting ways.

Each chapter begins with a **Dear Reader** letter that introduces in personal and engaging ways the topics to come. This book, built entirely on authentic classroom experience, will empower future teachers to *explore* content and classrooms, *reflect* on their learning, and *develop* an image of the teacher they aspire to be.

NEW TO THIS EDITION

NEW FORMAT: Pearson eText

This new third edition is available as an eText. Readers are able to access additional content not available through print, such as embedded videos of classroom teachers that bring content to life, audio versions of **Dear Reader** letters from the author, and direct links to related content on the Web.

Chapter 5: The Science, Art, and Service of Teaching

The *science* of teaching (curriculum, instruction, and assessment) is enhanced by the *art* of teaching, knowing when and how to teach concepts and skills based on our knowledge of students. In classrooms where the whole person is considered, effective teachers serve students and help them learn to serve others. This chapter includes an extensive section on teaching students to both serve and learn through serving.

Chapter 12: Professionalism in Relationships, Reality, and Reform

Being a teacher has its wonderful aspects and rewards layered on top of, and in between, the hard realities that make the profession challenging. But the benefits and satisfaction of effective teaching are more than just layers: They are *foundational* when we understand that what we do day-to-day both makes our country stronger and our way of life richer, and gives opportunities to children and adolescents that only education can provide. Professionalism must be woven through our relationships, realities, and reform efforts. Realities and reforms addressed in this third edition include bureaucratic overload, changing demographics, budget issues, value-added teacher evaluation, and performance-based pay.

NEW FEATURE: The Opinion Page

In each chapter you are introduced to authentic opinion editorials addressing content discussed in the chapter. These *Opinion Page* pieces are from newspapers across the country, some in urban areas, and some in suburban and rural areas. Following each feature, you are prompted by questions that are opportunities for you to respond to the piece and express your own opinions.

THE OPINION PAGE

This *Opinion Editorial* appeared in the *CantonRep*, the online newspaper of Canton, Ohio, on December 26, 2012.

What is a Teacher Really Worth?

by Charita Goshay

Goshay is a staff writer and regular opinion contributor for the CantonRep.

In recent months, teachers, first responders and other public employees have been whipping boys for people who think they enjoy too much compensation for their services. So what, exactly, is the dollar value of a teacher who saves the lives of 15 first-graders? How about one who sacrifices her life in an effort to save them? Which part of the faculty handbook advises a teacher on how to deal properly with unmitigated madness?

For those people who actually know a teacher, the heroism and sacrifice demonstrated by the educators in Newtown, Conn., are the least surprising aspects of the tragedy. Teachers don't just teach. The good ones inspire, challenge and change the lives of their students every day. They open up worlds of knowledge and introduce children to possibilities they otherwise wouldn't know existed. They go into their own pockets to level the playing field. They worry about "their kids," particularly those who they know have turbulent lives, even years after they move on.

Our culture has become such that we don't even blink or flinch at the news that someone will earn $10 million a year for throwing a ball or running a corporation into the ground. But a teacher gets flayed for failing test scores, even when the reasons are multifaceted and complicated.

These days, a lesson plan isn't enough. Teachers frequently must also be psychiatrists, substitute parents and bouncers. They're caught between uncooperative and irresponsible parents, ever more complicated school policies, a cynical taxpaying public that demands to know why schools aren't doing better, and kids

who are expected to miraculously rise above the chaos and instability in which they live. Even children from affluent and stable, supportive homes can have struggles that they bring with them to school. Because of all of this, no one in his or her right mind would become a teacher simply for a paycheck and a pension.

Being a public servant is a calling, one as compelling and clear as entering the clergy or becoming a physician. If teachers were compensated based on what they contribute to society, we couldn't afford them. The annual minimum salary for a National Hockey League rookie is $525,000. For baseball, it's $390,000. In the NBA it's $473,604. The average elementary-school teacher makes $40,283 a year, what many major-sport athletes make in a month.

Despite this bargain, we still find reasons to complain about teachers, ignoring the irony that if it were not for teachers, we'd be unable to express ourselves very well. Who has time to decipher someone else's cave-drawing rant? Not me. As we saw in Connecticut and as is demonstrated virtually every day, a teacher's dedication is immeasurable.

Copyright ©2012 CantonRep.com

This The Opinion Page piece covers a lot of ground with respect to teachers' dedication to the well-being of students. She also writes about the relative absurdity of salary discrepancies between teachers and professional athletes. Write a well-developed paragraph in response to each of the following questions.

1. Why, in Ms. Goshay's opinion, would our country not be able to pay teachers enough for what they do? Do you agree? Explain.

2. What is your response to the multiple roles teachers have in the lives of students? Have you considered how all encompassing teaching can be? Does this knowledge overwhelm you? Excite you?

NEW FEATURE: SocialMEdia

The astonishing and rapidly growing quantity of social media is part of everyday life for most of us, so why not employ it in the classroom? In each chapter you will learn how to use a variety of social media tools to enhance teaching and learning. In addition, these features offer suggestions for teaching students to use social media wisely and safely.

SocialMEdia

Cybercitizenship is a recently coined term referring to the responsibilities of those who use social media. A recent survey by the National Cyber Security Alliance showed that over 90% of the adults in K–12 schools believe we should teach students how to be safe and ethical cybercitizens. In 2012 the federal government passed the Children's Online Privacy Protection Act (COPPA), a bill designed to make more transparent the operations of Web sites that cater to children. But, as with so many societal issues, legislating safety must be accompanied by both common sense and vigilance. The American Academy of Pediatrics (2011) tells us limited self-regulation and susceptibility to peer pressure put children and adolescents at risk when using social media.

The immediacy and instant gratification of social media, coupled with the vulnerability of children and adolescents, make safety hazards likely and our involvement absolutely necessary. Many lists of safety/ethics rules have been written by private organizations, nonprofit groups, school districts, and even the FBI. When examined side-by-side they all include basically the same advice. Here's a summary of the most common tips for helping students stay safe as they use the Internet.

1. Always abide by school and home guidelines for when and how to use the Internet.

2. Treat people that you don't know on the Internet as strangers. Get to know your "online friends" just as you get to know all of your other friends.

3. Do not give out any personal information related to your family, friends, or yourself like passwords, addresses, and phone numbers.

4. Always tell an adult if you see something online that you know is wrong or that makes you feel uncomfortable. Never respond to such messages.

5. Never send out your picture without your parents' permission.

6. Don't respond when offered something such as gifts or money.

7. Don't ever accept a gift or an offer that involves having someone visit your house.

8. Never agree to meet someone you've met online in person unless you discuss it with your parents and an adult goes with you.

9. Never respond to provocative, rude, obscene, or threatening messages.

10. Always check with parents before downloading or installing software or doing anything that may jeopardize anyone's privacy.

NEW FEATURE: Dear Reader

The author speaks directly to you in letters written in conversational language to introduce the concepts in each chapter. This new feature will engage you in the content to come.

NEW SECTION: Common Core State Standards Initiative

You are introduced to the Common Core—how and by whom the standards were developed, the perceived benefits, government involvement, and more. You will see clearly the arguments both for and against the implementation of the Common Core State Standards through a detailed Q&A feature and an "Advocates and Critics" feature.

Aligned to New InTASC Teacher Preparation Standards

The new InTASC standards for teachers are concise and comprehensive. It's important for you to understand the profession's expectations of you.

Seven New Tables Detailing Laws and Their Implications for Teachers

Future teachers need to have a basic understanding of how laws affect them, their students, and their profession. The seven tables will help you comprehend implications of multiple case law rulings through common-sense explanations, written in easy-to-understand language.

Numerous New Tables and Figures Depicting the Societal Context of Children and Adolescents

Future teachers need a realistic picture of the dilemmas and life circumstances of the children and adolescents who will fill their classrooms.

Increased Emphasis on Bullying Prevention

It's vital for teachers to know the signs and symptoms of bullying in its many forms—including cyberbullying. You will learn productive ways to approach the bully, the bullied, and the bystander.

VITAL TOPICAL COVERAGE

- **Partnership for 21st Century Skills** This vibrant organization is influencing teaching and learning in U.S. schools: Chapter 1

- **Teacher Effectiveness Research** Recent research from *Teach for America* links particular teacher qualities and actions to increased student learning: Chapter 1

- **Changing Demographics** Shifts in student populations result in both challenges and benefits: Chapters 2, 9, and 12

- **Racial and Ethnic Diversity** How public schools address the issues: Chapters 2, 7, and 9

- **Cultural Pluralism** How teacher responsiveness increases the positive potential of diversity to enhance teaching and learning: Chapter 2

- **Language Minority Students** Ways of addressing the needs of students for whom English is not the first language: Chapter 2

- **Religious Diversity** The issues and how to handle them lawfully and with respect: Chapters 2 and 10

- **Recognizing Child Abuse** A frank discussion of this ever-present threat, including an extensive chart of what teachers should look for: Chapters 2 and 9

- **Charter Schools** The number of these public schools, freed in specific ways from the typical regulations required of other public schools, is rapidly increasing: Chapter 3

- **School Choice** The possibilities, as well as the pros and cons: Chapter 3

- **Common Core State Standards** Issues such as how and by whom the standards were developed, the perceived benefits, government involvement, and more: Chapters 4 and 12

- **Controversy and Curriculum** Examples addressing controversial issues including intelligent design, Eurocentrism, and sex education: Chapter 4

- **Social Media as Teaching Tools** The explosion of the use of social media to enhance teaching and learning: Each chapter

- **Trends in the International Math and Science Study and the Progress in International Reading Literacy Study** New test results: Chapter 4

- **High-Stakes Testing** The uses and abuses of state test results: Chapter 4

- **Life and Career Skills** Methods to incorporate 21st century life and career skills into the classroom: Chapter 6

- **Philosophy of Education** Interactive methods to help teacher candidates discover and define their philosophies: Chapter 8

- **Homelessness** Ways to recognize and better meet the wide-ranging needs of children in poverty and those who are homeless: Chapter 9

- **Childhood Obesity** The recent dramatic increase and imminent threat to student well-being: Chapter 9

- **Bullying** What teachers can do to heighten awareness and stem harmful relationally aggressive behavior: Chapter 9

- **Dropouts** The shocking data now available due to standardization of definitions, and what teachers can do to help students stay in school: Chapter 9

- **Recognizing Ethical Dilemmas** Multiple scenarios bringing to life the day-to-day ethical dilemmas teachers face in their classrooms and schools: Chapter 10

- **Religious Expression** What's lawful for students and teachers, in an easy-to-understand Q&A format: Chapter 10

- **Sexual Harassment** Recognizing and addressing sexual harassment: Chapter 10

- **School Funding** Controversy about how to finance public education, addressed through the continuing funding dilemmas faced by California residents: Chapter 11

- *A Blueprint for Reform* The next reauthorization of the Elementary and Secondary Education Act, as proposed by President Obama: Chapter 12

- **Teacher Evaluation and Performance Pay** Controversial proposals to evaluate and pay teachers based on student test results: Chapter 12

- **Professional Relationships** Practical ways to cultivate and maintain professional relationships: Chapter 12

- **Barriers to Families' Involvement** Exploration of why families are not school partners in education and ways to remedy the dilemma: Chapter 12

- **Mismatch Between Teacher Prep and Classroom Reality** Ways to respond when expectations are not met: Chapter 12

- **The Irreplaceables** Keeping the best teachers in the classroom: Chapter 12

- **Professional Responses to Reform** How to view and respond professionally to reform efforts: Chapter 12

Explore

EXPLORE AUTHENTIC CLASSROOMS

The focus teachers, students, and schools of this text are discussed throughout. You'll have many specific opportunities to meet and get to know these important people. Look for the *Teaching in Focus* headings to alert you to opportunities to get acquainted.

TEACHING IN FOCUS

- As each chapter opens, you'll get a glimpse of one of our focus teachers addressing chapter concepts in his or her classroom.
- We revisit classrooms of the teachers you come to know as they talk about specific topics that affect their classroom teaching in *Teaching in Focus* features throughout each chapter. Each in-chapter *Teaching in Focus* feature is accompanied by a picture of the teacher speaking to us in his or her own words.
- Watch the interviews, room tours, and lessons you read about in these.

Explore Your Own Positions on Education

WHERE DO I STAND?

These fascinating inventories begin each of the book's four parts by asking you to think about the concepts before reading. This not only engages you in what's to come, but also helps you personalize information you are asked to examine and reexamine as each chapter progresses.

Reflect

REFLECT ON YOUR EVOLVING UNDERSTANDING OF YOURSELF AS AN EDUCATOR

Points of Reflection features ask you to pause and think through what you've read and apply the ideas to your own notions of teaching and learning. You will find Points of Reflection throughout each chapter.

Develop

DEVELOP YOUR OPINIONS ON DIFFERENT ISSUES IN CONTEMPORARY EDUCATION

NEW! The Opinion Page features in each chapter explore issues in education through opinion editorials published in newspapers, asking you to consider the opinions, the issues, and your own opinions, and then to respond to items related to The Opinion Page piece. The context is set by the chapter content, along with background information about the particular topic or issue involved.

DEVELOP YOUR SENSE OF YOURSELF AS AN EDUCATOR

Developing Professional Competence This end-of-chapter feature probes the issues of classroom teaching and helps prepare you for licensure exams by posing a case, again featuring the focus teachers you have come to know. Following the case are multiple-choice and essay questions that connect classroom issues with pertinent standards, providing an excellent study tool.

⬤ The eText for this title is an affordable, interactive version of the print text that includes videos in every chapter, audio versions of **Dear Reader** features, author-led animations, and links to additional information. The play button appears where video, audio, or animations are available, while hyperlinked words provide access to other related websites.

To learn more about the enhanced Pearson eText, go to www.pearsonhighered .com/etextbooks.

Develop Grade Level and Content Understanding

Throughout this text, your attention is drawn to these basic levels: early childhood, elementary, middle school, and high school. Regardless of the school grade configuration, student growth and learning generally move along a continuum that we address within these four broad levels. We approach teaching and learning differently based largely on the developmental level of the students. A first grade teacher in a primary school and a first grade teacher in an elementary school both teach children in the phase of early childhood. Similarly, sixth grade students in an elementary school and sixth grade students in a middle school are all young adolescents in the middle level phase of development. The following table indicates where you can find grade-level specific information about a range of content in the text.

CHAPTER	EARLY CHILDHOOD	ELEMENTARY	MIDDLE SCHOOL	HIGH SCHOOL
Chapter 1: Teachers and the Teaching Profession	11: *Teaching in Focus* 11–12: Traditional Paths to Teacher Preparation	11–12: Traditional Paths to Teacher Preparation	6: *Teaching in Focus* 11–12: Traditional Paths to Teacher Preparation 22: *Teaching in Focus*	8: Interest in Subject Matter 11–12: Traditional Paths to Teacher Preparation
Chapter 2: Student Similarities and Differences	43: Developmental Characteristics by Level 50–54: Language Diversity	42: *Teaching in Focus* 43: Developmental Characteristics by Level	43: Developmental Characteristics by Level	32: *Teaching in Focus* 43: Developmental Characteristics by Level 50–54: Language Diversity 52: Bilingual Education 64–65: *Getting to Know Trista*
Chapter 3: Schools	72: *Teaching in Focus* 84–85: Structure and Organization	85–88: Structure and Organization	88–89: Structure and Organization	75: *Teaching in Focus* 89–90: Structure and Organization
Chapter 4: Curriculum, Assessment, and Accountability	104: *Teaching in Focus* 120–121: Assessment of Dylan	122: *Teaching in Focus*		114: *Teaching in Focus*
Chapter 5: The Science, Art, and Service of Teaching	145: Instruction	136: *Teaching in Focus* 145–146: Instruction	146: Instruction	146: Instruction

Supplements for Instructors

The following supplements to the textbook are available for download under the Educator tab at www.pearsonhighered.com. Simply enter the author, title, or ISBN, and then select this textbook. Click on the "Resources" tab to view and download the supplements detailed below.

ONLINE INSTRUCTOR'S MANUAL WITH TEST ITEMS

An expanded and improved online Instructor's Resource Manual (0-13-356337-5) includes numerous recommendations for presenting and extending text content. The manual consists of chapter overviews, focus questions, outlines, suggested teaching strategies, and Web resources that cover the essential concepts addressed in each chapter. You'll also find a complete chapter-by-chapter bank of test items.

ONLINE TEST GEN

The computerized test bank software, Test Gen (0-13-356339-1), allows instructors to create and customize exams for classroom testing and for other specialized delivery options, such as over a local area network or on the web. A test bank typically contains a large set of test items, organized by chapter and ready for your use in creating a test, based on the associated textbook material. The tests can be downloaded in the following formats:

- **TestGen** Testbank file—PC
- **TestGen** Testbank file—MAC
- **TestGen** Testbank—**Blackboard 9**
- **TestGen** Testbank—**Blackboard CE/Vista (WebCT)**
- **Angel** Test Bank
- **D2L** Test Bank
- **Moodle** Test Bank
- **Sakai** Test Bank

ONLINE POWERPOINT LECTURE SLIDES

These lecture slides (0-13-356335-9) highlight key concepts and summarize key content from each chapter of the text.

Acknowledgments

As a teacher and teacher educator for more than four decades, I found the writing of this text to be a labor of love. I have experienced extraordinary professional development opportunities through this project as I have probed deeply the many and varied issues involved in teaching PreK–12 children and adolescents.

Numerous people have been instrumental in the revision of this text. Here are some to whom I owe special thanks:

- Jeff Johnston, Pearson Vice President and Editorial Director, for his consistent professionalism.
- Ann Castel Davis, Executive Editor, for her insight, wisdom, and faith in me.
- Bryce Bell, Development Editor, for his expertise, professional guidance during the revision process, and his kind, thoughtful spirit throughout.
- Kerry Rubadue, Project Manager, for prompt and efficient attention to the details of production.

- Lynn Steines, Project Editor, S4Carlisle Publishing Services, for cheerfully overseeing the copyediting, proofreading, and indexing of this edition.
- Mark Kwicinski, copyeditor, S4Carlisle Publishing Services, for his keen eye for detail and thoughtful suggestions throughout the text.
- Darcy Betts-Prybella, Senior Marketing Manager, for her expert sense of what professors and students need and want, in addition to her generous spirit.
- Principals Laura Hill, Mike Larsen, Carol Bartlett, and Maria Romero, for opening their schools to me.
- Brandi Wade, Renee Ayers, Chris Roberts, Brenda Beyal, Tim Mendenhall, Traci Peters, Deirdre Huger-McGrew, Craig Cleveland, Derek Boucher, and Angelica Reynosa, the text's focus teachers, for opening their classrooms to me and sharing their wisdom with teacher candidates.
- Dylan Todd, Sherlonda Francis, Amanda Wiley, Hector Mancia, Josie Ford, Patrick Sutton, David McBeath, Trista Kutcher, Guillermo Toscano, Mayra Reyes, Khamanny Douangsavanh, and Hugo Martinez, the text's focus students, for teaching me so much.
- Melinda Ratchford, Benette Sutton, Judith McDonald, Laura Campbell, Tara Galloway, Lisa O'Neill, Amanda Kloo, and Brenda McCraw, my colleagues and dear friends at Belmont Abbey College, for their dedication to the preparation of future teachers that continually inspires me.
- Rus, my husband, for his unwavering support throughout, as well as the many hours of brainstorming and editing.
- In addition, I want to thank the professors who contributed time and thought in their feedback:

  Shelly Anderson, Central Texas College; Sharry Kimmel, Broward College; Robert Lake, Georgia Southern University; Ellen Nuffer, Keene State College; and Mary Ann Pangle, Tennessee State University.

Brief Contents

Contents

Part 4 Realities of Teaching and Learning 241

Chapter 9 The Societal Context of Schooling in the United States 245

Chapter 10 Ethical and Legal Issues in U.S. Schools 281

Chapter 11 Governing and Financing Public Schools 315

Chapter 12 Professionalism in Relationships, Reality, and Reform 341

Special Features

The Opinion Page

SocialMEdia

Teaching in Focus

1

Teachers, Students, and Schools

This book consists of four parts. In **PART I** we explore teachers—who they are, why they teach, and their role in the classroom and in the profession; students—their similarities and differences; and schools—in a variety of configurations, at four different levels, and in rural, suburban, and urban settings.

Each part begins with an inventory to help you begin thinking about the topics to be addressed and your personal experiences associated with them. Don't skip over these inventories; they are not busy-work or fluff. A wise teaching strategy is referred to as *activating prior knowledge and experiences*. This is an excellent way to begin any lesson because when our brains are engaged in a topic before we attempt to learn more about it, the whole teaching and learning experience is enhanced. Carefully complete each **Where Do I Stand?** feature to prepare you for what's to come!

Where Do I Stand?

This is the first of the self-exploration inventories you will complete at the beginning of each of the four Parts of the text. Through them you'll explore the world of teachers and teaching. Your responses are based on your opinions and your knowledge. As you explore the content of your course and this text, some of your initial responses will likely change. This is how we grow. We consider what we know and what we think. Then we explore and learn more and more, leading to inevitable changes of opinions and broadening of perspectives. Exciting prospect, don't you think?

This first inventory helps you explore your personal reasons for considering teaching as a career. Read each item and decide how meaningful it is to you. If an item resonates very strongly within you, then choose "4: I strongly agree." Reserve a choice of "4" for those items you genuinely care most about. If you agree with a statement, but are not overly enthusiastic about it, then choose "3: I agree." If you really don't care one way or the other about a statement, choose "2: I don't have an opinion." If you simply disagree with a statement, choose "1: I disagree." If you feel adamantly opposed to a statement, choose "0: I strongly disagree." In this inventory, **there are no right or wrong answers, just differing experiences and viewpoints.** Following the inventory are directions for how to organize your responses and what they may indicate in terms of where you stand.

4   I strongly agree
3   I agree
2   I don't have an opinion
1   I disagree
0   I strongly disagree

1. Some of my fondest memories involve experiences working with children/teens.
2. The health insurance and retirement benefits of teaching mean a lot to me.
3. In K–12 school I enjoyed and excelled in a particular subject.
4. As a teacher, I look forward to growing professionally.
5. At least one member of my family is an educator.
6. I am considering teaching because I believe education has necessary societal value.
7. Teaching is most worthwhile because of the opportunity to influence students.
8. Although I may be interested in other professions, the stability of a career in the public school system draws me to teaching.
9. Both the daily work hours and the yearly schedule of a teacher appeal to me.
10. Doing the same thing in the same way repeatedly does not appeal to me.
11. My desire to teach is based on my love of a particular subject.
12. There was a teacher in my K–12 experiences who had a profound impact on my life.
13. My family is pleased with my decision to teach.
14. A teacher's primary task is to help students become productive citizens.
15. Being with children/adolescents is something I enjoy and look forward to.
16. I am anxious to read whatever I can about the teaching profession.
17. A major reason for choosing the teaching profession is the appeal of having holidays and spring break time off.
18. Being a teacher means always having a job.
19. Education is necessary for the continued success of our country.

20. I have very fond memories of my relationship with one or more teachers in K–12 school.
21. Having a long summer vacation means a lot to me.
22. I have been drawn to a particular subject area for years.
23. Professional self-growth motivates me.
24. I am interested in teaching because I want to work with children and/or adolescents.
25. I plan to teach because someone in my family is encouraging my choice.
26. I want to teach because of the promise of job security.
27. Being a camp counselor appeals to me.
28. I want to teach to positively benefit society.
29. Content knowledge is the primary goal of education.
30. Someone in my family enjoys teaching and relays positive stories about the profession.
31. I would like to be able to personally thank a former teacher for influencing me to be a teacher.
32. I like the idea of having days off when my own children will also have time off.
33. I have a passion for a content area.
34. Even in difficult economic times, the fact that teachers will always be needed appeals to me.
35. My family values education and emphasizes the worth of teachers.
36. My career goal is to emulate a teacher I have known.
37. Without quality public education our society suffers.
38. I am still in touch with at least one of my K–12 teachers.
39. Being home by about 4 P.M. is important to me.
40. Teaching appeals to me most because I love to learn new things.

In the table, record the number, 0 to 4, that you responded for each indicated item. Then find the sum for each column's responses.

ITEM #	MY #	ITEM #	MY #	ITEM #	MY #	ITEM #	MY #	ITEM #	MY #	ITEM #	MY #	ITEM #	MY #	ITEM #	MY #
1		6		3		12		9		5		2		4	
7		14		11		20		17		13		8		10	
15		19		22		31		21		25		18		16	
24		28		29		36		32		30		26		23	
27		37		33		38		39		35		34		40	
Sum A		Sum B		Sum C		Sum D		Sum E		Sum F		Sum G		Sum H	

Now it's time to graph your responses. Mark and then shade your sums on the Choosing to Teach *bar graph. The results show how much you value, relatively speaking, eight reasons for becoming a teacher that we discuss in Chapter 1. Your instructor may ask you to share your graph with others as part of the exploration of teachers and the teaching profession.*

By the end of this book you will have explored many aspects of the teaching profession in very personal ways. As teachers, the better we know ourselves, the closer we come to understanding our students and finding ways to address their needs to help them grow.

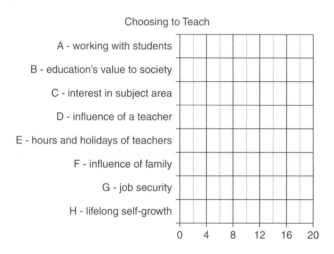

Choosing to Teach

A - working with students
B - education's value to society
C - interest in subject area
D - influence of a teacher
E - hours and holidays of teachers
F - influence of family
G - job security
H - lifelong self-growth

0   4   8   12   16   20

Teachers and the Teaching Profession

Dear Reader

No African tribe is considered to have warriors more fearsome than the Masai. Even with this reputation the traditional greeting between Masai warriors is *Kasserian ingera,* which means "And how are the children?"

This traditional tribal greeting acknowledges the high value the Masai place on their children's well-being. Even warriors with no children of their own give the traditional answer, "All the children are well," meaning that peace and safety prevail; that the priority of protecting the young, the powerless, is in place; and that Masai society has not forgotten its proper function and responsibility, its reason for being. "All the children are well" means that life is good.

When teachers hear the word *multitasking*, most teachers just grin, knowing that they are, and always have been, expert multitaskers. It's nothing new, it's not something they have to practice—it is simply how teachers do their work day in and day out. The hundreds of decisions that teachers make each day; the ever-changing scenarios that confront them hour to hour, minute to minute; and the faces of the students they serve, 20 to 120 at a time, create multiple roles that teachers fill simultaneously—all for the well-being of the children and adolescents in their care.

If we greeted each other with the Masai's daily question, "And how are the children?" how might it affect our awareness of children's welfare in the United States? If we asked this question of each other a dozen times a day, would it begin to make a difference in the reality of how children are thought of and cared for in the United States?

If everyone among us, teacher and nonteacher, parent and nonparent, comes to feel a shared sense of responsibility for the daily care and protection of all the children in our community, in our town, in our state, and in our country, we might truly be able to answer without hesitation, "The children are well. Yes, all the children are well."

Among the many questions to consider about teachers and teaching, here are some we address:

- Who teaches in the United States and why?
- How do we prepare to teach?
- Is teaching a profession?
- What is teacher professionalism?
- What are the characteristics of effective teachers?

Teaching in Focus

Traci Peters teaches seventh grade math at Cario Middle School in Mt. Pleasant, South Carolina. By all accounts she's an excellent teacher—just ask her principal, her colleagues, and, most importantly, her students. Outside school Traci enjoys a very happy home life with husband Dwayne and young son Robert. The seventh graders in Traci's classes know all about these two very important people in her life, and that's the way Traci wants it. Although math is the subject she has chosen to teach, she is conscious of the fact that her responsibilities go well beyond fractions and equations. She views each student as an individual with relationships and often complex growing-up issues. Traci reveals herself to them, and they, in turn, feel comfortable enough to share with her.

In a prominent place in the classroom Traci has a "Mrs. Peters" bulletin board on which she displays, among other things, family photos (from her childhood to the present), her favorite poems and book titles, her own seventh grade report card, and her 5×7 middle school picture. Traci says her students spend lots of time examining the board's contents, laughing and asking questions.

Traci sees herself as a role model of a healthy, positive adult who makes good choices and tries to make a difference in other people's lives. When asked if she would just as freely share with students the not-so-positive aspects of her life, she replies "Yes." When she's not feeling well, she lets her students know. If her son Robert is sick and she needs to stay home to care for him, she tells her students.

Traci attends her students' basketball games, concerts, spelling bees, Odyssey of the Mind competitions—the typical year-long parade of events. She views this as a tangible way to show her students she is interested in them, their growth, and their lives. Watch **Traci's interview** to get to know her better.

You are considering the most challenging and exhilarating career, one that is absolutely necessary for the preservation and enhancement of our way of life in America. Think about this: Teachers make every other profession possible. Most people join the teaching profession purposefully. In a large-scale survey of teachers with fewer than 5 years in the classroom, only about 12% said they "fell into teaching by chance." Some enter directly upon graduation from college, and some become teachers after pursuing one or more other careers. This same survey found that most teachers possess a strong inclination toward their career choice: 86% of the surveyed teachers believe that teaching requires a "sense of calling," and 96% say that teaching is work they love to do. The inference is that entering the teaching profession requires a commitment beyond that required by many other careers and, once in the profession, relatively new teachers overwhelmingly view teaching in positive ways (Public Agenda, 2003).

Who Teaches in the United States and Why?

Teaching is the largest profession in the United States, with almost 4 million teachers in both public and private schools (National Center for Education Statistics [NCES], 2012). Examine Figure 1.1 to see who teaches in the United States. Most teachers are white and female. There is considerable need for more diversity and gender balance in the teaching force. Do we want to discourage white women from becoming teachers? Absolutely not. Is there a need for more male teachers and teachers from minority population groups? Absolutely yes.

DECIDING TO TEACH

Helping you first make the decision to teach and then find your teaching identity is at the heart of this book. Exploring why other people choose to teach may help you clarify your own thoughts and desires. In 2006 the National Education Association (NEA, 2010) surveyed almost a thousand teachers, asking why they chose the teaching profession. The teachers were given a list of 21 possible reasons and asked to choose their top 3. Our discussion of the reasons for choosing to teach is organized around the eight reasons most often chosen by the teachers in the survey, beginning with the four chosen by at least 25% of the responders. As you read, think about your own reasons for considering teaching as your career.

Figure 1.1 U.S. teachers

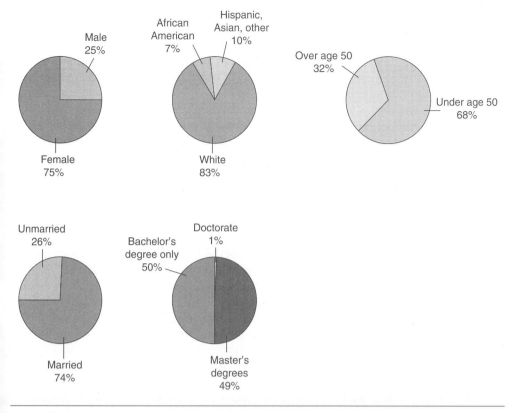

Source: National Education Association. (2010). Status of the American public school teacher 2005–2006. Retrieved August 17, 2013 from http://www .breakthroughcollaborative.org/sites/default/files/NEA%20-2005-06-Statusof%20Public%20School%20Teachers.pdf.

Desire to work with young people. A desire to work with young people was chosen by 71% of the surveyed teachers, with 77% of elementary, 67% of middle, and 61% of high school teachers choosing this option.

Because 6 to 7 hours of a teacher's day are spent in direct contact with students, enjoying their company is a must. Getting to know the students we teach allows us to become familiar with their emotional and social needs as well as their cognitive needs. You may hear teachers talk about teaching the **whole child**. This simply means attending to all their developmental stages and needs, along with teaching them grade-level and subject-area content. When we view the whole child, we realize the depth of our responsibilities as classroom teachers.

Value of education to society. The value or significance of education to society was the next most frequently chosen response at 42%. It's interesting to note that minority teachers were more likely to choose this response (49%) than white teachers (41%).

Education is widely viewed as the great equalizer. This means that differences in opportunity and privilege diminish as children reach their potential through quality education. In other words, the achievement gap narrows with the increased educational success of the students who historically underachieve. An **achievement gap** is a disparity among students, as some excel while

Traci Peters values young adolescents as individuals and develops strong positive relationships with them.

others languish with respect to learning and academic success. Through teaching you will make a difference in the lives of individuals and thereby benefit society as a whole.

Interest in subject matter. Interest in a subject-matter field was chosen by 39% of the surveyed teachers, with 62% of high, 48% of middle, and 22% of elementary school teachers choosing this reason. Also, 46% of males chose this reason, as opposed to 36% of females. Another interesting fact is that 48% of responders from the Northeast chose interest in subject matter, over 10% more than any other geographic area.

An intense interest in a subject area is important if you are going to teach that subject all day. Middle school is a happy compromise for people who have both a strong desire to work with students and a passion for a specific subject. Most middle school teachers teach one or possibly two subjects all day to students whose development is challenging and intriguing.

Influence of teachers. The influence of a teacher in elementary or secondary school ranked fourth (31%) among the reasons to become a teacher. Minority teachers (38%) were more likely to choose this reason than white teachers (30%).

Can you name the last five vice presidents of the United States? How about the current Miss America? Who represents your home district in the state legislature? Who was your fifth grade teacher? Who taught your favorite class when you were a freshman in high school? The last two questions are the easiest, aren't they? That's because teachers influence us. They are uniquely positioned to shape students' thoughts and interests during the formative years of childhood and adolescence.

Other frequently chosen reasons. A joke that's been around for a long time goes like this: "What are the three best things about teaching?" Answer: "June, July, August." Here's another: "What's the best time to be a teacher?" Answer: "Friday at 4." Within our ranks we smile at these harmless jokes. But the *schedule and hours of teachers* attract some to the field. Those who have not taught, or don't understand the pressure of having 15 or 25 or even 100 students dependent on them for at least part of each day, may view the schedule of a teacher as excessively punctuated with days off. However, time away from school is well deserved, even if it is used to catch up on teaching-related tasks. The change of pace is refreshing, allowing opportunities for revitalization.

Aside from summer vacation and days off, other aspects of scheduling make teaching a desirable choice for many. During the school year most teachers do not have students after about 3:30 in the afternoon. To people who work 8-to-5 jobs, 3:30 seems like a luxury. However, most teachers spend additional time either at school or at home planning for the next day and completing necessary administrative tasks. The teaching schedule allows for this kind of flexibility. A teacher's schedule is also ideal for families with school-age children. Having a daily routine similar to that of other family members has definite benefits.

Most of us who consider being teachers grew up in families that valued education and respected teachers. If there are teachers in your family who are energetic and enthusiastic about their careers, they may influence you to follow in their footsteps. Many teachers cite the *influence of family* as a factor in the decision to teach.

Teaching offers an *opportunity for a lifetime of self-growth*. Teachers experience growth, both personally and professionally, in many ways: through relationships, reading, attending conferences, and the wide variety of professional development opportunities available. Few careers are as exciting or as rewarding on a daily basis, including the satisfaction of positively impacting the future of children. Teaching is not a stagnant career; rather, it continually presents new experiences, all of which offer opportunities for self-growth.

We will always need teachers. *Job security* is attractive to many who choose to teach. Those who are competent are generally assured positions, even in difficult economic times. Other benefits related to job security include the availability of group health insurance and a reasonable retirement plan. It's unlikely that a career in teaching is chosen because of salary, although some districts and states are making progress in raising teachers' pay to be competitive with other fields that require a bachelor's degree. Table 1.1

TABLE 1.1 Teacher salaries by state

Rank Based on Average Salary	State	Average Salary	Beginning Salary	Percent 10-Year Increase
1	New York	$72,708	$44,370	41
2	Massachusetts	$70,752	$40,462	45
3	Connecticut	$69,165	$42,450	31
4	California	$67,871	$41,131	29
5	New Jersey	$66,612	$48,101	28
6	Illinois	$64,509	$36,636	34
7	Maryland	$63,960	$43,003	39
8	Michigan	$63,940	$34,724	24
9	Alaska	$62,918	$42,928	30
10	Rhode Island	$60,923	$39,006	25
11	Pennsylvania	$60,760	$41,192	22
12	Delaware	$57,934	$39,099	23
13	Ohio	$56,715	$33,035	32
14	Oregon	$56,503	$33,241	25
15	Wyoming	$56,100	$43,053	61
16	Hawaii	$55,063	$38,479	38
17	Wisconsin	$54,195	$33,170	28
18	Minnesota	$53,680	$34,025	27
19	Nevada	$53,023	$35,449	31
20	Washington	$52,926	$36,474	25
21	Georgia	$52,815	$33,673	25
22	New Hampshire	$52,792	$33,871	37
23	Indiana	$50,801	$33,574	17
24	Vermont	$50,141	$34,704	31
25	Iowa	$49,844	$32,895	36
26	Colorado	$49,228	$32,095	25
27	Louisiana	$49,006	$38,655	45
28	Kentucky	$48,908	$35,075	33
29	Virginia	$48,761	$36,737	21
30	Texas	$48,638	$34,234	26
31	Alabama	$47,803	$36,201	28
32	Arizona	$47,553	$31,689	27
33	Idaho	$47,416	$29,915	27
34	Nebraska	$47,368	$30,086	38
35	Maine	$47,182	$31,580	29
36	Montana	$47,132	$26,734	41
37	South Carolina	$47,050	$31,685	24
38	Utah	$47,033	$33,268	29
39	New Mexico	$46,888	$32,092	38
40	North Carolina	$46,605	$30,779	12
41	Kansas	$46,598	$32,964	29
42	Arkansas	$46,500	$32,478	34
43	Tennessee	$45,891	$33,287	22
44	Florida	$45,732	$35,236	19
45	Missouri	$45,321	$29,857	28
46	North Dakota	$44,807	$31,065	45
47	Oklahoma	$44,343	$31,600	28
48	West Virginia	$44,260	$32,435	23
49	Mississippi	$41,975	$31,187	31
50	South Dakota	$39,850	$29,308	31

Source: TeacherPortal.com. Retrieved August 18, 2013 from http://www.teacherportal.com/salary.

Figure 1.2 Additional reasons for choosing to teach

Desire to engage in intellectual work
Belief in the democratic potential of public education
Anger at the current conditions of education
Sense of mission
Empathy for students
Enjoyment of improvisation
Comfort with uncertainty
Passion for social justice

Source: From S. Nieto (2009). From surviving to thriving. *Educational Leadership, 66*(5), 8–13.

ranks states based on average salary, with the beginning teacher salary for each state also included. The final column shows the average percent of increase a teacher will experience after teaching 10 years in a state.

In almost all states and school districts, teachers are paid for both longevity in the profession and levels of education completed. A beginning teacher with a master's degree will likely receive a higher salary than a beginning teacher with a bachelor's degree. Two teachers with bachelor's degrees will be paid differently if one has 3 years of teaching experience and the other has 15 years in the classroom. In most cases, the fact that the teacher with 3 years can point to contributing to outstanding verifiable improvement and student achievement whereas the more experienced teacher has little to show with regard to influencing measurable student learning makes no difference in compensation. Is this fair? No. Have we found ways to measure student growth and pay teachers accordingly? Some ideas exist. School systems have tried for decades to pay teachers based on performance, or merit, but without the kind of success that perpetuates merit pay to the satisfaction of those affected, the teachers themselves. Performance pay is a hot topic in education, with education leaders at district, state, and federal levels proposing plans for paying teachers based on a variety of variables including student success on standardized tests.

We explore performance-based pay in depth in Chapter 12.

When considering salary, investigate the cost of living where you want to live. For example, thousands of experienced teachers in the suburbs outside New York City make more than $100,000 a year (Fessenden & Barbanel, 2005). However, an examination of the cost of living in such places as Westchester County, New York, shows that $100,000 there is equivalent to a much lower salary in most of small-town America.

Sonia Nieto (2009), a respected educator and writer, offers additional, and perhaps more intriguing, reasons for becoming and remaining a teacher in Figure 1.2. Nieto's reasons are somewhat more complex than the eight we just explored and they require thoughtful consideration. All of the reasons for choosing to teach are positive, of course. Yet, to only discuss all the benefits and rewards of teaching presents a picture that's out of balance. No career is without challenges; no career is without frustration. Teaching has its share of both, as we discover while considering the many aspects of teaching throughout this book.

Points of Reflection 1.1

We've looked at reasons for choosing teaching as a career. Given the eight reasons discussed and Nieto's additional eight in Figure 1.2, which are your top three reasons for considering the teaching profession, and why?

Brandi Wade, one of our focus teachers at Summit Primary School in Summit Station, Ohio, tells us that perhaps we don't choose teaching, but rather teaching *chooses us*. Read about her philosophy in ***Teaching in Focus***.

How Do We Prepare to Teach?

You may have heard it said of someone, "He's just a natural-born teacher." There's some truth in this statement. Teaching comes more naturally to some than to others. With varying degrees of natural talent and inclination for teaching, we all have much to do to prepare to effectively make the teaching and learning connection. Our nature-given attributes must be enhanced by the knowledge and skills gained through

We examine the influence of nature on who we are in Chapter 2.

Teaching in Focus

Brandi Wade, kindergarten, Summit Primary, Ohio. *In her own words. . . .*

It may not so much be that you choose teaching, but that teaching chooses you. It will be in your heart and on your mind constantly. Although it's never easy for more than 5 minutes at a time, teaching is the most important profession you can pursue. I am truly blessed to be a kindergarten teacher. I get to teach a different lesson, meet a different challenge, and see life from different perspectives every day in my classroom.

Laugh with the children, laugh at yourself, and never hold a grudge. Don't be afraid to say "I'm sorry" to a child when you have done something unprofessional or hurtful. If children do hurtful things, just hug them a little more tightly and make them feel safe. Children learn best when they feel safe and loved no matter what.

I don't teach to be remembered, although it's nice to think that you'll never be completely forgotten. I teach so that I can remember. I remember their personalities and how they grow. I remember the times we struggled with learning and succeeded, as well as those times when we fell short of our goals. I remember the laughter and the tears we shared.

Some people say, "Leave school at school." The best teachers I know often lose sleep thinking about and worrying about their students. It's worth every toss and turn!

Watch **Brandi's room tour** to get to know her better.

studying content, learning about theory and methods of teaching, being mentored, reading, observing, practicing, and reflecting.

Each state has its own preparation requirements for those who teach in public school classrooms. Most states require a prospective teacher to pass a test before they grant certification or licensure. The most widely used tests are part of the **Praxis Series** published by the Educational Testing Service (ETS). The state issues a teaching certificate or license when a teacher candidate is determined to be sufficiently qualified. Let's examine two broad paths to initial teacher preparation: traditional and alternative.

TRADITIONAL PATHS TO TEACHER PREPARATION

The traditional paths to initial teacher preparation come through a university department of education. National and state organizations carefully scrutinize university programs and evaluate how teacher candidates are prepared. About two thirds of states require university teacher education programs to be accredited (authorized to prepare teachers) through the **Council for the Accreditation of Educator Preparation (CAEP)**.

All three initial teacher preparation paths—bachelor's degree, fifth-year program, master's degree—include one or two semesters of **student teaching**, also called **clinical internship**. During this extended fieldwork, teacher candidates teach lessons and, for a designated time frame, take over all classroom duties. A classroom teacher serves as the **cooperating teacher** (host and mentor) while a university instructor supervises the experience.

> Student teaching is discussed in more detail in Chapter 12.

Bachelor's degree. A 4-year undergraduate teacher preparation program consists of a combination of general education courses, education major courses, and field experiences. Most early childhood and elementary teacher preparation programs result in a degree with a major in education. Many programs in middle-level education result in a degree with a major in education and two subject-area concentrations (15 to 24 hours each). To teach in high school, most programs require a major in a content area and a minor, or the equivalent of a minor, in education coursework.

Fifth-year program. Some universities offer a fifth-year teacher preparation program. Teacher candidates complete a major other than education and stay for a fifth year for more education coursework plus student teaching. For instance, a teacher candidate interested in science may major in biology and then stay a fifth year to become a certified, or licensed, teacher. Some of these programs include a master of arts in teaching degree rather than an extended bachelor's degree.

Master of Arts in Teaching. People who have a bachelor's degree in an area other than teacher education may pursue teacher preparation through a Master of Arts in Teaching (MAT) degree. Most early childhood and elementary MAT programs consist of all teacher education courses and fieldwork, whereas middle-level MAT programs typically require 18 to 24 hours of subject-area coursework in addition to education courses. High school MAT programs generally require a degree in a content area or the accumulation of enough content hours to be considered a concentration.

ALTERNATIVE PATHS TO TEACHER PREPARATION

There is a growing movement toward alternative paths to teacher preparation. In the 1980s alternative certification began as a way to address projected teacher shortages. Since the first efforts, we have seen various models for recruiting, training, and certifying people who already have at least a bachelor's degree and want to become teachers.

Since 1983 the number of teachers entering the classroom through alternative means has rapidly increased. Now all 50 states offer one or more of over a hundred different programs offering alternative certification/licensure, with some estimates stating that as many as a third of new teachers are using alternative routes to the classroom. Adults who decide that teaching is for them after having other careers are likely to enter the profession through alternative paths (Feistritzer, 2009).

Many alternative programs grow out of specific needs and are developed and coordinated through partnerships among state departments of education, school districts, and university teacher education programs. Their structures vary widely, and they tend to be controversial. Some people doubt that teacher preparation is as effective outside the realm of university-based programs.

Perhaps the most widely known alternative path to the classroom is through the nonprofit organization Teach for America (TFA). Teach for America is dedicated to expanding educational opportunity for children facing the challenges of poverty. TFA recruits individuals who are college seniors, recent graduates, and professionals who agree to teach in high-needs rural or urban schools for at least 2 years and become life-long leaders in the effort to end educational inequity. Teach for America teachers receive the same salary as other beginning teachers in their district and also, as AmeriCorps members, may receive student loan forbearance. In the 2012–13 school year, more than 10,000 TFA teachers taught about 750,000 students (Teach for America, 2013).

GETTING TO KNOW SCHOOLS, TEACHERS, AND STUDENTS

Regardless of the route you take to become a teacher, the more experiences you have in schools with teachers and students, the better prepared you will be to have a classroom of your own. The more experiences you have, the more certain your decision will be concerning whether teaching is for you. Experience in classrooms will also lead to more informed decision making about your teaching identity.

Most preparation programs require field experiences throughout. You may begin with observations in one course and then work with individual students and small groups in another, and then teach whole group lessons before and during student teaching/clinical practice. These experiences may hold many surprises for

Preparing to teach requires reflection on the many roles involved in the profession.

you. Having a 5-year-old nephew you enjoy seeing several times a year is very different from working all day with 20 five-year-olds in a kindergarten classroom. Your memories of senior advanced placement literature that inspired you to want to teach high school English may be a romantic picture of students paying rapt attention as the sonnets of Elizabeth Barrett Browning are discussed. However, this may be a far cry from an actual freshman English class. If you fit the profile of most teachers and are a white woman from suburbia, chances are that classrooms in urban America will expand your view of what it's like to be a teacher. Although you can read about differences in settings and students in this and other books and be somewhat informed, seeing for yourself brings reality into view.

There are other ways to gain insights into the classroom. Finding opportunities to have conversations with teachers is an excellent way to learn more about the realities of the classroom. Volunteering at schools, places of worship, and community organizations will present opportunities both to get to know kids and to observe adults interacting with them. Being a summer camp counselor, tutoring in an after-school program, and coaching in community recreation leagues all provide valuable experiences. This text provides opportunities to get to know 10 real teachers in 4 real schools teaching 12 real students.

MEET THE FOCUS TEACHERS

"You just had to be there!" we often exclaim when words aren't enough. Learning about teachers, students, and schools is one of those situations when photos or video clips can help convey what a thousand words cannot. Is it as good as being there? No, but it helps.

Throughout this text you will learn about 4 schools, 10 teachers, and 12 students. These people and places are real. Our 10 teachers are introduced in this chapter, our 12 students are introduced in Chapter 2, and their four schools are introduced in Chapter 3.

Is Teaching a Profession?

This text repeatedly refers to teaching as the *teaching profession*. Whether a particular job or career qualifies as a **profession** depends, in large measure, on who is making the determination. We hear references to the plumbing profession, the culinary profession, and the cosmetology profession, but there are established guidelines for determining if a career or job is universally considered a profession. These characteristics of a profession will likely not affect common usage of the word, but examining teaching with regard to them helps spotlight aspects of what we do that may need to be strengthened.

CHARACTERISTICS OF A PROFESSION

For decades authors have delineated the characteristics of a "full" profession. For equally as long, educators and others have debated whether teaching is indeed a profession. This debate is healthy because, as we consider the characteristics of a profession and measure teaching by them, we see what teaching is and is not, what teachers have evolved into, and what teachers may still need to become. A summary of a full profession's characteristics, from both a historical perspective and a modern one, is presented in Figure 1.3. Let's look briefly at these 10 characteristics and think about whether each applies to teaching.

Considering that in the United States children ages 5 through 16 are required to receive a formal education, and that most do this through public schools, a dedicated teaching workforce can collectively deliver this *essential service* (1). Members of this teaching workforce agree that teaching requires *unique knowledge and skills* (2), whether acquired through traditional or alternative paths. On-the-job *training, ongoing*

(*text continues on page 18*)

Figure 1.3 Characteristics of a full profession

1. Provides an essential service no other group can provide.
2. Requires unique knowledge and skills acquired through extensive initial and ongoing study/training.
3. Involves intellectual work in the performance of duties.
4. Individual practitioners are committed to service and continual competence.
5. Identified performance standards guide practice.
6. Self-governance in admitting, policing, and excluding members.
7. Allows for a considerable amount of autonomy and decision-making authority.
8. Members accept individual responsibility for actions and decisions.
9. Enjoys prestige, public trust.
10. Granted higher-than-average financial rewards.

Source: *Foundations of American Education* by L. D. Webb, A. Metha, and K. F. Jordan (2013). Upper Saddle River, NJ: Pearson.

Focus Teachers

Brandi Wade

Kindergarten teacher

Summit Primary School, Summit Station, Ohio

Teaching experience: Grades 5–6 (2 years)

Preschool and K (14 years)

Brandi says she has found her place in life. From her family to her friends to her teaching career, everything fits for this exuberant kindergarten teacher. One look around her classroom and one brief conversation are enough to know that 5- and 6-year-olds who spend time in Brandi's care are fortunate children.

Brandi believes in active involvement of children. She finds ways to teach the Ohio kindergarten curriculum standards through lots of movement, music, hands-on experiences, and play. Each year she spends whatever time is necessary to help her 15 to 25 kindergarten students

per class form positive habits so the necessary routines of the classroom take care of themselves. She knows that classroom management and learning go hand in hand.

"My heart is where the children are" is a phrase Brandi says and lives. She believes that children must feel comfortable and loved in their environment before they can learn and thrive. She laughs and cries with her students, allows herself to be vulnerable to their needs, and provides a warm, developmentally appropriate setting in which children learn and grow.

Brandi and her husband have two sons, a Jack Russell terrier, and two turtles. Brandi enjoys swimming, camping, reading mysteries, and going to movies.

Renee Ayers

Second grade teacher

Summit Primary School, Summit Station, Ohio

Teaching experience: Reading teacher (2 years)

First grade (3 years)

Second grade (4 years)

Renee exudes enthusiasm for life. From the soccer field to the energy she puts into teaching second grade, Renee's personality shines through. She says summers as a camp counselor influenced her teaching philosophy of infusing active learning and fun into instruction.

Renee is a reflective teacher who spends time in her classroom diagnosing student needs. She says her biggest challenge is to design learning experiences for each child that take into account what the child already knows and is able to do. She believes strongly in

individualizing assignments even when her instruction is geared toward the whole class. The children in Renee's class are learning to be reflective too. She saves samples of work from the beginning of the school year and periodically shows the samples to the students so they can compare and recognize their own progress. This is a simple process that's good for children.

At the end of the school year a very shy little boy said, "Mrs. Ayers, can you go to third grade with us?" The children pull at her heartstrings. All the effort is worth it.

Renee and her husband have a baby daughter, the delight of their lives. In addition to her adult women's soccer league, Renee enjoys skiing, snowboarding, mountain biking, and taking evening walks with her family.

Focus Teachers

Tim Mendenhall

Third, fourth, and fifth grade teacher

Rees Elementary School, Spanish Fork, Utah

Teaching experience: Fifth–eighth grade science (4 years)

Multiage third, fourth, and fifth grade (11 years)

Tim Mendenhall's ready laugh sets the tone for his classroom where third, fourth, and fifth grade students enjoy being actively involved in their own learning. Tim's comfortable manner allows his students to get to know him and one another in his multiage classroom.

Tim's approach to science is to provide interesting objects and books to grab his students' attention. Nothing compares to the excitement generated by the classroom's pet tarantula, Rosie. As Tim teaches his kids how to hold her, Rosie playfully crawls up and down his arm and onto the hand of a willing student (with a little coaxing from Tim!).

The reading area in Tim's classroom is surrounded by bookshelves. Inside the area are couches and pillows. Tim says the arrangement is his *kiva,* a Native American meeting space that traditionally was hollowed out with room for seating all around and reserved for important and/or spiritual gatherings. In Tim's reading kiva, his students find a comfortable place to enjoy his collection of varied and interesting books.

Before deciding to teach, Tim was a forestry major. His wife and three sons share his love of the outdoors. Tim finds ways to balance a wonderful family life with his responsibilities as a classroom teacher. Teaching school may not be the most lucrative profession, but it's what Tim loves to do.

Chris Roberts

Third, fourth, and fifth grade teacher

Rees Elementary School, Spanish Fork, Utah

Teaching experience: Special education (14 years)

Multiage third, fourth, and fifth grade (13 years)

Chris Roberts's adventurous spirit and active lifestyle permeate both his personal and his professional life. Chris has climbed Mount Kilimanjaro, rafted his way through the rapids of the Grand Canyon, and explored the shores of remote islands.

Chris brings his treasures to the classroom and shares his adventures with his students. Listening to real-life stories of scuba-diving encounters with giant sea rays and six-foot eels makes learning about ocean life and geography pure joy! Imagine spending three straight years in Mr. Roberts's class!

Chris is a fan of all kinds of art. He has posters of some of his favorite paintings on the walls of his classroom along with inspirational

poems, essays, and even cartoons. Chris infuses lessons in math, science, social studies, and language arts with a sense of curiosity and elements of critical thinking. One of his goals is for his students to see beyond the classroom walls, beyond Spanish Fork, and beyond Utah and the United States, to learn there's a whole world to experience.

Chris's family all share his love of adventure. Chris and his wife raised their children without television. He says there's nothing inherently wrong with television, but it distracts people from doing more worthwhile things like reading and experiencing life rather than just watching other people experience it.

Brenda Beyal

Third, fourth, and fifth grade teacher

Rees Elementary School, Spanish Fork, Utah

Teaching experience: Third grade (8 years)

Multiage third, fourth, and fifth grade (13 years)

The teaching profession is very personal to Brenda Beyal, and she approaches it with a sense of calling. The classroom environment she creates is warm and inviting.

Brenda's favorite subject to teach is language arts. She views literature as a child's window on the world, and reading as a way of experiencing both events and points of view. When her class of third, fourth, and fifth graders read a book together, they explore meanings, not just words. They enjoy finding out about the author and rereading the story for deeper meaning. They write in their journals about story themes and act out sequences.

(continued)

Focus Teachers

Brenda Beyal—continued

The fact that Brenda is Native American brings extra richness to her classroom. The wisdom of generations of her ancestors influences her. She has meaningful Native American objects and posters in her classroom and feels it's important for her to share parts of her heritage with her students. As they grow and encounter other Native Americans, Brenda wants her students to recall, "I know a Native American. I like the kind of person Ms. Beyal is. I'd like to get to know this person I have just met."

Brenda's family time with her husband, son, and daughter is very meaningful to her. She also enjoys drawing, sculpting, and collecting Native American artifacts.

Traci Peters

Seventh grade math teacher

Cario Middle School, Mt. Pleasant, South Carolina

Teaching experience: Seventh grade math/science (6 years)

Seventh grade math (2 years)

Traci's classroom is filled with math—the shelves, the walls, the tables—math is everywhere. The seventh graders in her classes know they'll be actively involved in tasks that help them understand concepts. From geoboards to examine perimeter and area, to paper triangles they tear apart to prove the angles add up to 180 degrees, problem solving becomes something they do, rather than something they just read about. One of Traci's primary goals is to show students that learning math can be lots of fun.

Traci offers her students before-school tutoring to help with concepts that may be difficult. The sessions also help students who

have been absent to get caught up. The tutoring not only gives an academic boost, but it also gives Traci and her students time to get to know one another better.

Traci believes it's important for teachers to reveal some of their personal selves to students. She freely talks about her son and proudly shows students pictures of him as she encourages students to talk about their families and what they like to do in school and out of school.

Traci is married and has a 2-year-old son. She says she loves the fact that she is his first teacher. Walking on the beach, traveling to see family and friends, and spending everyday time with her husband and son make life a real joy for Traci.

Deirdre Huger-McGrew

Sixth–eighth grade language arts, social studies teacher

Cario Middle School, Mt. Pleasant, South Carolina

Teaching experience: First, fourth, fifth grade (7 years)

Sixth–eighth grade language arts, social studies (4 years)

Deirdre Huger-McGrew has taught a variety of grade levels and subjects. She says each one is interesting and challenging, but none so much as her current assignment on a two-person team charged with implementing a new program at Cario Middle School called CARE: Cario Academic Recovery and Enrichment. The program is designed to assist low-achieving sixth, seventh, and eighth graders in working toward grade-level competency.

Deirdre and her teaching partner, Billy, have been given a unique opportunity to begin a program and design it in ways that are responsive

to their students. Principal Carol Bartlett has given them a good deal of professional autonomy. Deirdre says she is thriving in this situation even though her students are among the most challenging at Cario.

Deirdre's ability to talk with students about their interests, hopes, fears, and dreams makes her the ideal teacher for CARE students. She's the "mom" figure for the students.

Deirdre not only has students at Cario to care for, but her own home is brimming over with children. She and her husband have six children, all under 19 years old. Deirdre's attitude is "the more, the merrier." She says she's a teacher 24 hours a day! In her little free time, she enjoys writing and pursuing art activities.

Focus Teachers

Craig Cleveland

History, government, economics

Roosevelt High School, Fresno, California

Teaching experience: History, government, economics (18 years)

Every day, during lunch as well as in the five-minute passing periods between classes, students gather in Mr. Cleveland's classroom to play a tune on his piano or strum a chord or two on his guitar. Several other students sit on desks and listen or participate. This doesn't happen by accident. It happens because Craig Cleveland welcomes students to express themselves, to be comfortable finding their own voice in his classroom and in his presence.

Craig's philosophical stance concerning teaching and learning involves his belief that students learn best when they are interested and involved through authentic reading, writing, speaking, and listening activities. The lessons he plans in his history, government, and

economics classes include reading materials that push students to think and to interact with the text and one another. Students form opinions and write about them. Students speak to both question and persuade, to communicate in order to learn. The first rule of thumb in Craig's planning is "Give the students something worth thinking about."

Craig is an avid observer of human nature and the learning process both at school and in his home. He considers the home a fascinating lab for learning as he and his wife delight in watching their five daughters read, draw, create skits, and solve problems. Craig enjoys playing tennis and writing songs.

Derek Boucher

History, reading

Roosevelt High School, Fresno, California

Teaching experience: History (12 years)

Reading intervention (4 years)

Derek Boucher is an intense teacher whose conscientious involvement in the teaching profession sets a standard for all of us. His background in social sciences and his initial years in teaching led him to the realization that until students can read with fluency and comprehension, they will not be the kind of lifelong learners he would hope for them to be. Although high school may seem much too late to learn to read, the reality is that many 15- to 18-year-olds can read only well enough to barely pass classes, and some not even to that extent.

English-language learners often have even more difficulty.

Derek involves the students in all his classes in current events that impact their lives. He helps them put events and ideologies in context. They explore issues such as media influence and bias. He pushes them to think through issues, form opinions, and then find ways to express their opinions. He teaches them to be wise consumers of information.

Derek and his wife enjoy family time with their two sons and daughter. Derek is an avid reader of professional literature. He also contributes to it by writing opinion editorials in the local newspaper, the *Fresno Bee*, and articles in professional journals.

Angelica Reynosa

Modern World History

Roosevelt High School, Fresno, California

Teaching experience: World history (3 years)

Angelica Reynosa's tenth grade bilingual modern world history class is filled with enthusiasm. There are 34 students in the class, all of whom have been in the United States for less than two years. Angelica is a young Latina whose fluency in both Spanish and English makes her an ideal teacher at Roosevelt High School.

The students' enthusiasm for the class is enhanced by the fact that Angelica teaches in both Spanish and English. But language is not the only reason students are engaged. Angelica says her goal is to make every day enjoyable, memorable, and meaningful for all her students. She admits that it can be difficult to continually search for interactive, hands-on activities for teaching history, but the effort is worth it.

With a master's degree in school counseling, Angelica sees herself teaching several more years and then becoming a guidance counselor. She has aspirations to pursue a doctoral degree and plans to be part of the education profession for a long time.

Something that is particularly enjoyable for Angelica is the fact that she married a high school history teacher who teaches at a nearby school. Angelica says their conversations are filled with empathy because they each understand the other's dilemmas and can listen attentively and make helpful suggestions when challenges arise.

We follow these 10 teachers through interviews, room tours, and lesson clips in *Teaching in Focus* features throughout the book.

study (2), and development are encouraged, but not necessarily required, although most teachers must renew their teaching certification/license every 5 years or so by completing graduate coursework or by participating in other forms of professional development.

Teaching definitely *involves intellectual work* (3). Teachers pass along intellectual concepts and skills, which is the very heart of what teachers do. To enter and remain in a teaching career requires a *commitment to service* (4) and, hopefully, *continual competence* (4) as guided and measured by *performance standards* (5). The word "hopefully" is included because teachers rarely *police their own ranks* (6) to the point of excluding someone who does not live up to accepted teacher standards. If policing occurs, it is generally accomplished by administrators.

When the classroom door closes, teachers have a great deal of *autonomy* (7), sometimes approaching isolation. However, public school teachers must accept any student placed in their classrooms and must teach a set curriculum over which they have little or no control. Even with certain constraints, we are *decision makers* (7), and we must *accept individual responsibility* (8) for the decisions we make.

A great level of *trust* (9) is placed in teachers. After all, for 7 to 10 hours a day, families allow teachers to have almost exclusive control over their children. In most communities, teachers enjoy a degree of positional *prestige* (9), but they are rarely *granted higher-than-average financial rewards* (10).

As you can see, not all 10 characteristics of a full profession apply to teaching. We still have few mechanisms for policing our own ranks (6), and the financial rewards of teaching are not higher than average (10). Teachers should continue to work together to perpetuate each of the eight characteristics we exemplify while exploring ways to incorporate the other two. Many associations and organizations are helping teaching to be a profession by allowing teachers through collaborative efforts to set common goals, speak with a collective voice, and build research-based foundations to support what we do and how we do it.

PROFESSIONAL ASSOCIATIONS

National and regional professional associations provide leadership and support for teachers. Some serve the general teacher population; others are specific to a grade span or subject area. Most associations solicit members, hold annual conferences, publish materials, provide information, and advocate for those who teach and those who learn. Participating in professional organizations is a positive step toward growing as a professional.

The **National Education Association (NEA)** and the **American Federation of Teachers (AFT)** are the largest professional education associations in the United States, with a total of more than 5 million members, including teachers, administrators, professors, counselors, and other educators. Both organizations are unions and represent their members in **collective bargaining,** or negotiating with employers and states to gain additional benefits for their members. Large nonunion professional organizations such as **ASCD Learn. Teach. Lead., Kappa Delta Pi (KDP)**, and the **Council for Exceptional Children (CEC)** serve a wide spectrum of educators. Most national organizations have regional and state affiliate associations. These more local groups provide easily accessible face-to-face opportunities for interaction among members.

Interstate Teacher Assessment and Support Consortium (InTASC) standards address what teachers should know and be able to do and provide the framework for teacher performance standards.

We explore professional organizations in Chapter 4.

Each subject area has a professional organization that provides guidelines for what to teach, sponsors annual conferences, publishes relevant books and journals, represents subject areas in educational and political arenas, and both encourages and disseminates research on teaching and learning. Table 1.2 lists some of the professional associations available to teachers to assist with their professionalism. Visiting their Web sites will give you valuable insight into just how important these and other professional organizations are and can be.

TABLE 1.2 Professional organizations

Teacher Unions

AFT	American Federation of Teachers	www.aft.org
NEA	National Education Association	www.nea.org

Subject-area organizations

AAHPERD	American Alliance for Health, Physical Education, Recreation and Dance	www.aahperd.org
ACTFL	American Council on the Teaching of Foreign Languages	www.actfl.org
IRA	International Reading Association	www.reading.org
MTNA	Music Teachers National Association	www.mtna.org
NAEA	National Art Education Association	www.naea-reston.org
NBEA	National Business Education Association	www.nbea.org
NCSS	National Council for the Social Studies	www.ncss.org
NCTE	National Council of Teachers of English	www.ncte.org
NCTM	National Council of Teachers of Mathematics	www.nctm.org
NSTA	National Science Teachers Association	www.nsta.org
RIF	Reading Is Fundamental	www.rif.org

Level-specific organizations

ACEI	Association for Childhood Education International	www.acei.org
AMLE	Association for Middle Level Education	www.amle.org
NAEYC	National Association for the Education of Young Children	www.naeyc.org

Need-specific organizations

CEC	Council for Exceptional Children	www.cec.sped.org
InTASC	Interstate Teacher Assessment and Support Consortium	http://www.ccsso.org/documents/2011/intasc_model_core_teaching_standards_2011.pdf
NAGC	National Association for Gifted Children	www.nagc.org
SCA	Speech Communication Association	www.isca-speech.org
TESOL	Teachers of English to Speakers of Other Languages	www.tesol.org

General associations

ASCD	ASCD Learn. Teach. Lead.	www.ascd.org
KDP	Kappa Delta Pi	www.kdp.org
PDK	Phi Delta Kappa	www.pdkintl.org

What Is Teacher Professionalism?

Professionalism is a way of being. It involves attitudes and actions that convey respect, uphold high standards, and demonstrate commitment to those served. Fulfilling responsibilities and making the most of growth opportunities are core aspects of teacher professionalism. Patricia Phelps, former academic editor of the *Kappa Delta Pi Record* (a publication of KDP), presents a philosophical framework within which characteristics of teacher professionalism may be placed. Phelps (2003) states that teachers achieve greater levels of professionalism when they are willing to do what it takes, to

Advocating for students is important at all grade levels. Renee, a second grade teacher, and her twin sister, Tara, a high school physics teacher, both advocate for their students in developmentally appropriate ways.

Points of Reflection 1.2

Does the commitment to put students first sound like something you are willing to do? Explain the reason(s) for your answer.

do what must be done. In other words, professionalism involves hard work. This hard work requires commitment in three broad areas.

COMMITMENT TO MAKE STUDENTS OUR FIRST PRIORITY

Student welfare and learning must be paramount. Ask yourself, as a Masai might, "And how are the children? Are they all well?" Putting students first requires that we become advocates for their welfare.

Advocating for students. To be an **advocate for students** is to support and defend them, always putting their needs first. How do we become advocates for our students? Here are some components of advocacy to consider:

- Understand that advocacy takes multiple forms with individuals, groups, or causes, in both large endeavors and small actions.
- In all conversations, with educators and noneducators alike, keep the focus on what's best for students.
- Take an informed stance on issues that affect children. Actively promote that stance to have widespread impact.
- Support families in every way possible.

Advocacy guides our efforts and decisions directly toward our goal—improving students' learning, which, ultimately, improves students' lives.

Making wise decisions. As teachers we continually make decisions. Some of the decisions are made on autopilot, especially those that have to do with routines in the classroom. The quality of other decisions often rests on common sense and maturity, characteristics that are enhanced by preparation and experience. It's important to remember that our decisions have consequences and require thoughtful consideration to make sure we are advocating for our students and maintaining a classroom climate that is conducive to learning.

Determining classroom climate. Our classrooms can be respectful environments that promote learning, or not. The sobering words of Haim Ginott (1993, p. 15), a respected teacher and psychologist, should occupy a prominent position in both your classroom and your consciousness.

> I've come to a frightening conclusion. I am the decisive element in the classroom. It's my personal approach that creates the climate. It's my daily mood that makes the weather. As a teacher, I possess a tremendous power to make a child's life miserable or joyous. I can be a tool of torture or an instrument of inspiration. I can humiliate or humor, hurt or heal. In all situations, it is my response that decides whether a crisis will be escalated or de-escalated, a child humanized or de-humanized.

COMMITMENT TO QUALITY

Quality should characterize our knowledge of content and our relationships and interactions with students, colleagues, administrators, and families. Phelps (2003) tells us that "modeling quality is the most significant way to motivate others to put forth the same effort" (p. 10). Modeling quality requires that we have positive and productive values leading to teaching that facilitates learning.

Facilitating learning. Making the teaching and learning connection is the primary role of a teacher. Learning is why students are in school, and teaching is how we guide and facilitate learning. Our effectiveness as teachers should be measured by how much and how thoroughly students learn.

We can categorize the responsibilities involved in facilitating learning in a number of valid ways. Perhaps none is more important than evaluating each of our actions in terms of its contribution to academic rigor and developmental appropriateness. **Academic rigor** refers both to teaching meaningful content and to having high expectations for student learning. **Developmental appropriateness** means that our teaching addresses students' physical, cognitive, social, emotional, and character development. Academic rigor without developmental appropriateness will result in frustration for teachers and foster discouragement and defeatism in students. Developmental appropriateness without academic rigor will accomplish little in terms of student learning. Neither concept is mutually exclusive. In fact, they shouldn't be exclusive at all, but rather should interact in supportive ways and balance one another as they guide our decision making.

Developing dispositions. **Dispositions** are composed of our attitudes, values, and beliefs. They powerfully influence our teaching approaches and actions. Dispositions that are favorable to effective teaching include, among many others:

- I believe all students can learn.
- I value student diversity.
- I respect individual students and their families.
- I am enthusiastic about the subjects I teach.
- I value other teachers as colleagues and partners in teaching and learning.
- I believe families are important in making the teaching and learning connection.

Points of Reflection 1.3

Are these dispositions part of your personal beliefs? What other dispositions do you think contribute to being a teacher who promotes academic rigor and development appropriateness?

COMMITMENT TO CONTINUAL GROWTH

Teacher effectiveness is enhanced when a lifelong learning orientation is in place. A commitment to continual growth provides a powerful model for students.

Becoming a reflective practitioner. We grow when we reflect on our teaching practices. As discussed earlier in this chapter, **Reflection** with regard to teaching is thinking about what we do, how we do it, and the consequences of our actions or inactions, all with the goal of being better teachers. To be **reflective practitioners** means that we deliberately think about our practice, that is, what we do as teachers. We do this with the purpose of analysis and improvement. Sounds pretty automatic and unavoidable, doesn't it? But it's not. A teacher can repeatedly go through the motions of planning, teaching, and assessing throughout a career yet seldom engage in reflection that results in improved practice.

John Dewey (1933), one of the great American educators, described reflection using words such as *active, persistent*, and *careful*. So how do we become reflective practitioners who actively, persistently, and carefully think about how we teach? Here are some concepts to consider:

- Reflective practice requires conscious effort.
- Self-knowledge is vital and can be aided by thoughtfully completing the *Points of Reflection* throughout this text.
- Reading about and researching aspects of teaching will ground our practice and provide subject matter on which to reflect.
- Talking with other educators will both inform and strengthen what we do and how we do it.
- Being deliberate—doing what we do for a reason—will result in better decisions based on reflection.

21st-century knowledge and skills. Teachers committed to continual growth are determined to increase their knowledge and skills to keep up with current research and thought concerning teaching practices. During the first decade of the 21st century some major forces both inside of, and external to, the education community recognized and espoused the need for knowledge and skills that reflect the realities of the 21st-century world. Perhaps the most influential source of information about teacher and learner characteristics for the new century is the Partnership for 21st Century Skills (P21).

In 2013 there were 17 states officially and voluntarily aligned with the Partnership for 21st Century Skills: Arizona, Illinois, Iowa, Kansas, Kentucky, Louisiana, Maine, Massachusetts, Nevada, New Jersey, North Carolina, Ohio, South Carolina, South Dakota, Vermont, Wisconsin, and West Virginia. The Partnership for 21st Century Skills is a national organization that advocates for student acquisition of 21st century knowledge and skills. To help the United States compete in a global economy, P21 and its member states provide tools and resources that stress critical thinking and problem solving, communication, collaboration, creativity, and innovation. In doing so, P21 has emerged as the leading advocacy organization for infusing 21st century skills into education. To strengthen their focus, P21 brings business and education leaders together with policymakers to define and implement a vision for 21st century education (Partnership for 21st Century Skills, 2011).

The Partnership for 21st Century Skills outlines characteristics of teachers that help them teach students in ways that lead to success, including:

- Critical thinker
- Problem solver
- Innovator
- Effective communicator
- Effective collaborator
- Self-directed learner
- Information and media literate
- Globally aware
- Civically engaged
- Health conscious
- Financially and economically literate

These characteristics for teachers are developed and improved throughout the career of a professional teacher. A commitment to continual growth requires it.

Deirdre Huger-McGrew expresses her views about continual professional growth in *Teaching in Focus*.

Points of Reflection 1.4

Do you have a desire to continually grow professionally and personally? If so, how do you know? If you are hesitant to answer this question, what areas of your own motivation do you think you need to consider?

Teaching in Focus

Deirdre Huger-McGrew, language arts/social studies, Cario Middle School, South Carolina. *In her own words. . . .*

Throughout my 12 years as a teacher, I've taken many courses beyond my initial teacher training. I have been involved in teaching-related projects, most by choice and others as directed by my principal to achieve school and district goals. I have taken my professional development personally because I feel it is a part of my responsibility to nurture my growth as a teacher. It is my identity. It is who I am as a teacher. Seeking to enhance my skills makes a difference in my classroom. I take delight in embracing changing views and trying strategies that have the potential to improve my teaching.

What makes athletes, doctors, or lawyers the best in their fields? I believe it is their desire and ability to seek ways to improve what they do as professionals. This gives them an edge. Teachers should want the same. I want to continually accomplish growth-enhancing professional goals.

SocialMEdia

Yes, you read it correctly . . . the ME is emphasized because your use of social media both inside and outside the classroom is, in large measure, up to you. Few schools dictate the use of social media as an instructional tool, while many schools discourage, or even prohibit, the use of some tech devices if they are in the hands of students. So this is a personal issue, largely within your control. What will you do with your decision-making power?

In the not-too-distant past, textbooks such as this contained pages of instructions on how to utilize computers, word processing, and the Internet in the classroom. Most of today's teachers, and practically all of today's students, take these features of technology for granted and assume their use. So let's move on.

The astonishing and rapidly growing quantity and quality of social media devices make comment on them almost obsolete before a book can be published. However, widespread use of social media devices as *instructional tools* occurs at a much slower pace. Sharing innovations in teaching and learning tools has value, even if the particular piece of technology is several years old.

Social media is part of everyday life for most of us, so why not employ it in the classroom? Throughout this text you will read teaching strategies that include iPods, iPads, wikis, digital photography, blogs, Twitter, Skype, and handheld devices in features titled **SocialMEdia.** In addition, these features will offer suggestions on how you can teach students to use social media wisely and safely.

In this chapter we look at **Webinars**, the name given to Web-based seminars. The effectiveness of a Webinar is in its interactivity possibilities, with participants receiving and giving information in a discussion format. Many school districts and state departments of education offer professional development through Webinars. Is this kind of conferencing as effective as face-to-face interactions? Probably not, but Webinars are both cost- and time-efficient.

- One of the most inclusive sites for Webinars, both for a schedule of what's ahead and an amazing archive of recorded Webinars, is provided by ASCD Learn. Teach. Lead. The site is completely free and available to anyone.

http://www.ascd.org/professional-development/webinars.aspx

- Edtechteacher offers free Webinars to help teachers incorporate technology in the classroom. Anyone can register for these informative, interactive sessions.

http://edtechteacher.org/index.php/teaching-technology/webinars

Try a Webinar! While there are sometimes glitches in getting everyone on board, webinar technology is constantly improving. The learning is well worth the effort.

In each chapter you will read a feature titled *SocialMEdia*. As professionals we can't ignore the proliferation of **social media** in our world and in our schools. This feature highlights specific social media tools and how they may enhance teaching and learning.

This text will continue to refer to a career in teaching as the *teaching profession* and to teachers as *professionals*. Commitment to students, quality, and growth—everything a professional teacher does can be placed within this framework. Remember these three commitments as we examine what it means to be an effective teacher.

What Are the Characteristics of Effective Teachers?

"From the moment students enter a school, the most important factor in their success is not the color of the skin or the income of their parents, it's the person standing at the front of the classroom." This powerful statement was made in a speech to the Hispanic Chamber of Commerce in 2009 by President Barack Obama. Sobering, isn't it? The president of the United States is stating what recent research corroborates. Teachers make the most difference when it comes to student learning. Our effectiveness, or lack of it, matters.

The search for a neatly packaged description of an effective teacher dates back for centuries, even millennia. The best we can come up with are lists of characteristics based on observation and available data, along with narrative anecdotal descriptions. There's a lot to be learned from considering a number of perspectives.

Standards for teachers describe expectations for what they should know and be able to do to ensure learners reach their learning goals (InTASC, 2011). All teacher education standards address teacher effectiveness. School-level organizations such as the **Association for Middle Level Education (AMLE)** and the **Association for Childhood Education International (ACEI)** prescribe standards for new teachers. The 10 standards of the Interstate Teacher Assessment and Support Consortium (InTASC) describe what effective teachers should know and be able to do regardless of the level they teach. An overview of these standards is in Figure 1.4. The InTASC Standards are

---

Figure 1.4 InTASC standards

<u>The Learner and Learning</u>

Standard #1: Learner Development.
The teacher understands how learners grow and develop, recognizing that patterns of learning and development vary individually within and across the cognitive, linguistic, social, emotional, and physical areas, and designs and implements developmentally appropriate and challenging learning experiences.

Standard #2: Learning Differences.
The teacher uses understanding of individual differences and diverse cultures and communities to ensure inclusive learning environments that enable each learner to meet high standards.

Standard #3: Learning Environments.
The teacher works with others to create environments that support individual and collaborative learning, and that encourage positive social interaction, active engagement in learning, and self motivation.

<u>Content</u>

Standard #4: Content Knowledge.
The teacher understands the central concepts, tools of inquiry, and structures of the discipline(s) he or she teaches and creates learning experiences that make the discipline accessible and meaningful for learners to assure mastery of the content.

Standard #5: Application of Content.
The teacher understands how to connect concepts and use differing perspectives to engage learners in critical thinking, creativity, and collaborative problem solving related to authentic local and global issues.

<u>Instructional Practice</u>

Standard #6: Assessment.
The teacher understands and uses multiple methods of assessment to engage learners in their own growth, to monitor learner progress, and to guide the teacher's and learner's decision making.

Standard #7: Planning for Instruction.
The teacher plans instruction that supports every student in meeting rigorous learning goals by drawing upon knowledge of content areas, curriculum, cross-disciplinary skills, and pedagogy, as well as knowledge of learners and the community context.

Standard #8: Instructional Strategies.
The teacher understands and uses a variety of instructional strategies to encourage learners to develop deep understanding of content areas and their connections, and to build skills to apply knowledge in meaningful ways.

<u>Professional Responsibility</u>

Standard #9: Professional Learning and Ethical Practice.
The teacher engages in ongoing professional learning and uses evidence to continually evaluate his/her practice, particularly the effects of his/her choices and actions on others (learners, families, other professionals, and the community), and adapts practice to meet the needs of each learner.

Standard #10: Leadership and Collaboration.
The teacher seeks appropriate leadership roles and opportunities to take responsibility for student learning, to collaborate with learners, families, colleagues, other school professionals, and community members to ensure learner growth, and to advance the profession.

Source: Council of Chief State School Officers. (2011, April). Interstate Teacher Assessment and Support Consortium (InTASC) Model Core Teaching Standards: A Resource for State Dialogue. Washington, DC: Author.

divided into four general categories to help us understand them. The full document detailing the standards is a valuable tool for conceptualizing the effective teacher.

The **No Child Left Behind Act of 2001 (NCLB)**, a reauthorization of the Elementary and Secondary Education Act of 1964, was the most sweeping school legislation in decades. One of the major aspects of NCLB was the requirement that teachers be **highly qualified,** meaning that they have a standard of content knowledge and specialized preparation for their chosen level. The federal government set guidelines for the quality of teachers in public schools, but each state determines its own policy for what teachers must do to be considered highly qualified. Experienced teachers have options in terms of how to meet the highly qualified stipulations.

Throughout this book you will read editorial opinions that have been published in newspapers, both print and online, that express opinions of people who may be staff writers for the papers or guest columnists. In most cases these pieces are logically constructed and easy to understand. They are written by people who feel strongly, even passionately, about an issue. At the end of each **The Opinion Page** feature are prompts or questions to help you think through your own opinions. As you respond, you are doing what good teachers do—reflecting on issues and ideas and then recording your own thoughts with the purpose of professional growth.

When a lone gunman broke into the school and murdered 26 students and staff at Sandy Hook Elementary School, America was stunned. Discussions of school safety, gun control, and how we approach mental health were renewed that day in December 2012. In the midst of national debate, one incontrovertible truth was evident—teachers and administrators care for students. Read this chapter's *The Opinion Page* feature and respond to the items that follow it.

WHAT PARENTS SAY ABOUT TEACHER EFFECTIVENESS

In *The 41st Annual Phi Delta Kappan/Gallup Poll of the Public's Attitudes Toward the Public Schools*, parents were asked to rank nine teacher traits. From most important to least, the parents polled chose the following:

1. Dedication to, and enthusiasm for, the teaching profession
2. Caring about students
3. Intelligence
4. Ability to communicate, to understand, to relate
5. High moral character
6. Friendliness, good personality, sense of humor
7. Ability to discipline, to be firm and fair
8. Patience
9. Ability to inspire, motivate students (Bushaw & McNee, 2009)

A surprising and welcome statistic to come from the 2009 poll is that 7 of 10 parents report that they would like their children to become public school teachers. This whopping 70% is the highest percentage to respond favorably concerning their own children becoming teachers in over 30 years.

In the 44th annual Phi Delta Kappan/Gallup Poll titled *Public Education in the United States: A Nation Divided*, parents were asked to describe a teacher who had a positive impact on them. In order of frequency, the descriptors include:

Caring

Encouraging

Attentive/believed in me

Strict/tough/discipline

Challenging/demanding

Good/great teacher

Committed/dedicated

THE OPINION PAGE

This Opinion Editorial appeared in the CantonRep, *the online newspaper of Canton, Ohio, on December 26, 2012.*

What is a Teacher Really Worth?

by Charita Goshay

Goshay is a staff writer and regular opinion contributor for the CantonRep.

In recent months, teachers, first responders and other public employees have been whipping boys for people who think they enjoy too much compensation for their services. So what, exactly, is the dollar value of a teacher who saves the lives of 15 first-graders? How about one who sacrifices her life in an effort to save them? Which part of the faculty handbook advises a teacher on how to deal properly with unmitigated madness?

For those people who actually know a teacher, the heroism and sacrifice demonstrated by the educators in Newtown, Conn., are the least surprising aspects of the tragedy. Teachers don't just teach. The good ones inspire, challenge and change the lives of their students every day. They open up worlds of knowledge and introduce children to possibilities they otherwise wouldn't know existed. They go into their own pockets to level the playing field. They worry about "their kids," particularly those who they know have turbulent lives, even years after they move on.

Our culture has become such that we don't even blink or flinch at the news that someone will earn $10 million a year for throwing a ball or running a corporation into the ground. But a teacher gets flayed for falling test scores, even when the reasons are multifaceted and complicated.

These days, a lesson plan isn't enough. Teachers frequently must also be psychiatrists, substitute parents and bouncers. They're caught between uncooperative and irresponsible parents, ever more complicated school policies, a cynical taxpaying public that demands to know why schools aren't doing better, and kids who are expected to miraculously rise above the chaos and instability in which they live. Even children from affluent and stable, supportive homes can have struggles that they bring with them to school. Because of all of this, no one in his or her right mind would become a teacher simply for a paycheck and a pension.

Being a public servant is a calling, one as compelling and clear as entering the clergy or becoming a physician. If teachers were compensated based on what they contribute to society, we couldn't afford them. The annual minimum salary for a National Hockey League rookie is $525,000. For baseball, it's $390,000. In the NBA it's $473,604. The average elementary-school teacher makes $40,283 a year, what many major-sport athletes make in a month.

Despite this bargain, we still find reasons to complain about teachers, ignoring the irony that if it were not for teachers, we'd be unable to express ourselves very well. Who has time to decipher someone else's cave-drawing rant? Not me. As we saw in Connecticut and as is demonstrated virtually every day, a teacher's dedication is immeasurable.

This Opinion Page piece covers a lot of ground with respect to teachers' dedication to the well-being of students. She also writes about the relative absurdity of salary discrepancies between teachers and professional athletes. Write a well-developed paragraph in response to each of the following questions.

1. Why, in Ms. Goshay's opinion, would our country not be able to pay teachers enough for what they do? Do you agree? Explain.

2. What is your response to the multiple roles teachers have in the lives of students? Have you considered how all encompassing teaching can be? Does this knowledge overwhelm you? Excite you?

Over 70% of the parents surveyed have trust and confidence in their children's teachers, implying that they believe their children are having experiences similar to the ones they had with the teachers who positively impacted them (Bushaw & Lopez, 2012).

WHAT TEACH FOR AMERICA HAS DISCOVERED ABOUT EFFECTIVE TEACHERS

While attempting to determine why some teachers are significantly more effective than others in facilitating student learning, **Teach for America** has systematically observed and analyzed the results achieved by TFA teachers. They found some intriguing characteristics linked to teachers who facilitate student learning beyond what might be predicted for the mostly poor, mostly minority student population taught by TFA teachers. Effective teachers tend to . . .

1. set high, long-term goals for their students
2. perpetually look for ways to improve their effectiveness
3. constantly reevaluate what they are doing
4. recruit students and their families into the teaching and learning process
5. maintain focus, making sure everything they do contributes to student learning
6. plan exhaustively and purposefully
7. refuse to surrender to poverty, bureaucracy, and budgetary shortfalls
8. establish efficient classroom routines
9. possess a relentless mind-set of perseverance
10. reflect on their performance and adapt accordingly
11. show signs of contentment with their lives
12. have a history of personal goal achievement
13. know the content they teach (Ripley, 2010)

Although not necessarily a trait appropriate for this list, Teach for America tells us that a predictor of a TFA teacher's classroom success is the grade point average (GPA) in the last two years of college, rather than the overall GPA. In other words, a GPA that starts out mediocre and then improves appears to be associated with greater teacher effectiveness than a 4.0 all four years. Another interesting point is that the more college extracurricular accomplishments, the better the teacher. These are areas you can work on *right now* that will help shape the teacher you will become. Encouraging, isn't it?

WHAT STUDENTS SAY ABOUT TEACHER EFFECTIVENESS

Emphasis has shifted recently from the teacher to the pupil as the focal point for defining teacher effectiveness. Very simply stated, the "ultimate proof of teacher effectiveness is student results" (Stronge, 2002, p. 65). But what results? What seems like a simple statement has complicated nuances because accurately assessing student learning is itself complex. Do we judge the effectiveness of a teacher solely by the standardized test scores of students? That would be easy if standardized test scores told the whole story.

In a survey of about 400 urban, low-income middle and high school students conducted by Corbett and Wilson (2002), all of them identified their teachers as the main factor in determining how much they learned. They listed a variety of characteristics of the diverse teachers most effective in helping them learn, all of which fit into the following six categories. Effective teachers . . .

1. push students to learn
2. maintain order
3. are willing to help
4. explain until everyone understands
5. vary classroom activities
6. try to understand students (pp. 19–20)

EFFECTIVE TEACHERS MAKE A DIFFERENCE

"Substantial research evidence suggests that well-prepared, capable teachers have the largest impact on student learning" (Darling-Hammond, 2003, p. 7). This is not to say that other factors we discuss throughout this book do not significantly

Points of Reflection 1.5

Think about the teachers you have had. What made some effective and others relatively ineffective?

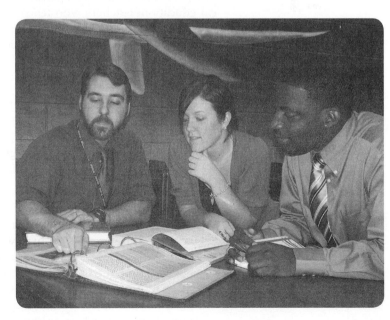

Effective teachers purposefully and collaboratively plan for instruction.

influence student learning. However, Linda Darling-Hammond, a noted expert on teacher quality, and others contend that an effective teacher can overcome many of the circumstances in students' lives and positively impact student learning. When the outside influences on student learning result in an achievement gap, Kati Haycock (2003), director of the Education Trust, tells us, "If we insist on quality teachers for every student, we can dramatically improve the achievement of poor and minority students and substantially narrow the achievement gap" (p. 11). Reiterating the need for effective teachers, James Stronge (2002), another respected educator, writes, "Teachers have a powerful, long-lasting influence on their students. They directly affect how students learn, what they learn, how much they learn, and the ways they interact with one another, and the world around them" (p. vii).

Teachers can be effective using very different approaches. You can probably name two teachers in your own experience who were effective but who had different traits. Stronge tells us "teaching effectiveness draws on a multitude of skills and attributes in different combinations and in different contexts to produce the results that define effectiveness" (2002, p. 64).

An important factor to understand when it comes to the characteristics of effective teachers and teaching is that much of what makes teachers effective comes through experience in the classroom. This is not to say that new teachers can't be effective. Of course they can! But think about this: Teaching is a profession that expects a brand-new teacher to do the same job as an experienced veteran (Johnson & Kardos, 2005). Don't count on someone saying, "Hey, it's okay if only half your kids learn about half of what you attempt to teach. After all, you're new." David Berliner (2000), a noted leader in teacher education, estimates that it takes about 5 years to "get smart about teaching" (p. 360). Some of the characteristics of effectiveness take time to develop, that is, it takes time to be able to make decisions with automaticity and to draw on experience to supplement formal training.

Throughout this text you are urged to ask repeatedly, as the Masai do, "And how are the children? Are they all well?" However, when you are a novice teacher, your primary question may often be "How am I doing?" In *Educating Esme: Diary of a Teacher's First Year*, Esme Codell (1999) reveals that with experience, the question "How am I doing?" increasingly becomes "How are the children doing?"

Effective teachers, regardless of whom or what they teach, share many common characteristics. Teacher professionalism is a thread that binds them all. But although there are many similarities, the day-to-day responsibilities may vary in many ways. Teachers of students with special needs; teachers who specialize in art, music, or physical education; teachers who teach all or most subjects to one group of students; and teachers who teach the same content area each day to several groups of students—all have specific preparation requirements and position responsibilities.

CONCLUDING THOUGHTS

Learning to be a teacher . . . teaching so others learn . . . learning to be a better teacher—this life-affirming cycle can be yours. Think of the cycle as a wheel that gathers momentum and takes you on a profound journey. You have begun to grow toward the profession. As a teacher, you'll grow within the profession. Read what becoming a teacher meant to one young man, Jamie Sawatsky, a seventh grade history teacher in Chantilly, Virginia.

I noticed the change in myself the first time I walked into my classroom. I was no longer Jamie. That was the name of the young man who had delivered pizzas or worked at the office. My newfound teaching life had metamorphosed me into "Mr. Sawatsky." My previous work experiences had taught me a variety of skills, but accepting the title of teacher has cast me into a world where I am charged with the awesome responsibility of sculpting young minds and preparing students for positive participation in their community. When asked why they entered the profession, many teachers respond, "I wanted a chance to make a positive change in the world." In my case, perhaps selfishly, I wanted to be in a profession that would make a positive change in me. With my first year of teaching about to conclude,

I can say that I am happy to be a teacher and happy to be "Mr. Sawatsky." (Tell, 2001, p. 18)

After reading the **Chapter in Review,** interact with Traci Peters in this chapter's **Developing Professional Competence.**

Chapter in Review

Who teaches in the United States and why?

- Teaching is the largest profession in the United States.
- Most teachers are white women, leading to a need for more men and people of color in teaching.
- Almost 90% of teachers believe teaching requires a "true sense of calling."
- The most common reasons for choosing to teach include the desire to work with young people, the value of education to society, interest in a subject, the influence of a teacher or of family, the teaching schedule, job security, and the opportunity for a lifetime of self-growth.

How do we prepare to teach?

- States issue a certificate or license to teach in public schools based on their own criteria.
- The traditional path to becoming a teacher is through a university-based teacher preparation program.
- Alternative paths to teacher preparation provide timely, but somewhat controversial, routes to teacher certification.
- There are many ways to get to know teachers, students, and schools, including field experiences through teacher preparation programs, volunteer opportunities, watching movies about teachers, and participating online through this and other texts.

Is teaching a profession?

- A profession is an occupation that includes extensive training before entering, a code of ethics, and service as the primary product.
- Teaching meets most of the criteria generally agreed upon for a full profession.
- Numerous professional organizations support teachers and teaching.
- Teachers can and should make contributions to the knowledge base of the teaching profession.

What is teacher professionalism?

- Teacher professionalism involves a commitment to make students the first priority.
- Teacher professionalism involves a commitment to quality in both our work and our relationships.
- Teacher professionalism involves a commitment to continual growth.

What are the characteristics of effective teachers?

- Effective teachers may have very different styles of teaching.
- The most important factor in determining teacher effectiveness is the extent of student learning.
- There are established standards for teacher effectiveness through organizations such as the Interstate Teacher Assessment and Support Consortium and the National Board of Professional Teaching Standards.
- Both individuals and organizations have opinions about what makes a teacher effective. There is much to learn from the differing viewpoints.

Developing Professional Competence

Thoughtfully reading this scenario and responding to the items that follow it will help you prepare for licensure exams.

You met Traci Peters in the beginning of this chapter. She is the math teacher on her four-person interdisciplinary team at Cario Middle School. In March one of her teammates, Melanie Richardson, announced that her husband was being deployed overseas and that, without his help with their five children, she was going to have to move to another state where her parents live. Melanie teaches English-language arts and has been on Traci's team, the Dolphins, for 3 years. This is a big blow to Traci and her two other teammates. Melanie will leave Cario in mid-April. The Dolphin team teachers are very easy to work with and have enjoyed a collegial relationship with Melanie.

Carol Bartlett, principal of Cario, understands the importance of finding the right person to fill the position, but she is told that a teacher from another school will be placed in Melanie's classroom for the remainder of the school year. Ms. Bartlett knows the teacher the district personnel office plans to place on the Dolphin team. Linda Merchant's reputation is that of a veteran teacher who does not collaborate, sits behind her desk during class, and consistently finds ways to undermine administrators. Ms. Bartlett suspects her position was purposefully eliminated at the other school and the district just needs to find a place for her. Ms. Bartlett is certain the Dolphin teachers will not be pleased with the district's choice.

1. Which of the following attributes of a full profession does this scenario directly violate?
   a. A full profession enjoys prestige and public trust.
   b. A full profession admits, polices, and excludes members.
   c. A full profession provides an essential service no other group can provide.
   d. A full profession involves intellectual work in the performance of duties.

2. Which of the following statements applies least to this situation?
   a. The three teachers on the Dolphin team will likely have to put out extra effort to keep their students from being affected by what they anticipate will be substandard teacher performance.
   b. The three teachers are likely most concerned about InTASC Standard 10: "The teacher fosters relationships with school colleagues, parents, and agencies in the larger community to support students' learning and well-being."
   c. The three teachers will continue to instill academic rigor while making their classrooms developmentally appropriate.
   d. Ms. Merchant has a master's degree in education, so the rumors about her are very likely exaggerated.

3. As they have always done, the Dolphin teachers take individual responsibility for the success of their team of students. Which of the following would not be evidence of this?
   a. They use opportunities to say positive things about their students in the community.
   b. They don't get involved in decisions that affect their students because they believe that designated experts know best.
   c. They invite families to come to school to discuss areas of concern for their children.
   d. They consistently talk about and act on what they believe to be best for their students.

Now it's time for you to respond to two short essay items involving the scenario. In your responses, be sure to address all the dilemmas and questions posed in each item. Each response should be between one half and one full double-spaced page.

4. Traci and her teammates understand that Ms. Merchant will be a temporary member of their team, or at least that's their hope. They have been assured by the school district that they will be able to interview candidates for the English-language arts position and that a new teacher can be in place by August. This helps them get through the remainder of the school year. As they look to the future, what are three qualities you would recommend they look for as they, along with Ms. Bartlett, choose a new teacher for their team?

5. U.S. Secretary of Education Arne Duncan (2009) believes that teacher evaluation is broken. The seventh grade team at Cario is about to experience some of the consequences of a system that not only fails to discriminate between effective and ineffective teachers, but also allows ineffective teachers to remain in the classroom. How would meaningful ongoing teacher evaluation help fix the system? How would you recommend the results of the evaluation be used?

2

Student Similarities and Differences

Dear Reader

It's all about the kids . . . schools, teacher preparation, lesson plans, activities, professional development, and so on. Our focus must always be on learners, those children and adolescents who enter our classrooms and live within our care at least 180 days a year. A teacher's entire career is an adventure in observing and interacting with whole—yet still developing—people; their needs and gifts and challenges keep the classroom fresh and vibrant as long as we positively approach our responsibilities as teachers. What a wonderful profession!

In this chapter we look at how students are both similar and different. A quick look at the pages tells you that we give differences much more attention than similarities. The primary similarity is that kids are kids—regardless of how they may differ from one another, they are first and foremost kids. Once that's established, we need to understand that each learner is complex, a composite of multiple factors, many of which we'll explore in this chapter. Each child has learning preferences, life circumstances, a personality, potential, and gifts, and each deserves our best efforts. This is in no way a comprehensive look at student diversity, but it's a good way to begin. Our responses to "And how are the children? Are they all well?" will be more meaningful when we see them as whole people, developing every day.

In this chapter we explore the student population in the United States by looking at aspects of similarity as well as aspects of diversity. Here are some questions we focus on in Chapter 2:

- How are we similar?
- How are gender differences manifested in schools?
- How are cultural and language diversity manifested in schools?
- What is the impact on students of family structure, religion, and socioeconomic status?
- How are learning differences manifested in schools?
- Who are students with exceptionalities, and how do we serve them?

Teaching in Focus

As Craig Cleveland looks around his classroom at Roosevelt High School in Fresno, California, while his second-period U.S. History students are making their way to their seats, he sees 32 adolescents—7 sophomores, 21 juniors, and 4 seniors. They are chatting as they make themselves comfortable in the crowded second-floor room. Their primary languages tell much of their ethnic stories—15 speak Spanish, 10 speak Hmong, 6 speak English, and 1 speaks Laotian. Thirteen of the 32 speak very little English, and write even less.

All 32 students qualify for free or reduced-price meals. Craig knows that students from low-income families struggle more to achieve academically. When measured by standardized tests with "basic" as average, over half are considered "below basic," or "far below basic," in both English language arts and math. In addition, 19 of the 32 have impairments of some kind that are recognized by the school and require special accommodations by teachers.

Craig's challenge today is to pique every student's interest in the question, "Is separate ever really equal?" To do this, Craig must find ways to define the issues, present background information, make it relevant to his heterogeneous class, and then facilitate an activity that engages every student.

The students in Craig's class are alike in many ways: They are all adolescents, most are from low-income homes in the same geographic area, and they have all gone through similar developmental stages to become 15-, 16-, 17-, and 18-year-olds. They also have many differences: Some are male, and some are female; some were born in the United States, whereas others are recent immigrants; some are Catholic, some Protestant, and some Buddhist. When viewed as a group, Craig's students are a wonderful but challenging example of diversity in the American classroom. Watch **Craig's interview** to get to know him better.

In the time it takes you to read a few pages in this book, a whole classroom of students will be born. That's right—statistically, 30 babies are born in the United States every 8 minutes. Your entire future kindergarten class, third grade class, middle school social studies class, or high school algebra class may be coming into the world right now.

Statistically, we can predict that of these 30 future students, 14 will be considered a racial minority, 8 will be born into poverty, and 9 will be born out of wedlock. Of these 30 children, 17 will have parents who divorce before the students graduate from high school, 5 will serve jail sentences, 5 will be victims of violence, 4 will commit a violent crime before age 16, and almost half will drop out before finishing high school (National Center for Education Statistics [NCES], 2011; U.S. Census Bureau, 2012). "And how are the children?"

Chances are your classroom won't mirror the statistics you just read. Classroom populations vary from little cultural or socioeconomic diversity to a challenging mix. You may teach in a school with students whose families are financially well off, or one with families that move when the rent comes due. You may teach in a stable rural community with conservative values and lifestyles, or you may teach in a suburban area that affords a great variety of opportunities and educational options, but where students tend to move often.

The 30 new lives that have begun in this 8-minute time frame may appear to be diverse, but they are actually more similar than they are dissimilar. They are individual beings with unique attributes and a variety of needs. But the most important thing to remember is that they are children, all worthy of our best efforts. Mark Twain said that children are born every day who could change the world. We just don't know who they are yet.

How Are We Similar?

We begin our look at similarities with a brief discussion of nature and nurture, the two sources of the influences that make us who we are. Then, through the views of Maslow, we look at the needs every human shares. We follow with an exploration of physical, cognitive, emotional, social, and character development.

NATURE AND NURTURE

There has been much debate on the question of what has the greater influence in determining who we are—nature or nurture. These two concepts are generally presented as oppositional: nature *versus* nurture. **Nature** refers to genetically inherited influences. Not only are certain physical characteristics, such as eye color, skin tone, and adult height, determined by nature, but also some aspects of our intelligence and personalities are established genetically as well. **Nurture** refers to the influences of our environment, encompassing everything that cannot be accounted for genetically. For instance, the people we meet, the schools we attend, and our economic status are all part of nurture.

Many older students agree that what they learned during the rapid brain growth period before first grade continues to influence them.

Each child arrives in the world with predispositions, or tendencies, accounted for by nature and over which we have no control. However, teachers do have some influence over nurture that can positively impact what students receive through nature. That's why we create classroom environments that stimulate growth—physical, intellectual, emotional, social, and moral. To more fully realize why we need to create these environments, let's examine the importance and relative priority of human needs that we all share.

MASLOW'S HIERARCHY OF NEEDS

Psychologist Abraham Maslow (1908–1970) proposed that all human beings experience the same needs. Figure 2.1 shows his classic **hierarchy of needs,** which is widely accepted as an accurate depiction of the order, from bottom to top, in which needs have to be met for healthy and full human development.

Maslow proposed that basic needs for survival and safety must be met first. Once these needs are satisfied, humans are motivated to move up the pyramid toward

Figure 2.1 Maslow's hierarchy of needs

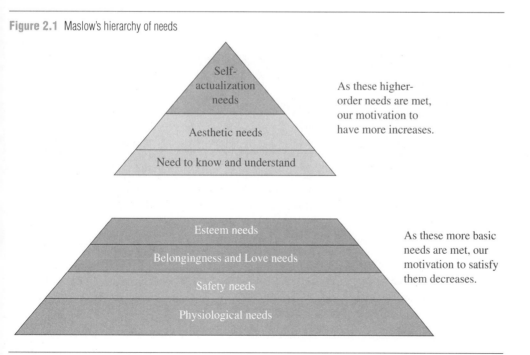

As these higher-order needs are met, our motivation to have more increases.

As these more basic needs are met, our motivation to satisfy them decreases.

higher-order needs. Makes sense, doesn't it? If students don't have food and shelter, or if they feel physically threatened, it's unlikely they will be concerned about understanding the Pythagorean theorem. Providing opportunities and support for needs fulfillment and promoting positive student development will help them ascend Maslow's pyramid and develop in positive ways.

STUDENT DEVELOPMENT

Most children progress through predictable age-related stages of development. The more we know about these developmental stages, the more empathy and support we can offer. In this section we meet 12 children and adolescents at various stages of development who are students of our focus teachers at our four focus schools. Take the time necessary to not only read the brief descriptions of the students, but to also look carefully at the photos of these real learners. Consider them as you read about five developmental areas: physical, cognitive, emotional, social, and character.

Focus Students: **Early Childhood**

Dylan Todd

Kindergarten

Summit Primary School, Summit Station, Ohio (student of Brandi Wade)

Dylan is the only child of Brandon and Lisa Todd. Their pride is obvious as they talk about what a delightful little boy he is. When Dylan smiles, everyone smiles. When he giggles, his pure expression of joy is contagious.

Dylan is in his second year as a kindergarten student. During his first year, Dylan made progress and perhaps could have gone on to first grade. However, in consultation with the school staff, Mom and Dad decided it would benefit Dylan to experience another year of kindergarten, giving him time to mature a bit more socially.

We meet Dylan in the middle of his second year of kindergarten. His teacher, Brandi Wade, says that he has made wonderful progress in learning to read. In terms of the reasoning ability needed for progress in math, Brandi says Dylan is continuously growing and learning.

Sherlonda Francis

Second grade

Summit Primary School, Summit Station, Ohio (student of Renee Ayers)

Sherlonda's personality shines. The challenge is to help her develop academically and find success in school so high school graduation will be in her future. Renee Ayers, her teacher, is afraid that if Sherlonda doesn't experience academic success soon, her penchant for socializing may actually get in the way of her success.

Sherlonda is doing fine in second grade. However, in first grade she had some difficulty paying attention and staying on task. Although this isn't unusual for early childhood students, it was chronic enough to concern the Summit Primary staff. Renee talked extensively with Sherlonda's first grade teacher, and they worked together to plan Sherlonda's second grade experience so she would experience success.

Sherlonda's mom is the sponsor of her church dance group, and her dad is very active in Sherlonda's life, saying his daughter loves to learn new things and figure out how things work. Both parents say they have always read to Sherlonda, and now she is reading to them.

Focus Students: **Elementary**

Amanda Wiley

Third grade

Rees Elementary School, Spanish Fork, Utah (student of Tim Mendenhall)

Amanda's mom, president of the Rees Elementary PTA, describes Amanda as "just plain fun." All it takes is five minutes of classroom observation to know the description fits. Amanda loves school now, but reading did not come easily for her, and first grade proved to be very challenging. Toward the end of second grade, things began to click for Amanda. Now in third grade, she is an avid reader.

Amanda is crazy about math. Mom says Amanda doesn't behave like a stereotypical girl. She would rather be involved in rough-and-tumble play than do what most girls want to do. Amanda is the middle of three sisters and doesn't seem to have time for relationships with other girls.

The summer before going to third grade, when Amanda would be in Tim Mendenhall's homeroom, she talked her family into letting her be the caretaker of Rosie, the class pet. As it turns out, the class pet is not a cuddly guinea pig or a cute little rabbit, but a large hairy tarantula.

Hector Mancia

Fourth grade

Rees Elementary School, Spanish Fork, Utah (student of Chris Roberts)

Hector's smile would warm the heart of any teacher. As a fourth grader, he is a fluent English speaker, vibrant, curious, and determined to succeed. Hector's family came to Utah from Mexico. One of his biggest challenges is to help his family learn English. Mrs. Mancia understands and speaks some English, but his dad and older brother do not.

Hector enjoys school. He fits right in with other third, fourth, and fifth graders in Chris Roberts's multiage class at Rees Elementary. Hector tells us that he really enjoys reading, sports, recess, and lunch—pretty typical of fourth graders. His mom tells us he enjoys basketball, school, and cleaning his room. This last may seem surprising, but Hector likes to please those around him.

Hector enjoys Mr. Roberts's lessons and says his teacher's travels add a lot to the classroom. Chris Roberts's teaching style draws him in and keeps him excited about school.

(*continued*)

Focus Students: **Elementary**

Josie Ford

Fifth grade

Rees Elementary School, Spanish Fork, Utah (student of Brenda Beyal)

At age 10, Josie loves school, reads fluently, enjoys math, and is quite proficient on the computer. She thrives in a multiage setting with children in grades 3, 4, and 5. She enjoys spending her days with her classmates, sharing the social aspects of children her own age and younger, and she enjoys as well the academic challenge of learning fifth grade standards, the guidelines for what students learn in each grade level, while assisting third and fourth grade students learn their standards. When Josie was a third grader she was assisted by the older children in her multiage classroom. Josie enjoys helping in the same way she was helped.

Josie has a well-rounded life and lots of advantages, evident both in her school performance and her home life. Mom tells us they have an active, outdoor-oriented family. She and her sister and parents often go on adventures in the Utah desert and mountains.

Focus Students: **Middle School**

David McBeath

Sixth grade

Cario Middle School, Mt. Pleasant, South Carolina (student of Deirdre Huger-McGrew)

At 6 feet and 195 pounds, David doesn't appear to be 12 years old. However, looking at his childlike face and hearing his soft voice, you realize he is a young adolescent whose emotional and social development are yet to catch up with his physical growth. David wants teachers to be friendly and organized. What he doesn't like are teachers who are boring or who cover material too quickly.

David enjoys music. He plays the bass guitar with a church rock band several times a week. David's mom tells us he hummed before he spoke. Music is his favorite pastime and a way of expressing himself. This kind of interest and talent are particularly important for students with learning disabilities, diagnosed early in David's academic life.

David's mom makes the most of his auditory skills by encouraging him to listen to books on CD and follow the words in the printed book as he does so. For the next six years, David will need all the help he can get to succeed in public school because of his academic difficulties, which display most readily in his reading achievement level.

Focus Students: **Middle School**

Patrick Sutton

Seventh grade

Cario Middle School, Mt. Pleasant, South Carolina (student of Traci Peters)

Patrick is a very self-assured 13-year-old seventh grader who likes school. He enjoys being with friends the most and doing homework the least (no surprise here!). He says he likes teachers who challenge him and dislikes teachers who are mean and yell at kids. Patrick says he would like to join the NFL. But if that's not in his future, he would like to be an architect.

Patrick's mom tells us he is a delight at home. She says he is independent, easy to be around, loves his family, and enjoys attention. The main challenge Patrick has faced is that the family has moved often. Patrick has had to make new friends and start over several times in his eight years of schooling. Mom thinks this has made him stronger and a better student. Her hope for him is that he will retain his love of learning and be true to himself.

Focus Students: **High School**

Trista Kutcher

Ninth grade

Wando High School, Mt. Pleasant, South Carolina (former student of Traci Peters)

Trista is as friendly as any high school freshman could be. She thrived at Cario Middle School. Wando High School students pass her and smile when they say hello. Trista is a cheerleader and an athlete—and she has Down syndrome.

Trista's coach and fellow cheerleaders tell us they anticipated problems because of Trista's disability. They soon discovered that their fears were not justified. Trista has proven to have both the skill and the attitude to be an asset to the squad.

Trista, her parents ReBecca and Joe, and her two sisters form a loving, supportive family. ReBecca and Joe are both teachers. When Trista was at Cario Middle School, ReBecca was there to make sure she had every advantage possible in a public school setting. At Wando High School, Joe is her homeroom teacher. Their interest and involvement have played a major role in Trista's success.

(continued)

Focus Students: **High School**

Mayra Reyes

Tenth grade

Roosevelt High School, Fresno, California (student of Derek Boucher)

Mayra was born in the United States and is fluent in both Spanish and English. Friends are at the center of her life. Mayra would much rather be at school than at home. She enjoys going out with friends and playing sports. She says she didn't like to read before enrolling in Derek Boucher's class. Now that she has read her first real book, she says she reads better and faster and enjoys it.

On the day that Mayra's mother had agreed to come to school to talk, Mom didn't show up because of a domestic dispute involving her boyfriend that led to a visit to the emergency room. Mayra's dad has been out of her life for years, and she doesn't understand how he can stay away. She confided that one of her fondest wishes is to be reunited with her father. Her home life often lacks the support that would help her be successful.

Mayra receives support at school through a program for Hispanic students focused on the arts called Folkloria. When asked about her future, she says she would like to be either a teacher or a nurse.

Guillermo Toscano

Eleventh grade

Roosevelt High School, Fresno, California (student of Craig Cleveland)

Guillermo represents the first generation in his family to go to high school. In conversation, his maturity and thoughtful demeanor are engaging. Guillermo tells us his dad came to the United States to give his family a better life.

Guillermo says he learns best when he experiences the concepts and content to be learned through class activities. He enjoys lots of teacher-student interaction.

Mom says Guillermo is always pleasant and kind. In fact, she affectionately calls him her "gentle bear." She says he enjoys school but is sometimes a little lazy. She lets us know with a giggle that even this trait endears Guillermo to her. He loves sports, both playing them and watching them. Mom hopes Guillermo will go to college and get into a business of his choice. She quickly adds that she hopes he can do all this right there in Fresno so he will be close to her. What a loving environment!

Focus Students: **High School**

Hugo Martinez

Eleventh grade

Roosevelt High School, Fresno, California (student of Angelica Reynosa)

Hugo is a 17-year-old junior with a very outgoing personality. Are you wondering why there's only one school picture of him? When Hugo, his mom and dad, and three brothers crossed the Mexican border into California 18 months ago, they only brought the clothes they were wearing.

Angelica Reynosa, Hugo's bilingual teacher, interprets the question about what he would like to do in the future. He responds in English, "I have a dream in my life." Then in Spanish he says he wants to graduate from high school, go to college, and be a doctor or a teacher. Hugo's mom and dad, with Angelica interpreting, express their pride in Hugo and say he is responsible, does his chores and

homework, and is well rounded. Their hope is that Hugo's teachers will be positive and continue to motivate him.

Perhaps the biggest roadblock for Hugo is his lack of U.S. citizenship. This precludes him from receiving grants and government loans. Without financial assistance, Hugo will likely not go from high school to college.

Khammany Douangsavanh

Twelfth grade

Roosevelt High School, Fresno, California (student of Craig Cleveland)

Khammany speaks fluent English at school but only Laotian at home. She participates consistently and demonstrates an appreciation for the value of education. As a learner, Khammany says interest in a subject is the key to motivating her to succeed. Khammany says she likes history in Craig Cleveland's class because there's so much in the past to think about and so much in the future to predict.

Khammany's mom, who speaks no English and relies on Khammany to interpret, is very emotional when she says she wants her daughter to receive a good education to help her succeed. This is especially important since the death of Khammany's dad about a year ago. Mom views her daughter as the hope of their family. She's bright and determined, and her mother is obviously proud of her.

Khammany will be the first in her family to graduate from high school and would be the first to enter college. However, she will likely feel compelled to help support her mom and extended family, making four years of college fairly elusive.

Physical development. Physical development involves how our bodies appear and how they function. Patterns of physical development are orderly in that the progression is generally predictable. Body parts mature at rates that make physical development the most obvious of the five areas of development.

Although each child follows a distinct growth curve, the most rapid growth occurs in early childhood, with steady growth through elementary school. In early adolescence there may be an explosive growth rate, leveling off in late adolescence. Girls often experience puberty as much as 2 years earlier than boys, but boys generally grow taller and heavier than girls by late adolescence (McDevitt & Ormrod, 2012). Watch focus student Guillermo's interview that includes his mother. He has always been big for his age, according to Mom.

Cognitive development. Cognitive (intellectual) development is considered the primary focus of school. Changes in cognition are just as profound—but often much more subtle—than outward physical changes. Yet the brain grows faster than any other part of the body. By age 5, the brain has reached approximately 90% of its full size while the body is only 30% developed (Feldman, 2011).

Jean Piaget (1896–1980) was one of the most renowned cognitive development theorists. Piaget recognized distinct differences in children's and adolescents' responses to questions that directly correlated to their chronological ages. This was the beginning of his research into the four **stages of cognitive development,** encapsulated in Figure 2.2.

Although Piaget's work is still held in very high esteem, researchers have concluded that he based much of his theory on children's deficits rather than on their strengths. Children may be more capable at younger ages than Piaget believed. Teachers may benefit from knowing about Piaget's stages, but should never use them to limit how and when the intellectual capabilities of students are stretched.

Rather than looking at their deficiencies, noted Russian psychologist Lev Vygotsky (1896–1934) advocated determining children's intellectual abilities and then providing opportunities for intellectual growth. He proposed that a child's cognitive development increases through exposure to new information and that learning takes place within the individual's **zone of proximal development**. This zone is the level at which a child can almost, but not completely, grasp a concept or perform a task successfully. As learning takes place, the zone widens. This theory is akin to **scaffolding**, a concept widely accepted within education that takes its name from the construction term for temporary supports placed around a structure to allow work to be completed. Vygotsky viewed learning scaffolding as the support given to children to help them move through progressive levels of learning.

Additionally, Vygotsky believed that children's learning is shaped by the culture and society around them. The more interactions, the greater the learning, as a child moves forward within an ever-expanding zone of proximal development (Feldman, 2011).

Focus student Dylan Todd repeated kindergarten, a situation his teachers and parents decided was best. Dylan's cognitive development was not the reason for repeating the grade level, but rather his social development. Watch Dylan's interview with teacher Brandi Wade and his parents.

Emotional development. Human experiences are given meaning through emotions. Both our emotions and our responses to them become more complicated with time. Children and adolescents experience a wide array of emotions, including happiness, anxiety, anger, fear, sadness, shame, and pride. For young adolescents, all these

---

Figure 2.2 Piaget's model of cognitive development

Sensorimotor intelligence (birth to 2 years of age)

Children primarily learn through their senses as their motor capabilities develop. Children in this stage don't actually "think" conceptually.

Preoperational thought (2–7 years of age)

Children begin to use symbols and their grasp of concepts develops rapidly. They begin to think about things and people outside their observable environment. Their viewpoint is generally limited because they have little ability to see things from different perspectives.

Concrete operations (7–11 years of age)

Children begin to think logically. They understand the concept of conservation, that quantities don't change because they are moved. Through manipulation of concrete objects they understand concepts such as number, space, and causality. They begin to see things from varied perspectives and draw conclusions.

Formal operations (11 years of age and on)

Adolescents progress from concrete thinking to the capability of thinking abstractly. They are able to make predictions, experience metacognition (thinking about thinking), and appreciate and use the structure and subtleties of language.

Source: McDevitt, T. M., & Ormrod, J. E. (2012). *Child development and education.* Upper Saddle River, NJ: Merrill/Pearson Education.

emotions—and more—may be experienced in one class period. Teachers need to be able to identity emotions as well as know how and when to respond to them.

In 1995, Daniel Goleman wrote *Emotional Intelligence: Why It Can Matter More Than IQ*, in which he proposed that a person's **emotional intelligence quotient (EQ)** may be the best indicator of future success in life. An emotional intelligence quotient involves a set of skills that accompany the expression, evaluation, and regulation of emotions. A high-level emotional intelligence quotient indicates an ability to understand others' as well as one's own feelings, respond appropriately to them, and, in general, get along.

Social development. Learning to get along with others is a process that begins when young children sit next to each other in **parallel play,** agreeably sharing the same space but not communicating. When children begin to share toys and verbally communicate, they are engaged in **associative play**. Progressing to **cooperative play,** children actively coordinate ways to keep the interaction going. When you think about it, these stages of socialization describe how we relate to others regardless of our age. Relating to others and thinking about them (and ourselves) is called **social cognition**. Whether we are simply coexisting (parallel play), communicating when necessary (associative play), or actively engaging with others (cooperative play), we are social creatures.

High school students' sense of identity develops during adolescence.

Relationships matter to us; adolescents are, at times, consumed with them. Relationships are part of America's youth culture, much of which revolves around groups that inevitably form as adolescents search for their identities. It's quite easy to see which youth subcultures appear to fit most easily into the traditional school setting—generally it's the "cool kids," the "jocks," and the "preppies." Other students may exhibit different developmental patterns and be labeled "nerds," "stoners," "loners," "goths," and so on. The names may change, but the subgroups live on. As teachers, our challenge is to connect with all our students and let them know we care about them, regardless of their social affiliations. Helping students develop positive and productive relationships within society is a major aspect of what teachers do.

Second grade teacher Renee Ayers's focus student, Sherlonda Francis, has a very social nature that may be a source of difficulty in achieving academic success. Watch **Sherlonda's interview** with teacher Renee Ayers and Mom and Dad, as they describe life with Sherlonda.

Now read focus teacher Tim Mendenhall's words in *Teaching in Focus* about forming relationships, adjusting what we do in the classroom based on who our students are, and making our classrooms fun.

Character development. A discussion of character, or moral, development can easily become value laden, depending on particular religious or ethical beliefs. Even so, certain character traits are considered positive by almost everyone, including honesty, trustworthiness, fairness, caring, and citizenship.

Noted developmental psychologist Lawrence Kohlberg contends that people pass through **stages of moral reasoning** as illustrated in Figure 2.3. Kohlberg's stages are based primarily on observations of males in Western culture and have been criticized for not being more universal or sensitive to gender differences. A psychologist and colleague of Kohlberg, Carol Gilligan (1993), suggests that differences in the way girls and boys are raised (nurture) can lead to differences in how they view moral dilemmas. According to Gilligan, boys tend to view morality in terms of broad principles of justice, whereas girls tend to view morality in terms of responsibility to individuals. We look more closely at gender differences in the next section.

A brief summary of development stages is shown in Table 2.1. Now that we've established some of the ways we are the same, let's think about ways we may be different.

Teaching in Focus

Tim Mendenhall, grades 3–5, multiage classroom, Rees Elementary School, Utah. *In his own words. . . .*

I would first encourage you to follow your heart. Trust yourself and do what you feel needs to be done for your students. Education is messy. You will try things and fail. That's how we learn.

Second, more than reading and math, teaching your students to be lifelong learners is your ultimate goal. Make your classroom fun. If you don't like a book or an activity, why do you think they will? Love what you are doing, and they will learn to love learning.

Finally, stay at teaching long enough to get the REAL pay. This could be a child bringing you a Cherry Coke (instead of an apple) every Friday. Or a former student running off the football field to talk with you when he is quarterback and supposed to be leading a play. Or a parent coming back and telling you that you are still their child's favorite teacher (even after all the years and they are now graduating from high school). The pay is great; you just have to wait for it sometimes.

Figure 2.3 Kohlberg's stages of moral reasoning

Stage 1: A rule is a rule, and people obey rules to avoid punishment.

Stage 2: Rules are followed or disobeyed based on rewards.

Stage 3: People obey rules because it's what others expect of them.

Stage 4: Society's rules are what's right, and people conform to expectations.

Stage 5: People follow rules out of obligation to what is agreed-upon behavior in their society. Laws and rules can be changed if society sees a compelling need.

Stage 6: People follow rules that agree with universal ethics. If a law doesn't, they feel free to disobey it.

Source: Adapted from Kohlberg, L. (1984). *The psychology of moral development: Essays on moral development.* San Francisco: Harper & Row.

How Are Gender Differences Manifested in Schools?

"It's a boy!" "It's a girl!" These are the exclamations heard in every delivery room in the United States. Whereas the anatomical differences between males and females determine sex, **gender** is the sense of being one sex or the other. Boys and girls, men and women—the differences are undeniable and are as fundamental as life itself. By age 2, children understand that they are either boys or girls, and they label others as well (Campbell, Shirley, & Candy, 2004).

It is common in U.S. households for girls to be encouraged to engage in what are considered gender-appropriate activities, such as playing with dolls and cooking on make-believe stoves; boys are encouraged to play with cars and throw balls. Household chores are often assigned by gender, with girls asked to wash dishes and boys asked to cut the grass. Boys and girls sense very quickly that there are expectations based on gender. **Gender stereotyping** occurs when perceived gender differences are assumed for all people, as in assuming that the play and chores previously described are always appropriate for one gender or the other. Generalizations about gender differences appropriately begin with phrases such as *tend to.* These two words indicate generalizing, as opposed to stereotyping. **Gender bias** is the favoring of one gender over the other in specific circumstances.

The federal government recognized gender bias in schools in 1972 when Congress passed **Title IX of the Education Amendments Act**, which states, "No person in the United States shall, on the basis of sex, be excluded from participation in, be denied the

TABLE 2.1 Developmental characteristics by level

	Early Childhood	Elementary	Middle	High
PHYSICAL	• Dramatic changes in appearance and abilities • Boundless energy • Rapid brain growth • Healthiest time of life	• Coordination increases • Dexterity improves • Steady growth • Significant differences in size among children	• Onset of puberty • Sudden growth spurts may change appearance • Specialized gross and fine motor skills develop • Some risk-taking behaviors exhibited	• Sexual/reproductive maturity is reached • Girls complete growth spurt; boys continue to grow • High level of physical risk-taking activities exhibited
COGNITIVE	• Piaget's preoperational stage • Very intense brain activity • Increased ability to speak with coherence, understand organization and patterns, and learn prerequisites for reading	• Piaget's concrete operational stage • Increased ability to think logically, apply learning strategies, view multiple perspectives, decode phonetically, and read aloud	• Beginning of Piaget's formal operational stage • Often self-absorbed • Increased ability to reason, solve complex problems, and use varied learning strategies	• Capacity for adult-like thought • Increased ability to reason abstractly, make decisions with more realism, and discern which learning strategies are effective
EMOTIONAL	• Self-concept develops and is influenced by family and society • Self-conscious emotions such as guilt and pride develop	• Self-concept becomes more complex and differentiated • Coping skills develop • Emotional ties beyond family develop	• May be emotionally volatile • Drop in self-esteem • Strong emotional ties with friends develop • Frequent mood changes • Begins to establish a sense of identity	• Sense of being invulnerable • May be prone to depression • Seeks independence and a sense of control • Sense of identity develops
SOCIAL	• Relationships with adults centered on direction, care, and protection • First friendships are developed • Types of play change from individual to cooperative • Becomes aware of other people's feelings	• Increasingly concerned with making and keeping friends • Becoming more assertive • Groups are generally same-gender • Capable of empathy • Awareness of social conventions and rules	• Conflicts with parents and other adults likely • Peers become more influential than adults • Popularity, or lack of it, becomes very important • Awareness develops of sexuality and gender-related relationships	• Identity crisis may lead to social dysfunction • Mixed-gender groups • Conformity with others decreases • Desire for self-reliance • Often overwhelmed with demands of relationships
CHARACTER	• Rules are rigid • Begins to understand intentionality • Aggression declines as language develops • Beginning awareness that actions may cause others harm	• Rules come from shared knowledge • Increased awareness of others' problems • Experiences guilt and shame over moral wrongdoing	• Strong sense of fairness • Desire to help those less fortunate • May value social approval over moral conviction	• Understands the need for rules to promote society • Increased concern about fulfilling duty to benefit others

Sources: Feldman (2011); Gallahue and Ozmun (2012); Goleman (1995); McDevitt and Ormrod (2012); Powell (2011); Richardson and Norman (2000).

benefits of, or be subjected to discrimination under, any education program or activity receiving Federal financial assistance." Title IX has helped correct inequitable treatment of males and females in schools, most notably in athletic programs involving teams.

SOCIAL ASPECTS OF GENDER

During early childhood, children are friends with whoever is convenient at day care, in preschool, or in the neighborhood. During the elementary school years children begin choosing friends of the same gender who have similar interests. With the advent of puberty, friends of the opposite gender begin to be included, and this trend continues through high school.

Boys tend to base their play on activities, whereas girls tend to base their play on talking. In group play, boys tend to play in more adventurous ways, such as acting out battles and physically challenging each other, whereas girls tend to take on roles that are calm, such as playing house or school. Research shows that boys tend to be more aggressive than girls, at least in physical ways. Boys most often show what researchers call **instrumental aggression,** or aggression based on attempting to meet a specific goal, such as grabbing a toy or establishing dominance in an activity. Girls may be as aggressive, but they usually learn to be so in more subtle ways that may be more emotional than physical. This type of aggression is known as **relational aggression** and may include name-calling, gossiping, or saying mean things just to be hurtful.

ACHIEVEMENT AND GENDER

Points of Reflection 2.1

Does the information in Table 2.2 ring true for you? If so, explain how you are or have been impacted. If not, what have you observed that may validate the information?

In general, researchers have found that boys tend to set higher goals than girls and attribute their achievement to ability. When they fail, they tend to attribute their failure to lack of effort. In contrast, when girls meet their goals, they tend to attribute their success to effort. When they fail, they tend to attribute their failure to lack of ability (Vermeer, Boekaerts, & Seegers, 2000). This generalization, illustrated in Table 2.2, is significant for teachers to understand. It indicates that one gender may be conditioned to view failure as the result of a lack of effort, which is easily corrected. The other gender may see failure as the result of a lack of ability, which is not easily corrected.

Until recently, it was generally held that boys scored higher than girls in almost every area tested. In the last 20 years, this academic gender gap has been closing. Although girls as a group may lag behind boys in some areas of science and upper-level math, they are outpacing boys in reading and writing, are more likely to be inducted into the National Honor Society, and are more likely to attend college (Glazer, 2005).

In classrooms many teachers call on boys more often than girls, allow boys to call out answers while scolding girls for doing so, give boys more encouragement to attempt difficult tasks, and generally have higher expectations for boys than for girls. This subtle discrimination is almost always unintentional, but it nevertheless has an effect on classroom participation.

SEXUAL ORIENTATION

Sexual harassment is addressed in Chapters 9 and 10.

The sex to which a person is romantically or socially attracted determines a person's **sexual orientation**. Estimates of the percentage of Americans who are gay or lesbian (attracted to the same sex) range from 5% to 10%. It is reasonable to assume that these estimates apply to the American student population as well. Although it has achieved a measure of acceptance, homosexuality remains in many instances the basis of discrimination and focus of hateful attitudes and actions. The two places that we like to think of as safe and supportive—home and school—are often the very places where the most hurtful slurs and overt rejection of gay and lesbian students occur.

Although acceptance of differences in sexual orientation remains elusive in some communities, others are stepping up and openly expressing support for students who are gay, lesbian, bisexual, or transgender, or who are questioning their orientation. One such community is Springfield, Illinois, as we see in this chapter's **The Opinion Page** feature.

Gender diversity: Implications for teachers. In 2012, 116 of the 506 public schools offering single-sex education opportunities were completely either all-boy or all-girl settings. Note that when schools and classes are discussed by the National Association for Single-Sex Public Education, the label goes from *gender* to *sex*. The word *sex* is used rather than gender because it is a more readily definable attribute.

TABLE 2.2 Boys' and girls' perceived reasons for success and failure		
Perceived Reason for	Boys	Girls
SUCCESS	High ability	High effort
FAILURE	Low effort	Low ability

Source: Vermeer, H. J., Boekaerts, M., & Seegers, G. (2000). Motivational and gender differences: Sixth-grade students' mathematical problem-solving behavior. *Journal of Educational Psychology, 92,* 308–315.

This Opinion Editorial appeared in the State Journal-Register, *Springfield, Illinois, on August 9, 2012.*

New SHS Student Alliance a Great Idea

by staff writer

For a lot of men, hurling gay epithets or having them tossed at you was an unfortunate rite of passage in junior high and high school. As our culture becomes more sensitive to sexual orientation and bullying in general, such incidents hopefully will be fewer and further between regardless of your gender.

But adults telling teenagers how they ought to treat each other can only go so far toward solving the problem. They are far more likely to respond to their peers' attitudes and behaviors. That's why it was heartening to hear about the effort to form a gay-straight student alliance at Springfield High School.

Madisen Morhet, a 15-year-old SHS student, was surprised at the vitriol of the name-calling when she arrived there as a freshman, particularly the kind directed at openly gay teens or those perceived to be. Morhet decided, along with her friend Emily Abate, to circulate petitions to start a club aimed at providing a support system for those being bullied because of their sexual orientation. "I don't think it's fair for students to come to learn and have to be treated that way," Morhet said.

She got 342 signatures from students and teachers, and principal Mike Grossen will review the petition once he receives it. He should seriously consider the idea. We also commend the Springfield School Board for adding sexual orientation to language in its policy manual to protect gay students and staff from discrimination. Board president Susan White said the lack of protection for people based on their sexual orientation was not intentional and had "just been left out." Board vice president Bill Looby asked that it be included. "Clearly, it's something that at least should be addressed in terms of discrimination language and in sending a message that we are tolerant," he said.

Regardless of your moral views regarding someone's sexual orientation, the time has long passed in our country where it is acceptable to pick on, make fun of or discriminate against someone because of the gender they are attracted to. The change in policy at the district is long overdue and should be made in other school districts' policy manuals if it already hasn't.

This Opinion Page piece approves the formation of a student support group for those whose sexual orientation differs and commends the school board's recognition and condemnation of bullying aimed at students who are questioning or expressing their sexual orientation. Write a well-developed paragraph in response to each of the following questions:

1. Do you agree with the writer's statement that teenagers are more likely to respond to their peers than to adults? If so, what might adults do in schools to provide support for student efforts to right wrongs?

2. Madisen Morhet's reason for circulating the petition lets us know that there's a real problem at SHS. With 342 signatures of those who agree with the formation of a gay-straight alliance, how might these "bystanders," who hear the cruelty but have not stepped up to try to stop it, now express their disapproval of bullying?

3. What statement will the principal make if he approves the formation of this alliance? If he does not approve, how might Morhet and other students proceed to change the culture of Springfield High with regard to acceptance of different sexual orientations?

When the National Association for Single-Sex Public Education (NASSPE) was founded in 2002, there were fewer than 20 public school single-sex education opportunities (NASSPE, 2013). You can see this is a growing trend.

We can't deny that girls and boys are different in some ways, whether the differences stem from nature, from nurture, or from the inevitable combination. With awareness, we can diminish gender-biased behaviors and attitudes in our schools. The most important contribution we can make toward alleviating gender bias in our classrooms is to treat our students as individuals, realizing that each is unique. In modeling this behavior we will help promote it in our students.

Our goal in creating **gender equity,** the fair and balanced treatment of boys and girls, is to provide learning environments where all students are free from limitations that might accompany gender stereotyping of what they can or should accomplish. Addressing the following questions will help foster gender equity in the classroom:

- Do I use examples of males and females in all roles and occupations?
- Do I encourage girls as well as boys to explore science and math?

Points of Reflection 2.2

Have you ever felt discrimination based on gender? If so, explain. Are you aware of discrimination in a school setting based on sexual orientation? If so, explain. Have you considered teaching in an all-boy or all-girl setting?

- Do I encourage boys as well as girls to read for pleasure and to participate in poetry writing and drama?
- Am I careful to include historical contributions of both males and females?
- Do I have a way of assuring that I call on boys and girls in equal numbers during class discussions?

How Are Cultural and Language Diversity Manifested in Schools?

Classrooms that were once populated with White students, Black students, and perhaps a few students with other cultural identities are now filled with students of many races and ethnicities. Along with this diversity come more and more students whose first language is not English. Figure 2.4, representing more than 63 million children and adolescents in 2010, shows projections for the changing student population ages 5 to 19. Note the trend of White students comprising diminishing percentages while the Black student percentage remains relatively stable and the Hispanic percentage steadily increases. Also increasing are Asian students, found in the 2010 census to have the most rapidly increasing percentage of growth, though still relatively small in total population.

Teachers in the United States are overwhelmingly White; only about 5% are Black and only 5% are Hispanic, Asian, and other races combined. Add this information to the fact that by 2025 less than half of children and adolescents in the United States will be White, and you can see that appreciating, acknowledging, and altering our curriculum and instruction to be responsive to the students in our classrooms will be increasingly challenging. Knowing our students well is imperative.

Teacher characteristics are discussed in Chapter 1.

CULTURAL DIVERSITY

A widely accepted definition of **culture** states that it is a "dynamic system of social values, cognitive codes, behavioral standards, world views, and beliefs used to give order and meaning to our own lives as well as the lives of others" (Delgado-Gaitan & Trueba, 1991, p. 3). Culture, and the complex combination of elements that compose it, should have a prominent place in any discussion of American education. Geneva Gay (2000) tells us that "culture is at the heart of all we do in the name of education" (p. 8).

Figure 2.4 Projections of U.S. population, ages 5–19

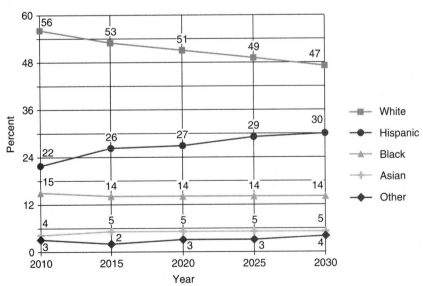

Recent research suggests that culture affects perceptions of the characteristics of intelligence. In the study "Who Are the Bright Children? The Cultural Context of Being and Acting Intelligent," Sternberg (2007) tells us that "different cultures have different views of intelligence, so which children are considered intelligent may vary from one culture to another" (p. 148). He contends that teachers' acceptance and understanding of the differences can affect how well students learn. Intriguing idea, isn't it?

Gollnick and Chinn (2013) contend that culture has three primary characteristics. First, culture is *learned*. The language, the ways we behave, the social rules, the expectations, the roles—all these aspects of a culture are learned from family and others who influence our daily lives. The second primary characteristic of culture is that it is sustained and strengthened because it is *shared*. To learn how to "be" in a culture requires mentors, those who share the culture and, in doing so, perpetuate the culture. Third, a culture is *adaptive* to its environment. The culture of a large group of people changes, or adapts, over time in response to many variables.

The characteristics that apply to cultures of groups also apply to cultures of individuals. Each of us has a cultural identity.

Cultural identity. The interactions of many factors, including language, religion, gender, socioeconomic status, age, values, beliefs, race, and ethnicity, form a person's **cultural identity**. This identity is adapted throughout a person's life in response to his or her experiences.

The words *race, ethnicity,* and *culture* are often used interchangeably, but they do not have the same meaning. As teachers, we need to understand the meanings of the terms to better navigate the complexities of our students' lives. Although the color of our skin (race) and the country of our origin (ethnicity) may contribute strongly to our cultural identity, neither encompasses the total concept of culture. Let's consider race and ethnicity separately.

Racial component of culture. The word **race,** when applied to a group of people, simply categorizes them according to the physical characteristics they have at birth, such as skin color and facial features. Characterization by race is a social, political, economic, and psychological reality (Mukhopadhyay & Henze, 2003). Some researchers say there are actually as few as three races, whereas others claim there are more than 300 (Gollnick & Chinn, 2013). Not a very precise way to categorize people, is it?

The federal government uses race to categorize people in the United States. For census taking, five races are designated: White, Hispanic, Black, Asian/Pacific Islander, and American Indian/Eskimo/Aleut. We still refer to races other than White as minorities. Table 2.3 lists the 2009 minority student populations by state. Note the wide range, with Vermont at 7% and the District of Columbia at 93%.

Categories of race are indistinct, without consideration of family or country of origin. Beginning in 2000, the census form allowed people to check more than one race. Because race is based solely on physical characteristics, what box would a person check whose mother is Chinese and father is Cuban? Half of Asian immigrants' children marry non-Asians, and 35% of Latino immigrants marry members of other races (Diversity Data, 2000). According to the 2000 census, about 7 million people indicated they were multiracial by marking more than one of the five races listed.

Ethnic component of culture. We will use the word **ethnicity** to mean simply an individual's country of origin (Gollnick & Chinn, 2013). Even if families are two, three, or more generations removed from their ancestral country, they may still strongly identify with both the country and the people who share their ethnicity. The category of ethnicity often reveals much more about our students than race. Knowing that a student is Hispanic (race) doesn't necessarily tell us much, but knowing that the child is of Cuban, Chilean, or Mexican heritage may be much more revealing and much more personalized.

Khammany, one of our focus students at Roosevelt High School, is Laotian, while most of the Asian students at the school are Hmong or Cambodian. Cultural

TABLE 2.3 Percentage of public school students by race and state, 2009

Rank by Percentage of Non-White Students	State	White	Black	Hispanic	Asian/ Pacific Islander	American Indian/ Alaska Native	Other	Percentage of Non-White Students
1	District of Columbia	6.7	80.2	11.5	1.6	0.1	—	93
2	Hawaii	19.7	2.3	4.6	72.7	0.6	—	81
3	New Mexico	25.5	2.1	59.9	1.3	10.4	0.8	75
4	California	27.0	6.9	50.4	11.6	0.7	3.4	73
5	Texas	33.3	14.0	48.6	3.7	0.4	—	67
6	Nevada	41.4	11.4	37.5	8.2	1.5	—	60
7	Arizona	44.1	6.0	41.4	3.1	5.5	—	56
8	Georgia	45.0	37.4	11.3	3.3	0.3	2.8	55
9	Maryland	45.5	37.9	10.0	6.1	0.4	—	55
10	Florida	45.9	23.9	27.2	2.7	0.4	—	54
11	Mississippi	46.1	50.1	2.2	0.9	0.2	0.5	54
12	Louisiana	48.5	46.0	3.2	1.5	0.8	—	52
13	New York	50.8	19.1	21.7	8.0	0.5	—	49
14	Delaware	51.6	33.3	11.3	3.5	0.4	—	48
15	New Jersey	53.0	17.1	20.6	8.6	0.2	0.4	47
16	Alaska	53.2	3.8	5.8	8.0	23.0	6.2	47
17	South Carolina	53.7	38.4	5.8	1.6	0.4	—	46
18	North Carolina	53.9	31.0	11.1	2.6	1.4	—	46
19	Illinois	54.2	19.5	21.7	4.3	0.2	—	46
20	Oklahoma	56.4	11.0	11.2	2.2	19.3	—	44
21	Virginia	57.7	26.2	9.7	6.1	0.3	—	42
22	Alabama	58.7	35.0	4.3	1.3	0.8	—	41
23	Colorado	60.6	5.9	28.6	3.7	1.2	—	39
24	Connecticut	63.7	13.9	17.6	4.4	0.4	—	36
25	Arkansas	65.3	21.9	9.2	1.8	0.7	1.0	35
26	Washington	66.1	5.8	16.5	9.1	2.5	—	34
27	Rhode Island	68.0	9.2	18.6	3.4	0.9	—	32
28	Tennessee	68.2	24.3	5.5	1.8	0.2	—	32
29	Kansas	68.8	7.7	15.7	2.5	1.2	4.0	31
30	Massachusetts	69.1	8.2	14.8	5.4	0.3	2.2	31
31	Oregon	70.0	2.9	20.3	4.8	2.0	—	30
32	Michigan	71.1	20.3	4.9	2.7	0.9	—	29
33	Pennsylvania	73.1	15.8	7.9	3.1	0.2	—	27
34	Nebraska	73.8	8.0	14.3	2.2	1.7	—	26
35	Minnesota	75.0	9.7	6.7	6.3	2.2	—	25
36	Missouri	75.7	17.8	4.1	2.0	0.5	—	24
37	Wisconsin	76.0	10.4	8.4	3.7	1.5	—	24
38	Indiana	77.8	12.8	7.4	1.7	0.3	—	22
39	Ohio	78.1	17.0	3.0	1.7	0.1	—	22
40	Utah	79.1	1.5	14.6	3.3	1.4	—	21
41	Idaho	80.4	1.2	15.0	1.8	1.7	—	20

Rank by Percentage of Non-White Students	State	White	Black	Hispanic	Asian/ Pacific Islander	American Indian/ Alaska Native	Other	Percentage of Non-White Students
42	South Dakota	81.3	2.6	2.8	1.4	12.0	—	19
43	Wyoming	81.4	1.2	12.1	0.9	3.2	1.2	19
44	Iowa	82.2	5.1	8.1	2.1	0.5	2.0	18
45	Montana	83.1	1.1	2.8	1.2	11.8	—	17
46	Kentucky	84.3	11.0	3.3	1.3	0.1	—	16
47	North Dakota	84.5	2.4	2.5	1.2	9.4	—	16
48	New Hampshire	90.8	2.0	3.5	2.5	0.3	0.7	9
49	West Virginia	92.4	5.3	1.0	0.7	0.1	0.4	8
50	Maine	93.4	2.9	1.2	1.7	0.7	—	7
51	Vermont	93.5	1.8	1.2	1.6	0.2	1.7	7
	U.S. total	**54.1**	**16.8**	**22.1**	**5.1**	**1.2**	**.7**	**46**

Source: U.S. Department of Education, National Center for Education Statistics, Common Core of Data (CCD), "State Nonfiscal Survey of Public Elementary/Secondary Education," 1999–2000 and 2009–10. National Center for Education Statis, n.d.

differences exist among Asian students that are important for teachers to understand. Watch Khammany's interview with focus teacher Craig Cleveland.

Cultural pluralism. We often hear the United States referred to as a *melting pot*, a metaphor that conjures up visions of a big caldron into which we all jump, are warmed to the melting point, and stirred with a big spoon that blends us together until we lose unique and characteristic traits. This pretty much describes **assimilation,** the process of bringing persons of all races and ethnicities into the mainstream by having them behave in ways that align with the dominant culture. Some assimilation is inevitable, and even productive, but the notion that to be successful we all must look, think, and act in similar ways is unhealthy in a nation that values individualism and human rights.

Cultural pluralism involves the recognition that our nation is populated by a rich variety of people of varying races and ethnicities—and thus cultures—all with the potential to positively contribute to our common goal of a productive, free society. So what would a school that purposefully promotes cultural pluralism look like? Such a school would teach a curriculum that includes the history and contributions of a variety of cultures; would encourage the expression of cultural traditions in the school setting; would work toward closing achievement gaps that exist among racial, ethnic, and cultural groups; and would assure that no student is excluded from participation in school activities based on race, ethnicity, or any other aspect of culture.

Cultural diversity: Implications for teachers. Three broad concepts have implications for effective teaching and learning with regard to cultural diversity.

Global awareness and 21st-century skills. One of the themes of the Partnership for 21st Century Skills (P21) is global awareness, not just for inclusion in what we teach students but as a vital component for teachers themselves. **Global awareness** involves understanding the environmental, societal, cultural, political, and economic concepts and issues that impact our world. We must know what's happening on our planet and understand—as well as respect—the fact that there are many worldviews and perspectives among people (Partnership for 21st Century Skills, 2011). Not being globally aware is a disservice to our students.

Points of Reflection 2.3

What is your race? What is your ethnicity? How would you define your cultural identity?

Multicultural education. The response of many U.S. educators to the fast-paced growth of diversity is **multicultural education,** an approach that celebrates diversity and promotes equal educational opportunities. James Banks (2004), an expert in the field, tells us that multicultural education has several goals, including

- the creation of equal opportunities for students of all cultures
- the development of knowledge, attitudes, and skills needed to function successfully in a diverse society
- the promotion of communication and interaction among groups that work for the common good

Unfortunately, many teachers attempt to include multicultural education by simply observing February as Black History Month or including a social studies unit on Native Americans. Chances are these lessons have little impact on the day-to-day lives of students. Some people actually oppose any attempt to address cultural diversity, fearing that multicultural education will divert attention from more important curriculum or weaken the sense of continuity and tradition in a school. According to Banks, those who promote the inclusion of multicultural education neither approve of shallow inclusion of concepts nor intend for it to in any way weaken U.S. schools.

Sonia Nieto (2003), a leading author on the topic of multicultural education, is concerned about the simplistic ways in which multicultural education is taught in schools. She proposes that multicultural education permeate all areas of schooling. Nieto says that if we ask ourselves the following four questions and then spend our careers as educators answering them, facing the answers, and making continual corrections, we will take multicultural education where it needs to go:

- "Who's taking calculus?" (student population in challenging courses)
- "Which classes meet in the basement?" (distribution of the best resources and facilities)
- "Who's teaching the children?" (distribution of the most effective teachers in our profession)
- "How much are the children worth?" (issue of funding—where the money for education goes and why) (pp. 8–10)

Cultural responsiveness. To make multicultural education a reality in the classroom requires culturally responsive teaching. A culturally responsive teacher is sensitive to diversity and regularly asks questions such as these:

- Do I know the culture of each of my students beyond their obvious race and ethnicity?
- In what ways might I help my students see their similarities as clearly as their differences?
- How can I help validate the cultures represented in my classroom?
- How can I promote communication among all students?
- How can I assure equal opportunities for learning for all students?

LANGUAGE DIVERSITY

We have looked at race and ethnicity as major contributors to our cultural identity. These two factors are largely based on nature and can't be changed. Our language, however, is rooted in nurture and can be changed. **Language** is our primary means of communication; through it, we transmit knowledge. Assimilation in terms of language, with all students becoming proficient in English, has benefits because most public school classrooms are conducted in English. Few would argue with the notion that communicating proficiently in English is a major factor for academic success in the United States. The dilemma, however, is how to ensure this for all students.

Although some immigrants are already English proficient, for most English is not their first language. Some immigrant students arrive in the United States with strong records of academic achievement in their native languages, but most do not. Some students may have mastered conversational English in that they can speak and understand it, but they lack the ability to use English to keep up with grade-level coursework (Short & Fitzsimmons, 2007). School settings require **Standard English**, a composite of the language spoken by educated middle-class people in the United States. There are two forms of Standard English: one that's spoken in our everyday lives, and a more formal version that is written and considered grammatically correct (Gollnick & Chinn, 2013).

But even within the English language there are variations. In the United States there are at least 11 regional **dialects,** or deviations from standard language rules used by identifiable groups of people. You may have been the brunt of jokes when you traveled outside your region, or you may have poked fun at someone in your college dorm who spoke with a regional dialect unlike your own. Black English, sometimes referred to as **Ebonics,** is one of the best known and most controversial dialects in the United States. In most school settings, Black English, along with Hawaiian Pidgin and Appalachian English, are associated with lower levels of both intelligence and social class (Gollnick & Chinn, 2013).

Focus students Guillermo, from Mexico, and Khammany, from Laos, are part of the rich fabric of diversity at Roosevelt High School in Fresno, California.

English-language learners. Students with **limited English proficiency (LEP)** may speak and understand some English but not enough to be successful without additional assistance in classes taught in English. Non-English speakers and students with LEP are referred to as **English-language learners (ELLs).** So LEPs are ELLs. The five most frequently spoken non-English languages in the United States are Spanish, French, Chinese, Vietnamese, and Tagalog, a language spoken by many Filipinos (U.S. Census Bureau, 2010).

We serve ELLs through TESOL, ESOL, ESL, SEI, and any number of bilingual education program configurations whose acronyms seem to multiply on a regular basis. Confused? If your answer is "yes," you are more than justified. The dilemma faced by students who do not speak English well enough to learn at adequate levels in a timely fashion in U.S. schools is both recent and rapidly growing. Not only are we unsure about how best to serve this population, but also our vocabulary pertaining to this situation hasn't solidified either, with overlapping and indistinct definitions.

Whether in the mall or filling out a job application, the value of fluency in English is obvious to students who are ELLs. Children in immigrant families often believe that continuing to speak their native language will hurt them in school settings, where often language is the most obvious characteristic that sets them apart. Another phrase used to refer to students whose native language is other than English, regardless of their current level of English proficiency, is **language minority students**. Figure 2.5 is a snapshot of language minority students. An interesting fact to consider is that in 1910, 97% of immigrants to the United States were from Europe or Canada. One hundred years later, only about 10% of the immigrants to the United States are from these parts of the world (Rance-Roney, 2009).

Hector Mancia, one of our Rees Elementary focus students, is fluent in English, but in his home, Spanish is the predominant language. Watch Hector's interview with focus teacher Chris Roberts and Mom.

Craig Cleveland's class roll in Table 2.4 mirrors the ethnic mix at Roosevelt High School in Fresno, California. Although Craig is fluent in Spanish and that's very helpful,

Figure 2.5 Snapshot of language minority students in U.S. public schools

There are more than 14 million language minority students in K–12 schools.

Children from immigrant families comprise most of the language minority students.

About 1 in 5 children ages 5 to 17 in the United States are from immigrant families.

The population of children in immigrant families is growing faster than any other group of children in the nation.

Almost 80% of children from immigrant families were born in the United States, making them U.S. citizens.

Immigrant families continue to be concentrated in California, Texas, New York, Florida, Illinois, and New Jersey, but many states are now experiencing sharp increases.

English language learners in the United States speak more than 350 languages, with more than 75% speaking Spanish.

Language minority students are more likely than native English-speaking students to come from low-income families.

Language minority students tend to be more transient than native speakers, with families trying out different housing options or moving to build closer family connections.

English language learners with fluently bilingual and culturally responsive teachers tend to perform better in school than those without such teachers.

Source: National Center for Education Statistics (2011); Migration Policy Institute (2010); Rance-Roney (2009).

notice that most of the designated LEP students are of Asian ethnicity. To meet this challenge head on, Craig involves all his students by

Role-play is discussed in Chapter 5.

- giving them as many curricular and instructional choices as possible
- having them talk to each other in their native languages about class content
- using role-play to reinforce concepts
- reading picture books that make concepts more transparent
- using written materials in students' native languages when available

You don't have to be in an urban area to have ELLs in your classroom. One of our focus schools, Summit Primary, in Summit Station, Ohio, has gone from a mostly White, all English-speaking school to one with the 17 languages listed in Figure 2.6. Summit Station, considered rural just a decade or so ago, is now more like a suburb of the urban city of Columbus.

Services addressing ELL. The acronyms mentioned earlier indicate the variety of ways we attempt to meet the needs of English-language learners. Let's look briefly at three approaches to delivering ELL services to students: bilingual education, English as a second language (ESL), and structured English immersion (SEI).

Bilingual education. One of the primary responses of public education to the needs of English-language learners is **bilingual education,** the delivery of instruction in two languages. Attempts are made to preserve native language abilities as students acquire skills in English. Perhaps the greatest barrier to bilingual education programs is the lack of teachers who speak both English and another language fluently. In addition to speaking two languages fluently, however, teachers in bilingual programs must also be qualified to teach math, science, social studies, reading, writing, and other subjects. Angelica Reynosa, one of our focus teachers at Roosevelt High School in Fresno, California, teaches bilingual classes. In Angelica's lesson she switches between Spanish and English as she engages her students in their own learning.

English as a second language. In **English as a second language (ESL)** programs, students receive individualized assistance once or twice a week for about an hour each session. Unlike bilingual education, ESL services are delivered only in English. With

ESL, little or no emphasis is placed on preserving native language or culture, and ESL teachers do not need to speak another language. ESL programs are far less expensive than bilingual programs for school districts to implement if they have limited numbers of students to serve.

TABLE 2.4 Craig Cleveland's second period class roll

Name	Grade	Primary Language
1. Acevez, Miguel*	12	Spanish
2. Avelar, Margarita	11	Spanish
3. Chavez, Jennah	11	English
4. Conriquez-Reyes, Dan	11	Spanish
5. Douangsavanh, Khammany	12	Laotian
6. Esqueda, Meagan	12	English
7. Garcia, Alberto	11	Spanish
8. Garcia, Diana	11	Spanish
9. Garcia, Guadalupe	11	Spanish
10. Hurtado, Cassandra	11	Spanish
11. Lopez, Crystal	12	Spanish
12. Maldonado, Sarah	11	English
13. Martinez, Andrew Jame	11	Spanish
14. Perez, Yvonne	10	Spanish
15. Rodarte, Silvia	10	Spanish
16. Rodriguez, Antonio	11	Spanish
17. Rodriguez, Daniel	12	Spanish
18. Romero, Norma	11	Spanish
19. Sanchez, Javier*	11	Spanish
20. Sepulveda, Elizabeth	11	English
21. Toscano, Guillermo	11	English
22. Valles, Leanna Marie	10	English
23. Vang, Doug*	10	Hmong
24. Vang, Ka Yeng*	11	Hmong
25. Vang, Mong Her*	11	Hmong
26. Vang, Pa*	11	Hmong
27. Vang, Sandda*	11	Hmong
28. Vang, Xoua*	11	Hmong
29. Vang, Zoua*	11	Hmong
30. Yang, Don*	11	Hmong
31. Yang, Gloria*	10	Hmong
32. Yang, Tom*	11	Hmong

* Considered limited English proficient (LEP).

Figure 2.6 Native languages at Summit Primary School, Ohio

English	Russian	French
Somali	Macedonian	Creole
Ohomo	Serbo-Croatian	Korean
Bosnian/Albanian	Spanish	Japanese
Sierra Leone/Creole	German	Tagalog/Filipino
Chinese/Cantonese	Croatian	

Structured English immersion. In response to observations that we may be teaching *in* English, but possibly not *teaching* English itself, **structured English immersion (SEI)** was developed. This approach includes significant amounts of the school day dedicated to the explicit teaching of the English language, including other content to support instruction, but not as the primary focus. In SEI, students and teachers speak, read, and write in English. Teachers treat English as a foreign language and apply instructional methods used by teachers of foreign languages. Students are expected to transition out of SEI programs on a specified timetable with the skills necessary to be successful in English-only classes. SEI may be the logical solution, or partial solution, to helping groups of students who speak many different languages become proficient in English.

Points of Reflection 2.4

Is English your primary language? If not, what is? Has language ever been a barrier for you? Do you know people who are English-language learners?

As of 2009, three states—California, Arizona, and Massachusetts—had passed laws requiring the development of SEI programs to replace many of the existing bilingual programs. SEI is perhaps the least understood of the three approaches. States and districts are creating SEI programs, given their student populations and resources available (Clark, 2009). Figure 2.7 is a schedule for students in the SEI program at George Washington Elementary School in Madera, California, which enrolls more than 500 English-language learners in grades K to 6.

Language diversity: Implications for teachers. Language diversity presents a major challenge for educators in the United States. As we welcome increasing numbers of English-language learners to U.S. schools, both teaching and learning are affected. Here are some questions to keep in mind as you consider teaching in a language-diverse classroom:

- How can I make my classroom an academically, emotionally, and socially safe place for students who are ELLs?
- How can I include the cultures of students who are ELLs in my classroom?
- What resources will I need to communicate subject-area concepts to all students?
- How will I communicate with families who are ELLs?
- What community services might benefit students who are ELLs and their families?

The influx of diverse cultures with varied languages can be a source of richness for the United States rather than a phenomenon that is feared or avoided. Striking a balance between preserving native cultures and helping students adjust to life in a basically English-speaking environment is a worthy goal. Hugo Martinez, one of our Roosevelt High School focus students, is an English-language learner and his parents speak little or no English. Watch **Hugo's interview** with focus teacher Angelica Reynosa and his parents.

Now we turn our attention to the impact of diversity in family structure, religion, and socioeconomic status on students.

Figure 2.7 Structured English immersion sample schedule

Emphasis/Activity	Time Allotted
Pronunciation and listening skills	20 minutes
Vocabulary	30 minutes
Verb tense instruction	20 minutes
Sentence structure	20 minutes
Integrated grammar skills application	20 minutes
English reading and writing	60 minutes
Math (specially designed academic instruction in English)	40 minutes
Science, social science, P.E.	40 minutes

Source: Clark, C. (2009). The case for structured English immersion. *Educational Leadership, 66*(7), 45.

What Is the Impact on Students of Diversity in Family Structure, Religion, and Socioeconomic Status?

Students come to school wrapped in all the influences of family, religion, and socioeconomic status. They are whole people with complex factors that impact their attitudes toward, and achievement in, school. The more we understand about these influences, the better able we are to meet student needs.

FAMILY DIVERSITY

The 1970s *Brady Bunch* television situation comedy introduced many Americans to the concept of the blended family. Today, blended families come in a variety of configurations. Many students live with people other than their biological parents. With the divorce rate over 50%, single-parent homes have increased more than 300% since 1980. In 2011, 35% of K–12 students lived in single-parent homes, with Mississippi at 47% and Utah at 21% representing the range of state percentages (National Kids Count Program, 2013).

The increasing mobility of American families also adds to the instability of students' home lives. Consider, for example, the increasing influx of both documented (legal) and undocumented (illegal) immigrants and the rapidly growing migrant population. These families may move two to four times a year, with children changing schools, enrolling and withdrawing from the same school multiple times, or simply not going to school. Not only is all this mobility potentially harmful for students, but it can also wreak havoc on classroom teaching and learning.

Family diversity: Implications for teachers. Knowing with whom our students live can give teachers insight into behavior and achievement patterns. Ideally, families are our partners in educating children and adolescents. If this is going to be a reality in classrooms, our tactics for gaining and maintaining family support must be sensitive and flexible. Here are some questions to consider for your classroom:

- How can I restructure volunteer opportunities to include evenings and weekends?
- Are options available for child care that might lead to greater parental participation?
- Can the school provide easily accessible transportation to boost family involvement?
- Can I be more inclusive by practicing simple tactics such as addressing correspondence with "Dear family" rather than "Dear parents"?

In Chapter 9 we look more closely at societal issues as they relate to families, and in Chapter 12 we discuss teachers' responsibilities toward students' families.

RELIGIOUS DIVERSITY

Religion and faith have considerable daily influence on many of our lives. Over 230 million people, or about 4 out of 5 of us, affiliate with a religious group. About 96% of Americans who practice a religion align with Christianity. However, religious diversity exists in urban, suburban, and rural areas in every state; among Americans who align with a religion, about 1.4% are Jewish and about 0.5% align with each of Islam, Hinduism, and Buddhism (Pew Forum, 2010). Freedom to practice a religion, or not, is central to our common political, social, and cultural heritage.

Private schools are often established to cater to and promote a particular religion. Public schools are open to all and are obligated to serve all. Although separation of church and state is the official stance, religion has considerable influence on what we do in schools. Most of the issues teachers face in terms of religious diversity can be dealt with positively simply through awareness.

Religious diversity: Implications for teachers. Our response to religious diversity must be within legal bounds and delivered with sensitivity. Here are some questions classroom teachers should consider concerning religious diversity:

- How do I make sure tolerance is modeled in my classroom?
- How can I guard against being offensive to students of varying faiths?
- How should holidays be observed?
- How can I best respond to the community in which I live and teach?

Points of Reflection 2.5

What do you remember about family support, or lack of it, in your own K–12 experience? How did your religious affiliation and beliefs impact you and your school experiences?

The last question will be very important to you. Although singing "Jesus Loves Me" at nap time in a Southern kindergarten might be not only tolerated, but encouraged, singing the same song in a kindergarten in suburban Denver might be seen as offensive and grounds for dismissal.

SOCIOECONOMIC DIVERSITY

One in five U.S. school-age children lived in poverty in 2010 (U.S. Census Bureau, 2011). This means almost 16 million students are part of an area of diversity that not only transcends differences in gender, culture, language, family, and religion, but also has widespread impact on success in school. Although **socioeconomic status (SES)** involves more than income level, the major determinant of SES is how much money a family makes. The gap between the haves and the have-nots is wider in the United States than in most other industrialized nations. We might call this a **privilege gap**. In 2010, over 15 percent of U.S residents lived below the poverty line, the highest poverty rate since 1993 (National Poverty Center, 2013). The poverty line includes some often-complex variables, but may be simplified by looking at income threshold levels. In other words, the government has determined the maximum pre-tax income a family may have to be considered living in poverty. Table 2.5 provides an overview of the threshold levels for single- and two-parent incomes with one to five children.

Using the table we see that a family of four—two parents and two children—that earns less than about $22,811 a year is considered to be in poverty. A commonly used measure of a school's socioeconomic status is the percentage of students who qualify for free meals. A student is entitled to free meals if the family's income is below 130 percent of the annual income poverty level guideline. So the two children in our family of four would still qualify if the family makes less than 130% of $22,811, or $29,654. Students with family incomes below 185 percent of the annual income poverty level guideline are eligible for a reduced-price lunch. For our family, that's $42,200. Of the five billion meals provided to 31 million students in the 2011–12 school year, 59% were free of charge and 9% were reduced price (New American Foundation, 2013).

Challenges of low SES. The federal government acknowledges there are unique challenges in teaching students living in low-income settings. Title I funding, which is additional money given to public schools when more than 40% of the students qualify for free or reduced-price meals, is the government's attempt to make school experiences equitable (U.S. Department of Education, 2011). These funds are intended to help educators better meet the needs of students in low-income settings who often are students with histories of low achievement.

TABLE 2.5 Maximum income to be designated in poverty					
	Children in Home				
Adults	1	2	3	4	5
1	$15,504	$18,123	$22,891	$26,434	$29,494
2	$18,106	$22,811	$26,844	$30,056	$33,665

Source: U.S. Census Bureau, Poverty Thresholds for 2011.

A major study of children in poverty (Hernandez, 2011) confirmed what educators and researchers have recognized for years about the importance of students reading by third grade. Here are some important findings published by the Annie E. Casey Foundation (2010):

Points of Reflection 2.6

How has your own SES affected your school experiences? Were you aware of socioeconomic differences among your classmates? Did this affect how you viewed your own circumstances or the circumstances of other students?

- One in six children who do not read proficiently in third grade do not graduate from high school on time, a rate four times greater than the rate for proficient readers.

- 22% of children who have lived in poverty do not graduate from high school, compared to 6% of those children who have never been poor. If a child spends half or more of life in poverty, the percentage of non-completion of high school rises to 32%.

- 26% of children who were poor for at least a year *and* were not reading proficiently in third grade don't finish school, more than six times the rate for all third grade–proficient readers.

SES diversity: Implications for teachers. Ruby Payne (2008) tells us that teachers are in a position to support students and families in poverty by attending to their resource needs, which include:

- emotional resources—the stamina to withstand difficult and uncomfortable emotional situations
- mental resources—the ability to learn; to read, write, and compute
- spiritual resources—a belief that help is available through a higher power that alleviates hopelessness
- physical resources—having a healthy body
- support systems—knowing who to turn to for everyday and future needs and information

We discuss families and SES in Chapter 9 and religion in Chapter 10.

- relationships/role models—having people around who demonstrate appropriate relationships and successful living
- knowledge of unspoken rules—knowing how to get along in a particular group (pp. 17–18).

How Are Learning Differences Manifested in Schools?

The revered **intelligence quotient (IQ)** affixes a number to intelligence that—in one single freeze-frame—labels us for life. Scores on IQ tests may provide useful information, but they are no longer considered the final answer in determining a child's intellectual capacity. We have moved beyond the notion that intelligence is a fixed attribute. Researchers now believe that **intelligence**, a capacity for knowing and learning, can change and is manifested in various ways, as illustrated in Figure 2.8.

MULTIPLE INTELLIGENCES THEORY

Harvard psychologist Howard Gardner (1983) added an *s* to the word *intelligence* and revolutionized how we view the concept. He theorized that intelligence is multidimensional and that our individual brains work in ways that give each of us our own personal intelligences. He called this **multiple intelligences (MI) theory**. The nine designated intelligences proposed by Gardner are not meant as a complete list and there is little research to validate them. Their value lies in the implication that we learn differently. Gardner (1999) tells us that the intelligences can be activated and connected in very individual ways. Table 2.6 lists the nine intelligences and suggests ways to address them when planning for instruction.

Figure 2.8 How our views of intelligence have changed

TABLE 2.6 Multiple intelligences and planning for instruction

Disposition/Intelligence	Plan Lessons That Include
Verbal-Linguistic Intelligence	Speaking, writing, listening, reading, communicating
Logical Mathematical Intelligence	Finding patterns; making calculations; formulating hypotheses; recognizing cause and effect; working with numbers and reasoning
Spatial Intelligence	Representing ideas visually; creating mental images; noticing details; drawing; working puzzles; using colors and shapes
Bodily-Kinesthetic Intelligence	Activities requiring touch, movement, strength, speed, flexibility, hand-eye coordination, balance, and physical expression
Musical Intelligence	Listening, singing, and playing an instrument; using tone, beat, tempo, melody, pitch, and sound to create music
Interpersonal Intelligence	Working with others; understanding body language, moods, and feelings
Intrapersonal Intelligence	Setting goals; assessing personal abilities; reflecting on one's own strengths and weaknesses
Naturalist Intelligence	Identifying and classifying living things and natural objects; analyzing ecological and natural situations; learning from living things; working in natural settings
Existentialist Intelligence	Considering the big picture; imagining very large or very small quantities; seeking answers to seemingly unanswerable questions

Source: Silver, H. F., Strong, R. W., & Perini, M. J. (2000). *So each may learn: Integrating learning styles and multiple intelligences.* Alexandria, VA: Association for Supervision and Curriculum Development.

LEARNING STYLES

Whereas Gardner's theory of multiple intelligences helps explain different forms of intelligence with implications for how we learn, theories of **learning styles** give us more explicit insight into the variety of ways in which the learning process happens. The validity of learning styles theory has fallen out of favor in some education circles, but the basic information is helpful as just one piece of the puzzle of how we are different as learners. Perhaps the simplest way to characterize learning styles is through the four commonly accepted **learning modalities,** or preferences: auditory (hearing), visual (seeing), tactile (touching), and kinesthetic (moving). We use all four in the process of learning, but each individual tends to favor one or two over the others. Traditional classrooms rely most heavily on auditory and visual modalities, such as lectures and visual supports, especially in the upper grades, while active learning techniques such as hands-on manipulatives and group work activate tactile and kinesthetic modalities and may engage some students more effectively. Figure 2.9 helps us understand students who learn best through hearing, seeing, touching, or moving.

Differences in how we learn: Implications for teachers. Incorporating what we know about multiple intelligences and learning styles into our plans for instruction helps meet the learning needs of more students. Here are some questions to keep in mind when considering these challenges:

- Do I view the students in my classroom as a collection of individuals, each with unique ways of being smart?
- Do I continually seek to understand the ways in which my students learn best?
- Do I plan some experiences that address and incorporate each of the multiple intelligences?
- Does my awareness of my students' various learning styles change how I teach?

Acknowledging that there are many ways to learn leads us to understand that some students have particular difficulties learning, while others learn more quickly and perhaps more deeply. These are students with exceptionalities.

Points of Reflection 2.7

With which of Gardner's intelligences do you most closely align? Did your teachers accommodate your particular ways of being smart? Describe how the learning modalities impact how you learn best. How do you think you might strengthen the modality you use least?

Figure 2.9 Learning styles and learner preferences

Auditory learners tend to. . .
    Enjoy reading and being read to.
    Be able to explain concepts and scenarios verbally.
    Like music and hum to themselves.
    Enjoy both talking and listening.
Visual learners tend to. . .
    Have good spelling, note-taking, and organizational skills.
    Notice details and prefer neatness.
    Learn more if illustrations and charts accompany reading.
    Prefer quiet, serene surroundings.
Kinesthetic learners tend to. . .
    Be demonstrative, animated, and outgoing.
    Enjoy physical movement and manipulatives.
    Be willing to try new things.
    Be messy in habits and surroundings.
Tactile learners tend to. . .
    Prefer manipulatives when being introduced to a topic.
    Literally translate events and phenomena.
    Tolerate clutter.
    Be artistic in nature.

Source: From *Introduction to Middle School* (2nd ed., p. 59), by S. D. Powell, 2011, Boston: Allyn & Bacon. Copyright 2011.

Who Are Students with Exceptionalities and How Do We Serve Them?

Learners with abilities or disabilities that set them apart from other learners are often referred to as **students with exceptionalities**. Heward (2013) tells us that exceptional children

> differ from the norm (either below or above) to such an extent that they require an individualized program of special education and related services to fully benefit from education. . . . Thus, *exceptional children* . . . refers to children with learning and/or behavior problems, children with physical disabilities or sensory impairments, and children with superior intellectual abilities and/or special talents. (p. 7)

Some exceptionalities are the result of nature; others may be the result of injury or illness, aspects of nurture. Two factors are especially important when we consider the education of students with exceptionalities:

- Identification: Deciding who has what exceptionality and to what degree
- Intervention: Determining how best to meet their educational needs

STUDENTS WITH DISABILITIES

The categories of student exceptionalities considered to be disabilities, along with the percentage of all disabilities that they represent, are shown in Table 2.7. Considering all the categories, about 12% of American students receive **special education services**, services provided by schools to help students function and learn in ways optimal to the individual.

Many disabilities, especially those that impair daily functioning such as orthopedic disabilities and hearing, sight, and disease-related impairments are diagnosed before children enter school. However, disabilities that are more subtle, and perhaps academic, are often officially identified through a team of educators equipped with expertise and diagnostic tools.

A designation of **learning disabled (LD)**—accounting for almost half the students receiving special education services—includes a general category of students with disorders involving problems understanding or using language that result in significant differences between learning potential and achievement (Turnbull, Turnbull, Wehmeyer, & Shogren, 2013). Misdiagnosis or the absence of a diagnosis is problematic. Many students develop coping strategies that mask their learning problems for years and very possibly for life. Students with learning disabilities may

- have difficulties with word recognition and text comprehension
- feel overwhelmed by the idea of getting started
- struggle to organize and use the mechanics of writing
- have difficulty differentiating numbers or copying shapes
- have difficulty identifying, using, and monitoring problem-solving strategies (Turnbull et al., 2013)

Intervention for students with learning disabilities may include time each day with a special education teacher, often referred to as a **resource teacher,** who will help them develop strategies for school success.

Identification of **attention deficit hyperactivity disorder (ADHD)** may be as problematic as identification of learning disabilities. Students with ADHD demonstrate three defining characteristics: inattention, hyperactivity, and impulsivity. ADHD is defined by the American Psychological Association (APA, 2000) as the frequent existence of these three characteristics in a persistent pattern that is more severe than in others of the same age. The APA estimates that 3% to 7% of students in an average class have ADHD, which falls within the "Other health impairments" category of Table 2.7. The intervention for students with ADHD may include specific strategies to help modify

TABLE 2.7 Categories of disabilities and percentages of students served

Disability	Percentage of Total Students Receiving Special Services
Learning disabilities	42.3
Speech or language impairments	18.8
Other health impairments	11.6
Intellectual disability	7.8
Emotional disturbance	6.9
Autism	5.7
Multiple disabilities	2.1
Developmental delay	1.8
Hearing impairments	1.2
Orthopedic impairments	1.0
Visual impairments	0.4
Traumatic brain injury	0.4
Deaf-blindness	< 0.1

Source: U.S. Department of Education. (2011). Individuals with Disabilities Education Act (IDEA) data (Table 1.3). Washington, DC: Author.

behavior or medication. They receive services through special education only if they qualify through impairments other than ADHD (Turnbull et al., 2013).

LEGAL SUPPORT FOR STUDENTS WITH DISABILITIES

Until recently, students with disabilities were often isolated in a room at the end of a hallway—out of sight, out of mind—unless they happened to be seen walking as a group or boarding one of those short buses designed to hold that "special" group of kids. Prior to 1975, most students with disabilities, designated as special education students, weren't even in the same facilities as other students; there were no provisions for them to attend public schools. In 1975 the landmark legislation **Public Law 94-142 (PL 94-142)** changed all that.

Today special education is viewed as a service rather than a place to send children. The **Education for All Handicapped Children Act (PL 94-142)** opened all public schools to students with disabilities and mandated that students with disabilities be given the opportunity to benefit from special education services at no cost to their families. The law established six governing principles, listed in Figure 2.10, that apply to the education of students with disabilities.

In 1990, PL 94-142 was amended and renamed the **Individuals with Disabilities Education Act (IDEA)**. Students with autism and traumatic brain injury were added to those entitled to services under PL 94-142. A change in attitude and philosophy became evident in the law when the language changed from "disabled individuals" to "individuals with disabilities." The person comes first, with the disability secondary. In 2004, IDEA was reauthorized as the **Individuals with Disabilities Education Improvement Act**. This latest reauthorization is the most comprehensive yet, including all U.S. laws affecting children with disabilities in one statute (Heward, 2013).

Students without disabilities often form close relationships with students who have disabilities. These relationships are mutually beneficial.

Figure 2.10 Six principles governing the education of students with disabilities

1. **Zero reject**: A rule against excluding any student.
2. **Nondiscriminatory evaluation**: Requires schools to evaluate students fairly to determine if they have a disability and, if so, what kind and how extensive.
3. **Appropriate education**: Requires schools to provide individualized education programs for each student based on evaluation and augmented by related services and supplementary aids and services.
4. **Least restrictive environment**: Requires schools to educate students with disabilities alongside students without disabilities to the maximum extent appropriate for the students with disabilities.
5. **Procedural due process**: Provides safeguards for students against schools' actions, including a right to sue in court.
6. **Parental and student participation**: Requires schools to collaborate with parents and adolescent students in designing and carrying out special education programs.

Source: Turnbull, R., Turnbull, A., Wehmeyer, M., & Shogren, K. A. (2013). *Exceptional lives: Special education in today's schools* (7th ed.). Upper Saddle River, NJ: Merrill/Prentice Hall.

INDIVIDUALIZED EDUCATIONAL PROGRAMS

Serving students with disabilities (ages 3 to 21), regardless of the setting or combination of settings, requires an **individualized educational program (IEP)** as prescribed by Principle 3 of PL 94-142. An IEP is developed by educators, the family, and others as appropriate and involves a detailed plan to reach specific goals. A student's IEP must be revisited annually and the student's progress evaluated. Although IEP formats may vary, the required elements are listed in Figure 2.11.

An important part of an IEP is the designation of where and with whom students with disabilities will spend their school time. Principle 4 of PL 94–142 explicitly states that students with disabilities will be in the **least restrictive environment (LRE)** possible. The LRE is generally a setting with students who do not have disabilities that also meets the educational needs of the students with disabilities. This is often the regular education classroom.

INCLUSION

Whether or not you are interested in teaching students with disabilities, you may be doing exactly that in a regular inclusive classroom setting if a student's IEP designates it as the LRE. **Inclusion** means that "students attend their home school with their age and grade appropriate peers, participate in extracurricular activities, and receive special education and support services, to the maximum extent possible, in the general education classroom" (Rosenberg, O'Shea, & O'Shea, 2006, p. 14). If inclusion is not appropriate, chances are that a student with disabilities is served in a self-contained setting with other students with disabilities for much of the day, served by teachers with specific training to work with students with disabilities.

Simply placing students with disabilities in a regular classroom does not mean inclusive practices are in place or that a rigorous learning environment will be maintained. Teachers still must effectively focus on individualized objectives for every student, facilitate interactions and cooperative learning among students at every learning level, and maintain collaborative relationships with students, parents, and special educators. Given this approach, inclusion can be a healthy and positive experience for students without disabilities as well (Heward, 2013). There is a growing trend toward co-teaching, involving a regular classroom teacher and a special educator in a single classroom.

Inclusion is not embraced by all. Some parents believe their students with disabilities are better served in smaller, special education classrooms where they are more likely to receive one-on-one attention from teachers specifically trained to work with them. Some regular education teachers are wary of having a student with disabilities placed in their classrooms, an understandable hesitation if they receive little or no training in meeting the emotional, social, and cognitive needs of the student. Although the Council for Exceptional Children (CEC), which is the professional organization of special

Figure 2.11 Components of an IEP

An IEP must include a statement of:

1. student's present level of academic achievement and functional level
2. measurable academic and functional annual goals
3. how the student's progress toward meeting the annual goals will be measured
4. special education and related services to be provided to the student
5. extent to which the student will not participate with nondisabled students and the regular classroom
6. accommodations necessary to measure the student's achievement on state assessments
7. date of beginning services
8. postsecondary goals and transition services at age 16

Source: Turnbull, R., Turnbull, A., Wehmeyer, M., & Shogren, K. A. (2013). *Exceptional lives: Special education in today's schools.* Upper Saddle River, NJ: Merrill/Prentice Hall.

education, endorses inclusion, the official stance is support for a continuum of services with inclusion as a desirable goal, but not the only appropriate option for all students with disabilities. Focus student Trista Kutcher benefits from an inclusive environment. Read **Getting to Know Trista** carefully to see all the possibilities she embodies.

ASSISTIVE TECHNOLOGY

The Technology-Related Assistance to Individuals with Disabilities Act of 1988 authorized funding for **assistive technology** devices and services. These devices and services benefit students with disabilities by helping them communicate, increasing their mobility, and aiding in multiple ways that enhance their capacity to learn. The range of assistive technology includes wheelchairs, voice-activated and touch-screen word processors, sound-augmenting devices, and closed-captioned television (Turnbull et al., 2013). Technology is making it possible for students with disabilities to function and learn at levels unimaginable only a decade ago.

STUDENTS DESIGNATED AS GIFTED AND TALENTED

Characteristics of students who are **gifted and talented** include phrases such as

- evidence of high performance capabilities
- intellectual, creative, artistic, or leadership ability well beyond average
- excelling in specific academic fields

Identification of students who are gifted and talented can be objective or quite subjective, depending on the criteria accepted by a particular school district. When IQ is used for identification, the threshold number is 125 to 130, achieved by only about 2% to 3% of the general student population. However, evaluating creativity along with IQ testing allows more students to benefit from gifted and talented services.

Services for students who are gifted and talented vary significantly and include pull-out programs with students working on projects or an accelerated curriculum. In-school options such as grade skipping, concurrent enrollment in two levels of schooling, curriculum compacting (faster pace), and advanced placement courses (rigorous high school courses with possible college credit for completion) enhance the opportunities of students designated as gifted and talented. There are also specifically designed magnet schools for them.

When students who are gifted and talented are in regular classrooms—and most are—we can better meet their needs by

- being flexible
- accepting unusual ideas and encouraging alternative solutions to problems
- not being intimidated by the intellectual and creative capabilities of students who have IQs that exceed our own
- differentiating instruction often

Differentiated instruction is discussed in Chapter 4.

GETTING TO KNOW TRISTA

Trista Kutcher is one of our focus students. She is a very special young lady. Her happy life and remarkable accomplishments are evidence of what dedicated parents and sensitive, knowledgeable education professionals can do to help children, even those with disabilities, realize their potential. Trista has Down syndrome.

Trista's mom, ReBecca, teaches eighth grade English language arts at Cario Middle School in Mount Pleasant, South Carolina, and Trista's dad, Joe, teaches math at Wando High School, where Trista is a freshman. Trista has two younger sisters, Suzanna, age 12, and Samantha, age 4. As a member of the 2003 USA Special Olympics gymnastics team, Trista won five medals at the Dublin, Ireland, games. She is a cheerleader at Wando High and is included in many regular education classes. Read this poignant story written by ReBecca, Trista's mom.

We Danced

by ReBecca Kutcher

Joe and I had the perfect life. . . . We dated in high school and married right out of college. Life was grand! We got pregnant and things were sailing along as we **danced** through life. People would often ask, "What do you want—a boy or a girl?" I never said more than my prayer that the baby would be healthy! Joe's response was that we just wished for "10 fingers and 10 toes." Deep down, however, I really wanted a little girl with blond hair and blue eyes who would **dance** in a recital, **dance** on the beach, and **dance** into everyone's heart!

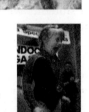

The pregnancy was perfect, as was the delivery. Joe and I held Trista Sue and cooed over her late into the night.

A few hours later the music stopped. The doctors told us our little blond-haired, blue-eyed Trista Sue had Down syndrome. Joe and I no longer felt like **dancing.**

Knowing breastfeeding was important for her in many ways, I wanted to continue her feeding schedule, even though she was still in the hospital. I would wake up during the night at 1:00 and 5:00 and travel to the hospital to nurse her. I would waltz around the room with her in my arms. How wonderful those **dances** were . . . just us, loving each other.

I decided I was going to get Trista involved in activities that every "normal" girl does. At age two I took her to Tapios School of Dance and Gymnastics. I asked the owner if Trista could enroll in her tap and ballet classes. She welcomed her with open arms and taught her to dance with grace and poise.

Around this time Trista's sister, Suzanna, was born. How proud she was to be a big sister! Oh, the mischief they could get into together. Eventually, Trista and Suzanna were in a dance recital together, Trista 6 and Suzanna 3. Suzanna was amazed at the lights and people in the audience. She completely forgot her dance. Big sister to the rescue! Trista decided this was unacceptable and took matters into her own hands. Trista marched across the stage, positioned herself behind Suzanna, and proceeded to move her arms and legs for her. The audience roared with laughter while Trista made Suzanna **dance.**

When Trista started school, we decided she should be included in the regular classroom. Speech was definitely a concern and having her with the other kids would be great modeling. Each of her accomplishments was celebrated by kids in the class and by teachers who were initially worried about how they would teach her.

Through elementary and middle school Trista thrived, making friends and showing all of us what she could do, rather than what she couldn't do. In high school she eats, drinks, and sleeps cheering during the fall and, like her gymnastics, loves it dearly. The other girls could not be more accepting and supportive of her.

Along with regular gymnastics competitions, Trista competed in Special Olympics gymnastics. She was the state champion from the age of 8. Being involved provided many opportunities for independence and pride. During the summer of 2002, she received another very important letter. It asked her to be a part of the Special Olympics Team USA for the 2003 World Games. As she opened that letter she beamed from ear to ear. This adventure was one of meeting the governor and the mayor, being featured in a commercial, being on the news and in the newspaper regularly, and having an official day in Mt. Pleasant proclaimed by the mayor as Trista Kutcher Day! Everywhere we went people knew her. Suzanna began to make a joke about all of us being her entourage! Never did we think we would be **dancing in her shadow!** She was leading us on the adventure of a lifetime!

The competition in Ireland was tough but she was ready! She won five medals, two of which were gold! As she stood on the podium, she cried and told me later that she was so proud because "She did it!" After the awards ceremony, the audience flooded the gym floor, joined hands, and **danced the Irish jig.** What a celebration!

The **dance** has been wonderful. The music has played nonstop for 15 years! Our dance began with three people on the floor . . . and ended with **a whole community kicking up its heels!**

Poem Written by Trista's Sister

Trista-
Famous, idol,
Likes to run, jump, and play,
Annoys me when she says she is right when she is wrong.
She can do cartwheels—I wish I could.
She wishes she could play basketball like me.
I do not like to go to the same parties as she does
Because then I feel like I have to look after her
and I cannot have fun.
It amazes me when she does flips and is not scared.
It makes me sad when she says hi to someone
and they do not respond back to her.
I am proud to tell my friends about all the gold medals she has.
I like when she smiles and her nose crunches up . . . it is so cute.
She has Down syndrome.
She is my sister!

By Suzanna Kutcher
12 years old

Now watch **Trista's story** to meet Trista and some of the people who impact her life.

Students with exceptionalities: Implications for teachers. The most important aspect of teaching students with exceptionalities is to recognize that each student is an individual with both learning potential and at least part of his or her mind "amply equipped to thrive" (Levine, 2003, p. 13). Seeing and seeking a student's strengths before, or concurrently with, our acknowledging limitations helps us embrace possibilities for each individual, whether in an inclusive classroom or in a special education setting.

Now that you know more about how students differ, consider the impact of social media on communication and teaching and learning. Social media tools, and the variety of ways of using them, are growing exponentially. When thinking about using social media in the classroom, we recognize our responsibility as teachers to help students become wise consumers of technology, understanding the need for vigilance to stay safe in cyberspace. This chapter's *SocialMEdia* feature addresses safety concerns.

Including students with exceptionalities in the classroom is beneficial to all students because instruction is delivered in a variety of ways to engage diverse learners. To do so successfully, teachers need support and time for planning, as well as an appropriate curriculum, materials, and resources. Ongoing professional development is essential.

Here are some questions teachers of inclusive classrooms need to ask:

- Do I take the time to get to know each student as an individual?
- Do I look for the strengths and abilities of all my students?

Points of Reflection 2.8

Were you diagnosed with a disability while in PreK–12 school? If so, explain. Did you know students who were diagnosed with a disability while in PreK–12 school? If so, describe one.

Were you designated as gifted and talented? If so, what do you remember about being set apart from other kids?

In Chapter 9 we address the dangers inherent in social media, such as cyberbullying.

SocialMEdia

Cybercitizenship is a recently coined term referring to the responsibilities of those who use social media. A recent survey by the National Cyber Security Alliance showed that over 90% of the adults in K–12 schools believe we should teach students how to be safe and ethical cybercitizens. In 2012 the federal government passed the Children's Online Privacy Protection Act (COPPA), a bill designed to make more transparent the operations of Web sites that cater to children. But, as with so many societal issues, legislating safety must be accompanied by both common sense and vigilance. The American Academy of Pediatrics (2011) tells us limited self-regulation and susceptibility to peer pressure put children and adolescents at risk when using social media.

The immediacy and instant gratification of social media, coupled with the vulnerability of children and adolescents, make safety hazards likely and our involvement absolutely necessary. Many lists of safety/ethics rules have been written by private organizations, nonprofit groups, school districts, and even the FBI. When examined side-by-side they all include basically the same advice. Here's a summary of the most common tips for helping students stay safe as they use the Internet.

1. Always abide by school and home guidelines for when and how to use the Internet.

2. Treat people that you don't know on the Internet as strangers. Get to know your "online friends" just as you get to know all of your other friends.
3. Do not give out any personal information related to your family, friends, or yourself like passwords, addresses, and phone numbers.
4. Always tell an adult if you see something online that you know is wrong or that makes you feel uncomfortable. Never respond to such messages.
5. Never send out your picture without your parents' permission.
6. Don't respond when offered something such as gifts or money.
7. Don't ever accept a gift or an offer that involves having someone visit your house.
8. Never agree to meet someone you've met online in person unless you discuss it with your parents and an adult goes with you.
9. Never respond to provocative, rude, obscene, or threatening messages.
10. Always check with parents before downloading or installing software or doing anything that may jeopardize anyone's privacy.

- Is cooperative learning used frequently in my classroom?
- Do I continually diagnose the progress of my students and adjust my instruction appropriately?

During your field experiences, look closely for evidence of inclusion. Ask teachers to help you understand more about students with exceptionalities.

CONCLUDING THOUGHTS

Now that we have looked at how students are similar and how they are different, perhaps the concept that all students can learn seems elusive to you. How, indeed, do we make "all children can learn" a reality given the circumstances that pervade some children's lives?

Understanding the uniqueness of each of us calls for an absolute commitment to individuality. Thomas Jefferson expressed the thought that there is nothing so unequal as the equal treatment of unequals. All children are equal in terms of their right to fulfill their own promise, but certainly children are unequal in the many ways we have discussed. The spirit of inclusion draws them all in; the unwavering determination to meet their needs requires attention and action based on each individual.

Yes, all children can learn. This statement is logically followed by these complex questions:

What can they learn?

When can they learn it?

In what ways will they learn it best?

As always, "And how are the children?" should be the center of our focus.

After reading the *Chapter in Review*, interact with Craig Cleveland in this chapter's *Developing Professional Competence*.

Chapter in Review

How are we similar?

- As human beings, we are more similar than dissimilar.
- Nature (genetics) influences human traits we are born with.
- Nurture (environment) influences who we are through every aspect of our lives that nature does not determine.
- Human beings share the same basic hierarchy of needs.
- We all experience physical, cognitive, emotional, social, and character development.

How are gender differences manifested?

- Anatomical differences between males and females determine sex, whereas gender is the sense of being male or female.
- Gender determines many of the choices we make and the expectations others have for us.
- Homosexuality is often the basis of discrimination.

How are cultural and language diversity manifested in schools?

- Race, although a social, political, economic, and psychological reality, is based solely on physical characteristics.
- Racism is a form of prejudice stemming from a belief that one race is superior to another.
- Ethnicity refers to a person's country of origin.
- Culture has many components and is learned, shared, and adaptive.
- Cultural identity relies on many factors, such as race, ethnicity, language, gender, religion, income level, values, and beliefs.
- Multiculturalism involves beliefs concerning the value of looking at the world through the eyes of people who are different from us.
- To be most effective, multicultural education needs to permeate all areas of schooling.
- Language is an aspect of cultural identity that can be augmented and enhanced.
- Bilingual education involves instruction delivered in two languages.
- English as a second language (ESL) is a pull-out program assisting English-language learners in English only.
- Structured English immersion (SEI) includes significant amounts of the school day dedicated to the explicit teaching of the English language, with other content secondary.

What is the impact on students of diversity in family structure, religion, and socioeconomic status?

- Blended families and family structures other than two biological parents and children are becoming more prevalent.
- The increasing mobility of American families potentially harms students and wreaks havoc on classrooms.
- Religion and faith have considerable influence on lifestyles and choices.
- The religious beliefs of families and communities influence decisions that relate to school issues.
- The gap between the haves and have-nots is wider in the United States than in most other nations.
- Low-income settings often contribute to lower achievement.

How are learning differences manifested in schools?

- There are many different ways to be smart and to exhibit intelligence.
- We all have learning style preferences.

- Students with exceptionalities include those with disabilities and those considered gifted and talented.
- A designation of learning disabled accounts for about half of students receiving special services.
- The concept of least restrictive environment means that students with disabilities are to be placed in the highest-functioning setting possible, usually the regular education classroom.
- Students considered gifted and talented are most likely to be included in the regular education classroom and pulled out for special classes for brief periods of time.

Developing Professional Competence

Thoughtfully reading this scenario and responding to the items that follow it will help you prepare for licensure exams.

In this chapter we learned about one of Craig Cleveland's classes. Craig's student teacher this semester, Jenny Langley, grew up in the suburbs of Fresno and attends Fresno State. Jenny never attended a Title I school and her PreK–12 school experiences were ideal by most standards, complete with advanced placement classes, a stable group of friends, and extracurricular activities that rounded out her high school years. In a conversation several weeks before her student teaching semester began, Craig discovered that Jenny's peer group had little diversity—although Jenny told him she had lots of experience with diversity because she was in the International Baccalaureate program and she knew two exchange students, one from Japan and one from Russia. Craig smiled to himself as she talked about her open-minded approach with those who are different from herself, knowing she was about to begin one of the most turbulent experiences of her young life.

Think through this scenario and answer the following multiple-choice questions:

1. Guillermo, one of our focus students, is a really good-hearted young man with acceptable English skills and a desire to help other people. Before and after class, Jenny might be able to best learn more about students with LEP by:
   a. Asking Guillermo to help her talk more easily with students whose primary language is Spanish.
   b. Staying close to Guillermo and listening to his casual conversations in both English and Spanish.
   c. Talking with Guillermo about what he knows about students who are ELLs.
   d. Watching Guillermo's easy demeanor with other students and trying to develop the same persona.

2. Craig explains Khammany's situation to Jenny by telling her about Khammany, Mom, and younger brother moving into a project apartment with only two rooms and the difficulties they face since Dad died last year. Khammany, one of our focus students, has to work at least 30 hours a week to help support the family. Which of the following benefits of longer blocks of class time will Craig probably say is most important to Khammany?
   a. During the 100-minute class, Khammany has more time to concentrate on history.
   b. The longer blocks afford more time for a variety of participation activities.
   c. The block allows for time to begin homework assignments with Craig available to assist.
   d. Khammany can earn eight credits per year.

3. Remember Craig's class list? Which is the least important reason that longer blocks of class time benefit ELLs?
   a. They get to spend more concentrated time on one subject with one teacher.
   b. There is more time to fully develop a concept, using a variety of communication methods.
   c. There are fewer subjects to learn at a time.
   d. Fewer passing periods limit opportunities to be involved in turf issues among diverse groups of students.

4. What do you think will be the best way for Jenny to begin to acclimate to her student teaching situation?
   a. Study the culture of the students she will encounter at Roosevelt.
   b. Spend at least 5 days simply shadowing Craig.
   c. Jump in and begin working with students.
   d. Spend the month before student teaching brushing up on her Spanish-language skills from taking 2 years of Spanish in high school.

5. Jenny has started her 16-week student teaching experience with enthusiasm based on the fact that she had 2 years of Spanish in high school. Which reason most likely causes her enthusiasm to quickly dim?
   a. She can read and write in Spanish to a moderate degree, but conversational Spanish is another story.

b. There aren't many written resources in Craig's classroom that are in Spanish.
c. Most of the students with LEP are Hmong.
d. Craig's class is not designated as a bilingual class.

Now it's time for you to respond to three short essay items. In your responses, be sure to address all the dilemmas and questions posed in each item. Each response should be between one half and one full double-spaced page. As you consider your responses, think about how these standards may apply.

National Board of Professional Teaching Standards, Proposition 1: Accomplished teachers recognize that in a multicultural nation students bring to schools a plethora of abilities and attitudes and aptitudes that are valued differently by the community, the school, and the family.

InTASC Standard #1: Learner Development

The teacher understands how learners grow and develop, recognizing that patterns of learning and development vary individually within and across the cognitive, linguistic, social, emotional, and physical areas, and designs and implements developmentally appropriate and challenging learning experiences.

InTASC Standard #2: Learning Differences

The teacher uses understanding of individual differences and diverse cultures and communities to ensure inclusive learning environments that enable each learner to meet high standards.

6. Jenny is walking into a world that is foreign to her. Explain two reasons why she may be apprehensive or even fearful.

7. As a suburbanite from a middle-income family, Jenny is now experiencing adolescents who live in poverty. What characteristics might the students display that will require Jenny to adjust her attitudes and expectations to meet their needs effectively?

8. Given what we know about the students at Roosevelt, which of the three methods for serving their language needs (bilingual education, ESL, SEI) would you recommend, and why?

Dear Reader

We live in a country where formal schooling of some sort is mandatory for children and adolescents. We have all participated. Whether in a public or private facility, or in a home, our experiences with schooling have a real impact on our viewpoint of what it means to be a student. In this chapter we consider a range of purposes of schooling. But first, we take a look at the differences between schooling and education. Mark Twain once said, "I have never let my schooling interfere with my education." This scathing view of formal schooling should drive us to be teachers who enhance, rather than impede, learning.

As we examine public and private K–12 schools in a variety of settings, think about whether teaching is a career you want to pursue and, if so, what your teaching identity might be. Take your time considering the information about schools and, in particular, our four focus schools introduced in this chapter. Can you envision yourself in a suburban elementary school? How about a middle school in a rural area or an inner city high school? Perhaps early childhood education is your choice. The world of teaching is wide open for you!

In this chapter we explore schools in the United States by addressing these focus questions:

- What are the purposes of public schools in the United States?
- What is the culture of a school?
- How do school venues differ?
- What is school like at different levels?
- What are the three principal settings of U.S. schools?
- What is an effective school?

Schools are centers of our communities, foundations of our citizenry, targets of political and ethical debate, mirrors and shapers of our society, and keepers of the hopes and dreams of parents and children. Without exception, the greeting "And how are the children?" should be on the lips and in the hearts of every adult in every U.S. school. Mandatory attendance makes some form of schooling a common factor in our society. As such, we have all experienced schools. But as with all human endeavors, our perspectives differ. Perspective, however, isn't the only reason we view schools differently—the schools themselves are different. Let's begin our exploration of schools in the United States.

Teaching in Focus

Brandi Wade teaches kindergarten at Summit Primary School in Summit Station, Ohio. She has witnessed many changes at her school as families have moved into the once rural area just outside Columbus. Housing developments have sprung up all around the school, and change has been ongoing for several years. The small town of Summit Station is now surrounded by a thriving suburban-like area, and there are no signs that growth is slowing down. The Licking Heights School District continues to build more and bigger schools to accommodate the influx of families.

Summit Primary is the only K–2 school in the district. This is a purposeful configuration. Principal Laura Hill says she likes the format because she has every kindergarten, first grade, and second grade teacher in the district right in her building. This lends a great deal of consistency to how children are taught and what and when they learn as Summit Primary retains its specialty of early childhood education. The grade-level teachers work together as teams to provide instruction that is developmentally appropriate for young children.

Along with the growth has come diversity. Once a school comprised of predominantly White children with a relatively small Black population, all English speaking, Summit Primary now serves children with a variety of heritages who speak any of 17 different languages. This diversity of languages presents a major challenge for the Summit teachers. In Brandi's two kindergarten classes, five languages other than English are represented, along with twin boys from Somalia. A special teacher works with these learners who speak limited or no English to help them acquire the English they need to make learning kindergarten skills an easier and more natural process. Brandi's dedication to all children in her kindergarten classes, regardless of their background, is evident in her interactions with, and conversations about, "her kids." Watch **Brandi's interview** to get to know her better.

What Are the Purposes of Public Schools in the United States?

We begin our discussion of the similarities and differences among schools by considering distinctions between education and schooling. We then consider the purposes of **public schools** in the United States, those funded *by* the public, and accountable *to* the public, through local, state, and federal governments.

DISTINCTIONS BETWEEN EDUCATION AND SCHOOLING

Remember in geometry class when the teacher told you that a straight line on the chalkboard wasn't a line but rather a line segment? You may have rolled your eyes and mumbled, "What difference does it make?" Well, for the content of the geometry class (and the inevitable test), it certainly mattered. But did your English teacher ever ask you to draw a *line segment* under a prepositional phrase in a sentence? Probably not. Outside the context of geometry class, most of us find it unnecessary to make a distinction between a line and a line segment.

So it is with the words *education* and *schooling*. As teachers, we need to understand the differences. Once we do, although we may use the words interchangeably in some contexts, we are always aware that distinctions do exist.

Education. Although it may not seem obvious, there is a distinct difference between education and schooling. **Education** is the lifelong process of learning. Every day of our lives, in every possible setting, we learn. When we see, hear, feel, or sense, we are learning. This is education—our lifelong formal and informal process of learning.

Schooling. One specific, formalized element of education is **schooling**. Schools are institutions specifically designed to educate in formal ways. They involve organization and structure, both of which should be determined primarily by the needs of those who learn, as well as those who teach.

A discussion of American schools is often called a discussion of American education. That's fine. It's understood that we are talking about what goes on in school settings. The hope is that the education occurring in school is productive and accurate in nature, but, regardless, learning of some kind is taking place just like it does continually in every walk of life. As teachers we are called educators. As long as we recognize and acknowledge that the whole world educates children, we may continue to interchange the words *education* and *schooling,* and *educator* and *teacher.*

COMPLEMENTARY PURPOSES OF PUBLIC SCHOOLS

There's no need to settle on—or settle for—narrowly defined purposes for public schooling. Although there are many, we will consider eight. These purposes may be best understood and put into perspective using the concept of balance. Each pair of purposes discussed is more complementary than oppositional. They balance each other.

Transmitting society and reconstructing society. Both of these purposes deal with societal knowledge and values. On the more conservative side, *transmitting society* involves public schools both reflecting and supporting our American society. This is a process called socialization. **Socialization** occurs through a variety of influences including home, family, place of worship, print and electronic media, peers, and of course, school. Students are influenced through the subjects we offer and the content of those subjects, as well as through our instruction, both actions and words. Transmitting society means promoting the concepts that preserve our democratic way of life and discouraging concepts that oppose it. Transmitting society is unifying, emphasizing what we have in common rather than our differences.

Teachers walk a fine line when it comes to achieving the purpose of transmitting society while continuing to respect the students and their families who bring differing societal views with them into the classroom. What many of us take for granted may be new and unusual to a growing number of our students. A democratic way of life involves acceptance of differences; in American schools, acceptance should escalate to the embracing of differences. This in itself is transmitting a society that preserves democracy.

The complement of transmitting society is *reconstructing society,* challenging knowledge and values with an eye toward improvement. The concept of social reconstruction involves teaching students to recognize what needs to change, identifying the means of change, and encouraging students to work proactively for a common goal. Rather than only passing down knowledge and values to preserve society's status quo, students are urged to examine different aspects of our society, keep what is worthwhile, and seek to change or discard what isn't.

As you can see, transmitting society and reconstructing society do not have to be opposing purposes. When they are balanced, it is possible to pass on the best of society while questioning and changing other aspects of society for the better.

Participation in society and academic learning. Preparing students to *participate in society* involves socialization plus the teaching of survival skills that will help them to get along with others; obtain and keep employment; be politically, morally, and socially proactive; and be productive members of a community, with a sense of responsibility. Public schools, along with other institutions and groups, certainly help prepare students for participation in society.

At the same time as we prepare students to participate in society we facilitate *academic learning.* Every subject area includes a body of knowledge that is, by and large, "society free," or independent from what's going on at the time within society. For instance, mathematical formulas, classic literature, history, and geography all have academic aspects that change little with time. Plato maintained that this kind of academic knowledge is the foundation for seeking truth that is not dependent on, or influenced by, current society, and that seeking of truth is a necessary purpose of education.

He encouraged students to look at possibilities through the lens of formal academic learning and to question the world around them.

In *A Place Called School*, Goodlad (1984) looked at many documents that have addressed the question "What is the purpose of schooling?" He concluded there are four broad goals:

1. Academic: Imparting knowledge and intellectual skills
2. Vocational: Preparing for the world of work
3. Social and civic: Participating in a democratic society
4. Personal: Developing self-expression and talent

Goal 1 obviously fits into the academic learning purpose, whereas the other three prepare students to participate in society.

Individual needs and collective needs. These two purposes most certainly go hand in hand. A citizenry of formally educated individuals serves the collective good. American public schools provide opportunities for children to reach their learning potential. Some schools make this opportunity more feasible and more readily attainable than others.

Meeting the *individual needs* of students is sometimes referred to as the development of *human capital*. These words seem mechanistic and cold until we consider them separately. The word *human* describes us. The word *capital* in this sense is a noun meaning the knowledge and skills derived from education, training, and experience. The development of human capital is directly related to the well-being of individuals. It takes groups of people—the collective—to preserve our democratic way of life.

To serve *collective needs*, then, is to view the purpose of American schools as ensuring strong, free communities by teaching knowledge as well as values such as honesty, hard work, civility, respect, compassion, and patriotism. The goals for the collective include economic prosperity, maintenance of our national security, and the development of a sense of both humanity and democratic ideals.

In American public schools we teach individual students who, together, form the collective of our country. The stronger the collective, the more opportunities there are for the individual.

These two purposes of public education are complementary and interdependent.

Sustaining for today and preparing for tomorrow. Schools *sustain for today* by providing a set of experiences for students. Yes, many of them will be successful in school. Some will go on to college and most will have productive careers. But some will not. Not because American public schools want it to be so, but because the reality is that not all students will make the transition from school to adulthood and become citizens who contribute in positive ways. Some will drop out of school and lack the knowledge, skills, and/or credibility to fulfill their potential in adult life. Some will experience debilitating life circumstances or even death before they complete high school. What we need to remember in terms of schools serving to sustain for today is that children—regardless of what their futures hold—deserve a warm, caring, nurturing environment where they have opportunities to learn and grow. Ideally, home and family provide this environment. Whether that's the case or not, American public schools should provide this environment day after day, year after year, as we ask one another, "And how are the children?"

Points of Reflection 3.1

With which pair of the eight complementary purposes of public schools do you identify most? Explain your choice.

Elliot Eisner (2004), one of our most influential educators, wrote, "Preparation for tomorrow is best served by meaningful education today" (p. 10). American public education that sustains for today, *prepares for tomorrow*. It's a building process, a self-perpetuating cycle.

Preserving our democratic way of life is accomplished through the fulfillment of these eight purposes and other related goals. Craig Cleveland writes about the learning

Teaching in Focus

Craig Cleveland, history teacher, Roosevelt High School, California. *In his own words. . . .*

Much of what you need to know about effective teaching and learning is found within yourself already. The environment and circumstances in which you learned powerful and life-changing lessons may have been in school or elsewhere in life. The relevant and meaningful lessons your students learn will need to be both inside and outside the school if education is going to have the power to transform them into thoughtful mature people.

Essential to creating a learning environment in the classroom is a researched and clearly articulated philosophy about how learning happens. When such a philosophy is in place, teachers are able to make sound and reliable instructional decisions and refinements.

Continuing my education in a graduate program, reading professional literature, regularly reflecting on my teaching with an eye toward improvement, and having ongoing conversations with friends and colleagues help make more concrete my beliefs about how learning happens. A ninth grade student of mine made the insightful statement, "Learning is natural." I believe learning is natural when the learner has interest and a voice as a participant within the learning environment of school.

that occurs both inside and outside of school, the education that you, as teacher candidates, are experiencing. He tells us that both education and schooling, as defined earlier, lead to learning for our students. He advises us to continue to develop as professionals in his *Teaching in Focus* feature.

Now let's look inside schools in the United States to examine both their commonalities and some of their differences, beginning with what may seem like an intangible but actually can be sensed in every aspect of schooling: the culture of a school.

What Is the Culture of a School?

School culture is the context of learning experiences; it's the prevailing atmosphere of the school. As places where people work together and learn together, schools function according to their cultures. Noted educator Roland Barth (2001) tells us, "A school's culture dictates, in no uncertain terms, 'the way we do things around here.' Ultimately, a school's culture has far more influence on life and learning in the schoolhouse than the state department of education, the superintendent, the school board, or even the principal can ever have" (p. 7).

A school's culture can be a positive force for learning or a negative influence that interferes with learning. It is important to recognize elements of a school's culture, both the forces that created it and those that perpetuate it. If the culture is positive, acknowledging the influential forces and then reinforcing them keeps the culture vibrant and growing. If the culture is negative or apathetic, altering it begins with looking closely at the influential forces and finding ways to begin the change process.

From a new teacher's standpoint, a positive school culture may be evident when experienced teachers consistently ask how things are going and offer to help with lessons, materials, managing student behavior, paperwork, and so on. Hearing teachers talking and laughing together, sharing what works in their classrooms, and speaking of students with caring and concerned attitudes demonstrates positive culture. On the other hand, when a school seems to have a territorial atmosphere with cliques of teachers criticizing other teachers and the principal, when offers of assistance are few, when students are spoken of primarily in critical terms, a new teacher will likely sense a negative culture. Because teachers comprise most of the adults in a school, their influence on school culture is immense.

TEACHERS AND SCHOOL CULTURE

Teachers' instructional skills and professionalism either improve a school's culture or keep it stagnant or negative. The level of respect teachers engender among their colleagues and in the community either builds a positive culture or serves to drag it down. This level of respect has much to do with the relationships that exist among a school's adults, which, in turn, influence the ways teachers relate to students. Because all teachers, experienced and new, have considerable influence on school culture, they must be instrumental in maintaining a positive culture or helping to change a negative culture into a more positive one.

CHANGING SCHOOL CULTURE

A school's culture can change. Can it change quickly or easily? Definitely not when improvement is the goal. Positive culture shifts require strong leadership, ownership of the problems and potential solutions by the adults in the school, and a steady, conscious influx of both attitudes and actions that produce the desired results. In contrast, changing a school culture from positive to negative may only require apathy and neglect.

All components of American education discussed in this text influence a school's culture. For instance, what is taught in a school can be dynamic and challenging, or mediocre and boring. Not only *what* is taught, but *how* it is taught, influences culture. The level of respect teachers and students have for one another influences school culture as does the level of teacher expectations for student success. Remember that the context of schools is complex; schools are living systems. Because students, teachers, parents, communities, policies, and politics all potentially influence school culture, many variances exist among schools, even those with the same basic structure.

How Do School Venues Differ?

U.S. schools vary greatly, from the traditional neighborhood public school to the ultimate private school: the home. This section looks at **school venues**, the variety of ways American students are educated in the more than 130,000 schools in the United States (National Center for Education Statistics [NCES], 2010).

PUBLIC SCHOOL VENUES

The vast majority of educational settings in the United States are public schools, with most of the funding to support them coming from some form of taxation. Public schools are accountable to the community through elected or governmental officials who have policy and oversight responsibilities.

School governance is addressed in Chapter 11.

Public schools come in all shapes and sizes. They are not only open to every student regardless of socioeconomic status, disability, race, or religion, but in fact they must provide a school setting for every child—that's part of being public. The number of public school students has hovered right around 50 million since 2006, with private school enrollment at about 5 million students.

Traditional public schools. The traditional, or **neighborhood, school** is still the predominant form of public schooling in the United States. **Traditional public schools** have no admission criteria, other than perhaps residency in a particular attendance zone. Their educational programs are designed to meet the needs of almost all students, with the possible exception of some with severe physical or mental disabilities. Over 45 million—of the more than 55 million students in grades K to 12 in both public and private schools in the United States—attend traditional public schools (Snyder, Dillow, & Hoffman, 2009).

A traditional public school that provides a comprehensive program of education and includes student and community services, such as after-school and family-education programs, may be considered a **full-service school**. Many of the components of a full-service school are made possible through community partnerships with businesses, health care providers, foundations, and government agencies. These services help students and their families cope with a variety of dilemmas. The goals of a full-service school may include the following:

- Meeting students' needs, both academic and nonacademic, through extended-day programs, counseling groups, homework assistance, and the like
- Increasing family stability through parent education
- Creating a safe haven for the community
- Providing role models for all family members
- Responding to physical and psychological needs
- Providing easy access to government services
- Involving community members from all walks of life in public education

Three particular venues of public schools draw specific groups of students. Each has a structure that uniquely matches the needs and interests of its student population.

Magnet schools. A school with a specific emphasis or theme may be known as a **magnet school**. The curriculum and/or instructional program of a magnet school are tailored with unique opportunities that attract certain students. A magnet school's focus may be math or science (or both), performing arts, technology, or high academic expectations requiring specific student qualifications. For example, a magnet school with an emphasis on preparation for a career in the trade arts, sometimes called a vocational magnet, would attract students interested in careers in construction, mechanics, cosmetology, culinary arts, and so on.

Magnet schools are more expensive to operate than traditional neighborhood schools. Their special programs may require funds for career-related equipment, performance studios, staff with specific expertise, smaller teacher-to-student ratios, and transportation beyond immediate neighborhoods. As parents and students seek more specialized environments, more and more magnet schools are opening and drawing specific groups of students out of the traditional neighborhood schools.

In 2010 about 2% of public schools were magnets. Their population accounted for about 3% of students enrolled in public schools (NCES, n.d.-a), serving about 1.5 million students.

Charter schools. A **charter school** is a public school that is freed in specific ways from the typical regulations required of other public schools. Charter schools are publicly funded, but independently operated. For instance, teachers and administrators in charter schools usually have more control than their counterparts in traditional public schools over how they spend their funds and the kinds of classes they offer. Charter schools must, in most cases, be approved by a state department of education and are open to all students within a specific school district. Charter school students take all state-mandated standardized tests and the schools are accountable for the quality of teaching and learning through test results.

Charter schools are created by those who see a need or an opportunity to fix a problem, such as declining student achievement, or to enhance a particular area, such as student abilities in the arts. Themes may revolve around a subject area, particular teaching techniques, a social problem, specific grade levels, or other issues the creators view as important. To attract students, leaders of charter schools must get the word out to the public and convince parents that the charter can better meet the learning needs of their children. Then, to keep students coming back year after year, they must follow through with their plans and goals. Government funding follows students to charter schools, which operate financially based primarily on per student allocations. Charter schools may be started from scratch or converted from preexisting schools. Once approved and in operation, charter schools are usually governed through **site-based management**, meaning that the school is in the hands of those closest to it, generally teachers, administrators, and parents.

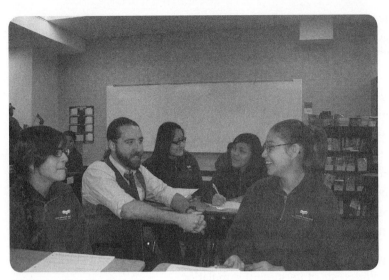

STRIVE Prep World Studies teacher Jesse White enjoys a positive relationship with his 7th grade students.

Responding to the public's desire for school choices, the number of charter schools has increased exponentially in the last decade. In 2010 there were almost 5,000 charter schools in 41 states. Charter student enrollment quadrupled between 2000 and 2010, when over 1.6 million students attended charter school. Today about 5% of public schools are charter schools, with about 3.5% of U.S. students enrolled in them (NCES, 2012).

Although most charter schools are independent, stand-alone schools, others are part of a larger system. Perhaps the best known of all charter school systems is the **Knowledge is Power Program (KIPP)**, a national network of 125 free, open-enrollment charter schools in 20 states serving more than 41,000 K–12 students. About 90% of KIPP students are eligible for free or reduced meals and about 95% are African American or Hispanic. Kipp's successes include a high school graduation rate of 90%, with 80% of KIPP graduates attending college (Knowledge is Power Program, 2013). This is quite a success story!

A smaller, locally successful charter system is the **STRIVE Preparatory Schools** in Denver, Colorado. STRIVE serves a population with disadvantages similar to those of the KIPP schools' population, and was originally established to primarily meet the needs of Hispanic children in the Denver area. The system is growing and establishing new schools each year, focusing on students who need additional attention to succeed, regardless of race or ethnicity. Since the inception of STRIVE Prep in 2006, STRIVE middle schools have achieved top academic honors for the state of Colorado—an amazing feat, considering their students are primarily poor and are from homes where English is not the first language (STRIVE Preparatory Schools, 2013).

Just as some regular public schools are effective and others are not, many charter schools are effectively educating students, but some are not. Because states have the right to support or close charter schools, some people are calling for closer supervision of the charters and more heavily monitored accountability, so that students and parents aren't lured in by promises that aren't fulfilled. Since charter schools receive state funding just like regular public schools, every time a student chooses a charter, the local public school loses funding. Charter schools remain somewhat controversial because of perceptions of lax accountability and funding dilemmas.

Alternative schools. Magnet and charter schools are both alternative forms of school organization. However, in public education, the term *alternative school* takes on a unique meaning. If a school is called an **alternative school**, more than likely it is a school designed for students who are not successful in a traditional school setting. Because school districts can't exclude students and attendance is compulsory until age 16, alternative settings have emerged that may be categorized in two ways: *remedial* and *last chance.*

Students who require more focused attention to be successful than what the traditional school can provide are in need of remediation: academic, social, emotional, or some combination of the three. Once remediation is completed, a student may return to a more traditional setting. Often students who are characterized as being **at risk**—those in serious danger of not completing school and who may be heading toward nonproductive or counterproductive lifestyles—are strongly urged to attend remedial alternative schools. Students who are not successful in a remedial setting may attend public alternative schools that are considered last-chance schools. In most cases the students have gotten into significant trouble in a traditional or remedial school; have been suspended multiple times; have consistently been disruptive in the classroom; or generally have not benefited from other, less intrusive programs. The SEED Public Charter Schools in Washington, D.C., and Maryland qualify both as charter

TABLE 3.1 Public school venues

Venue	Definition	Admission Criteria	Advantages	Disadvantages
Traditional	Neighborhood school	None	Close to home; sense of ownership	May not have programs of interest or that meet specific student needs
Full-service traditional school	School that offers student and community services that go beyond academics	None	Draws families in; provides services such as health promotion and community education	None
Magnet	School with specific emphasis or theme	Interest; talent; academic achievement	Specialized curriculum or instruction	May exclude some students; requires more funding
Charter	School freed from some district or state regulatory control	None; generally first come, first admitted	Site-based decision making; specialized curriculum or instruction	May lack sufficient oversight; danger of "ends justify means" mentality
Alternative	Usually a school for students who are not successful in other public school settings	Behavioral or academic problems	Can provide specialized assistance for students who need it most	May neglect some aspects of school while targeting specific needs; may stereotype or stigmatize students

schools because of their vision and unique structure, and as alternative schools because they were developed to meet the needs of students at risk of not succeeding in traditional public schools. The SEED Public Charter Schools are the only public boarding schools in the country.

The wide variety of public schools provides opportunities and choices. Table 3.1 summarizes the commonly available public school options.

PRIVATE SCHOOL VENUES

The two elements that make schools public—public funding and public accountability—are both absent in **private schools**. About 10% of students in the United States attend private schools (NCES, 2012). Families choose private education for a variety of reasons. Some choose private schools for potential benefits such as smaller class size, specific instruction to meet the needs of students with learning disabilities, or travel and extracurricular opportunities. Still others may choose private education because of family history. In some cases, generations of family members have attended a particular private school.

Some families choose private schools because of negative perceptions about local public schools. They may consider public schools inferior or inadequate. Still others want their children to have religious instruction or believe that their children's specific mental or physical needs require a private setting. Then there are other families who perceive that a private school may be more prestigious than the available public schools.

In most instances, public and private schools exist side by side in a community with little rancor. Yet there may be differences in underlying philosophy that cause friction. Unlike their public school counterparts, private schools are not obligated to educate all students, but are able to both selectively admit and dismiss students. Thus their classrooms typically have fewer behavior problems, a smaller teacher-to-student ratio, and stronger parental support. Some private school teachers see this as a trade-off because most of them are paid less than teachers in public schools.

Parochial schools. Most private schools are affiliated with a particular religious sect (denomination) and are often called **parochial schools**. Most religion-affiliated schools are aligned with the Catholic faith.

Private schools that are not aligned with a religious group exist in many forms and cater to a wide spectrum of student and family needs and wants. They may resemble charter schools with themes and areas of emphasis, but they are free from all government regulation because they are privately funded.

Points of Reflection 3.2

Did you attend public schools? Were they traditional neighborhood schools, magnet schools, charter schools, or alternative schools? If you attended a variety of public school venues, what differences among them did you experience?

Single-gender schools. Some private schools are **single gender**, enrolling either all boys or all girls. Although some public schools have opted for some single-gender classes and campuses under No Child Left Behind stipulations, most single-gender opportunities come through private schools.

Homeschooling. Students who receive most of their academic instruction in their homes are considered to be **homeschooled**. Although it's hard to pinpoint an exact number, we know there were over 2 million homeschooled students in the United States in 2010 (Ray, 2011). This figure represents about 3.6% of the total U.S. student population. The reasons for parents choosing homeschooling vary but are similar to parental reasons for choosing private over public school venues.

Homeschooling has become a social movement, with parents involved as political activists, organizers of national networks, and developers of curriculum and instructional materials. As you can imagine, the quality of the education received in the home varies widely. However, on standardized academic achievement tests homeschoolers tend to score 15 to 30 percentile points higher than students in public schools (Ray, 2011). How students fare socially has not been measured, only openly speculated about. A concern is that children who are homeschooled may miss out on the civic perspective and experiences gained only through going to school with students who are not like themselves in religious beliefs, racial or cultural background, socioeconomic status, or academic aptitude.

Homeschooling has always been part of the human experience. Some notable homeschooled students include Florence Nightingale, Thomas Edison, Margaret Mead, Charles Dickens, Benjamin Franklin, Orville and Wilbur Wright, Woodrow Wilson, and former U.S. Supreme Court Justice Sandra Day O'Connor.

For-profit schools. Nonreligious private schools are often **for-profit schools**. These schools are managed by some entity that receives a percentage of the money generated. Even some public schools may be for-profit. For years, public schools have contracted with private companies to provide some aspects of schooling such as transportation, custodial work, and food services. However, when companies contract with states or districts to take over all aspects of schooling and make money by doing so, then it's capitalism in the schoolhouse. These for-profit schools are given the federal, state, and local money per pupil that a public school receives and are referred to as **Education Maintenance Organizations, or EMOs** (the educational equivalent of HMOs in health care). Public schools run by private companies are controversial because they may make claims of increased student learning, with some of their data calculations often questioned by those who oppose privatization. Another controversial claim made by opponents of privatization is that when profit is the bottom line, services to the students with special needs may be neglected. More research is needed to determine the efficacy of for-profit companies managing public schools.

As you consider the variety of schools in both Table 3.1 and Table 3.2, keep in mind that what some may view as advantages may be considered disadvantages by others, and vice versa.

Both public and private schools create choices for families. Let's explore how school choice is manifested in U.S. schools.

SCHOOL CHOICE

School choice—letting parents and students decide which schools meet their needs—has a very democratic feel, doesn't it? Reasons for choice among schools include increasing parental involvement, providing learning environments more suited to individual students, attempting broader integration, accommodating particular interests and talents, and affording more desirable settings to at-risk or underprivileged students.

Let's consider school choice in the context of competition. Marketplace theory says that competition leads to improvement. But does this apply to schools competing for student enrollment, when more students mean more money? If all schools were high performing and differed only in theme or focus, then competition would simply mean

Points of Reflection 3.3

Did you attend private schools? If so, were they religiously affiliated? If you attended more than one venue of private school, what differences did you experience? Did you attend a combination of public and private schools? If so, what differences did you experience between public and private schools?

TABLE 3.2 Private and for-profit school venue

Venue	Definition	Admission Criteria	Advantages	Disadvantages
Religious	School with a religious affiliation	Agreement to either uphold or not interfere with the principles of the affiliation	Allows parents and religious groups to include their traditions and beliefs	Not accountable to any government agency
Nonreligious	School without a religious affiliation	Interest; can afford tuition; students may be rejected for any reason	Specialized curriculum or instruction	Not accountable to any government agency
Single gender	School for boys only or girls only	Must be gender of school; generally first come, first admitted	May better meet specific learning styles of either boys or girls	Not accountable to any government agency; may not mirror reality of the coed world
Homeschooling	Students are taught at home or in a home environment	Family member	Provides very specific one-on-one instruction in a manner desired by parents	Not accountable to any government agency; may isolate student from other cultures and viewpoints; may neglect some aspects of what is commonly agreed upon as necessary curriculum
For-profit	Schools run by individuals or corporations that make and keep monetary gain	Any criteria set by school managers	Can be very specialized	If private, not accountable to any government agency

appealing to student interests or learning preferences. But when certain schools gain enrollment while others lose because of real or perceived failures to meet the needs of students, the failing schools are left in an even more untenable situation. If we close them down, we may be eliminating the possibility of improving the predominant public school setting, the neighborhood school. However, no child should be in a school that is not making progress toward improved levels of learning. Answering the question, "And how are the children?" becomes even more complex and important.

For any choice plan, there are two key ingredients for success: information and transportation. Without provisions for both, a choice plan only gives choices to families who seek out information and have the capability to provide transportation out of their neighborhoods. Figure 3.1 illustrates three ways that public school choice may be manifested.

Public-to-public school choice. Allowing for choice among public schools occurs in a variety of ways. The option of attending magnet, charter, and alternative schools versus a traditional neighborhood school within a district is by far the most common manifestation of school choice. Taking this option a step further, **open enrollment** allows students to choose from among all the schools in a school district

Figure 3.1 School choice options supported by government funding with a few exceptions, such as magnet schools with specific student qualifications and alternative schools with student enrollment controlled by the district. Open enrollment may extend across district lines as well.

Elementary and Secondary Education Act. In 1965 President Lyndon B. Johnson proposed, and Congress passed, the **Elementary and Secondary Education Act (ESEA)** as a part of the "War on Poverty." The ESEA emphasizes equal access to education and establishes high standards and accountability (U.S. Department of Education, 2010). The ESEA was reauthorized as the No Child Left Behind Act (NCLB) in 2001. One provision of the act is that parents and students have school choice under certain conditions. The act includes guidelines for grading schools based on their progress toward reaching designated goals dealing with, among other factors, student achievement on standardized tests and attendance. Schools are evaluated and given report cards called **Adequate Yearly Progress**, or simply AYP reports. After 2 years of failing AYP, students at schools with a high percentage of students in poverty may transfer to schools with passing AYP reports. The school district has the responsibility to provide at least two designated recipient schools that passed AYP for each student and to make transportation available for students.

Are parents and students likely to take advantage of the choices provided by ESEA? Maybe, maybe not. More will if they are informed of the options in a timely fashion, if they are comfortable that long bus rides won't be necessary, and if the students are not socially committed to staying with their neighborhood friends who opt not to move. These are powerful "ifs." Here's another to consider: *If* their parents do not explore options, students will likely remain in schools designated as failing.

As of 2011, most states had asked for waivers from various NCLB regulations that have been granted by the Obama administration, many of which affect school choice (U.S. Department of Education, 2012).

Vouchers. Perhaps the most controversial of current efforts to provide school choice is the **voucher**, a government-issued form that represents part of the state's financial contribution for the education of a student. Parents choose a school and present the voucher, and the government allocates funding accordingly to the school.

Some vouchers are only for students living in poverty, allowing them to choose a school that perhaps better meets their needs. Other vouchers are awarded to any student within a designated area to use within a school district, or even across district lines. Some vouchers may be used only in public schools, whereas others may be applied to private school tuition or even to schools with a religious affiliation. The viability of voucher plans often sparks debates in state legislatures.

Consider this. Private schools are free to admit or refuse any student. They can decide not to take vouchers from students who don't fit in for any reason, including gender, race, past or potential achievement, or disability. Likewise, they can recruit and admit the most motivated, highest achieving students. Public money in the form of vouchers thus has the potential to become a tool of discrimination.

The use of vouchers to attend schools with a religious affiliation is perhaps the most controversial aspect of the program. Many people consider it a violation of the separation of church and state, and this obstacle may lead to the demise of vouchers as school choice alternatives.

Points of Reflection 3.4

Does a particular school venue appeal to you? If so, what elements of the particular type of school make it a possible career choice?

Advocates and critics of school choice. School choice, regardless of the format, has its advocates and its critics. If we simply pose the question, "Should parents have the right to choose a school that best meets the needs of their children?" most Americans would say yes. Table 3.3 lists several opposing views of school choice.

Even with all the variety of schools and choice options, the needs of some learners are still not being met. This reality deserves urgent attention and our best efforts. In this chapter's **The Opinion Page** feature we find praise for vouchers that appear to have benefitted children in New York City, with implications for other communities.

TABLE 3.3 Advocates' and critics' views of school choice

Advocates	Critics
Competition raises the standards, and consequently the performance, of all schools.	Competition destroys cooperation among teachers, schools, communities.
Competition gives parents decision-making power to choose for their children.	Only parents who are vocal advocates for their children will take advantage of options.
Competition forces low-performing schools to go out of business.	Students remaining in low-performing schools suffer.
Choice better accommodates diversity.	Choice leads to the possibility of further segregation.
Choice provides equal opportunities.	Choice exacerbates inequities.

THE OPINION PAGE

This Opinion Editorial appeared in the Florida Times-Union *on September 4, 2012.*

Low-Income Parents Deserve a School Choice, and Other Opinions

by the Times-Union editorial staff

What is a low-income family to do with failing schools and the inability to move to a better school system? Too often, a stifling bureaucracy means that change won't happen soon enough for the students trapped in the system.

One alternative has been to create vouchers that allow students to take their funding to private schools. Much controversy surrounds them for understandable reasons.

Just fix the public schools, critics say. Easier said than done, and usually of no use to students who don't have many years to waste. Now a study shows that vouchers can provide better education, especially in low-income neighborhoods. A study from the liberal Brookings Institution and the conservative Hoover Institution has documented the benefits in New York City.

The study included groups of students from kindergarten in 1997 to college enrollment in 2011. The researchers followed students who won a voucher lottery with a group who did not, the control group. This is the gold standard of research. The result: An African-American student who used a voucher to attend a private school was 24 percent more likely to enroll in college than one who did not.

"We know of no other voucher study that has been as successful at tracking students over such a long period of time," wrote Mathew Chingos of the Brookings Institution and Paul Peterson of the Hoover Institution in The Wall Street Journal.

Vouchers can provide an escape from a failing school system as well as pressure the public schools to improve. The largest provider of private schools in the New York study was the Catholic archdiocese, which has a history of educating low-income students without regard to race and creed. But this is no panacea, either, since Catholic schools often are under their own pressures.

Vouchers can help point out that there are options for educating low-income students that the public schools should be emulating. In the final analysis, there is no replacement for a good public school system. However, vouchers can help show the way and provide an outlet for families.

Copyright © 2012 Florida Times-Union.

This Opinion Page piece makes the point that choices are necessary for the success of students who don't have time to wait for us to "fix" public schools that are not meeting their needs. Write a well-developed paragraph in response to each of the following questions:

1. We know that some of our public schools are failing to meet the needs of many children. Does this fact justify the use of public money to fund vouchers used for private school education? What dilemmas might this involve?

2. Now that you know more about school choice, what other solution besides vouchers may meet the needs of low-income families and their children who are "trapped" in low-performing schools? Explain.

3. The writer states, "Vouchers can help point out that there are options for educating low-income students that the public schools should be emulating." Do you believe that school choice can lead to improvement for all schools? If so, what do we need to do to make this a reality?

What Is School Like at Different Levels?

U.S. schools are organized and structured in four basic levels: early childhood, elementary, middle, and high school.

STRUCTURE AND ORGANIZATION OF EARLY CHILDHOOD EDUCATION

Early childhood education is commonly divided into three basic age spans: preschool, kindergarten, and primary grades. Educators tend to agree that early childhood settings should be characterized by warmth, sensitivity, and nurture. Learning through play, with healthy doses of experimentation and discovery, describes a commonly held and balanced early childhood education philosophy. Let's briefly explore some of the structural and organizational components of early childhood educational settings.

Preschool. Experiences of 3- and 4-year-olds in the United States vary enormously. Some children stay home with a parent; some are provided simple child care. Others have a more structured **preschool** environment housed within a primary or elementary school. In this setting, often designated as a prekindergarten for 4-year-olds, care is enhanced by exposure to basic educational concepts. Preschool education may follow many different models.

The **Montessori** approach to early childhood education, with mixed-age grouping and self-pacing, is growing in popularity and has the reputation of being high quality when faithfully implemented (Morrison, 2008). Teachers in a Montessori setting are primarily guides, with children acting independently to choose learning activities. The **HighScope** approach, widely used in preschool through early elementary settings, is built on consistency and few transitions during the day as children construct meaning for themselves in problem-solving situations within learning centers. The **Reggio Emilia** approach to early childhood education for ages 3 months to 6 years is based on relationships among children, families, and teachers. Close long-term relationships are built because the teachers in each classroom stay with the same children for up to 3 years (Kostelnik, Soderman, & Whiren, 2004). **Head Start** is the largest provider of government-funded preschool education, serving over one million students each year across the U.S. Most students are served in heavily regulated centers. Children attend for half or whole days (U.S. Department of Health and Human Services, 2012).

Kindergarten. Once considered an optional bridge between preschool, or no school at all, and the beginning of formal education in first grade, **kindergarten** (meaning "child's garden") has become part of almost every 5- to 6-year-old child's educational experience, some for half a day and others for the entire day. However, full-day kindergarten is mandatory in only 10 states, with 34 states requiring that full-day kindergarten be offered in every school district. Some districts offer half-day kindergarten free of charge and will extend to full-day for a fee (Children's Defense Fund, 2012).

What occurs in both whole-day and half-day kindergarten classrooms across the country varies. In some kindergarten classrooms, children are involved in literacy-building activities; in others, there's little evidence of any emphasis on literacy. Some kindergartens are housed in K–5 or K–6 elementary schools, while others are in primary school settings that may include prekindergarten or kindergarten through grades 2 or 3. Figure 3.2 displays a possible schedule for half-day kindergarten, with teachers following a similar schedule twice a day. The step from kindergarten to first grade is a giant one, so it is crucial that the term *readiness* has become a major part of the vocabulary of early childhood education.

Some children enter kindergarten with many readiness skills; others do not.

Figure 3.2 Sample half-day kindergarten schedule

9:25–9:40	Arrival, morning exercises
9:40–10:40	Learning centers
10:40–10:50	Cleanup
10:50–11:10	Outdoor or gym play/snack
11:10–11:30	Whole group instruction
11:30–11:45	Small group time, cooperative activity
11:45–12:00	Art projects
12:00–12:15	Closing exercises/dismissal

Repeat with another group of children 1:20–4:05

Primary grades. Teachers in **primary classrooms**, grades 1 through 3, are faced with the challenge of meeting the needs of children with widely varying levels of both readiness for learning and acquired knowledge and skills. Imagine a first grade classroom with 5 children who have received very little home encouragement for learning and did not attend kindergarten, 10 children who attended three different kindergartens that varied widely in their approaches, and 4 students who are reading independently. The challenge is to engage them all in learning based on where they are today, with a view of their unlimited potential. Figure 3.3 shows a general schedule for a primary classroom.

Summit Primary, our early childhood focus school in Summit Station, Ohio, does not have a preschool program. Children must be 5 years old to enter one of Summit's three levels of kindergarten. The *Boost* class is for children who need more basic guidance and instruction. The *Average* class is for most of the children. The *Enrichment* class is for children who have already mastered some of the typical kindergarten skills, such as recognizing and writing the alphabet, reading one-syllable and often-used sight words, recalling a story orally in correct sequence, counting to 100, and making and explaining simple graphs. Some children go directly from one level of kindergarten to first grade, and others have the opportunity to stay in kindergarten for another year to build a stronger foundation for first grade. In addition to kindergarten, Summit Primary offers first and second grade. Focus teachers Brandi Wade (kindergarten) and Renee Ayers (second grade) teach at Summit Primary School.

STRUCTURE AND ORGANIZATION OF ELEMENTARY EDUCATION

Elementary classrooms may be **self-contained**, meaning that one teacher has responsibility for one group of children most of the school day. In some schools, teachers may share responsibility for a group of children, each specializing in one or two subject areas. A sample schedule for a self-contained third grade classroom is provided

Points of Reflection 3.5

Now that you know more about early childhood education, can you envision spending your days with the youngest students in American schools? What aspects appeal to you? What aspects do not appeal to you?

Figure 3.3 Sample primary grade schedule

8:50–9:10	Arrival, daily business, opening activities
9:10–9:30	Whole group instruction in literacy
9:30–10:30	Small groups rotate through reading and writing centers
10:30–10:45	Recess
10:45–11:45	Math instruction
11:45–12:15	Lunch
12:15–12:30	Read aloud
12:30–1:15	Science (physical education on Tuesday and Thursday)
1:15–1:30	Silent reading
1:30–2:15	Social studies (art on Monday; music on Wednesday)
2:15–2:45	Center time
2:45–3:10	Whole group review of day, clean-up, dismissal

Focus School

in Figure 3.4. A sample schedule for a fourth grade classroom with a team of three teachers, each teaching a core subject area, is provided in Figure 3.5. A team of three teachers would accommodate three classes of fourth graders.

Our three focus teachers at Rees Elementary School in Spanish Fork, Utah, have multigrade, or **multiage classrooms**, where children in three grade levels learn together. Chris Roberts, Brenda Beyal, and Tim Mendenhall each have homeroom classes made up of third, fourth, and fifth graders. They teach all four **core subjects**—language arts, math, science, and social studies—to their own classes, but each specializes in a fine arts area. Chris teaches movement and dance, Brenda teaches visual

---

Figure 3.4 Sample third grade schedule (self-contained)

8:50–9:15	Whole class morning meeting
9:15–9:35	Small group reading
9:35–9:55	Whole class instruction in writing/spelling
9:55–10:20	Reading and writing activities
10:20–10:40	Recess and snack
10:40–11:15	Whole group math instruction/activities
11:15–12:00	Alternating physical education (M), art (T), physical education (W), music (Th), physical education (F)
12:00–12:35	Lunch, recess
12:35–1:15	Alternating social studies and science
1:15–1:45	Alternating computer and library time
1:45–2:00	Read aloud
2:00–2:30	Free choice centers
2:30–2:50	Reading and writing activities
2:50–3:10	Whole group class meeting
3:15	Dismissal

Figure 3.5 Sample fourth grade schedule (three-teacher team)

8:50–9:05	Whole class meetings in homerooms
9:05–10:10	Block time:
	Group 1: Math
	Group 2: English language arts
	Group 3: Science/social studies
10:10–10:30	DEAR (Drop everything and read) in homeroom
10:30–10:50	Journal writing in homerooms
10:50–11:10	Recess and snack
11:10–12:15	Block time:
	Group 1: English language arts
	Group 2: Science/social studies
	Group 3: Math
12:15–12:35	Lunch
12:35–1:00	Computer or library time
1:00–2:05	Block time:
	Group 1: Science/social studies
	Group 2: Math
	Group 3: English language arts
2:05–2:40	Physical education
2:40–3:00	Alternating art and music
3:00–3:10	Whole class meetings in homerooms
3:15	Dismissal

arts, and Tim teaches theater to all three classes. Let's consider Brenda's class as an example of a multiage classroom. In the beginning of the school year, she has third graders who are new to her class, fourth graders who have already been in her class 1 year, and fifth graders who have already been in her class 2 years. At the end of the school year, the fifth graders move on to middle school after having been in Brenda's class for 3 years, and a new group of children who have finished second grade will be assigned to their first year with Brenda. One third of her class will be new each school year.

Focus School

Rees Elementary School

Spanish Fork, Utah

Kindergarten–fifth grade

Principal: Mike Larsen

Rees Elementary is a school for kindergarten through fifth grade students in Spanish Fork, Utah, just south of Salt Lake City. Located in a suburban area at the base of the Wasatch Mountains, Rees incorporates an emphasis on the arts supported by an experienced and enthusiastic faculty. Although each grade level provides traditional classrooms, Rees also has a dynamic team of three teachers who spend their days in multiage classrooms of third, fourth, and fifth grade students, all learning together.

To learn more about the structure and organization of Rees Elementary, where Brenda Beyal, Chris Roberts, and Tim Mendenhall teach, watch **Principal Mike Larsen's school tour and interview.**

Rees Elementary School, Spanish Fork, Utah.

Points of Reflection 3.6

Does teaching all subjects to the same group of elementary children sound like something you would enjoy? Elementary schools provide opportunities for professionals who are guidance counselors, media specialists, and teachers of students with special needs. Do these fields interest you?

Another possible elementary school teacher-student configuration with benefits similar to those of multiage grouping is **looping**, which occurs when a teacher stays with a particular group of students for more than 1 year. As the students go, for instance, from first to second grade, the teacher moves with them. Among the many positive reasons to loop are the following (Roberts, Kellough, & Moore, 2006):

- A consistent relationship develops between teacher and students and lasts for 2 or 3 years.
- Student learning styles, strengths, weaknesses, interests, behavior patterns, potential, family circumstances, and the like, are well known to the teacher.
- The last few weeks of the school year are often used more productively, with summer reading and project assignments more meaningful.
- The beginning of the school year requires fewer getting-acquainted and routine-practicing experiences.

STRUCTURE AND ORGANIZATION OF MIDDLE LEVEL EDUCATION

Some schools that serve sixth, seventh, and eighth graders are **departmentalized**, with teachers teaching their own subjects and meeting occasionally with other teachers who teach the same subject. For instance, with departmentalization, a teacher has Jamal in math but does not collaborate with Jamal's social studies or science teacher. The math teacher may not even know who Jamal has for social studies or science. According to the Association for Middle Level Education, the preferred organizational structure for middle level education is the student-teacher team, known as an **interdisciplinary team**. A team generally includes four core subject area teachers and the 80 to 100 or so students they share. If Jamal is on a team, all his teachers know exactly who teaches him each core subject. The team of teachers meets at least three times a week to plan together and discuss student progress and concerns. This kind of teaming is developmentally appropriate for **young adolescents** (National Middle School Association, 2010).

In some **middle-level schools**, students attend six or seven classes a day, each 50 to 60 minutes long. These classes include the core subjects, as well as other subjects that are considered **exploratory** or **related arts courses**. These may include art, music, physical education, industrial arts, languages, drama, and computer education, among others. Figure 3.6 shows both a traditional six-period student schedule and a schedule allowing for longer class periods, commonly called a **block schedule**.

Figure 3.6 Middle school student schedules

Traditional schedule (5 minutes to change classes)	
8:00–8:10	Homeroom
8:15–9:10	Math
9:15–10:10	English language arts
10:15–11:10	Band/art/foreign language/drama (9 weeks each)
11:15–11:45	Lunch
11:50–12:45	Science
12:50–1:45	Computer education/physical education (one semester each)
1:50–2:45	Social studies
2:50–3:00	Homeroom
3:00	Dismissal
Block Schedule	
8:00–8:15	Homework
8:20–10:00	English language arts block
10:05–10:55	Related arts rotation
11:00–11:30	Lunch
11:35–1:15	Math block
1:20–2:10	Science and social studies (rotating days)
2:15–3:05	Related arts rotation
3:05	Dismissal

Focus School

Cario Middle School

Mt. Pleasant, South Carolina

Sixth–eighth grade

Principal: Carol Bartlett

Cario Middle School serves sixth, seventh, and eighth grade students and is located in Mt. Pleasant, South Carolina, a medium-size city just across the Wando River from historic Charleston. Cario provides young adolescents with the foundational components of a true middle school, including teams of teachers who teach specific groups of students, close teacher-student relationships, high expectations, and a support network that boosts both academic and personal growth.

To learn more about the structure and organization of Cario Middle School, watch **Principal Carol Bartlett's school tour and interview**.

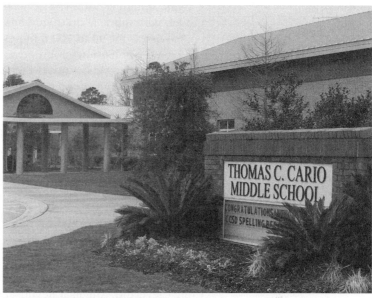

Cario Middle School, Mt. Pleasant, South Carolina.

Teaming is successfully implemented at Cario Middle School in Mt. Pleasant, South Carolina, where focus teachers Traci Peters and Deirdre Huger-McGrew teach. At Cario, each core class is taught for 70 minutes. The students also have one class period for a variety of special classes that are rotated every 9 weeks. They have a 30-minute lunch period and 5 minutes to go from class to class. Cario teachers provide a rich array of clubs and after-school activities from which students may choose.

STRUCTURE AND ORGANIZATION OF HIGH SCHOOL EDUCATION

High school may be a very recent experience for you, or it may have occurred decades ago. Virtually everyone agrees that high school represents a unique time of life. The four years of 9th, 10th, 11th, and 12th grade provide vivid memories—memories that many of us choose to relive every 10 years or so as we make our way back to reunions to reminisce, to see what and how our classmates are doing, or perhaps to show off or embellish our own accomplishments. Then there are those of us who would rather forget that time of our lives. Regardless of our feelings or memories from both an academic and a social perspective, high school experiences have a significant and long-lasting impact on most of us.

High school teachers typically specialize in one major subject and teach different areas or levels of that subject. All teachers of a subject form a department and meet periodically to discuss issues such as course materials, innovations and dilemmas in the subject field, and professional development opportunities. Departmentalization is the primary organizational structure of high schools.

Some high schools adhere to a traditional schedule of six or seven classes a day, each about an hour long. Students attend these classes for two semesters to earn a credit in each. However, alternative schedules are gaining popularity. Some schools are choosing to use blocks of 90 to 100 minutes per class that allow for more complete cycles of learning, such as completion of labs, reading and reflecting on literature, and proving as well as applying math theories.

Points of Reflection 3.7

Does teaching young adolescents on an interdisciplinary team in a middle-level setting appeal to you? Would you prefer teaching a core subject area or perhaps a special area such as a foreign language, art, or choral music? Does working as a guidance counselor, media specialist, or teacher of students with special needs interest you?

Block schedules may take one of two forms. Each has benefits. One form is composed of four classes per day of 90 to 100 minutes, every day, thus allowing four courses to be completed in a semester. One of the major benefits of this type of schedule is that students have only four subjects to study at a time, rather than six or seven. With four courses per semester, students have the opportunity to earn 32 credits in 4 years of high school. The other basic form of block scheduling is the alternating-day model. With this schedule, students also receive credit for eight courses a year, but each course meets for 90 to 100 minutes every other day for two semesters.

Our focus high school, Roosevelt High in Fresno, California, is actually two high schools in one. Most students (about 2,100) attend the comprehensive program, and about 500 students attend the arts magnet school, Roosevelt School of the Arts. The student population of Roosevelt High School, primarily Hispanic and Asian, is not typical of most high schools in the United States but is more common in California, Texas, and Florida. Most of you did not attend high schools that mirror Roosevelt. Most of you will not teach in high schools like Roosevelt, but some of you will. The majority of Roosevelt's students are from low-income homes. The majority of you are not. So why is Roosevelt our focus high school? There are several reasons. First, you need to see that effective teachers engage students in interesting and relevant lessons in all schools, regardless of the student profile or school setting. Second, because the high school that is so fresh in many of your memories is most likely a rural or suburban high school with families in middle- to upper-income brackets, you need to be exposed to a high school that is outside most of your zones of awareness and comfort. And, perhaps most important, adolescents are adolescents. Similarities outweigh elements of diversity. Focus teachers Craig Cleveland, Angelica Reynosa, and Derek Boucher teach at Roosevelt High.

We often return to discussions of school levels as we address various aspects of the teaching profession. Each time we do so, the information will build on previous topics so you will have a view of the big picture of what teaching is like in each level. Regardless of the level you decide to teach, your school will be in one of three principal settings.

Points of Reflection 3.8

Does teaching in a high school appeal to you? Is there a teacher who had a profound influence on the direction of your life that you would want to use as a model for your own teaching?

Focus School

Roosevelt High School

Fresno, California

Ninth–twelfth grade

Principal: Maria Romero

Roosevelt High School in Fresno, California, is a large urban school for ninth through twelfth graders. The student population of Roosevelt is predominantly Hispanic and Asian. Many of the Roosevelt students are children of migrant farm workers, and a significant number have only recently moved to the United States. The dedicated and creative faculty of Roosevelt High provide rich learning opportunities for all students, regardless of race, ethnicity, primary language, or socioeconomic status.

To learn more about the structure and organization of Roosevelt High School, where Craig Cleveland teaches, take a school tour with Assistant Principal John Lael and watch **Principal Maria Romero's interview**.

Roosevelt High School, Fresno, California.

What Are the Three Principal Settings of U.S. Schools?

When it comes to schooling, geography has a major impact. Sometimes a mile or two is significant with regard to educational experiences. Although the federal government has a new, more complicated system of classifying schools, the commonly accepted categories of schools—rural, suburban, and urban—exist in all 50 states and probably conjure up certain images in your mind that are generalized impressions of what each embodies. This section refines those images.

A focused view will reveal some generalities about the context of schooling in each of three areas: rural, suburban, and urban. The day-to-day realities of children within these three settings, both in and out of school, may be vastly different in terms of home, socioeconomic circumstances, and school opportunities. These differences may reflect the expectations held by parents, the community, and educators of what children can do and can be. Most teachers can do little to alter the out-of-school realities faced by their schools and schoolchildren. However, what teachers can alter are the ways they view students and their potential. It's a matter of values—both teachers' and students'. Before looking at each setting separately, let's examine some overall statistics.

Table 3.4 provides an overview of the percentages of schools and students in the three major public school settings, along with some perceived advantages and challenges of each. It's interesting that there are more rural schools than urban schools, but schools in urban settings serve almost twice as many students. This tells us that urban schools are considerably larger than rural schools.

The distribution of traditional public schools, public charter schools, and private schools in the urban, suburban/town, and rural settings is displayed in Table 3.5. Some points to note include:

- There are more public charter schools in urban settings than in suburban/town and rural school settings combined.

Points of Reflection 3.9

Did you live in a rural, suburban, or an urban setting? How would you describe the setting(s) of your PreK–12 experiences? If you had the opportunity to live in more than one setting, what do you recall about the differences?

TABLE 3.4 Overview of public schools settings, 2009

School Setting	Number of Public Schools	Percent of U.S. Public Schools	Percent of U.S. Public School Students Served in Each Setting	Some Perceived Advantages	Some Perceived Challenges
Urban	25,767	26%	35%	Possibility of making large gains in student learning	Low socioeconomic status of many families; problems associated with low expectations; low levels of parental/family education
Suburban/town	41,027	42%	46%	Families with higher socioeconomic status; relative ease of hiring qualified teachers	Satisfying various factions in the community; making continuous improvements
Rural	31,946	32%	19%	Smaller schools; community ownership	Inadequate tax base for funding; difficulty hiring qualified teachers; geographic isolation
U.S. total	98,740	100%	100%		

Source: U.S. Department of Education, National Center for Education Statistics. (n.d.-a). Common Core of Data (CCD), "Public Elementary/ Secondary School Universe Survey," 2009–10 (version 1b) and U.S. Department of Education, National Center for Education Statistics. (n.d.-b). Common Core of Data (CCD), "Public Elementary/ Secondary School Locale Code File," 2003–04, and "Public Elementary/Secondary School Universe Survey," 2003–04.

TABLE 3.5 Percent of public traditional, public charter, and private schools by setting 2009–2010

School Setting	Percent of Public Traditional Schools	Percent of Public Charter Schools	Percent of Private Schools
Urban	25%	55%	32%
Suburban/town	42%	29%	45%
Rural	33%	16%	23%
U.S. total	100%	100%	100%

Source: U.S. Department of Education, National Center for Education Statistics. (n.d.–a). Common Core of Data (CCD), "Public Elementary/ Secondary School Universe Survey," 2009–10 (version 1b); and Private School Survey (PSS), 2009–10.

- There are twice as many private schools in suburban settings than in rural settings.
- There are more traditional public schools in rural settings than in urban settings.

RURAL SCHOOLS

About a third of schools across the United States are in rural communities. In Montana, over 70% of the state's schools are rural. Twenty percent of Alaska's schools employ three or fewer teachers each, indicating how rural they are (Carter, 2003).

Most **rural schools** are smaller than urban and suburban schools. However, some draw students from an area that may encompass hundreds of square miles and have large student populations. A single primary school, elementary school, middle school, and high school, each with more than 800 students, may serve such a large geographic area.

Geographic isolation often means that students may have few of the opportunities and experiences found in more populated areas, such as museums and performing arts. Even basic services that people in suburban and urban areas take for granted, such as hospitals and large libraries, may not be readily available.

School financing is discussed in Chapter 11.

A high school of 100 to 200 students that is over an hour away from a medium-size town may have difficulty offering ample opportunities for what is commonly viewed as a well-rounded education. Think about it. To offer adequate coursework, a high school must employ certified subject-area teachers. Supporting an Algebra II class of 6 costs just about as much as supporting a class of 28, but districts must do so with much less financial support due to a low student enrollment count. Regardless of class size, the course requires a teacher and a classroom. Small high schools face similar constraints in offering extracurricular opportunities. It may be difficult to offer French club, debate team, football and basketball teams, and orchestra.

Points of Reflection 3.10

When you graduate with teacher certification, would you consider moving to an isolated rural area where you may be needed, but where there are no shopping malls, no theaters, and few single people under age 50? Does this lifestyle appeal to you? If so, why? If not, why not?

Hiring and retaining qualified teachers in small or large rural schools is a significant problem, even though the schools may be community-oriented centers in safe, scenic places. However, the benefits that may accompany a rural area such as ready access to recreation and natural beauty may outweigh any perceived drawbacks.

SUBURBAN SCHOOLS

Suburban schools most often serve students who live in single-family homes with grassy yards in areas dotted with shopping centers, places of worship, and recreational facilities. Apartment complexes and townhouses are scattered among the well-lit paved streets. Every few miles or so, there's a school. Town schools most closely resemble suburban schools; data from both categories are combined in this chapter.

Many people who live in the suburbs are likely to be in the middle-class to affluent socioeconomic spectrum. Their communities are basically safe places with adequate public services that provide a generally comfortable lifestyle. The schools, even in tight state budget situations, generally continue to operate at acceptable levels with tolerable class sizes, textbooks for each child in most subjects, and satisfactory building maintenance. Within suburban schools, students generally experience organization and order, extracurricular opportunities, and some degree of community participation and approval. These factors don't necessarily mean that students are learning at optimal levels, but there are some obvious advantages.

Many families choose to live in the suburbs and in small- to medium-size towns primarily because of what the schools offer their children. Real estate agents have long known that the public school options for specific residential areas have much to do with property appeal. Families desire stability and a satisfactory free education. If they can afford it, they buy homes in locations that will fulfill these desires. Do they get what they pay for? Most families would probably say "Yes."

Points of Reflection 3.11

Did you grow up in a suburban area? Do you enjoy the conveniences these areas generally afford? Is this type of location where you want to spend your teaching career? If so, why? If not, why not?

URBAN SCHOOLS

Most **urban school** settings are in sharp contrast to those of suburban schools. The facilities tend to be older, part of the fabric of downtowns that may or may not continue to be vibrant community areas. Although architecturally appealing, the older buildings are generally more expensive and difficult to maintain, and may be in a state of disrepair more often than suburban school buildings.

A few miles can make a significant difference in the school experience of students. At Wells High School in San Francisco, students look out the window to see Alamo Hill and the city skyline. Just 30 miles north of the city, students look out the window of Bolinas-Stinson Elementary at sea lions in Bolinas Lagoon.

Points of Reflection 3.12

Can you see yourself nurturing and guiding students who may depend on you for encouragement to see beyond their current circumstances? Is this the kind of challenge you might want to tackle?

Urban schools are likely to serve many students who live in low-income settings. As Jonathan Kozol poignantly related in *Savage Inequalities* (1991), funding differences certainly exist between some urban and suburban areas. However, some urban schools actually receive more funding per student than do suburban schools. One reason for this is that the federal government has programs that provide extra money for schools with student populations living below certain economic levels. Research supports the assertion that students from low-income families require more resources to perform at the same levels as students from middle-income families.

Many urban school settings present some unique challenges. The students in urban schools more often come to school with greater needs than can be met by the curriculum alone (Scherer, 2005). Still, there are schools in urban settings that make effective teaching and learning connections.

Regardless of the school setting, the explosion of technology and social media devices is undeniable. Rather than denying the impact of this situation, some schools and school districts are embracing it with programs now commonly referred to as Bring Your Own Device (BYOD) or Bring Your Own Technology (BYOT), explored in this chapter's *SocialMEdia* feature.

What Is an Effective School?

Effective schools meet the learning needs of the students who attend them. What are the characteristics of an effective school? Theorists and practitioners have attempted to measure schools' effectiveness for decades. Grappling with what elements characterize

SocialMEdia

Bring Your Own Device (BYOD) is a relatively new initiative spreading across the country. Some schools now allow students and staff to use personal mobile devices on their wireless networks for instructional purposes. Advocates say every school is participating in BYOD, but some admit it and others don't; the student devices are in schools. The choice is either to embrace and manage their use, as messy as the process may be, or to continue to try to keep the devices out of the classroom under threat of punishment.

In BYOD schools, laptops, netbooks, smart phones, tablets, iPods, and more are being used to take notes, complete assignments, create study tools, and work collaboratively with teachers and other students. As with any new initiative, there are benefits and challenges to consider. As BYOD becomes more widespread and schools and teachers share what works and what doesn't, the process will become manageable and productive.

Students may benefit from BYOD because they are:

- Already familiar and comfortable using their own technology so they can focus on actually learning with their devices rather than learning how to use them.
- More likely to have remembered their beloved mobile devices than textbooks or notes.
- More likely to continue learning outside of school hours.
- More likely to have limitless access to information and resources.

- Engaged by technology and more likely be more enthusiastic and excited about learning.

Challenges of BYOD include:

- Creating a BYOD policy that is manageable is difficult.
- The need for teacher professional development in order to optimize BYOD possibilities.
- Mobile devices that can overload a school's wireless network.
- Greater opportunities for cheating.
- The possibility that students may be more easily distracted while working on their own mobile devices.
- Students forgetting their devices or forgetting to charge them. Will there be "loaner" devices?
- Students who do not own the devices, creating an equity gap. Again, will there be "loaner" devices?
- Increased possibility of loss and theft.
- The need for parents to buy into BYOD and agree that students may take expensive technology devices to school.

If BYOD is going to be part of the teaching and learning strategies of a school, it's important to make sure that the end justifies the means. Mobile devices can change the way teachers teach and students learn if used appropriately. Schools and teachers must work to create motivating and engaging instructional strategies that lead to increased learning. "How to" advice and lots of opinions are available on the Internet.

effective schools keeps the conversation alive. The minute we say, "Okay. This is it. If a school does this list of things in these ways, it is effective," we will box in our thinking and become stagnant. Still, although characteristics may vary in many ways, we need a picture of what effective schools may look like and what students and teachers do in them.

CHARACTERISTICS OF EFFECTIVE SCHOOLS

In 1966, the Equality of Educational Opportunity Study, commonly referred to as the **Coleman Report**, concluded that family and community factors such as poverty and parental levels of education prevented some children from learning, and that no matter what the schools did, some children would not be successful. Appalled by this assertion, many in the education community adopted the mantra "All children can learn." President Lyndon B. Johnson responded to this problem in the 1960s with landmark legislation, the Elementary and Secondary Education Act. Among other things, this act provided extra funding, called **Title I funding**, for schools with high numbers of children from low-income homes. In the 1970s, President Gerald Ford expanded equal educational opportunity by signing **Public Law 94-142**, making special education services a right, not a privilege.

The **Effective Schools Movement** of the 1970s was initiated based on the belief that all children can learn. This movement was designed to locate schools deemed effective for all children and to identify common characteristics among these schools, including:

- Clear and focused mission
- High expectations for success
- Instructional leadership
- Frequent monitoring of student progress
- Opportunity to learn and student time on task
- Positive home-school relations

Lists of characteristics of effective schools are usually quite similar. An especially comprehensive list comes from a 2007 research study in Washington state (Shannon & Bylsma, 2007).

The characteristics include:

1. Clear and shared focus
2. High standards and expectations for all students
3. Effective school leadership
4. High levels of collaboration and communication
5. Curriculum, instruction, and assessments aligned with state standards
6. Frequent monitoring of learning and teaching
7. Focused professional development
8. Supportive learning environment
9. High level of family and community involvement

Effective schools may be found in rural, suburban, and urban areas. They may be early childhood, elementary, middle, or high schools, or any combination of grade level configurations. They serve any range of colors, classes, and ethnicities of students. School effectiveness exists where students are learning and experiencing positive personal growth, facilitated by teachers who make a difference.

In 2012, Routman (pp. 56–61) proposed that there are principles and practices that have been proven to be most critical for effective teaching and learning. She tells us that teachers act professionally in ways that increase school effectiveness by following these principles and practices:

1. *Rely on strong principal leadership.* Without strong principal leadership, it is rarely possible to have long-term improved student achievement.

2. *Raise expectations for what's possible.* High expectations are evident when teachers, among other things, do not waste instructional time, teach students to self-monitor learning and behavior, and give relevant assignments.

3. *Participate in professional learning communities.* A **professional learning community (PLC)** is a school-based group of teachers and administrators who work collaboratively to share practices and data analysis of student progress to improve teaching and learning.

4. *Develop shared beliefs.* Sharing beliefs is important to the relationships formed and the consistency of academic rigor.

5. *Apply an optimal learning model.* Taking learners from watching teachers do something to doing it themselves is a proven model of effective teaching and learning.

6. *Participate in effective coaching experiences.* Effective teacher coaches must, first of all, be experts in content and instruction, able to demonstrate strategies and help teachers become independent practitioners.

7. *Work toward becoming a self-sustaining school.* A self-sustaining school is one where there is a high level of collaboration and trust, where adults rely on one another to observe and give advice, and where adults are willing to work together for the benefit of students.

WE MAKE A DIFFERENCE

We make a difference when we ask ourselves and one another "And how are the children?" in conjunction with our best efforts to facilitate learning. According to Kati Haycock, director of The Education Trust, what schools do makes a huge difference in whether students learn. She asserts that what matters most is good teaching (Haycock, 2003). Quality teachers for every student will enhance a school's effectiveness. The education of quality teachers, the hiring and retention of quality teachers, and the continuing professional growth of quality teachers are key elements of effective schools, where a balance exists between students' academic achievement and personal development.

CONCLUDING THOUGHTS

George Albano, 25-year veteran principal of Lincoln Elementary School in Mount Vernon, New York, can answer "And how are the children? Are they all well?" by stating that 99% of his school's fourth graders scored at or above basic skill levels in English, math, and science even though more than 50% are eligible for free or reduced-price lunch and 60% are African American or Hispanic. He leads an effective school where the achievement gap is nonexistent and students are in the care of competent teachers who make them feel valued. Albano puts it this way, "Success comes down to hard work; great and dedicated teachers; an integrated curriculum; lots of art, music, and physical education; the willingness to bend and break rules occasionally; and the complete refusal to let any child fail to learn" (Merrow, 2004, p. 456).

Your challenge is clear. Be the generation of teachers who figures it out—the teachers who bring us closer to quality, effective education for all students.

After reading the **Chapter in Review,** interact with Brandi Wade in this chapter's **Developing Professional Competence.**

Chapter in Review

What are the purposes of public schools in the United States?

- Although often used interchangeably, there are distinctions between education and schooling. Education happens continually through all of life's experiences, whereas schooling is the formal structure of teaching and learning.
- Transmitting and reconstructing society are two complementary purposes of U.S. schooling.
- Teaching students how to participate positively in society while facilitating academic learning are two complementary purposes of U.S. schooling.
- There is no conflict between meeting individual student needs and collective student needs.
- Although schooling in the United States sustains students for today, it also prepares them for tomorrow.

What is the culture of a school?

- The culture of a school is the context of the learning experiences, as well as adult and student behaviors and attitudes.
- A school's culture can be a positive force for learning, or a negative influence that interferes with learning, and all shades in between.
- Teachers have an enormous impact on a school's culture.

How do school venues differ?

- There is a great variety of schools in the United States, from the traditional neighborhood public school to the ultimate private school, the home.
- Traditional public schools have education programs that suit most students.
- Full-service schools attend to the academic, health, and social service needs of students and families, and, in many cases, of the community.
- A magnet school is a public school with a specific theme or focus.
- A charter school is a public school that is publicly funded and independently operated. Charter schools are free from many of the regulations that apply to other public schools.
- Alternative schools are schools designed to meet the needs of students who are not successful in traditional schools.
- Private schools may or may not be affiliated with a religious organization.
- Single-gender schools, most of which are private, are schools for boys only or for girls only.
- Homeschooling is a growing trend in the United States.
- For-profit schools are run by management companies. The concept is controversial when applied to public schools.
- School choice plans provide students and parents with options in both the public and private sectors.

What is school like at different levels?

- Early childhood education spans birth through age 8, or roughly through third grade.
- Elementary education may include a variety of grade levels, with K–5 or 6 as the most common. Early childhood and elementary overlap on the low end; elementary and middle overlap on the high end.
- Middle school education usually includes grades 6 to 8.
- High school education includes grades 9 to 12.

What are the three principal settings of U.S. schools?

- Urban settings are cities with large downtowns and a dense population. Urban schools are likely to have a high percentage of minority students from low-income homes.

- Suburban/town settings are distinct locations that include neighborhoods and shopping/service/cultural facilities. Suburban/town schools are likely to have a lower percentage of minorities, with most students coming from middle- or upper-income homes.
- Rural settings are areas with sparse populations and few retail stores and services. Rural schools may be all White, all minority, or integrated to some extent, depending on the area.

What is an effective school?

- Effective schools are those that meet the learning needs of the students who attend them.
- Effective schools may have a variety of characteristics, with quality teaching as the most important common element.

Developing Professional Competence

Thoughtfully reading this scenario and responding to the items that follow it will help you prepare for licensure exams.

Brandi Wade enjoys the fact that as a kindergarten teacher she benefits from having all the other district kindergarten teachers in her building. Recall that as a K–2 school, Summit Primary houses all the kindergarten, first grade, and second grade classes in the Licking Heights, Ohio, School District. However, as the district grows and diversifies, community members and individuals on the school board are talking about creating neighborhood schools, five for grades K to 5, three for grades 6 to 8, and two high schools for grades 9 to 12.

Think about this dilemma from the perspectives of a variety of **stakeholders**, or those who have legitimate involvement and stand to gain or lose from the situation. Answer the following multiple-choice questions:

1. Brandi and the other kindergarten teachers think their teaching is more effective because of their collective expertise. They want to stay together. All of the following support the teachers' desire to stay together except:
   a. They can share ideas among nine teachers, rather than two or three that would result from structure changes.
   b. If there is a problem student, they have more options for classrooms for him or her.
   c. New programs are easier to implement because they can help each other.
   d. Materials are easier to manage.

2. Teachers of grades 3 to 6 in the intermediate school next door see the value of smaller schools that would be created if the county divides into school zones and also moves grade 6 to the middle school. With four grade levels, they have over 1,000 children in one building, with projected growth to 1,300 by next fall if nothing changes. Which rationale is the least important to their desire to see the district change grade-level configurations?
   a. There is no place large enough to gather all the students for special events.
   b. Research shows there is more violence and bad behavior in large schools than in small schools.
   c. Research shows that children feel a greater sense of belonging in a small school than in a large school, regardless of class size.
   d. Having grades K to 5 in one building may lend to more family stability, especially for those with several children in the grade range.

3. Teachers in the current middle school that now includes grades 7 and 8 think that participation in after-school activities would increase if kids lived closer to the school they attend. It's very difficult to have after-school clubs and sports when most students are bused to school from all across the county. From a student's standpoint, which of the following would be the least important reason for creating schools that are physically more accessible to all students who attend?
   a. A school with fewer students, based on a smaller geographic area, will allow students more opportunities to be involved in a variety of activities.
   b. The schools would be more ecologically friendly because more students could walk to them.
   c. Students could go to school with others in their immediate vicinity, making it more likely that their friends live close enough to socialize on weekends or after school.
   d. In smaller schools students tend to know each other and their teachers better.

4. Many community members, including parents, believe that smaller schools with wider grade bands located throughout the county will be best for the Licking Heights district. In the proposed plan, Summit High School, which is now a full-service school with a health clinic and adult education classes, would be divided into two smaller schools. Why might two high schools, strategically located in the county, benefit students and their families more?
   a. High school sports teams would have competition within the district, allowing for more playing time for athletes.
   b. Competition between the two high schools would increase enthusiasm in the community.
   c. Research has shown that higher percentages of students in small schools get involved in activities than students in larger schools.
   d. A full-service school with a health clinic in a central location at the large school has not proven to be useful.

5. Some parents and alums are opposed to breaking up Summit High School into two schools. Which of the following may explain some of their reasons?
   a. A large county high school has a better chance of having an excellent record of athletic championships.
   b. A larger school provides more curricular opportunities for students.
   c. Both a. and b.
   d. Neither a. nor b.

Now it's time for you to respond to two short essay items involving the scenario. In your responses, be sure to address all the dilemmas and questions posed in each item. Each response should be between one half and one full double-spaced page.

6. Brandi and several other kindergarten teachers plan to present their case for keeping the district schools in their current configuration at a school board meeting. What do you think their three strongest arguments will be?

7. Do you predict the district will reconfigure the schools? If so, explain why. If not, explain your reasons for thinking the schools will remain in their current configuration.

2

The Work of Teachers

In **PART II** we explore the work of teachers. In Chapter 4 we discuss the curriculum, or the "what" of teaching, and assessment, ways to determine if students are learning. In Chapter 5 we take a broad view of teaching by considering three major facets that are vital to teacher effectiveness—science, art, and service. The *science* of teaching is instruction, or the "how to"; the *art* of teaching involves knowing when and how to use what strategy to teach so that students learn; and the *service* of teaching is that sometimes intangible approach to all that we do to enhance the lives of students, their families, and our communities. In Chapter 6 we address the development and maintenance of a classroom environment that is both positive and productive.

Where Do I Stand ?

The purpose of this inventory is to determine where you stand concerning what is taught and how it is taught in PreK–12 schools. After reading an item, indicate your level of agreement by choosing a number and placing it in the blank before the statement. Following the inventory are directions for how to organize your responses and what they may indicate in terms of where you stand.

4   I strongly agree
3   I agree
2   I don't have an opinion
1   I disagree
0   I strongly disagree

▶ **Click Here to Complete Survey**

____ 1. What students learn in school is basically what the school plans for them to learn.

____ 2. Teaching in ways that meet the needs of students with differing aptitudes is important.

____ 3. Much of what is learned in schools is unintentional on the part of teachers.

____ 4. Most of what is taught in school should be stable and not swayed by society.

____ 5. If only English language arts, math, science, and social studies were taught, schools would still fulfill their primary purposes of educating children and adolescents.

____ 6. Basing learning on real-world situations is an excellent way to teach.

____ 7. Projects provide ideal learning opportunities.

____ 8. Teacher-led class discussion is one of the most effective teaching strategies.

____ 9. The expectations of society should guide what is taught in schools.

____ 10. Although interesting, classes that don't directly address English language arts, math, science, and social studies are not important in fulfilling the primary purposes of U.S. schools.

____ 11. After-school clubs and organizations are important to the education of students.

____ 12. The teacher should be the focus of attention in the classroom.

____ 13. In the classroom, we teach who we are.

____ 14. Our vision of the future should heavily influence what is taught in U.S. schools.

____ 15. Some students should be allowed to go through some topics more quickly than other students.

____ 16. Music, visual arts, and dance should be part of a public school education.

____ 17. Teaching reading and writing is the responsibility of all teachers at all levels.

____ 18. Concentrating on one subject at a time is best for student learning.

____ 19. What is taught in schools should not be impacted by cultural diversity.

____ 20. Lecture is a preferable way to teach for maximum learning.

____ 21. There are benefits associated with student collaboration.

____ 22. It is more important to master the basic subjects than to learn how to think critically.

____ 23. There is a core of knowledge that should dominate what is taught in PreK–12 school.

____ 24. Student learning opportunities depend on what teachers teach.

Now let's analyze your responses. Remember, **there are no wrong answers**. Find six sums, A to F, based on your responses to the numbered items as indicated.

ITEM #	MY VIEW	ITEM #	MY VIEW	ITEM #	MY VIEW	ITEM #	MY VIEW	ITEM #	MY VIEW	ITEM #	MY VIEW
1		3		2		8		4		6	
5		11		7		12		19		9	
10		13		15		20		23		14	
18		16		21		24		Sum E		Sum F	
22		17		Sum C		Sum D					
Sum A		Sum B									

If sum A is larger than sum B, you believe there is a basic group of subjects that should dominate what is taught. The learning experiences are carefully planned and little is left to spontaneity. Courses or experiences other than what are planned are secondary.

If sum B is larger than sum A, you believe in a broader scope of what should be part of student experiences. Teacher personality and demeanor figure into student learning, as do classes not considered basic and after-school activities.

If sum C is larger than sum D, your preferred approach to teaching and learning is student centered.

If sum D is larger than sum C, your preferred approach to teaching and learning is teacher centered.

If sum E is larger than sum F, you believe that what is taught in schools should be stable and not altered based on societal changes.

If sum F is larger than sum E, you believe that at least some of what is taught in schools should be responsive to societal changes.

Curriculum, Assessment, and Accountability

 Dear Reader

Classroom teachers are curriculum designers and assessors of learning. Although teachers don't actually determine the curriculum, or what content and skills to teach, being a curriculum designer means they use a set of guidelines called standards to tell them what is appropriate at a particular grade level in a particular subject. They then develop plans for teaching and learning and they design students' days so that there are opportunities to learn and practice the knowledge and skills of the prescribed curriculum.

One of a teacher's most challenging tasks is determining when and how much students learn. If we don't assume the role of assessor, we might design and teach lessons that we think are leading to learning when, in fact, the students aren't "getting it." To avoid unproductive teaching, we need to continually look for signs of learning—or the absence of them—to direct our teaching and improve student learning.

Who's responsible for student learning? Although common sense tells us the answer involves lots of people, including teachers, students, parents, and community members, teachers tend to get a disproportionate amount of "blame" when students don't succeed academically. Is this fair? No, of course not, since the factors that contribute to a child's success are many and complex. We are responsible for much of the process that leads to learning and we gladly acknowledge this. However, when you dedicate yourself to the teaching profession, you take on the burden of being in the public eye as the keeper and dispenser of knowledge, sharing the praise for successful student learning, but reaping the lonely blame for

failure. The challenges and satisfactions of teaching make this fact a small price to pay for being one of the most important people in the lives of many children and adolescents!

Here are the focus questions involving curriculum, assessment, and accountability that organize Chapter 4:

- What is the formal curriculum?
- What other curricula do we teach in U.S. schools?
- What is involved in classroom assessment?
- How do teachers evaluate student learning and assign grades?
- What are standardized tests, and how are their results used?
- Who is accountable for student learning?

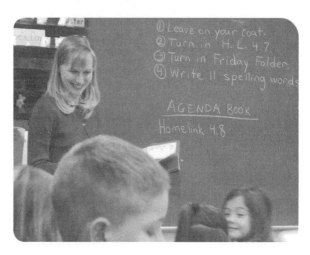

Teaching in Focus

Renee Ayers believes that ongoing assessment is vital to her teaching. The progress her second graders are making at Summit Primary, in Summit Station, Ohio, is recorded and analyzed in multiple ways. She even finds ways for her students to view their own progress.

One of Renee's favorite uses of student self-assessment involves writing. She asks her second graders to write their best about any topic they choose during the first week of school. She then tucks these little masterpieces away until the last week of second grade, when the students again choose a topic and write about it. Renee surprises her students by giving them their first week's writing to compare. She says it's one of the most joyous celebrations a 7- or 8-year-old can experience. The looks on their faces and their obvious pride in recognizing their progress are priceless!

Renee keeps anecdotal records on her students in two distinct and user-friendly ways. One method involves a clipboard and note cards. She tapes the first card to the board so the bottom of the card and the bottom of the clipboard are even. She writes a student's name on the bottom of the card. Then she tapes another card so that its lower edge lines up just above the name on the first card and writes another student's name on the bottom of that card. She continues this process, taping cards up the board to the clip. She carries this board around as she talks with students about their reading or math or a project they may be working on. In doing so she is practicing teacher observation with the added benefit of recorded notes.

Renee uses another clipboard to hold pages of sticky-back labels. She writes students' names, the date, and her observations about student learning on the labels. Later she simply puts the labels in a notebook on pages designated for each student. This is a quick way to record informal assessments all day and then easily organize them.

Of course Renee also does more formal assessments similar to what most early childhood teachers do. But she feels that her informal assessments help her develop the kind of rapport with her students she values and give her clear insights concerning their learning.

Renee models both attitudes and techniques that promote the use of assessment as an integral part of classroom practice. She takes seriously her responsibility to understand her students' strengths and weaknesses, to know their learning profiles, and to monitor their continual progress. Her innovative approach contains ideas you can adapt to your own classrooms. Watch **Renee's lesson and interview** to learn more about her innovative approaches containing ideas you may want to adapt to your own classrooms.

Curriculum is the educational term for what students experience in schools. Effectively determining what students know and are able to do involves **assessment**. Considering who bears the responsibility for student learning is referred to as **accountability**. Curriculum and assessment are, or should be, interdependent and inseparable. Our mantra should be "We teach what we test, and test what we teach." Curriculum should drive assessment. It should be that simple, but it isn't. In this era of politicized accountability, we find that assessment often drives curriculum. Tests with far-reaching consequences dictate what we teach, rather than the other way around. In this chapter we learn about the Common Core State Standards Initiative, a reform effort intended to standardize what is taught in language arts and math across the country. Teachers and others are writing and sharing assessments that address these standards. The plan is to make what we teach the same as what we assess in a more seamless way.

What Is the Formal Curriculum?

The **formal curriculum** encompasses what is intentionally taught within the stated goals for student learning. The formal curriculum, sometimes referred to as the **explicit curriculum**, is what teachers are expected to teach, what students are expected to learn, and what society expects of schools. The formal curriculum is based on three foundations: the needs of the subject, the needs of students, and the needs of society (Estes, Mintz, & Gunter, 2011). These three needs align with what John Dewey conveyed in two of his most important books, *The School and Society* (1900) and *The Child and the Curriculum* (1902). The titles speak volumes, as do the texts, about the interconnectedness of society, students, and the subject matter itself. Dewey (1938) also emphasized that formal curriculum is dynamic, meaning that it is continually changing and evolving. Later in the chapter we explore three other kinds of curricula that contribute to the experiences of students in schools: informal, extra, and null.

As we consider the formal curriculum, we must acknowledge the guiding contributions of Ralph Tyler (1949), one of Dewey's students. Tyler developed what is now called the **Tyler Rationale**, proposing four questions that should be asked throughout the process of curriculum development.

1. What educational purposes should the school seek to attain?
2. What educational experiences can be provided that are likely to attain these purposes?
3. How can these educational experiences be effectively organized?
4. How can we determine whether these purposes are being attained?

Before about 1990, broad guidelines for what to teach were developed primarily by state planning committees and were based largely on textbook content, federal educational goals, and a "this is the way it's always been" attitude. Individual schools and teachers refined the state or school district guidelines to suit their particular circumstances. However, in 1989 curriculum development moved abruptly into what might be called the **era of standards** when the National Council of Teachers of Mathematics (NCTM) published math standards for grades K to 12, the first official set of standards written for a core subject area (NCTM, 2000).

More information on John Dewey and Ralph Tyler is in Chapter 7.

STANDARDS INFLUENCE WHAT WE TEACH

Content standards define what students should know and be able to do relative to subject areas at specific grade levels. Standards help organize and guide teaching and learning in the classroom.

Following NCTM's lead, the professional organizations of other subject areas developed subject-specific content standards. Each professional organization is quick to say that its standards are not the curriculum but should be used to develop a cohesive plan for what is taught. When we discuss the individual subjects of the formal curriculum, we learn more about professional organizations and the standards that guide what teachers teach and students learn within specific disciplines.

Two other types of standards influence curriculum. **Performance standards**, or **benchmarks**, designate the level of the knowledge or skill that is considered acceptable within a particular grade level. Some standards documents also include **process standards** that support content learning by explaining both how the content might best be learned and how to use the content once it is acquired. For example, the five broad areas of NCTM content standards—number and operations, algebra, geometry, measurement, data analysis/probability—are accompanied by five process standards: problem solving, reasoning and proof, communication, connections, and representation.

Because the Constitution does not specifically address education, what is taught and learned in U.S. schools is largely left up to individual states. By the beginning of the 21st century, virtually every state had content standards in place, leading to what is called the **standards-based reform movement**, another way of expressing the era of standards.

Although most state standards are based on professional organization standards, there are variations among them. When the 2001 No Child Left Behind Act, the reauthorization of the Elementary and Secondary Education Act, required accountability, state standards and the associated standards-based testing became key to meeting this mandate. The pressure was on to show student achievement and improvement. The competitive nature of states, with their test results stacked up against one another, inevitably lead to comparisons between state-determined results and results from the National Assessment of Educational Progress (NAEP), often referred to as the "nation's report card." This comparison reveals major discrepancies, indicating that some state standards and tests are not as rigorous as others. Some states report high levels of proficiency among their students only to have NAEP results imply that the state's students are not measuring up. In other words, it's easier to look good with regard to test results

Points of Reflection 4.1

Did your teachers refer to standards in your PreK–12 experiences? Are you aware of any ways standards impacted your learning experiences? If so, briefly explain what you remember.

when standards are lower and tests are easier. This accounts, at least in part, for the increasing support for common standards.

Common Core State Standards. In this second decade of the 21st century, efforts aimed at the adoption of a set of common standards are in full swing. The work toward common standards, which would mean a national common curriculum in a practical sense, was initiated by two organizations that are made up of representatives from all of the states: the **National Governors Association** (NGA) and the **Council of Chief State School Officers** (CCSSO). These organizations have joined together to work on the Common Core State Standards Initiative.

The NGA and CCSSO (2010) tell us that the Common Core State Standards

- are aligned with college and work expectations
- are clear, understandable, and consistent
- include rigorous content and application of knowledge through high-order skills
- build upon strengths and lessons of current state standards
- are informed by other top-performing countries, so that all students are prepared to succeed in our global economy and society
- are evidence and research based

Adoption of the Common Core State Standards in K–12 English language arts and math is voluntary for states and most have done so. Although the federal government did not write the standards, mounting research indicating state-to-state differences in standards and testing prompted the federal government to put funding on the line. President Obama and Secretary of Education Arne Duncan are spearheading **Race to the Top**, an initiative that challenges states to make bold efforts to improve teaching and learning. Over $4.35 billion in federal money is available through grant funding to states and school districts, with areas of improvement for individual states and districts linked directly to alignment with common, internationally competitive standards and testing.

It's important for teachers to understand how the Common Core State Standards were developed and how they will be implemented. Frequently asked questions (FAQ) about the standards are in Figure 4.1. Take a few minutes to get a broader view of the common standards through careful reading of the questions and answers. The Common Core State Standards will likely play a major role in your teaching career.

As with all reform efforts, there are people who are in favor of Common Core State Standards and others who object to them. Table 4.1 presents a variety of views of both advocates and critics.

Objections to standards. Although grade-level-specific, subject-based standards have brought unprecedented organization to what is taught and when it is taught, they are not perfect documents. The Common Core State Standards provide a measure of relief from the following flaws often cited for state-developed content standards:

- Excessive coverage—the sheer volume of standards in any content area may be overwhelmingly impractical.
- Fragmentation of learning—isolated bits and pieces of knowledge and skills may not be connected and may, therefore, lack context and meaning.
- Details that obscure major ideas—too many details may keep students and teachers from "seeing the forest for the trees."
- Broad concepts that are too nebulous—standards written in broad generalities can be open to many interpretations.
- Lack of consistency—state standards and subsequent standards-based testing are uneven, with some more demanding than others.

Figure 4.1 Common Core State Standards

What are the Common Core State Standards?
The Common Core State Standards are standards written for K–12 English language arts and math to provide consistency of learning expectations across states. Before these standards, each individual state developed its own standards and standardized exams, resulting in widely varying topic emphases and levels of rigor in American public schools.

Who is leading the Common Core State Standards movement?
The Common Core State Standards are the result of collaboration between the Council of Chief State School Officers (CCSSO) and the National Governors Association Center for Best Practices (NGA). The CCSSO and NGA are state-based organizations that brought together teachers, school administrators, subject area experts, and education organizations from across the country to develop a common core of state standards for K–12 English language arts and math.

Why are the Common Core State Standards believed to be a valuable reform in K–12 education?
The developers of the common standards tell us they want every child to receive an education that provides tools necessary to succeed in college and beyond, no matter where they live. Because standards varied widely from state to state, consistency can only be accomplished through a set of common rigorous standards that provide clear expectations for how students, parents, administrators, education policy makers, and the community can work together toward providing the tools for success.

The Common Core State Standards make it easier for states to work together on ways to meet the standards and share helpful information and resources.

Common standards prompt textbook and digital media producers to concentrate on one set of standards and improve the resources available to all teachers and students.

The standards provide a measuring stick for student learning that is consistent from state to state. This is important for policy makers and education leaders who watch for progress on a national level.

Now that the English language arts and math standards are written, will they ever change?
Yes. The standards for K–12 English language arts and math are considered dynamic documents, meaning that they will be revised based on feedback as teachers use them and discover ways to improve them.

Will the common core state standards prevent teachers from making decisions about how to teach?
No. The standards provide expectations for the knowledge and skills needed for student success. Teachers, principals, and others will decide how to help students meet the standards. Teachers will write lessons that address both the standards and student needs in their own classrooms.

Did teachers help create the common core state standards?
Yes. Teachers participated in the development of the standards through multiple organizations including the National Education Association (NEA), American Federation of Teachers (AFT), National Council of Teachers of Mathematics (NCTM), and National Council of Teachers of English (NCTE). The CCSSO and NGA continually ask for comments and feedback.

Will more standards mean more tests?
No. The CCSS allow states to develop and share appropriate assessments. A test based on individual state standards is replaced by a test based on the common standards.

Will common standards be developed for other subjects?
No, that's not part of the plan. English-language arts and math were chosen because they are considered the basic subjects necessary for learning all subjects. Other subject areas are very important to education, but NGA and CCSSO will not develop standards in other subjects. States will continue to develop and revise rigorous and effective standards for other subjects with the help of organizations such as the National Coalition for Core Arts Standards, National Art Education Association, National Research Council, the National Science Teachers Association, the American Association for the Advancement of Science, the National Council for the Social Studies, the American Alliance for Health, Physical Education, Recreation and Dance, and the American Council on the Teaching of Foreign Languages.

Are the Common Core State Standards an attempt by the federal government to control public education?
The creation of the CCSS is a state-led endeavor, not a result of federal government efforts. However, the federal Department of Education agrees in principle with a common set of standards and uses financial incentives to encourage states to adopt the Common Core State Standards.

Source: National Governors' Association Center for Best Practices, Council of Chief State School Officers. (2010). *Common Core State Standards.* Retrieved January 1, 2013, from http://www.corestandards.org.

TABLE 4.1 Advocates and critics of common core standards

Advocates Believe that Common Core Standards	Critics Believe that Common Core Standards
Provide clear and consistent goals for learning, regardless of where in the United States students may live	Take away states' rights to determine what is taught and learned
Prepare U.S. children for success in college and work	Are premature and that state standards have not had sufficient time to succeed
Unite teachers and students across the United States as a cooperative effort	Do not allow for local educational values and use of local resources
Provide common ground around which strategies and programs may be shared	Detract from individualism of states and teachers
Build on strengths and lessons of current state standards	Are unwieldy and will not be enforceable
Level the academic playing field for all students	Will bring all states' standards down to the lowest common denominator

- A less flexible way of teaching—many experienced teachers find adherence to sets of standards inhibiting when compared to a curriculum that gives more choices.
- High-stakes accountability—standards lead to testing, the results of which determine student grade-level retention, school status, teachers' jobs, and availability of funds, among other major consequences.
- Decisions influenced by disagreeing factions—liberals and conservatives, religious and nonreligious, all battle for inclusion and exclusion of content, making standards "political footballs."

All of these objections and more are to be expected because any reform measure that changes the way teachers teach and students learn is bound to be controversial. The debate is healthy and keeps the process alive and dynamic. Regardless of the controversy, standards give teachers information about what students should have learned in the past and must learn in the future. Using grade-level-specific standards for planning helps teachers fit their expectations into the bigger picture of student learning over time.

Along with standards, another major factor that impacts what is taught on a daily basis is the textbook.

TEXTBOOKS

Historically, one of the most influential determiners of what we teach has been the *textbook*. Now that adherence to standards in the content areas is mandated by states, textbooks have lost a little of their power to shape curriculum. However, textbooks are likely to guide teaching on a daily basis if a textbook publisher responds to the standards movement by aligning content and skills with Common Core State Standards for English language arts and math as well as state standards for other subjects.

Textbooks in the classroom. Quality textbooks, whether paper-based or electronic, help organize and sequence course content. They provide a logical progression of topics, with content and skills that build on prior understanding and skills mastery. For instance, a social studies text will be organized chronologically so learners see how certain events impact subsequent events. A math textbook helps learners build on prior knowledge and skills in logical ways as they move, for instance, from recognition of geometric shapes to finding perimeter and then area in elementary geometry.

Teachers base up to 90% of classroom assignments and homework on textbooks and the accompanying supplements (Jones, 2000). Supplementary materials may provide options for enrichment, remediation, extension, application, and practice of skills. They may also provide lesson plans to guide teachers, online assistance, workbooks, tests, and a variety of other resources for both students and parents. These options allow teachers to more easily tailor content to student needs and readiness.

Limitations of textbooks. We should be aware that, although textbooks can be powerful—and generally positive—influences on what we teach and students learn, they may also pose the following problems:

- Textbook content may not match standards.
- Textbooks may include too many topics, with few in adequate depth.
- There may be readability issues as the textbooks attempt to be readable for a range of abilities.
- Textbook authors may avoid interesting but controversial topics to please constituent groups.
- Textbooks may lack content or be of poor quality, problems perhaps masked by concentration on making the books colorful and appealing.
- Textbooks may exhibit bias related to conservative or liberal ideology, culture, race, gender, and the like, either overtly or by omission.

You probably will not have much choice when it comes to textbooks available for your use. Be conscious of both their value and their limitations, knowing that textbooks have a significant impact on what we teach and what students learn in the subject areas of the formal curriculum. But although standards and textbooks have considerable influence on what we teach, the various levels of government also have influence because our public schools are precisely that—public.

Points of Reflection 4.2

What do you remember about using textbooks in your PreK–12 experiences? Were they major determinants of what was taught and learned? Were they interesting to read? Did they help increase your understanding and skills?

GOVERNMENT INFLUENCES WHAT WE TEACH

Because almost everyone in the United States has attended school, most of us think we know a lot about what should be taught, as well as how to teach it. This attitude, in part, leads to the continuing influence of all levels of government on education.

Local government generally has little to do with standards and textbooks, but involved local citizens serve on school boards and, as such, have some say in how schools function. The state level of government, however, exerts a great deal of influence because most standards and other curricular decisions are made at the state level. Governors, legislators, and officials within state departments of education influence what is taught and learned in public schools.

The federal government, although not directly dictating standards, has significant influence on how schools educate students through federal legislation, most notably after the Russian *Sputnik* launch in 1957 created a sense of urgency in terms of improving U.S. education in a competitive world. Once the National Defense Education Act of 1958 created math, science, and foreign language priorities, other federal legislation was passed in rapid succession that continues to influence what we teach and how we teach it, including the following:

- The Economic Opportunity Act of 1964 made vocational training a priority.
- The Civil Rights Act of 1964 prohibited discrimination, with the stated goal of equal access to quality education.
- The Elementary and Secondary Education Act of 1965 established Title I status, intended to increase funding in schools with large populations of economically disadvantaged children.
- The Bilingual Education Act of 1968 ensured the teaching of the curriculum in native languages as students learned English.
- The Title IX legislation of 1972 provided enhanced opportunities for girls to participate in athletics.

Curriculum, Assessment, and Accountability   109

- The Individuals with Disabilities Education Act of 1975 made participation in public education by students with disabilities a right rather than a privilege.
- The No Child Left Behind Act of 2001, one of several reauthorizations of the Elementary and Secondary Education Act of 1965, required states to maintain curricular standards, test all students on the standards' knowledge and skills, and report on student achievement in disaggregated ways (separating various groups so their scores may be compared).
- A Blueprint for Reform is President Obama's proposed reauthorization of the Elementary and Secondary Education Act and replacement for the No Child Left Behind Act of 2001. This legislation highlights five basic reform areas, including:

1. College- and Career-Ready Students
2. Great Teachers and Leaders in Every School
3. Equity and Opportunity for All Students
4. Raise the Bar and Reward Excellence
5. Promote Innovation and Continuous Improvement

In Chapter 11 we explore school governance and the impact of federal, state, and local government on how schools operate.

ADDITIONAL INFLUENCES ON CURRICULUM

In addition to the influences previously discussed, other groups and ideologies influence the formal curriculum.

Parents and the community. Every community has a unique identity by virtue of the citizens who live within it, including parents who send their children to public schools. What gets the attention of the community is often a controversial issue that strikes a dissonant chord among community members. What may be considered mainstream in Miami, Florida, could be controversial in Boise, Idaho.

Parental and community involvement in schools is discussed in Chapter 12.

Parents and community members can exert influence on curriculum in a variety of ways including voicing opinions to school personnel and school board members or local media, refusing to allow children to participate in certain activities, suggesting alternative curricular approaches, and serving on textbook adoption committees.

Partnership for 21st Century Skills. As we have already discussed, the knowledge and skills made explicit in the P21 documents are not necessarily new, but when packaged in this organization's format they make a compelling case for inclusion in the curriculum. The states that have officially become partners are all working toward including the P21 framework of knowledge and skills in their curriculum plans. Even with the development and implementation of Common Core State Standards, the Partnership for 21st Century Skills will likely continue to impact what is taught and learned in U.S. schools.

Colleges and universities. Students enter the doors of colleges and universities with knowledge and skills determined by the PreK–12 curriculum. Simultaneously, colleges and universities affect the direction of what is taught and learned in schools primarily through the preparation of teachers, research conducted by faculty, and faculty involvement in standards development. Because of this, higher education is in the unique position of being both a recipient and a molder of curriculum.

Points of Reflection 4.3

Before reading further, think about your own experiences with English language arts, math, science, and social studies. Which content area appealed to you most? How did the teacher's level of enthusiasm and teaching strategies influence the appeal of the subject for you?

SUBJECTS OF THE FORMAL CURRICULUM

We generally consider English language arts, math, science, and social studies as the core subject areas. In early childhood and elementary settings, classes outside the core curriculum are built into the day either within the individual classroom or in special classes that meet perhaps weekly. Most middle and high schools require students to take a specific number of courses that are not part of the core. These courses, known as **related arts**, **exploratory**, or **encore courses**, are valuable components that enhance the formal curriculum and include physical education, technology, world languages, music, home arts, theater, and more.

Core subject areas. The subjects designated as core have basically been the same for over a century. Although much of the content has changed, English language arts (ELA), math, science, and social studies are consistently taught in early childhood, elementary, middle, and high schools.

English language arts. The National Council of Teachers of English (NCTE) and the International Reading Association (IRA) tell us that language development includes reading, writing, speaking, listening, viewing, and study of media. In early childhood, elementary, and middle school, much of the ELA curriculum focuses on skills, including reading, grammar, spelling, mechanics of punctuation and capitalization, editing, and basic research. Traditionally, reading through the fourth grade has consisted mainly of fiction (short stories and simple books). However, the Common Core State Standards for ELA call for an equal mix of fiction and nonfiction in early childhood and elementary schools, along with an increased emphasis on writing skills. In middle school, the focus is on a variety of literary forms and writing. High school ELA is primarily literature based, with continued emphasis on writing skills and research. Communication skills such as oral presentation and persuasive speech have figured more prominently in ELA classes at most levels in recent years.

Mathematics. According to the National Council of Teachers of Mathematics (NCTM, 2000), the need to understand and use math in everyday life has never been greater. From making purchasing decisions to interpreting tables and graphs, math is a vital part of the present and will be increasingly important in a more complex future. Children in early childhood settings now explore concepts involving algebra, geometry, and data analysis. Elementary and middle level students are asked to use problem-solving strategies involving multiple variables. An increasing number of high school students are taking advantage of advanced placement math courses for college credit.

By viewing math as something students do and connect to real life, NCTM standards ushered in a shift in math education from memorizing procedures to understanding concepts, and from emphasizing isolated mechanical ways of finding solutions to problem solving. The Common Core State Standards for math continue the emphasis on problem solving.

Science. The vision of the National Science Teachers Association (NSTA) is for all students to regularly experience science education that revolves around unifying themes such as order, organization, models, change, measurement, and function. To do this, teachers emphasize that science is a process involving observation, inference, and experimentation. This is a major shift away from content-specific facts toward understanding concepts through process and inquiry, with students asking questions and searching for answers. For instance, when science is taught through themes, young children learn what it means to measure and how to use measurement tools. In middle and high school, they examine how and why measurement is important in every aspect of science (NSTA, 2005).

Social studies. The National Council for the Social Studies (NCSS) tells us that the "primary purpose of social studies is to help young people develop the ability to make informed and reasoned decisions for the public good as citizens of a culturally and demographically diverse society in an interdependent world" (2005, p. 1). This is a definite shift from the way social studies was approached for much of the last century. Before the influence of NCSS and the curricular changes prompted by standards, social studies was dominated by names and dates to be memorized, with little or no application of concepts to local, national, or international dilemmas.

Science comes alive for students like Amanda at Rees Elementary when they are encouraged to observe and interact.

The NCSS standards are based on 10 themes that are addressed in all school levels but approached differently based on the developmental level of the students. For instance, for standard 1 (culture), students in early childhood and elementary settings may explore food, clothing, and shelter in places that represent the ethnicities of the students in a class. In middle grades a unit on the culture of a country may involve examining the lifestyles of the people and the environment and completing comparative writing exercises. A high school social studies class may address culture through a unit on religious expression in schools in which students consider different faiths, examine relevant case studies, argue opposing views, freely voice opinions, and develop supporting rationales (NCSS, 2005).

Related arts. Related arts courses complement and enhance the core curriculum. Let's take a look at some that are frequently offered.

Technology. The International Society for Technology in Education (ISTE) is a professional organization whose mission is to provide "leadership and service to improve teaching and learning by advancing the effective use of technology in education" (ISTE, 2005). The standards for technology are organized into categories such as basic operations, communication tools, and ethical issues. Almost all schools have computer labs used for classes in **information literacy**, a broad phrase involving recognition of when information is needed, knowing how to access information, and judging information credibility. In these labs, designated technology teachers teach whole classes of students at a time.

Foreign languages. The statement of philosophy of the American Council for the Teaching of Foreign Languages (ACTFL) tells us that "the United States must educate students who are linguistically and culturally equipped to communicate successfully in a pluralistic American society and abroad" (2005, p. 2). To accomplish this mission, high schools and most middle schools offer courses in a variety of world languages, most commonly Spanish and French. Because of the recognition that young children acquire a second language more readily than do young adults, many early childhood and elementary schools offer opportunities to learn a second language.

The Standards for Foreign Language Learning are organized according to five goals that ACTFL calls the "Five C's of Foreign Language Education": communication, cultures, connections, comparisons, and communities (ACTFL, 2005, p. 2).

Physical education and health. Leaders of physical education (PE) and health education strongly advocate for more time spent in physical activity and health-related instruction. Supporting standards are provided by the National Association for Sport and Physical Education (NASPE) and the American Association for Health Education (AAHE).

Physical education in early childhood and elementary schools may be unorganized play time, often the responsibility of the classroom teacher, or there may be a designated PE teacher who conducts whole class sessions two or three times a week for each grade level. In middle school, PE and health are likely to be rotated courses, perhaps covering 9 weeks each year, with health taught by either the PE or science teacher. In high school, students are usually required to take only one or two courses in PE and not even that many in health. Given the health risk factors associated with adolescence in society today, implementation of the NASPE and AAHE standards is especially important for teenagers.

> In Chapter 9 we look at how societal health issues add urgency to the uniform implementation of PE and health standards.

Arts. The National Standards for Arts Education define what students should know and be able to do in the four arts disciplines: music, dance, theater, and the visual arts. The standards essentially state that by the end of high school, students should be able to communicate at a basic level in the four disciplines and be proficient in at least one art form. The availability of art experiences in music, dance, theater, and visual arts in PreK–12 schools varies tremendously. In early childhood and elementary schools, the classroom teacher may be responsible for the art curriculum, or the school may have an art specialist. In middle and high schools, students usually have a variety of arts classes from which to choose and perhaps a limited number of arts activities.

It is an unfortunate fact that when the budget is tight in schools and districts, the arts are often the first to go. After all, standardized tests don't even mention forms of dance, genres of paintings, composers and their works, or elements of drama.

Career and tech-prep courses. Career and tech-prep cover a broad category of courses that are usually offered in high school. Some courses are of general interest, such as basic industrial or home arts classes, while some are career oriented, such as auto mechanics and cosmetology. The federal government supports a program called **School-to-work**, initiated to bring real-world work-related skills and understanding to students through courses that introduce them to career possibilities.

Before discussing the remaining types of curricula, let's look briefly at three aspects of the formal curriculum that cross subject-area boundaries: integrated curriculum, culturally responsive curriculum, and arts-infused curriculum.

IMPORTANT CONCEPTS THAT ADD VALUE TO CURRICULUM

There are some important concepts to consider as we explore curriculum. If we think of the formal curriculum as a cloth that covers the school day with learning opportunities, these concepts may be thought of as threads that weave in and out of the subjects and add value, as illustrated in Figure 4.2.

Integrated curriculum. Continuing the cloth analogy, the strength of cloth comes from weaving the threads in different directions so that the cloth holds together. When teachers include content and skills from a variety of subjects in lessons—and weave them together in meaningful ways—they are incorporating **integrated**, or **interdisciplinary**, **curriculum**. An integrated curriculum basically involves approaching a concept from different perspectives to create learning opportunities based on connections. This is often accomplished through the use of a unifying topic or theme. Early childhood and elementary teachers do it all the time. Second grade teachers may weave a study of farm life throughout the year, aligning core and related arts subjects with the theme whenever possible. Math problems may deal with farming scenarios and science may revolve around light, rain, and soil, along with zoology. The history of farming and literature about farming and farmers may be taught.

In middle school, teams of teachers may weave whole days, or even weeks, around a theme that brings together research involving real-world events and phenomena. Curriculum integration is least common in high school. However, even though high school teachers are usually organized into subject-area departments, this in no way prevents an ELA teacher from teaching about literature through short stories, poems, and novels that reflect a topic addressed in the social studies curriculum for the grade level. For instance, if U.S. history is a course taken by most sophomores, the sophomore ELA

Points of Reflection 4.4

What do you remember about related arts classes? Which ones did you particularly enjoy and why? Were there related arts classes you did not want to take? If so, which ones and why? Do the related arts classes you took in PreK–12 impact how you spend your time now? If so, how?

Figure 4.2 Fabric of curriculum

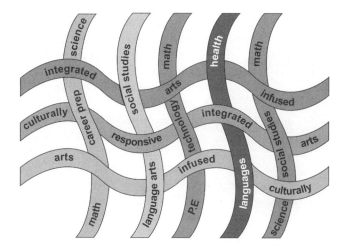

Points of Reflection 4.5

What do you recall about your teachers' efforts to connect subject areas? Did you experience thematic units of study? If so, describe what you remember.

teachers could incorporate period literature that coincides with the progressive history of the United States as taught by the history department faculty.

Connecting subjects of the formal curriculum can occur at a variety of levels of complexity. From merely mentioning in a geometry lesson that the word *symmetry* is also important in art and then showing a painting that exhibits the concept, to a well-planned series of lessons with subject-area boundaries blurred by real-world context, our efforts to make connections within the curriculum pay big dividends in terms of student interest and learning.

Culturally responsive curriculum. As diversity in U.S. schools increases, the importance of, and demand for, a culturally responsive perspective grows. When we approach curriculum in **culturally responsive** ways, we incorporate a **multicultural curriculum** that purposefully includes contributions and viewpoints from the perspectives of different cultures, ethnicities, races, genders, socioeconomic levels, or any other way we may differ. At its best, a multicultural curriculum is accurate, timely, and sensitive while avoiding tokenism or a sense of forced inclusion (Banks, 2003).

The methods used to demonstrate cultural responsiveness and to infuse a classroom with a multicultural curriculum will depend on the grade level and subject area. In early childhood and elementary settings, celebrating historical events and holidays of a variety of cultures helps create awareness of values and traditions within the various cultures. In middle and high school, making a variety of perspectives part of your classroom discussions, and asking students to research and report on issues of interest to them that include various perspectives, can help forge an understanding of people of different cultures. One of the most effective tools for including a variety of perspectives is an emphasis on current events.

Considering our cloth analogy, think of culturally responsive curriculum as adding a rich texture to the cloth, perhaps a tapestry effect, as connections are made among subject areas. Read focus teacher Derek Boucher's philosophy about a teacher's relationship to the curriculum, making curriculum relevant, and furthering our knowledge and skills in *Teaching in Focus*.

Arts-infused curriculum. Including the arts in the curriculum requires awareness of opportunities, along with purposeful determination to include music, theater, dance, and the visual arts whenever possible. You don't need to be an artist or musician to display art or play music in the classroom. Encouraging students to create their own works of art to enhance a project takes exactly that—encouragement.

We explore student diversity and multicultural curriculum in Chapter 2.

Points of Reflection 4.6

What do you remember about your teachers' efforts to be culturally responsive? Were various holidays acknowledged or did you study contributions of a variety of people of different races and ethnicities? If so, what do you recall? How did you experience the arts as part of your PreK–12 experiences?

Teaching in Focus

Derek Boucher, History and Reading, Roosevelt High School, Fresno, California. *In his own words* . . . .

After 12 years working in an urban, public high school in the Central Valley of California, I still firmly believe that teaching is a noble profession. Allow me to share the components that have made the biggest difference in my life as a teacher.

Love your content area. Engage in reading, writing, research, discussions, and even travel in your content area. The passion these activities generate comes across to students and changes lives.

Developing a philosophy of education will serve you better than learning multiple strategies. From a rich philosophy, great strategies emerge. Strategies apart from

a philosophy come and go. In 1995 my teacher education program pushed me to think deeply about my philosophy of teaching and learning. For example, I believe that curriculum should be relevant and meaningful to students as often as possible. Humans are innately curious. I believe that faith in the learner is imperative.

Go to graduate school. After 5 years in the profession, I enrolled in graduate school and studied in the area of reading/language arts. This experience changed my life as a professional and benefited me infinitely more than school district training has ever done. Find the most progressive graduate program around and go for it! You'll never regret it.

"The arts are the great equalizer in education. Regardless of native language, ability or disability, music, art, and drama are accessible to all" (Gregoire & Lupinetti, 2005, p. 159). As an equalizer, the arts can provide both expression and success for all students, regardless of the diversity they may display. Consider these four reasons for integrating the arts:

- Arts provide a natural view into the contributions and perspectives of other cultures.
- Arts are primary means of communication.
- Arts provide opportunities for achievement that may not otherwise be available.
- Arts may focus on alternative ways to assess and evaluate (Cornett, 2003).

Brenda Beyal, the multiage teacher at Rees Elementary in Spanish Fork, Utah, who infuses both visual arts and drama into the curriculum, encourages her students to express themselves in unique ways through what she calls a *squiggle*, a randomly drawn curvy line that forms the basis for artistic expression. Each student is given a piece of paper with the same squiggle on it and is asked to use imagination and creativity to fashion a drawing around the basic structure. While they work on their masterpieces, music plays in the classroom. Does this activity distract from the formal curriculum? Brenda views experiences such as the squiggle as enriching her classroom by creating a sense of ownership on the part of her students that ties them more closely to the formal curriculum they will encounter during the day. Watch Brenda's room tour not only to see the squiggles, but also to understand how this wonderful teacher organizes her classroom. Recall that when we toured Rees Elementary with Principal Mike Larsen, the arts emphasis was obvious on the walls of the school.

Although it's hard to imagine objections to infusing arts into the curriculum, there are groups who oppose arts on the grounds that their inclusion detracts from the core subjects. Controversy and curriculum are never far apart.

CONTROVERSY AND CURRICULUM

In a society that values opposing views and encourages diversity, the curriculum is sure to be debated. The dynamic nature of this debate is healthy, but it can also be frustrating at times for educators. Religious beliefs, censorship for a variety of reasons, and philosophical differences all influence what's included in the formal curriculum. Here are a few examples of issues that are controversial in some school districts and states with regard to what is taught in public schools:

- There is an ongoing debate over the exclusive teaching of evolution to explain the origin of human beings. **Intelligent design**—proposed by some parents and community members who practice Christianity and oppose the teaching of evolution—includes a belief that certain features of the universe and of living things are best explained by an intelligent being (God), not by the process of natural selection espoused by evolution. Some people argue for an evolution-only curriculum; others argue for intelligent design only. Still others propose the teaching of both as theories, incurring the disapproval of many in the scientific community, including most colleges and universities, where evolution is considered factually based.
- Earlier we discussed multicultural curriculum, or the purposeful inclusion of contributions of persons of diversity and traditions that are not considered mainstream America (a loosely conceived concept). One of the arguments for more cultural responsiveness is that U.S. curriculum is too **Eurocentric**, meaning that contributions and traditions that do not originate in Europe are underrepresented. For instance, in 2010 there was ongoing debate in the Texas legislature about whether or not Hispanics should be added as historic characters to the public school curriculum considering that about 40% of the Texas population is Hispanic. Some proponents of a core knowledge curriculum

argue there is already enough to learn about basic ideas, classic literature, scientific knowledge, and so forth without including efforts to be culturally responsive that may take away valuable classroom time.

- Whether schools should teach sex education, and, if so, what should be taught, and when should topics be introduced, are questions about which many in the United States feel strongly. The whole issue of sex education is value laden and emotionally charged. Many believe that the responsibility to teach children and adolescents about sex falls squarely on the home and religious organizations, while others contend that the school is the appropriate venue because it impacts the most students over a long period of development. With the goal of reducing teen pregnancies and sexually transmitted diseases, courts generally uphold the rights of schools to provide sex education. But the mere legality of a controversial issue such as this does not equate with widespread benign acceptance, nor does it alleviate the burden of deciding what to teach and when to teach it.

Societal circumstances and pressures that may affect curricula, including health and sex education, are discussed in Chapter 9.

Teachers have an outlet for developing a voice about controversial aspects of teaching and learning as they share information and opinions. In this chapter's *SocialMEdia* feature, we learn more about teacher blogs. In Chapter 3 we discussed professional learning communities and the value of teachers working together to share knowledge, skill, and resources. Many teachers consider blogging as a way to connect to other teachers to develop informal learning communities. Read the feature, explore some blogs, and see if this may be a way for you to grow into and in the teaching profession.

What Other Curricula Do We Teach in U.S. Schools?

We've learned what goes into creating the formal curriculum for U.S. schools. Now let's look at other kinds of curricula that are part of what teachers do. Although not as obvious in as many ways as the formal curriculum—and certainly not as regulated by standards and policies—the informal, extra, and null curricula nonetheless impact teachers and students.

SocialMEdia

There's probably no need to define a blog, but there are some considerations of interest, including:

- The word *blog* is short for web log.
- As a noun, a blog is an online record of opinions and information. As a verb, to blog is to post entries on the Web site.
- Blogs have been around since the mid-1990s and, by some estimates, almost 200 million blogs are active worldwide.
- Blogs may be individual or have multiple contributors, and most are interactive, allowing anyone to post comments and questions.

Many teacher blogs exist and serve to share information, strategies, philosophies, and frustrations. Most are initiated to communicate with other teachers outside the immediate accessibility of the blogger. Blogging can be an excellent tool of reflection. In a very real way, teacher blogging takes courage—the courage to frequently post without necessarily overthinking an issue and to honestly reflect on the profession, as well as individual days in the classroom.

Sometimes raw, revealing initial opinions, questions that prompt problem-solving, and sharing of successes and failures lead to improved teaching and learning. In addition to sharing ideas and strategies, teacher blogging can amount to self-analysis under the watchful, and hopefully helpful, eyes of readers and contributors.

Gauging from teacher appraisals on the Internet, blogging is a very positive extension of teaching. For many teachers, blogging is an excellent source of professional development, enhancing professional growth and practice, and a means of resource sharing. Here is just a sampling of blogs to explore. You will find many more that may interest you.

http://teachpaperless.blogspot.com/2009/09/why-teachers-should-blog.html
http://mscassidysclass.edublogs.org
http://thespian70.blogspot.com
http://www.sciencefix.com
http://learningismessy.com/blog
http://whatedsaid.wordpress.com

INFORMAL CURRICULUM

The **informal curriculum** is what teachers and schools teach and what students learn that is not part of a lesson plan, a curriculum guide, or standards. It encompasses what is learned by students through attitudes, values, and various types of informal teaching situations, such as in the hall between classes, at recess, and on field trips when conversations are casual. This informal learning may be positive or negative and is often unintentional. When the formal curriculum is referred to as the explicit curriculum, the informal curriculum may be called the **implicit curriculum**, meaning that often it is implied and subtle. You may also hear informal curriculum and **hidden curriculum** used interchangeably. There is a distinction, however, because the informal curriculum has positive connotations, whereas the hidden curriculum has more of a negative sense, implying there may be teacher motivations that are somehow less than positive.

Another phrase equated with the informal curriculum is **wayside teaching**. John Lounsbury (1991), a noted middle-level educator and advocate for young adolescents, as well as the name-sake of the John H. Lounsbury College of Education at Georgia College and State University, tells us that wayside teaching is the teaching we do inside and outside the classroom through our attitudes, values, habits, interests, and creation of classroom climate. Regardless of what students learn in terms of content and skills through the formal curriculum, they learn *us*. They watch us, listen to us, and notice their surroundings; they learn more than we imagine.

As an illustration of the value of the informal curriculum, consider a middle school science teacher who, wrestling with the "What should I teach?" question, decided to ask her former students what they remembered about her class and what they believed were the most important lessons. She developed a survey and received responses from students she taught in each of her 9 years in the classroom. Their responses included the following:

> "The most important things I learned from you weren't in class, but during the Science Olympiad . . ."

> "The [finest] things I learned from you have nothing to do with science."

> "The most important thing I learned from you would have to be the ability to be nice to people even if you feel like screaming. . . . The way you acted toward our class and the compassion you showed to our class [taught me this]."

> "Self-confidence and how important it is."

> "How important science is to society."

> "How you encouraged everyone to do their best."

Several students responded that the books she read aloud to them (in science class!) changed their opinions on diversity (Little, 2001, pp. 62–63). What a powerful example of positively teaching the informal curriculum!

Additional elements of the informal curriculum are discussed in Chapter 5.

Points of Reflection 4.7

Think about how the informal curriculum affected you. What did teachers say and do that impacted you most? What attitudes did they display that spoke volumes to you as a learner? What informal lessons do you remember most from grades PreK–12?

Renee Ayers, second grade teacher at Summit Primary, develops caring relationships with her students. Here she and Sherlonda share secrets in the positive environment Renee maintains in her classroom.

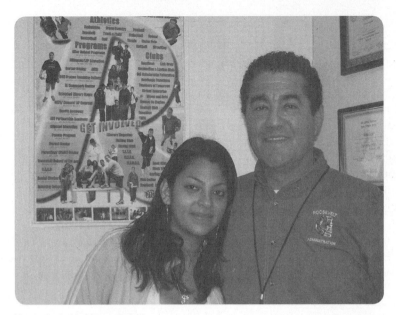

The poster behind focus student Mayra and Roosevelt Assistant Principal John Lael lists some of the extracurricular possibilities at RHS.

Points of Reflection 4.8

In what extracurricular activities did you participate? What did participation mean to you? In which activities did you want to be involved but for some reason were not?

EXTRACURRICULUM

Activities sponsored by the school but outside the limits of the formal curriculum are considered extracurricular. Although some elementary schools offer extracurricular activities, such as jump rope and craft clubs, most extracurricular opportunities begin in middle school and expand in high school.

Extracurricular activities provide opportunities for active involvement for students, and for sponsorship and coaching for teachers. Examples include:

- Odyssey of the Mind, math and book clubs
- debate, chess, and photography clubs
- band and choral activities
- athletics of all kinds, including cheerleading
- school newspaper, student government, and honor society

Recently there has been renewed interest in the factors that contribute to **school connectedness**, or student bonding and engagement. Lack of school connectedness may lead to disruptive behavior, substance abuse, emotional distress, absenteeism, and dropping out. The importance of doing what it takes to foster connectedness is magnified when we consider that approximately half of all high school students, whether urban, suburban, or rural, feel "chronically disengaged" from school. A major factor that influences school connectedness is participation in extracurricular activities. Researchers have found that extracurricular activities "provide all students—including at-risk and gifted students—an academic safety net" (Holloway, 2000, p. 88).

NULL CURRICULUM

The **null curriculum** is what *isn't* taught—content and skills that perhaps simply haven't been considered or are not considered important enough to teach. Content and skills may also not be taught simply based on tradition. "We teach what we teach largely out of habit" (Eisner, 2002, p. 103). The null curriculum also includes topics considered controversial, including almost anything dealing with religion, abortion, homosexuality, and other topics that are controversial in some areas but not in others.

The null curriculum may not be as important as the formal curriculum, the informal curriculum, and the extra curriculum, but it is certainly worth thinking about. What is *not* part of the school curriculum may never be considered by students, and therefore may have little to do with their futures. For instance, if we neglect to incorporate a culturally responsive curriculum, the failure to acknowledge and celebrate differences may contribute to prejudice and exclusionary attitudes in students.

The Partnership for 21st Century Skills promotes the teaching of some concepts that are not currently in most curricular plans. On the P21 Web site we are told that the challenge is to purposefully incorporate the broad literacies they support. A **literacy** involves the ability to analyze and apply knowledge and skills necessary to solve problems within a discipline. The Partnership recommends that schools promote financial, economic, business, entrepreneurial, civic, health, wellness, information, and communication literacies. In many schools, these broad disciplines are not addressed and therefore are part of the null curriculum. When schools incorporate them, they will become part of the formal curriculum.

Wolk (2007) tells us there are important concepts typically missing from school curriculum, thereby relegated to the null curriculum. He contends that students and society as a whole would benefit from the inclusion of, and emphasis on, knowledge of self; love of learning; caring and empathy; environmental literacy; social responsibility; global awareness; and money, family, food, and happiness.

Now that we have discussed curriculum in its different forms, let's explore how we know if, what, and when students learn the content and skills we teach.

Points of Reflection 4.9

Did you gain insight concerning any of Wolk's missing curricular pieces when you were in PreK–12 school? If so, through what part of the curriculum? What do you wish would have been included in your PreK–12 experiences?

What Is Involved in Classroom Assessment?

Classroom assessment encompasses all the possible ways teachers determine what students know and can do measured against standards or other learning goals. The assessments developed and used by individual teachers are **criterion referenced**, meaning that student results indicate levels of mastery of a subject and do not depend on how other students score. In its many forms, classroom assessment serves multiple purposes that are appropriate for the variety of curricula and instructional strategies used in U.S. schools.

PURPOSES OF CLASSROOM ASSESSMENT

Determining student achievement and reporting grades are the most commonly understood reasons for classroom assessment, but these are not the only purposes. The National Council of Teachers of Mathematics (NCTM) broadened our view of the purposes of assessment. Figure 4.3 illustrates NCTM's four purposes of assessment.

Monitoring student progress. Ongoing assessment allows teachers to be continuously aware of where students are in the learning process. Assessing student knowledge and skill levels before beginning a unit of study is called **diagnostic assessment** or, more commonly, **pretesting**.

The results of diagnostic assessment should be used to plan the daily lessons of the unit, including multiple **formative assessments** in a variety of formats that gauge student progress. Feedback is the key to making formative assessment effective. Feedback needs to be timely and specific enough to make students aware of not only where they are in the learning process, but also what they need to do to move forward.

Making instructional decisions. Assessment can be a waste of time and effort if it does not influence the content, the instructional strategies, and the pacing or sequencing of classroom experiences. Effective monitoring of student progress provides the information and insight needed to make instructional decisions that promote student growth. These decisions may involve reteaching or teaching differently to help more students master the unit content and skills.

Evaluating student achievement. Assessment allows teachers to measure if, and how much, students learn. Formative assessments and their results may have a part in

Figure 4.3 NCTM's four purposes of assessment

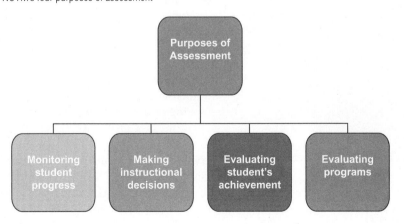

Figure 4.4 Diagnostic, formative, and summative assessment in the classroom

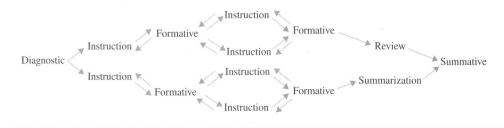

the measurement, but **summative assessment** is most often used to evaluate student achievement. A summative assessment is typically more formal than a formative assessment and involves judging the success of a process or product. Summative assessments most often occur at the end of a unit of study. Paper-and-pencil tests are traditional summative assessments, but they need not be the only format used. Students should be given opportunities to demonstrate what they know and are able to do in a variety of ways, such as completion of a project or performance of an authentic task, or one that actually applies the knowledge and skills. When students succeed, teachers can and should recognize accomplishments.

Look closely at Figure 4.4. Notice the flow from diagnostic to formative to summative assessment. The double arrows between formative assessment and instruction indicate that formative assessment helps teachers make decisions about instruction. There is fluidity between ongoing formative assessment and what is planned in the classroom. Summative assessment occurs at the end of the formative assessment/instruction ebb and flow.

Evaluating programs. The fourth purpose of assessment may extend beyond the classroom. Instructional materials and formalized programs such as Scholastic 180, the literacy program used by focus teacher Deirdre at Cario Middle School in Mt. Pleasant, South Carolina, are purchased by schools and districts. The components of these programs are monitored for effectiveness, and decisions are made regarding their value based on results of various forms of assessments.

FORMS OF ASSESSMENT

Students learn differently and should have a variety of opportunities to demonstrate what they know and can do. Varying the assessment format ensures that differing student learning styles and intelligences are accommodated.

Robert Marzano (2000), an educational researcher, compiled the seven basic forms of classroom assessment listed in Table 4.2. Read about each and think about whether and how it might serve a diagnostic, formative, and/or summative function.

One of the forms of assessment, teacher observation, is a given. We watch, we listen, and we make mental or written notes about student progress. One of our focus students at Summit Primary School in Ohio is repeating kindergarten, not so much for academic reasons as for social ones. Dylan Todd was a young 5-year-old when he started kindergarten. A bright little boy living in a comfortable

Forced choice, essay, and short written responses continue to dominate classroom assessment.

TABLE 4.2 Seven forms of assessment

Form of Assessment	Characteristics
1. Forced choice	• Multiple choice, matching, true/false, fill-in-the-blank • Can be scored objectively • Most common form of assessment • Choose from among alternatives given
2. Essay	• Good for assessing thinking, reasoning, and expression skills • Opportunity to demonstrate knowledge of relationships • Gives information on how students process knowledge • Scoring can be subjective
3. Short written responses	• Mini-essays • Brief explanations of information or processes • Scoring more objective than for essays
4. Oral reports	• Assess student speaking ability • Similar to essay but more impromptu • Require acute listening skills to score
5. Teacher observation	• Informal • Best for process-oriented and nonachievement factors • Good when linked to interview of student • Teacher notes used to record observation results
6. Student self-assessment	• Most underused form of assessment • Helps develop higher-order metacognitive skills • Assessment conference allows student to clarify own level of learning
7. Performance tasks	• Require student to construct responses, apply knowledge • Require more than recall of information • Can assess a variety of forms of knowledge and skills • Scoring dependent on task

Source: Marzano, R. J. (2000). *Transforming classroom grading*. Alexandria, VA: Association for Supervision and Curriculum Development.

socioeconomic status (SES) home with adoring parents, Dylan experienced expected academic growth in his first year at Summit Primary. But, as his teacher observed, he was still quite immature at the end of his initial year in kindergarten. Teacher observation, as we see in Table 4.2, is particularly effective when assessing nonachievement factors. In consultation with Mom and Dad, the decision was made to have Dylan repeat kindergarten, this time in the enrichment class. In this group designed for children who have mastered a set of basic skills, Dylan is thriving. Revisit Dylan's interview with teacher Brandi Wade and his parents.

Performance assessment. The last of Marzano's seven forms of assessment involves performance. This simply means that students actually show what they know and can do in ways that do not solely involve paper-and-pencil tests. **Performance assessment** may be a project, a demonstration, a creation, or anything that requires the application of knowledge and skills. You may hear the terms *alternative assessment* and *authentic assessment* used interchangeably with performance assessment. **Alternative assessment** is assessment that doesn't fall within Marzano's first three categories. **Authentic assessment** means that students show what they know and can do in a real-life setting or situation. Performance assessment is alternative assessment and may also be authentic.

Portfolio assessment. One way to put a variety of assessments together to reflect student learning is to use portfolios. To create a **portfolio**, students or teachers, or both, assemble a cohesive package of representative evidence of student learning. A portfolio may serve as

- A compilation of all the work a student does over a period of time. The student may feel a greater sense of accomplishment from reviewing a portfolio than from seeing individual assessments that are quickly discarded.
- A selected collection of work intended to show growth over time.
- A display tool for work samples that showcase the student's best work.

You are likely creating a portfolio, or will be soon, of products related to your education coursework. Your portfolio will show your professional growth. At some point your instructors will evaluate your portfolio and assign a grade that indicates your achievement.

ASSESSMENT OF 21ST-CENTURY KNOWLEDGE AND SKILLS

The Partnership for 21st Century Skills (2012) defines goals for assessment that reflect its philosophy and the practical advice you have read about in each of the preceding chapters. They endorse assessment that

- Promotes balance, including both standardized assessment and classroom formative and summative assessment.
- Emphasizes the role of feedback as part of learning.
- Uses technology and measures student mastery of 21st-century skills.
- Includes development of portfolios.

Points of Reflection 4.10

What forms of assessment do you remember from your K–12 experiences? Did you have preferences? If so, what aspects of the different assessments did you prefer? Why?

Given all the possible ways to assess what students know and can do, it is important to create a balanced assessment plan for the classroom. Each assessment method has appropriate uses and each has limitations. Paying close attention to which assessment is appropriate will help ensure assessments align with curriculum, instructional strategies, and the needs of students. In ***Teaching in Focus,*** Brenda Beyal, one of our three focus teachers at Rees Elementary School in Utah, gives valuable advice about balance in teaching and the merits of focusing on student learning.

Teaching in Focus

Brenda Beyal, Grades 3–5 Multiage Classroom, Rees Elementary School, Spanish Fork, Utah. *In her own words. . . .*

What a wonderful, scary, exhilarating, confusing, demanding profession you have chosen. Wonderful because you spend it with children. Scary because you have to teach them to become literate, capable human beings. Exhilarating because your creative juices have a place to flourish. Confusing when students come with baggage and with very little room for instruction, practice, and evaluation. And, finally, demanding because it takes hard work, perseverance, and commitment. To help with your journey, I offer the following five bits of advice.

1. Be present in your classroom. Be intellectually, emotionally, and socially present in your room. Pay attention to the students, what they are saying and doing. Keep yourself present.

2. Search out colleagues who will nourish you and your profession. Find the teachers who aren't protective and territorial over their teaching. Search out the ones who share, don't compete, and have a philosophy similar to yours.

3. Continue learning, read education journals, subscribe to a professional publication, and read for pleasure.

4. Focus on student learning and not on your teaching. Teach to see students grasp ideas and come up with their own ideas. You may have delivered a lesson that was outstanding, uses all the bells and whistles and the correct language you have been taught, and still not reach a child. Focus on student learning.

5. Live a rich life. Children need teachers who experience, explore, and discover. Take vacations, learn to knit, do it.

How Do Teachers Evaluate Student Learning and Assign Grades?

Now that we have discussed the purposes and forms of assessment, let's look at how we use assessment to evaluate student learning and, ultimately, assign grades. Recall that evaluating student achievement is one of the four purposes of assessment.

EVALUATION

The words *evaluation* and *assessment* are often used interchangeably, but they are not the same. Assessment is gathering evidence of student learning. **Evaluation** makes judgments about, and assigns values to, the results of assessments. For example, a student writes an essay about the effects of rail travel on the gold rush of the 1800s. The teacher uses the essay as an assessment of what the student learned in a unit on the events leading to the statehood of California. The assessment provides the evidence to evaluate the quality of student learning.

It is not necessary, or advisable, to evaluate all evidence of student learning. In our previous example, the teacher may assess the note-taking skills of the student by checking on the completeness of note cards the student filled out during research in the library (first formative assessment). This assessment and teacher feedback help the student make corrections in the research process and move forward with the project. The teacher may simply record a check in the grade book to indicate that student progress was assessed through an examination of note cards. There's no need to make an evaluation at this point. When the student submits an outline for approval, a second formative assessment occurs. Later the teacher may read through the essay rough draft and give feedback on it (third formative assessment), yet still not record an evaluation. In this scenario there are three formative assessments without evaluation. When the student turns in the completed essay, the teacher will use a rubric to do a summative assessment of this student's alternative performance, and then record an evaluation.

RUBRICS

One of the most productive innovations in assessment is the **rubric**, an assessment tool that makes explicit what is being assessed, lists the characteristics of the different degrees of quality, and provides a rating scale to differentiate among these degrees. Rubrics add consistency to subjective evaluation and serve several distinct, yet related, purposes:

- Rubrics provide clear expectations for assignments. Therefore, they are instructional tools as well as assessment tools.
- Rubrics allow teachers to differentiate consistently among performance levels.
- Rubrics provide guidelines for student improvement.
- Rubrics make grading more transparent and consistent.

There are two basic types of rubrics. A **holistic rubric** uses one scale for an entire project. In Table 4.3 you can see that a student may receive a score of 0 to 5 according to the descriptor that most closely matches the work being assessed.

An **analytic rubric** specifies separate parts of an assessment task, product, or performance and the characteristics of various levels of success for each. An analytic rubric gives much more information than a holistic rubric. The sample analytic rubric in Table 4.4 could be used to evaluate a demonstration lesson you may create and deliver in a teacher preparation class.

Along with numbers for scoring, most rubrics include descriptors of what the numbers mean. For instance, on a 0 to 5 scale, the numbers may be interpreted as follows:

TABLE 4.3 Sample holistic rubric

Score	Descriptor
5	Student clearly understands the assessment task and the product fulfills all the requirements accurately and completely.
4	Student understands most of the assessment task and the product fulfills the requirements.
3	Student understands just enough of the assessment task to fulfill most of the requirements.
2	Student has little understanding of the assessment task and fulfills a minimum of the requirements.
1	Student does not understand the assessment task and fulfills none of the requirements.
0	Student does not attempt the assessment task.

TABLE 4.4 Sample analytic rubric

Criterion	4	3	2	1	0
Topic choice	Relevant, interesting	Appropriate	Shallow, lacks interest	Very limited	Not appropriate
Planned assessment	Creative, matches instruction	Adequate and appropriate	Only addresses part of topic content/skills	Does not address topic	Not included
Standard(s) objective(s)	Appropriate, well written	Appropriate	Improperly written	Not appropriate	Not included
Lesson procedures	Clear, detailed, could be easily implemented by others	Clear and adequately detailed	Not detailed enough to be implemented by others	Unclear	Not included
Handout for class	Professional, detailed, few mechanical errors	Adequate detail, useful, few mechanical errors	Not enough detail, distracting mechanical errors	Not useful	Not included

5 – Advanced		5 – Highly accomplished
4 – Proficient		4 – Developed
3 – Adequate	or	3 – Developing
2 – Basic		2 – Emerging
1 – Below basic		1 – Preparing to begin
0 – Not attempted		0 – Not attempted

Many Internet sites provide templates for the creation of rubrics for multiple content areas and performance tasks. To take advantage of all the benefits of using rubrics to evaluate classroom assessment tasks, products, and performances, teachers should:

1. Create rubrics for as many tasks as appropriate.
2. Explicitly teach students how to read and use rubrics.
3. Distribute rubrics when the task is explained or assigned.
4. Refer to the rubric when giving directions, answering questions, guiding students, and so on.
5. Provide samples of work (sometimes called anchors or **exemplars**) that fit the various criteria for scoring so that students actually see what a product that earns a particular number looks like.
6. Inform families about the use and benefits of rubrics as assessment tools so they will understand the evaluation criteria and know how to help guide their students.

ASSIGNING GRADES

A **grade** is a judgment of assessment quality, or an evaluation, with a number attached to it. The wisdom of assigning grades has been questioned for decades by many who view grades as harmful to student self-esteem and detrimental to progress (Powell, 2011). Even so, Marzano (2000) states that "Americans have a basic trust in the message that grades convey—so much so that grades have gone without challenge and are, in fact, highly resistant to challenge" (p. 1).

Perhaps the most compelling reason for grades is that they are expected by students, families, administrators, and the public in general. In *How to Grade for Learning*, O'Connor (2002) summarizes reasons for grading as follows:

1. Instructional uses: Clarify learning goals, pinpoint strengths and weaknesses, motivate
2. Communication uses: Inform students and parents about achievement
3. Administrative uses: Promotion, graduation, honors, eligibility
4. Guidance uses: Help students and parents make educational and vocational plans

Guidelines for grading. There are guidelines that assist teachers in making grades fair and accurate depictions of student learning, including:

1. Relate grading procedures to learning goals.
2. Relate grades to an individual's achievement on learning goals, not an individual's relative achievement to other students.
3. Grade individual achievement only.
4. Include a sampling of student work, not all work, in a student grade.
5. Update grades to reflect how much learning occurs by the end of the grading period, not a compilation of scores when topics were new.
6. Carefully arrive at a final grade by considering the method of averaging to be used and the significance of zeros.
7. Base all grades on quality assessments.
8. Involve students in the grading process whenever possible and appropriate. (O'Connor, 2002, pp. 243–244)

As you consider implementing classroom assessment, remember this mantra: "Teach what you test; test what you teach." Return often to the four purposes of assessment discussed earlier in this chapter.

What Are Standardized Tests, and How Are Their Results Used?

A **standardized test** is one that is given to multiple groups of students, designed for specific grade levels, and typically repeated annually. These tests are administered and scored under controlled conditions, and their exact content is unknown to everyone except the test makers before they are administered.

Let's begin by comparing standardized tests and standards-based tests. A **standards-based test** is one that is devised according to the content of a specific set of standards. For instance, state standardized tests are also standards based because state content standards (now primarily the Common Core State Standards in ELA and math) are addressed in the writing of the test items. But to say a test is standardized doesn't necessarily mean that it is standards based. The content may be derived from textbooks or various curriculum guides but not necessarily from a specific set of standards.

In the previous section we discussed ongoing classroom assessment in varied formats that provide a broad view of learning over time. In contrast, standardized tests and their results tend to be more isolated snapshots of learning. These are often termed **high-stakes tests**—standardized tests that have far-reaching consequences, sometimes referred to as high-stakes consequences. A single test administered in one specific format once a year is very different from ongoing classroom assessment.

STANDARDIZED TESTS IN THE UNITED STATES

Standardized tests are given in some form in every public school in the United States. Let's explore four broad categories.

International Association for the Evaluation of Educational Achievement (IEA). The IEA was founded in 1958 and is an independent, international cooperative of national research institutions and governmental research agencies, conducting large-scale studies of educational achievement. In general, the two prominent IEA tests

- provide achievement data to show trends in performance over time
- foster public accountability
- allow achievement comparisons among countries

Trends in International Mathematics and Science Study. As the only international test of math and science that compares students worldwide, the **Trends in International Mathematics and Science Study (TIMSS)** has been administered every 4 years since 1995.

In 2011, 50 countries participated in TIMSS testing and the exams were given to sample populations of fourth graders and eighth graders. As with any standardized assessment, IEA attempts to monitor conditions under which the TIMSS exams are given to make sure nations follow the appropriate guidelines for randomly selecting students. Percentages of items answered correctly for the top 10 countries are in Table 4.5. It's interesting to compare math fourth and eighth grade averages. Internationally, the math average for fourth grade is 9 points higher than for eighth grade. In science, the international average for fourth grade is 6 points higher than for eighth grade. This has implications for the four years between fourth and eighth grade, or possibly has implications for the test given in fourth grade and the test given in eighth grade. Are expectations relatively higher for eighth graders than for fourth graders, or are the tests not an accurate reflection of the grade level expectations? Perhaps further research will reveal an answer. Here are some highlights from the most recent administration of the tests:

- The average mathematics score of both U.S. fourth graders and eighth graders was higher than those in 40 of the 50 other countries.
- The average science score of U.S. fourth graders was higher than those in 43 of the 50 other countries.
- The average science score of U.S. eighth graders was higher than those in 40 of the 50 other countries.
- All of the countries scoring higher than U.S. students in both fourth and eighth grade were Asian or European. (International Association for the Evaluation of Educational Achievement, 2012a)

Progress in International Reading Literacy Study. As the only international test of reading proficiency that compares students worldwide, the **Progress in International Reading Literacy Study (PIRLS)** was administered to fourth grade students only in 2001, 2006, and 2011. The PIRLS assessment tests proficiency in two specific types of reading, literary and informational. The percent of literary text items answered correctly by U.S. students on the 2011 exam was 70%, while the percent of informational text items answered correctly was 60%. These numbers align with the international averages, with correct answers on literary texts 59% and on informational texts 50%. It's important to note that results like these prompted the developers of the Common Core State Standards for English language arts to place equal weight on narrative, or literary, reading skills and on informational, nonfiction reading skills. Percentages of items answered correctly on the 2011 PIRLS for the top 10 countries are in Table 4.6. United States fourth graders scored the same as, or better than, 40 of the 45 nations participating in PIRLS in 2011.

TABLE 4.5 Percentage of items correct on TIMSS 2011 for the top 10 of 50 countries

Math						Science					
4th Grade			8th Grade			4th Grade			8th Grade		
Rank	Country	%	Rank	Country	%	Rank	Country	%	Rank	Country	%
1	Singapore	74	1	Republic of Korea	74	1	Singapore	66	1	Singapore	64
2	Hong Kong	74	2	Singapore	73	2	Republic of Korea	65	2	Chinese Taipei	59
3	Republic of Korea	74	3	Chinese Taipei	72	3	Finland	63	3	Republic of Korea	58
4	Chinese Taipei	71	4	Hong Kong	68	4	Japan	60	4	Japan	57
5	Japan	70	5	Japan	64	5	Russian Federation	59	5	Finland	56
6	Northern Ireland	65	6	Russian Federation	56	6	Chinese Taipei	59	6	Russian Federation	54
7	Belgium	62	7	Israel	51	7	United States	57	7	England	52
8	Russian Federation	61	8	Finland	49	8	Czech Republic	56	8	Hong Kong	52
9	England	61	9	Hungary	49	9	Hong Kong	56	9	Hungary	50
10	United States	60	10	United States	48	10	Hungary	56	10	United States	50
International Average (50 countries)		50	International Average (50 countries)		41	International Average (50 countries)		48	International Average (50 countries)		42

Source: TIMSS 2011 Assessment. Copyright © 2012 International Association for the Evaluation of Educational Achievement (IEA). Publisher: TIMSS & PIRLS International Study Center, Lynch School of Education, Boston College, Chestnut Hill, MA and International Association for the Evaluation of Educational Achievement (IEA), IEA Secretariat, Amsterdam, the Netherlands. Retrieved January 4, 2012 from http://timssandpirls.bc.edu/timss2011/downloads/T11_IR_M_AppendixE.pdf.

TABLE 4.6 Percentage of items correct on PIRLS 2011 for the top 10 out of 45 countries

Reading, 4th Grade		
Rank	Country	%
1	Hong Kong	69
2	Finland	68
3	Russian Federation	68
4	Singapore	68
5	Northern Ireland	66
6	United States	65
7	Chinese Taipei	65
8	Croatia	65
9	Denmark	65
10	England	64
International Average (45 countries)		55

Source: PIRLS 2011 Assessment. Copyright © 2012 International Association for the Evaluation of Educational Achievement (IEA). Publisher: TIMSS & PIRLS International Study Center, Lynch School of Education, Boston College, Chestnut Hill, MA and International Association for the Evaluation of Educational Achievement (IEA), IEA Secretariat, Amsterdam, the Netherlands. Retrieved January 4, 2012 from http://timssandpirls.bc.edu/pirls2011/downloads/P11_IR_AppendixE.pdf.

National Assessment of Educational Progress. Often called the nation's report card, the **National Assessment of Educational Progress (NAEP)** is the only standardized test systematically administered to a sampling of students across the United States. The NAEP is administered to fourth, eighth, and twelfth graders in math, reading, writing, science, history, economics, geography, civics, foreign language, and a variety of the arts. The grade levels and subjects are rotated so that not every subject is assessed in every grade each year. The results are not reported by student, school, or district, but only by race, grade level, and state. The NAEP

- allows for the achievement tracking of students at specific grade levels over time, both nationally and by individual states
- provides a basis for state-to-state comparisons
- allows for results tracking for a particular subject area and for comparisons among subject areas

Scores on the NAEP are divided into three categories: basic (partial mastery), proficient (solid performance on grade-level content/skills), and advanced (superior). Unfortunately, many students do not even achieve at the basic level. With a few exceptions, scores on the NAEP have remained about the same over the years. One exception occurred in 2005, when fourth and eighth grade math scores were the highest since NAEP testing began in 1969. However, in all subject areas except reading, the percentage of twelfth graders at the proficient and advanced levels is consistently lower than the corresponding percentage for fourth and eighth graders. Over the years, scores at all grade levels in social science subjects such as history, civics, and geography have been lower than the scores in other areas. In all subjects, significant gaps remain between the scores of white students and those of African American, Hispanic, and Native American students (National Center for Education Statistics, 2006).

General standardized tests. Mandatory testing of students using standardized tests has existed for decades. The most frequently administered general standardized tests include the California Achievement Test (CAT), the Comprehensive Test of Basic Skills (CTBS), the Iowa Test of Basic Skills (ITBS), the Metropolitan Achievement Test (MAT), and the Stanford Achievement Test (SAT). You may have taken one or more of these tests multiple times.

Many nationally published standardized tests provide detailed score reports for individual students that serve diagnostic purposes when studied by teachers. If given annually, it's possible to track a student's progress in a variety of content and skill areas within a subject.

A major thrust of national standardized tests involves comparing students, both individually and in groups. Comparison is possible because the tests are **norm referenced**, meaning that they are administered to a group of students selected because they represent a cross section of students. The scores of these representative students become the norm against which all other students are compared. Students receive percentile rankings. For instance, if Enrique's reading comprehension performance on the MAT is 78%, this means that 78% of students in his grade-level norm group scored lower than he did, and 22% scored higher. This does *not* mean that Enrique knows 78% of the content tested, only that he did better on the test than 78 of every 100 students who took the test. Recall that classroom assessment is criterion referenced, meaning the assessment actually indicates what students know and can do rather than providing comparison data.

Two important concepts of standardized assessment are validity and reliability. If a test has **validity**, it means that the assessment measures what it is intended to measure. If a test has **reliability**, it means that the assessment yields a pattern of results that is repeated and consistent over time. Makers of standardized tests expend much effort to ensure validity and reliability and to assure the users of the tests that both of these critical components are in place.

State standards-based standardized tests. The newest category of standardized tests in the United States is the state standards-based test, with items based on specific standards. All 50 states now have their own tests administered at a minimum to students in third through eighth grade. This widespread use of standards-based tests resulted from the No Child Left Behind Act of 2001, a reauthorization of the Elementary and Secondary Education Act. In the first decade of the 21st century, NCLB dramatically changed the public education landscape in the United States in a number of ways, notably in the area of assessment.

Test results in some states are not reported in ways that are useful to teachers as they make instructional decisions. For instance, many state tests simply place students in one of four categories, such as below basic, basic, proficient, and advanced. These types of results do not provide information about performance within a particular subject area. In science, for example, the tests do not reveal whether students lack understanding in earth science, biological science, or both. In other words, the results are evaluative and summative, not part of the learning process. "Educative feedback is immediate, relevant, and useful, and it promotes student learning" (Reeves, 2004, p. 9). Teachers and other educators have expressed disappointment that many state standards-based tests do not provide educative feedback.

State standards-based assessments are high-stakes tests because there may be drastic consequences associated with inadequate test results. For instance, the results are used to make decisions about funding and human resources, which students are promoted or held back, and who graduates and who doesn't (Stiggins, 2008). Based on standardized test results, states threaten (and sometimes follow through) to close schools, dismiss principals and teachers, and then reopen schools with new staffing and perhaps new programs.

Although most states have adopted the Common Core State Standards in English language arts and math, assessments of the standards still vary. States are collaborating as they implement the standards and write appropriate test items, some with the help of publishers experienced in test creation. Common testing practices will likely surface in the near future.

THE GOOD, THE BAD, AND THE UGLY OF STANDARDIZED TESTING

Many educators, parents, concerned citizens, and others loudly criticize standardized testing, particularly state standards-based standardized testing practices. Among the most well-known critics are James Popham, Susan Ohanion, Alfie Kohn, Anne Lewis, Richard Stiggins, and David Sadker. Critics of current standardized testing practices are not against assessments that are well-constructed tools for improving instruction. Their criticisms are directed at certain current practices. We hear them say, in essence, "You can't fatten cattle by weighing them," meaning that testing alone won't result in more learning.

In a series of focus groups in 2003, Public Agenda, an education watchdog organization, asked questions about accountability issues. The groups of teachers, parents, students, employers, and professors all overwhelmingly responded that using one test to judge what and how much is learned has questionable merit. They agreed that basing high-stakes consequences on the results of a single test is not appropriate (Johnson & Duffet, 2003). High-stakes consequences for those accountable for learning are attached to the results of most standardized tests, even while the tests are considered by many to be narrow measures of learning. In this chapter's **The Opinion Page** feature, we read about a school in California that, according to the writer, is meeting the needs of the student population while plagued by regulations that label the school, teachers, students, and community as underperforming. Read this opinion piece and then respond to the prompts that follow it.

There's an adage that says, "What we measure, we do." This means that assessment often determines and limits the curriculum. With test-based accountability and high-stakes consequences, this is probably inevitable. This approach is problematic because often what gets tested gets taught, and little else. For instance, announcements of which subjects will be tested at which grade levels influence how teachers allocate time, often leading them to exclude valuable curricular components for the sake of test preparation. In elementary schools in states where only math and language arts are tested, social studies and science are often relegated to 30 minutes or less in the late afternoon. This practice leaves obvious holes in the curriculum to which students are exposed. The consequences of ignoring standards that are not tested show up in later grades when students lack prior knowledge upon which the curriculum may depend. Do you recall the discussion of the null curriculum? What *isn't* taught can have far-reaching consequences.

Figure 4.5 contains statements about the good and the bad of standardized testing. Of course, the statements don't apply to all tests, just as the statements don't paint

Points of Reflection 4.11

Think about a school in your hometown or near your college that is perhaps in a similar situation as Truckee Elementary, in that the real picture of what occurs there is masked by testing results. Describe the school and the circumstances that led you to choose it.

This Opinion Editorial appeared in the Sierra Sun, a newspaper serving Truckee, North Lake Tahoe and the High Sierra of California, on February 28, 2012.

Truckee Elementary Draws Academic Strength through Diversity

by Alex Herrera

Herrera is co-president of the Truckee Elementary School Parent Teacher Organization.

Too often, trying to dispel stubborn myths can turn into an exercise in futility. But sometimes, the reality of a situation is so plain to see that correcting perception becomes a simple matter of communicating a few, basic facts. Such is the case when setting the record straight about Truckee Elementary students' scholastic achievements.

On the basis of the 2011 results for Standardized Testing and Reporting (STAR), Truckee Elementary School has been designated a Program Improvement school. It's an often scrutinized label that belies the reality of TES, one of a vibrant and diverse community school, steered by passionate teachers who continue to develop bright, high-achieving, and confident students. And ironically, it also obscures the truth about standardized testing results . . . that TES students actually produce some of the best test scores in the district.

The fact is in 2011, Truckee Elementary's English-Learner sub-group ranked first in English Language Arts (ELA) and second in mathematics (out of four reporting schools). And the English-Only sub-group ranked second in ELA and third in math (out of six reporting schools). That is, both sub-groups' scores ranked near the top in the majority of tests, and they were above average in all tests. Yet TES retains PI status [a Program Improvement school], while schools with lower performing sub-groups do not.

The reason? Many schools, including several in this district, are exempt from meeting progress goals set forth by the No Child Left Behind act, either because they do not receive federal Title 1 funds, or because their sub-groups are not deemed large enough to be considered "numerically significant."

Truckee Elementary is fortunate to receive Title 1 funds other schools don't. These substantial, incremental dollars alleviate some of the pain caused by cuts in ever-tightening budgets.

And as both the largest and most diverse elementary school in the district, we have more than just a handful of students in our sub-groups. As a consequence, Truckee Elementary is measured, while other schools with lower-performing sub-groups are not.

At Truckee Elementary, we don't believe any school should be measured solely by test scores. Standardized tests do nothing to reflect a child's social development, aspirations, dedication and self-esteem, factors that predict success in the real world at least as well as test scores. The strength of our school lies not in STAR rankings, but rather in the skills, passion and can-do attitude of our staff, the dedication and diversity of our student body, and the inexhaustible energy of our parents.

Still, when it comes to the unavoidable reality of mandated, standardized testing, scores do matter. And our school is not shying away from the challenge. Scores for our English Only and English Learner students sit near the top of their categories. Our school will continue to work hard to drive scores up even further, eventually dropping our Program Improvement status. That not only means maintaining the strength we've developed in core disciplines like mathematics, but in helping our English Learners close the achievement gap.

Truckee Elementary's diversity is its greatest strength, not its weakness. TES is — and will remain — a quality school our staff, students, parents, and the entire community can be rightfully proud of. However you choose to measure, there's simply no basis for any perception to the contrary.

This Opinion Page piece is an admirable balance of philosophy between those who completely malign standardized testing and those who say it is absolutely necessary. Write a well-developed paragraph in response to each of the following questions:

1. Why does Mr. Herrera believe that the results of STAR do not reflect the true nature of teaching and learning at Truckee Elementary School?

2. What opinion does Mr. Herrera voice that lets us know he doesn't object to measuring student achievement? Do you agree with his view?

3. Is Truckee Elementary the kind of school where you would want to teach? If not, explain. If so, write about your reasons.

a complete picture. The issues are much too complex to be examined adequately in a chart. For our purposes, however, Figure 4.5 serves as an overview.

Standardized testing is not going away. Recognizing that reality, and making classrooms positive places in spite of testing pressures, is the challenge facing us in this age of accountability. Classroom teachers can take the reality of standardized testing and use it in beneficial ways by

Figure 4.5 Pros and cons of standardized testing

Standardized testing is a *positive* component of public education in the United States because

- many tests align with acknowledged learning goals (standards) and measure progress toward those goals
- administering the same test to large numbers of students allows for comparisons to be made and resources to be allotted where they are most needed
- standardized tests are cost effective because they are administered and scored uniformly
- without testing on a grand scale there is no way to make sure schools and teachers are doing the jobs they are assigned

Standardized testing is a *negative* component of public education in the United States because

- the results are often misused, with consequences that are out of line with the relative importance or meaningfulness of the scores
- the tests are often poorly constructed, with items that are not grade-level or subject-area appropriate
- standardized testing often reduces the curriculum by requiring teachers to concentrate on what is tested and eliminate what is not
- inadequate evidence is available to show a correlation between raising scores on state standardized tests and learning as reflected on the NAEP, ACT, SAT, or other nationally published standardized tests
- test-taking skills have an undetermined effect on raising scores, making increased learning a questionable result of better scores
- low-income, mostly minority, students predictably score below students with higher socioeconomic status, validating the opinion that the tests may actually test what's learned, or not, outside school
- teachers generally support standards, but undue pressure from high-stakes standardized tests can undermine productivity
- standardized tests don't measure important concepts such as cooperation, creativity, and flexibility

- modeling mature and reasoned responses to the assessments
- encouraging positive attitudes in colleagues and students
- teaching students that life is full of challenges we may not like or agree with, but that we must meet head on with our best efforts

TEST-TAKING PREPARATION

"Teaching to the test" is a phrase almost always viewed negatively. Stop and think about it for a moment: If the test is a good one that aligns with standards and contains reasonable questions, then teaching to it is a positive thing, right? "Teaching to the test" means emphasizing particular content and format. There's nothing inherently wrong with this if the practice doesn't limit the curriculum more narrowly than the standards and if it doesn't inhibit the implementation of a variety of engaging instructional practices. However, these are big "ifs" and may constitute pitfalls in the name of accountability.

Test preparation is an expectation. However, "many teachers . . . experience a disconnect between their vision of a challenging and rewarding career and the day-to-day grind of test preparation" (Renzulli, Gentry, & Reis, 2004). It doesn't have to be this way. Creative teachers are able to weave test-preparation strategies throughout a rich curriculum and engaging instruction in ways that benefit students and expand their learning. Here are some examples of appropriate strategies:

- Practicing the format of a standardized test increases students' chances of success. If students are familiar with the way the test looks and the way answer choices are arranged on the answer sheet, the possibility of non-content-related errors is reduced, and the test itself becomes a more accurate assessment of student knowledge and skills. For instance, if students are accustomed to listening to directions and working in silence, test day will not seem quite so extraordinary.
- If an anticipated test is in multiple-choice format, it's a good idea to occasionally provide classroom assessments in multiple-choice format.
- If short written response items are anticipated, teaching students to compose succinct, logical answers to prompts should be part of a teacher's instructional strategies.

- Almost every state provides practice materials that supposedly align with state tests. Districts and individual schools often purchase commercially produced materials designed to prepare students for standardized tests and make them available to teachers, or even mandate that they be used. If used on a limited basis, this practice is acceptable.

Who Is Accountable for Student Learning?

When *A Nation at Risk* was published in 1983 by the National Commission on Excellence and Education (a commission appointed by President Reagan), America's public schools were painted as inadequate. Too many students were dropping out or graduating without basic literacy and math skills. People began asking who should be held responsible for student learning or the lack of it. Who should ask, "And how are the children? Are they all well?" and accept responsibility for the answer?

Students have the choice of listening, participating, behaving, and learning—or not. Given the finest and most equitable opportunities and full support from home, students should be held accountable for their own learning. And they are. Teachers grade them, and much of their future success rests on their school accomplishments. But students have very different starting positions when it comes to learning. Some have built-in family and community support and advantages, while others do not.

Parents and families bear a share of the accountability burden. If students are not supported in terms of adequate shelter and food, encouragement to value education, and physical and emotional surroundings conducive to studying, then families are not doing their part to promote student learning.

The adults who spend the most time with students outside the home are their teachers. Few teachers would ever deny that they are accountable for student learning, but most are quick to add they are not alone in their accountability. They expect their principals, as well as the other adults in the lives of students, to support their efforts in every way possible. Teacher evaluations often include their students' score reports from year to year. The days of assuming a teacher is effective based on pleasant personality or self-declaration of competency are over. It has become absolutely necessary for teachers to follow a curriculum that is standards based. If student scores on state standards-based standardized tests are not acceptable, or at least improving, then teachers do not meet expectations.

Local school districts and school boards are also accountable for student learning because they make financial, programmatic, and personnel decisions that affect schools and classrooms.

Points of Reflection 4.12

Who bears the heaviest load of accountability for student learning? If you do not believe that only one group is totally responsible, explain your view of balance with regard to accountability.

Communities are accountable for student learning. If financial support of schools and a fundamental respect for education are not present, then communities are failing to accept their portion of accountability. Elected representatives of communities—legislators, members of city councils, mayors, and governors—all play roles in accountability because they are responsible for policies that either promote or thwart student learning.

State and federal governments share in accountability for student learning. Both levels of government pass laws and deliver mandates that directly affect schools.

So we see that "Who's accountable?" may be answered, "All of us." In other words, "And how are the children? Are they all well?" should be asked and answered over and over by everyone in the United States.

CONCLUDING THOUGHTS

Now that you know more about curriculum—what it is and where it comes from—you understand the importance of both knowing content and being enthusiastic about it. In today's educational and political environment, accountability for student learning falls most heavily on teachers.

Whether student learning occurs, and to what degree, may be gauged through classroom assessment. However, for the sake of coordination of state and national goals, a standardized system is necessary. Both classroom and standardized assessment results should guide the decisions teachers make every day in terms of curriculum and assessment. A great deal of work is still required to create a fair and equitable system that does not stifle imaginative teaching and learning but does yield results teachers can use to plan effective teaching and learning experiences.

We began this chapter by looking at assessment through the practices of Renee Ayers at Summit Primary School in Ohio. Now as the chapter comes to an end, we join Renee as she decides to use portfolio assessment in her second grade class. Read through *Chapter in Review* to help refresh your memory of what we have discussed, and then interact with Renee as she plans for portfolio assessment in *Developing Professional Competence*.

Chapter in Review

What is the formal curriculum?

- The formal curriculum is what is intentionally taught and stated as student learning goals.
- Standards, defined as what students should know and be able to do, serve as the framework for much of the formal curriculum.
- Adoption of the Common Core State Standards in K–12 English language arts and math is voluntary for states and most have done so.
- Textbooks have a great deal of influence on the school and classroom curriculum.
- Various levels of government influence the formal curriculum.
- The formal curriculum includes both core and related arts subjects.
- An integrated curriculum involves linking curricular areas as their contents complement one another.
- A culturally responsive curriculum includes contributions and ways of viewing the world from perspectives of different cultures, ethnicities, races, genders, and socioeconomic levels.
- Infusing arts (music, theater, dance, and visual arts) into the curriculum provides opportunities for expression that motivate and engage students.
- There are multiple points of controversy related to curriculum.

What other curricula do we teach in U.S. schools?

- The informal curriculum is what teachers teach and students learn that is not part of the planned curriculum or standards.
- The extra curriculum consists of activities that are sponsored by the school but outside the formal curriculum.
- The null curriculum is what isn't taught.

What is involved in classroom assessment?

- The four major purposes of classroom assessment are to monitor student progress, make instructional decisions, evaluate student achievement, and evaluate programs.
- The three major kinds of assessment are diagnostic, formative, and summative.
- The seven basic forms of assessment are forced choice, essays, short written responses, oral reports, teacher observation, student self-assessment, and performance tasks.
- Both performance and portfolio assessment provide information on what students know and can do.
- 21st-century assessment promotes balance, includes feedback, uses technology, and encourages portfolio development.

How do teachers evaluate student learning and assign grades?

- To evaluate is to make judgments about quality and quantity.
- Rubrics are instructional and assessment tools that make expectations explicit.
- A grade is an evaluation with a number attached to it.

What are standardized tests, and how are their results used?

- Most standardized tests are high-stakes tests.
- The Trends in International Mathematics and Science Study (TIMMS) and Progress in International Reading Literacy Study (PIRLS) compare student achievement among countries.
- The National Assessment of Educational Progress is called the nation's report card because it allows comparisons to be made among states.
- State standardized tests are also standards based.
- There are both benefits and drawbacks to standardized testing.
- There are appropriate ways to prepare students for standardized tests in addition to providing a rigorous and standards-based curriculum.

Who is accountable for student learning?

- Teachers, principals, and schools bear much of the burden of accountability.
- Families, the federal government, and local and state administration are often viewed as less accountable for student learning.

Developing Professional Competence

Thoughtfully reading this scenario and responding to the items that follow it will help you prepare for licensure exams.

In the *Teaching in Focus* opening segment of this chapter you read about Renee Ayers's focus on using assessment as an avenue for growth for her second grade students. She understands the value of keeping track of growth over time. In her classroom, Renee has a filing system that allows her to conference conveniently with parents about their child's progress. With all these measures in place, Renee is ready to employ portfolio assessment in more formal ways with her students at Summit Primary School in Ohio.

Think through this scenario and answer the following multiple-choice questions:

1. Renee is most likely planning to use portfolios to
   a. Display each student's best products
   b. Substitute for traditional report card grades
   c. Primarily teach students how to be organized
   d. Show student growth over time

2. Knowing Renee as we do leads us to predict that compiling work will be done by
   a. Students alone to teach organizational skills
   b. Renee and students working together
   c. Renee alone because she knows which pieces best accomplish the purposes of portfolio assessment
   d. Renee, in conjunction with Principal Laura Hill

3. Given what you know about Summit Primary School, how will Principal Laura Hill get the word out to all the other second grade teachers in the district if Renee's experiment with portfolio assessment is successful?
   a. Ask Renee to explain what she experienced and her perceptions of results in a faculty meeting
   b. Report Renee's success in a district principal's meeting
   c. Invite all the district second grade teachers to a special portfolio showcase event at Summit Primary
   d. Ask Renee to write about her experiences for the district educator newsletter

Now it's time for you to respond to two short essay items involving Renee and portfolio assessment. Your responses should each be between one half and one full double-spaced page.

4. Given what you know about Renee and her classroom practices, why is portfolio assessment the next logical step for her?

5. Consider the National Board for Professional Teaching Standards Core Proposition 3, which says "Accomplished teachers . . . employ multiple methods for measuring student growth and understanding and can clearly explain student performance to parents." Explain how Renee's plan addresses this standard.

The Science, Art, and Service of Teaching

Let's begin thinking about this chapter's content with an analogy, and a delicious one at that! Baking chocolate chip cookies requires specific ingredients, all of which are necessary. Flour is a necessary ingredient, but flour is certainly not sufficient. Butter is necessary, but not sufficient. Chocolate chips are absolutely necessary, and the more the better, but they aren't sufficient. To bake delicious cookies, all the ingredients matter. Some ingredients taste better than others when sampled alone, but when they are blended in the right proportions, the result is delightful!

Applying "necessary, but not sufficient" to teacher effectiveness reveals that the *science* of teaching (curriculum, assessment, and instruction) and the *art* of teaching (knowing how and when to use particular strategies to teach the curriculum) are necessary, but not sufficient by themselves for optimal student development. The ingredient of *service*, when added in large and individualized measure, completes the teaching recipe.

In this chapter we explore a variety of teaching and learning instructional strategies, along with two additional components of teaching—the *art* of teaching and the *service* of teaching.

In Chapter 5 we focus on these questions:

- How is instruction implemented in U.S. schools?
- What is the art of teaching?
- How do teachers serve students?

Teaching in Focus

Chris Roberts is an adventurer. He travels extensively, climbs mountains, and rafts in white water. He could do lots of things with his life—and he does. But his career choice is teaching 9-, 10-, and 11-year-olds at Rees Elementary School in Spanish Fork, Utah.

It takes only a few minutes in Chris's multiage classroom to recognize how his energy and wide range of interests influence how he interacts with students. He teaches all the core elementary subjects, as well as the dance component of the arts emphasis at Rees. When asked what he gets out of teaching, Chris says, "I like to play, I love these kids, and learning is the most exciting thing in the world."

You won't find in his lesson plans any references to the fascinating displays in Chris's classroom. Nor will you find "Tell the kids about my last dive off the Yucatan" or "Let my students know that life is a wonderful adventure." When Chris infuses his hobbies, interests, and travel into his classroom, he is teaching what we defined earlier as the informal curriculum—lessons that aren't in the curriculum standards. The cartoons with philosophical messages, the inspirational stories and poems, the giant topographical map of Utah, the newspaper and magazine clippings about people who triumphed over unimaginably difficult circumstances, and the personal family photographs—all of it speaks to who Chris is and what he values. Watch **Chris Roberts' room tour** to learn more about his personality, interests, and philosophy that impact his interactions with students.

Teaching has been thought of as both *science* and *art* for decades. *The Art and Science of Teaching* (2007), written by educator and researcher Robert Marzano, has helped revitalize acknowledgment that teaching is more than just **science**, or a knowledge of the formal curriculum and assessment, accompanied by proficiency in the use of instructional strategies. Teaching is also **art**, involving decision making based on numerous variables leading to skillful application of instructional strategies to teach the curriculum and assess learning in ways that meet the varying needs of students. Science and art are both necessary, but not sufficient, for effective teaching and learning. A third dimension is required—service. The **service** of teaching involves attitudes and approaches that promote growth in mind, body, and spirit for the present, equipping students for their journey toward responsible, respectful, and informed life and citizenship in the future.

Teaching in 3D brings curriculum, instruction, and assessment alive for students.

The current craze in theaters is 3D, a process that adds depth that is visible when viewed through special lenses. Take a movie such as *Avatar*. In two dimensions, it's an enjoyable story with amazing computer-generated images. But when the third dimension is added, movie goers become part of the action—bobbing and weaving as objects and creatures appear close enough to touch. The audience becomes involved. *Avatar* works in 2D, but adding the third dimension enhances the perception of depth and helps make it an unforgettable adventure.

Teachers skilled in the two dimensions of teaching—science and art—are generally effective. They know the curriculum and how to teach and assess it. When the service dimension is added, students experience greater levels of cognitive, physical, emotional, social, and moral development. **Teaching in 3D**, with the whole child always in view through the lens of service, prompts students to be active participants in their own learning and growth.

How Is Instruction Implemented in U.S. Schools?

Just as curriculum is the *what* of teaching, instruction is the *how*. Without effective instruction that meets the needs of learners, the most thoughtfully and soundly designed curriculum would not lead to effective learning (Tomlinson & McTighe, 2006). We know there is not one single approach to instruction that works for every student in every subject all the time. Differing student intelligences, learning styles, abilities, societal contexts, and so on, make using a variety of instructional approaches necessary to meet students' needs. Therefore, building a large repertoire of instructional strategies is vital. No need to worry—instructional possibilities are practically limitless.

A teacher provides learning opportunities that fall within a spectrum ranging from teacher-centered to student-centered, depending on the topic or skill, the knowledge and skill level of students, the time frame in which instruction must occur, and the teacher's instructional style. There are circumstances when lecture (perhaps the most teacher-centered of all strategies) is appropriate, and there are other scenarios when student-centered exploration with guidance works best. You may hear the phrases *sage on the stage* and *guide on the side* as you continue your teacher preparation. When a teacher is a *sage on the stage*, there is a lot of telling and demonstrating going on. Strategies such as lectures and **mini-lectures** (shortened, focused versions of the lecture) and teacher demonstrations are examples of *sage on the stage* teaching that can be effective strategies within a teacher's broader repertoire of teaching techniques. When a teacher is a *guide on the side*, the teacher is setting expectations, providing instructions, and serving as a resource while students do the work and exploration that lead to learning. Guiding, or facilitating, student learning leads to increased active engagement.

BIG IDEAS OF INSTRUCTION

Let's explore some of the big ideas of instruction, along with some supporting instructional strategies that allow teachers to apply the big ideas in their classrooms. Each of the big ideas of instruction deserves, and indeed has had, entire books written about it. What you read here is an overview so you will be aware of some of the ideas that will likely be emphasized during your teacher preparation program.

Promote critical thinking. **Critical thinking** involves observing, comparing and contrasting, interpreting, analyzing, seeing issues from a variety of perspectives, weighing variables, and then making decisions and solving problems based on these thinking skills. Can we really teach children and adolescents to think critically as they learn the standards of the formal curriculum? The answer is *yes*. Teaching critical thinking and **problem solving** is not an addition to the curriculum but rather a way of approaching the knowledge and skills we teach.

Benjamin Bloom and others at the University of Chicago first published what is now referred to as **Bloom's taxonomy** of thinking skills in 1956. Simply put, **thinking skills** are those skills that aid in processing information. These skills grow in complexity and sophistication as they progress from Level I to Level VI of the taxonomy. Bloom's taxonomy has become an essential tool used by teachers as they plan and organize learning experiences. All the levels, as illustrated in Table 5.1, are necessary, and none should be neglected. Designing learning experiences that call only for knowledge and comprehension is cheating the minds of students who need to apply and analyze what they know, synthesize or create something new, and evaluate ideas and events. When planning lessons and assessments, teachers should use Bloom's taxonomy and the action verbs associated with each level. Questioning, an important strategy to promote student thinking, is enhanced by using the question *stems*, or question beginnings. In 2001 Anderson and Krathwohl revised Bloom's taxonomy by, among other things, using different words to describe some of Bloom's original levels and designating synthesis (creating) as a higher thinking level than evaluation.

TABLE 5.1 Bloom's taxonomy

	Categories	Key Verbs		Question Stems
Level I	Knowledge (Remembering)	Recognize Identify Recall Memorize	Retrieve List Define Duplicate	When did _____? Who was _____? Where is _____? Why did _____? Can you list four _____?
Level II	Comprehension (Understanding)	Interpret Summarize Infer Illustrate	Classify Compare Explain	How would you compare _____ to _____? What is the main idea of _____? What is meant by _____?
Level III	Apply	Implement Use Operate	Dramatize Illustrate Solve	How would you use _____ to _____? What approach would you use to _____? Can you _____ by _____?
Level IV	Analyze	Organize Integrate Focus	Categorize Differentiate Examine Test	What evidence can you find to conclude that _____? What does _____ have to do with _____?
Level V	Evaluate	Check Critique Judge	Monitor Defend Support	What is your opinion of _____? How valuable is _____ for _____? Why would you recommend _____?
Level VI	Synthesis (Creating)	Generate Plan Design	Construct Produce Develop	How would you change _____ to form _____? Can you propose a different way to _____? How would you design _____ to _____?

Source: From *Introduction to Middle School*, 2e (p. 206), by S. D. Powell, 2011, Boston: Allyn & Bacon. Copyright 2011 by Pearson Education, Inc.

Teach through inquiry. When students pursue answers to questions posed by others or developed on their own, they are involved in **inquiry learning**. Observation, questioning, hypothesizing, and predicting are all part of inquiry-based learning, which requires students to move beyond rote memorization to become independent thinkers and problem solvers. Teaching and learning through inquiry may involve real-world contexts and discovery, and it can be accomplished in such simple ways as providing scenarios for students to explore or objects for students to manipulate.

Inquiry-based instruction is not new. All discoveries have come about as the result of questioning and answer seeking. Before students can formulate questions on their own or search for answers, they need knowledge and skills as building blocks. Once these building blocks are in place, then students are ready to inquire and look for answers. Inquiry-based instruction is an effective way of teaching and learning because the ideas we create ourselves are the ones we tend to retain (Renzulli, Gentry, & Reis, 2004).

A common way of implementing inquiry-based teaching is to design experiences that require students to engage, explore, explain, elaborate, and evaluate. This is commonly called the **5-E lesson plan**. For instance, an elementary teacher can tell third graders the conditions necessary for bean plants to sprout and grow. The students can be tested and many will be able to recite the conditions, at least for the test. Using the 5-E plan, here's how the teacher might guide children through a cycle of inquiry learning:

- Take students outdoors and ask them to observe the plants in the schoolyard (engage and explore).
- Have students discuss with each other what they observed as the conditions for plants to grow and thrive (explain).

- Talk with students about the possibility of an experiment involving some beans that are given the conditions the students think are needed for plants to thrive, as well as other beans that are deprived of the conditions (elaborate).
- Assist students as they work together to create the desirable and undesirable conditions using real beans (elaborate).
- Guide students as they observe and record bean growth and come to conclusions about what contributes to bean plants thriving, and whether their predictions were correct (evaluate).

An important element of inquiry learning is the thinking skill of questioning. Asking students appropriate questions helps them examine concepts and phenomena. When a teacher asks thoughtful questions, students also learn how to frame questions that lead to meaningful learning.

Incorporate student collaboration. There can be significant benefits when students collaborate in a learning environment. Students may share responsibility for a project, discuss a question or prompt given by a teacher, tutor each other, help each other study for a quiz, or participate in a planned group activity. Most often student collaboration in schools is referred to as cooperative learning.

Loosely defined, **cooperative learning** refers to any instance of students working together. It was, however, more strictly defined in the 1980s when Roger and David Johnson designed the following cooperative grouping patterns:

- informal groups that meet together for a variety of tasks as needed
- formal groups that complete designated, often long-term, tasks
- base groups whose members support one another with remembering and completing assignments, studying, and sharing resources (Johnson & Johnson, 1999)

The Johnson brothers devised five requirements for effective student grouping practices:

1. *Positive interdependence*—setting group goals for which all members must work to achieve; shared rewards; roles for each member including facilitator, recorder, materials gatherer, timekeeper, and encourager
2. *Face-to-face interaction*—students work together to explain, complete assignments, solve problems, and so on
3. *Individual accountability*—students must complete individual tasks that contribute to the group
4. *Interpersonal skills*—students learn to work together in socially acceptable ways
5. *Group processing*—students reflect on how well they worked together and how effectively they accomplished their goals; students give teacher feedback on group functioning (Johnson & Johnson, 1999)

Cooperative learning is a big idea of instruction that can be successfully implemented in early childhood, elementary, middle, and high school. It's likely that you have been a member of many cooperative groups during your school experiences. Table 5.2 contains some ways teachers group and regroup students for learning.

Use technology. Today's students are referred to as the "Media Generation," digital learners in "techno-drenched atmospheres" that are "gizmo-intensive" (McHugh, 2005, p. 33). "No generation has ever had to wait so little to get so much information" (Renard, 2005, p. 44). **Educational technology** is any technology-based device that assists teachers in teaching and students in learning. Even though students are growing up in a techno-drenched atmosphere, they still need guidance

Points of Reflection 5.1

Think about the cooperative learning experiences that were productive and pleasant for you in school (including college), as well as those that either failed or were not enjoyable. What made them successful? What contributed to problems with group functioning?

TABLE 5.2 Cooperative learning strategies	
Strategies	**Description**
Think-Pair-Share (T-P-S)	T-P-S involves all students in nonthreatening ways. Teachers expose students to information, give a prompt, ask a question, or provide an experience and then challenge them to think about it in a particular way and perhaps record their thoughts on paper (T). Students then choose a partner (P) and share their thoughts (S). Pyramid T-P-S involves multiple pairs of students discussing the question/prompt.
Jigsaw	This strategy involves students becoming experts on particular topics within *expert groups* and then teaching those topics to the other students in their *base groups*. Jigsaw is a powerful tool that actively involves students both in their own and other people's learning.
Role Play	Getting students up and moving as they dramatize a scenario can make a point or prompt students to think in divergent ways. Role playing becomes more effective with practice.
Tableau	Similar to role play, tableau involves students assuming a freeze-frame position that illustrates an event in a short story, book, or historical event. While students pose, another student in the tableau group reads a narrative that is being dramatized.

in navigating educational technology. They need to learn how to access what they need and decide what is important and relevant from among the seemingly endless flow of information. Students are so used to instant gratification from "on" switches that they are often frustrated when problem solving takes more time and intensive searching. Teachers are responsible for helping students make sense of technology tools, along with ways of using them to be academically productive in our technology-rich society.

The International Society for Technology in Education (ISTE) provides detailed descriptions of the knowledge and skills related to technology use appropriate for children and adolescents. Virtually all major subject-area organizations join ISTE in promoting technology use in the classroom, as do professional organizations representing the various levels of PreK–12 education.

In looking at technology available in schools, the two broad categories to consider are teaching tools and tools for teachers. Technology *teaching tools* are resources that enhance curriculum, instruction, and assessment when used by teachers to teach and by students to learn. Some of the available technology teaching tools are in Table 5.3. This chapter's **SocialMEdia** segment features the use of smartphones as educational technology. Technology *tools for teachers* are those that expedite and/or enhance the work of teachers and, consequently, curriculum, instruction, and assessment in the classroom. Examples include websites that allow for sharing of ideas, software that helps with lesson planning, and electronic gradebooks. Many technologies accommodate both categories.

The ability to share information quickly and easily is possible through classroom technology.

Integrate reading and writing across the curriculum. Reading and writing are vital skills, without which life is both difficult and limited. Regardless of the subject or grade level, all teachers need to be

SocialMEdia

A smartphone can be an effective teaching and learning tool. Today's phones allow for audio, image, and video capabilities. Smartphones are different from a computer lab because the devices are personal. Students have invested lots of time and energy in learning how to use them and exploring possibilities. Additional reasons for using smartphones as educational technology tools include:

- Use can be engaging and motivating
- Learning on the smartphone can extend beyond the school walls
- Smartphones incorporate familiar technology

There are dilemmas involved in classroom smartphone use, including:

- Not all students have a smartphone
- Some phones will support fewer applications than others
- Some students may take advantage of anonymity to use phones inappropriately
- Loss and theft
- Possible distractions and interruptions

The use of smartphones as educational technology is a continually developing phenomenon. Sample uses include:

- Using a site like www.polleverywhere.com, students can respond to questions and teachers can track instant answers. This particular site is free for classrooms of 30 or fewer.
- Accessing prerecorded teacher-developed information and materials to prepare for class
- Taking advantage of the thousands of educational apps as supplements
- Collecting data and recording audio, photos, and video from experiments, field work, voice messages, and so on
- Making podcasts, picture blogs, twittering, and more
- Learning and communicating collaboratively
- Accessing podcasts
- Creating mini-documentaries using the in-phone camera
- Recording field trips

Regardless of a school's smartphone use policy, chances are that middle and high school students have them stowed away in a backpack, purse, or pocket, or perhaps left in a locker or car. Bringing this social media tool into plain sight and using it appropriately for teaching purposes may make sense for you, as long as you have a plan and permission from your administrator.

TABLE 5.3 Technology teaching tools

Technology Tool	Value in the Classroom
Word processing software	Built-in support for writing and publishing
PowerPoint	Popular presentation program used by teachers in their classrooms to deliver instruction and by students to demonstrate skills and display project products
Smart technology	Interactive white boards with Internet accessibility that engage learners
Streaming video	Allows students to view video that is either stored on a site, or live, as it downloads on the computer
Instructional software	Used to learn about concepts and/or practice skills; five categorizes of instructional software: drill-and-practice, tutorial, simulation, instructional games, and problem solving (Roblyer, 2013)
Tablet computers	Also known as notebooks; smaller, more portable than laptop computers; used to access Internet, send and receive e-mail, take photos and shoot videos, and play music
Internet	Most widely used network: World Wide Web (WWW)
Podcast	Like creating a radio program and then distributing it on the Internet; virtual publishing
Electronic books	e-media; iBooks; eTexts
Distance learning	Acquisition of knowledge and skills through instruction delivered using technology; learning is not place based
Digital games	Attention getting and interactive; simulations

teachers of reading and writing. Infusing the curriculum with reading and writing learning and practice opportunities is often referred to as *reading across the curriculum* and *writing across the curriculum*.

Reading. An old adage says that children "learn to read" through third grade and "read to learn" from then on. If only that were true. In early grades when teachers expect to teach reading, they emphasize emergent literacy (getting ready to read) and beginning reading (letter/word recognition and story patterns), and often their efforts are supported by reading specialists whose sole responsibility is teaching children to read. However, many students are not proficient readers by the end of third grade. Even if they are proficient, reading expectations become more stringent and complex, creating the need for specific literacy instruction beyond third grade. The Common Core State Standards ELA guidelines call for increased emphasis on nonfiction text throughout K–12, a step in the right direction toward literacy. In middle and high school there is currently a devastating lack of reading proficiency. More than half of the ninth graders in the 35 largest cities in the United States read at the sixth grade level or below (Vacca, 2002). The average student in a high school classroom is reading below the level of content-area texts and 25% of adults are functionally illiterate (Moats, 2001). Some ideas for promoting reading skills are presented in Figure 5.1.

Access to books, recreational reading, and silent reading all lead to improved skills in both decoding and comprehension (Krashen, 2002). Fluent readers have the skills to be fluent writers. Conversely, students who struggle to read will struggle to write as well.

Writing. Techniques for effective writing in multiple genres have not received as much attention or classroom time as reading instruction. Writing can be meaningfully integrated into all subjects at all grade levels and may be descriptive, creative, factual/informative, or expository. Teaching students to write involves many components, including sentence formation, punctuation, capitalization, word usage, style, and spelling.

Students will benefit from keeping notebooks or journals in multiple subjects to build both reading and writing skills, to increase note-taking proficiency, to record questions about content, to reflect on learning, and so on. Writing essays, biographical sketches, descriptions of events, stories, poetry, and answers to prompts fit naturally into ELA and social studies classes. Writing narrative explanations of science and math procedures deepens and extends understanding.

Now that we have considered some big ideas of instruction and some strategies that bring the big ideas to life in the classroom, we are ready to explore how teachers plan for instruction.

PLANNING FOR INSTRUCTION

We discuss assessment in depth in Chapter 4.

Curriculum is meaningless without instruction to convey it and instruction is useless without curriculum. Assessment, the gathering of evidence of student learning, is a third component of teaching and learning that is interdependent with curriculum

---

Figure 5.1 Ways to promote reading skills

- Give students access to student-friendly, inviting, content-rich reading materials (books, magazines, newspapers, etc.).
- Read aloud to students at all grade levels to show them how to navigate through difficult text.
- Provide opportunities for silent, oral, and recreational reading.
- Use appropriate before (explain vocabulary, predict), during (graphic organizers, note taking, integrating prior and new knowledge), and after-reading strategies (summarizing, checking for understanding).
- Take a "textbook journey" as a class to help students understand the way the pages are set up, the purposes of the illustrations and data representations, the length and structure of the lessons and sections, the activities and exercises that follow sections, the glossary, and so on.

and instruction. All three components are vital in planning learning experiences for children and adolescents.

Backward design. In their 2005 book, *Understanding by Design*, Wiggins and McTighe introduced educators to a concept that links curriculum, instruction, and assessment in meaningful and interconnected ways. This approach to planning for teaching and learning to accomplish understanding is called **backward design**. The word *backward* is used because the approach is in contrast to the way many teachers approach planning, which is to think of activities before considering the desired results of using those activities. Backward design starts with step 1—deciding on the desired learning results (curriculum); then step 2—identifying how to collect the evidence necessary to know if the results have been achieved (assessment); and, finally, step 3—proceeding to choosing how to help students acquire the desired knowledge and skills (instruction). These three stages, as illustrated in Figure 5.2, constitute backward design. Although some teachers view backward design as revolutionary, others call the concept just plain common sense and say they have used some version of it to plan their work for years.

Diagnostic, formative, and summative assessment compose step 2 of backward design, identifying how to collect the evidence necessary to know if desired results have been achieved. Diagnostic assessment is only possible when desired results have been identified and a plan for collecting evidence has been made, the first two stages of backward design. For instance, a teacher may plan a unit of study based on the Industrial Revolution. The teacher decides on the major concepts (content) and skills the students should understand and be able to do. The teacher then decides how to determine when the students have mastered the major concepts and skills using formative and summative assessment. A diagnostic assessment is then formulated that will diagnose what the students may already know about the topic. The teacher uses this information to plan instruction, step 3 of backward design.

In addition to introducing the concept of backward design and expanding our view of understanding, Wiggins and McTighe (2005) contend there is too much for teachers to teach and for students to thoroughly understand in content standards. They advise us to prioritize the standards within three categories. The most vital knowledge and skills are in the first category and are referred to as the big ideas and core tasks, defined as those that give "meaning and connection to discrete facts and skills" (p. 5). The next category consists of the knowledge and skills that are important to know and be able to do. The third category, and the one where some content may simply be mentioned or possibly eliminated altogether, consists of the knowledge and skills that may be worthy of being familiar with but don't rise to the category of being important to know and do. This is good advice.

Levels of planning. In early childhood and elementary classrooms, a daily **lesson plan** may mean planning experiences involving reading and math, with perhaps some social studies and science, a little art, and maybe some music and physical activity.

Figure 5.2 Stages of backward design

Stage 1 Identify desired results (curriculum)

Stage 2 Determine acceptable evidence (assessment)

Stage 3 Plan learning experiences (instruction)

In middle and high school, a daily lesson plan may mean planning for two English classes and two literature classes. Daily lesson planning is the planning that links teaching and learning every day in U.S. schools.

A daily lesson plan should build on the lessons of previous days in cohesive ways. To assure this, daily lesson plans should be conceived within weekly plans or unit plans. A weekly lesson plan is just that, 5 days of sequential lessons. A **unit of study** usually involves a theme, with daily plans within the unit addressing aspects of the theme. Weekly and unit plans should be conceived within **long-range plans** that may encompass a 9-week time frame, a semester, or a year. The best way to plan is with the entire school year's worth of standards in focus. Many schools and school districts provide **pacing guides** that outline what should be taught and when it should be taught, designating the order of concepts and skills. There are also online resources to assist in all levels of planning.

Components of a lesson. Many types of lesson plan formats exist. A common one is shown in Figure 5.3. Subject-area organizations recommend specific components and particular formats that you will learn about as part of your teacher preparation program. Regardless of the format, there are lesson components that are usually considered necessary for effective instruction. Keep in mind that not every lesson will include each component, but over the course of a week, teachers generally incorporate all the components in some way.

Here is a brief explanation of each of the lesson components in Figure 5.3:

- *Standards*—Standards basically set the curriculum and determine what teachers teach and students learn.
- *Objectives*—These are concise statements about what students are expected to learn and be able to do as a result of the lesson.
- *Lesson opening*—The lesson should begin in a way that captures students' attention and creates interest. The opening can be a time to figure out what students already know about the lesson content (their prior knowledge). The information teachers gather requires them to be flexible as they adapt the lesson based on student knowledge and skill.
- *Procedures*—This is the step-by-step plan for how students will learn/explore a topic and/or skill. Procedures may include a variety of models including cooperative learning, inquiry-based instruction, technology integration, and more, with combinations of strategies that include reading and writing and contribute to project- and problem-based learning. Class discussion, questioning, note taking, demonstration, and so on, are traditional teaching genres that may be part of the lesson procedures.
- *Plan for differentiation*—All of the ways that instruction may vary based on a number of factors, primarily differing student learning needs.
- *Opportunities for **guided practice** with feedback*—It's important for students to have opportunities to work independently on applying knowledge in a

---

Figure 5.3 Sample lesson plan format

Standard(s) to be addressed:
Lesson objective(s):
Lesson opening:
Procedures:
Plan for differentiation:
Opportunities for guided practice with feedback:
Independent practice:
Assessment of learning:
Closure of lesson:
Materials and resources:

nonthreatening setting (without being graded). Feedback from the teacher (or as part of an online program) as to whether the student is on the right track will prevent students from practicing incorrectly.

- *Independent practice*—This can be in or out of class and often takes the form of **homework**.
- *Assessment of learning*—How do we know if students have learned what we have articulated in the lesson objective(s)? There are multiple ways of assessing student learning.
- *Closure of lesson*—Providing a way for students to summarize what has been learned is a good way to close a lesson. The bell should not end the class period; there should be a plan to logically draw the class session to a close.
- *Materials and resources*—Planning a lesson includes gathering everything necessary for the lesson to proceed.

Planning for instruction is a vital part of what teachers do. Knowing our students and their developmental levels allows us to plan our teaching appropriately to facilitate their learning.

Not every instructional strategy is appropriate for every grade level. Early childhood is not the place for note taking, and high school is not the place for graphing solely with pictures. Some strategies, however, are appropriate for all levels of school. For instance, demonstration and cooperative learning can be used effectively in early childhood, elementary, middle, and high school classrooms.

Early childhood instruction. *Active engagement* is absolutely necessary in early childhood classrooms. Early childhood teachers need to be masters of engaging children in meaningful activities and providing an environment for creative and cooperative play. In PreK, children learn prereading strategies and the meaning of numbers, among other basic concepts. In kindergarten through third grade, children *learn to read* and perform basic *problem solving*.

In Brandi Wade's lesson, the *objective* is for students to make judgments about the concepts of *less than*, *greater than*, and *equal to* as they manipulate objects. Because Brandi works with the children every day, she knows that their *prior knowledge* includes awareness of the symbolism involved with the concepts and how to count to at least 20 by assigning a number to an object (one-to-one correspondence). Brandi uses what the students already know to engage them in an activity. Here are some strategies Brandi uses in her lesson:

- *demonstrates* counting, sorting, writing numbers, choosing correct symbols
- uses candy M&Ms as manipulatives, or objects to illustrate a concept
- encourages children to work at tables where they can observe and help each other (*cooperative learning*)

Brandi uses the natural social nature of children to encourage them to work together with real objects to accomplish the lesson objective.

Elementary instruction. For students in elementary classrooms, reading takes on new purposes beyond learning to decode words and reading fiction. Reading becomes a tool for acquiring new knowledge in language arts, math, social studies, science, and other subjects. Although *active engagement* remains vital, elementary children can be expected to read, study, and complete assignments with some measure of independence for brief periods of time.

In Brenda Beyal's lesson, the students experience *tableaus*, discussed earlier in Table 5.2. Here are some strategies Brenda uses to support the tableau lesson:

- delivers a *mini-lecture* on author Eve Bunting
- *reads aloud* portions of *Smoky Night*

- uses a graphic organizer to explain what a *tableau* involves
- incorporates *cooperative group work* as a vital part of the tableau
- *facilitates* the work of groups

Brenda knows that her students are able to read *Smoky Night* silently and answer questions about its content. However, she wants her students to be more deeply involved with the book and, among other things, understand the author's motivations, become knowledgeable about the period of history in which the story takes place, understand the societal implications of the story, and experience some of the emotions of the characters. She chose the tableau strategy to accomplish her instructional *objectives*.

Middle-level instruction. Young adolescents typically respond positively to *active learning* opportunities. They are eager to be involved in meaningful experiences that require *inquiry* and creative *problem solving*. They also respond to more traditional strategies such as *mini-lectures* and *note taking* if they have been taught to actively listen, record, and organize what they learn. Variety and frequent shifts in strategies are key to engaging middle-level students.

In Traci Peters's lesson, the students review topics. They complete a worksheet and both respond to *teacher questions* and *take notes*. The new learning in this lesson involves students discovering the sum of the measures of the angles of a triangle, and then writing generalizations about what they have learned. Here are some strategies Traci uses to support the day's lesson:

- begins class with checking *independent practice* (*homework*) to support and review concepts
- *demonstrates* and *questions* using overhead projector
- uses *manipulatives* to discover concepts
- facilitates *cooperative learning* to check for understanding
- requires *written explanation* of learning
- *facilitates* small group work

Traci knows the value of *inquiry-based learning*. She knows that if her young adolescents *discover* the sum of the angles of a triangle they will understand the concept and remember what they learn.

High school instruction. Students in high school respond to *active learning* opportunities. They work best when the content interests them and when they interact with the subject or topic in ways that require them to be *problem solvers*.

In Craig Cleveland's lesson, students are engaged in a thought-provoking class discussion after Craig reads a picture book to them about discrimination. The students then read a series of Jim Crow laws, with the purpose of developing role plays that illustrate a particular law. The students act out their role-play scenarios, and then the class discusses what they have seen. This kind of active involvement is excellent for promoting *critical thinking*. Here are some of the strategies Craig uses in his lesson:

- *reads aloud* to students
- facilitates *class discussion*
- delivers a *mini-lecture*
- uses quotation to provoke *critical thinking*
- assigns *role play*
- incorporates *cooperative groups*

Points of Reflection 5.2

Can you imagine being the teacher in Brandi's classroom? Brenda's classroom? Traci's classroom? Craig's classroom? Which lesson and style appeal to you most?

Craig knows his students well. He understands that the study of discrimination through Jim Crow laws will appeal to them because of the *real-world context*. He also knows that language barriers in his classroom may be partially bridged through *role play*.

What Is the Art of Teaching?

"At its heart, teaching involves being able to 'unpack' something one knows well to make it accessible to and learnable by someone else" (Ball & Forzani, 2011, p. 41). This statement expresses the **art of teaching**—the ability to logically, and in a variety of ways, divide content and skills into manageable components and create experiences that lead to student learning. We've established that the science of teaching involves knowing the curriculum, honing instructional strategies, and becoming skilled in a range of assessment tools. Now let's explore ways to implement the science of teaching to meet the needs of individual students. Doing so is truly an art!

There isn't a formula for effective teaching. We can't say, "I have 24 students, 13 girls and 11 boys. Two have been retained a year, six have either an IEP or a 504 plan, and three are designated as gifted. I'll plug this information into a formula and out will come curriculum content; sequencing; diagnostic, formative, and summative assessment practices; and the right mixture of instructional strategies." Wouldn't it be great to have a teaching input-output machine? But no such machine exists. Every student is different, making every classroom of students different. Teachers are artists, directing learning experiences choice by choice, day by day.

New teachers may master much of the science of teaching and may instinctively, on occasion, incorporate the art of teaching in their classrooms. However, much of the art of teaching comes with experience. But learning from experience doesn't necessarily lead to increased artistry; the learning must be intentional (Barth, 2006). Purposefully observing students and how we interact with them and the content leads to increased artistry and awareness of what works and what doesn't. Marzano (2011) tells us that "Deliberate practice involves more than just repetition, it requires activities that are designed to improve performance, challenge the learner, and provide feedback" (p. 82). Deliberate development of the art of teaching is a continual growth process involving serious reflection on classroom practice, perhaps journaling and conversations with other educators, and meaningful professional development. That's what makes it so exciting. There's always more to learn and do.

DIFFERENTIATION AS ARTISTRY

Approaching instruction in a variety of ways to provide multiple paths for students to both learn the content and develop the skills of the curriculum is artistry. In 1999, Carol Ann Tomlinson gave this philosophy and practice a name: **differentiation of instruction**. Tomlinson (2010) tells us that teachers who differentiate instruction strive to do whatever it takes to meet student needs in terms of affect, readiness, interests, and learning profile. Student *affect* involves "how students' emotions and feelings impact their learning" (p. 16). Student *readiness* refers to "a student's proximity to specified knowledge, understanding, and skills" (p. 16). Student *interest* includes "that which engages the attention, curiosity, and involvement" (p. 16). A student's *learning profile* is determined by many factors, including learning preferences, gender, and culture.

The artistry of differentiating instruction involves an array of content, a variety of processes, and choices of products when possible. The *content* is what the students should know, understand, and be able to do. *Process* consists of the ways students make sense of content, typically through activities and practice. A *product* shows what students know and are able to do; it may be, for example, a project, demonstration, test, or display.

Tomlinson wisely cautions against trying to differentiate too much, too quickly. She advises us to start slowly by recognizing one need (affect, readiness, interests, or learning profile) in our classroom, changing one part of a lesson (content, process, or product), and implementing this differentiated strategy followed by reflection on the results. As our ability and comfort levels grow in diagnosing the affect, readiness, interests, and learning profiles of our students, we can incorporate more and more instructional practices that more effectively meet their needs. However, tackling too many differentiated strategies too soon in a teacher's career, or in a particular student setting, can lead to

Points of Reflection 5.3

Do you recall teachers who attempted to teach the same content in different ways? If so, what type of strategy addressed your learning profile most? If not, what is one strategy you wished you could have experienced more in K–12?

doing an activity for the activity's sake and the sacrifice of solid, well-designed teaching (Tomlinson, 1999). Great advice.

Taking Tomlinson's advice and starting small may involve simply incorporating **manipulatives**, or objects, to represent numbers or concepts in a lesson on fractions. Differentiating may involve prompting pairs of students to complete an assignment together, allowing students to teach each other. Or perhaps differentiation will consist of giving students choices about how they want to work on the week's vocabulary words, with some individually writing definitions and others quizzing each other quietly in a corner of the room. Tomlinson's view, in general terms, of what teachers do in differentiated classrooms is outlined in Figure 5.4.

The realization that every student behavior indicates affect, interest, readiness, and learning profile, and that reading these behaviors is part of the art of teaching, can be staggering. Most new teachers find themselves concentrating on the lesson being taught with a sort of tunnel vision that may make them oblivious to student reactions. Over time, comfort with lesson procedures increases and a teacher's vision widens to include student behaviors. In other words, our classroom peripheral vision increases. At this point it's possible to use the *art of teaching* to increase the effectiveness of *the science of teaching*.

HIGH EXPECTATIONS AS ARTISTRY

The art of teaching leads us to make decisions centered on students and their needs. For decades, research has indicated that teacher expectations determine how they interact with students. High expectations for some students lead teachers to treat them differently than the students for whom they have low expectations. Expectations matter.

Addressing expectations as part of the art of teaching is vital. It's easy to say "I have high expectations for all my students" and then behave very differently toward individuals. Here's what we need to realize . . . *high* expectations do not necessarily mean the *same* expectations. When teachers are realistic, they know that student aptitudes and readiness vary greatly. Having the same expectations for all students isn't fair to any student. Our expectations should be based on all the variables that contribute to learner differences: affect, readiness, interests, and learning profile. Expectations should be individualized and always set high for each student, with a clear vision of growth and success. We must be cautious, however, to avoid stereotyping when we consider variables such as socioeconomic status or race, factors that may lead to unfair and debilitating lower expectations.

All teacher behaviors communicate expectations to students and, in turn, influence students' expectations of themselves. Teacher expectations of a student often become a self-fulfilling prophecy. Teacher and author LouAnne Johnson tells us, "When my students believe that success is possible, they will try. So my first priority in any class is to help my students believe in themselves and their ability to learn" (2005, p. xiii).

Points of Reflection 5.4

Were you aware of your teachers' expectations of you? If so, how did you know? Did teacher expectations have anything to do with your effort to be successful?

Figure 5.4 Differentiation of instruction

When teachers differentiate instruction they . . .

- begin where students are
- accept and build upon the premise that learners differ
- engage students through different learning modalities
- ensure that a student competes against himself more than he competes against other students
- believe that students should be held to high standards
- ensure that each student realizes that success is likely to follow hard work
- use time flexibly
- are diagnosticians who prescribe the best instruction for their students

Source: Tomlinson, C. A. (1999). *The differentiated classroom: Responding to the needs of all learners*. Alexandria, VA: Association for Supervision and Curriculum Development.

Marzano (2011) tells us there are four distinct steps we can take to both be aware of our expectations and to purposefully adjust our behavior. The first step is to *identify students for whom we may have lower expectations*. Second, he urges us to *identify similarities among students* so that we recognize potential. This leads us to identify possible biases that should not impact expectations. Once we've done this soul-searching, the third step is to *identify how we treat the students from whom we expect less*. Then as the fourth step, we do what's necessary to *behave toward students based on our high and thoughtfully individualized expectations*.

High, individualized expectations for each and every student impact not only academic achievement, but also student social-emotional health and well-being. While developing and maintaining these expectations, teachers are using artistry that assumes the best of students and "enables us to treat both our students and ourselves with respect and dignity . . ." (Smith & Lambert, 2008, p. 18). When we do so, we are serving the whole student, cognitively, physically, emotionally, socially, and morally.

Expectations are explored in more detail in Chapter 6.

How Do Teachers Serve Students?

Teaching is a service profession. Although service takes on a variety of definitions depending on context, for our purposes, the **service dimension of teaching** involves an attitude that approaches students as complete human beings, with cognitive, physical, emotional, social, and moral components. In other words, an approach to teaching from a service point of view is all-inclusive rather than focused only on academic and cognitive progress. Teachers also have the opportunity to engage students in service, as they learn about real-life issues and personal and collective responsibility. **Service-learning** occurs when student experiences combine service with a purposeful learning component.

TEACHERS SERVING STUDENTS

Most teachers naturally see students and their profession through a service lens, but to do so intentionally increases the potential impact of this third dimension of teaching. Note that a service approach does not in any way conflict with academic learning; the service dimension is not anti-accountability. It's not an add-on, but rather an integral part of a teacher's day. Service primarily manifests itself in the unplanned, spontaneous, and unavoidable area of the curriculum that is rarely written in a lesson plan, but which strongly influences every part of teaching and learning—the informal curriculum.

The informal curriculum is discussed in Chapter 4.

Like it or not, who we are and what we do impact our students. By virtue of being the teacher, our words, actions, nonverbal communication, and attitudes become part of every academic lesson we plan and implement, as well as every teacher-student encounter and interaction. We impact the informal curriculum, both intentionally and unintentionally. We might go so far as saying teachers *are* the informal curriculum. If we are positive, caring, excited about learning, fair, and organized, students learn that

- optimism is more productive than pessimism;
- cooperation and empathy matter;
- structure and enthusiasm enhance learning; and
- responsibility is personal and valuable (Powell, 2010).

On the other hand, if we are negative, lack interest in students and subjects, or exhibit a general disdain for our work, students are likely to mirror these qualities. If our classrooms are a mess, if the school building is dilapidated, and if the community is unsupportive, students learn that they may not matter very much.

There are as many aspects of the service dimension of teaching as there are instructional strategies and combinations of strategies. Although we focus here on six ways teachers serve students, once you understand the service dimension, you will naturally add to them based on your personality and the students you serve. After we explore these six ways, we discuss the purposes and methods of involving students in service and service learning.

1. Form relationships. Relationships matter. Robert Pianta, author of *Enhancing Relationships Between Children and Teachers*, writes, "Although instruction-oriented interactions with adults have the goal of increasing the child's skill in a particular area, these interactions nonetheless occur in the context of the relationships in which they are embedded—and they are influenced by the qualities of those relationships" (1999, p. 81). Promoting positive relationships means making connections with students with an interested mind and a caring heart. Relationships happen between individuals; viewing students as individuals is necessary. This means, to the extent possible, we should get to know our students, and, in turn, allow them to get to know us. We need to be real people with dreams, flaws, and lives outside school.

Positive relationships may be formed through simple acts such as quickly learning student names, greeting students with a smile, having real conversations, acknowledging circumstances that affect student lives, and demonstrating care at every turn. Teacher-student relationships are also fostered when students know they can count on us to protect them—academically, emotionally, and socially. Refusing to tolerate any sort of harassment among students builds the trust necessary for positive relationships.

Empathy, as the capacity to see situations from another's point of view, is something we should both exhibit and teach. The better we know our students, the greater our capacity for empathy. The more we model empathy and talk about it with students, the more likely they are to empathize with each other and with us, making relationship bonds stronger and more beneficial.

Building relationships leads to increased student engagement and achievement (Stipek, 2006). When students sense they are valued in classroom relationships, they are more willing to cooperate and engage in the classroom (Jensen, 2005). Students who sense they belong have more inner resources to use to be successful (Osterman, 2002). Nel Noddings, a highly respected teacher and researcher, tells us that caring about students leads to their sense of belonging. Moreover, Noddings (1992, p. 27) maintains that "Care is the bedrock of all successful education." In this very important way, teaching as service complements the formal curriculum.

2. Create a climate of respect. A climate of respect begins with a teacher deliberately modeling acceptance. It's obvious to students when a teacher accepts all students for who they are and where they are in their growth journey; it's also obvious to students when a teacher doesn't. Unconditional acceptance fosters self-acceptance and leads to students accepting each other. Fried (2001) tells us that only when people feel they can be themselves without ridicule or alienation will they be willing to take risks, make mistakes, and keep growing.

When students sense acceptance, they are more willing to express themselves. A climate of respect exists when a teacher values what students have to say, or **student voice**. Giving students choices, asking for their opinions, teaching them to reflect on their own learning, and giving meaningful writing assignments help develop student voice. When students are treated with respect, two valuable things happen: their self-worth grows and they are more likely to respect the teacher.

3. Model productive habits. When you think about how many waking hours students spend in school from kindergarten through high school, it becomes clear that they spend as much, if not more, time with teachers as with family members during their formative years. Students watch us as we work and express our personal interests. It's a valuable service for teachers to model productivity.

In an article "Watching Us Work," Tomlinson (2012, p. 92) tells us that teachers who model productive habits of successful, well-adjusted adults and use opportunities to prepare students for their futures

- respect students;
- assume students have abilities;

- hold high expectations;
- teach students to work smart; and
- discuss stepping stones to successful futures.

As we teach the prescribed knowledge and skills, it is possible to boost development of students into fulfilled citizens with productive work ethics.

4. Emphasize civics and citizenship. The most recent National Assessment of Educational Progress (NAEP, n.d.) results show civics education ranks last among the subjects tested. We need not only more direct teaching about government and the principles of democracy, but also opportunities for students to practice these principles, along with the empowerment to do so.

The habits of good citizenship must be modeled in our schools by the adults who inhabit them. Civics education can enhance these habits. This is not the sole responsibility of social studies teachers; just as with reading and writing, all teachers share this responsibility. Every day in every newspaper across the country we find articles about how "we the people" live together and make decisions. Be informed and talk about topics that are current and interesting. This may take as little as a 30-second mention or a 10-minute discussion. Bring up issues and ask for student opinions and solutions. This is practicing citizenship. Damon (2012) tells us that there are at least four commonsense ways to foster civics and citizenship knowledge and action:

1. Talk about current, as well as past, civic leaders. Yes, we can learn from George Washington and Nathan Hale, but how about from Hillary Clinton and Colin Powell?
2. History courses shouldn't necessarily be chronologically based. How about using concepts and themes to blend the past and the present?
3. Foster patriotism by emphasizing the best of America's traditions.
4. Make sure students know how our government works. Knowledge is power in the development of civic participation and pride.

Retired U.S. Supreme Court Justice Sandra Day O'Connor says, "Knowledge of our system of government is not handed down through the gene pool . . . The habits of citizenship must be learned . . . But we have neglected civic education for the past several decades, and the results are predictably dismal" (Coley & Sum, 2012). In 2009, O'Connor founded *iCivics*, combining her passion for civics and the availability of technology for teaching. *iCivics* is a nonprofit group providing free online educational games and lesson plans focusing on structures of government, citizenship rights and responsibilities, and the Constitution. Teachers across the country are taking advantage of *iCivics* resources to engage students.

5. Promote character building. School-wide emphasis on character development has gone in and out of favor for decades, depending in large measure on school leadership and community expectations. Three-dimensional teachers help students build character, regardless of school programs intended to do so. Many components of character education are accepted as valuable to most Americans. Very few would be opposed to students learning to be more honest, hard-working, and responsible. These desirable traits support academic learning, and they may be even more long-lasting and beneficial than the subject-area standards in the curriculum.

One character trait addresses desirable student-to-student interactions—**civility**. When we practice civility, we treat others the way we want to be treated. Defining civility, pointing out instances of civility and examples of incivility, and modeling civility by not tolerating any form of harassment in our classrooms are part of a teacher's service to students.

Character education is addressed in Chapter 2.

A classroom and school climate of civility will only exist when students are empowered to do what's right, both individually and collectively. Because most student-to-student interactions occur outside the hearing of adults, we need to help students understand that when two, three, or more of them stand up against harassment, bullying of any kind, or inequities, they become a force for civility. To demonstrate the power of standing together, pick up a student's wooden pencil and break it with both hands. Then gather five or six pencils from students and try to break them, together, in the same way. You won't be able to. Chances are students will remember this demonstration of strength in numbers when civility is practiced together.

6. Communicate positively. Teachers communicate all day long, verbally and nonverbally. Nonverbal communication may be body language, gestures, eye contact, touching, writing, or electronic in expression. What we say, what we don't say, and the constant stream of messages we convey impact students. These messages are powerful: A careless or sarcastic comment may slip and be forgotten by us, yet may cut to the heart of a student. A disdainful look read by a student as a comment on his worth may long be remembered.

On the other hand, a thoughtful question asked with genuine interest or a smile in the hall and a friendly greeting may make a student's day. Simple gestures like a pat on the shoulder, an e-mail sent to mom saying project work is going well, eye contact during a conversation . . . this communication takes very little time or effort, but could change the direction of a day or a lifetime for a child in crisis.

To communicate with optimum effectiveness requires an element we often neglect—listening. There's a difference between hearing and really listening. Simply hearing will not give us the clues we need to thoughtfully and appropriately respond. When communicating with students, a disposition of service requires us to *respond* rather than *react* to words and events. This takes self-control, and lots of it. Reactions are quick and brash. Responses take more time to formulate, with both reason and thoughtfulness. Remember, however, that sometimes all a student wants is a listening ear and some validation of feelings and concerns. In this regard, listening is a form of communication; silence can be powerful.

Points of Reflection 5.5

Do you recall a teacher who obviously served students in one or more of the six ways discussed? Describe how you responded to the extra effort of the teacher.

We have discussed just six aspects of the service dimension of teaching. This chapter's **The Opinion Page** feature is based on one of the most appealing aspects of the teaching profession. We get to "start over" every school year! Aspects of the previous year that worked well can be enhanced and implemented again. Approaches that were less than successful may be changed or abandoned. In "Let's resolve to improve school year" the guest writers give valuable advice for beginning a new school year. Because the service dimension of teaching should grow and develop with experience, it's valuable to consider additional ways to be three-dimensional teachers.

SERVICE-LEARNING

There is a difference between volunteerism and service-learning. **Volunteerism** entails choosing to give time or effort to serve or support a cause without the expectation of receiving anything in return. Volunteerism is noble; there are many avenues for all of us to volunteer. We want students to see us modeling volunteerism as we encourage them to do the same. **Service-learning**, however, goes beyond volunteering, and, indeed, may not be voluntary on the part of students. When a planned learning component is added to service, we have created a service-learning opportunity with the goal of enhancing students' social, academic, and civic skills and sensibilities.

On the **National Service-Learning Clearinghouse** website, we read "Through service-learning, young people—from kindergarteners to college students—use what they learn in the classroom to solve real-life problems. They not only learn the practical applications of their studies, they become actively contributing citizens and community members through the service they perform" (2012). To illustrate the difference between volunteerism and service learning, the website uses this example. If students volunteer to serve the community by cleaning out a streambed, this is certainly a service. But if the students collect the trash and debris, analyze what they find to determine polluting effects, and then share the results with the community, they are learning while serving and providing valuable information that may solve a community problem.

This Opinion Editorial appeared in the Omaha World-Herald on August 8, 2012.

Let's Resolve to Improve School Year

by Gene A. Budig and Alan Heaps

Budig, a McCook, Neb., native, was president/chancellor of three major state universities. Heaps is a vice president of the College Board in New York City.

According to the academic calendar, it's a new year. August and September are the months when K–12 and higher education institutions gear up for the start of school.

Here in the United States—as well as in many other countries—the beginning of the new year is accompanied by a number of traditions. One of the most popular is the making of resolutions: promises to ourselves and others that we will behave well (or better) in the months ahead.

The practice of making new year's resolutions is not a new one. Four thousand years ago, the Babylonians started each year by paying their debts and returning borrowed objects. Two thousand years ago, the Romans asked forgiveness from their enemies. Five hundred years ago, medieval knights took a vow to reaffirm their commitment to chivalry.

In recent times, the new year's tradition has been altered to favor a more tailored approach to resolutions, each of us focusing on behavior that fits our individual situation. According to a U.S. government website, popular resolutions here in America include to drink less alcohol, eat healthier food, enroll in more education, find a better job, get fit, lose weight, manage debt, reduce stress, quit smoking, do more recycling, save money, take a trip and/or volunteer to help others.

It is estimated that almost half of adult Americans make new year's resolutions. It is also estimated that one-quarter drop their resolutions within a week. One-third drop their resolutions within one month. Slightly more than half (54 percent) drop their resolutions within six months.

In the spirit of new beginnings, we talked with a few colleagues and developed a list of educator resolutions for the upcoming academic year.

Be innovative: Our world is rapidly changing. In many ways, possibilities are limited only by our imaginations. But many of our schools look and work the way they did a hundred years ago. We need to implement bold ideas for improving our classrooms.

Be students ourselves: All of us can find something to learn, whether it's about new teaching methods, classroom technology or even a new personal hobby. Let's be continuous learners so we can see the teaching process through the eyes of students.

Broaden the enterprise: We live in a world where the many parts of our lives are interconnected. This is also true of students, all of whom have intricate and powerful ties to their communities, families and personal histories. Let's reach out to student families and community members.

Lead the discussion: No one knows education better than educators. While our judgment is far from infallible, we need to better assert our opinions and knowledge. Let's lead the debate by raising the issues we believe important.

Admit our weaknesses: There are problems in education, and some of them are of our own making. Let's admit this and work to fix them.

Communicate more: Teachers are good at talking to teachers. Counselors are good at talking to counselors. Principals are good at talking to principals. But we're not as good at communicating among the levels and with others. Let's communicate with the broad spectrum of educators and others.

Be role models: Students look not only to what we say but also to what we do. They emulate our behavior in things both big and small. Let's behave in ways we would want our students to follow.

Set high expectations: Our students are a pretty remarkable group. They can achieve almost anything with the right supports. Let's give all students the credit and respect they deserve.

It's about the students: Most importantly, this year, let's remember that education is not about the teachers, the administrators or the lawmakers. It's about the students. If we keep our focus on the students and their welfare, we will have done much to improve the conversation about our schools.

These resolutions are tough ones. But educators are committed to their profession and their students. We hope that educators will work hard to be in that 46 percent who keep their resolutions for more than six months.

Much of the content of this Opinion Page piece relates directly to what you have read in this chapter. Choose three of the nine resolutions and write a well-developed paragraph for each, discussing aspects of the chapter that support them.

Guidelines for service-learning. The National Youth Leadership Council recommends that service-learning experiences include the eight specific components in Figure 5.5. The individual components may exist within a project to varying degrees, but should be part of the design for service-learning projects. Many school districts believe so strongly in the benefits of service-learning that they are making participation in the experience a requirement for graduation. For instance, the Service-Learning Initiative of Chicago Public Schools (2002) requires 40 hours of service-learning experience as part of what's necessary for high school graduation. Chicago Public Schools (2002) simplified guidelines for acceptable service-learning experiences into three components. Within these three components we see implications for the more rigorous standards in the National Youth Leadership Council.

1. Students *prepare* by
   - learning about issues
   - building the skills they will need
   - developing an action plan for service
2. Students *act* by
   - engaging in meaningful service
   - making a difference in their community
   - realizing connections to classroom curriculum
3. Students *reflect* by
   - analyzing and making sense of their experiences
   - discussing, journaling, and presenting

Service-learning opportunities vary based in part on the age of students; interests of teachers and students; collaborations in place among schools and community organizations; and, of course, community need. There are ongoing needs such as homeless shelters, park and road clean-up, and nursing homes. There are also crises to which students and teachers can find ways to respond. In October 2012 Hurricane Sandy devastated much of the Northeast, destroying homes, roads, and schools; about six weeks later, 26 children and adults were killed in a horrific attack on Sandy Hook Elementary. Sandy, then Sandy Hook . . . our hearts broken twice in a matter of weeks. As teachers, we should create service-learning opportunities for ongoing community needs, but also be ready to act quickly to help our students be aware of crises (age-appropriately), providing meaningful ways to help students respond as they serve in some capacity. For instance, if you teach on an 8th-grade team you may have a year-long recycling service-learning project. Suddenly in April, a community suffers massive damage from a tornado and rainstorm, leaving a middle school flooded with no classroom supplies. Your team could organize a campaign to collect school supplies and get them to the students meeting in a makeshift school in an abandoned strip mall. Each student could

Figure 5.5 National Youth Leadership Council service-learning guidelines

Service-learning should:

1. Be meaningful and personally relevant service.
2. Link to curriculum to meet learning goals and content standards.
3. Incorporate reflection that leads to analysis of self and individual relationships to society.
4. Promote understanding of diversity and mutual respect among all participants.
5. Provide participants with a strong voice in planning, implementing, and evaluating projects.
6. Be collaborative with the intent of being beneficial and meeting community needs.
7. Include ongoing monitoring of progress.
8. Have sufficient duration to result in specific outcomes.

National Youth Leadership Council. (2008). K–12 Service-Learning Standards for Quality Practice. Retrieved from http://www.nylc.org/sites/nylc.org/files/files/Standards_Oct2009-web.pdf.

write a personal note expressing their best wishes to the students who are victims of the storm. The victims, in turn, may be encouraged to express their thanks for the well wishes and the supplies. Could the school district afford to provide school supplies for the rest of the year? Yes, probably. But the human desire to help, and the human desire to show gratitude, will both be enhanced as students learn organization and communication skills.

Service-learning possibilities are many, with some of the more common projects listed in Figure 5.6. An outstanding source of projects and lesson plans is the Service-Learning Ideas and Curricular Examples (SLICE), a resource provided by the National Service-Learning Clearinghouse. Service-learning projects may also be conducted within the framework of an established organization or movement, with examples in Figure 5.7.

Some schools have an annual *Day of Service*. Teachers prepare students for the day by facilitating their research in the area of service; using guest speakers; taking field trips; and, in general, helping students understand what they will experience and why it's important. A day of service may involve road or parks clean-up, a walk/run to raise money for a cause, or a day spent with senior citizens. First Lady Michelle Obama is the chairperson of Youth Service America's *Global Youth Service Day* occurring every April. This is the largest service event in the world. Teachers and students can plan service projects with the help of Youth Service America.

Benefits of service-learning. The benefits of service-learning are numerous for both the community and the students who participate. Members of the community may receive valuable assistance with ongoing or crisis-related problems, become the recipients of additional assistance because of the spotlight created by student attention, and be encouraged to make needed changes as a result of student enthusiasm and innovation. Students who participate in service-learning may experience life-long

Points of Reflection 5.6

What service-learning projects were you involved with in K–12? Describe one project and how participation affected you.

Figure 5.6 Examples of service-learning

Need:	Project:	Possible learning components:
Deteriorating buildings, homes, neighborhoods	Paint structures or create murals to beautify town, neighborhood, or school buildings	– Planning project – Scale drawing
Loneliness of elderly	– Write letters, make holiday cards – Choral or instrumental concerts – Visits with residents of nursing facilities – Reading to seniors – Create oral histories	– Communication skills – Knowledge of history
Homelessness	– Tutor children after school – Collect school supplies and clothes – Collect toys and books for clinics near homeless shelters	– Organization skills involved in project planning – Knowledge of economy – Understand job requirements and availability – Understand housing options and dilemmas
Hunger	Plant, maintain, and harvest a community garden; give food to needy	– Knowledge and skills for plant growth – Understanding environmental concerns – Math skills needed for garden design – Respect for growing systems
Hunger	Collect and distribute food	Verbal and writing skills to communicate need and collection plan

Organization	About the organization	Contact information
Alex's Lemonade Stand Foundation (ALSF)	Alex (1996–2004) started a front yard lemonade stand to raise money for cancer research; now a national fundraising movement	http://www.alexslemonade.org/
Project Learning Tree	Program of the American Forest Foundation; uses the forest to engage students in environmental concerns and solutions	http://www.plt.org/
Veterans History Project	The American Folklife Center collects, preserves, and makes accessible the personal accounts of American war veterans	http://www.loc.gov/vets/
National Student Campaign Against Hunger and Homelessness (NSCAHH)	Largest student network fighting hunger and homelessness in the country	http://learningtogive.org/papers/paper199.html
Service for Peace	Established in 2002 by international youth volunteers from across the U.S. to help participants develop a sense of responsibility for others, confidence in their own ability to make a difference as they work together with people from different backgrounds to their own	http://www.serviceforpeace.org/
PeaceJam	International education program originating in Colorado in 1993; purpose is to create young leaders committed to positive change in themselves, their communities and the world through the inspiration of Nobel Peace Laureates	http://www.peacejam.org/
Project Linus	Founded in 1996 to provide blankets for children who are seriously ill or have experienced trauma	http://www.projectlinus.org/

personal and academic benefits that align with 21st century knowledge and skills such as collaboration, communication, and leadership. They may

- develop critical thinking and problem-solving skills
- increase their understanding of the curriculum
- gain hands-on experience
- explore values and beliefs
- increase their exposure to, and understanding of, diverse cultures and communities
- learn more about social issues, both their causes and possible remedies
- discover skills and interests in a potential career path
- make connections that could lead to jobs or internships
- increase their commitment to serving others

With an impressive list like this, it's hard to imagine *not* planning service-learning opportunities for students. Read about a very meaningful service-learning emphasis at Chardon Middle School in Figure 5.8.

Figure 5.8 Chardon Middle School service-learning experience

On Tuesday morning, September 11, 2001, the United States came under attack as four commercial airplanes were hijacked. The unsuspecting airliner crews and passengers became victims of suicide missions carried out by 19 al-Qaeda terrorists, members of an Islamist militant group founded by Osama bin Laden in 1988. Three of the planes were used to strike targets on the ground, including the World Trade Center buildings in New York City and the U.S. Pentagon. Nearly 3,000 people tragically lost their lives.

The fourth plane, United Airlines Flight 93, was in route from New Jersey to San Francisco when four al-Qaeda terrorists hijacked the plane by breaking into the cockpit and redirecting the flight toward Washington, DC, with the intent of crashing into the White House. Several passengers were able to call family and friends on the ground and learned of the hijacker's intentions. They courageously fought the hijackers and, in the process, Flight 93 crashed near Shanksville, Pennsylvania. Because of the actions of the 40 passengers and crew aboard the plane, the attack on the U.S. Capitol was thwarted.

Let's look at how Tim Bowens and his colleagues and students have used service-learning to learn more about, and memorialize, Flight 93 heroes. In his own words, Tim tells us how this particular service-learning emphasis fits within the Chicago Public Schools service-learning guidelines.

1. Students *prepare:*
   - Every year in Chardon, Ohio, our middle level students learn about the horrific events of September 11, 2001. Annually our 6th graders visit the Flight 93 Memorial in Pennsylvania where they learn about the importance of the heroism of the passengers and crew of Flight 93 through presentations at the site by families of passengers and crew members, as well as students who were in nearby schools on 9/11.
2. Students *act:*
   - After years of visiting temporary memorials for Flight 93, students and their community raised over $10,000 to help build the permanent memorial now at the site of the crash.
   - During the 2010–2011 school year we worked with a local arts organization to create an oral history project. Nearly 30 individuals were interviewed concerning the events of 9/11, and specifically about Flight 93. The interviews were transcribed and made into a theater production.
   - In 2012 teachers and students worked with artist Augusto Bordelois to create two murals made of thousands of pieces of colored mosaics. The murals are on permanent display on two staircases in Chardon Middle School. One represents 9/11 and the other is dedicated to Flight 93. Mr. Bordelois spent time preparing the students by showing how art and history are connected. He relayed examples of how important historical events (ex. Washington crossing the Delaware) have been interpreted by artists. He also demonstrated the significance of monuments and memorials. This tied beautifully to our 6th grade curriculum as we study ancient civilizations and their enduring impact/contributions. Look no further than the Egyptian pyramids for meaningful symbols and memorials.
3. Students *reflect:*
   - Since the murals are there for all to see (the artist feels they will stand even if the school was demolished-that's how well-constructed they are), students can take pride in them as they walk by in the years to come. They know that future generations of students will learn from their service-learning project.
   - Teachers can use the murals as an introduction to 9/11 and for instruction prior to visiting Shanksville each spring.
   - One of the more moving aspects of being at the Memorial occurs when we leave the site. We ask students to be silent and just quietly reflect on all they see. Now when students return to school, the murals bring that back.

Source: From e-mail communication with Tim Bowens, November 24, 2012.

CONCLUDING THOUGHTS

John Goodlad, following his landmark study of American high schools, wrote that the typical classroom is a site where "boredom is a disease of epidemic proportion" (1984, p. 9). What a devastating indictment.

Can you picture a classroom full of students deeply immersed in learning rather than entrenched in boredom? Asking, "And how are the children? Are they all well?" leads us to make engaging teaching that leads to optimum student learning our ultimate goal. Now that you know more about instruction—its limitless variety and potential— your ability to envision student engagement has increased. Recognizing that the art of teaching involves knowing how and when to apply instruction based on student needs and preferences, and understanding that teaching is a service profession, helps us become 3D teachers, ready to address the cognitive, physical, emotional, social, and moral development of our students. We began this chapter by considering Chris Roberts and his classroom at Rees Elementary in Utah. Now as the chapter comes to an end, we join Chris as he uses his knowledge of curriculum and instruction to support multi-age grouping. Read through *Chapter in Review* to help refresh your memory of what we have discussed, then interact with Chris as he confronts a challenge in *Developing Professional Competence*.

Chapter in Review

How is instruction implemented in U.S. schools?

- Backward design is an approach to planning for teaching and learning that starts with deciding on the desired learning results, then identifies how to collect the evidence of learning, and concludes with choosing appropriate instructional strategies.
- Content priorities include first, vital knowledge and core tasks; then, what is important to know and do; and finally, what is worth being familiar with.
- There are big ideas of instruction that serve to ground and provide a framework for teaching and learning.
- Multiple strategies of instruction allow for variety in how the curriculum is taught.
- Thoughtfully planning for instruction is vital for effective teaching and optimal student learning.
- Some instructional strategies are appropriate for students of all levels.
- Choosing instructional strategies for each of the four levels of school requires thoughtful consideration.

What is the art of teaching?

- The art of teaching is the ability to logically, and in a variety of ways, divide content and skills into manageable components and create experiences that lead to student learning.
- There is no formula for effective teaching. Every student is different, making every classroom of students different.
- The artistry of differentiating instruction involves an array of content, a variety of processes, and choices of products when possible.
- Expectations should be based on all the variables that contribute to learner differences: affect, readiness, interests, and learning profile. Expectations should be individualized and always high for each student, with a clear vision of what constitutes growth and success.

How do teachers serve students?

- The service dimension of teaching involves an attitude that approaches students as complete human beings, with cognitive, physical, emotional, social, and moral components.
- Teachers serve students when they form relationships, create a climate of respect, model productive habits, emphasize civics and citizenship, promote character building, and communicate positively.
- Service-learning occurs when student experiences combine service with a purposeful learning component.
- Service-learning requires students to *prepare* by learning about issues and developing an action plan, then to *act* by engaging in meaningful service and realizing connections to classroom curriculum, and to *reflect* by analyzing and making sense of their experiences.
- The benefits of service-learning are numerous for both the community and the students who participate.

Developing Professional Competence

Thoughtfully reading this scenario and responding to the items that follow it will help you prepare for licensure exams.

The district school board where Chris Roberts teaches is considering doing away with multiage classrooms. We read about multiage classrooms in Chapter 3 as we explored a variety of configurations for teaching and learning in U.S. schools. We also know from the interviews with Chris and his teammates Brenda and Tim that they have successfully taught for years in classrooms occupied by third, fourth, and fifth graders. We hear Chris admit in his interview, however, that he doubts he gets to all the content standards of the three grade levels as he teaches in a multiage setting each year.

Chris believes strongly in exposing students to the world through a variety of means. His extensive travels, his love of the arts, and his selection of books for the classroom provide opportunities for him to infuse teaching and learning with real-world context. Through this context Chris knows that his students are learning valuable lessons.

It will be difficult to defend multiage grouping to the school board, but Chris is convinced the configuration works for his teaching team.

Think through this scenario and answer the following multiple-choice questions:

1. Chris states that he probably doesn't get to all the state standards in his classroom. He may be able to clarify which, if any, of the standards he doesn't address by
   a. reading summaries of the standards provided in the state document
   b. matching the textbooks he uses to the standards
   c. taking the time to look very closely at the standards for each grade level and create one document that sequences the standards
   d. asking someone from the state to observe his classroom

2. Chris knows that he will be questioned about the range of ages in his classroom. Which of the following statements is *least* appropriate for making a case for multiage grouping?
   a. My teaching style works because kids will learn what interests them.
   b. Chronological age does not necessarily determine learning readiness.
   c. Sometimes students learn much from each other and the age disparities often work in favor of peer teaching.
   d. In multiage classrooms teachers can guide learning over a 3-year period to make sure there is consistency and continual progress.

3. All of the following will likely be helpful to Chris as he prepares to make his case before the school board except for which one?
   a. Brenda and Tim
   b. Parents of students in his class
   c. Mike Larsen, the principal
   d. Utah Superintendent of Education

4. What information might be *most* convincing if he had time to research it?
   a. The number of other schools using multiage grouping
   b. A comparison of the success in sixth grade of the students from multiage grades 3–5 settings and the students in self-contained classes in grades 3 to 5
   c. A survey of parents of children in grades K to 2 to see how many will request a multiage setting when their children reach third grade
   d. A comparison of how Utah fares relative to other states on the NAEP exam

5. Which combination of big ideas of instruction should Chris emphasize as the *most* powerful justification for having third, fourth, and fifth graders in one classroom?
   a. Promoting critical thinking and differentiating instruction
   b. Incorporating student collaboration and promoting critical thinking
   c. Differentiating instruction and incorporating student collaboration
   d. Teaching through inquiry and using technology

Now it's time for you to respond to two short essay items involving the scenario. In your responses, be sure to address all the dilemmas and questions posed in each item. Your responses should each be at least one well-developed paragraph.

6. Chris has decided that he will attend the next school board meeting and present his reasons for continuing multiage grouping. This item is about his preparation. Who should he speak with to help him prepare to do this? What elements of his classroom practice should he emphasize? About what should he be very knowledgeable before addressing the board? Consider the following InTASC Standards and how Chris might use them as he prepares to address the school board:

Standard #2: The teacher uses understanding of individual differences and diverse cultures and communities to ensure inclusive learning environments that enable each learner to meet high standards.

Standard #3: The teacher works with others to create environments that support individual and collaborative learning, and that encourage positive social interaction, active engagement in learning, and self motivation.

Standard #4: The teacher understands the central concepts, tools of inquiry, and structures of the discipline(s) he or she teaches and creates learning experiences that make these aspects of the discipline accessible and meaningful for learners to assure mastery of the content.

Standard #5: The teacher understands how to connect concepts and use differing perspectives to engage learners in critical thinking, creativity, and collaborative problem solving related to authentic local and global issues.

Standard #7: The teacher plans instruction that supports every student in meeting rigorous learning goals by drawing upon knowledge of content areas, curriculum, cross-disciplinary skills, and pedagogy, as well as knowledge of learners and the community context.

Standard #9: The teacher engages in ongoing professional learning and uses evidence to continually evaluate his/her practice, particularly the effects of his/her choices and actions on others (learners, families, other professionals, and the community), and adapts practice to meet the needs of each learner.

7. Chris knows how important his introduction is in terms of getting the board to listen to him and find him credible. What should he say in his opening remarks?

Creating and Maintaining a Positive and Productive Learning Environment

 Dear Reader

Students are motivated to learn when the learning environment is positive and productive. The converse is also true. The absence of a positive and productive learning environment stifles motivation and learning. Thinking through the concepts in this chapter is a vital first step in creating a classroom environment that engages students and enhances learning.

We used to talk about *classroom management* as the task that involved corralling students into a state of attention and then directing them to do what we wanted. Not so long ago, the picture-perfect scenario of good classroom management was 30 students all seated in rows; all with sharpened pencils, tablets (paper ones!), and textbooks opened to page 234; and all giving rapt attention to the person standing in the front of the room. That worked for some of us as learners, but won't work in most classrooms today. The concept of *learning environment* is so much broader and richer than classroom management.

Learning is messy. Student engagement in their own learning is crucial. Creation of a learning environment that is stimulating, structured to include participation, marked by respect and civility, and lead by a teacher who is both 100% present and armed with comprehensive lesson plans and differentiated strategies will make the environment positive and productive. It's not too soon to begin thinking about the learning environment you want to create in your future classroom as

you continue your journey toward becoming a teacher. In this chapter we explore answers to these questions:

• How do teachers create a positive learning environment?

• What routines contribute to maintaining a productive classroom environment?

• How do teachers establish expectations, incentives, and consequences?

• How can I develop a classroom management plan?

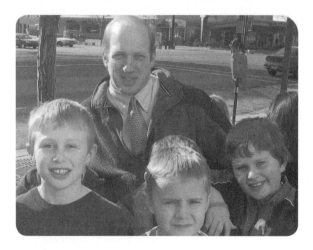

Teaching in Focus

When Jeff walked into Tim Mendenhall's multiage classroom at Rees Elementary School, Utah, in late September, he had one of those "I don't want to be here" looks. His entrance was more of a shuffle than a walk, and his demeanor was obvious to other students as well as to Mr. Mendenhall. Jeff had just moved to Spanish Fork from Los Angeles. He was 12 and entering fifth grade for the second time. Tim sensed that Jeff would prove to be quite a challenge. When it was time for the third, fourth, and fifth graders in Tim's multiage class to go out for recess, Tim asked Jeff to spend the time with him so they could get to know each other. Jeff's first words were "Why do I have to be in here with all these babies?"

Fortunately for Jeff, he had come to a school and a homeroom with structure, and a teacher with a classroom management philosophy that responds to students as individuals. Tim applies a theory that might be called game therapy. He believes in playing with kids—on the field and in the classroom. He tells us, "If you earn the kids' respect by being respectful, consistent, and fun, there are few problems. If you make learning enjoyable and meaningful, then students stay on task and want to be with you. Wanting to learn, wanting to be with you, and wanting to do whatever you have planned is motivation enough to behave."

Tim had his work cut out for him. Jeff had no intention of joining in. The first week or so he sat silently and sullenly. He resisted any kind of group work and refused to take part in classroom and outside games until Tim tossed a basketball his way. He threw it back. Tim shot at the basket and missed. Jeff picked up the ball, made the basket, and grinned. That's all Tim needed to plan his strategy. Back in the classroom he placed a three-ring binder filled with basketball player cards on Jeff's table.

Jeff had the potential to be very disruptive to the classroom community Tim had so carefully built. By being sensitive and purposeful, Tim was able to avoid power struggles and give Jeff a behavioral comfort level. Although his behavior didn't become a problem, Jeff continues to struggle academically. That's the challenge Tim faces daily. However, Tim has cleared a major hurdle because he has won Jeff's respect and Jeff wants to be with him. Watch **Tim's lesson and interview** to get to know him better.

Creating and maintaining a positive and productive learning environment is complex and compelling—complex because there are multiple variables to consider, and compelling because without a positive and productive learning environment, teaching has little effect. New and experienced teachers alike are often puzzled by the whole process. They sometimes think of the learning environment in narrow terms of student cooperation and student misbehavior. But the learning environment is so much more. When teachers expand their view to include the elements discussed in this chapter, it becomes clear that creating and maintaining a positive and productive learning environment is indeed a puzzle, one with many interlocking pieces that depend on one another to form a complete, stable picture.

How Do Teachers Create a Positive Learning Environment?

Some of the most important pieces of the learning environment puzzle are shown in Figure 6.1. A positive and productive learning environment that includes these vital components doesn't just happen. It takes planning, continuous effort, and a watchful eye.

PHYSICAL SPACE

A welcoming, well-organized, student-friendly environment goes a long way toward helping accomplish both learning and affective goals. John Dewey's wisdom concerning the physical surroundings of learning includes his statement that "any environment is a chance environment so far as its educative influence is concerned unless it has been deliberately regulated with reference to its educative effect" (1944, p. 19). This statement tells us that our classrooms themselves matter. The learning environment

Figure 6.1 A positive and productive learning environment

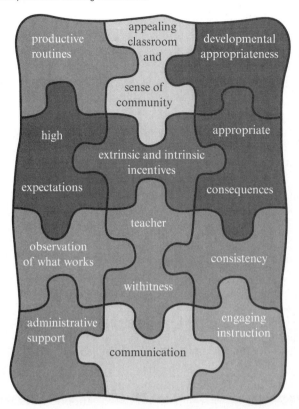

can actually enhance teaching and learning when we deliberately and thoughtfully arrange and decorate with student well-being in mind.

Teachers seldom have much to say about which classroom they are assigned or the general condition of the school building. You may have gone to school in well-kept, relatively modern buildings; in older stately surroundings; or in dilapidated structures beset with never-ending maintenance problems. Your teachers may have had clean, comfortable spaces to decorate, or they may have fought off bugs and fungus in a dingy, poorly lit room plagued with a leaky roof. Teachers are responsible for making the most of room assignments. Even under dismal circumstances, designing a classroom can be both challenging and fun. Do it for your students, and do it for yourself. The classroom truly is "home away from home."

Home away from home. As a teacher you will spend 8 to 9 hours a day for almost 200 days every year in your classroom. Early childhood and elementary students will spend almost all of their days in the classroom with you, whereas middle and high school students will generally spend about a sixth of their school time in any one classroom. The classroom atmosphere is important for all students, but it is particularly influential for students who may, through circumstances beyond their control, find that school and their classrooms are the cleanest, most welcoming environments in their lives.

Deirdre's classroom at Cario Middle School takes on a home-like appearance with the addition of furniture other than desks.

If space allows, adding a comfortable couch, chairs, lamps, rugs, plants, curtains, and other homey items does wonders for inviting students in to learn. Focus teacher Deirdre Huger-McGrew of Cario Middle School, South Carolina, created a reading center in her classroom with a couch, chairs, tables, and lamps, as you can see in her room tour. Watch **Deirdre Huger-McGrew's room tour** to see how she uses her classroom space.

Seating arrangement. The arrangement of desks and tables in a classroom depends on a number of variables, including the level of the school, the subject(s) taught, and available floor space and furniture. Traditional rows of desks are fine for whole group instruction, whereas clusters of desks or students sitting together at tables work well for group work. Ideally, the arrangement will be flexible so seating can accommodate various instructional strategies.

Proximity. Whatever the seating arrangement, one vital element to keep in mind is **proximity,** the accessibility of teacher to students. The teacher needs to be able to approach each student quickly and easily, without having to negotiate narrow pathways that could lead to stumbling or a complex maze that makes it difficult to work one-on-one with students. Students also need to have visual access to boards and screens.

Wall space and interest centers. Creative teachers often find ways to entice students to come into the classroom and browse. Walls and tables offer tremendous opportunities to create spaces that students will want to explore just to see what's up. At Roosevelt High School, Angelica Reynosa's and Derek Boucher's room tours display Hispanic cultural items and reveal an extensive classroom library.

A simple yet potentially powerful use of wall space is the organized display of student work. Preprinted posters may be appropriate on classroom walls, but they should not be used to the exclusion of regularly updated student work. Displaying student work fosters student ownership of the classroom. Some teachers only display exemplary work, such as tests that received As or perfectly colored maps. This practice stops short of being optimally effective if half or more of the students never see their work displayed because their achievement on traditional assignments never rises to the top of the class. Ingenious teachers who know students well incorporate creative assignments that give average and even below-average achievers opportunities to excel. It is well worth the time to arrange physical classroom space thoughtfully, which will shape in many ways the interactions of the people who inhabit the classroom and contribute to building classroom community.

Points of Reflection 6.1

Think about the classrooms in your PreK–12 experiences. Were they inviting and conducive to learning? Why or why not? How do you envision your future classroom's appearance?

BUILDING COMMUNITY

The concept of classroom climate is introduced in Chapter 1.

A **classroom community** is not just a place but also a way of actively learning together. Dewey (1944) expands on this thought by telling us that people in a community are "like-minded," having common beliefs, understandings, and aims (p. 4). Maintaining what Dewey calls like-mindedness can be thought of as maintaining **classroom climate,** the everyday environment in which teachers and students work together.

Let's look at four ways teachers can maintain a classroom climate that builds community among themselves and their students:

1. Demonstrate care.
2. Develop trust.
3. Teach unconditionally.
4. Embrace social media.

Demonstrate care. A teacher must care about curriculum, instruction, assessment, society, the past, the present, the future, and—most of all—about students. Nel Noddings, noted educator and author, strongly believes that care is the vital foundation for building community. She tells us, "Caring is the very bedrock of all successful education" (1992, p. 27). As Angela Lumpkin writes, "When students know that their teachers genuinely care, they respond by exerting greater effort to reach their potential" (2007, p. 158). Craig Cleveland

Figure 6.2 Ways to develop student-teacher relationships

- talking informally with students before, during, and after class about their interests
- greeting students outside of school, such as at extracurricular events or at stores
- singling out a few students each day in the lunchroom, and talking to them
- being aware of and commenting on important events in students' lives, such as participation in sports, drama, or other extracurricular activities
- complimenting students on important achievements in and outside of school
- including students in the process of planning classroom activities, soliciting their ideas and considering their interests
- meeting students at the door as they come into class and saying hello to each child, making sure to use each student's name

Source: Marzano, R. J. (2003). *What works in schools: Translating research into action* (pp. 100–101). Alexandria, VA: Association for Supervision and Curriculum Development.

at Roosevelt High School obviously cares for his students and treats them with respect and genuine interest. Observe this in Guillermo's interview with Mr. Cleveland.

A caring classroom centers on relationships—between teacher and students and among the students themselves. Taking a personal interest in students is the first step in developing caring relationships. Respectfully approaching students as individuals is key to this process. So how do we get to know individual students? Early childhood and elementary classrooms of 15 to 30 students allow teachers to know students and their families well. The numbers are manageable, and teachers have most of the day, every day, to develop relationships. Middle and high school teachers are challenged by both numbers and time because they may have 60 to 120 students a year in their classes for only a small portion of each school day. Marzano (2003b) suggests a number of ways teachers can get to know students, shown in Figure 6.2.

Develop trust. For a classroom community of learners to function optimally, trust is an absolute necessity: trust between teacher and students, and among students. A safe environment—academically, emotionally, and physically—is necessary. Maslow's hierarchy of needs indicates that physiological needs, safety, love, and belongingness form the basis for meeting higher-order needs. All of these needs must be met by a classroom characterized by trust.

> Maslow's hierarchy of needs is discussed in Chapter 2.

In a trust-filled classroom, students are more comfortable with the environment and willing to take risks that lead to learning. They know that if they attempt a task and don't succeed, they will be encouraged to try again and given tools that increase the likelihood of success. They are more willing to answer questions and to pose them as well, knowing they won't be ridiculed or demeaned in any way. Trust fosters learning. In *Teaching in Focus*, Craig Cleveland at Roosevelt High School, California, tells us that teacher-student relationships characterized by trust and respect encourage students to take more risks that lead to learning.

Teach unconditionally. When we practice **unconditional teaching** we accept students for who they are, not for what they do. It's an attitude that conveys clearly to students that they matter to us, no matter how many times they may fail to achieve or misbehave. Unconditional teaching requires that we allow students to begin fresh, that we don't take their misbehavior or lack of effort personally. We are adults who do what we can to help students grow. Alfie Kohn (2005) tells us that unconditional teaching involves

- showing students we are glad to see them
- showing students we trust and respect them
- displaying an appealing informality
- spending time with students even when we don't have to
- asking about students' lives outside school and remembering their answers
- finding something appealing about each student

Teaching in Focus

Craig Cleveland, history teacher, Roosevelt High School, Fresno, California. *In his own words. . . .* Educators first teach who they are. Their dispositions, views of life, and how they perceive their students is picked up on and learned by the students before the first quiz. The opportunity for excellent student performance in the classroom is directly related to how the teacher interacts with the students. I believe that teachers must be fair, have no favorites, and be liberal in providing needed help. Kindness is the fundamental rule for communication between student and teacher. Kindness is hopeful, encourages students to do better, and shows respect for others. Both Guillermo and Khammany *[two of our focus students]* come from supportive families where they are loved. They thrive in a classroom environment where their ideas are listened to and respected. I believe that students are more willing to take risks in class when they know that their contribution will be appreciated.

Embrace social media. It has been estimated that in approximately 1 minute, 42,000 people will update their Facebook status, 36,000 tweets will be sent, and 15 hours of video will be uploaded to YouTube (Ray, 2010). Throughout this text you read about social media and how to use the tools to enhance professional development and in classroom teaching strategies. Social media is part of our lives, whether we choose to recognize it or not. In addition to Facebook, Twitter, and YouTube, social media tools outside of school such as Ning communities, Google Groups, Etherpad, Wordle, and VoiceThread, to name a few, are connecting both adults and students.

Marc Prensky (2010), author and founder of Games2train, tells us that when we think that virtual relationships, or those that exist online, are somehow less real or important than face-to-face ones, we are barriers to our students' progress by limiting their relationships and harming the learning community. Computers, to be of optimal value, must be personalized so they become extensions of the student's personal self and brain, customized to be tools of expression and communication.

Checking technology tools at the door of the school or telling students to keep smartphones turned off while in the school building is not going to stop texting and other technology-enhanced communications from happening. Smartphone communication is the new form of note passing. Try as we might to prevent it, note passing persists, just in ever-changing formats. To fight it is to lose.

School-provided technology, typically classroom computers, have filters in place with the purpose of protecting students from admittedly dangerous situations. But once students leave school, the filters are gone and they face the perils alone. Steve Johnson (in Ray, 2010) advises teachers to teach students about the devastating possibilities of **cyberbullying,** for instance, by teaching them **cybercitizenship**. Using an abstinence stance when it comes to social media cheats our students of wisdom we could convey.

> Cyberbullying and cybercitizenship are addressed in Chapter 9.

As teachers, we should be open and willing to learn as we explore the possibilities presented by social media that can help build community in creative and ever-expanding ways. This chapter's *SocialMEdia* feature introduces Twitter as a teaching and learning tool.

KOUNIN'S PHILOSOPHY

As a result of observation and analysis, Jacob Kounin (1970) described what effective classroom managers do. To create and maintain a positive and productive learning environment, teachers must practice *withitness*. This term refers to awareness of what's going on in the whole classroom that enables the teacher to step in when needed to keep the environment positive. Teacher withitness often surprises students because they perceive the teacher must have eyes in the back of his or her head. Withitness allows teachers to do what Kounin calls **overlapping**, which means multitasking, or

SocialMEdia

The learning environment is most effective when all students are engaged and participating. Teachers can use a variety of social media to make this a reality, including Twitter.

Twitter is a micro-blogging communication network made up of participants using messages of up to a maximum of 140 characters, called Tweets. Teachers have experimented for several years with ways to use Twitter for teaching and learning. There are hundreds of comments online about Twitter in the classroom, so there is no shortage of ideas. Twitter is useful in and out of the classroom because it can be used with any Internet-connected computer as well as on Internet-accessible mobile devices. For this reason, Twitter may be the most democratizing of current social media tools because it's readily available and does not require specific tools. With the 140-character restriction, students who lack confidence in their writing skills are not as intimidated by Twitter. Keep in mind, however, that this restriction is not just motivating, but also challenging in many circumstances because students are forced to express themselves with economy of words. It's very often more difficult to say something meaningful in fewer, rather than more, words.

Organizations like *ASCD Learn. Teach. Lead.* use Twitter for a wide variety of purposes including spreading information about professional development opportunities, keeping participants posted about what's happening at conferences, communicating among teachers about teaching and learning, and following noted educators to learn about their most current ideas and research projects.

Here are 10 ideas for using Twitter in K–12 learning environments:

- Encourage students to work together, sharing ideas and completing projects
- Bring current events into the classroom in real time
- Reach out to experts in particular fields
- Practice communicating in a new language, including English for English language learners
- Communicate assignments and changes in plans
- Ask students to read an article or chapter and then summarize it in 140 characters
- Pose a prompt and ask students to tweet responses
- Create a discussion group using a hashtag so all are included
- Follow a famous person connected to the curriculum and report on his/her life to class
- Develop "Twitter pals" with students tweeting another student in a different location or with different demographics to learn about diversity

In addition to all the learning environment benefits, Twitter can also be a great way to communicate with other teachers to share questions and ideas. Getting started with any new technology is usually the most difficult step. Excellent information regarding every aspect of Twitter is available at

https://support.twitter.com/articles/215585#.

---

taking care of several things at once. A teacher who has withitness and the ability to overlap can help a small group with an assignment, see a student pestering another student, and give a "cut-it-out" look while answering a question and checking the clock to see how much time remains in the class period.

In addition, Kounin says effective classroom managers understand the **ripple effect** that occurs when one action leads to or directly affects another action. He tells us that the cut-it-out look given to one student may help deter another student from the same off-task behavior. This is a positive ripple effect. Similarly—but with negative results—if the teacher interrupts the whole class, loudly saying, "Jeremy, stop that right now. You do nothing but continually disturb," other students may perceive that the teacher overreacted and begin to display the same pestering behaviors (Lemlech, 2010).

Kounin's research has yielded the commonsense view that teachers who know what's going on, who can switch from one activity to another smoothly, and who can maintain positive momentum will be successful in maintaining a productive classroom environment. As you continue reading this chapter, keep withitness, overlapping, and the ripple effect in mind.

Points of Reflection 6.2

Do you recall teachers who appeared to have withitness? Describe one of these teachers and why you believe withitness was part of his or her style.

USING TIME WISELY

One constant in schools is time itself; however, how we spend that time is variable. Although some communities have increased the length of the school day, and even the number of days in a school year, most have 180 school days a year, and about 7 hours a day, for impacting students. This 180/7 configuration is based on tradition and not necessarily on what we know about teaching and learning. The length of the school year and the hours in a school day are often political pawns and are not likely to change before you enter your first classroom as a teacher.

Our challenge is to maximize the time we have with students. Early childhood and elementary teachers may have 7 hours a day with students, but that doesn't mean they have 7 hours of **instructional time,** the time available for teaching and learning. Middle and high school teachers may have 65 minutes in each class period, but that doesn't mean they have 65 minutes in which to actually implement instruction. If we are not careful, too much time is spent in nonproductive ways or at least in ways that do not promote academic learning. Given administrative demands such as collecting lunch money, taking attendance, responding to interruptions, and getting students where they need to be throughout the day, we often sense that the amount of time available for instruction is limited. Recess, transitions from class to class, lunch, and so on—all legitimate uses of time—further limit instructional time.

One study yields some fairly shocking results concerning the breakdown of the time allotted for the school day. The minimum school day in most elementary schools consists of 6 hours, or 360 minutes. After subtracting time for recess, lunch, and transitions, the time left for academics is about 4.5 hours, or 270 minutes. In the schools studied, researchers found that teachers actually used about 3 hours, or 180 minutes, for actual instruction. Of these 180 minutes, only about 120 resulted in productive learning time, or **time on task** (Weinstein, Romano, & Mignano, 2011). What this amounts to is about 2 hours a day, out of 6, spent on meaningful application of the formal curriculum. This is not acceptable. But before we view this finding too negatively, keep in mind that the informal curriculum is also very important. Interaction time between a teacher and students has positive effects on student learning in terms of relationship building and motivation, two concepts we know make a positive difference in student learning. However, a teacher's goal must be to spend more than a third of a school day in meaningful teaching and learning. Be very conscious of our responsibility to maximize the valuable commodity of time in the classroom.

> The formal curriculum and the informal curriculum are discussed in Chapter 4.

What Routines Contribute to Maintaining a Productive Classroom Environment?

A **routine,** sometimes referred to as a procedure, is an expected action that occurs in a given circumstance to accomplish a task efficiently. When routines are in place in the classroom, teachers have more time to teach, and students have more time to learn.

PRACTICING ROUTINES

It is important to practice routines in the first weeks of school. In this way, the routines become habits. Three important reasons for using routines that help preserve instructional time are: getting student attention, responding to interruptions, and transitioning from one activity to another.

Student attention. When students are engaged in class activities, and the teacher wants to make an announcement, give directions, or remind students of the time, an attention getter is necessary. Some teachers turn the classroom lights off and on or simply speak loudly enough to be heard. An excellent method for getting attention involves the teacher raising a hand and students doing likewise. Students know to stop talking as their hands go up. Once there is silence, the teacher talks while students listen. If rehearsed repeatedly during the first weeks of school, this method (and a variety of others you'll observe in field experiences) will become automatic. Having one method, practicing it, and consistently using it will return big dividends.

Responding to interruptions. Class interruptions constitute a real frustration for teachers. The most frequent culprit is often the public address (PA) system. The routine of students instantly "freezing" will allow the announcement to be heard and any necessary action to be taken quickly.

Students at all levels have legitimate reasons for leaving a particular class to go somewhere else in the building. Perhaps it's a resource class, a special counseling group, a remedial reading class, or a gifted and talented program. The students involved need to practice the routine of watching the clock and leaving when it is time or watching the doorway for someone who may arrive to escort them. These comings and goings should not be allowed to interrupt the whole class. Students occasionally need to go to the restroom or get a drink of water during class time. Teachers should establish routines for these occasions as well.

When a visitor (an administrator, teacher, student, or parent) enters the classroom, the routine of students noticing and working more quietly will allow the teacher to respond without interference. This routine will not come naturally for students; it must be practiced.

Transitions. When students change activities or locations they are in **transition,** the time when most classroom disruptions happen. In early childhood and elementary schools, children may transition between learning activities three or four times before going to recess or a special area class such as music or physical education. Then it's back to the classroom until lunch, perhaps followed by another recess, then back to class. Teachers typically have routines for all these transitions.

In middle and high schools the transitions between classes provide opportunities for misbehavior. Students may be in crowded, rushed circumstances, where social dilemmas can easily surface. A routine for *teachers* that can decrease the likelihood of misbehavior involves merely standing outside their classroom doors during transitions.

ROUTINES IN THE FOUR LEVELS OF SCHOOL

The nature and number of classroom routines vary depending on the school level. Early childhood and elementary classrooms have many more elements to which routines apply than middle school classrooms, and high school classrooms have even fewer. But there are some elements at all four levels that call for routines. For instance, attendance must be taken one or more times daily. Distribution of materials and entering and leaving the classroom also occur daily. Let's take a look at some of the routines of our focus teachers.

Early childhood. Brandi Wade and Renee Ayers, teachers at Summit Primary, Ohio, implement routines in their classrooms for activities such as

- paying attention
- gathering supplies
- moving about the room
- working in groups
- playing with, and putting away, games and toys
- reacting to interruptions
- going to the rest room
- lining up and moving through the building
- sharpening pencils
- keeping desks in order
- filing and retrieving folders

Brandi and Renee provide a personal routine for each student in the form of classroom jobs that help develop responsibility. These routines/jobs make life in the classroom run more smoothly and increase instructional time. Some of the jobs include board eraser, floor patrol (uses small broom and dust pan), computer helper (turns off computers at the end of the day), and gardener (waters plants).

Renee tells us that her classroom space is limited and she needs to use every inch of it in optimal ways. Routines and classroom jobs for her students maximize efficiency.

Creating and Maintaining a Positive and Productive Learning Environment   **169**

Early childhood and elementary classrooms should be cheerful and organized for learning. This one includes clusters of desks and supplies for group work, a cubby and coat hook for each student, plants to care for, a word wall, and more.

Each morning Renee follows a routine that organizes her students. She uses a pocket chart (plastic hanging chart with clear pockets) to display her daily classroom schedule in terms second graders can read. She changes the activities as needed so the students know ahead of time what to expect. A sample of the contents of Renee's pocket chart is shown in Figure 6.3. Watch Renee's room tour to see how she uses her classroom space.

Elementary. Many elementary teachers deal with classroom elements that require routines similar to those found in early childhood classrooms. Students in grades 3 through 5, however, are developmentally able to adhere to more complicated routines and to do them without direct prompting from the teacher. Chris Roberts, Tim Mendenhall, and Brenda Beyal work as a team at Rees Elementary, Utah. They have established similar routines because they share students throughout the day. Chris, Tim, and Brenda expect their students to come and go between classrooms and throughout the school responsibly. Within each classroom the routines vary, but basically, they deal with these activities:

- gathering/using materials
- turning in homework assignments
- borrowing library books
- dismissal procedures for walkers, bus riders, and car riders

Tim has a schedule on a bulletin board in his classroom. He tells us his students look at it every day and, if he doesn't keep it current, they readily remind him. Tim not only thinks that a schedule is important, but also that it emphasizes the organization of the classroom. He makes it easy for routines to be followed by providing resources and everyday supplies in bins that are clearly labeled. His students know where to go to get what they need, and how to do so in an orderly way. Watch Tim's room tour to see how he uses his classroom space.

Middle school. Because Deirdre Huger-McGrew at Cario Middle School, South Carolina, has one small group of students half a day and another small group for the

Figure 6.3 Second grade pocket chart schedule

9:30 Welcome/Morning Work
Calendar/Morning Message
Self-Selected Reading
Working with Words
Rest Room Break/Snack
Writing
11:55 Music
12:35 Lunch
1:05 Recess
Guided Reading
Rest Room Break
Math
Science/Social Studies
4:00 Dismissal

Source: From Renee Ayers' classroom at Summit Primary School in Ohio.

other half, she finds it relatively easy to get the students to follow routines that make the classroom run smoothly. These routines revolve around the following activities:

- computer use
- gathering and returning materials
- rest room and water breaks

Traci Peters, seventh grade math teacher at Cario, believes in the value of structure. The routines she establishes include:

- passing in and handing back papers
- borrowing supplies from the bins in the room
- obtaining rest room passes, used only during the first and last 5 minutes of class

Traci is extremely organized. Each desk has a number; each critical math resource has a number. A student in Traci's class knows that his seat number must match his calculator, protractor, and ruler number. There is a chart on Traci's wall assigning students to write a summary of the day on the "What did I miss?" board, to which absent students go when they return to class. These routines save valuable instructional time in Traci's classroom. Watch Traci's room tour to see how she uses her classroom space.

High school. Students in high school can be expected to understand routines. There are generally fewer to deal with, but they are no less important than in the earlier grades. Craig Cleveland, Derek Boucher, and Angelica Reynosa, teachers at Roosevelt High School, California, have routines addressing these activities:

- entering and leaving class
- paying attention
- working in groups
- checking out and returning materials
- responding to class interruptions, such as announcements, hand-delivered messages, and visitors

Craig's classroom routines revolve around group work and his classroom library. Students practice working together in the beginning of the school year, learning to collaborate and cooperate. Craig teaches them. Then for the rest of the school year the students know the routine and follow it. They also know where to go in Craig's classroom to get the reading material that interests them or that is assigned. There are books on every wall in the classroom. Craig uses house gutters mounted on the wall to serve as book shelves, making book and magazine covers visible to attract students. Watch Craig's room tour to see how he uses his classroom space.

Establishing developmentally appropriate routines and then teaching and practicing them increases the effectiveness and efficiency of the classroom. Also necessary for classroom effectiveness and efficiency are developmentally appropriate expectations, incentives, and consequences.

How Do Teachers Establish Expectations, Incentives, and Consequences?

When you read the title of this chapter, you may have thought it was just a fancy way to refer to a chapter on **classroom management,** the establishment and enforcement of rules and disciplinary actions. You should now see that creating and maintaining a positive, productive learning environment encompasses much more than the traditional notion of classroom management. There is no single recipe for effective classroom management that works all the time in every classroom. Teachers have always struggled with this part of their work.

Expectations, a word with positive connotations, will be used in place of *rules,* a word with negative connotations. **Incentives** will be used in place of the overused and value-laden word *rewards.* The word *consequences* implies more natural ramifications for wrongdoing than does the word *punishment,* which can be arbitrary. The three concepts of expectations, incentives, and consequences are interdependent. However, for the sake of organization and clarity, they are addressed separately here.

Before discussing expectations, incentives, and consequences, think about the concepts of prevention and intervention. When it comes to student misbehavior, teachers have only two options: *They can either prevent it, or they will need to intervene.* Obviously, prevention is more desirable. Remember that the best way to prevent behavior problems in the classroom is through engaging instruction.

Engaging instructional practices are discussed in Chapter 5.

EXPECTATIONS

Teacher expectations impact students in significant ways as they affect students' academic performance and behavior. Teacher expectations may become self-fulfilling prophesies for some students. Therefore, it is vital to set and communicate high expectations.

Establishing behavioral expectations. How do teachers establish expectations that are foundational, including physical norms for preserving the health and safety of students, moral norms pertaining to respect for others, and societal norms for politeness and individual responsibility? The answer, in large measure, depends on the developmental stages of the students. With young children, most expectations have to be made very explicit—for example, "Don't bother classmates," "Share materials," and "Don't tease one another." For older children and adolescents, many expectations can be summed up with statements such as "Treat one another with respect."

Establishing behavioral expectations is generally a teacher task. However, proponents of what is sometimes called a **democratic classroom**—one that promotes choice, community, authentic learning, and relevant, creative curriculum—encourage student participation in the establishment of behavioral expectations. Other influences affect the task, including expectations previously established by the school district and those held by the grade level or the whole school staff. There are few circumstances in which an individual teacher should set expectations less stringent than grade-level, team, or whole-school expectations. However, teachers can certainly add to, or make more stringent, their own classroom expectations. For instance, if school expectations include a "no gum" rule, then a teacher cannot allow gum chewing in the classroom. But if there is no school-wide rule against gum chewing, a teacher may nonetheless establish the expectation that students will not chew gum in a particular classroom.

Here are some examples of behavior, some mild, some moderate, and some severe, that fall short of most teachers' behavioral expectations:

- talking or moving around the classroom at inappropriate times
- disturbing others (of course, there are thousands of ways students might do this!)
- tardiness and excessive absences
- off-task behaviors (missing materials, working on an assignment that is not the current task, daydreaming, or sleeping)
- leaving the classroom without permission
- cheating, lying

This teacher should establish behavioral expectations to help maintain productive routines such as class transitions.

- using obscene or vulgar language
- defacing property
- verbal or physical noncompliance (refusing to do what is asked)

- theft and vandalism
- fighting or inflicting violence
- being under the influence of illegal substances

Sample expectations. Some teachers choose to keep their lists of expectations short and general, as illustrated in Figure 6.4. Notice that none of the sample lists of expectations mentions cheating, lying, vulgar language, vandalism, theft, substance abuse, or violence. As stated earlier, most teachers lump preventing all of these negative actions under the word *respect*, assuming that if students show respect, they won't engage in any of these behaviors.

Why would students choose to live up to classroom expectations? Many do so because they are accustomed to living up to expectations at home or in other settings. Some students require specific incentives to comply with expectations. Most students fall somewhere in between.

INCENTIVES

An incentive is a reason for doing something. For instance, a first grade student may stay in line while walking to music class (expectation) because the teacher told the class if everyone stayed in line, the music teacher would be pleased (incentive). Keep in mind that incentives that motivate one individual may have little effect on another. If the first grade student doesn't like music or the music teacher, pleasing that teacher would not serve as an incentive. Teachers are responsible for understanding their students well enough to provide the bases for incentives that will motivate students in terms of behavior, academics, and personal growth.

The two basic kinds of incentives are extrinsic and intrinsic. **Extrinsic incentives** are those that are imposed or that originate outside the individual. **Intrinsic incentives** are those that come from within and result from students' natural drives.

Extrinsic incentives. Most theorists (and indeed probably most of your professors) downplay the value of extrinsic incentives in the classroom. And they are right. Extrinsic incentives are less desirable than intrinsic incentives. Extrinsic incentives depend on people other than the student. For instance, if a fourth grade teacher offers a popcorn party on Friday if the class has fewer than five names recorded for misbehavior during the week, then students depend on one another to behave and on the teacher to keep

Points of Reflection 6.3

What classroom expectations, or rules, do you remember in your K–12 experiences? Were they clear and rational, or were they ambiguous and nonsensical? On what do you base your opinion? What is the most important expectation for your future classroom?

Figure 6.4 Sample lists of classroom expectations

1. Pay attention.
2. Listen when others talk.
3. Treat each other with courtesy.

---

1. Work all class period.
2. Complete all assignments.
3. Stay in the area you are assigned.
4. Show respect at all times.

---

1. Respect each other and the teacher at all times.
2. Talk quietly so as not to disturb others.
3. Ask for help by raising your hand.
4. Follow all classroom procedures.

---

1. Arrive on time for class every day.
2. Have all materials needed to participate fully.
3. Maintain a respectful attitude.

---

1. Respect yourself.
2. Respect others.
3. Respect property.

his or her word. They apply peer pressure, again external, to achieve the Friday incentive. Do you think the students will be just as motivated to behave acceptably the next week without the promise of a popcorn party? Probably not. When extrinsic incentives are taken away, positive results are less likely to be reinforced. When teachers employ extrinsic motivation, they are taking on the full responsibility for motivating their students. Even so, extrinsic incentives are common in all levels of school.

In early childhood and elementary classrooms extrinsic incentives may include:

- extended time for recess
- a movie at the end of the day or week
- special food treats
- free time for students to explore classroom centers on their own
- music to accompany an activity
- more time to engage in a favorite activity
- stickers, certificates

At some point in your field experiences you will likely encounter extrinsic incentives in the form of a **token economy,** a system of distributing symbolic rewards (tokens) for appropriate behavior and withholding or taking away rewards for inappropriate behavior. At a designated time, students can exchange their tokens for something they value. Principal Susan McCloud at T.C. Cherry Elementary School in Bowling Green, Kentucky, reports that the culture of Cherry changed remarkably when her teachers began concentrating on positive behavior and incentives rather than negative behaviors and punishment. One major aspect of the change was the establishment of a token economy, in which students accumulated Cherry Pit Points that they could later "spend" at the Cherry Pit Store. Principal McCloud says this token system gives the students a sense of power and control when they think, "'Hey, I can behave and if I do, I get things that I want'" (2005, p. 49).

A primary influence for young adolescents revolves around friends. Many middle-level teachers capitalize on this developmental trait by promising socializing time at the end of a class period or at the end of a week in exchange for appropriate behavior. High school teachers take advantage of adolescent tendencies in the same way. In middle and high school, extrinsic incentives tend to be less tangible and more social in nature, such as the use of praise as a motivator.

Young adolescents and peer influence are discussed in Chapter 2.

Praise. Praise may be a powerful extrinsic motivator for some students. It is extrinsic because it depends on someone else, the praiser. There are important guidelines for optimizing the value of praise. Specific praise is more effective than general praise. For instance, saying to a student, "Your participation in today's activity helped your whole group stay on task. Thanks, Marcus," is more valuable than simply saying, "Nice work" as Marcus's group leaves the classroom. Using the student's name is important. Whether to praise in private or in public depends in large measure on the developmental level of the students. Most early childhood and elementary students enjoy being praised in front of their classmates. Young adolescents and high school students are often embarrassed by public praise. A compliment in private is generally more motivational and increases the likelihood of the desired behavior being repeated.

Logic of extrinsic incentives. In a perfect world, extrinsic incentives would not be necessary. We would all behave appropriately because it's the right thing to do. We would all work hard to reach our potential and to benefit others. Real teachers in real school settings understand the theories that reject extrinsic incentives; they also understand that much of society runs as smoothly as it does because of extrinsic motivation. Ask how many people who work in service industries (fast-food restaurants, dry cleaners, etc.) actually get out of bed and go to work because they are internally motivated to do their jobs. How they do their jobs—their attitude, attention to quality, and drive to be successful—may indeed be intrinsically motivated. But chances are that most go to work to earn money.

Ideally, students complete assignments and behave appropriately because they want to (intrinsic motivation). But there are tasks (drill and practice, assignments with no readily apparent value) and behaviors (walking in a straight line, being quiet when a visitor enters) that simply may not be internally motivating for some students in some settings. When it comes to extrinsic and intrinsic incentives, most teachers use a mixture to meet the real needs in their real classrooms.

Intrinsic incentives. For lasting results intrinsic incentives, such as the satisfaction of completing an assignment that is challenging, or behaving appropriately in an assembly, have the most value. Helping students understand why a particular behavior is desirable builds an internal "want to" that is motivating. When an individual behaves appropriately because of intrinsic motivation, chances are the desired behavior not only lasts but spreads to other aspects of life with positive results.

The best classroom management involves **student self-monitoring**. This is the ultimate intrinsic incentive because when students assume control of their own behavior, they develop a sense of ownership. Sounds good, doesn't it? We all want this for our students and our classrooms. However, helping students move toward this ideal when they may be accustomed to being told what to do, when to do it, and how to do it, with the promise of rewards for compliance, is a difficult task. Teaching for obedience is much easier than teaching for responsibility. Methods of accomplishing student self-monitoring are beyond the scope of this text, but this discussion may plant the seed that will give you the intrinsic motivation to think about, read about, and plan for a classroom full of self-monitoring students.

Akin to intrinsic motivation is the concept that when student needs are met, misbehavior is less of an issue. When student needs are met, students behave appropriately because (1) they want to, and (2) there's little need to do otherwise. Glasser's *Choice Theory* (1998) says that five basic needs constitute the source of all intrinsic motivation: survival, love and belonging, power, freedom, and fun. Glasser contends that giving students what they need will get teachers what they want: student responsibility and more appropriate behavior. Erwin (2003) tells us that when teachers understand these needs, it is possible to "transform your classroom into a place where students . . . behave in respectful, responsible ways" (p. 21). Figure 6.5 includes ways in which teachers can address Glasser's five basic needs.

Figure 6.5 Addressing Glasser's five basic needs

Survival
- provide opportunities to get food, water, fresh air
- maintain behavior guidelines that promote safety and respect
- develop routines that add a sense of order and security

Love and Belonging
- learn names and personal information quickly
- greet students as they enter the classroom
- let students know you personally
- teach cooperation
- engage students in ways that show them they are valued

Power
- give students a voice in the classroom
- be conscious of a variety of learning styles
- teach personal responsibility
- allow for second and third chances to demonstrate learning

Freedom
- give choices
- use a variety of instructional strategies

Fun
- use games in instruction
- engage students in brain teaser activities

Source: Erwin, J. C. (2003). Giving students what they need. *Educational Leadership, 61*(1), 21–23.

As with other aspects of teaching, teachers must remember that their classrooms are likely to include diverse groups of students. What is valued and what is motivating may be quite different from classroom to classroom, and student to student. Knowing students well—their cultures, their home settings, their disabilities, and more—is vital in understanding how to help them behave in respectful and responsible ways. We'll look more closely at this issue later in the chapter.

Now let's turn our attention to what takes place when students do not respond favorably to incentives.

CONSEQUENCES

Points of Reflection 6.4

What do you remember about consequences in your K–12 experiences? Which appeared to be effective and why? What kinds of consequences make sense to you?

Proactive prevention strategies, coupled with a system of incentives that helps students self-monitor their behavior, is the best approach to classroom management. But when expectations are not met, and prevention isn't enough, teachers must intervene. Intervention usually involves consequences. There are two guidelines teachers should follow to help ensure that consequences are reasonable, fairly applied, and not overly reactive, punitive, or exclusionary. First, *consequences should match the inappropriate behavior.* Second, *consequences should focus on the behavior, not on the person*, thus preserving both the student's dignity and the teacher-student relationship.

Matching consequences to misbehavior. Consequences should match misbehavior both in appropriateness and in severity. Although it would be impossible to design a distinct consequence for every type of misbehavior, teachers should attempt to match consequences whenever possible. For instance, if a student writes on desks or lockers, an appropriate consequence would involve cleaning during a school-required detention. If a student wastes class time, spending free time making up class work would be appropriate. If teasing and hurt feelings are involved, perhaps an apology and reading a short story about how hurtful teasing can be may be effective. Most schools have a standard list of consequences ranging from mild to severe. As with expectations, these consequences need to be applied in the classroom. Teachers can go beyond school-wide agreed-upon consequences by developing and implementing consequences tailored to the misbehavior of their own students.

Unobtrusive interventions. The variability of both students and misbehavior dictates a wide range of consequences, beginning with consequences that do not disrupt instruction. There are both nonverbal and verbal ways to address relatively minor behavior problems such as student inattention; minor off-task behaviors like daydreaming, doing something other than what is expected, and not using proper materials; leaving a designated area; pestering another student; and many others.

Nonverbal **unobtrusive interventions** include moving closer to the offending student (proximity), giving a disapproving look, stopping mid-sentence for a moment to gain student attention, and making an established gesture. To be effective, nonverbal interventions take thought and proactive behavior on the part of the teacher. The best way to learn about nonverbal interventions is to watch and listen carefully as experienced teachers make them work. You'll have opportunities to do this during field experiences in your teacher preparation program. Chances are that unobtrusive intervention will be enough for most students, most of the time, if the environment is respectful and students are engaged in learning.

What Mr. White expects of you:

I expect you to....

1. Take responsibility for your work and grade.
2. Respect your teachers, peers, and surroundings.
3. Follow ALL directions.
4. Raise hand before speaking.
5. Come in quietly and ready to learn.

What you can expect from Mr. White:

(Positive Consequence)

You can expect....
1.) a smile.
2.) verbal praise.
3.) a positive call home.
4.) tangible rewards (candy, pencils, etc).

OR

(Negative Consequence)

You can expect....
1.) a warning.
2.) a minor referral for lunch or after school detention
3.) a negative call home.
4.) a major referral.

Setting expectations and consequences, and then making them public and explicit, helps bring order and civility to the classroom.

Verbal interventions can resolve minor problems if delivered quickly, calmly, and in ways that match the offense. From saying, "Everyone needs to listen," to using the offending student's name in a classroom scenario, to a class discussion about why a particular behavior is inappropriate, teachers' words can make a difference. Whatever is said should purposefully lead students back to focus on instruction or learning activities.

Simply asking a student to move to another part of the classroom temporarily, or permanently, may solve some minor misbehavior problems. Withdrawing privileges is another tactic some teachers use successfully.

Teacher-prescribed consequences. Teachers must move beyond unobtrusive nonverbal and verbal intervention when misbehavior warrants. The timing of this escalation depends on a number of variables, including school level, student needs, and assessment of possible damage or danger involved with the misbehavior.

Time-out is a consequence often used in early childhood and elementary classrooms. Students are isolated, usually within the classroom, and not allowed to participate in whatever is going on. Time-out works well as a consequence if not overused and if classroom instruction and activities are engaging, making isolation undesirable.

Detention is a consequence often used at all grade levels. It is most effective when it involves isolation and requires the student to give up time he or she would rather spend elsewhere. Some teachers, teams of teachers, and whole schools find that lunch detention works well. Students assigned to lunch detention are separated from others and required to eat lunch alone in silence. After-school detention is typically used for completion of assignments or for school-related chores such as cleaning or helping in some way. Weekend detention, sometimes called Saturday school, is generally reserved for more serious or repeated offenses.

Boynton and Boynton (2005) describe the concept of sending a student out of the classroom for the purpose of reflection and to consider better choices as **processing**. Students may be sent to another classroom, the hallway, the library, or a designated room, sometimes called a behavior improvement room (BIR). An important part of processing is what Marzano (2003a) refers to as "written self-analysis" (p. 84). He recommends that students analyze what part they played in the misbehavior, how others contributed, how it should be resolved, and what might prevent it from happening again. Processing is appropriate for minor misbehavior that occurs repeatedly or student disruptions that aren't resolved through unobtrusive nonverbal or verbal interventions.

Serious consequences. Some misbehavior calls for consequences beyond what an individual teacher may assign. Misbehavior involving physical violence, loud or threatening verbal abuse, vandalism, theft, and possession of illegal substances or weapons dictates the involvement of building-level administrators who may elect to involve law enforcement. Such serious misbehavior often results in suspension, either in school or out of school, or expulsion. Classroom teachers should not attempt to handle such misbehavior alone. A supportive and decisive administrator can be one of the most valuable assets to teachers and the classroom management process.

Chances are that most in America would be surprised to know that **corporal,** or physical, **punishment** is still allowed in 22 states today (Farrell, 2010). Interestingly, the perceived need for such punishment dates back to the early days of the United States. Figure 6.6 provides a portion of a teacher's journal dated 1776 that describes a "bad boy" and the philosophy of the day about "curing" the student. Most teachers will recognize at least some of the traits described by Master Lovell in at least a few of the students they have known. Reviewing the history of educational practices provides a perspective showing that the struggles teachers face in today's classrooms are not necessarily new.

The first state to ban corporal punishment was New Jersey in 1867. Many large cities in the Northeast banned corporal punishment before their states. Notably, New York City banned the practice in 1870, whereas the state of New York did not ban it until 1985. Educators may use paddling, the most common form of corporal punishment, in all the Southern states, plus others. The last state to ban the practice was Ohio in 2009. Of the remaining states, paddling takes place most often in Texas, Mississippi, Tennessee, Arkansas, and Alabama. The total number of incidents has decreased sharply from

Figure 6.6 Master Lovell's journal

A Bad Boy is undutiful to his father and mother, disobedient and stubborn to his master, and ill natured to all his playmates. He hates his books and takes no pleasure in improving himself. . . .

He is always in mischief, and when he has done a wrong, will tell twenty lies to clear himself. He hates to have anyone give him good advice, and when they are out of sight, will laugh at them. He swears and wrangles and quarrels with his companions, and is always in some dispute or other. . . .

He is frequently out of humor, and sullen and obstinate, so that he will neither do what he is asked, nor answer any question put to him. In short, he neglects everything that he should learn, and minds nothing but play and mischief. He grows up a confirmed blockhead, incapable of anything but wickedness and folly. . . . [T]o make a bad boy into a good one, he should be thrashed daily for some reason or other, and locked securely in a closet. There he can meditate upon his sins and thus avoid his fate.

Source: Loeper, J. L. (1973). *Going to school in 1776.* New York: Macmillan.

about 3% of the student population experiencing some form of corporal punishment in 1976 to only 0.5% of students in 2003 (Farrell, 2010).

School districts that practice corporal punishment must follow guidelines governing its use that have resulted from court cases. These guidelines include giving specific warnings that a behavior may result in physical punishment, having more than one adult present, and ensuring that the punishment is reasonable and humane (Dunklee & Shoop, 2002). Although corporal punishment has vocal critics and its practice has fallen out of favor with most districts and educators, some people still believe it is warranted.

Focus on the behavior, not the person. Children and adolescents are developing and growing. Their misbehavior often results from fleeting moods, spontaneous impulses, and poor decision making linked to immaturity.

Constructive correcting. Assigning consequences in ways that serve as student learning experiences is both productive and constructive—productive in that students sense that they are viewed as individuals, and constructive in that students may use the experience to build their understanding of why certain behaviors are unacceptable. Correcting students in constructive ways can turn something negative into a growth experience. For instance, a consequence for using the word *retard* in a joking manner may be viewing a video about children with Down syndrome that explains their intellectual disabilities and the coping strategies they are taught. The disrespect shown by using *retard* as a slang word will hopefully be corrected with increased understanding.

Boynton and Boynton (2005) tell us that the goal of correcting students should be to have them reflect on their actions, be sorry for their misbehavior, and determine to make better choices next time. How teachers correct students makes a difference. If done constructively, the chances of a student walking away hating the teacher and planning to misbehave again, but not get caught, are diminished. Steps to use when correcting a student and assigning a consequence are listed in Figure 6.7.

Figure 6.7 Steps to use when correcting students

1. Review what happened.
2. Identify and accept student's feelings.
3. Review alternative actions.
4. Explain the building policy as it applies to the situation.
5. Let the student know that all students are treated the same.
6. Invoke an immediate and meaningful consequence.
7. Let the student know you are disappointed that you have to invoke a consequence to his or her action.
8. Communicate an expectation that the student will do better in the future.

Source: Boynton, M., & Boynton, C. (2005). *The educator's guide to preventing and solving discipline problems.* Alexandria, VA: Association for Supervision and Curriculum Development.

Starting fresh. When focus is placed on the misbehavior, and not on the student, it is possible for the student to see beyond the incident and consequence to the possibility of a fresh start. Chris Stevenson (2002), noted expert on middle-level education, advises us to have an attitude that says to students, "Redemption is always close, not closed" (p. 219). In other words, when a student misbehaves and a consequence is assigned, the student deserves to be given a fresh start. This helps students build **resilience,** the ability to bounce back and meet life's challenges.

Family communication. When communicating with the family of a student who misbehaves, it is vital to focus on the misbehavior, not the person. In essence, if a student is maligned rather than the misbehavior, then the family is maligned, with a negative effect on the family-school relationship. A wise teacher emphasizes the positive and the potential before discussing the misbehavior.

If a teacher has already had a positive family communication, such as a complimentary note sent home or a pleasant meeting at Back-to-School Night, then a phone call about a behavior problem may work wonders. For some students, just the threat of a call is enough. For other students, a call home is meaningless. For instance, parents may not be available for a call (and students know this) or parents may have received many such calls and may not care or may feel helpless to remedy the situation.

We look more closely at family conferences in Chapter 12.

Parent or family conferences can be effective if they are handled professionally and result in an agreed-upon, enforceable plan to correct the problem.

This chapter's **The Opinion Page** feature is about a principal who obviously understands the big picture of expectations and consequences. Teachers can learn a great deal from this principal's design of a consequence that fits the misbehavior.

THE OPINION PAGE

This Opinion Editorial appeared in the Inter-Mountain, a newspaper serving the Potomac Highlands area of West Virginia, on May 30, 2012.

Students Must Learn from Their Mistakes

by staff writer

Next month, a group of Pendleton County High School graduates will host a Fun Day for area youth to raise money for the custodian staff and fire department. They'll also spend two days of their summer vacation helping clean up around the school.

This is the same group of 25 to 30 students who, a few weeks ago, broke into their school, scattered corn, straw, and yarn, wrapped toilets in Saran wrap and tin foil, and smeared Vaseline and shaving cream throughout the building. What started out as a planned prank of decorating some classrooms with balloons and streamers got "out of hand" the students and their Principal Tim Woodward say. The school's custodian described the result as "a mess, a total mess."

Classes were canceled the following day to allow time for cleanup.

Law enforcement isn't pressing charges, unless school system officials decide otherwise. Some parents think their children deserve a stern punishment.

Woodward decided against suspending the students, saying that would cause them to miss their graduation. Instead, he elected to impose "restorative discipline restitution"—hence the additional summer projects. This, he says, "actually teaches the student."

Had they been suspended from graduation, they may have felt remorse on that day or regret in years to come. They may even have quite a tale in explaining why they didn't get to attend the ceremonies. What they would be without is a lesson of value.

While many may not agree with Woodward's decision, it appears he is on the right track. There's no excuse for what the students did. It was simply wrong. Now, it's in their best interest and that of those who affiliate with them in the future to learn from their mistakes. It may even be something they can teach their children.

Copyright © 2012 Inter-Mountain.

This Opinion Page piece commends an act of common sense on the part of the principal. Write a well-developed paragraph in response to each of the following questions:

1. In what ways does the consequence fit the misbehavior? Why do you think some parents did not agree with the principal's choice?

2. How does the principal demonstrate consideration for the whole child? What does this have to do with resilience?

3. In what ways does the punishment contribute to constructive correcting? Explain the use of the phrase "restorative discipline restitution."

Now that we have considered ways to create a positive learning environment; how routines contribute to a productive learning environment; and some of the basics of expectations, incentives, and consequences, we are ready to explore developing a classroom management plan.

How Can I Develop a Classroom Management Plan?

Considering elements that contribute to a successful classroom management plan will create an awareness of what to look for in field experiences throughout your teacher preparation program as you observe teachers dealing daily with learning environment issues.

This section looks briefly at what selected theorists and researchers have to say about classroom management; the necessity of considering students' special needs, societal context, and developmental stages; and some general guidelines for planning and implementing classroom management.

PROMINENT THEORIES OF CLASSROOM MANAGEMENT

If you presented a classroom management scenario to a room full of teachers and asked them how they would respond, you'd no doubt hear as many solutions as there were teachers. A single foolproof recipe for classroom management simply doesn't exist. Many new teachers are dismayed to hear this because a recipe or formula would make life much easier. But take heart! Teachers can take advantage of what experienced theorists like those in Table 6.1 have to say, as well as research-based strategies, to garner ideas to consider in developing personalized classroom management plans.

TABLE 6.1 Overview of selected theories of classroom management

Theorist	Model	Basic Beliefs
Skinner	Behavior modification	Teachers use positive and negative reinforcements or rewards and punishments to modify or shape students' behavior.
Glasser	Choice therapy and quality schools	Schools help satisfy students' psychological needs and add quality to their lives. Teachers teach, manage, provide caring environments, and conduct class meetings in a way that adds quality to students' lives.
Gordon	Teacher effectiveness training	Teachers teach self-discipline, demonstrate active listening, send "I-messages" rather than "you-messages," and teach a six-step conflict resolution program.
Canter	Assertive discipline	Teachers and students have rights in the classroom. Teachers insist upon responsible behavior and use a hierarchical list of consequences to manage behavior.
Kounin	Instructional management	Teachers use effective instructional behaviors (teaching techniques, movement management, and group focus) to influence student behaviors.
Curwin and Mendler	Discipline with dignity	Teachers protect the dignity of students. Teachers are fair and consider individual situations (as opposed to rigid rules), list rules that make sense to students, and model appropriate behaviors.
Gathercoal	Judicious discipline	Teachers provide behavioral guidelines for property loss and damage, threats to health and safety, and serious disruptions of the educational process. They also demonstrate professional ethics and build a democratic classroom.

Source: Manning, M. L., & Bucher, K. T. (2013). *Classroom management: Models, applications, and cases.* Boston: Pearson Education, Inc.

CONSIDER THE STUDENTS

We have already discussed the importance of considering all aspects of students' lives when planning for curriculum, instruction, and assessment. This outlook is equally important in planning for the learning environment.

Special needs. Students with special needs, those requiring unique services to optimize their learning potential, usually also require specific guidelines for classroom management. The best way to find out what the guidelines are for a student with special needs is to talk with the person in your school who has oversight responsibility for the student's education, most often one of the special educators in your building. You will be referred to the student's Individualized Education Program, which will contain information about any variances from what are considered normal, reasonable incentive-and-consequence systems necessitated by the student's disability. The Individuals with Disabilities Education Act (IDEA) includes provisions for the development of a management plan through a team of educators using a process known as **functional behavioral assessment (FBA)**. FBA looks for events and actions that may lead to misbehavior and devises strategies to help students abide by classroom expectations.

> In Chapter 2 we discuss students with special needs, related services, and IEPs.

Societal context. Students don't leave their home lives on the schoolhouse steps at 8 A.M., to be picked up again at 3:30 P.M. as they leave the classroom. The societal context in which they are growing up colors their attitudes, aptitudes, and reactions. You name it, they bring it with them into the classroom. The answer to the familiar questions, "And how are the children? Are they all well?" should guide the development and implementation of a classroom management plan.

What motivates one child to follow routines and expectations may be meaningless to another. Students' perceptions—regardless of whether the source may be culturally or socioeconomically based—influence their reactions to expectations, incentives, and consequences. Some of the everyday areas about which perceptions may differ include eye contact, physical closeness to others, competition, and receiving attention (Manning & Bucher, 2013).

To understand this issue of differing perspectives, examine what experienced educators and sociologists have to say about sensitivity and insightful management options. Some of the best sources of information, including Ruby Payne, Lisa Delpit, Alfie Kohn, and Jonathan Kozol, remind us that diversity exists within specific groups, as well as among groups. This diversity and resulting issues may impact the day-to-day functioning of classrooms as teachers strive to match their classroom management systems to students' developmental levels.

> In Chapter 2 we discuss student diversity, and in Chapter 9 we examine the societal context of our students and schools.

Developmental appropriateness. Understanding human development is absolutely essential when writing and implementing a classroom management plan. Let's take a look at how some of our 10 focus teachers maintain learning environments through classroom management plans that both match their personal styles and respond to the developmental stages of their students.

Early childhood. Brandi Wade at Summit Primary, Ohio, works to create a safe, loving, consistent environment for kindergartners. She attempts to match misbehavior with logical consequences. For instance, if during group time on the classroom carpet a child is disruptive, the child must go back to his or her desk, continuing to listen, but not sitting with the rest of the children.

Brandi uses a system that is theme related, and her expectations for student behavior increase as the year progresses. For instance, her expectation in September may be for students not to argue as they form lines to leave the room. If students "earn" 15 apples in their class apple basket for meeting this expectation, they may enjoy an apple-tasting party.

When planning for classroom management, always consider your students and their developmental needs.

Elementary. Chris Roberts, multiage teacher at Rees Elementary School, Utah, has a classroom management/learning environment philosophy best related in his own words:

> Maintaining a positive environment really boils down to a quote I follow by Ron Miller, "Our work is not about curriculum or a teaching method. It is about nurturing the human spirit with love." I do my best to have unconditional love for my students. I think my students feel that and do their best to work hard and learn all they can. We don't have "rules," but we do have "agreements." I believe that language change is important. Kids are smothered in rules. We meet together a lot in the beginning of the year and do experiential activities to build teamwork. We talk about how we want our village to be. We write down our discussions and sign an agreement that we will do our best to show respect for ourselves, others, and property. We continually assess how we are doing all year long. I write a lot of letters to my students telling them I appreciate the positive things they are doing. (From e-mail communication with Chris Roberts, November 11, 2005)

In the opening scenario of this chapter you read about Tim Mendenhall and a new student who came into his classroom with a history of misbehavior and poor academic performance. Tim applied his classroom management plan to help Jeff acclimate to Rees Elementary and make behavioral progress, a necessary step toward academic success. The general guidelines of Tim's management plan are presented in Figure 6.8.

Middle school. Focus teacher Traci Peters at Cario Middle School, South Carolina, invests a lot of time in getting to know her students and attending school events to support their participation. Building relationships is foundational to Traci's classroom management plan.

Traci and her students abide by the five basic behavior guidelines agreed on by the entire staff of Cario Middle School and listed in Figure 6.9. The Charleston County School District requires teachers to give conduct grades for each student in every 9-week grading period. Employing a system commonly found in many schools, Traci gives demerits for misbehavior. She has a system for converting demerits into letter grades. She also uses a "three strikes, you're out" policy, meaning that after three demerits in her classroom in a quarter, a student goes outside her classroom management plan and talks with a building-level administrator. Traci says, "Basically, I give kids a chance to be kids,

Figure 6.8 Tim Mendenhall's guidelines for classroom management

1. Build trust from the moment students walk through the door.
2. Protect trust all year long.
3. Play with students on the field and in the classroom (sports, checkers, educational games, etc.).
4. Don't send students away to be disciplined unless absolutely necessary. If you do, you give away their respect for you and your role.
5. Don't ever be degrading. This ruins your relationship with students.
6. Set up clear expectations with consequences that apply when students make bad choices.
7. Make students take responsibility. Keep their problems, their problems.
8. Be sympathetic but firm, fair, and consistent.

Source: From e-mail communication with Tim Mendenhall, November 12, 2005.

Figure 6.9 Cario Middle School student expectations

1. Conduct yourself in an orderly manner.
2. Be on task.
3. Respect yourself and others.
4. Take care of all property.
5. Promote safety in everything you do.

but at the same time I expect them to respect me and those around them." She tells us that parent communication is a major help in managing a middle school classroom.

High school. A high school administrative team and staff with expectations for respect and consistent consequences can generally run a positive and productive campus. Most high school students understand behavioral expectations and the rationale behind them. If adolescents ages 15 through 19 are disruptive in the classroom, they know exactly what they're doing and, in some cases, do it because they know they can get away with it or perhaps because they want to be suspended. Students who are disruptive in high school are often sent out of the classroom, instructed to see an administrator, and may be given **suspension,** or sent off school grounds, for a specified length of time. This severe consequence should be reserved for extreme cases.

Roosevelt High School, California, publishes school rules as well as its Student Code of Conduct in a student handbook. The school rules on which Roosevelt teachers build their classroom expectations are shown in Figure 6.10. The Code of Conduct covers expectations for a safe environment, closed-campus rules and exceptions, the necessity of ID tags, absences, the use of electronics, and a sexual harassment policy. In addition, the Fresno Unified School District maintains a zero-tolerance policy for possession of firearms, weapons of any kind, explosives, controlled substances, and attempted or actual harm to another person. Immediate suspension occurs for these violations, many times resulting in **expulsion,** or permanent removal from school.

Our three focus teachers at Roosevelt High, Craig Cleveland, Derek Boucher, and Angelica Reynosa, seldom have misbehavior in their classrooms that a certain look or a private word won't remedy. They are instead often faced with the dilemma of students not engaging in learning. So rather than overt misbehavior, a lack of desire or enthusiasm for the whole educative process often challenges them. This can be an even more perplexing problem than dealing with students who are disruptive.

INCORPORATE 21ST-CENTURY SKILLS

We have discussed the Partnership for 21st Century Skills (P21) in the context of curriculum, instruction, and assessment while addressing the first three 21st-century outcome categories: Core Subjects; Learning and Innovation Skills; and Information, Media, and Technology Skills. P21's philosophy is that mastering the first three outcome categories is not enough to be successful in life. The fourth outcome category is *Life and Career Skills.* The five major components of Life and Career Skills are listed in Figure 6.11. Let's briefly examine each component.

Points of Reflection 6.6

Do the behavior and classroom management dilemmas of early childhood sound like something you might find intriguing? If so, in what ways?

Can you envision yourself managing an elementary classroom? If so, what appeals to you about this age group?

Does managing a classroom of unpredictable, yet wonderful, young adolescents appeal to you? If so, why?

Do you have the desire to establish caring relationships with maturing adolescents who wish to be treated as adults but who may not have the self-control or self-motivation to match? If so, explain.

Figure 6.10 Roosevelt High School behavior guidelines

Roosevelt High School students are required to conduct themselves in an appropriate, acceptable manner at all times when present in school, in classrooms and hallways, on school grounds, and at school-sponsored events. Students are to:

1. Treat others with consideration and dignity.
2. Respect the property of others.
3. Be punctual and prepared for class.
4. Follow the direction of all staff.

Figure 6.11 21st-century life and career skills

- Flexibility and adaptability
- Initiative and self-direction
- Social and cross-cultural skills
- Productivity and accountability
- Leadership and responsibility

Flexibility and adaptability. Being flexible and adaptable doesn't mean passively going with the flow. P21 suggests that we teach students to respond to change in ways that make growth a priority and to use feedback constructively. This means that students need to develop resilience that helps them deal with both praise and criticism. Teaching students to be adaptable involves giving them experiences in different roles, responsibilities, and schedules.

Although we can control many elements in the classroom, it is inevitable that something will interrupt the flow of teaching and learning. For instance, in an elementary classroom a teacher may purposefully orchestrate a disruption in an event students helped plan, like an afternoon outdoors looking for plant samples. The teacher might lead the students to plan the event on a day when she knows the field is scheduled to be mowed. When she tells the students about the mowing on the morning of their planned outing, they will be disappointed. She can have the students get into small groups and brainstorm how they might be flexible and adaptable and still accomplish their goals. Then students should share and discuss their possible alternatives. This is a life skill that is very much a part of a productive classroom environment.

Initiative and self-direction. The components addressed in these life and career skills include managing goals and time, working independently, and being self-directed learners. All of these components play major roles in maintaining a positive and productive learning environment. Independent, self-directed learners will be able to manage time as they accomplish their goals. Helping students become this ultimate vision of who we want them to be isn't necessarily something that becomes part of daily lesson plans. It is a teacher attitude that weaves in and out of every formal and informal encounter we have with students. For instance, a high school civics teacher may plan for students to complete a semester-long project. Many steps are built into the project, beginning with a whole-class activity involving brainstorming, followed by small group work for those with similar interests. Then the individual student, armed with skills from working with two different size groups, sets off independently to work through the assignment step by step at his or her own pace. The teacher is deliberately creating experiences that lead to independence and self-direction.

Focus student Patrick Sutton is a good example of a student who is self-motivated and self-confident. Watch **Patrick's interview** with teacher Traci Peters.

In Chapter 2, we discuss student diversity.

Social and cross-cultural skills. This area is all about relationships and communication, two vital aspects of a classroom community. Showing respect in a variety of circumstances and with a broad spectrum of people—based on age, gender, ethnicity, abilities, political persuasions, religion, and all the ways we may differ—is key. Every day in the classroom, teachers have the responsibility to model acceptance and respectful communication. They model when to speak and when to listen, when to be open minded, and then when to stand on reasoned ground.

One way to foster social and cross-cultural skills is purposefully grouping and re-grouping students in ways that expose them to all the diversity a particular setting can offer. Some demographics are rich in diversity; others are not. Even where race and socioeconomic circumstances are similar, students display diversity in learning styles, abilities, motivation, and achievement. Teachers need to look beyond the obvious and into the subtle, and then group students, teaching them how to communicate and work together in positive and productive ways.

Productivity and accountability. Producing results and fulfilling responsibilities, or being accountable, are vital attributes of success. When students experience success through being productive and accountable, success will likely lead to more success. It's a cycle we often have to orchestrate the first or second time around until students experience what it's like to actually be productive. We certainly have to be close guides for younger students to first succeed, and then recognize success in the form of productivity so they understand the cycle and will want to replicate it. But adolescents often need this close guidance as well. Our hovering will have to take different forms to be effective, but that's part of understanding the development of our students. If adolescents have little experience with productivity and accountability, we have to make the elements obvious, actually *plan* for them to succeed, and then help them reflect on the big picture of the relationship between hard work and success.

Leadership and responsibility. There's a reason why social studies standards begin with the study of self and family in kindergarten; extend to the study of neighborhoods and community in first grade; and then progress to an overview of local, state, and national dimensions before concentrating on U.S. History in fifth grade. From there, a broad view of history is tackled, followed by in-depth study of how our world works regarding people, geography, politics, and so on. Children and adolescents develop from a narrow perspective on life and their world to an understanding of interdependence, built in large measure through the guidance of their teachers.

Integrity and ethical behavior, two attributes we hope will be part of all aspects of leadership, don't necessarily happen naturally. Pointing out moral dilemmas and then prompting students to make choices and act in responsible ways is a positive and healthy part of the informal curriculum. For instance, when a dispute arises on the playground—and it most certainly will—rather than assigning a consequence based on what appears to be a rule infraction or simply a child being mean, a teacher might plan a class debriefing of the situation with students asking questions of the kids involved in the dispute, attempting to get at the cause of the problem. In this way, students begin to think through situations, look at possible causes and solutions, recognize volatile circumstances, and learn to take responsibility and lead others in that direction as well. Although this all sounds quite straightforward and simple, it takes incident after incident, solution seeking over and over again, to internalize the lessons. As adults, this is a lifelong learning task, and for children, we can't start too soon to help them develop leadership and responsibility skills.

> We discuss appreciation for moral dilemmas in Chapter 1 and the informal curriculum in Chapters 4 and 5.

GENERAL GUIDELINES FOR DEVELOPING A CLASSROOM MANAGEMENT PLAN

We have discussed some of the most important elements of developing and implementing a classroom management plan. Figure 6.12 presents some commonsense guidelines that Jones (2011) tells us are supported by current research.

Certain guidelines are nonnegotiable when establishing a classroom management plan. Although it is impossible to address all of them within the scope of this book, here are several important ones:

- *Always stay within school and district policies and guidelines.*
- *Use positive rather than negative statements when establishing expectations.* Students need to know what they *should do*, not just what they *shouldn't do*. For instance, the expectation "We will show respect for others when working together or apart" is more likely to gain compliance than "We will not be disrespectful of others when working together or apart." Plant positive thoughts in students' minds to promote productive habits of appropriate behavior.

Figure 6.12 Components of effective, comprehensive classroom management

1. Understand students' personal and psychological needs.
2. Create an affirmative classroom climate that fosters positive relationships.
3. Involve students in a commitment to on-task behavior.
4. Use effective instructional methods that lead to optimal learning.
5. Respond to unproductive behavior with respect and promote development of cooperative skills.

Source: Jones, V. (2011). *Practical classroom management.* Boston: Pearson Education, Inc.

- *Consistently apply expectations and consequences.* Some teachers set an expectation and have different consequences based on the number of times a student's behavior is outside the expectation. This sort of consequence layering in no way undermines the consistency of consequences.
- *Look for students' redeeming characteristics.* We all have them. Looking for the good in students helps us like them more and perhaps find some things in common with them.
- *Explore conflict resolution and peer mediation.* This approach involves students trained as go-betweens to help other students work through their differences and agree to disagree amicably. Look for such programs as you observe and interact in schools.
- *Communicate and document.* Once established, a teacher's classroom management plan should be explicitly taught to students, the building administrators should receive a written plan, and parents and families should be informed of it. An aspect of communication often neglected by teachers is documentation, or record keeping. When a consequence is applied, document it.
- *Ask for help.* There are some behavior issues that classroom teachers should not handle alone. Physical violence, overt bullying, and verbal abuse of students or adults cannot be tolerated in a classroom setting. Episodes of this nature must be dealt with immediately by administrators.

DON'T BE PART OF THE PROBLEM

Think back to your days in prekindergarten through 12th grade. Can you remember a classroom behavior problem actually getting worse because of something a teacher did or didn't do? Were you ever in a class when student misbehavior escalated so that it was almost out of control even as the teacher yelled for attention? How about out-of-control behavior in the presence of a teacher who repeatedly used "shhhh" to ask for silence? Neither approach works.

Purposefully embarrassing students should never be a teacher tactic. The result may be serious psychological damage to the student. Another likely result is the student's loss of respect for the teacher who has displayed his or her own version of misbehavior.

Avoid making threats without following through. This practice can have disastrous results in a classroom. A teacher repeatedly saying, "If you don't stop that I'll . . ." may cause the immediate misbehavior to escalate, and it guarantees future problems because students won't believe the teacher will follow through.

Teachers should never allow a classroom confrontation to escalate into a power struggle. When a student loses control of his or her temper and directs remarks at a teacher, and the teacher reacts in kind, the opportunity to be a mature, reasonable role model is lost. No one wins. Giving a student time to calm down and gracefully save face will provide a chance for student and teacher to talk about the situation. In some exaggerated cases, avoiding a power struggle prevents physical violence and gives time for administrators to get involved in a resolution.

As a last bit of advice, don't take student behavior personally. Remember that students come into our classrooms with all that nature and nurture has dealt them. Although our actions and attitudes can in large measure determine the classroom learning environment, human beings at times defy prediction. When a student lashes out at you or a classmate or a circumstance, chances are the behavior is due, at least in part, to life outside the classroom walls. We do our best to prevent behavior problems, we respond in ways that stem escalation, and still there will be times when we feel as though we have failed. Students are not acting out to show their dislike or disdain for us or the curriculum . . . don't take it personally.

CONCLUDING THOUGHTS

Students learn much more than academic subjects in our classrooms. They learn how to exist in society. They learn the limits of what they can and can't do in terms of behavior. A positive and productive learning environment is safe—physically, emotionally, and academically. When students feel safe they are more likely to participate, learn, and grow.

Creating and maintaining a positive and productive learning environment is hard work. Teachers can learn how to cultivate appropriate relationships with students, how to establish routines that foster productivity, and how to thoughtfully develop classroom management plans that are effective. With diligence and consistent monitoring, a positive and productive learning environment can be maintained.

Well-managed classrooms are marked by civility. Some students come to school without a clear idea of what civility looks like because they don't live in the midst of it. Teachers must model civility, orchestrate an environment that fosters it, and then expect nothing less of students.

After reading the ***Chapter in Review,*** interact with Tim Mendenhall as he struggles to mentor a new teacher in this chapter's ***Developing Professional Competence.***

Chapter in Review

How do teachers create a positive learning environment?

- The physical layout, appearance, usefulness, and overall appeal of the classroom either enhance the learning environment or detract from it.
- Care and trust help teachers and students build a sense of community.
- Teacher awareness, ability to multitask, and recognition that one action directly affects another are valuable assets in creating a positive learning environment.
- Time is a constant that should be used wisely to promote learning in schools.

What routines contribute to maintaining a productive classroom environment?

- The types of routines needed vary by school level, but their importance at all levels cannot be overemphasized.
- Students need to practice routines so they become productive habits.

How do teachers establish expectations, incentives, and consequences?

- Successful classroom management is a prerequisite for successful teaching and learning.
- The best prevention of behavioral problems is engaging instruction.
- Many issues and situations require teachers to establish behavioral expectations, incentives for achieving these expectations, and consequences for not fulfilling them.

How can I develop a classroom management plan?

- Prominent theories and classroom observations provide background and strategies for new teachers to use to formulate management plans.
- Teachers should consider student needs and development when formulating a plan.
- Classroom management plans are most effective when expectations are stated positively; when expectations, incentives, and consequences are applied consistently; and when teachers model appropriate behavior.

Developing Professional Competence

Thoughtfully reading this scenario and responding to the items that follow it will help you prepare for licensure exams.

Tim Mendenhall is an experienced teacher who values relationships with students and has confidence in his classroom management procedures. He was asked by Principal Mike Larsen to mentor a new teacher. She came to Rees with a very strong academic record that included graduating with a 4.0 GPA and a master's degree in teaching reading. Mr. Larsen was very excited to give her an opportunity to teach a self-contained fourth grade class as her first teaching assignment. Tim was happy to be her mentor, but when Elizabeth arrived at Rees she wasn't keen on the idea of someone actually assigned to help her be successful, and she let others know it.

Tim was friendly and offered to help her set up her room and to go through the fourth grade curriculum and materials she would use. She politely listened but showed little interest. For classroom management she posted preprinted posters with rules and warnings. Tim explained that Rees has basic expectations that involve respect and that she may want to meet with her students to talk about what respect might look like in the classrooms and allow the kids to have some input. To that she said no, and told Tim that her training was as a Skinnerian behaviorist.

One afternoon in October, after hearing repeatedly from students that Elizabeth's kids were not happy and several parents had complained to Mr. Larsen, Tim overheard a conversation in the hallway. Elizabeth told Marcus that she was at the limit of her patience, that he was nothing but trouble, that she now knew how to treat him for the rest of the year, and that his parents would be very disappointed in him. Tim knew it was time to talk with Elizabeth even though she had resisted his attempts before.

Think through this scenario and answer the following multiple-choice questions:

1. Which guideline for developing positive teacher-student relationships do you think Elizabeth most likely violated in her encounter with Marcus?
   a. Strong content instruction
   b. Clearly defined parameters of acceptable student behaviors
   c. Use of effective monitoring skills
   d. Appropriate consequences

2. Elizabeth told Tim that she is a Skinnerian behaviorist. This means that:
   a. She must have studied Skinner and believes that children will behave if they understand what's right.
   b. In her study of Skinner she learned that rewards and punishment will shape student behavior.
   c. In graduate school she learned that B. F. Skinner believed in verbally reprimanding students and humiliating them to gain obedience.
   d. She is a trained specialist in behavior management.

3. Based on what he heard in the hall, Tim is afraid that Elizabeth's style of classroom management will possibly destroy which quality he believes in building?
   a. Resilience
   b. Self-determination
   c. Students' love of learning
   d. A healthy sense of competition among students

Now it's time for you to respond to three short essay items involving the scenario. In your responses, be sure to address all the dilemmas and questions posed in each item. Your responses should each be between one half and one full double-spaced page.

4. Refer to Tim's guidelines for classroom management in Figure 6.8. Name two guidelines for which it is likely too late for Elizabeth and this year's fourth graders. Name two guidelines that Elizabeth may have in place, given what you know from this scenario. Explain why you selected each of the four guidelines.

5. What problems does Elizabeth invite for the rest of the year by telling Marcus that she knows how she will treat him? Explain.

Foundations of Education

The topics addressed in **PART III** are typically thought of as the foundations of education. In Chapter 7 we explore the history of education in the United States, spanning from before our country was officially formed all the way into the 21st century. Throughout the chapter, events in the history of our country are examined for their impact on education. In Chapter 8 you learn about five basic philosophies that apply to education. You are asked to begin articulating your own philosophy of education.

Where Do I Stand ?

This inventory helps you begin thinking about elements of your philosophy of education. After reading an item, indicate your level of agreement by choosing a number and placing it in the blank before the statement. Following the inventory are directions for how to organize your responses and what they may indicate in terms of where you stand.

4   I strongly agree
3   I agree
2   I don't have an opinion
1   I disagree
0   I strongly disagree

▶ **Click Here to Complete Survey**

_____ **1.** It is vital that we teach personal responsibility in school.

_____ **2.** Students must be disciplined hard workers in order to learn.

_____ **3.** The classroom should be a model of democracy.

_____ **4.** Memorization is a learning strategy that should be employed frequently in classrooms.

_____ **5.** Schools should use intense study of the classics to strive for excellence in students.

_____ **6.** Making a lesson interesting to students is important to their learning.

_____ **7.** Learning is worthwhile only if it increases a student's sense of self.

_____ **8.** The school and teachers should determine what is learned, without regard for student interests.

_____ **9.** A major goal of public education is positive social change.

_____ **10.** Choices and electives have no place in the curriculum.

_____ **11.** A teacher should be a facilitator of learning.

_____ **12.** Rules are very important in the classroom and must be adhered to at all times.

_____ **13.** Teachers teach the whole child, not just the intellectual aspects.

_____ **14.** An important part of teaching involves instilling students with a sense of responsibility for humanity.

_____ **15.** Part of the responsibility of a teacher is to be an intellectual and moral role model.

_____ **16.** Active engagement is important for learning.

_____ **17.** Curriculum should be established that does not easily or often change, but may shift because of changes in society.

_____ **18.** Cooperative learning is an instructional tool that should be used often in the classroom.

_____ **19.** There is a set curriculum of basic core knowledge that all Americans should know.

_____ **20.** Individualism and freedom of choice are paramount in successful classrooms.

_____ **21.** Teachers are primarily dispensers of knowledge.

_____ **22.** Learning takes place through experiences.

_____ **23.** The wisdom students need may be obtained through study of the writings of great thinkers down through history.

_____ **24.** Standards and testing are of the utmost importance in schools.

_____ **25.** Traditional teaching methods, primarily those that are teacher directed, work best.

_____ **26.** Choices in what and how to learn are important.

_____ **27.** Curriculum should be established that does not change regardless of shifts in society.

_____ **28.** Standardization, tracking, and testing should have a minor role, if any, in the classroom.

_____ **29.** Student differences are not important when determining what and how to teach.

_____ **30.** Exploration and discovery are major factors in student learning.

Place the number you chose representing your level of agreement beside each of the following item numbers. Then find the sum of each column.

ITEM	MY #	ITEM	MY #
2		1	
4		3	
5		6	
8		7	
10		9	
12		11	
15		13	
17		14	
19		16	
21		18	
23		20	
24		22	
25		26	
27		28	
29		30	
Sum A		Sum B	

- If Sum A is larger than Sum B, your views of schools and teaching tend to be more **teacher centered**. We examine two philosophies within the teacher-centered category.

- If Sum B is larger than Sum A, your views of schools and teaching tend to be more **student centered**. We examine three philosophies within the student-centered category.

You may sense a need to alter some of your responses as you learn more, and that's a very healthy thing to do. The more we know, the more we grow.

History of Education in the United States

Dear Reader

History is neither dull nor dry. Real people in real places used problem-solving techniques to address real issues as they arose—and made history in the process. These people were as alive as you are today. History is nothing but problem solving, a skill often relegated to math class only. But think about it . . . life presents dilemmas and we deal with them, or problem solve. This then leads to more dilemmas as the results of our previous actions confront us and we gain more insight. This is history in the making!

You've probably heard the saying, expressed by many in various ways, that if we don't pay attention to history, we are doomed to repeat it. Educators tend to be among the worst perpetrators of proving the truth in this saying. We seem to recycle old ideas every 30 years, or less, even though they didn't work the first time around. One reason for this sad state is that we, as teachers, fail to know the history of our profession and the practices that are part of it.

Learning about and from our past needs to be purposeful. As a new teacher, you will have limited specific knowledge of the history of teaching and learning practices. However, the longer you teach, the more frequently you will say to yourself, "Didn't we do that a few years ago, but back then it was called something else?" At that point you should do your homework and question the viability of what you are being asked to do, always keeping the question "And how are the children?" in your view. This is the only way we will move forward—rather than in circles—when it comes to doing what's most needed by students in the teaching and learning process.

The major questions guiding this chapter include:

- What were the major influences, issues, ideologies, and individuals in 17th-century American education?
- What were the major influences, issues, ideologies, and individuals in 18th-century American education?
- What were the major influences, issues, ideologies, and individuals in 19th-century American education?
- What were the major influences, issues, ideologies, and individuals in 20th-century American education?
- What major influences, issues, ideologies, and individuals are we experiencing in 21st-century American education?
- How are U.S. schools addressing racial and ethnic diversity in the 21st century?
- How can I be aware of education history in the making?

Teaching in Focus

Angelica Reynosa, a world history teacher at Roosevelt High School, California, knows that her task of helping sophomores understand historic events and their impact on today's world is a complex one. Most of the 31 students in Angelica's class are new to the United States. Some of them may have picked up English through classes at Roosevelt or simply from living in Fresno. Many live in homes where only Spanish is spoken. These students haven't grown up steeped in the U.S. social studies curriculum and reciting the Pledge of Allegiance each morning since they were 5 years old. As a second-generation American herself, Angelica understands at least some of her students' challenges.

Angelica has always loved to study history. She views the subject she teaches as a living, breathing entity that's filled with problem-solving scenarios and intrigue. Her teaching philosophy dictates that she engage her students, not merely give out reading assignments. The objective of the lesson shown in the video is "Students will participate in an activity that will help them grasp the reasons for the rise of Marxist theory. They will experience the 'haves' and 'have-nots' of the capitalist system and critically evaluate the benefits and drawbacks of capitalism and socialism." That's an ambitious objective, one that takes lots of thought and planning.

Many of Angelica's students fall into the have-nots, similar to the people Angelica describes in her lesson. They may be in the United States illegally, crowded into the homes of extended family while their parents look for work or hold low-paying jobs. There's so much Angelica wants them to understand about the world. Watch **Angelica's lesson and interview**.

This chapter is an overview of the history of education in America. Knowing the major influences, issues, ideologies, and individuals will give you some perspective as you explore education in the United States. Every philosophy and trend that guided educational processes was forged or in place because of what theorists and teachers thought was right at the time. You will likely find some of what you will read to be antiquated, or worse, immoral. But remember that every generation has a perspective that the previous one did not. We have not always considered equal opportunities for all children to be a guiding force in what we do in schools. Earlier eras were impacted by segregation—and even refusal to provide opportunities to learn to read and write—for some races as well as for children with disabilities. For example, the Puritans, who founded the Massachusetts Bay Colony with a zealous need for religious freedom, were themselves intolerant of other beliefs. They considered children to be little sinners who could only be saved by reading about, and obedience to, Biblical principles. Racial segregation was the norm throughout our history until 1954, when state laws mandating or permitting segregation were declared unconstitutional. We still struggle with integration issues. It took us until 1975 to legislate the rights of children with disabilities to an education in the least restrictive environment, rather than an education, considered a mere privilege, given when it was convenient to the schools. Study the history of education in America, learn from it, and contribute to solutions to its challenges, rather than repeating the mistakes of the past, as we move forward.

What Were the Major Influences, Issues, Ideologies, and Individuals in 17th-Century American Education?

Schools in the 17th century were established by the Europeans who settled along the east coast of what would become the United States of America.

CONTEXT FOR CHANGE

The founding of Jamestown, Virginia, in 1607 by roughly 100 men is used to mark the formal beginning of North America's colonization. Previous voyages to the New World were mostly prompted by the hope of finding riches. The English Puritan religious sect that settled in Plymouth, Massachusetts, 13 years later included men, women, and children. Families came to begin new lives in a place where they hoped to be free to worship their God in their chosen ways. Culturally, the first colonists had their roots in England; religiously, the first colonists opposed the Church of England because it lacked tolerance for any doctrine other than its own. The Church of England in the 17th century was an extension of the English government. To escape being forced to abide by the Church of England's doctrine, the Puritans, who held that the Bible in its literal (or pure) form is the source of all wisdom, sought to establish English-style colonies with their own biblical interpretations to guide them. However, they were not particularly more tolerant than the Church of England they had escaped. For instance, because one of the prominent Puritans of the 17th century, Roger Williams, espoused separation of church and state, he was banished from the Massachusetts Bay Colony to what is now Rhode Island.

The Puritans believed that people were basically sinful and that children would remain so if they could not ward off Satan by reading the Bible and faithfully upholding its principles. To the Puritans, children were merely small adults who needed to learn scripture. Play was considered a waste of time, and discipline was stern (Pulliam & Van Patten, 2013). This attitude carried over into early American schools.

Some of the events of the 17th and subsequent centuries are depicted on the timeline in Figure 7.1. Notice that selected events of American history are depicted alongside momentous events in U.S. public education to provide context for what you read in this chapter. Refer to Figure 7.1 often as you progress through the centuries.

17TH-CENTURY AMERICAN SCHOOLS

The early colonists recognized the need to provide schooling for their children, at least for their male children. They also knew that learning a trade was perhaps best accomplished by working with an expert artisan. Later, as colonies flourished in New England, the Middle Atlantic area, and the South, more formal types of schools grew in both number and variety.

Early colonial schools. Having left England and suffered the hardships of the transatlantic voyage to the New World, the Puritans established an early type of schooling influenced both by European theorists, some of whom are listed in Table 7.1, and by Puritan religious beliefs and social customs. Although the first colonial schools were established for religious purposes, by teaching students to read and write they

TABLE 7.1 Influence of major theorists on early American education	
Theorist	**Summary of Influence**
Erasmus (1466–1536)	Need for systematic training of teachers; liberal arts education includes classics
Luther (1483–1546)	Education necessary for religious instruction; education should include vocational training; need for free and compulsory education
Calvin (1509–1564)	Education serves religious and political establishments; elementary education for all; secondary education for leaders; emphasis on literacy
Bacon (1561–1626)	Education should advance scientific inquiry; provide rationale for development of critical thinking skills
Comenius (1592–1670)	Learning must come through the senses; general body of knowledge (paideia) should be possessed by all
Locke (1632–1704)	Goal of education is to promote the development of reason and morality to enable men to participate in the governing process

Source: Webb, L. D., Metha, A., & Jordan, K. F. (2012). *Foundations of American education* (7th ed.). Upper Saddle River, NJ: Pearson Education, Inc.

Figure 7.1 U.S. education in historical perspective

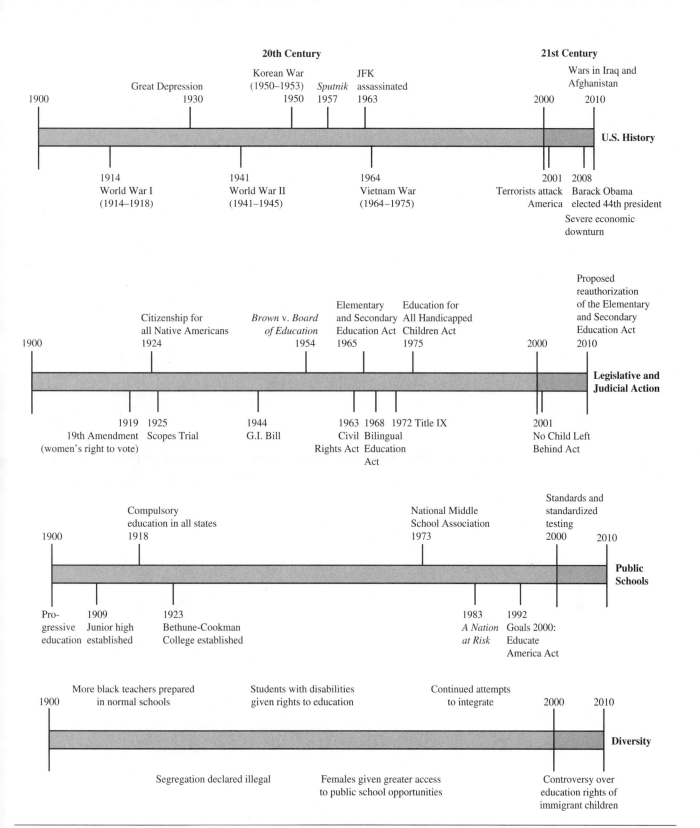

20th Century

U.S. History

- 1900
- Great Depression 1930
- Korean War (1950–1953) 1950
- *Sputnik* 1957
- JFK assassinated 1963
- **21st Century** — Wars in Iraq and Afghanistan 2010
- 2000

- 1914 World War I (1914–1918)
- 1941 World War II (1941–1945)
- 1964 Vietnam War (1964–1975)
- 2001 Terrorists attack America
- 2008 Barack Obama elected 44th president / Severe economic downturn

Legislative and Judicial Action

- 1900
- Citizenship for all Native Americans 1924
- *Brown* v. *Board of Education* 1954
- Elementary and Secondary Education Act 1965
- Education for All Handicapped Children Act 1975
- 2000
- Proposed reauthorization of the Elementary and Secondary Education Act 2010

- 1919 19th Amendment (women's right to vote)
- 1925 Scopes Trial
- 1944 G.I. Bill
- 1963 Civil Rights Act
- 1968 Bilingual Education Act
- 1972 Title IX
- 2001 No Child Left Behind Act

Public Schools

- 1900
- Compulsory education in all states 1918
- National Middle School Association 1973
- Standards and standardized testing 2000
- 2010

- Progressive education
- 1909 Junior high established
- 1923 Bethune-Cookman College established
- 1983 *A Nation at Risk*
- 1992 Goals 2000: Educate America Act

Diversity

- 1900
- More black teachers prepared in normal schools
- Students with disabilities given rights to education
- Continued attempts to integrate
- 2000
- 2010

- Segregation declared illegal
- Females given greater access to public school opportunities
- Controversy over education rights of immigrant children

helped the secular aspects of society develop and prosper as well. These students, overwhelmingly white boys, then had the skills to participate in commerce.

The earliest Puritan settlers educated their children within their own homes, but **dame schools** soon became common. Dames were respected women who had learned to read and write, usually without formal schooling, and who turned their homes into schools where parents paid to have their children educated. Some children went from a dame school, which was essentially the first American elementary school, or from no schooling at all, to an apprenticeship that required them (virtually all boys) to move into the home of a master. The master taught them a trade and often also taught them basic literacy skills. Girls usually stayed home and learned homemaking skills from their mothers.

As education moved from individual homes into schools throughout colonial America, notable differences in education emerged among colonies in different geographic areas. Figure 7.2 is a map of colonial America showing the three basic geographic areas we discuss next.

Schools in the New England colonies. In 1630 the Massachusetts Bay Colony was established, followed by Rhode Island, Connecticut, and New Hampshire. These four colonies made up early New England. Their inhabitants tended to be very much alike, sharing the Puritan faith and English roots. They tended to settle in towns that made formal education a relatively easy endeavor. Dame schools were commonplace for New England children, who learned basic reading, writing, and arithmetic skills, all within a religious context. Girls in New England were allowed to attend the dame schools, although their curriculum was different and focused primarily on homemaking. The elementary education of a dame school was generally the extent of what girls received in terms of formal schooling for much of the colonial period.

In 1635 the first **Latin grammar school** was established in Boston for boys whose families could afford education beyond the dame school. The word *grammar* is

---

Figure 7.2 The 13 original colonies

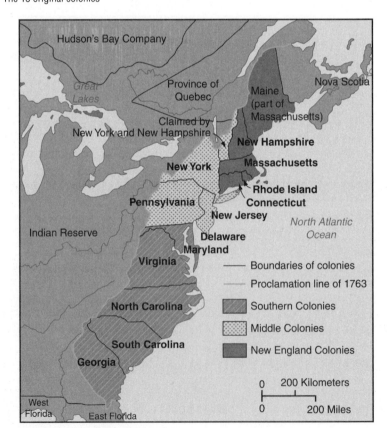

associated with elementary school today but was a term for secondary schools in the 17th century. Students learned higher levels of reading, writing, and arithmetic, along with classical literature. The Latin grammar schools were considered the forerunners of modern high schools and specifically prepared boys to attend Harvard University, established in 1636 (Tehie, 2007).

Only the wealthiest New Englanders went beyond dame schools. Schooling opportunities and apprenticeships for white boys from poorer families were either less desirable or nonexistent. Girls, African Americans, and Native Americans had even fewer opportunities for educational advancement.

Some Puritan leaders recognized the benefits of educating all children, at least all white children. The **Massachusetts Act of 1642** was the first **compulsory education law** in the New World. Although the law required all white children to attend school, it did not specify how or where children would get an education. Nor did the law provide funding, making it the first **unfunded mandate**, a legally enforceable law without provision for monetary support. Five years later, the Massachusetts Act of 1647, also known as the **Old Deluder Satan Act** because education was considered the best way to fight the devil, established that every town of 50 or more households must provide a school. Again, no funding was attached, and either parents or the whole community contributed to supporting a school and teacher. These two acts, along with Puritan determination, led to the New England colonies having about the same literacy rate as England by 1700 (Cohen, 1974).

The *New England Primer* was first published in 1690 for children in upper elementary and secondary levels. The book was a perfect example of the interrelatedness of education and religion in colonial New England. Published for over 150 years with few substantial changes over its lifetime, the *New England Primer* included a spelling guide based on the alphabet denoted in brief rhymes and pictures. The *New England Primer* also included the Lord's Prayer, the Apostles' Creed, the Ten Commandments, a list of the books of the Bible, and the numbers 1 to 100. Figure 7.3 contains a sample from the *New England Primer*.

Schools in the middle colonies. New York, New Jersey, Pennsylvania, and Delaware made up the middle colonies. Their population was much less homogeneous than that of New England. Settlers came from Sweden, the Netherlands, Germany, France, and other parts of Europe, along with people of the Quaker faith who primarily settled in Pennsylvania.

No one kind of school could satisfy the diversity of the middle colonists. Each religious sect established its own brand of schooling: Lutherans, Presbyterians,

Parochial schools are discussed in Chapter 3.

Figure 7.3 New England Primer

Jews, Mennonites, Catholics, Quakers, Baptists, Huguenots, and so on. The colonies attempted to license schools but did not provide financing. The middle colony schools were mostly private, or *parochial*, a term typically associated with religion. These parochial schools often taught a greater variety of subjects than the New England schools and included topics such as business, bookkeeping, and navigation.

Points of Reflection 7.1

What evidence are you aware of that leads you to believe that where students live today affects their educational opportunities?

Schools in the southern colonies. Like the middle colonies, the southern colonies were settled by diverse groups, but the settlers were even more widespread geographically. In Virginia, Maryland, Georgia, and the Carolinas, more so than in New England or the middle colonies, opportunities for education were based almost exclusively on social class. Children of plantation owners and wealthy merchants either attended private schools or were taught at home by tutors. These privileged students went from elementary to secondary schools either in the South or in Europe. Children who lived on small farms or children of laborers experienced whatever education was available through charity schools run by people who believed education should be more widely available, apprentice programs, or church schools. The children of slaves received no formal education in the southern colonies during the 17th century.

TEACHERS IN COLONIAL AMERICA

During the 17th century there was no formal system of teacher preparation. The closest parallel would have been apprentices assigned to Quaker teachers, who themselves lacked formal training in the education of both children and teachers. In dame schools the teachers were widows or housewives who could read and write to some unspecified degree of proficiency. Men who taught in the first elementary schools often did so for very short periods of time before beginning official training for the ministry or law.

Many teachers were indentured servants who taught in exchange for passage to the New World. Often people were teachers because they were not successful in other occupations; some were even of questionable character or conduct (Pulliam & Van Patten, 2013).

Teachers in the secondary schools (Latin grammar schools) enjoyed more status than those in elementary-level schools. They often had more education themselves, and many had college training (Ornstein & Levine, 2006).

Many teachers in both the 17th and 18th centuries participated in the curious custom of *boarding 'round*. To save lodging money, towns required teachers to live with the families of their students for 1 week at a time. This practice did nothing for the dignity of the teacher or the profession. Pay was low, about what farmhands made, and without permanent homes, teachers often thought of themselves as expendable part-time employees.

Today, the majority of what students know about history is taught by K–12 teachers. Far from expendable, teachers use every resource at their disposal to enhance student learning. One social media tool that is proving useful in all subjects, but particularly in teaching history, is *Google Docs*. Through this Internet tool teachers can create virtual packets of information, including primary source documents, videos, photos, lists of resources, and so on, to go with the standards they are teaching. *Google Docs* are instantly available to all students on a variety of Internet-accessible devices. Read more about *Google Docs* in this chapter's **SocialMEdia** feature.

What Were the Major Influences, Issues, Ideologies, and Individuals in 18th-Century American Education?

The first half of the 18th century was characterized by geographic expansion on American soil and the maturation of the economic and political climate. In perspective, it was relatively calm in terms of history and schools when compared to the second half.

SocialMEdia

Google Docs, a free web-based suite of services offered by Google, was introduced to the public in 2010. This productive tool allows you to create and edit documents online while collaborating in real-time with other users. It's simple and intuitive to use. There's no software to purchase and never a charge for creating or uploading documents, presentations, spreadsheets, forms, and drawings that may be kept personal, shared for others to view, or shared for others to work on collaboratively with you. There's even a chat feature.

For teaching and learning, there are many ideas for using *Google Docs* in the classroom, including:

- Teachers can load primary sources and photos and students have access to them instantly.
- Students can work on writing projects, with peers and/or teachers adding comments and edits.

- A team of students can work on a project from anywhere in real time, with all participants seeing additions and questions at the same time.
- Surveys and forms can be easily created and completed, with results available on a spreadsheet.
- *Google Docs* includes thousands of templates for drawing, forms, surveys, and so on.
- Collaborative brainstorming is possible, with participants adding information in creative webs to show connection of ideas.
- Students can do homework and assignments together.
- Student Drop Boxes can collect student work and organize it for teachers.

A YouTube *Google Docs* tutorial is available at http://www.youtube.com/user/docs

CONTEXT FOR CHANGE

Representatives to the First Continental Congress (1774) in Philadelphia met originally to discuss how to claim their rights as British citizens in America. However, the Declaration of Independence soon followed, as did the writing of the Constitution, and then the Bill of Rights. The United States of America was rapidly taking shape (Boyer & Stuckey, 2005).

Future leaders, such as Benjamin Franklin (1706–1790) and Thomas Jefferson (1743–1826), were born and grew up not only to pave the way for the new nation, but also to influence the direction in which 18th-century education was heading.

18TH-CENTURY AMERICAN SCHOOLS

In 1751 Benjamin Franklin established the Franklin Academy, a school that was oriented toward real-world, useful learning. The Franklin Academy offered mathematics, astronomy, navigation, accounting, bookkeeping, French, and Spanish. One significant contribution of the Franklin Academy was its provision for students to choose some courses, the forerunner of today's electives.

Private **academies** sprang up across America. These schools were designed to teach content intended to prepare students to participate in business and trade. They met not only intellectual needs but also economic needs. In addition to these academies, **town schools** were established for whole communities. Although some schools still limited curriculum to reading, writing, and the classics, specialized schools in the form of academies became popular.

Benjamin Franklin (1706–1790)

A pudgy, bookish man with long curly hair and little square glasses, flying a kite in the middle of a thunderstorm, is the image most have of Ben Franklin. Inventor and philosopher extraordinaire, Franklin contributed to American education in many valuable ways. In the mid-18th century he espoused educating America's youth in the practical and useful arts and trades. In addition to the traditional study of reading and math, he was the first to propose the study of history that included not just past politics and wars but also customs and commerce. He founded the Library Company of Philadelphia in 1731 to promote reading by subscription to help tradesmen and farmers become as intelligent as gentlemen of other countries. In his *Proposals Relating to the Youth of Pennsylvania* (1749), Franklin said that wise men view the education of youth as "the surest foundation of . . . happiness" (Franklin, 1931, p. 151).

Franklin (1749/1931); Good (1964).

Thomas Jefferson (1743–1826)

As author of the Declaration of Independence and the third president of the United States (1801–1809), Thomas Jefferson believed that only through education could people preserve freedom and promote their own happiness. Historian S. Alexander Rippa (1997) said of Jefferson that "none has so consistently viewed public education as the indispensable cornerstone of freedom" (p. 55). Jefferson believed that government must be by the consent of the governed, and he wanted those governed to read. In fact, he suggested to President John Adams that anyone who was given the opportunity to learn to read but didn't, should not be allowed to vote. President Adams disagreed with this idea.

Disappointed by the Virginia House of Burgesses's refusal to pass his Bill for the More General Diffusion of Knowledge, Jefferson spent the years following his presidency establishing the University of Virginia (UVA). It was truly his university in the beginning. He designed both the curriculum and the buildings, bought the trees and designed the landscaping, purchased the library books, chose the faculty, and admitted the first class of students. Thomas Jefferson died on July 4, 1826, 1 year after UVA opened and exactly 50 years following the adoption of the Declaration of Independence.

Good (1964); Rippa (1997).

Thomas Jefferson had political, practical, and intellectual motives for his interest in and attention to education. He believed that education was essential to the maintenance of a viable republic. Education, in Jefferson's view, would increase production and preserve health. In 1779 he proposed the Virginia Bill for the More General Diffusion of Knowledge, which provided for broader availability of education for more children. Jefferson's bill did not pass the Virginia legislature, but it raised awareness of the need and potential value of education among both lawmakers and the public (Good, 1964).

In the 18th century many Quakers came to America. They believed that education should be all-inclusive. In 1770, Quakers in Philadelphia established a school for elementary students that included girls, African Americans, and Native Americans. In the South, however, formal education for African and Native Americans was nonexistent, despite a high literacy rate for white men and women. In Virginia, for example, 9 of 10 white men, and 2 of 3 white women were able to read (Button & Provenzo, 1989).

Noah Webster (1758–1843) had a profound influence on 18th-century American schools, particularly because of his writing. His most important work was the *American Spelling Book*, published in 1783. Some scholars say Webster had more influence on American education than anyone else in the 18th century and have referred to him as "Schoolmaster of the Republic" (Webb, Metha, & Jordan, 2012).

Several colleges were established in the colonies prior to the American Revolution, among them Yale University in 1701, the University of Pennsylvania in 1753, Brown University in 1764, and Dartmouth College in 1769. At first, theology was the most popular degree; later, other majors such as law, medicine, and commerce increased in popularity (Cohen, 1974).

18TH-CENTURY TEACHERS

As was true in the 17th century, teachers in the 18th century continued to be undervalued in most of colonial America. In Loeper's (1973) *Going to school in 1776,* we find accounts of teachers who plowed fields and did menial tasks during the summer to support themselves in the winter while teaching. One in particular, Mistress Robbins, was hired to be a teacher at the age of 17 because she could read from the Old Testament without stumbling over the big words. Once hired, she found her responsibilities included physically taking care of the schoolhouse. She had to resort to severe corporal (physical) punishment to control the older boys whom she reported as threatening, lawless, and profane. She was forced because of low pay to live with her students' families or, as it was called, to board 'round.

EDUCATION AS A PRIORITY

Education received a boost in priority with the passage of the **Northwest Land Ordinance of 1787**, which divided federally owned wilderness land into townships and required the building of schools. Article Three of the Ordinance proclaimed "Religion, morality, and knowledge being necessary to good government and the happiness of mankind, schools and the means of education shall be forever encouraged."

Education is not directly mentioned in the U.S. Constitution ratified in 1788. However, the Tenth Amendment in the Bill of Rights states, "The powers not delegated to the United States by the Constitution, nor prohibited by it to the states, are reserved to the States respectively, or to the people." Thus, from the inception of the United States to the present, except for the occasional federal mandate, states have grappled independently with educational issues.

As the new nation of the United States of America approached the 19th century, a surge of energy was directed toward education. Leaders and policies emerged that would place American education squarely in the foreground of thought and action.

What Were the Major Influences, Issues, Ideologies, and Individuals in 19th-Century American Education?

The 19th century was one of unprecedented growth, both geographically and governmentally.

CONTEXT FOR CHANGE

In 1800 American geography lessons included maps showing 17 states. By the end of the century maps of America boasted 45 states. During this century the United States established a functioning and flourishing economy, endured a protracted test of the strength of its union (the Civil War), and matured into a stable, respected political entity.

With the election of President Andrew Jackson in 1828, the birth of the Democratic Party brought changes to American politics, turning a nation governed largely by an aristocratic society to one based in greater measure on government of, by, and for the people. Westward expansion propelled by the continuing desire for individual independence and opportunity took the growing nation all the way to the Pacific Ocean.

Cultural and economic differences between an increasingly industrialized North and an agrarian South grew and festered in the 19th century. The rift erupted into the Civil War in 1861 as southern states seceded from the Union and formed the Confederacy.

Although the most commonly perceived reason for the Civil War is slavery, other actual issues surrounding the onset of hostilities revolved around states' rights and economics. Over 600,000 Americans on both sides lost their lives before the North and South were reunited in 1865.

Of all the issues facing the American population as the 19th century drew to a close, the most significant were associated with the Industrial Revolution. Poverty-level wages, a workforce that would soon include too many children, unchecked immigration, and abysmal working conditions all reflected poorly on the country's ability to cope with the abuses actually brought about by its wonderful spirit of inventiveness. Each of these issues would have to be faced and solved, and the educational system revamped to meet the needs of the more commerce- and industry-based society that was on the horizon.

19TH-CENTURY AMERICAN SCHOOLS

The 19th century in the United States was characterized by a wide variety of schools. There were town schools, primarily in the northern states; charity schools, run by churches and philanthropic groups; and widely varying dame schools serving as small

Horace Mann and the common school movement made it possible for some African American children to be educated in public schools.

venues for local education. Religious schools grew as families banded together with others of the same denomination and country of origin. Academies of all descriptions, some prestigious and some humble, flourished in the first half of the 19th century. In the South most educational opportunities still belonged to the wealthy; in the West most frontier children did not attend school. The obvious lack of consistency and opportunity did not mirror the ideals of America's founders, who saw education as a means to accomplish the goal stated in the Preamble of the U.S. Constitution to "promote the general Welfare."

On the post–Civil War education front, one fact was crystal clear: Both the classical educational system popular in the Northeast and the one-room schoolhouse approach adopted during western frontier days were increasingly incapable of meeting the needs of the country. Let's look at some of the categories of schools developed in 19th-century America.

Common schools. The system of free public schools that exists today had its beginnings in the common schools movement, first established about 1830. **Common schools** were community-supported elementary schools for *all* children established in response to a variety of economic, social, and political factors. This was a radical departure from previous schooling that catered primarily to wealthy males. Think about it . . . *all* children. Because free public education for all children was a new concept, common schools were debated, with many citizens seeing their value and others remaining skeptical, as illustrated in Table 7.2. Horace Mann was the champion of common schools. In fact, he was widely regarded as a champion of children in general and of the basic American ideal of opportunity for all.

In common schools, and most other schools of the 19th century, the works of William Holmes McGuffey had the most significant impact on what children learned. McGuffey's books differed from the unimaginative literature of previous centuries and included stories that promoted truth, honesty, and hard work.

Points of Reflection 7.2

How would you compare the views of businesspeople and politicians today concerning public schools to the views held by businesspeople and politicians in the 19th century concerning common schools, the first public schools?

TABLE 7.2 Merits of and objections to the common school from various viewpoints

Group	Merits
From the viewpoint of . . .	**Common schools provided . . .**
the working class	avenues for social and economic mobility
some in business and industry	an increase in the supply of literate and trained workers
social groups	means of controlling crime and social unrest
people of the frontier	symbols of civilization and ways to keep literacy and citizenship alive in the wilderness

Group	Objections
From the viewpoint of . . .	**Common schools were objectionable because . . .**
private school proponents	free schools meant fewer private school students
some in business and industry	they decreased the workforce of children who opted for school instead of jobs
some political leaders	of their apprehensions that an overeducated citizenry might question authority

As common schools increased in number, their inconsistencies became more and more apparent. Some were housed in acceptable buildings with adequate supplies and appropriate heating and lighting. Other common schools were housed in dilapidated, poorly heated and lit, filthy surroundings.

Secondary schools. When the English Classical School opened for young men in Boston in 1821, it marked the beginning of the public high school. In 1824 the school's name was changed to the Boston English High School. In 1838 a coeducational high school opened in Philadelphia. This school offered three tracks: a classical (Latin) curriculum (4 years), a modern language curriculum (4 years), and an English curriculum (2 years) (Webb et al., 2012).

Before the Civil War, high schools were almost exclusively found in the North and always in cities. Because children could learn to read in common schools, and reading was considered sufficient education by many citizens, high schools were slow to grow in number.

In the aftermath of the Civil War, with Reconstruction and rapidly growing industrialization, economic growth spurred the establishment of more schools—not just common schools, but also secondary schools. High schools began to flourish about 1850 and by 1870 had replaced academies as the dominant secondary school. In 1874 a case in the Michigan Supreme Court called the **Kalamazoo case** established that the legislature could tax for support of both common and secondary schools, propelling public high schools into school systems in every state (Ornstein & Levine, 2006).

> More court cases are discussed in Chapter 10.

Kindergarten. Early childhood education in the United States developed after elementary (common schools) and high schools (secondary schools). In Europe, Swiss educator Johann Pestalozzi (1746–1827) developed the theory of child-centered education and the concept of individual differences among children. German educator Friedrich Froebel (1782–1852) agreed with Pestalozzi, but he took child-centered education further. Froebel was a proponent of an activity-based curriculum in an early childhood setting, where children are encouraged to be creative and expressive. This setting was called a kindergarten, or "children's garden." The first kindergarten in the United States was established in 1860 in Boston. By 1873 kindergartens had become part of many public school systems (Chartock, 2004).

> Early childhood education is discussed in Chapter 3.

With the establishment of kindergarten, common school, and high school, the need for specially prepared teachers grew.

TEACHER PREPARATION

Before Horace Mann's proposal that teachers receive special training, few completed any form of secondary education. Teachers were inadequately and inconsistently prepared. Notable exceptions were the

Horace Mann (1796–1859)

Widely known as the Father of American Education, Horace Mann had a profound influence not only on early American schools but also on modern schools. He believed that regular attendance in schools with quality teachers would serve to equalize opportunities for poor, African American, and disabled children. He vigorously advocated for common schools.

As attorney and state legislator turned education advocate, Mann established the first **normal school** in 1839 in Lexington, Massachusetts. Normal schools proved to be incredibly important as 2-year colleges specifically designed to prepare teachers. Mann was not afraid of controversy as he pushed for separation of church and schools, not a popular stance in 19th-century America. Even as an avowed religious man, he was often criticized from church pulpits. As the first secretary of education for the Massachusetts Board of Education, which he helped establish in 1837, and throughout his life, Horace Mann spoke eloquently and worked tirelessly as a champion of schools and students.

Not only was Horace Mann an advocate for free quality education, but he also worked for the abolition of slavery and the limiting of alcohol as a social problem and was a vocal supporter of women's rights.

Chartock (2004).

W. H. McGuffey (1800–1873)

Far from the overly pious and drab books that first appeared in American schools and painted a dreary picture of the worth of children, W. H. McGuffey's six-volume set of *McGuffey's Readers* included stories and poetry that appealed to the interests of students. The volumes were geared to specific levels and paved the way for the separation of elementary school into grade levels. The volumes sold over 1 million copies between 1836 and 1906 and helped students learn to read and study while instilling in them virtues such as patriotism, morality, and a work ethic. McGuffey, as a minister, professor, and college president, indelibly left his mark on American education.

McNergney and McNergney (2009); Webb et al. (2012).

Friedrich Froebel (1782–1852)

When the first English-speaking kindergarten in the United States opened in Boston in 1860, it was the direct result of the work of Friedrich Froebel, widely viewed as the father of the kindergarten or "children's garden." Froebel thought of young children as flowers that would blossom into healthy adults if given the opportunity to be creative in an active curriculum. His emphasis on self-development and self-expression is the theoretical basis for early childhood education.

Johnson, Musial, Hall, Golnick, and Dupuis (2011).

Emma Willard (1787–1870)

While boarding schools were teaching girls how to be polite, proper wives who could serve tea and make gentile conversation, Emma Willard was formulating plans for a school to teach girls and women useful, solid skills in homemaking as well as content and pedagogy to enable them to be teachers or to enter other professions. In 1821 she established the Troy Female Seminary, the first institution of higher learning for girls. Before the first normal school was established in 1839 by Horace Mann and others, the Troy Seminary had prepared over 200 teachers. Emma Willard is also credited with the establishment of home economics as a legitimate subject area. Willard wrote textbooks, traveled extensively, and was a lifelong activist for women's rights.

Chartock (2004); Good (1964); Webb et al. (2012).

Catherine Beecher (1800–1878)

Although Catherine Beecher's sister, Harriet Beecher Stowe, author of *Uncle Tom's Cabin*, may have more name recognition, Catherine had a great impact on the establishment of teacher training schools, or normal schools. In 1832 she established the Western Institute for Women, partially because she saw a need for better educated teachers. The institute was not publicly funded and did not prepare teachers exclusively, but it spawned other institutions of higher learning for women. In 1839 Beecher, along with Horace Mann and others, started the first publicly supported normal school for teacher preparation.

Holmes and Weiss (1995).

teachers prepared at the Troy Female Seminary, the first institution of higher learning for women in the United States, established in Troy, New York, in 1821 by Emma Willard (1787–1870).

The first normal school, a publicly funded institution dedicated exclusively to preparing teachers, was established 18 years later, in 1839 in Lexington, Massachusetts. Catherine Beecher (1800–1878), along with Horace Mann, was instrumental in making teacher preparation a priority in normal schools.

As these first specially prepared teachers entered their classrooms, they seldom encountered children with disabilities, children of color, or children of poor immigrants. This situation would change with time.

19TH-CENTURY EDUCATION FOR CHILDREN WITH DISABILITIES, MINORITIES, AND IMMIGRANTS

The 19th century was marked by meager, yet important, advances in education for children with disabilities, children of color, and children of poor immigrants.

Children with disabilities. Social mores of the day demanded that any educational opportunities for children with disabilities be separate from those for children without disabilities. A few innovative schools were established in the 19th century for students with certain disabilities. In 1817 Thomas Gallaudet established the first school for the deaf in Hartford, Connecticut. In the mid-19th century, physician Samuel Howe was influential in the establishment of the first school for blind children, the Perkins School for the Blind in Watertown, Massachusetts (Cubberly, 1934). Mental and behavioral disabilities were not addressed in 19th-century schools.

Native American children. In 1824 the U.S. government established the Bureau of Indian Affairs and began placing whole tribes of Native Americans on reservations. Most of what little formal schooling Native American children received was provided by missionaries, whose efforts were fueled by a desire to convert the children to Christianity. The missionary schools were not consistently organized or maintained (Chartock, 2004).

A further goal of most efforts to educate Native American children in the 19th century was **assimilation**, the attempt to make the children more like white children, the dominant culture, or, in the terms of the time, "civilizing" them. The American government built boarding schools in the latter part of the 19th century and forced thousands of Native American children to leave their homes and live in these boarding schools where attempts were made to diminish their culture in favor of the white, English-speaking social norms of the time. The boarding schools proved to be complete failures with Native American students running away or returning to their reservations immediately after graduation (Webb et al., 2012).

Mexican American children. At the end of the Mexican American War in 1848, vast territories comprising what are now Arizona, California, Colorado, Nevada, New Mexico, and Utah came under U.S. control. The Mexican families who stayed in these territories after the United States took over suffered discrimination much like the Native Americans. Like Native Americans, Mexican Americans were targets of efforts at assimilation. For much of the 19th century most Mexican American children had few, if any, educational options. When they did attend school, teachers generally tried to Americanize them, or assimilate them into the dominant culture by insisting they learn and use English and give up some of their customs (Webb et al., 2012).

Prudence Crandall (1803–1889)

Way ahead of her time, and incredibly courageous, Prudence Crandall believed strongly in the rights of African American students to an education. Her Quaker roots and her own education under a noted abolitionist, Moses Brown, helped shape her steadfast belief in equal opportunity. In 1830 Crandall founded a school for neighborhood girls in Canterbury, Connecticut. When she admitted an African American girl, Sarah Harris, Crandall and her school became the target for vandalism and ostracism. White parents withdrew their daughters. When Crandall established a school populated entirely by African American girls, it was destroyed by outraged whites. Sarah Harris went on to teach many years in Louisiana, thus carrying on Prudence Crandall's legacy.

Pulliam and Van Patten (2013).

African American children. Although the education of Native American and Mexican American children was far from ideal and was inconsistently implemented, at least it didn't face legal objection by state or federal governments. The education of African American children in the 19th century did. For example, when Prudence Crandall admitted an African American student, Sarah Harris, to the school she founded in Connecticut in 1830, the school was forced to close. Crandall reopened the school for girls and enrolled 15 African American students from other states. The Connecticut legislature subsequently passed the **Black Law**, a law that specifically forbade schools intended to educate African Americans from other states without the permission of local authorities.

Prior to the Civil War, **Black Codes** were enacted, predominantly in the South, prohibiting the education of slaves. Some white people feared that educating slaves would give the slaves a sense of self-importance and they might begin to think they were created equal and had certain inalienable rights—as stated in the Declaration of Independence. In 1850, with increasing numbers of free African Americans in the North desiring education, the Massachusetts Supreme Court upheld the decision in *Roberts* v. *City of Boston* that separate-but-equal schools did not violate the rights of African American children. This ruling solidified the practice of *separate but equal*, meaning that separate schools for black and white children supposedly offered the same opportunities for all children. This assumption proved to be false, with schools for African American children receiving less funding and being housed in inferior facilities (Kaplan & Owings, 2011). At the end of the 19th century, the practice was reinforced by the ruling in a similar case, *Plessy* v. *Ferguson*.

The doctrine of *separate but equal* was evident in the United States until well past the middle of the 20th century.

Following the Civil War, the Bureau of Refugees, Freedmen, and Abandoned Lands, more commonly referred to as the Freedmen's Bureau, made efforts to help African

Booker T. Washington (1856–1915)

As a steadfast believer that education was the way to advance socially and economically, Booker T. Washington spent his life furthering educational opportunities for African American students. First graduating from, and then teaching at, the Hampton Institute, Washington later founded the Tuskegee Institute in Alabama in 1881. Throughout his career, Washington promoted his message that African Americans needed vocational skills to get and keep good jobs. Washington led the Tuskegee Institute until his death in 1915.

Chartock (2004); McNergney and McNergney (2009).

Americans find ways of making a living and settle into a free lifestyle. The Freedman's Bureau opened 3,000 schools in the South to educate African American children. By 1869 about 114,000 African American students were being educated in these schools. Along with typical school subjects, these new schools added industrial training in an effort to prepare African American students for employment (Gutek, 2005). In addition, many ex-slaves formed their own education associations that sponsored schools exclusively for African American children, staffed exclusively by African American teachers. By 1870 southern African Americans had established over 500 of these schools, resembling the earlier common schools movement (Kaplan & Owings, 2011). Hampton Institute, founded in 1868, was an institution of higher education that emphasized industrial skills and teacher preparation for African Americans.

The most famous graduate of the Hampton Institute was Booker T. Washington. Following graduation he became Hampton's first African American teacher. Washington was a major supporter of vocational education for African Americans. He viewed learning practical skills as a way of advancing socially and economically in the United States. In 1881, Washington founded the Tuskegee Institute in rural Alabama. By 1890 Tuskegee had 88 faculty members and more than 1,200 students, making it one of the larger colleges in the South (McNergney & McNergney, 2009).

Asian American children. Although their numbers were smaller than immigrants from Mexico, there were children of Asian parents in U.S. schools in the 19th century. Most were Chinese, who began to arrive midcentury and filled a need for laborers in an increasingly industrialized America. The Immigration Act of 1882 slowed the arrival of people from China. In the latter part of the century traders from India began arriving, mostly on the East Coast of the United States. Until 1886 people from Japan could not leave their country. Once the restriction was lifted, Japanese (mostly men) moved to the United States and began to fill the void for inexpensive labor created by the Chinese government's crackdown on emigration. (Note that to *emigrate* means to leave one's country. When people emigrate, they become *immigrants* in their destination country.)

Children of poor immigrants. The United States is a nation of immigrants. The country's motto, *E Pluribus Unum*, means "from many, one." The issue of how to educate the *many* and have a strong *one* is not new. From 1870 to 1900, the United States experienced an influx of almost 12 million immigrants, many from Mexico, Asia, and Eastern Europe, and many whose primary language was not English (Boyer & Stuckey, 2005).

Many immigrants were very poor, but their skills were needed in the rapid industrialization of the United States. As the economy grew, so did the tax base for supporting free elementary schools and high schools. The number of free public schools increased dramatically as the country attempted to cope with its industrial growth and, with the many coming to its shores, to become one nation (Gutek, 2005; Takaki, 1993).

Most poor immigrants in the 19th century had no means of providing for their families when they first arrived in the United States, generally in the already heavily populated cities of New York and Chicago. **Settlement houses** were established by reformers to address the problems of urban poverty. These were community service centers that provided educational opportunities, skills training, and cultural events. Jane Addams (1860–1935), who was raised in a wealthy Quaker home, established Hull House, the most famous of the settlement houses, in Chicago in 1889.

HIGHER EDUCATION

In 1862 President Lincoln signed a congressional bill called the **Morrill Act**. Through this act the government granted states 30,000 acres of land for every senator and representative it had in Congress in 1860. The income the states could generate from this land was to be used to support at least one college. The Second Morrill Act of 1890 further stipulated that no grants would be given to states where college admission was denied because of race unless the state provided a separate-but-equal institution. As a result of the Morrill legislation, 65 land-grant colleges were established, including the universities of Maine (1865), Illinois (1867), and California (1868); Purdue University (1869); and Texas A&M (1871) (Rippa, 1997).

Jane Addams (1860–1935)

Raised in a wealthy home with an abolitionist Quaker father, Jane Addams set her sights on becoming a doctor. However, because of back problems, she quit her studies and determined to dedicate her life to helping the urban poor. She founded Hull House in an old, rundown Chicago mansion. Located in the middle of an immigrant neighborhood, Hull House provided education for both children and adults. Addams recruited college-educated young women to work at Hull House. Many later used what they learned there to propel them to make their own contributions to social reform. For years Hull House served as a model for other successful settlement houses, which numbered almost 100 by 1900.

Addams tirelessly promoted women's suffrage (right to vote) and was president of the Women's International League for Peace and Freedom from 1919 until her death in 1935. In 1931 she received the Nobel Peace Prize.

Boyer and Stuckey (2005).

As colleges flourished, more progressive ways of educating children and adolescents also began to grow. The discussion of 20th-century education begins with progressive education, first introduced at the close of the 19th century.

What Were the Major Influences, Issues, Ideologies, and Individuals in 20th-Century American Education?

Varying population patterns, American inventiveness, wars, and technology made the 20th century one of extremes.

CONTEXT FOR CHANGE

In the 20th century, America survived two world wars; numerous regional conflicts in Korea, Vietnam, and elsewhere; and a protracted period of dire economic stress. It also thrived in years of unprecedented economic prosperity. The populace of the United States grew increasingly aware of its own diversity. Periods of rampant racial tension necessitated healing and both legal and educational responses on a national level.

Technological advances took us to the moon and beyond, enhanced communication of all sorts, and brought about global awareness unimagined in other centuries. In schools, the beginning of the century ushered more of the components of John Dewey's progressive education into classrooms.

PROGRESSIVE EDUCATION

In 1896 John Dewey established the first laboratory school at the University of Chicago to test the principles of **progressive education**. The progressive method was very different from the traditional 19th-century approach to education. What started with students learning in cooperative groups and letting their interests guide what they learned about traditional subjects grew into a major movement with far-reaching implications. The influence of John Dewey was tremendous as the United States moved from the 19th to the 20th century.

The progressive movement gained momentum during the first quarter of the 20th century and flourished until the end of World War II. The influences of progressivism

There's more information about progressivism in Chapter 8.

Points of Reflection 7.3

Do your views align with some of the basic principles of progressive education in Figure 7.4? If so, which ones and why? Do your views differ from those of progressive education? If so, how?

FIGURE 7.4 Basic principles of progressive education

1. Education is life, not just preparation for life.
2. Learning should be directly related to the interests of the child.
3. Learning through problem solving should be emphasized more than rote memorization of subject matter.
4. The role of the teacher is to facilitate learning more so than to direct it.
5. Cooperation among students should be emphasized more than competition.
6. Democracy should be practiced to encourage the free interplay of ideas that leads to growth.

Source: Kneller, G. F. (1971). *Introduction to the philosophy of education.* New York: Wiley.

are still evident in the 21st century. The basic principles of progressive education are summarized in Figure 7.4. These principles show the sharp contrast between the philosophy of progressivism and the established ways of conducting school discussed earlier. John Dewey's primary focus was the implementation of schooling as a means of social reform and the improvement of life for Americans.

John Dewey (1859–1952)

Think about all the things that happened in the United States during John Dewey's life, from the Civil War to the Korean War. He lived and wrote a very long time. In terms of education, many consider Dewey the most influential American of the 20th century. He was a professor of philosophy and pedagogy at the University of Chicago and at Columbia University. In Chicago, Dewey's son attended a school run by an ardent follower of Pestalozzi and Froebel. Dewey was so impressed with the approach of the school that he began researching, thinking, and writing about it. What we know today as progressive education was given an intellectual foundation by Dewey.

Dewey wrote more than 500 articles and 40 books, among which *The School and Society* (1900) and *The Child and the Curriculum* (1902) had perhaps the greatest impact on American education. In his laboratory school at the University of Chicago, he implemented progressive education and introduced projects such as carpentry, weaving, sewing, and cooking into the curriculum. Dewey believed that education should be experiential and child centered, rather than subject driven. He proposed that education is best served when the whole child is considered, including all the aspects of development.

John Dewey believed that democracy should be practiced not only in the governance of the United States but also in the day-to-day life of a school. Children should be free to question, investigate, and make changes in their environments. Learning the principles of democracy early in life would serve them well later as adults.

Dewey (1956); Rippa (1997).

JUNIOR HIGH AND MIDDLE SCHOOL

The need for a bridge between elementary and high school became apparent as the high school developed into a 4-year institution and the courses taught there became more standardized in content. Educators began to delineate the kinds of preparation necessary for high school success. High school teachers and administrators asked for basic preparation in algebra and English before high school. Writers such as G. Stanley Hall began recognizing a period of life called adolescence and acknowledging that adolescence was different from childhood. This new viewpoint led to a change in the configuration of schools; elementary schools shifted from eight grades to five or six, and the remaining two or three grades became junior high schools. Later in the century, junior high most frequently encompassed grades 7 through 9.

In the 1960s, another concept of schooling was formed to meet the unique needs of young adolescents: the middle school. Rather than viewing grades 5 to 8 or 6 to 8 as merely a time of preparation for high school, middle school philosophy called for recognition of the unique developmental qualities of young adolescents and use of developmental appropriateness in the school, in both curriculum and instruction.

MONTESSORI METHOD

Montessori philosophy is discussed in Chapter 3.

Although Maria Montessori (1870–1952) was developing a philosophy of early childhood education in Italy and other parts of Europe in the beginning of the 20th century, the Montessori method was not widely implemented in the United States until the 1950s. Today many Montessori principles can be found in early childhood settings across the United States.

INFLUENTIAL AFRICAN AMERICAN LEADERS

W. E. B. Du Bois believed that African Americans should pursue higher education to become leaders in politics and education. He sharply disagreed with Booker T. Washington's philosophy that African Americans would best serve themselves and their race by pursuing vocational arts and skills to prepare them to compete with white people in the workplace.

Mary McLeod Bethune was influential in both education and government policy. Her long career as a teacher, as well as college instructor and founder, took her from her home in South Carolina to college experiences in Chicago; to Florida, where she founded Bethune-Cookman College; and all the way to Washington, D.C., where she served as an adviser to President Franklin D. Roosevelt in the 1930s (Chartock, 2004).

THE LAST FIVE DECADES OF THE 20TH CENTURY

1950s. The *Leave It to Beaver*, white-bread world of Ward and June Cleaver and their two sons was experienced by many families in the United States and was considered a desirable social paradigm during the period of unprecedented economic growth and prosperity following World War II. In 1957, however, the "all's right with the world" syndrome was shaken by the Soviet launch of *Sputnik*, the first satellite to venture into space. The **National Defense Education Act of 1958** called for strengthening of science, math, and foreign language programs. Teachers were given training in the use of new methods and materials in hopes of bringing American student learning up to, and beyond, the levels of learning in other countries.

Another major factor in the American schools of the 1950s was the increasing pressure to desegregate. After all the years of separate-but-equal schools, the Supreme Court upheld the complaints of the National Association for the Advancement of Colored People (NAACP) made on behalf of a Kansas family in the now famous ***Brown v. Board of Education*** ruling of 1954. Chief Justice Earl Warren declared that segregating children based solely on race was wrong and illegal. Some schools integrated

Maria Montessori (1870–1952)

A compassionate medical doctor, Maria Montessori established a children's house, a kind of school within a house, for poor children in early 20th-century Italy. As people recognized the transformation in these children, they began studying Montessori's methodology and opening other children's houses, later referred to as Montessori schools. As Maria Montessori herself said, "The task of the child is to construct a man [or woman] oriented to his environment, adapted to his time, place, and culture" (1967, p. xiv). She believed that children are capable of integrating aspects of the world around them through the use of their senses. Children ages 3 to 6 are the ideal participants in the Montessori method. Montessori insisted that children's environments be carefully constructed to allow them to sense their learning with materials, such as letters made of sandpaper and colored objects to count.

Chartock (2004); Good (1964); Montessori (1967).

W. E. B. Du Bois (1868–1963)

A champion of equality for Africans and African Americans, W. E. B. Du Bois spent his life as a scholar, a writer, and a reformer. In 1895 he was the first African American to earn a doctorate from Harvard. From 1895 through the 1950s he was a college professor and a civil rights activist. He organized worldwide conferences of black leaders. Du Bois considered Africa the homeland of all black people and wrote about the dual citizenry of black people who had left Africa in his 1903 book, *The Souls of Black Folks*. In 1907 he cofounded the National Association for the Advancement of Colored People (NAACP). Disillusioned by lack of progress for people of African descent in the United States, Du Bois embraced socialism. At age 93, he joined the Communist Party and moved to Ghana, where he died at age 95.

Boyer and Stuckey (2005).

Mary McLeod Bethune (1875–1955)

Born in South Carolina of former slave parents, Mary McLeod Bethune was educated in a Presbyterian mission school and attended Moody Bible Institute in Chicago. The school in her hometown of Mayesville was for whites only. Although Bethune originally wanted to be a missionary to Africa and was often quoted as saying the drums of Africa still beat in her heart, she dedicated her life to educating African American students. She established a school in Florida that became a normal school to train female African American teachers. Later the school evolved into Bethune-Cookman College, a 4-year coeducational college with mostly African American students.

In the midst of her work with education, Bethune became good friends with Eleanor Roosevelt, who drew her into government service—specifically the National Youth Administration (NYA), a branch of the Works Progress Administration (WPA) created by President Franklin D. Roosevelt. In 1935 Bethune founded the National Council of Negro Women, an umbrella group for all organizations working on behalf of African American women.

Boyer and Stuckey (2005).

This Opinion Editorial appeared in The Dallas Morning News, *on May 5, 2013.*

Choosing Separate and Unequal Texas Schools

by staff writer

Sunday's Page One story about the resegregation of public schools is sobering but can't be surprising to anyone who lives, breathes and sees. It's not something that has happened over-night or that is linked to racist policies. Rather, it is socioeconomic reality: Those with the means move away from problems and toward places where they believe their children can best succeed. To many, that means moving out of the struggling Dallas Independent School District to places such as affluent, far-northern Frisco. . . . When DISD was forced to desegregate in 1970, the district was 60 percent white. Now, it's less than 5 percent white. At a third of DISD campuses, whites make up 1 percent or less of the student body. In the last 15 years, the number of white students in DISD has dropped from 16,019 students to 7,417. Mean-while, during that same period, the white population at Frisco ISD has gone from 2,873 to 22,973.

This isn't as much about race and ethnicity as it is class and poverty. As the series points out, some minority parents are also making the choice to flee traditional public schools by enrolling their children in charter schools.

Unlike the segregationist policies that led to the landmark Brown vs. Board of Education ruling in 1954, this resegregation can't be addressed with a simple court ruling. It's not about laws that try to keep certain students out. It's about parents choosing to move students out. As DISD board President Lew Blackburn points out, "some racial overtones" may be part of the problem. But there's also a legitimate perception that districts such as DISD are doing a lousy job of educating students.

Regardless of the culprit, the result is the same: Kids from poorer families, who tend to be minorities, are relegated to un-derperforming schools because, unlike their better-off contem-poraries, they have few real educational options. Such divides threaten the cohesion of a well-functioning society. We know it doesn't have to be this way. Even within DISD, examples abound

of high-achieving schools with diverse populations, such as Woodrow Wilson High School and the School for the Talented and Gifted.

One part of the solution is adequate funding for schools, which the state Legislature has done a woeful job of providing. But that is just one piece of the puzzle, along with engagement by parents, commitment from students, higher expectations from teachers, and the most effective educational strategies from administrators. It underscores the need for effective education reforms, crafted around accountability, such as those being advanced by DISD Superintendent Mike Miles.

Desegregation in the 21st century won't be the result of court rulings, but rather, turning urban districts into centers of innova-tion that make them academic destinations parents want to move to, not away from. Texas Commissioner of Education Michael Williams emphatically states, "If we don't [close the racial achieve-ment gap], then those people who believe demographics is destiny will be right. But we're not going to allow them to be right. We can still be a state that is going to be more Hispanic, more African-American and still outperform every other state in the country."

This Opinion Page paints a realistic portrait of many urban school districts. It tells us schools in the Dallas Independent School Dis-trict have become more and more dominated by minority students as white families have moved to suburbs where they perceive their children will receive a better education. Write a well-developed paragraph in response to each of the following questions:

1. The writer says resegregation isn't linked to racist policies, but to socioeconomic reality. Prior to 1954, could this state-ment be made about segregated schools? Why or why not? What changed policy?

2. Why does the writer link school reform with accountability? How are the two interdependent?

3. What does "demographics is destiny" mean? Why is Com-missioner Williams so determined to not let the statement be true?

peacefully, but others did not. Still other segregated schools made little or no attempt to change at all.

In some parts of America, schools and school districts appear to be resegregat-ing, not because of laws or policies related to race, but because of socioeconomic differences. This chapter's **The Opinion Page** feature is written by an editor of a Dallas, Texas, newspaper who believes the urban Dallas Independent School District is a victim of socioeconomic segregation, resulting in the majority of white families mov-ing away from the city and into the suburbs.

While the launching of *Sputnik* triggered immediate changes in American education, and desegregation came to the forefront as an ongoing issue with significant moral implications, another, quieter, yet very important change was also taking place in the 1950s. Educators began to examine curriculum more carefully as a result of the thinking of Ralph Tyler (1902–1994). Tyler proposed that data concerning the needs of the learner, the needs of society, and the needs of the subject area should all be considered in the process of developing curricula. Tyler believed that learning should have both specific objectives and appropriate assessments.

Another influential person in American education, Benjamin Bloom (1913–1999), headed a group that composed what has become known as Bloom's taxonomy of learning objectives. The taxonomy was introduced in 1956 and continues to influence how educators think about and write learning objectives today.

1960s. The 1960s were characterized by a more outspoken U.S. citizenry. The election of a young, vibrant president, John F. Kennedy, gave rise to a sense of idealism among younger voters. After the assassination of President Kennedy in 1963, Lyndon Johnson attempted to continue in this vein with what he called the War on Poverty and the creation of the Great Society. Both the Kennedy and Johnson administrations allocated large amounts of money to break the cycle of poverty in the United States (Boyer & Stuckey, 2005). For example, the **Vocational Education Act of 1963** quadrupled the amount of money allocated for vocational education.

The following year, the **Civil Rights Act of 1964** stipulated that if schools discriminated based on race, color, or national origin, they would not be eligible for federal funding. Similarly, in a series of court battles, the Supreme Court continued to strike down school segregation.

In 1965 Congress passed the Elementary and Secondary Education Act (ESEA), which provided extra money for school districts with low-income families. Project Head Start was also established to boost the early learning of children ages 3 to 6 from low-income homes. The **Bilingual Education Act of 1968** (Title VII of the ESEA of 1965) validated children's native language and provided funds to assist non-English-speaking students, who were dropping out of high school at a rate of about 70%. The dramatic increase in numbers of Mexican and Mexican American children in the schools as a result of both legal and illegal immigration has created an ongoing challenge for educators that the Bilingual Education Act only partially addresses.

Ralph Tyler (1902–1994)

Upon his death, a news release from the Stanford University News Service called Ralph Tyler "the grand old man of educational research." Ralph Tyler's contributions to education were many, but his legacy is centered on curriculum development. Of the 16 books and over 700 journal articles he wrote, the one with perhaps the most impact was among his first, *Basic Principles of Curriculum and Instruction,* published in 1949.

Tyler's commonsense approach to curriculum development involved

- determining the goals of the school;
- selecting learning experiences useful in attaining the goals;
- organizing instruction around the experiences;
- and then deciding how best to evaluate the learning.

Tyler conducted a groundbreaking longitudinal analysis of 30 schools and the careers of their students called the Eight-Year Study (1933–1941). This study focused on the opportunities students had who stayed in school rather than joining the workforce during the Depression.

Tyler is also responsible for initiating the National Assessment of Educational Progress (NAEP) test in the 1960s, still the only test that evaluates the U.S. school system itself rather than the success of the students in it. Ralph Tyler was often heard to make two statements: "I never wanted to be anything but a teacher," and "I never met a child who couldn't learn."

McNeil (1995); Stanford News Service (1994); Tyler (1949).

Benjamin Bloom (1913–1999)

Following the 1948 convention of the American Psychological Association, Benjamin Bloom chaired a team that examined the cognitive, affective, and psychomotor domains of educational activity. From their work came what today is known as Bloom's taxonomy, discussed in Chapter 5. As part of his work at the University of Chicago, Bloom observed that about 95% of all classroom questions were at the knowledge (recall) level. The taxonomy provides a way to structure both activities and questions that run the gamut of intellectual processing.

Bloom also did extensive work in the area of assessment. He was influenced by Ralph Tyler and recognized that comparing students wasn't as important in terms of assessment as helping students master the learning.

Benjamin Bloom's work has been both condensed and expanded over the years by scholars and practitioners. His contributions to education are meaningful and enduring.

Bloom (1956); Eisner (2000).

Ralph Tyler and Benjamin Bloom are discussed in Chapter 4.

Immigration is discussed in more detail in Chapter 9.

1970s. During the first half of the decade, the country's attention was focused on the Vietnam conflict and the administration of President Richard Nixon. Public trust in establishment institutions was repeatedly shaken, resulting in a general lack of confidence in schools and teachers. The number of students in public schools decreased during the 1970s, while private schools and homeschooling grew. Public school students' test scores dropped. Many perceived a need to implement a back-to-basics curriculum, and demands for accountability increased.

At the same time, some good things happened in 1970s education. Title IX of the Education Amendment Acts, which prohibited sexual discrimination in any education program receiving federal funding, took effect in 1972. Additionally, in 1979 President Carter elevated the federal Office of Education to a department, making its secretary a member of his cabinet.

PL 94-142 and Title IX are discussed in Chapter 2.

PL 94–142, the Education for All Handicapped Children Act, passed in 1975. This important legislation granted children with disabilities the right to an education that meets their needs in the least restrictive environment.

It wasn't until the 1970s that the U.S. policy toward Native Americans changed from one of assimilation to fostering self-determination, encouraging Native Americans to take charge of their own education, whether on reservations or in other public schools. Today, even though there are more Native Americans under age 20, proportionally speaking, than in the general white population, a smaller percentage of Native Americans participate in formal education (Ornstein & Levine, 2006). In other words, in the whole Native American population, there is a greater percentage of people under the age of 20 when compared to the white population. Yet there is a smaller percentage of these young people in school when compared to white young people.

1980s. During the 8 years of Ronald Reagan's presidency (1981–1989), federal funding for elementary and secondary education declined by 17%. Even so, the quality of education received renewed attention for two basic reasons. The first reason was concern over economic competition with Japan. Many Americans believed that the United States had begun to compare unfavorably with Japan, in part because of inferior schools.

The second reason for the renewed attention to education was the release in 1983 of a report commissioned by President Reagan called *A Nation at Risk: The Imperative for Educational Reform*. The language of the report was strong, referring to public education in the United States as a "rising tide of mediocrity." In response, various proposals for reform and improvement surfaced. The *Paideia Proposal* (1982) by Mortimer Adler called for a core curriculum based on Great Books. The 1989 Carnegie Council on Adolescent Development report, *Turning Points: Preparing American Youth for the 21st Century,* validated the middle-level philosophy of the Association for Middle Level Education, which called for small learning communities, the elimination of tracking, and careful guidance.

Restructuring became a buzzword in education. Some of the efforts included year-round schools, longer school days, longer school years, and more funding for technology.

1990s. The 1990s could be labeled as the era of standards. Along with the standards came tests designed to determine whether students had met the standards. The emphasis shifted from the input of education (what teachers do, funding, support) to the output of education (student learning). President Bill Clinton brought increased attention to education as he promised to be an effective "education president." He formalized Goals 2000, an initiative begun by his predecessor George H. W. Bush during his administration (1988–1992). Although the goals were admirably lofty, they were also unrealistically high and have, for the most part, been unfulfilled.

Standards are discussed in detail in Chapter 4.

In the 1990s, teachers began taking on leadership roles in schools and in school districts. There was more collaboration among parents, the community, students, administrators, and teachers. Record enrollments resulted in a teacher shortage. President

Clinton, in addition to providing federal support for the recruitment of 100,000 new teachers, joined policy makers in asking states to raise teacher standards (Webb et al., 2012).

What Major Influences, Issues, Ideologies, and Individuals Are We Experiencing in 21st-Century American Education?

One full decade of this new century has passed. Our nation has experienced turbulence on every front.

CONTEXT FOR CHANGE

The new century was ushered in with fears that proved to be unfounded as we anticipated what was called Y2K, or Year 2000. Many gathered around televisions to watch as the year 2000 dawned in countries around the globe, complete with celebrations and massive displays of fireworks—and an eerie sense of anxiety about events such as worldwide computer blackouts and destruction of all sorts that were prophesized but never materialized.

Less than 2 years later, our worst fears did materialize in the form of the disastrous day now simply known as 9/11. When terrorists killed thousands of Americans on our own American soil, our way of life changed, both politically and practically. The subsequent conflicts and political unrest in Iraq and Afghanistan continued to take their toll. The administration of George W. Bush (2000–2008) was one of turmoil and intense disagreement over issues related to war, economics, and governmental controls. The economic downturn that began during the Bush years strangled American prosperity and perpetuated a downward spiral of failed businesses and unemployment that made life very difficult for many in the first decade of the 21st century. Rampant mistrust and suspicion plagued America.

The election in 2008 of America's first African American president, Barack Obama, brought jubilation for some and a newly expressed animosity for others. The abrupt change from a conservative Republican administration to what many viewed as a liberal Democrat occupant in the White House put American's political tolerance for bipartisan decision making and action to the test. Even with the election of President Obama for another term in 2012, the inability of the two major parties to work together continued.

NO CHILD LEFT BEHIND

The defining education-related legislation of the first decade of the 21st century was the No Child Left Behind Act of 2001 (NCLB). The act was the reauthorization of the Elementary and Secondary Education Act (1965) and called for accountability of schools and school districts to states, and of states to the federal government. No Child Left Behind was formulated as a response to evidence that students were being promoted without mastering concepts and were graduating without basic literacy skills.

NCLB is discussed in more detail in Chapter 4.

21ST-CENTURY KNOWLEDGE AND SKILLS

As noted in previous chapters, the Partnership for 21st Century Skills (P21) exerts considerable and growing influence in schools across the country. But it's not just an organization that is influencing what we teach and learn; it's the underlying concept that our world is changing and schools need to change as well.

In each Context for Change section in this chapter we get a sense for the complexity of life in the United States and around the world. The goal of teachers and schools should be to provide educational experiences that reflect this complexity as we equip students to live productively and positively. The present, and therefore history as well, is shaped by human responses to dilemmas. It's all about problem solving, a 21st-century skill that is more relevant now than ever before.

In the 21st century, information will continue to grow at exponential rates. Teaching students how to figure out what they need to know, where and how to access it, and then how to use it effectively, should be emphasized in teaching and learning. Then wrapping this package in appreciation for, and the ability to accomplish, collaboration will help students thrive in the 21st century.

21ST-CENTURY SCHOOLS

In most schools in the United States it would be difficult to recognize change between the 1990s and the first decade of the 21st century. In some schools the classrooms may not have changed much physically or in terms of learning experiences since long before 1990. Yet in others innovative technology such as SMART Boards, tablet and laptop computers, LCD projectors, and more tell the story of mushrooming technological advances.

Virtual education is becoming more widespread as educators use technology to deliver and reinforce teaching and learning. Books of all kind are available electronically, and communication with classrooms around the globe changes the way we view instruction. Although teaching is still viewed as place-based in a classroom for most educators, the possibilities of using whole communities and cyberspace as learning environments are taking education into uncharted dimensions. What an exciting time to become a teacher!

How Are U.S. Schools Addressing Racial and Ethnic Diversity in the 21st Century?

The short answer to this question is "Not very well," and certainly not with consistency. For instance, research shows that 55 years after the Supreme Court declared that separate is not equal in *Brown* v. *Board of Education*, U.S. schools are more segregated now than before the Court ruling (Orfield, 2009). Of the defining issues in American education, perhaps none is so challenging as finding ways to address racial and ethnic diversity. Table 7.3 shows the percentage of students by race and ethnicity in regions of the United States.

Although American public schools have been relatively successful in educating immigrants from Europe and Asia and helping them achieve at least middle-class status in the United States, our schools have been much less successful in doing so for those students from nonwhite communities—African Americans and Hispanics (Orfield, 2009).

AFRICAN AMERICAN STUDENTS

Laws have been passed and policies have been made with the intent of fully integrating U.S. schools. In our history, African American students were not treated as benignly as Native and Mexican Americans or any other racial/ethnic group. They have suffered

---

TABLE 7.3 Public school student enrollment percentages by region and race/ethnicity (2006–2007)

Region	White	Black	Latino/Hispanic	Asian	Native American and Other
West	44.6	6.4	38.7	8.3	2
South	48.9	26.5	21.5	2.6	.5
Northeast	64	15.4	14.9	5.3	.3
National	56.5	17.1	20.5	4.7	1.2

Source: Orfield, G. (2009). *Reviving the goal of an integrated society: A 21st century challenge*. Los Angeles: The Civil Rights Project/Proyecto Derechos Civiles at UCLA.

outright and purposeful discrimination, including laws that forbade their education. Today there are no such laws, and yet in some locations and in some circumstances we still find differences in opportunities for black students, compared with white students (Banks & Banks, 2010).

One of our focus students at Cario Middle School, Patrick Sutton, is an excellent student with what appears to be an intact sense of confidence. For Patrick, as an African American student, the doors of opportunity seem to be open wide. His positive experiences at Cario are what we should desire for all students, regardless of their race or ethnicity. Watch the interviews with **Patrick and with Patrick's Mom**.

HISPANIC AMERICAN STUDENTS

At the end of the first decade of the 21st century, there were over 45 million Hispanic people living in the United States. Some families have been in America for centuries, and the vast majority has come here to escape some form of oppression. They have come from many countries, and thus have a variety of ethnicities, as illustrated in Figure 7.5.

> The differences between race and ethnicity are discussed in Chapter 2.

The dilemmas for schools regarding the rapid increase of Hispanic students are complex. Perhaps the dilemma with the most impact on schools is that of language diversity. How do we teach the standards to children who can't understand what we say or write? Currently our schools attempt to answer this question through three basic programs: English as a Second Language (ESL), bilingual education, and Structured English Immersion (SEI). Our efforts are inadequate, particularly for any child raised in a non-English-speaking home. Read what focus teacher Angelica Reynosa has to say about her role as an advocate for Hispanic students in Teaching in Focus.

> Dilemmas of English-language learners are addressed in more detail in Chapters 2 and 9.

ASIAN AMERICAN STUDENTS

About half of the world's population falls into the broad category of Asian. They may live in China, Japan, India, Pakistan, Vietnam, Korea, Samoa, and many more countries. Asian Americans have vastly different experiences both before emigrating and when in the United States either legally or illegally (U.S. Census Bureau, 2009).

FIGURE 7.5 Hispanic subgroups in the United States

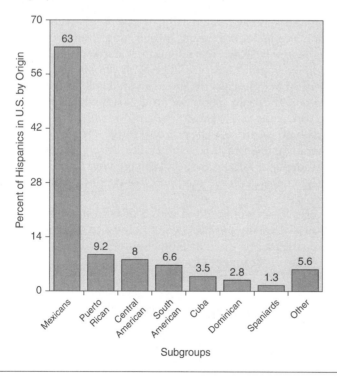

Source: U.S. Census Bureau. (2011). The Hispanic Population: 2010. Retrieved August 30, 2013, from http://www.census.gov/prod/cen2010/briefs/c2010br-04.pdf

Teaching in Focus

Angelica Reynosa, World History, Roosevelt High School, California. *In her own words. . . .*

I can't imagine being anywhere else professionally than in a school. My husband and I are both teachers. It is a wonderful life!

I teach in a school where minority populations are the majority. Most of my students, and indeed most of the students at Roosevelt, are Latino Americans. Some were born in America; others have been here for only a few weeks. Some have families with established careers; others have families who are undocumented workers. Regardless, they are the faces of an ever-growing Latino presence in America. Some of my students, like Hugo, have secure, loving homes headed by parents who risked their lives to come to America. Hugo will be successful. He knows it's his legacy. He attends school regularly, and he is learning English quickly.

I see my job as not only a teacher of a course for high school credit but also as an advocate for the well-being of my students, most of whom are in bilingual classes so they can learn their subjects while learning to be fluent in English. As a Spanish speaker, I am able to teach both history and coping skills in English communication. Find your special niche in education. You have unique talents and gifts that will be valuable to students. Search for those talents and develop them for the sake of the students. Revisit **Angelica's lesson**.

Students from China, Japan, and India generally achieve at high levels in U.S. schools, while students from Southeast Asian countries such as Vietnam and Cambodia tend to struggle. Many children who come to America from war-torn, trauma-filled areas find their problems within U.S. education exacerbated, or made worse, by their life experiences. Again, language is a major barrier to success. In large cities and small towns across America, teachers who speak only English work daily with children who speak a great variety of languages in their homes and struggle to communicate in English in order to learn even small bits and pieces of our curricular standards.

MIDDLE EASTERN AMERICAN STUDENTS

So often targets of prejudice in our post-9/11 world, students of Middle Eastern descent are entering our schools in increasing—yet still relatively small—numbers. They may be from countries including Egypt, Jordan, Iraq, Iran, Syria, Lebanon, and Saudi Arabia. Many are linked to Islam, the religion of people referred to as Muslims. But in reality, more Middle Eastern Americans align with Christianity than with Islam.

Cultural norms of Middle Eastern American students are often noticeably different from the mainstream. They may talk more loudly with what sounds like an odd intonation, hold hands with same-sex friends, not consider being late a sign of disrespect, not hold females in as high regard as males, and so forth. Because these norms are counter to what we generally expect in U.S. schools, life in school may be more difficult for some. Even so, students of Middle Eastern heritage tend to do quite well in school, go to college at a higher than average rate, and live productive lives in the United States (Banks & Banks, 2010).

Your future classroom will be filled with a diverse student population. Remember that students display diversity in many ways, not just in race or ethnicity. But chances are you will have at least two races or ethnicities represented. Welcome the challenge! Our differences make us stronger.

Points of Reflection 7.4

Do you anticipate a diverse classroom with a sense of excitement or a nagging dread? Explain your answer. Is there anything in your background that uniquely prepares you for a diverse classroom? If so, explain.

Ways that students display diversity are discussed in Chapter 2.

How Can I Be Aware of Education History in the Making?

Time gives us perspective. We can look at the history of American education and determine which of the various influences, issues, ideologies, and individuals have most affected the course of schools, teachers, and students. What is less than obvious is which of these influences, issues, ideologies, and individuals are making a difference or initiating significant change right now. Fifty or 100 years from now, it will likely be evident.

Education issues come and go, often in predictable cycles. The notable individuals involved in education at any given point are numerous. Sifting through them to determine who has significant and long-term influence generally only happens with time. The danger of listing contemporary movers and shakers in any field is the inevitable omission of names. Given that risk, Table 7.4 is an attempt to provide a partial list of individuals and their contributions that are currently influencing American education. You will no doubt hear and read about these people as you pursue a degree in teaching.

Reading professional journals, continuing to take courses, attending conferences, having conversations with colleagues—all of these activities will help you stay abreast of the individuals in the forefront of our work as teachers. History is in the making all around us. In classrooms across the United States, excellent teachers are the real heroes of education. If you decide to be a teacher, then the history of American education has been changed, perhaps not in ways that will make it into history books, but definitely in ways that will influence the lives of the hundreds, maybe thousands of students in your future classroom.

Points of Reflection 7.5

Which educators in your school experiences have had the most positive impact on you? Explain their impact.

TABLE 7.4 History in the making

Individual	Theory, Field of Research, Written Works
Mortimer Adler	Paideia Proposal; core curriculum based on Great Books
James Banks	Multicultural education
David Berliner	Educational researcher; teacher effectiveness
Marva Collins	Tireless advocate for all children; founder of Westside Preparatory School
James Comer	Comer Model; emphasis on social context of teaching and learning
Larry Cuban	Expert on change in education
Linda Darling-Hammond	*The Right to Learn*; teacher quality and preparation
Marian Wright Edelman	Children's Defense Fund; advocate for all children
Elliot Eisner	Arts education; curriculum reform
Jaime Escalante	Outstanding high school math teacher in urban Los Angeles
Paulo Freire	*Pedagogy of the Oppressed*; education gives power to the poor
Howard Gardner	Multiple intelligences theory
William Glasser	Choice theory of human behavior
John Goodlad	*A Place Called School*; democracy and education; teacher education
Maxine Greene	Existentialism; *Landscapes of Learning*
E. D. Hirsch	*Cultural Literacy: What Every American Needs to Know*
Ivan Illich	Social reconstructionism; *Deschooling America*
Herbert Kohl	*36 Children*; the value of teachers and teaching differentiated instruction
Jacob Kounin	Classroom management
Jonathan Kozol	*Savage Inequalities: Children in America's Schools*; study of urban children
Sonia Nieto	Multicultural and bilingual education
Nel Noddings	Caring in the classroom; teacher reflection
Theodore Sizer	Coalition of Essential Schools; necessity of community in school environment; *Horace's Compromise*
Robert Slavin	Success for All program; early intervention
Kay Toliver	Outstanding teacher in urban New York City
Carol Ann Tomlinson	Differentiated instruction
Grant Wiggins/Jay McTighe	*Understanding by Design*; development of curriculum, instruction, and assessment

CONCLUDING THOUGHTS

This brief look at the history of education in the United States has been written from a majority culture viewpoint (white, middle class) primarily using sources having the same lens. Encapsulating 400 years into one brief chapter involves choices that have inherent limitations. Be aware of this when you consider any aspect of history. Understand that there's always more to the story.

American education has been more reactionary than trailblazing, more foundational than earthshaking. In an ideal world educators would be ahead of dilemmas, and the teaching and learning in U.S. schools would lead the way toward solutions to our country's problems. And indeed this is true, but in a subtle way. The adage "Teachers make all other professions possible" elevates teachers to indispensable heroes, although they are largely unheralded as such.

The history of education in the United States parallels the history of the country. Although once relatively simple and perceived as manageable, education in the United States is now incredibly complex and often unwieldy, with issues to match. In spite of the lessons to be learned from studying the history of American education, there remain unacceptable conditions for learning in some schools, unequal opportunities for children based on such factors as socioeconomic status and race, and international test results that show mediocre performances by U.S. students. Together we will face many challenges as we strive to effectively build on the past to do a better job of educating in—and for—the future, always asking, "And how are the children? Are they all well?"

We began this chapter by considering Angelica Reynosa's classroom and teaching responsibilities at Roosevelt High School in Fresno, California. As she teaches world history, she is often reminded that the plight of many of her students resembles some in history who have suffered hardships but who also possessed hope for a better life. Now as the chapter comes to an end, we join Angelica as she considers ways to make history relevant for her students.

Read through *Chapter in Review* to help refresh your memory of what we have discussed, then interact with Angelica as she plans learning experiences for her students in *Developing Professional Competence*.

Chapter in Review

What were the major influences, issues, ideologies, and individuals in 17th-century American education?

- Many of the original colonists came to America seeking religious freedom and established schools to bolster their beliefs.
- Colonial schools primarily served white males.
- Education differed greatly among the New England, middle, and southern colonies.

What were the major influences, issues, ideologies, and individuals in 18th-century American education?

- Private academies served as secondary schools that went beyond what was taught in dame schools and town schools.
- Influential leaders such as Benjamin Franklin, Thomas Jefferson, and Noah Webster contributed to the expansion of educational opportunities.
- Education became a state responsibility by virtue of not being addressed in the Constitution.

What were the major influences, issues, ideologies, and individuals in 19th-century American education?

- Common schools were the first public, free American elementary schools.
- Following the Civil War, the first high schools began to flourish to meet the new economic demands of an increasingly industrialized United States.
- Kindergarten, with an activity-based curriculum, became common by the end of the 19th century.
- Teacher preparation institutions called normal schools were created to respond to the need for more teachers with increased and consistent preparation.
- Few educational opportunities existed for children with disabilities, children of color, or children of poor immigrant parents.
- Land-grant colleges were established as a result of the Morrill Acts.

What were the major influences, issues, ideologies, and individuals in 20th-century American education?

- John Dewey and the philosophy of progressive education fostered more active student participation in a school system based on democratic principles.
- Junior highs, and then middle schools, bridged the gap between elementary and high schools.
- Interest in science and math education increased following the launch of *Sputnik*.
- In 1965 Congress passed the Elementary and Secondary Education Act (ESEA), which initially provided extra money for school districts with low-income families, and now applies to a variety of education reforms.
- During the 1970s, the Education for All Handicapped Children Act and Title IX increased educational opportunities for all children.
- *A Nation at Risk* served as a wake-up call for education in the United States.
- Curriculum standards emerged in the 1990s as the defining criteria for the quality of teaching and learning.

What major influences, issues, ideologies, and individuals have we experienced so far in 21st-century American education?

- The first decade of the 21st century in America was filled with turmoil.
- The No Child Left Behind Act of 2001 called for increased accountability at local and state levels and emphasized the need for all children to learn.
- The Partnership for 21st Century Skills (P21) has exerted, and continues to exert, considerable and growing influence in schools across the country.
- Some schools have remained virtually unchanged for decades; others reflect the technology and strategies available for teaching and learning in the 21st century.

How are U.S. schools addressing racial and ethnic diversity in the 21st century?

- Although some strides have been made in a quest to provide equal opportunities for learning to all children in the United States, there is still much to do.
- African American students are more segregated now than they were at the time of *Brown* v. *Board of Education*, when *separate but equal* was designated as unlawful.
- The Hispanic student population is rapidly growing, but our ability to improve their learning and their language skills is not keeping up with their need.
- Students from China, Japan, and India generally appear to be achieving at high levels in U.S. schools, while students from Southeast Asian countries such as Vietnam and Cambodia struggle.
- Cultural norms of Middle Eastern American students are often noticeably different from mainstream Americans, necessitating an even greater need for understanding on the part of teachers.

• Teachers should assume the responsibility of staying current with major shifts in educational concepts and trends. Time provides perspective. As history unfolds, those most influential will emerge in prominence.

Developing Professional Competence

Thoughtfully reading this scenario and responding to the items that follow it will help you prepare for licensure exams.

Angelica Reynosa wants her students to see the big picture included in the world history curriculum and wants to help them grasp the significance of how various forms of government enhance or inhibit people's lives. She wants them to understand how knowledge of history is meaningful for their futures and how it can give them perspective about their roots and cultural struggles.

Think about Angelica and her students as you answer the following multiple-choice questions:

1. Why is the establishment of colonies in the 17th century in what is now the United States relevant to many of Angelica's students?
   a. The people who came to America from Europe did so to find refuge from a government that they found to be oppressive.
   b. It's been 400 years and we now have perspective on the early days of the United States.
   c. Many Hispanics came to America then as they do now.
   d. Mexico was experiencing a similar fight for independence in the 17th century.

2. Why is it important for Angelica's students to understand how various people throughout history have suffered oppression?
   a. They need to see that they are not alone.
   b. They will be encouraged to see how people have overcome difficulties.
   c. They need to understand it so they won't perpetuate it.
   d. It is vital to understand that history repeats itself.

3. In the lesson you observed, what purpose does the candy serve?
   a. The candy randomly given and taken shows students that they actually have very little control over their lives.
   b. They are learning to cleverly hoard candy and keep it from being taken away, much as they will need to do in a capitalistic country.
   c. The candy is an incentive to participate fully in the rock-paper-scissors activity.
   d. The candy is randomly given and taken away, showing that in governments without freedom there is little control over one's destiny.

Now it's time for you to respond to two short essay items involving Angelica and her students. In your responses, be sure to address all the dilemmas and questions posed in each item. Your responses should each be between one half and one full double-spaced page.

4. The class you observed is bilingual. How did Angelica approach the lesson to both teach the content and the English language? Why is Angelica's own ethnicity important to the teaching and learning process in her classroom?

5. As Angelica considers her students and her responsibilities, she reflects on these two NBPTS and InTASC standards. Why is each especially important to her, given that she teaches in a bilingual classroom?

NBPTS Standard 5   Teachers are members of learning communities.

InTASC Standard 9   Professional Learning and Ethical Practice

The teacher engages in ongoing professional learning and uses evidence to continually evaluate his/her practice, particularly the effects of his/her choices and actions on others (learners, families, other professionals, and the community), and adapts practice to meet the needs of each learner.

Dear Reader

When it comes to a philosophy of education, there's no avoiding it. Every decision, every action, and every interaction come from a philosophy, whether we've thought about it, written it, or never even considered it. One thing's for sure . . . we live it.

The Greek word *philo* means "love," and *sophos* means "wisdom." **Philosophy,** then, means "love of wisdom." Philosophy is a means of answering fundamental questions. It's not a boring, stuffy subject, but rather a vibrant way of discovering and expressing ways of being and behaving. A teacher's **philosophy of education** is the teacher's "love of wisdom" regarding teaching that expresses itself every day in the classroom.

This chapter provides only a very brief overview of some of the components of philosophy that apply to teaching and learning. Don't be put off by the terminology. Think about the meanings and implications of the words that label the areas of philosophy we discuss: essentialism, perennialism, progressivism, social reconstructionism, and existentialism. Consider the concepts seriously and internalize them. Each area has a down-to-earth definition and is illustrated with words that are familiar. Take it personally and pay attention to how each philosophy affects teaching and learning. You'll learn a lot about yourself. This won't happen with a quick read-through and a glance at the figures. The chapter is relatively brief, allowing

time to read it twice or even three times, purposefully reflecting on the content to make it personally meaningful.

Here are the major questions we address in Chapter 8:

- Why is a philosophy of education important?

- How do five prominent philosophies of education affect teaching and learning?

- How do I begin to develop my own personal philosophy of education?

Teaching in Focus

Brenda Beyal's passionate approach to teaching is evident in every aspect of her work—curriculum choices, teaching methods, relationships with students, interactions with colleagues, and the learning environment she has created in her classroom. In her interview, Brenda tells us she considers her choice to teach a "calling." She had planned to be an engineer until she took a course that addressed the needs of children with disabilities. That's when she knew teaching would be her life's work. She has taught for over 20 years, most of them spent in a multiage classroom at Rees Elementary, south of Salt Lake City, Utah.

Brenda's classroom is very student friendly, with tables and a couch rather than desks in rows; a large classroom library with books for all reading levels on a wide range of topics; multiple cabinets of art supplies; display boards of student work; and an area filled with Native American art, posters, and artifacts that have personal meaning to Brenda because of her Native American heritage.

Brenda was one of the originators of the multiage concept at Rees Elementary. She wanted to have longer term relationships with individual students. She saw the benefits of children at different stages of maturation being together for several years. She also liked the idea of collaborating with other teachers in creative ways. With colleagues Chris and Tim, Brenda maintains an arts-infused curriculum by teaching all three classes of multiage students an art form. Brenda's specialty is visual arts, evident by the amount of artwork in her classroom.

Each day is filled with opportunities, according to Brenda, who finds purpose and beauty all around her as she fulfills her calling. Later in the chapter we'll translate what we know about Brenda into a philosophy of education. To get a glimpse of her philosophy, watch **Brenda's interview**.

If you've ever considered questions such as "Who am I?" or "What's my purpose in life?" you have engaged in philosophical thought. Every attitude and action is determined by some deeper basic beliefs, conscious or unconscious. To bring a philosophy to the surface of your consciousness requires consideration of your values and views about life. It necessitates reflection on circumstances, reactions, assumptions, intentions, and so on.

Few teachers have a defined philosophy of education. If asked, most may shrug and say, "I've never thought about it," or, "I don't have time for that kind of stuff." But if you study a teacher's attitudes and actions over even a relatively brief period of time, you can probably make some accurate statements about the philosophy that impacts what you observe.

Why Is a Philosophy of Education Important?

A philosophy of education is a living, dynamic part of who we are in the classroom. Allan C. Ornstein (2003) expresses the far-reaching impact of a philosophy of education when he writes,

> Philosophy enters into every important decision about curriculum, teaching, instruction, and testing. . . . The methods and materials a teacher chooses to use in a classroom reflect a professional judgment, which reflects philosophy. When a teacher decides to increase the homework load or assign a particular author, he or she is acting on the basis of philosophy. In short, choices reflect philosophy—and whether we recognize our own philosophy in education, it is out there and it influences our behavior and attitudes in classrooms and schools. Philosophy then operates overtly and covertly, whether we know that it is operating or not. (p. 17)

Because teacher preparation puts you in a position to think about decisions relative to teaching, prospective teachers are usually asked to write a philosophy of education. This means you will look closely at established philosophical viewpoints, you will analyze what these viewpoints mean to teachers and their work, and then you will either state with which philosophy you agree or with which combination you most closely align. The philosophy of education you write before entering the classroom as a teacher

Figure 8.1 Karen Heath, 2005 Vermont Teacher of the Year

One of the ubiquitous rites of passage for preservice teachers is the completion of a philosophy of education. When I was a senior in college 22 years ago, having just completed my student teaching, one of the final requirements before being certified was to complete such a document. I was still a student, and much of what I thought about and wrote was largely theoretical. I wrote about the need for children's differences to be recognized, the importance of process in education, and freedom within a structured environment. "A Personal Philosophy of Education," as it was titled, went subsequently into a box in an attic while I ventured across the country and, a few years later, settled into a home in Vermont where the box was moved to a new attic, gathering dust with other college relics.

Last year when I was nominated to be Teacher of the Year, I was called upon once again to produce a philosophy of education. I sat down one weekend and wrote about what I believe to be the most important aspect of education—the heart. Years of experience have taught me that in order to be an effective teacher, my heart must be in it fully, from devotion to subject matter, to striving to keep up with best practices, and, most importantly, to having a heart connection to the children, as that is the only sure avenue to effective student learning.

It took a bit of digging, but I found the old college box, and at the very bottom of it lay my original philosophy of education. I took it like a treasure into the afternoon sun in our yard and carefully read not just a philosophy, but also the mind-set of an idealistic 21-year-old. Surprisingly, I still agreed with everything I had written, but there was a distinct lack of mention of anything having to do with relationships. I guess that is the aspect of teaching that I have truly learned over time.

Though my first written document sat untouched for 23 years and my newest one was just composed, I have always carried with me a philosophy of education. It brings stability to my work as initiatives and programs come and go. From a fairly benign population of children in a wealthy college town to an inner-city Boston high school, my philosophy is the backbone of what I do as a teacher. It directs what and how I teach and, most importantly, how I interact with my students. It is the core of who I am as a teacher.

Source: E-mail communication with Karen Heath, January 18, 2007.

will be based on limited experience and will be a work in progress. But it's a start, and an important one. A philosophy of education is a living, dynamic part of who we are in the classroom. It's healthy and productive for teachers to teach according to combinations of philosophies. This creates balance and produces commonsense, responsive decisions in the classroom.

People change and grow, often in response to personal experiences. Your philosophy will change and grow. In Figure 8.1, read about Karen Heath's experience of writing an initial philosophy of education as a college assignment and her subsequent experiences leading her to revisit her philosophy.

How Do Five Prominent Philosophies of Education Affect Teaching and Learning?

Exploring prominent philosophies will provide a framework for understanding what they mean for teaching and learning. The five philosophies featured in this section are not the only ones that directly impact the work of teachers. A few others are discussed briefly at the end of this section.

When we refer to an aspect of education as teacher-centered, the teacher is prominent in the choices of curricula and in the instructional strategies. When the curriculum and instructional strategies are student-centered, the students have choices concerning what to learn and the instructional strategies actively involve students in their own learning. The five philosophies discussed here fall neatly into these two categories. Essentialism and perennialism are teacher-centered approaches, whereas progressivism, social reconstructionism, and existentialism are more student-centered, as illustrated in Figure 8.2. Keep this in mind as you read about the five philosophies.

Teacher-centered and student-centered instruction are briefly discussed in Chapter 5.

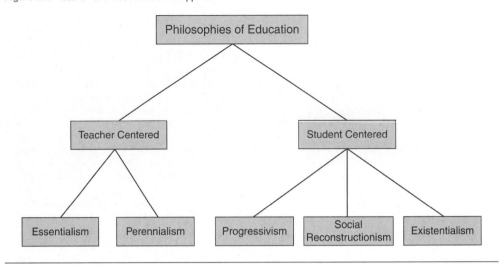

Figure 8.2 Teacher- and student-centered approaches

Also think about early childhood, elementary, middle, and high school classrooms as you consider each philosophy of education.

PHILOSOPHY TREES

The discussion of each philosophy is accompanied by a diagram of a tree. The analogy of a philosophy of education to a tree is appropriate in many ways. The tree trunk represents teaching. The root system is a particular philosophy of education, or a combination of philosophies, providing the strength and foundation of the tree: The philosophy literally grounds the tree. The branches of the tree represent the work of teachers. Each trunk-attached branch supports smaller branches with plentiful leaves that represent teaching and learning.

Many aspects of a tree's growth are directly analogous to teaching and learning. Do you recall seeing a cross section of a tree trunk? Elementary students learn that you can count the rings to determine the age of a tree because each year of growth not only takes a tree skyward but also wraps another layer of life around it. So it is with teaching experience. Each year, previous experiences aren't shed but rather are wrapped in new experiences.

Trees have two kinds of roots: anchor roots, which grow deeper with time and hold the tree upright against most winds, and feeder roots, which shoot out in all directions and draw in nourishment. Have you ever noticed a makeshift fence or stakes with colored tape around the base of a tree when construction was nearby? The purpose of this barrier was to let workers know that digging closer would likely damage the tree. Although a tree can survive the loss of some feeder roots, the diameter of the feeder and anchor root system is generally the same as the diameter of the canopy of the tree's branches and leaves. Cutting away feeder roots will diminish the canopy in like proportion. The size and stability of the philosophical root system determine the effectiveness of the teaching and learning canopy. Your anchor matters; your philosophy of education affects all aspects of your success as a teacher.

ESSENTIALISM

Essentialism is a philosophy of education based on the belief that a core curriculum exists that everyone in the United States should learn. This core can shift in response to societal changes but should always be basic, organized, and rigorous. When you hear someone praise the concept of "back to basics," chances are that person is an essentialist.

Essentialism is an ancient philosophy, but it grew in popularity in the 20th century in the United States as a backlash to progressivism, the educational philosophy begun by John Dewey. Whereas progressivism puts student interests at the center of

Figure 8.3 Essentialism tree

curriculum and instruction, essentialism puts little stock in what students want in terms of what and how they learn. Essentialism gained impetus from the launching of *Sputnik* by the Soviet Union in 1957 and again from the publication of *A Nation at Risk* in 1983. Supporters of the essentialist philosophy are vocal about their view that schools have dumbed down the curriculum with nonessential courses, resulting in lower test scores (Ravitch, 2000). Essentialists favor high expectations for students, along with testing to measure mastery of standards.

An essentialist philosophy of education puts the teacher front and center as an intellectual and moral role model. Direct instruction is encouraged, but other instructional methods are used if they prove effective. Students are expected to listen and learn as they follow the rules of the classroom.

One prominent proponent of essentialism is E. D. Hirsch (b. 1928), author of *Cultural Literacy: What Every American Needs to Know* (1987). Hirsch lists events, people, facts, discoveries, inventions, art, literature, and more that he believes all Americans should know about to be culturally literate. Another proponent of essentialism is Theodore Sizer (b. 1932), founder of the Coalition of Essential Schools, a group of about 200 schools that pledge to promote the essentialist goals of a rigorous curriculum based on standards. Sizer (1985) insists that Coalition of Essential Schools students clearly exhibit mastery of content as well as evidence of developing thinking skills.

Take a few minutes to study the essentialism tree in Figure 8.3. Visualizing how teachers might translate the elements of essentialism into their classrooms will help you understand this philosophy of education.

PERENNIALISM

Perennialism is a philosophy of education based on a core curriculum, and in that regard it is similar to essentialism. The difference lies in what constitutes the core. The word *perennial* means "everlasting" and is often used when talking about plants. A perennial flower blooms in season, is dormant for a time, and then blooms again, year after year. A flower that is not a perennial is an annual that must be replanted each year. Perennialism, as a philosophy of education, says there is a curriculum with themes and questions that endure and are everlasting. In contrast, the curriculum of

A Nation at Risk and *Sputnik* are discussed in Chapter 7.

Points of Reflection 8.1

Do you identify with some of the elements of essentialism? If so, which ones? Do some of the aspects of essentialism in the classroom, as illustrated in Figure 8.3, appeal to you as a prospective teacher? Are there some aspects that do not appeal to you? If so, which ones?

Figure 8.4 Perennialism tree

essentialism is considered basic and core, but its components may change as society changes and, as such, the essentialist curriculum is more comparable to an annual.

Perennialists believe that even as life changes and times change, the real substance and truths of life remain the same. The wisdom students need may be obtained through the study of **Great Books,** the writings of those considered to be the great thinkers through the history of Western civilization, such as Homer, Shakespeare, Melville, Einstein, and many others. Perennialists do not endorse choices in the curriculum or elective courses, and they ascribe to a rigid curriculum for elementary, middle, and high schools.

Teachers who practice perennialism as a philosophy of education want to be in control of the classroom. They dispense knowledge and lead discussions of classics that require rigorous, logical thought by students. Differences in students are rarely considered, as all are expected to learn from the classics (Webb, Metha, & Jordan, 2012).

Mortimer Adler (1902–2001), author of the *Paideia Proposal* (1982), is perhaps the best known recent proponent of perennialism as a philosophy of education. The word *paideia* refers to a state of human excellence. Adler said that schools should use intense study of the classics to strive for excellence in students (Pulliam & Van Patten, 2013). Adler founded the Great Books of the Western World program at the University of Chicago in 1930 (Adler, 1982).

Take a few minutes to study the perennialism tree in Figure 8.4. Visualizing how teachers might translate the elements of perennialism into their classrooms will help you understand this philosophy of education.

PROGRESSIVISM

Progressivism is a student-centered philosophy of education that focuses on a curriculum of interest to students. To progressivists, education is more than preparation for the future—it is life itself. The progressive philosophy of education endorses experiential learning full of opportunities for student discovery and problem solving.

Constructivism and pragmatism are philosophies of education that fall within the broader philosophy of progressivism. Constructivism, an inquiry-based way of approaching instruction, builds on progressivism because students are challenged to construct, or discover, knowledge about their environments. Process is valued in progressivism, often

Points of Reflection 8.2

Do you identify with some of the elements of perennialism? If so, which ones? Do some of the aspects of perennialism in the classroom, as illustrated in Figure 8.4, appeal to you as a prospective teacher? Are there some aspects that do not appeal to you? If so, which ones?

more than product. The theory is that students who learn through the processes of construction, discovery, and problem solving will be better able to adapt to a changing world. Another philosophy, **pragmatism,** says that student-centered perspectives that are integrated with firsthand experiences are the most effective (Chartock, 2004).

Teachers who ascribe to progressivism act primarily as facilitators of learning, serving as resources and guides to students who explore, gather evidence, and draw conclusions. Real-world problem solving is intended to promote individual student development (Gutek, 2005).

John Dewey (1859–1952) was the most prominent of all the proponents of progressivism, beginning in the late 19th century and continuing well into the 20th century. Dewey supported a balance between valuing established content with structured learning activities and planning experiences that interest, motivate, and actively involve students. Although progressivism fell out of favor in a call for more academic rigor in the late 1950s, many tenets of the philosophy continue to be part of today's most widely used instructional strategies. Many teachers are choosing to involve students in their own learning through technology tools. The use of tablets in the classroom is growing rapidly in popularity and potential effectiveness. This chapter's *SocialMEdia* feature looks at the benefits of classroom tablets, as well as the dilemmas their use may present.

Take a few minutes to study the progressivism tree in Figure 8.5. Visualizing how teachers might translate the elements of progressivism into their classrooms will help you understand this philosophy of education.

Encouraging students to engage in learning and express themselves is part of the philosophy of progressivism.

Points of Reflection 8.3

Do you identify with some of the elements of progressivism? If so, which ones? Do some of the aspects of progressivism in the classroom, as illustrated in Figure 8.5, appeal to you as a prospective teacher? Are there some aspects that do not appeal to you? If so, which ones?

Figure 8.5 Progressivism tree

SocialMEdia

Although public education is traditionally slow to adopt new technology, the use of tablets in the classroom is proving to be the exception. Some estimates put tablet sales to schools as doubling each year for several years. However, integrating them into the curriculum is still in the infancy stage. Teachers using tablets see them as valuable tools for teaching and learning, with potential to have greater impact with time.

Tablets make sense in every kind of school, but particularly in rural areas, providing virtual field trips, conversations with experts from around the world, advanced placement courses, and more. In some areas there aren't enough towers to make Internet access possible in homes. Even without Internet, programs can be loaded on tablets to give access to students in rural areas.

Let's look at some benefits of tablet use for teaching and learning:

1. Students are comfortable with the technology. Teachers may have difficulty adjusting to tablets, but students don't. Tablets are portable, colorful, connected, and interactive.
2. Tablets are now readily available, made by a number of companies, each with strong and weak points. Apple's iPad, Amazon's Kindle Fire, Barnes & Noble's Nook, Google's Nexus 7, and other Android tablets are among the most popular. The Microsoft Surface has some advantages because of its detachable keyboard, solving the typing issue of other touch-only tablets. Increased competition will likely drive prices lower.
3. Innovative software is continually being developed specifically for tablets. There are applications for tablets in all subject areas. For example, in science there are apps that allow students to explore and label the stars and constellations. Images from digital microscopes may be shared on tablets. Tablets can bring history to life through interactive e-books and videos, with primary sources accessible. Students can keep up with happenings around the world on tablets. For students with special needs, curriculum may be tailored through specific apps that help them learn in ways that suit their strengths.

4. Cameras on tablets allow individual exploration, creativity, and the capacity for more engaging presentations.
5. Because of access to the Internet, information on tablets does not go out of date as it does in a textbook.
6. Tablets can store thousands of books, allowing students virtually limitless data storage capacity.
7. Tablets provide class interactivity. Students can communicate with teachers and other students, share ideas, and work on projects.

There are drawbacks to using tablets in the classroom that will undoubtedly be remedied with innovation and time. Here are some of the challenges of classroom tablet use:

1. The initial cost of tablets for a whole school is expensive. When questioned, cost is a factor for most individuals in positions to make the tablet-or-no-tablet decision. However, a New York City Council member has suggested replacing textbooks with tablets for 1,700 schools. She contends that this can happen when New York City stops purchasing textbooks.
2. So far, most tablets do not have built-in keyboards. The touch screen is not considered efficient for lengthy writing. It is still more difficult for students to respond to data on a tablet than on desktop or laptop computers.
3. Monitoring student activity on tablets is a dilemma for many teachers that may be solvable using a tablet that is loaded with only what teachers want on them. The Kuno educational tablet allows content to be stored locally on the device. If a school doesn't want Internet access on the tablets, but only curriculum for the various subject areas, programs such as the CurriculumLoft, a web-based storage system for digital curriculum, will make this possible.
4. Breakage, loss, and theft pose dilemmas.

Perhaps the biggest challenge from a teacher's standpoint is finding ways to make tablets, or any technology for that matter, part of daily instruction, not just a motivating add-on. The possibilities are many. Chances are you will enter the teaching profession with classroom tablets both commonplace and productive.

SOCIAL RECONSTRUCTIONISM

More than any other philosophy of education, **social reconstructionism** looks to education to change society, rather than just teach about it. Social reconstructionism as a philosophy of education calls on schools to educate students in ways that will help society move beyond all forms of discrimination to the benefit of everyone worldwide. This philosophy addresses such topics as racial equality, women's rights, sexism, environmental pollution, poverty, substance abuse, homophobia, and AIDS. Proponents of other educational philosophies often avoid such topics, thus relegating the topics to the null curriculum.

The null curriculum is discussed in Chapter 4.

According to some educators, Theodore Brameld (1904–1987) founded the philosophy of social reconstructionism following World War II. Brameld (1956) based the philosophy on two premises: (1) people now have the capacity to destroy civilization,

Figure 8.6 Social reconstructionism tree

and (2) people have the potential to create a civilization marked by health and humanity. The basic tenets of social reconstructionism, however, go back to the early Greeks and, more recently, to Karl Marx, who called for a social revolution that would bring about equity among all people (Jacobsen, 2003).

Teachers who ascribe to social reconstructionism promote active student involvement in societal problems. They plan experiences for students to explore issues and possible solutions, but avoid moralizing. They promote democracy and the freedom to make choices while helping students discover the consequences of particular lines of reasoning and action. All of this occurs within an educational context that focuses on reading comprehension, research techniques, analysis and evaluation skills, and writing as a form of persuasive communication.

Major proponents of social reconstructionism as a philosophy of education include George Counts (1907–1974), Paulo Friere (1922–1987), and Ivan Illich (1926–2002). In his book *Dare the School Build a New Social Order?* (1932), Counts wrote about his view that schools should equip students to deal with world problems. Friere wrote in *Pedagogy of the Oppressed* (1970) about his personal experiences in working with poor illiterate peasants that led him to the philosophy that education is the key to empowering the poor to control and improve their lives. In his book *Deschooling Society* (1971), Illich promoted a radical view. He wrote that schools as we know them should be eliminated because they do nothing to decrease poverty. He contended that schools actually prevent what he saw as real education, a process he viewed as happening in more informal ways. Although "deschooling" American society is not likely to happen, the social reconstructionist views of Illich have prompted important questions about the role of public education (Chartock, 2004).

Take a few minutes to study the social reconstructionism tree in Figure 8.6. Visualizing how teachers might translate the elements of social reconstructionism into their classrooms will help you understand this philosophy of education.

Points of Reflection 8.4

Do you identify with some of the elements of social reconstructionism? If so, which ones? Do some of the aspects of social reconstructionism in the classroom, as illustrated in Figure 8.6, appeal to you as a prospective teacher? Are there some aspects that do not appeal to you? If so, which ones?

EXISTENTIALISM

The primary emphasis of **existentialism** is on the individual. As a philosophy of education, existentialism contends that teachers teach the whole person, not just math, reading, science, or any other particular subject. Each student searches for personal meaning and personal understanding. If learning about a subject increases a student's sense of self, then it's worthwhile. Practices such as standardization, tracking, and testing do not fit into an existentialist viewpoint. Because meaning is personal, each student has the freedom and the subsequent responsibility to make his or her own choices. Existentialism rejects traditional education. Few schools practice existentialism as an educational philosophy, and most that do are private. However, there are teachers in both public and private classrooms who practice some elements of existentialism.

The existentialist teacher honors individual students by arranging for learning experiences from which each student may choose. The classroom atmosphere is supposed to be stimulating and full of choices. The student's job is to make choices and then take responsibility for those choices. Teachers and students have a great deal of individual contact, participating in learning that is self-paced and self-directed (Greene, 1978). A teacher who follows existentialism as a philosophy of education teaches best by being a role model, and demonstrates the importance of a discipline by pursuing academic goals related to the subject area.

A. S. Neill (1883–1973) was one of the most influential proponents of existentialism. He founded the Summerhill School in England following World War I. Learning by discovery was the primary feature of Summerhill. The student as an individual was emphasized and exploration for the sake of learning had few restrictions (Neill, 1960).

Maxine Greene (b. 1917) is the most well-known proponent of existentialism. She refers to a heightened level of personal awareness as "wide-awakeness." Greene refutes critics of existentialism who say that the philosophy in practice allows children to run free and out of control. She maintains that freedom has rules that allow others to be free as well (Greene, 1995).

Take a few minutes to study the existentialism tree in Figure 8.7. Visualizing how teachers might translate the elements of existentialism into their classrooms will help you understand this philosophy of education. Then read what Chris Roberts, one of our focus teachers at Rees Elementary School, says that reflects his philosophy of education.

Points of Reflection 8.5

Do you identify with some of the elements of existentialism? If so, which ones? Do some of the aspects of existentialism in the classroom, as illustrated in Figure 8.7, appeal to you as a prospective teacher? Are there some aspects that do not appeal to you? If so, which ones?

Figure 8.7 Existentialism tree

Teaching in Focus

Chris Roberts, Grades 3–5 Multiage Classroom, Rees Elementary School, Utah. *In his own words. . . .*

I heard or read somewhere that "you teach who you are." I know, after teaching 29 years, that there is a lot of truth in those five words. I've had students return to visit me years after they've been in my class and I get invited to many of their weddings. As we catch up on the years that have passed, none of them talk about their reading or math; they tell me about me. Their memories don't focus on the great unit I taught on Native Americans, but rather on the time I told them about a trip I went on or a belief I have about life. I don't think you can be an excellent teacher if your own life is boring or "unexamined," as Henry David Thoreau would caution. Children will naturally be less interested in learning from someone they find uninteresting. Don't let the classroom, and pressures you will surely face, rule your life. Live a full life. Share with your students what you learn and experience on your amazing path.

OTHER PHILOSOPHIES

Other "isms" may impact educational philosophy. Let's look briefly at some of them.

Idealism is a philosophy based on the belief that ideas are the only reliable form of reality. Idealists believe that because the physical world changes continually, ideas are what should be taught. Taking the opposite stance, **realism** is based on the belief that some facts are absolutes whether recognized by all or not. Realists contend that the only way to know these absolutes is to study the material world.

Romanticism, or naturalism, contends as a philosophy of education that the needs of the individual are more important than the needs of society. Many early childhood and elementary educators incorporate into their classrooms the tenets of romanticism that state that young children are born good, pure, and full of curiosity, and that their individual interests should be validated with opportunities to explore and manipulate elements of their environment.

Postmodernism grew out of a sense that those in power control those who don't have power. Postmodernists believe this control is manifested through major institutions such as schools. The decades of the 1960s and 1970s were times of unprecedented outcries for justice and equality through the civil rights movement, the feminist movement, and a renewed concern for the poor. Postmodernist philosophy grew as a response to these cultural stirrings. The postmodern curriculum includes perspectives on history and literature by a variety of authors representing different lifestyles. Proponents of postmodernism contend they are attempting to strike a balance of power among all people and that intellectual growth from multiple perspectives is one avenue for doing so. Critics of postmodernism contend that the philosophy seeks to promote political purposes rather than intellectual purposes (Ozmon & Craver, 2008).

You will likely encounter other philosophies as you participate in future teacher preparation courses. The ones you have read about so far provide many choices for you to consider as you begin the process of forming your own philosophy of education. This chapter's **The Opinion Page** feature expresses a philosophy of education. The writer has definite opinions about a particular aspect of education that should be included in the opportunities afforded students.

How Do I Begin to Develop My Own Personal Philosophy of Education?

When it comes to developing a philosophy of education, balance is important. If you found yourself aligning with parts of one and parts of another as you read about the prominent philosophies of education, and thinking, "How will I weigh all this and decide?" you are certainly not alone. Very few educators can place themselves squarely

THE OPINION PAGE

This Opinion Editorial appeared in the Las Vegas Sun, *on January 15, 2012.*

Education Should Include Opportunities in Sports, Activities

Jocelyn Jordan commutes to Western High School to play for the girls' basketball team because her school doesn't have a squad . . . sometimes she makes it on time, sometimes she doesn't.

Jordan, a sophomore at Northwest Career Technical Academy, is at the mercy of public transit. Her journey requires her to catch two buses; she sometimes jogs in at the end of practice because of a late bus. When practice or games are over, which can be well into the evening, it's back to the bus stop to go home. She tries to do her homework on the bus so she isn't up too late after finally getting home.

Teammate Tenaya Williams, a sophomore guard at Western, understands that. She takes the bus home, a trip of 3.1 miles. She knows the distance because she has walked the route and measured it.

But, admirably, these young women aren't looking for sympathy—they know that's the price they have to pay for playing high school basketball.

"If you really care about something, you will walk 3.1 miles for it," Williams said. "It's cool. I don't mind having to take the bus or walk."

That is a commendable attitude. It certainly isn't easy for a student to try to juggle school and a sport, particularly when she knows she won't be home until late and may still have to cram in homework. It makes for long days and not much sleep. That's hardly a recipe for student success, and not too long ago, students had a better option. The Clark County School District used to provide bus service to help students who were staying late for extracurricular activities but that service was ended about a decade ago in a round of budget cutting.

The lack of bus service dampens student participation in sports and after-school activities. "I guarantee you a majority of the schools would get more kids involved if we had activity buses," [said] Ray Mathis, the district's executive athletic director. . . . "There are a lot of kids in that situation across the district."

Western is part of the district's "turnaround" effort. It is one of three low-performing high school campuses that are receiving extra money and attention as officials try to boost performance. As part of that effort, school officials should find a way to provide students the opportunity to participate in sports and extracurricular activities by offering some sort of way home.

This may not be a priority in a district that has struggled with low test scores, and it can be easy for some people to wave off sports and activities as "extras," saying schools should be focusing on the basics and raising student achievement. Academics is vitally important, and it's true that raising student performance has to be the priority. But that shouldn't be seen as exclusive of sports and activities. Sports and extracurricular activities are an important part of a student's education. Involvement in activities helps students connect with the school. They also teach important lessons that can't be replicated in a classroom—consider the friendships found among teammates or the bonds formed when students come together in a club to accomplish a task.

Without lessening the importance of academic achievement, life is much more than filling out the right bubble on a standardized test. Any turnaround won't be complete until students have the opportunity to receive a well-rounded education, and that includes the ability to participate in sports and extracurricular activities.

And sometimes that includes help getting there.

This Opinion Page piece expresses a philosophy of education, not necessarily one that fits neatly in one of our five philosophies, but rather a mix of philosophies. Write a well-developed paragraph in response to each of the following questions:

1. Choose two philosophies from this chapter that align with what The Opinion Page expresses. Write about each, briefly explaining why you chose it.

2. Do you support the opinion expressed in The Opinion Page? If so, why? Do you have personal experiences that lead to your support? If you do not agree with The Opinion Page, give your reason(s).

3. Do you agree that it's the school district's responsibility to provide transportation for students who choose to be involved in extracurricular activities? If so, why? If not, why not?

in one camp or another. Picking and choosing from among the components of several philosophies is referred to as taking an *eclectic approach*. This entails balance. It's natural for teachers to lean toward one philosophy or approach more than another, but subscribing to only one philosophy will not serve the needs of all children. Chartock (2004) states, "For every belief there is an equal and opposite belief and data to support both. That's why the field of education is never dull" (p. 136). Never dull, indeed.

As we established early in this chapter, we all have philosophies. They may be consciously held, or they may just be "how we are" or "what we think." But one thing's for sure, our philosophies become evident when we make decisions or when an issue arises. In Figure 8.8 we look at three of our focus teachers and their philosophical bents.

Figure 8.8 Philosophy of education and our focus teachers

The eclectic approach applies to our focus teachers. Now that you know more about progressivism, it's obvious that all 10 of our focus teachers exemplify large measures of this philosophy. Examining what we know about them, none appear to adhere to the perennialism philosophy. This philosophy is more likely to be exemplified by college instructors than by K–12 teachers. Let's consider the roles that essentialism, social reconstructionism, and existentialism play in the teaching of three of our focus teachers. Refer to the philosophy trees to better understand the explanation of how our focus teachers align with not only progressivism, but also another philosophy.

Derek Boucher and Essentialism

Watch Derek's interview, room tour, and lesson to help you think more clearly about his philosophy of education. Looking at the essentialism philosophy tree, let's think about which characteristics Derek displays in his approach to teaching and learning.

- Teacher branch: Derek definitely believes that his responsibilities include being an *intellectual/moral role model*. He expresses in his interview that teachers are role models and the importance of exemplifying good citizenship.
- Student branch: Derek emphasizes the need for *hard work* in order to achieve. He reminds his students regularly that what they learn depends on their determination and willingness to work.
- Curriculum branch: Derek's position as a reading teacher in a high school setting speaks to his belief that the *basics* are important. He knows that reading and writing proficiency is the key to a successful future for his students, many of whom are English language learners.
- Instruction branch: Derek has a strong interest in *proven methods* of instruction. He is adamant about doing what's research-based rather than whatever current fad is being promoted. In his interview we hear him express this.

Brenda Beyal and Social Reconstructivism

You watched Brenda's interview in the beginning of this chapter. Now watch Brenda's room tour and lesson to help you think more clearly about Brenda's philosophy of education. Examining Brenda's personal philosophy tree in Figure 8.9 and the social reconstructivism philosophy tree in Figure 8.6, we can easily see the similarities.

- Teacher branch: Brenda feels an intense need to help her students develop a *sense of personal responsibility* for themselves and for society. Her deeply-held pride in her Native American heritage influences this strong desire for students to understand that the world is bigger than just themselves and their immediate family and friends, and that unless we all work together, society will not thrive.
- Learning Environment branch: We see in Brenda's lesson that *community building* is important to her. The groups working on tableaus in the lesson have much to do together to accomplish their tasks. She provides choices and allows the students to take responsibility for the products of the lesson.
- Instruction branch: Brenda believes that given the tools to do so, students will discover or *construct knowledge*. Because she incorporates cooperative learning, she values *group work*.

Craig Cleveland and Existentialism

You watched Craig's interview, room tour, and lesson in Chapter 2. Reviewing all three brief videos will help you think more clearly about his philosophy of education. Looking at the existentialism philosophy tree, let's think about which characteristics Craig displays in his approach to teaching and learning.

- Teacher branch: Craig must teach the *whole child* because of, among other reasons, the language diversity in his classes. Also, we know that Craig welcomes students between classes to show he appreciates their *individuality* expressed outside class time.
- Student branch: In his lessons, Craig emphasizes to students that their *choices* matter. He helps students develop critical thinking tools to take *personal responsibility*, make decisions and communicate them.
- Learning Environment branch: In his lesson, Craig has students working collaboratively to develop a skit that portrays one of the Jim Crow laws. Students are encouraged to differentiate among the inequities the laws perpetuated and *democratic approaches*.
- Instruction branch: Students are given choices concerning their group approaches to the lesson assignment. They must weigh the choices and *make decisions*.

Figure 8.9 Brenda's philosophy tree

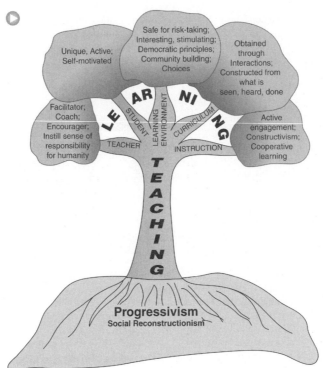

Aspects related to branches of philosophy that are addressed in Brenda's class include:

Epistemology—ways of knowing Brenda's "calling" as knowing based on divine revelation

Axiology—What is just and unjust?
Smoky Night theme

Axiology—How should we judge the quality of what we see, hear, and touch? art-infused curriculum

YOUR TURN

Now it's your turn to grow a philosophy tree. The root system will consist of an anchor philosophy, the philosophy with which you most closely align. There's no need to ascribe to every tenet of this anchor philosophy, but it should express most of your current beliefs about teaching and learning. Other philosophies may be part of the feeder root system. The branches and leaves of the tree's canopy will be a mix of what you believe about the roles of the teacher, students, the learning environment, the curriculum, and instruction. Keep in mind that the deeper and wider the philosophical root system, the stronger and more stable the trunk will grow and the richer and more extensive the canopy will be.

Figure 8.10 is a tree waiting for you to make it your own. Your philosophy tree can be a valuable component of the teaching portfolio you will no doubt develop as part of your teacher preparation.

One approach to help begin examining your own philosophy is to study the content of Table 8.1 carefully. Considering the responses to the important and broad questions in the table is a way to explore your own philosophical views. There are many questions that may be asked, with each philosophy of education contributing unique responses.

Another approach to growing your philosophy tree is to spend some time thinking about your favorite teachers in early childhood, elementary, middle, and high school. Why did you admire them? What made them special? Your answers need to go beyond "She was so nice" or "He just stands out in my mind." To help you think through the reasons particular teachers had positive effects on you, put a special teacher's name on the chart in Table 8.2. Then think about how this person appeared to view his or her roles as a teacher, including relationships with

Brenda, one of our focus teachers at Rees Elementary, demonstrates her skills during a field trip with her students.

Figure 8.10 My philosophy tree

TABLE 8.1 Sample questions and philosophical responses

Question	Essentialism	Perennialism	Progressivism	Reconstructionism	Existentialism
What is real?	Elements of core curriculum; may change	Elements of core curriculum; unchanging	What can be verified through the senses	What can be verified through research and analysis	Based entirely on the individual's perspective and experience
How do we acquire knowledge?	From a combination of the classics and science	From the never-changing classics	From individual experiences and discovery	From individual and group searches for meaning and justice	Through individual quests; making choices
What is valuable?	Core of knowledge that responds to some societal shifts	Changeless core of knowledge	Determined by individual interacting with own culture	Whatever makes society more just and equitable	Whatever leads to greater self-knowledge
What makes sense?	Classics provide generalizations; specifics are deduced; observation and analysis of specifics may lead to generalization	Deductive reasoning from truths of classics	Discovered through problem solving	Weighed against potential benefit or harm to society	Whatever enhances individual freedom and increases personal responsibility

TABLE 8.2 My favorite teachers' philosophical bents						
Teacher's Name	Teacher's Role	Interactions with Students	Learning Environment	Curriculum	Instruction	Aligned with Which Philosophy?

students, the creation of the learning environment, and approaches to curriculum and instruction. Table 8.2 will help organize your recollections.

A sincere, honest start to the development of a philosophy of education will help grow you into the teaching profession. Having opportunities to talk about your philosophy and listen to your classmates, your instructor, and teachers in the field will make you more comfortable articulating your stance. The more you think, talk, and listen, the more confident you will become that you are grounded in your reasons for how you approach your role, your students, the learning environment, curriculum, and instruction.

CONCLUDING THOUGHTS

Chances are that a philosophy of education is not something you've ever seriously considered. Now you have some background about major branches of philosophy, as well as philosophies of education. You have been prompted to think about, and tentatively declare, which philosophy represents your primary beliefs about teaching and learning. You also know that an eclectic approach is not only natural but will actually benefit the diverse groups of students you will no doubt encounter.

Thoughtful teachers are not necessarily swayed by gimmicks and fads. They have basic beliefs about teaching and learning that guide their practice, and they can articulate the bases for their decisions. These are teachers who will positively affect student learning throughout their careers. This applies equally to early childhood, elementary, middle, and high school teachers. A carefully considered philosophy of education provides a solid foundation for professionals in the classroom.

After reading the *Chapter in Review,* read more about Brenda and respond to items in this chapter's *Developing Professional Competence*.

Chapter in Review

Why is a philosophy of education important?

- We all have philosophies that guide our decisions, attitudes, and actions.
- A teacher's philosophy of education affects every decision about teaching.

How do the prominent philosophies of education affect teaching and learning?

- Essentialism is a philosophy of education based on the belief that there is a core curriculum that is responsive to the times and that every American should know.
- Perennialism is a philosophy of education based on the belief that there is a changeless core curriculum that every American should know.
- Progressivism is a philosophy of education that focuses on a curriculum of interest to students and experiential learning.

- Social reconstructionism is a philosophy of education that endorses a curriculum that benefits society by promoting equity.
- Existentialism is a philosophy of education that focuses on the individual's search for meaning.

How do I begin to develop my personal philosophy of education?

- Incorporating components of more than one philosophy of education into your personal philosophy is an eclectic approach.
- Growing an effective philosophy tree requires a strong root system with philosophical grounding to enhance both teaching and learning.

Developing Professional Competence

Thoughtfully reading this scenario and responding to the items that follow it will help you prepare for licensure exams.

Brenda Beyal ascribes to a very student-centered philosophy of education, as we have seen in her interview, room tour, lesson, philosophy tree in Figure 8.9, and what we have read in *Teaching in Focus*. She knows the content she teaches and works very hard to be the best teacher she can be. The one thing that continually bothers Brenda is the fact that we are in an era of standards, where curriculum is prescribed and teaching is on a fast-paced schedule. Add to this the week of standardized tests she must monitor every spring, and we find Brenda seeking balance for her students and innovative ways to accomplish what is expected of her while paying attention to individual student needs.

One of Brenda's favorite authors is Vito Perrone (1991). Here is an excerpt that is particularly poignant for her:

> To engage students constructively, the school day needs more continuities, not more fragmentation. Work that can truly be valued takes time, sometimes hours and days. It is hardly reasonable to expect a child to complete a fine piece of artwork in ten- or twenty-minute intervals, twice a week, or produce a well-organized, thoughtful description, a poetic or narrative story within ten minutes. Teachers know this but claim that in this current basic skills, testing, "academic" environment, they don't have the time any more for work of that quality. (p. 33)

Given what we know about Brenda, answer these multiple-choice questions:

1. What do you think Brenda considers a source of fragmentation of her teaching day?
   a. District administrative guidelines that outline the time to be spent each day on language arts, reading, math, science, and social studies.
   b. Her students go to dance/movement class with Chris Roberts in the morning and to music/theater class with Tim Mendenhall in the afternoon.
   c. She has an early lunch time with her class.
   d. Rees incorporates two recess times a day.

2. Brenda attributes her agreement with Perrone's point about what is valuable in schoolwork to her Native American heritage. What might be the best of these four options for Brenda to let students know about her opinion?
   a. She could teach the students some of the soothing chants and tunes Native American mothers sing to their children.
   b. She could share artifacts and talk with students about how they are preserved.
   c. She could tell them stories about patience and perseverance from Native American folklore.
   d. She could explain to students the meaningfulness of the sundial and how Native Americans have historically honored the sun.

Now it's time for you to respond to three short essay items involving Brenda. In your responses, be sure to address all the dilemmas and questions posed in each item. Your responses should each be between one half and one full double-spaced page.

3. Which do Brenda and Vito Perrone appear to value more: progress of a group or progress of the individual? Explain your response.

4. Perrone writes about "continuities." What kinds of activities do you think Brenda would put in this category? Explain two continuities you would expect to see in her classroom.

5. How might Brenda incorporate balance into the day as she teaches the standards while valuing quality and creativity?

Realities of Teaching and Learning

In **PART IV** we consider many of the realities of the teaching profession. Chapter 9 *is not* a happy chapter. In fact, the issues involved in the societal context of our students' lives will likely make you uncomfortable and sad. Nonetheless, understanding that many of our students come to us already psychologically—and perhaps physically—bruised and battered by poverty, violence, health issues, racism, and other issues that prove to be barriers to success in school is necessary to help us recognize the tremendous responsibilities involved in teaching. Chapter 10 deals with how laws and ethics affect what we do and how we do it. Chapter 11 presents governance and finance information all teachers should understand as engaged citizens as well as educators. Finally, Chapter 12 addresses the necessity of approaching relationships, realities, and reform in professional ways.

Where Do I Stand ?

This inventory focuses on professionalism, a way of life that should permeate your relationships, always be a reality for you, and propel reform that benefits teaching and learning. As you think through the following statements that prompt you to consider your own views, indicate your level of agreement by choosing a number and placing it in the blank before the statement. Following the inventory are directions for how to organize your responses and what they may mean in terms of where you stand.

4 I strongly agree
3 I agree
2 I don't have an opinion
1 I disagree
0 I strongly disagree

> ▶ **Click Here to Complete Survey**

_____ 1. Professionalism entails meeting responsibilities head on, as well as taking full advantage of opportunities involving teaching and learning.

_____ 2. One of the most valuable aspects of a teacher preparation program is the opportunity to spend time in schools.

_____ 3. Becoming a professional entails reflecting on field experiences in schools.

_____ 4. Upon graduation, a teacher candidate has time to develop professional attitudes and actions.

_____ 5. Being positive is a choice. It doesn't mean glossing over difficulties but rather approaching each day with possibilities in focus.

_____ 6. Core courses, although interesting, have little bearing on teacher preparation.

_____ 7. It is very important to respect the adults and students in your school.

_____ 8. Spending time in schools is peripheral to learning to be a teacher.

_____ 9. Becoming a professional involves field experiences that let you see reality, reflect on what you see, and formulate possible solutions to the dilemmas you observe.

_____ 10. Learning what not to do as a result of seeing its actual, or potential, damage is powerful.

_____ 11. Being realistic about schools is counter to being positive about the possibilities of quality education.

_____ 12. When we fulfill our responsibilities and take advantage of our opportunities involving relationships, we are doing so for the children and adolescents we teach.

_____ 13. We only learn valuable lessons in professionalism from positive role models.

_____ 14. Teachers who take responsibility for student learning take no excuses—from students, parents, or themselves.

_____ 15. Part of professionalism entails teaching the whole child, requiring that we accept students for who they are rather than what they do.

_____ 16. When conditions outside the classroom are severely impaired, making a positive difference for kids within our classrooms is close to impossible.

_____ 17. When we take responsibility for teaching all students unconditionally, regardless of the circumstances, we will necessarily have high expectations for them.

_____ 18. The way schools care about children is reflected in the way schools care about the children's families.

_____ 19. Parental involvement is actually an interference in many instances.

_____ 20. Parental involvement matters to student achievement.

_____ 21. Teachers need to grasp the reality of parental concern and tenaciously find ways to involve them.

_____ 22. Professional courtesy dictates that teachers not observe one another in their classrooms because of the possibility of being judgmental.

_____ 23. Whatever the barriers to parental involvement, teachers need to strive continually to break them down by cultivating an invitational attitude.

_____ 24. Part of being a professional teacher is knowing what is available and, along with administrators and counselors, making sure families are aware of how to access community services.

_____ 25. Although teachers have responsibility for the welfare of students in their classrooms while in school, they bear little responsibility for their relationships with students' families.

_____ 26. Professional growth is an absolute necessity for teacher effectiveness.

_____ 27. There is always something to be learned when teachers get together, regardless of the perceived quality or relevance of what is formally presented.

_____ 28. Teachers have a responsibility to join professional organizations to help build the teaching profession.

_____ 29. Classrooms and groups of children benefit from engaging lessons, but this does not promote the professionalism of teaching.

_____ 30. When a teacher tries an instructional strategy that works well with a particular topic, or with a specific group of students, sharing the experience with other teachers is an act of professionalism.

Now record your responses, find the sum of each column, and then divide each sum by 10 to determine A, B, and C.

ITEM #	MY RESPONSE	ITEM #	MY RESPONSE	ITEM #	MY RESPONSE
1		17		4	
2		18		6	
3		20		8	
5		21		11	
7		23		13	
9		24		16	
10		26		19	
12		27		22	
14		28		25	
15		30		29	
Sum=		Sum=		Sum=	
÷10=	=A	÷10=	=B	÷10=	=C

Now subtract C from 4 because C indicates levels of disagreement with negative concepts. This new number becomes D, a positive indicator.

Add A, B, and D and divide the sum by 3. Plot this number on the number line to see where you fall on a continuum of professional attitudes.

Does your place on the number line accurately reflect where you think you are with regard to teacher professionalism? If so, why? If not, why not?

The Societal Context of Schooling in the United States

Dear Reader

This chapter is about the realities that touch the lives of students in our classrooms. Although these issues don't affect all students or families in a negative way, they do reach into all settings—urban, suburban, and rural. They affect all races and all ethnicities in both affluent neighborhoods and impoverished ones. And they affect both U.S. citizens and noncitizens.

The issue of poverty has far-reaching negative effects on students and their success. It's hard for most of us to understand what it's like to move when the rent comes due. Yes, the negative influences of poverty can be overcome, but it's a difficult road to travel. Even so, teachers can help children and adolescents travel it more productively. Issues involving childhood and teen obesity, substance abuse, and risky sexual behavior are also serious challenges that will likely be with us for a long time. We are working on impacting student choices. The guarded good news is that drug, alcohol, and tobacco use, as well as many risky sexual behaviors, have either leveled off or are declining. Helping children and adolescents make wise choices continues to be a major teacher responsibility.

Brown v. *Board of Education*, the landmark case that led to school desegregation, was decided 60 years ago, and yet we still deal with issues revolving around race. All too often violence, theft, and bullying exist in society and in schools. Creating respectful environments of civility is the responsibility of teachers who are watchful and wise.

This chapter examines elements that make up the complex societal context in which schooling occurs, including responses to these questions:

- How do family, community, and society impact students in the United States?
- How does socioeconomic status affect students in the United States?
- How do health issues affect students in the United States?
- How does race affect students in the United States?
- What are the effects of bullying, theft, and violence on students and schools in the United States?
- How do truancy and dropping out affect youth in the United States?

Teaching in Focus

Her 14 years in the classroom have allowed Brandi Wade, one of our focus teachers at Summit Primary School in Ohio, to see her first group of kindergarteners graduate from high school—or not. She has watched her students progress through primary, elementary, middle, and high school. She has seen some cope and thrive, and others become involved in destructive lifestyles. One thing she knows for sure is that success is more likely for some than for others. Thus she continually adjusts and differentiates.

In early December Brandi decided that she needed to change some of her routines and instructional strategies. She had lived with her kindergartners 5 days a week for more than 3 months, and she knew some of them were not yet thriving. Her experience had taught her that treating these 5- and 6-year-olds equally was not going to meet their needs.

Brandi's decision to make some general changes in her classroom, including a new seating arrangement,

a new rule-and-consequence system, a heavier reliance on one-on-one instructional strategies, and a buddy plan, came as a result of her consideration of the students in her class.

Brandi's realistic view—that some of her students will struggle more than others—lowers neither her hopes nor her expectations for all her students. Regardless of the strikes against them, Brandi maintains that her children can and will learn. She knows that challenges for her children may come in many forms. Students raised in poverty face particular challenges. Children who are minorities face other challenges. Children who live in relative wealth, but with few restraints or little structure, are challenged in other ways. All of Brandi's students need academic and interpersonal skills, along with self-confidence and the ability to make reasoned decisions. All are, or will be, at risk in some way. Revisit **Brandi's room tour and interview** to hear again about her philosophy of education.

After reading the title of this chapter, you may be asking why the opening scenario would be about Brandi Wade, a kindergarten teacher. The answer is actually simple: Social issues do not suddenly appear in the lives of adolescents. The societal context of students' lives surrounds them from birth. By the time children are in kindergarten, many influences have already shaped them. Brandi is very aware of the fact that her students enter kindergarten with individual histories as well as their present circumstances. They do not come to her, as educators once believed, as blank slates. Many already have strikes against them not of their own making, such as poverty or a family that doesn't value education. Brandi understands the saying, "There's nothing so unequal as the equal treatment of unequals." Think about this.

How Do Family, Community, and Society Impact Students in the United States?

The most basic societal unit of humankind is the family. Families exist within communities, and communities make up the larger building blocks of any society. This relationship, as illustrated in Figure 9.1, creates a pattern of influence that is undeniable. When children are very young, the family has the most direct influence. As they grow, the community plays a bigger role in children's lives. The influence of society grows immensely stronger with age.

For some children, family life is idyllic and supportive; for others, it is not. Some children's families live in communities that are peaceful and caring; others live in the midst of destruction and violence. Although they all live within the same society, some children in the United States are shielded from some negative influences by family and community, and others are not.

FAMILY

Family diversity is discussed in Chapter 2.

Family is a source of diversity. Regardless of what a family may look like or the societal pressures the family may experience, members of families can support student success—or thwart it.

Figure 9.1 Individual, family, community, society

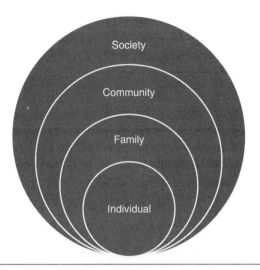

Many children and adolescents are victims of abuse and neglect, which places them squarely in the at-risk category. **Child abuse** is any act that results in death, serious harm, or exploitation; **child neglect** is a form of abuse resulting from a failure to act in the best interest of the child. Five children died each day in 2010 as a result of abuse or neglect. The United States has the worst record of child abuse–related deaths among all industrialized nations (ChildHelp, 2013). This fact should alarm all of us. Table 9.1 consists of percentages of child fatalities in 2011 by gender, age, race, and perpetrator. Tragic, indeed. Examining the data in Table 9.1 indicates that African American, Hispanic, and White children comprise about 90 percent of the fatalities, with African American children dying at the highest rate of almost four per 100,000. Remember as you review the table that the majority race of people in the United States is White, while the African American race comprises only about 12% of our population. Although the percentage of total 2011 child abuse and neglect fatalities is led by White children (41%), the actual rate (1.6 per 100,000) is lower than all other categories except for Asian and Pacific Islander children. Children of two or more races had the next highest number of fatalities after African American children with almost three per 100,000. More fatalities were male than female, and the perpetrators were 78% likely to be parents. It is also appalling to realize that over 90% of the fatalities due to child abuse and neglect in 2011 were predominantly those most vulnerable, children under the age of 8.

Allegations of child abuse and neglect received by agencies of the U.S. Department of Health & Human Services (DHHS) go through a screening process to determine if child maltreatment is likely. If it is, the allegation is turned over to Child Protective Services (CPS) and considered a report of child abuse or neglect. According to the National Child Abuse and Neglect Data System (NCANDS), more than two million reports of abuse and neglect were reported and investigated, with approximately 700,000 children victims of child abuse or neglect in 2011. Although this number is disturbing, NCANDS reports that it represents only the tip of the iceberg. For a case of abuse or neglect to be included in government statistics, it must be reported, meet the established definition, and be investigated. Some forms of neglect, as well as both sexual and emotional abuse, have few recognizable symptoms to a casual observer. The maltreatment can remain undiscovered for an entire childhood. The recorded cases could actually represent millions of victimized children and adolescents. By some estimates, as many as 60% of deaths by abuse are not reported as abuse cases (DHHS, 2011).

It is difficult to determine the scope of the toll that child abuse takes on children and adolescents in the United States. For many, it's hard to imagine the reasons or the results of such cruelty. For some students, teachers and school personnel are their most trusted adults. In fact, about 60% of child abuse and neglect incidents are reported by teachers, police officers, lawyers, and CPS staff, with 16% reported by teachers alone.

TABLE 9.1 Child abuse and neglect fatalities by gender, age, race, and perpetrator, 2011

Gender	Percentage
Male	59
Female	41
Age	
0–3 years	82
4–8 years	9
5–17 years	9
Race	
African American	28 (3.9 per 100,000)
American/Alaskan Native	1 (2.6 per 100,000)
Asian	1 (.4 per 100,000)
Hispanic	18 (1.9 per 100,000)
Pacific Islander	.1 (1.2 per 100,000)
White	41 (1.6 per 100,000)
Two or more races	4 (2.9 per 100,00)
Unknown	7
Perpetrator	
Father	15
Father and other	2
Mother	26
Mother and other	13
Father and mother	22
Other	22

Source: U.S. Department of Health & Human Services, 2011, *Child Maltreatment 2011*. http://www.acf.hhs.gov/sites/default/files/cb/cm11 .pdf#page=69

Points of Reflection 9.1

How familiar are you with child and adolescent abuse and neglect? Do you have personal experiences with abuse or neglect? Do you know people who were victims of abuse? Briefly explain.

What can schools and teachers do? School personnel are among those required to report suspected abuse. Also included are social workers, health-care workers, mental health professionals, child-care providers, medical examiners or coroners, and law enforcement officers. Teachers should report suspicions to administrators or guidance counselors. Any citizen may report suspicions of abuse to any Child Protection Services agency or to ChildHelp at 800-4-A-CHILD (800-422-4453).

As a teacher, you may be the adult who comes between a child and a lifetime of suffering or, worse, death. Knowing the signs of neglect and abuse is an important first step. Figure 9.2 lists the signs provided by Child Welfare Information Gateway. Read how focus teacher Tim Mendenhall sees his impact on families in ***Teaching in Focus***.

COMMUNITY AND SOCIETY

Previous chapters have discussed the concept of community as it refers to relationships in a classroom or school. In this section, **community** refers to the neighborhood, town, city, or county in which a student lives. The members of a community are those who live within a specific geographic vicinity, those with whom students

Figure 9.2 Recognizing child abuse

The following signs may signal the presence of child abuse or neglect.

In general, the **child:**

- Shows sudden changes in behavior or school performance.
- Has not received help for physical or medical problems brought to the parents' attention.
- Has learning problems (or difficulty concentrating) that cannot be attributed to specific physical or psychological causes
- Is always watchful, as though preparing for something bad to happen.
- Lacks adult supervision.
- Is overly compliant, passive, or withdrawn.
- Comes to school or other activities early, stays late, and does not want to go home.
- Is reluctant to be around a particular person.
- Discloses maltreatment.

In general, the **parent:**

- Denies the existence of—or blames the child for—the child's problems in school or at home.
- Asks teachers or other caregivers to use harsh physical discipline if the child misbehaves.
- Sees the child as entirely bad, worthless, or burdensome.
- Demands a level of physical or academic performance the child cannot achieve.
- Looks primarily to the child for care, attention, and satisfaction of the parent's emotional needs.
- Shows little concern for the child.

In general, the **parent and child:**

- Rarely touch or look at each other.
- Consider their relationship entirely negative.
- State that they do not like each other.

Here are the signs of child physical, sexual, and emotional abuse, as well as the signs of neglect.

Signs of Physical Abuse

Consider the possibility of physical abuse when the **child:**

- Has unexplained burns, bites, bruises, broken bones, or black eyes.
- Has fading bruises or other marks noticeable after an absence from school.
- Seems frightened of the parents and protests or cries when it is time to go home.
- Shrinks at the approach of adults.
- Reports injury by a parent or another adult caregiver.
- Abuses animals or pets.

Consider the possibility of physical abuse when the **parent or other adult caregiver:**

- Offers conflicting, unconvincing, or no explanation for the child's injury, or provides an explanation that is not consistent with the injury.
- Describes the child as "evil" or in some other very negative way.
- Uses harsh physical discipline with the child.
- Has a history of abuse as a child.
- Has a history of abusing animals or pets.

Signs of Neglect

Consider the possibility of neglect when the **child:**

- Is frequently absent from school.
- Begs or steals food or money.
- Lacks needed medical or dental care, immunizations, or glasses
- Is consistently dirty and has severe body odor
- Lacks sufficient clothing for the weather
- Abuses alcohol or other drugs

Consider the possibility of neglect when the **parent or other adult caregiver:**

- Appears to be indifferent to the child.
- Seems apathetic or depressed.
- Behaves irrationally or in a bizarre manner.
- Is abusing alcohol or other drugs.

(continued)

Figure 9.2 (*continued*)

Signs of Sexual Abuse

Consider the possibility of sexual abuse when the **child:**

- Has difficulty walking or sitting.
- Suddenly refuses to change for gym or to participate in physical activities.
- Reports nightmares or bedwetting.
- Experiences a sudden change in appetite.
- Demonstrates bizarre, sophisticated, or unusual sexual knowledge or behavior.
- Becomes pregnant or contracts a venereal disease, particularly if under age 14.
- Runs away.
- Reports sexual abuse by a parent or another adult caregiver.
- Attaches very quickly to strangers or new adults in their environment.

Consider the possibility of sexual abuse when the **parent or other adult caregiver:**

- Is unduly protective of the child or severely limits the child's contact with other children, especially of the opposite sex.
- Is secretive and isolated.
- Is jealous or controlling with family members.

Signs of Emotional Maltreatment

Consider the possibility of emotional maltreatment when the **child:**

- Shows extremes in behavior, such as overly compliant or demanding behavior, extreme passivity, or aggression.
- Is either inappropriately adult (parenting other children, for example) or inappropriately infantile (frequently rocking or head-banging, for example).
- Is delayed in physical or emotional development.
- Has attempted suicide.
- Reports a lack of attachment to the parent.

Consider the possibility of emotional maltreatment when the **parent or other adult caregiver:**

- Constantly blames, belittles, or berates the child.
- Is unconcerned about the child and refuses to consider offers of help for the child's problems.
- Overtly rejects the child.

Source: From Child Welfare Information Gateway, 2013. *What Is Child Abuse and Neglect? Recognizing the Signs and Symptoms.* Retrieved August 31, 2013, from https://www.childwelfare.gov/pubs/factsheets/whatiscan.cfm

Teaching in Focus

Tim Mendenhall, Grades 3–5 Multiage Classroom, Rees Elementary School, Utah. *In his own words. . . .*

I have found that my influence goes beyond the classroom. It overflows into the home as well. My relationships with students are built before and after school and in the hallways. Their siblings look forward to being in my classroom. I get to know parents through my students, at parent-teacher conferences, and while working with parent volunteers. I take the time to build relationships with parents. I have found that students and their families become fiercely loyal to teachers who care. It hit me when one of my student's parents said, "I feel I can come to you anytime with a problem with my child and you listen." Education is a partnership, and the more bridges we build, the more it benefits our students.

may come in contact through everyday activities like shopping or when seeking services.

Most towns, cities, and counties provide services such as medical facilities; utilities (electric, gas, and water); welfare and Medicaid; some form of counseling or assistance; law enforcement; recreation opportunities; and schools. The available services vary. Some students and their families live in communities that support healthy lifestyles. In these communities traditional measures of success—economic stability, nonviolent approaches to problem solving, and education—are valued and promoted.

Unfortunately, many students live in communities that not only are nonsupportive, but also may actually be harmful to them. Some neighborhoods and communities are filled with violence and drugs, where children and adolescents are exposed to unhealthy lifestyles. For many children, negative influences of society will be mitigated by positive forces, such as supportive families, higher socioeconomic status, or membership in the majority race. Other children will suffer proportionately more from negative societal influences due, at least in part, to poverty.

What can schools and teachers do? Regardless of the community in which a student lives, there are havens that provide private and government services. Teachers need to be knowledgeable about the services available to students and their families and provide them with information about how they can use those services to improve their lives.

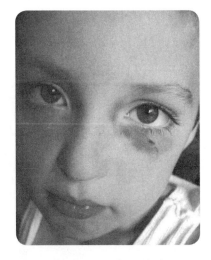

Teachers are obligated by law to report suspected child abuse. Some symptoms are more noticeable than others.

How Does Socioeconomic Status Affect Students in the United States?

We may think we know what "poor" looks like: the house, the car, the neighborhood, the need for a warm coat and school supplies, hunger, and meals supplied through Title I free breakfast and lunch programs. But Richard Rothstein (2008), a researcher who analyzes poverty's effects, tells us to look more deeply to see the multitude of effects that may accompany poverty. If two groups of students attend the same quality school, but one group is distinctly disadvantaged in terms of socioeconomic status (SES), the group with low SES will achieve at lower levels. This is true not only according to Rothstein but also according to statistics kept in almost every school setting. "Each of these disadvantages makes only a small contribution to the achievement gap, but cumulatively, they explain a lot" (Rothstein, 2008, p. 8). Rothstein lists some of the disadvantages, stating that children in low-SES settings may have:

- no routine medical and dental care, leading to more absences
- increased likelihood of asthma, often resulting in sleeplessness, irritability, lack of exercise
- lower birth weight, resulting in many possible health issues
- lead poisoning and iron-deficiency anemia, each leading to cognitive and behavioral difficulties
- more mobility when the rent comes due, resulting in less school continuity
- greater family stress due to employment uncertainty, often resulting in arbitrary discipline
- fewer adult role models with professional careers
- more likelihood of living in single-parent homes
- fewer family vacations, trips to museums and zoos
- fewer opportunities for dance lessons, music instruction, organized sports teams, cultural awareness, and other activities that build confidence

Keep in mind that these are generalizations, and not stereotypes. Individual students living in poverty may display some, all, or none of these characteristics. In addition, Eric Jensen (2009, p. 19), veteran educator and expert researcher concerning brain function, tells us that "children raised in poverty are more likely to display

- 'Acting-out' behaviors.
- Impatience and impulsivity.
- Gaps in politeness and social graces.
- A more limited range of behavioral responses.

- Inappropriate emotional responses.
- Less empathy for others' misfortunes."

Points of Reflection 9.2

Think about the community in which you spent all or a portion of your childhood. Was it a supportive community with people and services that contributed to your overall well-being? Or did you encounter situations that made it more difficult to grow and learn? Briefly explain.

Table 9.2 shows the percentages of children living in homes with incomes below the poverty line. Nationally, this percentage is 23%, with New Hampshire at the lowest percentage (12%) and Mississippi having the highest percentage (32%). Given that over 50 million children and adolescents are in public schools each day, that's about 12 million kids living in poverty in our classrooms. Some say that emphasis on the disadvantages of poor children gives educators excuses for why these children don't learn at the levels of other children. On the contrary, awareness of these and other disadvantages provides teachers a more realistic view of what our mission involves. Excuses are unacceptable; understanding is invaluable.

TABLE 9.2 Percent of children in families living in poverty by state, 2011

States		Percentage of Children Living in Poverty
New Hampshire		12%
Maryland		14%
Vermont Connecticut Massachusetts North Dakota	Alaska New Jersey Virginia Minnesota	15%
Wyoming Utah		16%
Iowa Delaware	Hawaii	17%
Colorado South Dakota Wisconsin	Washington Nebraska	18%
Kansas Maine		19%
Montana Pennsylvania	Idaho	20%
Rhode Island Nevada	Illinois Missouri	22%
Oklahoma Indiana	California New York	23%
Ohio Oregon		24%
Florida Michigan		25%
Tennessee West Virginia	Georgia North Carolina	26%
Kentucky Texas	Arizona	27%
Arkansas South Carolina	Alabama	28%
Louisiana		29%
New Mexico		31%
Mississippi		32%
United States Percentage		23%

Source: *The Annie E. Casey Foundation 2012 Kids Count Data Book*. Baltimore: Annie E. Casey Foundation, 2013.

Mark Rank, researcher in the area of poverty and children, tells us that half of all children in America will live in households that make use of food stamps at some time in their first 18 years of life. Even more startling is the fact that nearly 90% of African American children will have this experience. "Taken as a whole, the negative impact of poverty on children's overall health status is reflected in the fact that it has been estimated that poverty among American children raises the direct expenditures on health care by approximately $22 billion per year" (Rank & Hirschl, 2009, p. 998).

HOMELESS CHILDREN AND YOUTH

Perhaps the most devastating impact of poverty is homelessness. The United States has more homeless children and women than any other industrialized nation (Shine Global, 2012). The federal government defines homeless children and youth as those who lack a fixed, regular, and adequate nighttime residence. The children and youth may share overcrowded temporary housing (72%) or live in emergency or transitional shelters (18%) or in motels (5%) due to lack of alternative adequate accommodations. About 5% of the children in homeless families have little to no shelter and may spend nights in cars, parks, public spaces, abandoned buildings, substandard housing, bus or train stations, or similar settings (National Center for Homeless Education, 2012). Just reading this definition is troubling; imagine what life must be like for the children who live it.

In the 2010–2011 school year, the U.S. government estimates that there were more than 1 million homeless children enrolled in public schools. This number is an underestimate of the total homeless children population, with more than 41% of the entire homeless population composed of families (National Center for Homeless Education, 2012). The severe economic downturn of 2008 resulted in an 11% increase in the number of homeless children from 2008 to 2011. Many families that had homes in 2008 or 2009 lost them and became homeless. Causes of homelessness among children fall into three interrelated categories: family problems, economic problems, and residential instability. Regardless of the cause, recent evidence confirms that homelessness among families is increasing (National Coalition for the Homeless, 2009b).

The **McKinney-Vento Act** of 1987 is part of the federal government's response to homelessness. The act addresses the problems homeless children and youth face in enrolling, attending, and succeeding in school (National Center for Homeless Education, 2012). Because of this act, homeless students are assured of:

- equal access to the same free, appropriate public education
- a public preschool education
- comparable educational services, including transportation and meals
- a mainstream school environment, free from being stigmatized in any way

Homelessness is a devastating experience for families—it disrupts every aspect of family life, causes physical and emotional damage, interferes with children's education and development, and often results in the separation of children from parents. Figure 9.3 lists certain generalizations about the conditions in which homeless children live and the effects of homelessness on their parents.

Although generalizations may be useful for understanding children and planning learning experiences, it is important not to lump all low-income or homeless students together as a group and design programs based on only one element of their lives—their socioeconomic status (Landsman, 2006). This kind of categorizing flies in the face of all we know about student learning differences and the value of getting to know students individually.

What can schools and teachers do? Strategies for teaching students who live in low socioeconomic conditions are found in Figure 9.4. When we consider ways to meet the needs of children and adolescents living in poverty, Landsman tells us, "Teachers need to see assets and possibility where conventional eyes often see a dead end" (2006, p. 32). What excellent advice.

Points of Reflection 9.3

With what socioeconomic status (SES) group(s) are you most familiar? How did your own SES affect your school days?

Figure 9.3 Impact of homelessness on families

Homeless parents and their children are more likely to have experienced violence and to be separated from each other.

- Domestic violence is the second most frequently stated cause of homelessness for families.
- One out of three homeless teens has witnessed a stabbing, shooting, rape, or murder in their community.
- Homelessness is the most important predictor of the separation of mothers from their children.
- 34% of school-aged homeless children have lived apart from their families.
- 62% of children placed in foster care come from formerly homeless families.

Homeless children have less of a chance of succeeding in school.

- Homeless children are more likely than housed children to be held back a grade.
- Homeless children have higher rates of school mobility and grade retention than low-income housed children.
- Frequent school transfers are the most significant barrier to the academic success of homeless students.

Homeless parents suffer various impacts of homelessness.

- Over two thirds of homeless parents are unemployed.
- 53% of homeless mothers do not have a high school diploma.
- Over 50% of all homeless mothers have a lifelong mental health problem.
- Homeless adults in family shelters, when compared to the general adult population, have three times the rate of tuberculosis and eight times more HIV diagnoses.

Source: National Coalition for the Homeless. (2009a). Education of homeless children and youth. Retrieved May 11, 2013, from http://www.nationalhome less.org/factsheets/education.pdf

Figure 9.4 Strategies for teaching economically struggling students

- Assume that all students can learn complex and creative material.
- Create a classroom that gives students as much control as possible while maintaining safety and structure. Let students' interests drive the curriculum.
- Do not assume common behaviors or states of mind for all low-income students or parents.
- Focus on the assets that students bring to the classroom: resiliency, perseverance, flexibility, compassion, and hope.
- Understand that you cannot change the world but you can work within your classroom and community to effect change. Advocate for small class size.
- Build a network of colleagues who are finding ways to challenge low-income students. Meet in the media center on Fridays to talk about "what went right this week."
- Maintain your "other life" so that you can go into the classroom ready to meet kids wholeheartedly and without resentment.
- Find ways to provide the necessities, such as winter coats, art materials, and a place to wash clothes. Look in the community for resources—for example, a place for students to do homework.
- Find respectful ways to survey students about their home situations. Make yourself available for students to talk with you. Refer them for help when they share serious problems or speak of a lack of basic needs at home.
- Ask students to do jobs for you to help them feel important and in control of something in their lives.
- Do not single out kids or indicate in front of others that you know they are homeless or poor.
- "Cut deals" with students, helping them find realistic ways to meet work requirements.
- Convince students that "I believe you can learn and I will listen to you and give you meaningful work to do."

Source: Landsman, J. (2006). Bearers of hope. *Educational Leadership, 63*(5), 26–32.

We are also advised to be teachers who have "a practical awareness of the students' physical needs coupled with a passion for teaching" (2006, p. 28). Here are examples of educators who fit this description as they recognize the pervasive negative effects of poverty:

- Doug is a middle school science teacher who keeps granola bars in his desk drawer for students who are so hungry that they fall asleep in his class. He also goes to the cafeteria for free breakfast with students who are hungry but may be embarrassed to go in alone.

- George is a high school teacher who collaborates with social workers to get clothes for students who need them and allows homeless students to leave school materials with him.
- Mary is principal of a middle school where local businesses contribute classroom supplies instead of asking students and parents to provide them. For Christmas the staff gave bags to homeless students filled with practical items and gift certificates to grocery stores. They report that the toughest students soften and begin to trust the adults at school.

What we do in our classrooms to promote learning may indeed affect the future conditions of the students we teach and, ultimately, their children, the next generation of students. In a very real way, we *can* affect the economic conditions in which children grow. Jensen tells us that children who live in poverty have had major negative influences on their lives and feel hopeless. He contends that one of the most meaningful things we can do for children in poverty is to give them hope. "Hope changes brain chemistry, which influences the decisions we make and the actions we take. Hopefulness must be pervasive, and every single student should be able to feel it, see it, and hear it daily" (2009, p. 113).

One of our ethical responsibilities as teachers is to raise public awareness of our students' accomplishments and realities. In doing so we can help eliminate harmful stereotyping and inform our communities about ways they may help our children grow strong and healthy in mind, body, and spirit. Read about one educator's efforts to raise public awareness in this chapter's **The Opinion Page** feature.

How Do Health Issues Affect Students in the United States?

Some health issues pose immediate and obvious dangers to children and adolescents. For instance, underage alcohol consumption and abuse of both legal and illegal drugs alter mental states and lead to overt behavioral changes. Other health issues are just as insidious, but their effects are incremental; their negative consequences occur gradually and are generally not accompanied by alarm. For instance, tobacco use and obesity among children and adolescents rarely push adult panic buttons, but may lead to deadly consequences.

Rates of substance abuse—specifically of alcohol, legal and illegal drugs, and tobacco—are either decreasing or not rapidly rising. Early sexual experiences are declining, with a teen birth rate that has fallen dramatically in recent years. However, some health professionals say that the overall health of children and adolescents is worsening because of dramatic increases in obesity rates.

SUBSTANCE ABUSE

Substance abuse is a pattern of alcohol, tobacco, or drug use that can lead to detrimental and habitual consumption, very possibly with impaired functioning at school and work, along with legal difficulties. According to the National Institute of Drug Abuse survey conducted by Johnston, O'Malley, Bachman, and Schulenberg at the University of Michigan (2012), the guarded good news is that substance abuse among children and adolescents did not escalate between 2008 and 2012. The bad news continues to be that substance abuse is extremely dangerous and can be deadly. Even if the statistics show leveling or a decline, one child or adolescent harmed by substance abuse is one too many.

This Opinion Editorial was published in the La Crosse Tribune, *Wisconsin, on December 25, 2012.*

Poverty in Schools Is Community Problem

by Rick Blasing

Rick Blasing is a counselor at Lincoln Middle School, SOTA II and Coulee Montessori in La Crosse, Wis.

When you consider what it must be like to be a child living in poverty, what do you envision?

Do you visualize a sad, sullen young person, an individual who cannot even consider the possibility of a happy life for himself? Do you see an individual who may be poorly fed, ill-clothed or whose eyes reflect a profound sadness?

When we see this young person in the community, we cannot fully know whether the possible signs of poverty we observe are a consistent life-condition. However, in the schools and in our classrooms, educators quickly learn of the dire conditions in which far too many of our community youth exist.

Through daily contact, teachers quickly recognize the signs of those who might be lacking sleep or who might be disconnected from their peers. These children become quickly evident to the caring educator, who can recognize a youngster who lacks not only material things but also the essential components and necessities needed for a healthy brain and body, a sense of self-esteem and a positive vision for their future.

Students who live in poverty parachute into the school environment from their "other world" on a daily basis, always striving to display a semblance of normalcy. It can be a tortuous and damaging existence for them, and it can assault their young sense of self and distort what they see as their own value and place in society.

For many, the school and classroom offers at least a temporary respite from the fundamental things lacking in their young lives.

Our community is indeed rich in resources. We are wealthy beyond measure when it comes to the amount of dedicated people who work to make things better for others. Working in the schools, I'm often heartened by the degree of dedication and selfless generosity demonstrated by parents and guardians who contribute their time and talents, educational materials, and pantry items to help with the great work going on. It's truly humbling and encouraging to witness this.

It's exciting to see an increasing degree of collaboration between groups and agencies in our region, which are searching for new ways to help those children and their families in our community. At a gathering in August, the city of La Crosse, La Crosse County and the La Crosse School District hosted the La Crosse Community Summit: Rebuilding for Learning II community conversation.

This event brought together city and county professionals, educators and other community stakeholders with the goal of creating and implementing a web of organized learning supports to address those societal barriers to learning.

While children in poverty certainly have the ability to achieve at the same level and reach the same academic benchmarks as their peers, their initial ability to effectively focus and learn can be severely hampered when their basic human needs are not being met.

A more recent community conversation about children in poverty took place in October at Viterbo University. Co-sponsored by AMOS (a local interfaith community coalition), the D.B. Reinhart Institute for Ethics in Leadership at Viterbo, the La Crosse County Human Services Department and Family Policy Board, League of Women Voters of the Greater La Crosse Area, and the Wisconsin Council on Children and Families, this gathering provided a meaningful discussion involving strategies for helping children and families in poverty. Through these invaluable community conversations, we learn about the ways we can work together for greater common good.

During this season of giving and sharing, it's a timely reminder that we remain focused on those families in our society needing resources, assistance, job-training and employment opportunities to better their economic situation and prospects for the future. It is imperative we do what we can to provide the children with the necessary resources and nutrition so that they can effectively learn and grow while in our schools—giving them all of the benefits that a good education provides.

It has been said that it's the moral test of a nation in how it treats those who are in the dawn of life or in the twilight of life. Let us aspire to meet that moral test and, to that end, work to eliminate the poverty that hurts the lives of so many families and children in our community.

Copyright © 2012 *La Crosse Tribune.*

This Opinion Page piece is poignant and compelling. It is a statement of a community's dedication to ask "And how are the children? Are they all well?" They want to answer that they are doing what they can to give every child opportunities for positive development, regardless of their circumstances. Write a well-developed paragraph in response to each of the following questions and prompts:

1. Relate what you know about Maslow's hierarchy of needs to what Rick writes in this Opinion Page. Elaborate on which needs must be met first, and which will be met more easily as a result.

2. The imagery of students "parachuting" into the school environment makes a point. Why is this message so important for teachers to understand?

3. What are some ways you might make the most of what Rick calls the "temporary respite" of your classroom?

When do children and adolescents begin drinking alcohol and using drugs? Although most research studies begin with eighth graders, elementary teachers and principals know that experimentation with alcohol, drugs, and tobacco begins even earlier. The average boy takes his first drink at age 11; the average girl, at age 13. Nationwide, over 20% of students report drinking more than a few sips of alcohol for the first time before age 13 years (Centers for Disease Control and Prevention [CDC], 2012a). Despite recent lower rates of consumption as shown in Figure 9.5, alcohol usage remains widespread, with about 72% of high school seniors and 39% of eighth graders consuming more than just a trial taste. Binge drinking, defined as five drinks in a row at least once in 2 weeks, is reported for about 25% of seniors and 8% of eighth graders (Alcoholism Information and Resources, 2010). The rates of those who report being drunk in the past 30 days is much too high: 4% of 8th graders, 13% of 10th graders, and 25% of 12th graders (Johnston et al., 2012).

It is a heartbreaking fact that thousands of adolescents die each year as a result of underage drinking and driving.

The heartbreaking stories of automobile accidents involving intoxicated or high adolescents at the wheel spur groups such as Mothers Against Drunk Driving (MADD) and Students Against Destructive Decisions (SADD; formerly Students Against Drunk Driving) to continue their awareness campaigns. Teenage drunk driving kills about eight teens a day. Research published by Rutgers University shows that when teenagers first get their driver's license, they perceive the risk of drinking and driving to be high. With driving experience, the perceived risk decreases and illegal behaviors involving drinking and/or using drugs while driving increase (McCarthy & Brown, 2004). In other words, the longer they have a license, the more teenagers engage in dangerous activity. This implies that safe driving education needs to continue throughout high school, not just as a prerequisite for obtaining a license. Of all teen deaths in car accidents, 60% are related to alcohol or drugs. Statistics show that a teenage boy with a blood alcohol level of 0.05, below the level to be considered legally drunk, is 18 times more likely to be in a single car accident than nonimpaired boys. For girls the number is even worse. A girl with a blood alcohol level of 0.05 is 54 times more likely to cause a single-car crash (Alcoholism Information and Resources, 2010). Staggering statistics.

Figure 9.5 Percentages of use of alcohol in past 30 days: 8th, 10th, and 12th grades

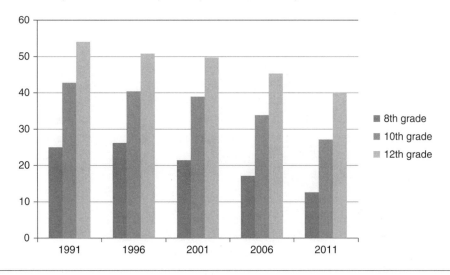

Source: *Monitoring the future: National results on adolescent drug use* by L. D. Johnston, P. M. O'Malley, J. G. Bachman, and J. E. Schulenberg, 2012. Retrieved January 28, 2013, from http://monitoringthefuture.org/pubs/monographs/mtf-overview2011.pdf

Both cigarettes and smokeless tobacco continue to pose health dangers for children and adolescents, although teenagers use less of both now than in the 1990s, as shown in Figure 9.6. Eighty percent of adult smokers begin the habit before the age of 18. Nicotine in tobacco affects the structural and chemical changes in developing brains of children and adolescents, making those who smoke more vulnerable to alcohol and drug addiction, as well as mental illness. In fact, research by the National Center on Addiction and Substance Abuse (CASA) at Columbia University tells us that teens who smoke cigarettes are 5 times more likely to drink, 13 times more likely to use marijuana, and 10 times more likely to develop alcohol and drug dependencies. Although we have known for a long time that smoking causes deadly cancers and cardiovascular and respiratory diseases, we now have a better idea of the long-term damage nicotine can have on brains that are still developing (National Center on Addiction and Substance Abuse, 2007).

Marijuana use by adolescents is up, as indicated in Figure 9.7, corresponding to the decreasing perception by teens that marijuana is harmful, or potentially harmful. Now

Figure 9.6 Percentages of use of cigarettes in past 30 days: 8th, 10th, and 12th grades

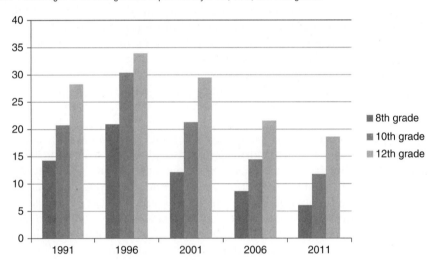

Source: *Monitoring the future: National results on adolescent drug use* by L. D. Johnston, P. M. O'Malley, J. G. Bachman, and J. E. Schulenberg, 2012. Retrieved January 28, 2013, from http://monitoringthefuture.org/pubs/monographs/mtf-overview2011.pdf

Figure 9.7 Percentages of use of marijuana in past 30 days: 8th, 10th, and 12th grades

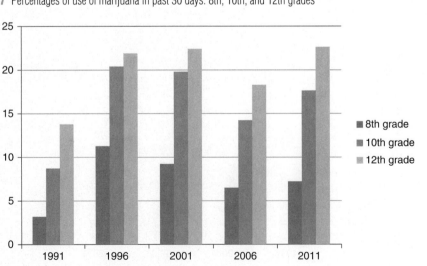

Source: *Monitoring the future: National results on adolescent drug use* by L. D. Johnston, P. M. O'Malley, J. G. Bachman, and J. E. Schulenberg, 2012. Retrieved January 28, 2013, from http://monitoringthefuture.org/pubs/monographs/mtf-overview2011.pdf

that at least two states are challenging the federal government's label of "illegal" for marijuana, coupled with the lack of generational memory of harmful side effects, teenage use is increasing. The National Institute on Drug Abuse (NIDA) tells us there is substantial research to prove that:

- Cannabis dependence leads to lower IQ.
- Heavy marijuana use before age 18 results in mental impairment.
- The risk of addiction when started in teens goes from 1 in 11 to 1 in 6.
- Reported problems with heavy use include impaired cognition, deteriorating social life, and reduced career potential (Johnston et al., 2012).

Other drugs are somewhat common among adolescents, but in much lower levels than alcohol, cigarettes, or marijuana. Synthetic marijuana, also known as K–2 or Spice, is sometimes more readily available than real marijuana. When manufacturers can't get a particular ingredient, they substitute chemicals, adding to the dangers of this synthetic drug. Abuse of inhalants—the drug of choice for some younger teens because of availability—is decreasing. However, according to a large-scale research report, 11% of students had sniffed glue, breathed the contents of aerosol spray cans, or inhaled paints to get high one or more times during their lives (DHHS, 2012). This year's National Institute on Drug Abuse (NIDA) survey showed reason for concern about a family of drugs referred to as "bath salts," containing an amphetamine-like stimulant often sold in drug paraphernalia stores. Abuse of prescription Vicodin has decreased slightly, while abuse of Adderall is increasing from 5.4 percent in 2009 to 7.6 percent in 2012 among 12th graders. The NIDA research continues to show that most teens who abused prescription medications are getting them from family members and friends. For the past few years the abuse of over–the–counter cough and cold medicines containing dextromethorphan has held steady at about 6 percent (Johnston et al., 2012). Over the course of their lifetimes, 3% of teens report trying heroin, and 8% report having used ecstasy or a hallucinogenic drug (e.g., LSD, acid, PCP, angel dust, or mescaline) (DHHS, 2012).

Children and adolescents often have an unfounded sense of immortality. Do you remember thinking, "Well, sure. Some people are hurt by this, but it won't happen to me"? The students in your future classrooms will likely often have this attitude. They grossly underestimate the serious consequences of abusing alcohol, drugs, and tobacco.

What can schools and teachers do? In 1995 the Supreme Court ruled that schools can arrange to randomly test student athletes for drugs. In 2002 another ruling included those who voluntarily participate in activities such as cheerleading, band, debate, and so on. Schools that conduct random student drug testing hope to decrease abuse among students in two ways. First, schools hope random testing will serve as a deterrent to drug use. Second, they hope to identify adolescents who already have drug problems and refer them for counseling and treatment (Johnston et al., 2012).

Teachers need to be informed about the warning signs—often sudden, negative changes in behavior and academic performance—of alcohol and drug abuse. We need to be articulate when it comes to describing the consequences of substance abuse of all kinds. We must take the problem seriously. Here are some suggestions for positively influencing students:

1. Develop strong relationships with students and understand their unrealistically optimistic perceptions concerning substance abuse.
2. Become a trusted mentor for individual students at risk for using alcohol, drugs, and tobacco.
3. Don't just give statistics. Expose students to graphic videos of the consequences of risky behavior, introduce them to families that have suffered the consequences of substance abuse, have students with recovery stories speak with your class, and so on.

4. Promote honest discussions about real-world issues, including substance abuse.

5. Use active instructional techniques such as role-playing to teach refusal skills.

6. Make information available about community services related to prevention and intervention of substance abuse.

SEXUALITY-RELATED CONCERNS

Fewer never-married 15- to 19-year-olds are having sexual experiences now than in the 1990s. They are starting later, and experiencing fewer partners. The use of birth control has remained disturbingly low, and is decreasing. Some trends of sexual intercourse among teenagers are in Table 9.3. By racial subgroups, the students reporting having intercourse before age 13 and in 9th through 12th grade are in Table 9.4.

Teen birthrate. Although pregnancy among girls ages 10 to 14 is especially tragic, only about 1 in every 1,000 girls in this age group becomes pregnant (Infoplease, 2009). As illustrated in Figure 9.8, except for the first half of the 1990s, the teen birthrate for 15- to 19-year-olds has declined since 1960, with slight increases in 2006 and 2007. A decrease in sexual intercourse among adolescents has contributed to the decline (Centers for Disease Control and Prevention, 2012d). A student population of sexually active teens who are more informed concerning the use of contraceptives is also contributing to lower pregnancy rates (Healthcommunities.com, 2010). Even with the incidences of teen births decreasing, the United States still has the highest teenage birthrate among developed countries. About 1 million teenage girls get pregnant annually, resulting in over 400,000 births. More than 4 of 5 teen mothers are unmarried, putting them and their babies at greater risk of living in poverty (Infoplease, 2004).

TABLE 9.3 Trends in sexual activity as reported by 12th graders (percentages), 1991–2011

Survey Question	1991	1995	1999	2003	2007	2011
Have you ever had intercourse?	54	53	50	47	48	47
Did you have intercourse before age 13?	10	9	8	7	7	6
Have you had intercourse with more than 4 people?	19	18	16	14	15	15
Did you use any form of birth control during your last intercourse experience?	17	16	15	14	15	13

Source: Centers for Disease Control and Prevention (2012b). *Trends in the Prevalence of Sexual Behaviors and HIV Testing National YRBS: 1991–2011.* Atlanta, GA: Author. Retrieved March 10, 2013, from http://www.cdc.gov/healthyyouth/yrbs/pdf/us_sexual_trend_yrbs.pdf

TABLE 9.4 Percentages of students reporting having had intercourse by race and grade level

Race	Before Age 13	9th Grade	10th Grade	11th Grade	12th Grade
White	6	27	38	51	63
Black	19	48	58	64	74
Hispanic	9	37	47	56	60
Asian	4	—*	24	34	44
Multiple Race	13	35	58	65	65

Source: Centers for Disease Control and Prevention. (2012c). *Sexual Risk Behavior Data & Statistics.* Retrieved March 10, 2013, from http://www.cdc.gov/healthyyouth/sexualbehaviors/data.htm
*not enough data

Figure 9.8 Pregnancy rates per 1,000 teens, ages 15 to 19, 1940–2011

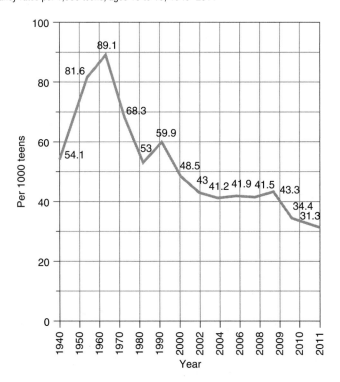

Sources: Centers for Disease Control. (2010). *Teen birth rates drop in 2008 following a two-year increase.* Atlanta, GA: Author; Hamilton, B. E., & Ventura, S. J. (2012). Birth rates for U.S. teenagers reach historic lows for all age and ethnic groups. *NCHS Data Brief, 89.* Hyattsville, MD: National Center for Health Statistics; Hamilton, B. E., Martin, J. A., & Ventura, S. J. (2012). Births: Preliminary data for 2011. *National Vital Statistics Reports, 61*(5). Hyattsville, MD: National Center for Health Statistics; Ventura, S. J., Mathews, T. J., & Hamilton, B. E. (2001). Births to Teenagers in the United States, 1940–2000. *National Vital Statistics Reports, 49*(10). Hyattsville, MD: National Center for Health Statistics.

There are, of course, many consequences of teenage pregnancy, including:

- Eighty percent of teen mothers must rely on welfare at some point.

- Teenage mothers are more likely to drop out of school, with only about a third of teen mothers obtaining a high school diploma.

- Teenage pregnancies are linked to increased rates of alcohol and substance abuse.

- Both teen mothers and teen fathers have lower educational levels and reduced earning potential.

- The annual cost in the United States of teen pregnancies from lost tax revenues, public assistance, child health care, foster care, and involvement with the criminal justice system is estimated to be about $7 billion (Healthcommunities .com, 2010).

Homosexuality. Homosexuality is not, in and of itself, a health concern. However, sexual orientation is an issue that evokes strong sentiments that spill over onto school grounds. "Tragically, public schools have become front lines in the culture war over homosexuality—and the biggest losers are the kids caught in the crossfire of incendiary rhetoric and bitter lawsuits" (Haynes, 2006, p. 3). In an effort to find a process that will allow educators and students alike to civilly discuss issues of sexual orientation, a document entitled "Public Schools and Sexual Orientation: A First Amendment Framework for Finding Common Ground" was endorsed in 2006 by organizations including the American Association of School Administrators and the Association for Supervision and Curriculum Development (First Amendment Center, 2006). Will documents such as this end teasing and harassment aimed at adolescents who are, or are perceived to

Homosexuality is discussed in Chapter 2.

be, homosexual? Perhaps eventually official documents will help. However, the effects will not come quickly enough to spare many hurt feelings and prevent acts of violence toward individuals.

What can schools and teachers do? Schools should provide health education courses for at least middle and high school students that include open and honest information concerning matters of sexuality, with a forum for asking and answering questions. Teachers should show informed sensitivity to students grappling with sexuality-related issues. As with substance abuse, refusal skills are important, and they are more likely to be demonstrated by students who perceive a sense of control over their lives. The physical and emotional dangers of early sexual activity, STDs and HIV/AIDS, and teen pregnancy can be communicated in nongraphic and noncontroversial ways, often couched in terms of self-respect.

In the classroom, treating all students with respect is vital. Not allowing students to use derogatory language about sexual orientation will help keep a respectful atmosphere. Among upper elementary and middle school students, saying "That's so gay" is a sign of disapproval. Students often use the phrase lightly, but its implications can deeply hurt those students who perceive themselves to be homosexual. Simply saying, "We don't use that phrase in this classroom or this school" and then sticking to it is an example of creating a more respectful atmosphere.

Some schools have established sex education programs and clinics that provide access to birth control information and devices; others primarily advise abstinence. Both programs are controversial. Many districts support special schools for pregnant students and new mothers. These schools help young women stay in school and graduate. Teenagers should be assisted in the development of skills in communication and sexual decision making so that sex does not just "happen." As teachers, we can help make teens aware of the consequences of sexually risky behaviors.

CHILDHOOD OBESITY

Americans rank obesity as a health problem second only to cancer. Childhood obesity has more than doubled in children and tripled in adolescents in the past 30 years. In 2010 over one third of children and adolescents in America were considered overweight or obese (CDC, 2013). The commonly held definition of **obesity** involves the body mass index (BMI), a measure of how much a person weighs relative to height, as illustrated in Table 9.5 (Paxson, Donahue, Orleans, & Grisso, 2006).

First Lady Michelle Obama has chosen childhood obesity as a cause to champion. Her program *Let's Move* is a nationwide campaign with the goal of solving the problem of childhood obesity in a generation and empowering children born today to reach adulthood at a healthy weight. "The physical and emotional health of an entire generation and the economic health and security of our nation is at stake" (2010).

Mrs. Obama is traveling the country promoting healthy habits in schools, communities, and families. She is asking school food services to cut calories and offer more fresh

Points of Reflection 9.4

Do you agree with including sexuality-related information in the curriculum? Why or why not?

Think about if, when, and how students should receive instruction on matters of sexuality.

Josie Ford is one of our focus students at Rees Elementary. She appears to be very young and naive. Watch Josie's interview with teacher Brenda Beyal and her Mom. Should Josie receive sex education as a fifth grader?

Points of Reflection 9.5

Use the BMI formula to determine your own weight status. Are you surprised by what you discover about yourself? Do you think it's wise to make children and adolescents face the reality of where they are on the scale? Why or why not? What difference might this knowledge make to them?

TABLE 9.5 Computing body mass index (BMI)

BMI	Status
Below 18.5	Underweight
18.5–24.9	Normal
25.0–29.9	Overweight
30.0–39.9	Obese
40 and above	Morbidly obese

Note: BMI = (weight in pounds × 703) ÷ [(height in inches) × (height in inches)].

Source: Craig, G. J., & Dunn, W. L. (2007). *Understanding human development* (p. 248). Upper Saddle River, NJ: Prentice Hall.

Figure 9.9 Factors contributing to childhood obesity

1. increases in television and computer game use that have led to a new generation of "couch potatoes"
2. the explosive proliferation of fast-food restaurants, many of which market their products to children through media campaigns that tout tie-ins to children's movies and TV shows
3. increases in sugary and fat-laden foods displayed at children's eye level in supermarkets and advertised on TV
4. schools that offer children junk food and soda while scaling back physical education classes and recess
5. working parents who are unable to find the time or energy to cook nutritious meals or supervise outdoor playtime
6. the exodus of grocery stores from urban centers, sharply reducing access to affordable fresh fruits and vegetables
7. suburban sprawl and urban crime, both of which keep children away from outdoor activities

Source: Paxson, C., Donahue, E., Orleans, T., & Grisso, J. A. (2006). Introducing the issue. *The Future of Children, 16*(1), 3–18.

produce. It is estimated that as many as half of school-age children eat about half their daily calories at school; what is served in the cafeteria matters.

What's considered normal weight for children and adolescents varies with their age. But take a look at a line of children walking down an elementary hallway or adolescents gathered around the school commons. It is obvious which students are grossly overweight or on their way to becoming so.

Researchers are studying the causes and consequences of childhood obesity. Figure 9.9 lists seven factors that contribute to what the authors of the study cited call an epidemic of childhood obesity.

The consequences of childhood obesity include serious health issues such as type 2 diabetes, heart disease, sleep disorders, asthma, joint dysfunction, and mental health problems. What used to be considered adult-only health problems are now serious health problems for adolescents and even children. As a result of weight issues, today's children may live shorter and less healthy lives than their parents (Paxson et al., 2006). Serious social and psychological problems are also consequences of childhood and adolescent obesity. Being teased, loneliness, low self-esteem, and other consequences result from being a severely overweight child or teenager.

Although researchers are not saying that obesity causes lower academic performance, the link between obesity and lower achievement may reveal serious academic consequences. Seriously overweight children are twice as likely to be in special education and remedial classes from an early age. A study of approximately 11,000 kindergartners found that overweight children had significantly lower reading and math scores when compared to children in the normal weight range. These academic difficulties continued through first grade (Story, Kaphingst, & French, 2006).

Mrs. Obama is quick to point out that childhood obesity is not the fault of the children themselves. The kids don't choose what's offered in the school cafeteria for breakfast and lunch. They are not responsible for foods loaded with sugar and fat or super-sized portions, nor do they determine how much time is allotted for recess and physical education. Yes, they may choose to watch TV and play video games or surf the Internet instead of running around outside, but it's the adults who make all of the alternatives available (Obama, 2010).

Physical activity, healthy food choices, and lessons relating to the dangers of obesity may help curb the alarming trend of childhood obesity.

What can schools and teachers do? In 2004 Congress passed the Child Nutrition Reauthorization Act, mandating that all schools participating in the federal school meal program develop comprehensive wellness policies focusing on the following:

1. What children and adolescents eat in school:
   - Provide more nutritious school breakfasts and lunches.
   - Limit à la carte items to healthier foods.
   - Reduce or eliminate vending machines or stock only nutritious foods.
2. How physically active students are in school:
   - Provide daily physical education (PE) in elementary and middle school.
   - Increase high school PE requirements and provide more extracurricular physical activity options.
3. In-school health and nutrition education

Teachers can encourage all of the elements of a wellness policy by serving as role models for healthy living. Eating nutritious, balanced meals and snacks in school and showing evidence of an active lifestyle that includes exercise will go a long way toward influencing students. Teachers can help prevent childhood and adolescent obesity by being vocal advocates for students' health. Chris Roberts is one of our focus teachers at Rees Elementary, Utah. Watch Chris's lesson to see him teach dance and movement to students on his multiage team. Not only does he live a very active life, he also requires his third, fourth, and fifth graders to participate in movement to music and to the beating of drums.

SUICIDE

The ultimate health issue and absolute tragedy for young adolescents (ages 10 to 14) and adolescents (ages 15 to 19) is suicide. Here are some facts to consider:

- In 2010, 1.3 per 100,000 young adolescents, ages 10–14, died of suicide.
- In 2010, 7.5 per 100,000 adolescents, ages 15–19, died of suicide.
- Suicide remains the third-leading cause of death among teens, trailing only accidents and homicide.
- Boys die 4 times as frequently as girls from suicide, even though girls attempt suicide much more frequently.
- The 3 racial groups of teenagers most likely to commit suicide are Native American/Alaskan Native (21 per 100,000), White (11 per 100,000), and Black 7 per 100,000).
- Firearms account for almost half of teen suicides.

(American Association of Suicidology, 2013).

Depression is a mental illness characterized by a deep sense of sadness and a loss of interest or pleasure in activities. Students who are depressed are 14 times more likely to make a first suicide attempt. In fact, over half of all adolescents who suffer from depression eventually attempt suicide (American Psychiatric Association, 2005a). Depression is one of the factors contributing to suicide attempts, as shown in Figure 9.10. One or more of the factors listed are usually present when an adolescent attempts suicide, but it is possible that none of them are evident. The American Psychiatric Association (2005b) tells us that "Teenagers who are planning to commit suicide might 'clean house' by giving away favorite possessions, . . . they may also become suddenly cheerful because they think that by deciding to end their lives they have found the solution" (p. 2).

Figure 9.10 Signs and symptoms of suicidal feelings

A teenager contemplating suicide may:
- change eating, sleeping, and personal grooming habits
- withdraw from friends, family, and pleasurable activities
- tend toward violent actions and drug and alcohol use
- exhibit marked personality changes including rebellion
- lose interest in school with declining quality of work
- frequently complain about symptoms, often related to emotions, such as stomachaches, headaches, fatigue, etc.
- express a sense of being a bad person and make statements such as "I won't be a problem much longer" and "Nothing matters anymore"
- give away favorite possessions and throw away things once considered important
- become suddenly cheerful after a period of depression
- experience hallucinations or bizarre thoughts

Source: Based on American Academy of Child and Adolescent Psychiatry. (2009). *Facts for families: Teen suicide.* Retrieved June 3, 2010, from http://www .aacap.org/cs/root/facts_for_families/teen_suicide

What can schools and teachers do? The American Psychiatric Association (2005b) advises that simply taking time to talk with troubled adolescents about their emotions and problems can prevent what they call the "senseless tragedy of teen suicide" (p. 2). Here are some guidelines for dealing with adolescents at risk for suicide attempts:

- Understand and recognize factors that may indicate suicidal tendencies such as those in Figure 9.10.

- If you suspect suicidal tendencies, always notify others such as a mental health professional or a school counselor who may, in turn, contact family members.

- Be willing to listen, rather than lecture.

- Find ways to involve students in service learning that takes them "outside" themselves.

- Reassure adolescents that depression and suicidal tendencies are treatable.

Points of Reflection 9.6

Has suicide touched your life? If so, in what way(s)?

OTHER RISKY BEHAVIORS

Over 15,000 students in 21 large urban areas responded to extensive surveys about their behaviors. The Youth Risk Behavior Surveillance Survey (YRBSS) is the largest public health surveillance system in the United States, monitoring a broad range of health-risk behaviors among high school students. Here are some facts that indicate ways we may influence the long-term health of our students. Obviously, many of these behaviors don't just magically begin when students step inside the high school hallways. Education and modeling will impact younger students and perhaps serve as preventive measures. High school students reported these risky behaviors over a 30-day timeframe:

- 88% who rode a bicycle did *not* wear a helmet.

- 8% *never*, or almost never, wore car seat belts.

- 24% had ridden in a car with a drunk driver (encouragingly, this is a decrease from 40% in 1991).

- 33% had texted while driving.

- 17% had carried a weapon (gun, knife, or club; 5% on school property).

- 6% of students had not gone to school on at least 1 day because they felt they would be unsafe at school or on their way to or from school.

- 90% of students did *not* wear sunscreen when outside for more than 1 hour on a sunny day.
- 69% of students did not get 8 or more hours of sleep on an average school night.
- 31% of students played video or computer games or used a computer for something that was not school work for 3 or more hours per day on an average school day.
- 32% of students watched television 3 or more hours per day on an average school day.

(U.S. Department of Health and Human Services, 2012)

It's important for teachers to recognize that our influence can extend across many risk areas.

How Does Racism Affect Students in the United States?

Even though race has been discredited as a legitimate, precise way to categorize people, "race and racism profoundly structure who we are, how we are treated, how we treat others, and our access to resources and rights" (Mukhopadhyay & Henze, 2003, p. 669). **Racism** is a form of prejudice that stems from a belief that one race is superior to another. Racism may be perpetuated by individuals or even by governmental policies (Gollnick & Chinn, 2013).

DISCRIMINATION

It's illegal to discriminate by race in American public schools. So that should be the end of the discussion, right? You will never find a public school policy that says, "If you are a racial minority, you must attend schools with peeling paint and inadequate, poorly maintained bathrooms," or, "If you are a child of color you may not experience advanced classes or be in gifted programs." No, this would be against the law.

However, official policies of nondiscrimination often do little to remedy discrimination in the day-to-day realities of the children and adolescents of color who make up about 40% of students in American public schools. Even in classrooms where a rich racial diversity exists, subtle forms of racism may be at play. The most subtle may be silence, with no ill intent on the part of the teacher. Polite and Saenger (2003) tell us that "the most pernicious and pervasive silence in . . . school classrooms is the silence surrounding the subject of race" (p. 275). Children are aware of physical differences of race at a very early age. Avoiding the subject doesn't make children's questions go away; they simply go unasked and unanswered. If children are not given opportunities to explore their own identities, as well as those of others around them, they will move from elementary to middle to high school carrying increasingly "complex feelings about race and racial issues, including pride, ignorance, anger, shame, ambivalence, and alienation" (Lewis-Charp, 2003).

Another subtle form of discrimination in schools is what has become known as the *soft bigotry of low expectations*. Whether these expectations are the result of an assumption about abilities and intelligence, of previous experiences with students of various races, or of some other factor, having low expectations for some students amounts to racism. Landsman (2006) says, "I believe that a true test of any country's morality is whether it gives all children a fair and equal chance to achieve their potential as human beings" (p. 29).

IMMIGRATION AND CLASSROOM SUCCESS

The presence of immigrant children and adolescents in our classrooms helps all students understand that people view the world differently. They contribute to our

Statistics about the racial makeup of U.S. schools are in Chapter 2.

Points of Reflection 9.7

What is your racial identity? How has this identity affected you as a student? How does your own racial identity impact your beliefs about, and attitudes toward, those with racial identities other than your own?

classrooms by increasing our knowledge and appreciation of diversity and by providing our classrooms with richer learning experiences.

One in every five students has a parent who was born outside the United States. A quarter of these children were also born outside the United States. By some estimates, immigration will account for 96% of the future increase in the school-age population over the next 50 years (U.S. Census Bureau, 2008). This is a societal fact that will affect, if it doesn't already, every teacher. Deb Perryman, an advocate for immigrant students, tells us about her experiences in Figure 9.11.

Teachers often need to make an extra effort to understand how immigrant children may respond to many aspects of school in the United States. Without sensitivity to differences, racism may become part of their classroom experiences. Ariza (2002) gives us some examples of differences that may be manifested in a classroom with children who are immigrants or the children of immigrants:

- Manes is a student from Haiti whose parents have gone to great lengths and considerable risk to ensure an education for their children. In Haiti, teachers rarely send communications home with students. Weeks after sending home notes that required parental attention and signatures, a frustrated teacher assumes Manes's parents don't care. However, they simply didn't know to look in Manes's book bag for notes and papers requiring their attention.

- Hong, a student from Southeast Asia, has had a cold and sore throat. A common ethnic remedy in her country of origin is to rub a coin up and down on an area that is causing illness to draw out the pain. When Hong arrives at school with what appear to be bruises on her neck, the teacher suspects child abuse.

- Mohammad, a son of recent immigrants from the Middle East, is Muslim. Normally an active, cheerful child, he became withdrawn and wanted to change

---

Figure 9.11 Deb Perryman, 2004 Illinois Teacher of the Year

I teach the very fine students of Elgin High School in Illinois. EHS is an urban school serving 2,200 students speaking 56 languages. Official records show that 50% of our kids are living at or below the poverty level.

I remember the stories my grandparents told me of the hard times they had coming to the United States from Ireland. They faced name calling and worked dangerous jobs for low wages. I am thankful for all of the risks they took because I have so many opportunities. I remember my great grandpa yelling at the top of his lungs during dinner. He wasn't mad but nearly deaf after many years working as a boiler maker. That is the first time I can remember thinking to myself, "I will never treat another person the way my grandparents have been treated."

The immigration process is very complicated. As of May 2005 Illinois has a law (HB 60) that is providing possibilities for thousands of students. It buys time for those students seeking citizenship to actually complete the process while continuing their education. It gives me hope and, best of all, gives hope to students who are children of immigrants.

I have a set of twins I am working with now. When they entered the United States from Mexico 10 years ago, their parents went to the Immigration and Naturalization Service and began their road to citizenship. They have diligently tried to meet every stipulation and deadline, only to find themselves basically still on square one because of the bureaucracy involved, along with our overloaded, and understaffed, naturalization system. Now the boys are ready for college and the family is threatened with deportation.

I will continue to champion the cause of protecting immigrant children from arbitrary harm. I will ask the hard questions. When will we accept the next wave of immigrants without prejudice? When will we realize that every generation before us has come to the land of opportunity to get/create jobs and live productively?

Source: From e-mail communication with Deb Perryman, January 13, 2007.

his name following the 9/11 tragedy in 2001 so that no one would associate him with his religion or with terrorists.

- Maria, a 7-year-old whose family is from Colombia, routinely carries a baby bottle filled with milk in her lunch box. Her classmates teased her, and her teacher asked if she had mistakenly put her baby brother's bottle in her lunch. She was humiliated. The teacher later discovered that it is both proper and commonplace in some areas of Colombia for primary school children to drink from bottles.

Immigration and the laws addressing it continue to be a major source of contention and animosity in the United States. Regardless of the political infighting and social stigmas, the immigrant children and adolescents in our classrooms are just that—children and adolescents. They deserve the same care and consideration teachers give to all other students.

What can schools and teachers do? Joseph White and James Cones, the authors of *Black Men Emerging* (1999), tell us there are three basic steps to confronting racism.

1. *Explore the issue of racism intellectually.* Read about racism and minority groups and discuss what you read with other teachers. Attend sessions at conferences that explore issues of racism and how to combat it in the classroom.
2. *Engage in dialogue about racism.* Start conversations with families, students, and the community about racial issues. Be open to frank talk and serious exchange of ideas.
3. *Immerse yourself in other cultures.* If you are white, attend an African American church service or a Kwanza celebration where you can join in and begin to understand traditions and perceptions. If you are Jewish, attend a Christian service. If you are non-Hispanic, join in Cinco de Mayo festivities.

In our classrooms we need to be sensitive to each and every student, listen to interactions and guard against racial slurs of any kind, hold high expectations for all students, and continually seek to understand and appreciate differences that may accompany race.

What Are the Effects of Bullying, Theft, and Violence on Students and Schools in the United States?

School is a relatively safe place to be. Considering that more than 55 million students attend school each day, the chances of one of them being a victim of a violent act are small. However, crimes against students by other students continue to be problematic, even though the occurrence of violence and theft in schools has decreased since the mid-1990s (Dinkes, Kemp, & Baum, 2009).

Recent data indicate that school-age students are victims of all kinds of minor crimes about as often at school as away from school. However, with serious violent crimes such as rape and murder, the difference between in-school and out-of-school victimization is dramatic, with school the least likely place for harm (Dinkes et al., 2009).

Physical threat is not the only aspect of victimization to consider. The insidious nature of bullying causes real harm to students who are bullied, to those who perpetrate the bullying, and even to the bystanders who see it happening and do nothing to help.

BULLYING

In the aftermath of the 1999 Columbine High School tragedy, people across the United States asked, "How could something like this happen?" Psychologists, counselors, principals, teachers, and parents, as well as the print and electronic media, began to speculate about what might have led Dylan Klebold and Eric Harris to kill their schoolmates and a teacher and then turn the guns on themselves. From conversations with people who knew Dylan and Eric, the conclusion was drawn that they were adolescents who felt alienated from other students and from school.

Although the extreme violence of Columbine cannot be entirely explained by examining student relationships, interest in interactions among students has grown. Bullying, often considered as simply "what kids do," has become a topic of concern. **Bullying,** or relationally aggressive behavior, is "a type of emotional violence where individuals use relationships to harm others. Examples include exclusion from a group and rumor spreading" (Ophelia Project, 2005, p. 3). In addition, bullying may involve physical aggression, such as shoving, tripping, and taking personal items. "Bullying is a weapon of people driven by the need for power. Bullying can be a single interaction—verbal, physical, or emotional—but it is always crafted to cause fear and to exert power" (White-Hood, 2006, p. 30). Bullying may be linked to current and future psychological and behavioral difficulties, including depression, dropping out of school, substance abuse, risky sexual behavior, abnormal eating habits, delinquency, and suicide. "Sticks and stones may break my bones, but words will never hurt me" may be the least accurate adage ever. Words hurt; inappropriate images ruin lives.

Almost everyone has been teased or called names at some point, and most people have teased others or been guilty of name-calling. When teasing becomes malicious and repetitive, when its intent is to embarrass, hurt, or isolate, it crosses the line into bullying. When rumors are intentionally spread to destroy the reputation of another, gossip becomes bullying. Most teachers can identify students who bully, as well as those who seem to be magnets for taunts and subtle forms of relational aggression. Figure 9.12 is an overview of the most frequent forms of bullying, according to students—one in three of whom report being bullied.

Cyberbullying. A particularly insidious form of bullying accomplished through social media sites, text messages, e-mail, chat, and websites is **cyberbullying.** The purpose of cyberbullying is to intentionally embarrass, harass, intimidate, or make threats through mean messages, rumors, pictures, videos, or fake profiles. Cyberbullying may happen 24 hours a day, 7 days a week and likely victimizes children and adolescents when they are alone. Messages and images can be either posted anonymously to one person or widely distributed, and may be harsher because the bullier is probably anonymous. Not knowing who the cyberbullier is can add to the anxiety. Here are some instances of cyberbullying:

- Tricking someone into revealing personal or embarrassing information and then sending it to others
- Posing as the victim and sending mean or untrue messages as him or her
- Forwarding mean messages
- Making fun of others on a website
- Using websites to rate others as sexiest, prettiest, ugliest, and so on, often in vulgar, insulting ways

---

Figure 9.12 Frequent forms of bullying

Being made fun of: 21%
Being the subject of rumors: 18%
Pushed, shoved, tripped, or spit on: 11%
Threatened with harm: 6%
Excluded from activities on purpose: 5%
Coerced to do something they did not want to do: 4%

Source: Dinkes, R., Kemp, J., & Baum, K. (2009). *Indicators of school crime and safety: 2009* (NCES 2010–012/NCJ 228478). Washington, DC: National Center for Education Statistics, Institute of Education Sciences, U.S. Department of Education, and Bureau of Justice Statistics, Office of Justice Programs, U.S. Department of Justice.

- Posting photos without consent
- Creating fake online profiles on websites such as Facebook, Myspace, Twitter, etc., to make fun of people

By definition, cyberbullying only occurs among children and adolescents. When adults exhibit similar behaviors, it's considered **cyber-harassment** or **cyber-stalking,** a behavior that can have legal consequences. The same groups of children and adolescents who are more susceptible to non-cyberbullying—those who are lesbian, gay, bisexual, or transgender (LGBT) youth and those with disabilities or who are socially isolated—are most likely to be victims of cyberbullying. However, many incidents involve students considered otherwise mainstream but who may be the object of jealousy or a grudge. This chapter's *SocialMEdia* feature addresses cyberbullying, a very real problem that deserves teacher vigilance to recognize, prevent, and teach responses that lead to cyber-safety.

The bully, the bullied, and the bystander. An excellent resource for teachers on the topic of bullying is Barbara Coloroso's book, *The Bully, the Bullied,*

SocialMEdia

Teachers should learn to recognize and prevent cyberbullying. They should help kids know how to respond when it occurs. Some instances are easy to recognize because the messages are direct and mean. Other instances involving impersonations, posting of personal information, and videos sent to a select group may be much more difficult and time-consuming to detect.

Some signs of cyberbullying may be similar to, or the same as, signs of other victimization or extreme stress. Even so, it's important for teachers to watch for symptoms and then determine their causes. A victim of cyberbullying may:

- be overly protective or secretive about online activities.
- turn off the screen when someone comes near.
- become withdrawn or show signs of depression.
- be anxious or overly stressed.
- stop using the computer and other technology.
- suddenly avoid or change friends.
- lose interest in activities or school.

The profile of someone who cyberbullies may not be overtly different than that of any other adolescent since the reasons for this harmful activity may be jealousy or a grudge, two things that are part of the human condition. A cyberbullier may:

- be overly protective or secretive about online activities (same as the bullied).
- turn off the screen when someone comes near (not unlike the bullied).
- appear nervous or secretive when using social media.
- spend excessive amounts of time on the computer.

Teachers may help prevent cyberbullying by:

- implementing and enforcing a school anti-bullying code of conduct.
- having students sign an anti-bullying and anti-cyberbullying pledge (to not participate and to speak up if someone is being bullied).
- creating a safe place for students to voice concerns or problems.
- talking with students about cyberbullying: what it is, the impact it has, and its consequences.
- making it clear that cyberbullying will not be tolerated.
- working with students to help raise cyberbullying awareness within the school through student-led clubs, assemblies, or posters. (National Crime Prevention Council, 2013)

Teachers should tell students to **never**. . .

- post or share personal information, or that of a friend, online (including full name, address, telephone number, school name, parents' names, credit card or Social Security number).
- share Internet passwords with anyone, except your parents.
- meet anyone face-to-face previously known only online.

If students suspect, or are certain, cyberbullying is occurring, teachers may advise them to:

- tell an adult they trust about what's going on.
- not delete any of the emails, texts, or messages. They can serve as evidence.
- keep a record of incidents.
- not forward any mean messages that spread rumors.
- not plot revenge because it won't solve anything.
- report the incident to the administrator of the website.

Cyberbullying hurts. It can be dangerous physically, emotionally, and socially. Cyber-safety is everyone's responsibility.

and the Bystander. The **bully** doesn't generate as much attention as the act of bullying, but perhaps should. Until we understand why and how a child becomes a bully, we will not be effective in deterring bullying. Bullies may have been, or are, victims of bullying themselves. For the most part, bullies are seeking power. They exert power by harming others, by intimidating, and by being dominant.

The **bullied** are victims of the act of bullying. We've all known them; perhaps you yourself were one. The bullied are targets. Some may be the youngest; the smallest (or largest); victims of previous trauma; submissive; outstanding in some way (often academically); the kid with low self-esteem; annoying; racially/culturally different; one with physical or mental disabilities; kids with acne or a hearing aid; those who are lesbian, gay, bisexual, transgender or who are questioning (LGBTQ) their sexual orientation . . . or simply the kid in the wrong place at the wrong time. In fact, a survey of LGBTQ students revealed that 9 out of 10 experienced harassment in school (DHHS, 2013). Whatever their situations, children and adolescents who are victims of bullying may

Bullying in middle school is a growing threat to the physical and psychological well-being of young adolescents.

- become withdrawn
- begin using alcohol and drugs as escape mechanisms
- skip school
- be unwilling to attend school or other activities
- suddenly stop caring about grades
- have lower self-esteem
- develop health problems

David McBeath, our 6th grade focus student at Cario Middle School, is very large for his age. In contrast, he is shy and soft spoken. His social skills are underdeveloped. Watch **David's interview** with both focus teacher Deirdre Huger-McGrew and his mom. Can you imagine other young adolescents bullying David? It doesn't have to be overt; simply finding ways to exclude him is a form of bullying.

The **bystander** is anyone who witnesses bullying. A bystander has choices to make: simply watch, walk away, join in, or intervene (Coloroso, 2008). As adults we think we would, of course, intervene and help the bullied. It's easier for us than it is for peers of the bully and the bullied. This is where the culture of a school or classroom either can make it tougher to bully or allow bullying to continue unchecked. A culture of openness, respect, and civility will make it harder for bullying to occur. A culture of free-for-all, disrespect, and empty threats will perpetuate bullying.

School culture is addressed in Chapter 3.

What can schools and teachers do?

In 2004 Congress amended the Safe and Drug Free Schools Act to include bullying and harassment. This addition requires all schools that receive federal funding to actively prevent bullying and to respond to all instances of it. School districts are developing policies and mandating antibullying programs. Books such as *Odd Girl Out: The Hidden Culture of Aggression in Girls* (Simmons, 2002) and *Best Friends, Worst Enemies: Understanding the Social Lives of Children* (Thompson & Grace, 2001) shed new light on the ramifications of relational aggression for both the aggressor and the victim. Books like these and established antibullying programs indicate that many times bullies were themselves bullied at some point or perhaps abused in some way by family members. Most scenarios are complex. Even when teachers don't understand all the circumstances and are not trained to work

Points of Reflection 9.8

Do you recall being bullied? If so, how did it happen? Did you know students who were relentlessly bullied in school? Did you know students who bullied others? How did you feel toward those who bullied others? How about toward those who were bullied?

through the psychological maze of causes for episodes of bullying, they can take steps to help prevent bullying in classrooms and schools. These steps include the following:

1. Watch for bullying and take it seriously. Don't be an idle bystander.

2. Train all adults in the school, including office and custodial personnel, bus drivers, and teacher assistants to recognize and respond when bullying occurs.

3. Be an obvious presence. Early childhood and elementary teachers should monitor the playground. Middle and high school teachers should be visible and vigilant in the hallways, at lunchtime, at bus drop-off areas, at extracurricular events, and so on.

4. Do everything possible to help students develop genuine self-esteem that will prevent bullying driven by the victim's lack of confidence. An intact self-esteem will also prompt victims of bullying to better withstand the torment and to seek assistance.

5. Incorporate lessons, formally or informally, that help students internalize the belief that bullying and relational aggression in all forms are harmful and absolutely wrong.

6. Implement prescribed antibullying programs with sincerity and purpose.

Research indicates that bullying may be the last significant step before the bully or the victim turns to more physically dangerous behavior, such as physical violence against other students.

VIOLENCE AND THEFT IN SCHOOLS

The most common forms of violence in schools are physical fights, with about equal fault among fighters, and simple assault involving a perpetrator and a victim. Both forms of violence involve boys about twice as often as girls. The good news is that between 1993 and 2009, the percentage of high school students reporting being in a fight on school grounds dropped from 16% to 11%. A larger percentage of Black and Hispanic students report being in fights than Asian and White students. Fighting is reported more often in urban settings than in suburban and rural settings (National Center for Education Statistics, 2011).

Incidents of theft in schools include purse snatching, pickpocketing, and taking of another's property from desks and lockers. In 1995 about 8% of middle and high school students reported something stolen from them while at school. The rate of theft in school has decreased steadily since then, with only 3% reporting theft in 2009 (U.S. Department of Justice, 2011).

Deaths at school due to violent acts are rare, considering that there are more than 55 million students in school each day. In 2009 there were 33 violent deaths in public schools. Even though the numbers are relatively small compared to the total population, 2012 proved to be an especially brutal year for violent deaths in schools. In February, a single gunman at Chardon High School, Ohio, fatally shot three students. In December, a young man armed with assault weapons killed 20 first grade students and six adult staff members at Sandy Hook Elementary in Newtown, Connecticut. These horrific events break our hearts and cause us to wonder what could possibly go through someone's mind that would lead them to commit a crime so heinous against students and their families. In our rage and despair we look more closely at counseling, at recognition of severe psychological problems, at the availability of weapons, increased school security, and so on, as we ask why something so awful could happen. Communities respond to their grief in a variety of ways, knowing that they are by and large helpless to find adequate remedies. In Figure 9.13 we read, in his own words, teacher Tim Bowens's account of one way the Chardon, Ohio, community responded to their February 2012 tragedy.

What can schools and teachers do? To help ensure the safety of students from early childhood through high school settings, schools have formulated a variety of

Points of Reflection 9.9

Have you experienced theft or violence as a student? Have you seen any of these activities take place in school? What consequences did the perpetrators face? What was your reaction to these crimes?

Figure 9.13 Chardon Middle School and Project Linus

On February 27, 2012, a former student of Chardon High School in Chardon, Ohio, entered the school and fatally shot three students and wounded several others. I was on bus duty one afternoon some time after the shootings at Chardon High School when I saw students walking by with blankets around their shoulders. There were multiple designs – soccer balls, rainbows, stars, and so on. Kids were being kids that day, and it was great to see. They found both comfort and peace from the blankets lovingly made by volunteers who were concerned for their well-being following the tragic events of that awful day in February. I learned this was a program called Project Linus that provided each student at Chardon High School with a blanket. When my colleague Julie Kenny and I began planning a Day of Service for our school, this seemed like a perfect service project. The shootings at Chardon High made all our students grow up quickly, and gave them empathy for others who experience trauma and tragedy. An ugly and unpredictable reality came to their doorstep. After the lockdown, when they left our building to the safety and security of their parents' arms, they learned about the tragedy that would change so many lives.

The goal in all of our projects has been for our students to see and reach beyond the walls of our school. During the Day of Service, students created blankets in small groups with the assistance from teachers. While creating the blankets, students had an opportunity to work together to make something special that would bring comfort to other students. It was especially fun to watch the 8th grade boys attempt something so foreign to many of them. It was important for our students to give back in light of all who reached out to our district and our students in the days following February 27. Our lovingly made blankets were delivered by Project Linus volunteers to children in area hospitals in hopes that they would bring a smile and some comfort to those who are suffering.

Source: From e-mail communication with Tim Bowens, November 24, 2012.

plans and policies, ranging from programs that foster respect among students to overt ways of increasing security, such as installing surveillance cameras and metal detectors, requiring ID badges, locking school entrances during school hours, and using drug-detection dogs in random sweeps. Some school districts have adopted **zero tolerance** policies, meaning there are nonnegotiable consequences for certain infractions. For instance, the consequence for fighting may be automatic suspension for 3 days. Possession of a weapon may result in automatic expulsion.

Between the horrific events at Columbine in 1999 and the 2007–2008 school year, many schools responded to the threat of violence. Controlled access to the building during school hours went from 75% to 90%, the requirement that students wear badges or picture IDs went from 4% to 8%, the use of security cameras went from 19% to 55%, the provision of telephones in most classrooms went from 45% to 72%, and the requirement that students wear uniforms went from 12% to 18% (Dinkes et al., 2009).

Individual teachers may have the greatest effect on school safety and security by being aware and watchful. Although violent episodes may occur, they are relatively infrequent. When students take weapons to school or there is a student fatality on school grounds, it is often front-page news—probably because it doesn't happen very often and, when it does, most people are appalled by it. Rather than being frightened day in and day out, think through how you would respond to a variety of scenarios, primarily how you would get help from nearby teachers, administrators, counselors, school security officers, and the like. Most schools have plans in place to address violence when it occurs.

Bullying and violence don't have a single source or cause. They originate from complex situations that didn't begin in an instant and won't be fixed quickly or with a single solution. A multifaceted approach is needed that emphasizes civility, tolerance, and respect for dignity and life, as well as the inclusion of commonsense security measures.

How Do Truancy and Dropping Out Affect Youth in the United States?

Dropping out of school has been called "the silent epidemic" by researchers at the Bill and Melinda Gates Foundation—"silent" because it has been covered up and ignored for decades, and "epidemic" because the problem has reached near-panic proportions (Bridgeland, Dilulio, & Morison, 2006). One of the most accurate predictors of dropping out is truancy.

TRUANCY

Nonattendance of compulsory education, not including excused absences generally granted for health reasons, is called **truancy** (Focus Adolescent Services, 2006). Truancy is often referred to as "cutting class" or "skipping school." According to the Los Angeles Office of Education, not only does truancy indicate who is most at risk for dropping out, but also it correlates strongly with juvenile delinquency. In Van Nuys, California, a 3-week sweep of the city for truant middle and high school students correlated with a 60% drop in shoplifting arrests. School officials concluded that when they're not in school, many truancy-prone students are committing crimes (Focus Adolescent Services, 2006).

On any given day, about 5% of students are absent from U.S. schools. At some schools, however, the rate is often closer to 20%. Absenteeism for any reason causes students to fall behind. With too many absences, students may feel lost in class, resulting in low self-esteem and a sense of resignation. Families suffer the consequences of truancy as they watch someone they love drift toward academic failure. Communities suffer, not just because of crime, but because of the possible loss of productive, self-sufficient citizens.

According to a study by the Center for Social Organization of Schools at Johns Hopkins University, when truant students were asked why they skipped school, about half said they just didn't want to go to school, about a fourth said they felt pushed out or bullied, and the remaining fourth reported external problems, many of them family related. The researchers found this information encouraging because they contend that 75% of the truancies, or all except those attributed to external problems, can be altered by school actions. We must give students schools that are safe and free of bullying (MacDonald, 2004).

What can schools and teachers do? Schools need to maintain accurate attendance records and communicate all absences to families. Although it sounds obvious, many schools do not pay attention to absences and do not call students' homes to ask about students who don't show up. Often parents and guardians don't know there's an attendance problem until it appears insurmountable.

Teachers must develop relationships with students that let them know they matter. Engaging, relevant instruction and a "we miss you when you're gone" attitude go a long way toward doing away with the "I just didn't want to go" syndrome expressed by so many truant students. Catching the problem in the truant stage will help prevent the travesty of dropping out.

DROPPING OUT

The reality is that each year over a million students who begin ninth grade with their peer group will not walk across the stage at graduation 4 years later. About 7,000 students drop out of school every single day (Alliance for Excellent Education, 2009). Honestly acknowledging how many students **drop out,** or do not graduate from high school in 4 years—and most will leave high school if they don't graduate in 4 years—is the first step to fixing the problem. And there definitely is a problem.

Prior to 2005, students who left school but indicated that they would seek a GED certificate or who simply never returned to school after numerous absences were not considered dropouts. For decades, states reported grossly inflated high school completion numbers, with most percentages above 80% and many above 90%. The U.S. Department of Education mandated in 2010–2011 that all states use the same definition of *graduation rate*, meaning students who successfully complete high school in four years. State graduation rates using this definition are in Table 9.6. Any data before 2011 undercounted dropouts and included inflated graduation results. Now we are able to

TABLE 9.6 High school graduation rates by state, 2010–2011

Rank	State	Graduation Rate	Rank	State	Graduation Rate
1	Iowa	88%	9	Arizona	78%
2	Vermont	87%	9	Delaware	78%
2	Wisconsin	87%	9	Kentucky	78%*
3	Indiana	86%	9	North Carolina	78%
3	Nebraska	86%	10	Minnesota	77%
3	New Hampshire	86%	10	New York	77%
3	North Dakota	86%	10	Oklahoma	77%*
3	Tennessee	86%	10	Rhode Island	77%
3	Texas	86%	11	California	76%
4	Illinois	84%	11	Utah	76%
4	Maine	84%	11	Washington	76%
5	Connecticut	83%	11	West Virginia	76%
5	Kansas	83%	12	Mississippi	75%
5	Maryland	83%	13	Colorado	74%
5	Massachusetts	83%	13	Michigan	74%
5	New Jersey	83%	13	South Carolina	74%
5	Pennsylvania	83%	14	Alabama	72%
5	South Dakota	83%	15	Florida	71%
6	Montana	82%	15	Louisiana	71%
6	Virginia	82%	16	Alaska	68%
7	Arkansas	81%	16	Oregon	68%
7	Idaho	81%*	17	Georgia	67%
7	Missouri	81%	18	New Mexico	63%
8	Hawaii	80%	19	Nevada	62%
8	Ohio	80%	21	Washington, DC	59%
8	Wyoming	80%			

* United Health Foundation. (2012). *United States high school graduation rates: 1990–2012.* Retrieved March 11, 2013, from http://www .americashealthrankings.org/all/graduation

Source: U.S. Department of Education. (2012). *Regulatory adjusted cohort graduation rate, all students: 2010–11.* Retrieved March 11, 2013, from http://eddataexpress.ed.gov/data-element-explorer.cfm/tab/data/deid/127/

compare state data and track progress over time. New graduation rates are also key elements of accountability in measuring the effectiveness of schools.

From a racial standpoint, Asian students topped the graduation rates, with 79% of Asian students finishing high school in four years, followed by White students at 76%, Black students at 60%, and Hispanic students at 58%. The Bureau of Indian Education, a division of the Bureau of Indian Affairs, is in charge of educating an estimated 41,000 American Indian and Alaska Native children in 183 elementary and secondary schools on 64 reservations in 23 states. The graduation rate of these students is 61% (U.S. Department of Education, 2012).

Why do students drop out of school? The reasons are often complex, with Figure 9.14 listing eight of them. You can mix and match the reasons to form plausible scenarios. For instance, boredom in a particular class may lead a group of students to identify with one another and to ditch school occasionally; skipped classes may then lead to academic problems, more absences, and finally dropping out. However, there's actually good news in Figure 9.14. The most cited reasons for dropping out are largely within our control; they are school related. Although we can't change much of the societal context of our students, we can change what happens within the walls of our

Figure 9.14 Top reasons dropouts identify for leaving school

High school dropouts say they . . .

- were not motivated or inspired to work hard (69%)
- found classes to be uninteresting (47%)
- were failing in school (35%)
- started high school poorly prepared (35%)
- would have been required to repeat a grade to graduate (32%)
- had to get a job and make money (32%)
- became a parent (26%)
- had to care for a family member (22%)

Source: Bridgeland, J. M., Dilulio, J. J., & Morison, K. B. (2006). *The silent epidemic: Perspective of high school dropouts.* Retrieved April 8, 2006, from http://www.ignitelearning.com/pdf/TheSilentEpidemic3-06FINAL.pdf

classrooms. In the following "What Can Schools and Teachers Do?" section, there are steps to take to increase graduation rates and, in doing so, have tremendous impact on the lives of our students as well as on the economic viability of our nation.

Dropping out often results from a slow process of disengagement, with costly ramifications that may last a lifetime. The negative consequences included in Figure 9.15 are primarily economic. However, the cognitive, social, emotional, physical, and moral impact of dropping out is often devastating for individuals, families, communities, and our country.

One of our focus students at Roosevelt High School in Fresno, California, is absent too often. Mayra Reyes's homeroom teacher, Derek Boucher, is concerned about her. She seems to have a very active social life with many friends and cousins, but her home life with her mom and mom's boyfriend is volatile. Mayra is a U.S. citizen and is a second-generation American. As such she can attend community college using government grants. Derek encourages her to think about her future as a way to keep her interested in school. He knows that truancy often results in dropping out and that nationally the dropout rate for Hispanic students is close to 50%. Watch **Mayra's interview** to get to know her better.

Dropping out of high school today is to a student's social health what smoking is to his or her physical health—an indicator of a host of poor outcomes to follow, ranging

Figure 9.15 Negative consequences of dropping out

- Nearly half of dropouts ages 16 to 24 are unemployed (Thornburgli, 2006).
- Dropouts typically earn less than graduates: The average earnings difference is estimated to be $9,000 a year and $260,000 over the course of a lifetime (Dynarski, Clarke, Cobb, Finn, & Rumberger, 2008).
- Dropouts in 2008 will cost the United States almost $319 billion in lost wages over their lifetimes (Alliance for Excellent Education, 2009).
- Dropouts contribute only about half as much in taxes as do high school graduates (Dynarski et al., 2008).
- If U.S. high schools and colleges raise the graduation rates of Hispanic, African American, and Native American students to the levels of white students by 2020, the potential increase in personal income would add more than $310 billion to the U.S. economy (Alliance for Excellent Education, 2009a).
- Increasing the graduation rate and college matriculation of male students in the United States by just 5% could lead to combined savings and revenue of almost $8 billion each year by reducing crime-related costs (Alliance for Excellent Education, 2009).
- Dropouts draw larger government subsidies in the form of food stamps, housing assistance, and welfare payments (Dynarski et al, 2008).
- Dropouts constitute a disproportionate percentage of all prisoners and of prisoners on death row; 67% of the latter did not complete high school (Thornburgh, 2006).
- Dropouts have worse health outcomes and lower life expectancies than high school completers (Dynarski et al., 2008).

Source: Alliance for Excellent Education. (2009). *High school dropouts in America.* Retrieved June 7, 2010, from http://all4ed.org/files/GraduationRates_FactSheet.pdf; Dynarski, M., Clarke, L., Cobb, B., Finn, B., & Rumberger, R. (2008). *Dropout prevention.* Retrieved June 8, 2010, from http://ies.ed.gov/ncee/wwc/pdf/practiceguides/dp_pg_090308.pdf; Thornburgh, N. (2006, April). Dropout nation. *Time*, pp. 30–40.

from low lifetime earnings, to high incarceration rates, to the likelihood that the dropout's children will also drop out of high school and start the cycle anew.

What can schools and teachers do? There are no simple solutions to the problem of students dropping out of school. But much of the dilemma is solvable with purposeful effort that focuses on the whole child. Addressing an isolated problem area will likely not be enough, but addressing several areas of concern may produce the desired result of keeping students in school.

In most instances, the students who drop out are capable of succeeding academically: Most are passing when they drop out, and 70% are confident they could complete the program of study (Education Vital Signs [EVS], 2006). Educators don't need to dumb down the curriculum. Efforts to retain students should center on some or all of the following suggestions:

1. Know the warning signs. For instance, sixth graders who don't regularly attend school, receive poor marks for behavior, or fail math or English for any reason have only a 10% chance of graduating (EVS, 2006). So, even a group of sixth graders can be targeted for intervention.
2. Establish ninth grade academies. Many schools have found success in separating ninth graders and providing them with extra counseling and support.
3. Consistently provide engaging curricula and instruction.
4. Maintain a safe environment and a welcoming climate.
5. Ensure an adult advocate for every student at every grade level. This person may be a classroom teacher, counselor, mentor, or administrator who has a specific responsibility to stay connected to the student.
6. Improve home and school communication.
7. Provide flexible school configurations of both time and space that address the preferences and developmental needs of students.

Points of Reflection 9.10

What experiences have you had with dropping out? Do you know students who dropped out? What have their experiences been?

CONCLUDING THOUGHTS

There's a saying "We cannot control the wind, but we can adjust our sails." The societal issues that negatively affect students are complex and multidimensional. They don't begin with us, and most won't be completely resolved through us. However, with that reality in view, we can begin to focus on positive steps to prevent or halt risky behaviors and their impact on children and adolescents. Controlling the wind may not be within our reach as teachers, but it is indeed possible to adjust both our own and our students' sails.

After reading the ***Chapter in Review,*** read about Brandi's dilemma involving child neglect and respond to items in this chapter's ***Developing Professional Competence.***

Chapter in Review

How do family, community, and society impact students in the United States?

- Families, communities, and society in general can support student success or thwart it.
- Children and adolescents who are victims of child abuse or neglect are at risk physically, emotionally, socially, and academically.
- Communities can provide vital services for students and their families.

How does socioeconomic status affect students in the United States?

- The privilege gap between the haves and have-nots is a societal dilemma with far-reaching ramifications for children and adolescents.
- Children in low-income settings have many disadvantages that affect achievement in school.
- The most devastating impact of poverty is homelessness.

How do health issues affect students in the United States?

- The rates of most forms of substance abuse have recently decreased, yet even one child or adolescent harmed by substance abuse is one too many.
- Children and adolescents often have an unfounded sense of immortality, which makes them feel they will not be harmed if they use substances such as inhalants, alcohol, legal and illegal drugs, and tobacco.
- Risky sexuality-related behavior can result in emotional distress, sexually transmitted diseases, and unplanned pregnancy.
- Teasing and harassment about homosexuality can be the root of distress for students in and out of school.
- Childhood obesity is near epidemic proportions and has long-term negative effects on students and society.
- Suicide is the third leading cause of adolescent deaths, with contributing factors that may be recognizable, leading to intervention.

How does race affect students in the United States?

- Racism is a form of prejudice stemming from the belief that one race is superior to another.
- Racism may take the form of inaction through silence or of low expectations for certain students.
- Immigrants and their children require special attention to ensure success in school.

What are the effects of bullying, theft, and violence on schools and students in the United States?

- Bullying can be verbal, physical, or emotional and is intended to exert power and cause harm.
- Violent acts in school include simple assault (usually fighting), sexual assault, and aggravated assault (definite perpetrator and victim) and occur most frequently in urban areas and among high school students.

How do truancy and dropping out affect youth in the United States?

- Truancy is a reliable predictor of dropping out.
- The dropout rate in the United States is over 30%, with long-term negative effects for students, families, communities, and the country.
- Reasons for dropping out are many and complex, with financial, self-esteem, and crime-related consequences.

Developing Professional Competence

Thoughtfully reading this scenario and responding to the items that follow it will help you prepare for licensure exams.

One thing Principal Laura Hill at Summit Primary School is adamant about is making sure there is a visible adult at home when her kindergarten students and first and second graders are dropped off by the bus after school. The drivers are instructed to bring children back to school if an adult does not appear in the yard or doorway. Consistently, an adult welcomes Caroline each afternoon.

Caroline is in Brandi Wade's kindergarten class. She is quiet and shy. As you read in the beginning of the chapter, in December Brandi rearranged physical aspects and instructional strategies in her class based on her observations of the children. During the first couple of months of the year her concern for Caroline grew. Although her mom came to Back-to-School Night and raised no red flags for Brandi, she sees some indications that all may not be well at Caroline's house.

In her 12 years as a classroom teacher she has seen bruises and burn marks on children and has reported them to the principal, who took appropriate action. After the fact she has known of sexual abuse of her students, but she has never had suspicions. Brandi sees no obvious signs of abuse with Caroline but rather subtle hints of something wrong. On the playground, there are times when she notices that Caroline appears to be sore when she walks. Brandi has also noticed that when a man is around, Caroline clings to her. One day during free drawing time, Caroline drew a picture of a man that was anatomically pretty accurate.

Think through this scenario and answer the following multiple-choice questions:

1. Because there are no overt signs of neglect, Brandi should
   a. continue to watch Caroline and document what she notices.
   b. talk with Principal Hill about her observations and leave it to her to pursue the situation.
   c. try to get Caroline to confide in her.
   d. ask a family in Caroline's neighborhood if they notice anything suspicious about the family.

2. One day Caroline mentions that her mother has a boyfriend who lives with them. Brandi's response to this should be to
   a. tell Principal Hill immediately.
   b. ask Caroline if she likes him.

   c. call Caroline's mom and ask for a parent conference.
   d. wait and see what else happens.

3. The children like to post their drawings on a large bulletin board in Brandi's classroom. She encourages them to do so. On the day she sees Caroline's drawing, how might she avoid having the picture of the man posted?
   a. She could ask the children to put their drawings in their desks and then take Caroline's after the children leave for the day.
   b. She could say she will choose drawings for the day that will be posted.
   c. She could post all the drawings in an effort to let Caroline know she has done nothing wrong.
   d. She could say they don't have time to post at the moment and she would just like to keep the children's drawings for now.

Now it's time for you to respond to two short essay items involving the scenario. In your responses, be sure to address all the dilemmas and questions posed in each item. Your responses should each be between one half and one full double-spaced page.

4. There is always a danger that stepping into a domestic problem will actually make it worse. Perhaps nothing wrong is taking place. Given this, should Brandi share her concerns about Caroline as the holidays approach or wait until the children return after winter break? Explain your response.

5. Brandi takes the portion of InTASC Principle 10 that follows very seriously. She always tries to understand the context of her students' lives. This particular situation with Caroline, however, is a new challenge and one that makes her feel inadequate to handle. What might Brandi do to help Caroline feel safe in school and not to fear the men who are part of the school environment?

InTASC Knowledge, Principle 10

The teacher seeks appropriate leadership roles and opportunities to take responsibility for student learning, to collaborate with learners, families, colleagues, other school professionals, and community members to ensure learner growth, and to advance the profession.

Ethical and Legal Issues in U.S. Schools

Dear Reader

Teachers hold a unique position in a community. In our trust are the children, the dearest resource of love and hope for each generation. It's an awesome responsibility and an opportunity for service, challenge, and fulfillment that few professions provide. Along with responsibility and opportunity come legal and ethical guidelines.

Please carefully consider the topics in this chapter. Even though very few teachers have legal issues over the course of their careers, avoiding problems and circumstances that may put your career in jeopardy requires a healthy dose of common sense and an understanding of the laws that directly relate to teachers and schools. We teachers are citizens and, as such, enjoy the same rights as other citizens. However, because teachers represent their schools, there are policies and expectations that affect what we do and what we say both inside the schoolhouse and in the community. The more we know about laws, policies, and expectations, the better.

Ethical guidelines are not legislated. Because teachers spend their days with children and adolescents who bring their experiences, families, and cultures to school with them, situations are often not simply black or white, but are tinged with subtle shades of gray. Most dilemmas and decisions you will make as a teachers have no laws, or even school policies, to guide you. This is where a sense of ethics will be very important.

This chapter explores ethical values involved in being a teacher, the nature of the relationship between ethics and laws,

and rights and responsibilities of both teachers and students. These are the questions we consider:

- What does it mean to be an ethical teacher?
- How do laws affect schools, teachers, and students?
- What are the legal rights of teachers?
- What are the legal responsibilities of teachers?
- How does the law impact the relationship between school and religion?
- What are the legal rights of students?

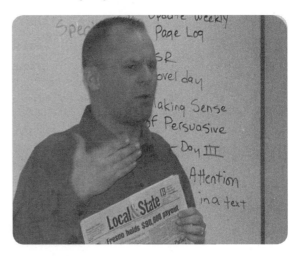

Derek Boucher teaches modern world history and U.S. history at Roosevelt High School in Fresno, California. He is also the reading intervention teacher for sophomores and juniors, many of whom are English-language learners. It is in this capacity that Derek feels a keen sense of responsibility toward building his students' literacy skills. He tirelessly searches for ways to engage his students in reading.

Derek believes that to transform students into readers, it is important to make reading both satisfying and focused on meaning. The nature of the content is what pulls students into the process. Consequently, Derek continually builds his classroom library. He selects books and magazines that will capture student imagination. He engages students in literature by selecting topics and sources that capture student interest yet contain embedded skills instruction. To draw students into his lesson, Derek is shown using a newspaper article that gives examples of sexual stereotyping.

Derek's passion for teaching compels him to grow professionally. He tells us, "Professional literature has changed my life as a teacher. That's why I'm an avid reader of books and journals that push me to think more deeply and conceptually about teaching and pedagogy." Derek regularly expresses his views on curricula and reading instruction by writing letters to the editor and opinion pieces for newspapers and magazines. He extends his influence in this way because he sees it as the right thing to do. Watch **Derek's interview** to get to know him better.

The United States has laws for a reason—they make it possible for people to live together as a nation. Laws prompt civility in neighborhoods, towns, cities, states, and across the country. We gain perspective and more fully understand how laws affect the daily work of teachers by examining actual people and events that have helped shape the fabric of laws that affect education. The cases in this chapter are not fictional. They are true. Read carefully and think about the implications for your future career in an early childhood, elementary, middle, or high school classroom. But first, consider how ethical standards play a major role in the teaching profession.

What Does It Mean to Be an Ethical Teacher?

Laws tell us what we can and can't do. **Ethics** tell us what we should and shouldn't do. Ethics are standards of conduct based on moral judgments. Because ethics are grounded in personal belief systems, what is ethical in one person's view might not be ethical from another's perspective. Although most of the time what is lawful is also ethical, and what is ethical is also lawful, this is not always the case from everyone's viewpoint. For instance, abortion is legal in the United States, but many U.S. citizens consider it unethical. For some people with strong antiabortion beliefs, acting on personal ethics may mean becoming involved in unlawful forms of protest against a legal activity.

PROFESSIONAL ETHICS

Most professions have codes of ethics. The largest teacher organization, the National Education Association (NEA), has a code of ethics you may read on the NEA website. The NEA Code of Ethics is divided into two sections: teacher commitment to students and teacher commitment to the profession. The code lists actions teachers "shall not" take to fulfill obligations to students and the teaching profession.

It is important for teachers to understand the "shall nots" of teaching that serve as guidelines to help us avoid unethical situations and their consequences. However, there are also many "shalls" involved in practicing ethical teaching, as we have discussed throughout this entire text. If these positive elements are internalized, practicing ethical teaching becomes habitual. Ethical teachers *shall*:

- purposefully serve as positive role models for their students
- put students' best interests ahead of other considerations
- involve families often and positively
- support colleagues and work collaboratively
- create and maintain a productive learning environment
- diversify instruction to address student differences

Laws do not dictate these actions; ethical attitudes and beliefs call for them. Similarly, Derek Boucher's attitudes and actions with regard to the teaching profession, both inside and outside the classroom, stem from his ethics.

Let's bring these concepts into the reality of the classroom by examining what it means to be an ethical teacher. Regardless of what else our students learn, they learn *us*. We either represent, or *mis*represent, ethical behavior in the classroom.

ETHICS FOR TEACHERS

An ethical teacher is guided by a set of beliefs that leads to attitudes and actions focused on what's best for students. Being ethical means taking the high road and behaving professionally in the midst of big issues as well as in everyday decision making in the classroom.

Howe (1996) tells us that six characteristics form a conceptual basis for making ethical decisions. The first characteristic, appreciation for moral deliberation, means understanding that situations are complex and that part of our obligation is to ensure that the rights of all involved are protected. The second characteristic, empathy, refers to the ability to put oneself mentally in the place of others to appreciate a variety of perspectives. Knowledge, the third characteristic, is necessary to have a clear view of the dilemma at hand. Dealing with knowledge requires reasoning, the fourth characteristic, and courage, the fifth characteristic, is needed to act on that reasoning. Finally, the sixth characteristic, interpersonal skills, allows teachers to communicate effectively with others about their ethical deliberations. These six characteristics are described in Figure 10.1. Characteristics 2 through 6 are self-explanatory. This doesn't diminish their value, but we know what they look like in practice more often than we do characteristic number 1.

Cultivating an "appreciation for moral deliberation," as Howe puts it, is a career-long area of growth for teachers. When we have big decisions to make, we generally see the right and wrong sides pretty clearly. We know there are consequences for our choices and we usually recognize many of them. This is a good thing. But what about the seemingly little decisions and actions, the things we do, or don't do, on a regular basis? Is it possible that these less-than-life-changing situations have "complex moral dimensions" and require that we have a "realization that care is needed to protect the rights of all parties"? Bringing higher-order thinking and problem-solving skills to bear on all dilemmas, big and small, is what teachers must do.

In Table 10.1 you'll find some sample attitudes and decisions leading to actions, along with questions a teacher might consider. Could a teacher be dismissed because

---

Figure 10.1 Six desirable characteristics for teachers as they make ethical judgments

1. Appreciation for Moral Deliberation—ability to see complex moral dimensions of a problem and realization that care is needed to protect the rights of all parties
2. Empathy—ability to "get inside the skin of another"
3. Knowledge—facts to enable us to put issues in context
4. Reasoning—reflecting systematically on an issue and moving step by step to a conclusion
5. Courage—the willpower to act in what we perceive to be the right way, rather than just the comfortable way
6. Interpersonal Skills—communicating about issues sensitively and tactfully

Source: Howe, K. R. (1996, May/June). A conceptual basis for ethics in teacher education. *Journal of Teacher Education, 37*, 6.

TABLE 10.1 Recognizing ethical dilemmas

Attitudes/Decisions/Actions	Thinking It Through
With a wink, I say to a few students that I think I'm coming down with something. I return 48 hours later with an obvious skier's sunburn.	Is it OK to indicate to students that I am going to call in sick when I'm really planning to go on a ski trip? What lesson are they learning from me about responsibility and honesty?
A spelling bee competition is planned for tomorrow in which all the students in each class must participate. I have three students who are English-language learners. I really want to win this bee because I am a candidate for my school's Teacher of the Year award. I casually mention to the three students that tomorrow would be a great day to stay home and enjoy the new-fallen snow because it's Friday before winter vacation and they won't miss much.	Have I let my desire to look good get in the way of doing what's right for my students? Without these three students, my fifth grade class has the best chance of winning our grade-level bee. Winning will be a big boost for my students. So am I justified in encouraging these three students to stay home? After all, it's Friday before winter vacation and not much will go on that's academic in nature besides the spelling bee. They won't miss much . . . or will they?
On a field trip to a local museum I decide to buy each student a cold drink from a vending machine. I drop in two quarters and out pops not just one soda, but three. I laugh and say this must be my lucky day.	It's only a dollar loss for the vending company, but am I setting a good example for students? If I think that cheating the system makes me lucky, what message am I giving my students?
I just started a landscaping business that hopefully will occupy my weekends and give me extra income. I have developed an advertising flyer that I will distribute in the community. Because I haven't made much money yet, I decide to use the school copier late one afternoon to make a thousand flyers.	The students will likely never know I did this. But if another teacher walks into the workroom and sees what I'm doing, will my reputation be somewhat affected?
A parent generously donated $200 for me to buy a classroom set of a novel to use in spring semester. She determined the donation amount by going to a local bookstore. Knowing that I would get a 10% teacher discount, she gave me a check rather than buying the books herself. I go online and find the books for $150 and order them. I decide that it was my ingenuity that resulted in the discount and decide to keep the extra $50 for my trouble.	It's unlikely that anyone will ever know about this, so why should I care? After all, I work very hard as a teacher and this is just a small perk. Is $50 worth living with a small voice inside that says I should have spent the money on something for my classroom?
It's time for the first-quarter grades to be submitted just as football season has become very exciting. Our team is looking promising as a contender for the district championship. Mike has a 68% in my class, making him ineligible to play in a big rivalry game Friday night. He's had a lot to do with practice every afternoon and he's a really good guy. I decide to make his grade a C– instead of a D.	I didn't make this adjustment for several other students who struggled, or maybe didn't struggle enough, to make a C–. Because I insist that all my students keep up with their grade averages, Mike will know that I changed his grade. What message am I sending him about doing just enough to get by and then receiving "gifts"? If he brags about this, what about the other students, both those who didn't get the extra boost and others who do fine in my class but will know that I fudged on Mike's grade? Will some parent discover what I have done and complain to my principal?
It's time once again to promote the sale of wrapping paper to earn money for school projects. I send a letter home encouraging parents to join in. I e-mail parents each day reminding them to help their students sell the paper. I promise the students a party, but only for those who bring in orders for $100 of paper. The students feel the pressure, as do the parents.	Because my class is composed of kids from a wide range of socioeconomic-level homes, am I unduly putting pressure on some families who don't know many people with discretionary money to spend on fancy wrapping paper? If I still like the party idea, how might I design the party incentive so that particular students would not be ostracized?
Because fund-raising efforts have been disappointing in recent years, and our school improvement team wants to landscape the courtyard, our principal decides to give each student who brings a $20 donation 10 points to be used on any test in any class during the quarter.	At first I buy into this plan, not considering the fairness or morality of it. Then a student comes to me and complains that being able to give $20 will be difficult. Suddenly I see this initiative as very unfair and fundamentally misguided. Should I express this to my principal? Should I tell my students that I won't honor the 10-point bonus?

of these? Maybe, but probably not. Would a teacher's reputation suffer in the eyes of some? Maybe, and probably so. Every teacher could name similar—as well as very different—scenarios from personal experience, if prompted to think about it. Perhaps there's the dilemma: *if prompted to think about it.* When our actions go unexamined, we are less likely to consider moral deliberation and therefore not be the ethical teachers we might otherwise become.

When we habitually apply ethical thinking and actions (the "shalls" referred to earlier) to situations, we are contributing to the development of students who ideally will do the same. As we model morally sound decision making, it is helpful to have a vision of desirable traits we want to promote in those we profoundly influence through ethical teaching. In writing about her vision of young adolescents, Donna Marie San Antonio (2006, p. 7) simply and eloquently describes some desirable traits. We want students to be

- smart but not arrogant
- flexible but not easily deterred from their hopes and dreams

- compassionate toward others but not overly accommodating
- self-confident but not too preoccupied with themselves
- proud but not exclusive

Helping students build these traits is a tall order and one we must fulfill with ethical attitudes, decisions, and actions. The results will be positive and cumulative.

Now that you have considered what it means to be an ethical teacher and some of the ways ethics guide classroom practice, it's time to look at more concrete guidelines.

Points of Reflection 10.1

What are your memories of teachers who promoted ethical behavior? Describe a scenario from your PreK–12 school experiences.

What are your memories of teachers who displayed unethical attitudes and actions? Describe a scenario from your PreK–12 school experiences.

How Do Laws Affect Schools, Teachers, and Students?

The U.S. government, its legal system, and the laws that affect schools, teachers, and students are based on a balance of rights and responsibilities. The government and legal system achieve a viable balance of power through the interaction of the three branches of government: executive, legislative, and judicial. Since the founding of the United States of America, four basic sources of law have directly impacted the everyday work of all teachers: the U.S. Constitution, federal laws, state and local laws and policies, and case law.

U.S. CONSTITUTION

The Constitution does not specifically mention education. However, certain amendments directly impact teachers and schools.

First Amendment. The First Amendment to the Constitution, shown in Figure 10.2, guarantees, among other things, freedom of speech and religion and prohibits government (i.e., public school) advancement of religion. The relationship between law and religion is discussed later in this chapter.

Freedom of speech, as guaranteed in the First Amendment, applies to schools. As you read this chapter you'll recognize how often the First Amendment is cited as a guide in decision making on educational issues. The Association for Supervision and Curriculum Development (ASCD) established The First Amendment Center to provide resources to assist schools in implementing the guiding principles of the First Amendment.

Fourth Amendment. The Fourth Amendment protects citizens from unreasonable search and seizure and, in doing so, protects the basic privacy and security of all people, including students' rights to privacy. For instance, do students have the right to keep whatever they want in a locker assigned to them? Under what circumstances can adults examine the locker's contents? This topic is discussed later in the chapter.

Fourteenth Amendment. The Fourteenth Amendment protects the rights of due process and guarantees equal protection to all citizens. For teachers, this amendment pertains to job security and the right to be heard if charges are made against them. Later in the chapter we examine how this amendment affects both teachers and students.

Figure 10.2 First Amendment

Congress shall make no law respecting an establishment of religion, or prohibiting the free exercise thereof; or abridging the freedom of speech, or the press; or the right of the people peaceably to assemble, and to petition the government for a redress of grievances.

The general guidelines of the U.S. Constitution, specifically the First, Fourth, and Fourteenth Amendments, provide the framework for the federal laws that affect schools, teachers, and students.

FEDERAL LAWS

The federal statutes written and passed by Congress (the legislative branch of the U.S. government) have a major impact on the daily work of teachers and the operation of schools.

Here are examples of federal laws impacting education:

- The National Defense Education Act (1958) established curricular priorities, placing math, science, and foreign languages at the top.
- The Civil Rights Act (1964) officially ended generations of overt racial segregation in public schools by declaring, "No person in the United States shall on the grounds of race, color, or national origin, be excluded from participation in or be denied the benefits of, or be subjected to discrimination under any program or activity receiving federal financial assistance." Unfortunately, however, segregation still exists in public schools in many areas.
- The Elementary and Secondary Education Act (1965) was originated to benefit children in low socioeconomic settings. This act created Title I funding and has been reauthorized several times.
- The Bilingual Education Act (1968) proposed that students be taught in their native languages while they learned English.
- Federal Title IX legislation (1972) opened many doors, specifically to girls, by prohibiting discrimination based on gender.
- The Individuals with Disabilities Education Act (1975, 1990, 2004) guarantees the rights of students with disabilities to a free education in the least restrictive environment.

Another federal law you've read about many times throughout this text is the 2001 reauthorization of the Elementary and Secondary Education Act, known as No Child Left Behind. This federal law has significantly impacted schools thus far into the 21st century.

STATE AND LOCAL LAWS AND POLICIES

The U.S. Constitution stipulates that anything not specifically addressed by it becomes a state issue. Consequently, laws and policies affecting education vary from state to state, and from district to district within each state. Some of the issues addressed by state and local laws and policies include curriculum standards and assessment mandates, as well as funding and governance. The guidelines for teacher certification are also left up to states, with some federal stipulations.

CASE LAW

Many legal decisions concerning education are based on precedents—what has been done in the past and what the judicial system has decided with regard to specific rights and responsibilities. The cases brought before the courts are deliberated and settled based on what the U.S. Constitution says, what federal law dictates, and what state and local governing bodies have established. All of these aspects are considered, ideally with heaping doses of common sense, as decisions are made by the courts.

Case law is based on the doctrine of *stare decisis,* a Latin phrase meaning "let the decision stand." This means that once a decision is made in a court of law, that decision sets a precedent for future cases of a similar nature until challenged or overturned. There is a large body of federal case law on which state and local cases rely for precedents. A decision made by the U.S. Supreme Court establishes case law until either the Supreme Court changes the ruling or an amendment to the Constitution alters the decision. Unfortunately, many school and local government officials have not abided by this principle. Because the Supreme Court doesn't have an enforcement arm, continued court action is sometimes necessary to bring school districts into compliance. For instance, the famous *Brown* v. *Board of Education* (1954) court decision ruled that separate schools are not equal and opened many schoolhouse doors for African Americans. Occasionally during the last 60 years, however, decisions have been made that do not comply with the *Brown* results, and more court action has been needed (LaMorte, 2012).

Throughout this chapter, discussions of the legal rights and responsibilities of teachers, the rights of students, and the relationship between schools and religion will cite sample case law. In this chapter's **The Opinion Page** feature, we read about actions that allegedly conflict with case law.

THE OPINION PAGE

This Opinion Editorial appeared in The Stamford Advocate, *Connecticut, on March 8, 2013.*

A Return to School Segregation?

by Wendy Lecker

Wendy Lecker is a columnist for Hearst Connecticut Media Group and is senior attorney for the Campaign for Fiscal Equity project at the Education Law Center.

From Brown vs. Board of Education to Connecticut's landmark case, Sheff v. O'Neill, to the language of the Connecticut constitution, the law has been clear. Children have a constitutionally guaranteed right to a public education that is not impaired by isolation based on race, ethnicity, national origin or disability. Therefore, it is unconstitutional to develop and fund education programs that intentionally or unintentionally limit access to educational opportunities based on racial or ethnic backgrounds, or disabilities. Yet recently, it was announced that schools exclusively for "gifted" children will be opening in Windham, New London, and Bridgeport. Whether intended or not, the proposal takes Connecticut back to the ugly era of school segregation.

These three districts plan to pull what they characterize as "gifted" children from their schools and create separate schools "to highlight and encourage the potential" of these particular students. The schools are modeled after the Renzulli Academy in Hartford, named for UConn professor Joseph Renzulli, and serving "gifted" children in kindergarten and in fourth through ninth grades.

Admission to this school is based on Connecticut Mastery Test scores, grades and a teacher recommendation, although a representative at the school explained that the scores are the "big part" of admissions. Decades of research have proven that standardized tests are an unreliable and inaccurate measure of student achievement and do not measure student potential. In fact, the data reveal that the strongest correlation is between test scores and socio-economic status.

The gross injustice of relying on these tests scores is apparent at the Hartford Renzulli Academy. In 2011, the school had no ELL (English Language Learners) or any students with disabilities. In 2012, the school had but one ELL student and only 6 of the 120 students were classified as students with disabilities. The notion that you cannot be "gifted" if you do not speak English or if you need special education services is absurd.

Beyond the faulty admissions criteria, segregating so-called gifted children into a separate school contravenes what we know about a child's educational development. Children blossom at different times. A child who may not display his gifts at 10 may develop them at 13, given the appropriate access to learning. Conversely, a child who may read at an advanced stage at age 5 may find that her classmates have caught up to her developmentally by age 7, thus erasing her perceived "gift." Cementing children into a classification at one age, and denying them access to higher-level learning deprives those in the lower level of that chance to blossom. Until now, even Joseph Renzulli asserted that his gifted pedagogy was designed to work in all school settings for all children.

The most disturbing issue of all is that creating separate schools for "gifted" children violates Connecticut law and policies prohibiting school segregation. While the equal protection clauses in most state constitutions only bar discrimination, Connecticut's expressly bans segregation as well as discrimination. In Sheff v. O'Neill, our Supreme Court ruled that segregation has pernicious effects on children whether that segregation is intentional or unorchestrated, and ruled that the state must act to prevent and eradicate school segregation.

Connecticut's state Board of Education recognized that segregation has a destructive effect on children's educational opportunities. In its 2010 resolution against tracking, the board wrote that grouping by ability "limits achievement and stifles expectation and opportunity for college and successful competition in the workplace" because it denies those in lower levels access to a more challenging curriculum and higher expectations. The board unanimously disapproved any practice that permanently groups students for instruction. As the board noted, the practice of tracking disproportionately burdens poor, African-American and Latino students.

(continued)

(continued)

The state board resolved that any school district that assigned students to a particular level based on assessed or perceived readiness had to disclose this fact to parents and report to the state the research proving that this separate placement was necessary, the length of time it planned to deny children in lower levels access to learning with higher-achieving peers, and the demographic characteristics of those children denied access to higher-achieving peers. Now, only three years later, officials stand silent as Connecticut abandons its commitment to desegregation. Indeed, it appears that our leaders are acting to speed re-segregation.

In recent years the state has dramatically increased funding for privately run charter schools that routinely exclude non-English-speaking students and students with disabilities. And now, we have a proposal for "gifted only" schools, equipped with "gifted only" water fountains, "gifted only" bathrooms and "gifted only" lunchrooms.

Something is very wrong here.

Copyright © 2013 *The Stamford Advocate*.

This Opinion Page piece is an impassioned statement against student segregation. The writer knows the law and is observing instances that she perceives as Connecticut schools not adhering to either the spirit or the letter of the law. Write a well-developed paragraph in response to each of the following questions:

1. Ms. Lecker expresses her dismay at the proposed admissions criteria for the three schools designed exclusively for gifted children based largely on results of Connecticut's state assessment, the Connecticut Mastery Test. Do you agree or disagree with her opinion of the use of this primary criteria? Why?

2. The 2010 resolution against tracking, or grouping by ability, was a bold step for Connecticut's Board of Education. What does the statement that tracking "disproportionately burdens poor, African-American and Latino students" mean? Did you experience tracking? If so, how did you feel about it? If you never experienced tracking, what is your opinion of the practice?

3. Who would most likely challenge the proposed schools exclusively for gifted children? Briefly explain three legally-based actions or events that will likely be persuasive in court.

Figure 10.3 Relationship of law and ethics

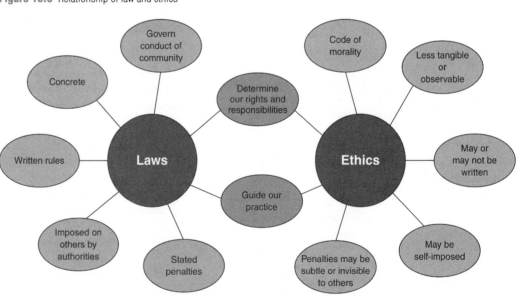

Before addressing the rights and responsibilities of teachers and students, consider the relationship between laws and ethics. Take a few minutes to examine Figure 10.3 that shows how laws and ethics differ in a number of ways, yet still share some qualities.

What Are the Legal Rights of Teachers?

Teachers in the United States are entitled to the same rights as other Americans. Most teachers will never find themselves in positions where their legal rights are threatened in any way. The day-to-day realities of teaching rarely involve legal challenges.

However, some rights are occasionally tempered by the opinions of either the community or the court when there is concern that teachers' individual rights may impact classroom effectiveness. In addition, certain legal rights apply specifically to the teaching profession.

EMPLOYMENT LEGALITIES

Being employed by a school district entails understanding your rights and responsibilities. You will sign a contract, possibly have tenure in your future, and have procedures for filing grievances if things go wrong or if dismissal is threatened.

Teaching contracts. A **contract** is an agreement between parties that states the rights and responsibilities of each. A teacher signs an initial contract and then signs again each year to continue in the same position. Teaching contracts typically include a formal offer of employment, the salary, and a description of the position. When you sign a teaching contract, you state that you will abide by district policies. It is very important to carefully read and understand the policies and the contract. Both are extensive and may be written in complex language. Don't hesitate to ask for an explanation.

Contracts are binding on both parties. If you sign a contract and then back out or take a different job, or if the district backs out, you or the district can be sued for damages involving **breach of contract**.

Tenure. Continuing contract status is known as **tenure**. Most districts require teachers to serve successfully for about 3 years before offering them a continuing contract, or tenure. During these first 3 years or so, teachers can be dismissed for suspected incompetence or because of a general **reduction in force** of the district teacher population. Such a reduction may result from lower student numbers, budget cuts, or program cancellations. Reductions in force (RIFs) may also apply to tenured teachers. However, the general rule of "riffing" is that the last hired are the first to go.

A teacher with tenure is entitled to a contract each year unless the district has reason not to renew it or the teacher decides to go elsewhere. In most states tenure doesn't guarantee a particular position in a particular school, but it does guarantee employment in the district.

Some object to the concept of tenure because it requires more steps to dismiss an ineffective teacher who has tenure. However, even teachers with tenure cannot keep their jobs if they are shown to be incompetent, display immoral behaviors, are insubordinate, or are involved in any of a wide array of behaviors considered unprofessional conduct.

Dismissal. Teachers have been dismissed for many reasons, some of which sound outrageous to us today. Historically, teachers have been dismissed for not attending a particular church, for wearing pants in public (a female teacher), for marrying or becoming pregnant during the school year, and even for moving to a neighboring town. More recently the courts have ruled for dismissal due to, among others, the following reasons:

- insubordination
- neglect of duty
- conduct unbecoming a teacher
- incompetence
- physical or mental health problems
- engaging in illegal activities
- causing or encouraging disruptions

Some teacher offenses are considered by the courts to be remediable, meaning that given assistance and time, a teacher may be able to correct the problem and be effective in the classroom. For instance, if a district begins dismissal procedures because a tenured teacher's classroom management skills are considered very poor, the court will likely say the teacher has a right to try to remediate those skills. On the other hand, some actions are considered irremediable in that they are so unprofessional that a district is not obligated to provide assistance. Conviction in a criminal case and having a sexual relationship with a student are two examples of actions for which districts may begin immediate procedures toward dismissal.

A teacher's role-model effectiveness is based both on work and personal behavior. It relates to your reputation among students, staff, and in the community. Here are two overriding questions asked when considering dismissal:

- Is the educational process significantly disrupted by the teacher's action?
- Is the teacher's credibility significantly harmed among students, colleagues, families, and the community?

Due process. When a tenured teacher is threatened with dismissal, the steps the district must take to pursue the charges against the teacher are called **due process.** Due process is an important principle that requires guidelines to be followed to ensure that individuals are protected from arbitrary or capricious treatment by those in authority. The procedures of due process vary by state, but generally a teacher must be:

1. notified of the proposed charges
2. given reasonable time to examine evidence
3. told who will be called as witnesses and given the right to legal representation
4. provided with a hearing before an impartial jury, panel, and/or judge
5. given the opportunity to call witnesses and cross-examine the district's witnesses
6. afforded a decision based on evidence
7. provided a transcript of the proceedings
8. given the right to appeal

Even though due process has been in force for many years and will likely continue to be part of the profession, outcomes of hearings based on due process may vary by location and according to the times (LaMorte, 2012).

Points of Reflection 10.2

How do you feel about teachers going on strike and removing themselves from the classroom for a period of time during which collective bargaining takes place? Should teachers be allowed to strike—knowing it means closing schools during the process—because of grievances about their work environment (salary, hours, class size, etc.)? Why or why not?

Unions and collective bargaining. Although not exclusively related to getting and keeping a job, collective bargaining is a right practiced in most states by teacher unions. States often allow unions to negotiate with school boards concerning elements of teacher contracts and working conditions. The two major teacher organizations that act as unions are the National Education Association (NEA) and the American Federation of Teachers (AFT). States have their own affiliates of NEA or AFT to represent teachers in more local ways. Individual teachers and groups of teachers can file **grievances**, or formal complaints against a district. NEA and AFT, or their state affiliates, often represent teachers who file grievances. NEA and AFT, as unions, can also call for teacher strikes when collective bargaining does not result in changes that satisfy the large groups of teachers who affiliate with the unions.

FREEDOM OF EXPRESSION

There are many ways to express opinions and beliefs, including symbolic, written, and verbal expression. Symbolic expression generally involves making a statement by what is worn—a style of clothing, a political button, particular colors, an armband, a ribbon. Some symbolic statements are socially acceptable, even desirable.

For instance, ribbons showing support for breast cancer research or bracelets commemorating important days in history are considered appropriate. However, wearing an armband to protest an ongoing war, or wearing a shirt with inflammatory or offensive words or pictures, may be legal outside school but ruled unacceptable in school. These acts can serve as possible grounds for dismissal. Wearing shirts with religious messages are also grounds for dismissal. In 2001, a case determined that a teacher could not wear a "Jesus 2000" shirt because of its religious message (*Downing* v. *West Haven Board of Education*). For teachers, freedom of symbolic expression has limits, especially if it disrupts the school or classroom or makes it appear that the school endorses a particular viewpoint.

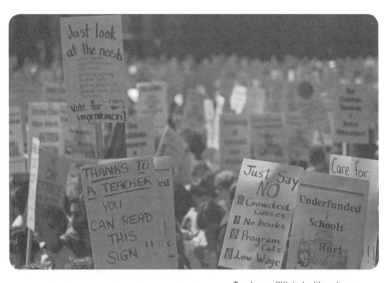

Teachers affiliated with unions may go on strike when collective bargaining does not result in satisfactory changes.

As with symbolic expression, written and spoken expression must not interrupt the education process. Teachers have the right to express themselves through letters to the editor, written articles, conversations, speeches, and debates. Since the often-quoted case of *Pickering* v. *Board of Education,* 1968, the courts have generally ruled on the side of teachers' rights to freedom of spoken and written expression, even when that expression involves harsh criticism of a school, district, or personnel connected to education. In *Pickering,* an Illinois teacher wrote a sarcastic letter to the editor criticizing the school superintendent and school board for funding practices. U.S. Supreme Court Justice Thurgood Marshall stated that the problem was one of balance between personal rights of the teacher and the district's right to promote efficient public service through its employees. The court ruled in favor of Pickering and his right to openly debate questions without fear of retaliatory dismissal.

If a teacher's expression is intended to incite unprofessional behavior, the courts may rule against the teacher, as in *Stroman* v. *Colleton County School District,* 1992. The teacher was dismissed because he asked other teachers to call in sick as a form of protest. The Supreme Court ruled in favor of the school district on grounds that encouraging others to lie is unprofessional.

ACADEMIC FREEDOM

Academic freedom is a form of expression that allows teachers to use their judgment in making decisions such as what to discuss, what to assign as readings, and what teaching strategies to employ. Like the other freedoms, academic freedom has limits that courts have upheld in many cases.

One recurring issue involves the courts' attempts to balance the right of academic freedom with a district's desire for students to learn a specific curriculum. Districts and states set the curriculum teachers must teach. When teachers exercise academic freedom and go beyond or eliminate parts of this curriculum, problems occur because either (1) including the additional topics does not leave time for the prescribed curriculum, or (2) the non-prescribed topics are controversial and may be deemed inappropriate.

In this era of standards and high-stakes testing, failing to teach the prescribed curriculum is likely to become evident when student test scores decline, but it may take years for a pattern of lower scores to emerge. The line between what is appropriate in the classroom, and what is not, is the most common cause of disagreements between districts and teachers with regard to academic freedom. Some of the topics deemed inappropriate in the public school classroom when they are not part of the curriculum include sexuality-related issues, gun control, abortion, some political issues, and any topic involving offensive language. For instance, in *Keefe* v. *Geanakos,* 1969, a Massachusetts high school English teacher assigned an article from the *Atlantic Monthly* that contained offensive language. He was fired because he would not agree to never give the assignment again. A court decision gave Keefe his job back and stated that because some of the school's library books contained the same words and students would likely not be shocked by them, parental complaints about the words did not dictate what was proper in the classroom.

Some teaching methods may be deemed inappropriate if a teacher cannot substantiate the approach using professional opinions and research. Even if the teacher takes a case to court to try to acquire the right to use a method and loses, dismissal is seldom based on the attempt to use the strategy. In *Murray* v. *Pittsburgh Board of Education,* 1996, a teacher used a motivational technique called "Learnball" with at-risk high school students involving dividing the class into teams. Competition between teams involved rewards, such as listening to the radio and shooting baskets with foam balls. The school board ordered the teacher not to use the method. Murray sued the board but lost. The courts determined that the school board had the right to set policy against particular teaching methodologies.

Table 10.2 consists of court cases and some thoughts about their implications for you as a teacher. The general direction of court cases today that consider dismissal tends more toward defending a teacher's personal liberty than in the past. Table 10.3 consists of cases decided in favor of the teacher. Don't dismiss a case because it seems to be from a long time ago. The alleged misconduct and subsequent court decisions are still relevant as case law. Take your time as you read about real cases and either court-sanctioned dismissal or court-ordered reinstatement.

TEACHERS' PERSONAL LIVES

A teacher has a right to a personal life. However, the concept that teachers are role models entails more limits than people in other professions experience. These limits have been upheld in the courts, with some limits more clearly defined than others. As late as the 1960s, teachers were quickly and without challenge fired for adultery, drunkenness, homosexual conduct, illegal drug use, unmarried cohabitation with the opposite sex, or becoming pregnant while single. Today a teacher's personal conduct must be shown to have a direct negative effect on job performance to result in dismissal.

Personal conduct and job performance. The notion that teachers can be automatically fired for what is considered by the community as immoral behavior was rejected by the California Supreme Court in *Morrison* v. *State Board of Education,* 1969. The court found that grounds for dismissal must include evidence that the personal conduct of a teacher adversely affects job performance. The court also said it was dangerous to allow the terms *immoral* and *unprofessional* to be interpreted too broadly. It was established that immoral conduct means vastly different things to different people. To some individuals, immoral behavior includes laziness, gluttony, selfishness, and cowardice, and unprofessional conduct for teachers may include signing controversial petitions, opposing majority opinions, and drinking alcoholic beverages. In Morrison, the court ruled that a teacher should not be fired because someone disapproves of the teacher's personal life unless it directly relates to his or her professional work, and that today's morals may well be considered absurd in the future. In recent decades, the courts have generally ruled that teachers have the right to privacy in regard to procreation, marriage, child rearing, and other activities in the home (Schimmel, Stellman, & Fischer, 2011).

Since 1969 other cases have been brought to courts by teachers who felt they were wrongly dismissed. The courts continue to look for evidence that particular conduct adversely affects job performance. In *Eckmann* v. *Board of Education,* 1986, an Illinois teacher was fired when she became pregnant while unmarried and decided to raise the

Points of Reflection 10.3

Are there issues about which a teacher should not talk or write if it means the community will be aware of his or her views? If not, justify your answer. If so, what is one issue and why?

If you felt strongly about teaching a particular topic in an advanced high school class, but the district said that you should not spend time on that topic even though it was not offensive, how would you respond?

TABLE 10.2 Teacher dismissal cases and implications

Case	Explanation	Implications for Teachers
Walthart v. *Board of Directors* Iowa, 2005	Teacher had knowledge that her minor son and his teenage friends were consuming alcohol on her property, but failed to intervene. Court held that her ability to be a role model was damaged.	This happens more frequently than we realize. Not only is it against the law, but, for a teacher, it represents incredibly poor judgment.
Nancy J. Zelno v. *Lincoln Intermediate Unit No. 12 Board of Directors* Pennsylvania, 2001	Teacher had 3 DUI offenses and 2 offenses for driving while her license was suspended. She was incarcerated on weekends during the school year and remained incarcerated through the summer until her sentence was completed.	Engaging in illegal activities by drinking while driving shows a blatant disregard for safety and teachers should never be in this position. Your personal life can indeed impact your reputation and status as a role model.
Gaylord v. *Board of Education, Unified School District, Morton County* Kansas, 1990	Teacher called in sick after his request for a day off was denied.	Not only is this *insubordination*, but it also shows a real lack of good sense. Teacher work schedules are reasonable when compared to most professions. Always try to arrange travel and activities on weekends or days designated as teacher holidays.
Stroman v. *Colleton County School District* South Carolina, 1992	Teacher circulated a letter to encourage his fellow teachers to engage in a "sick-out" to protest change in methods for paying teachers and perceived budgetary mismanagement.	This is a clear case of *causing or encouraging a disruption*. There are legitimate ways to express concern over policies that will garner respect for you and your colleagues when disagreements arise. Encouraging others to lie is unprofessional and a sure way to lose both respect and a teaching position.
Ware v. *Morgan County School District* Colorado,1988	High school music teacher took a misbehaving student outside and used obscene language to tell him he was a disgrace to the band.	This is wrong on so many levels and definitely *conduct unbecoming a teacher*. First, telling a student he is a disgrace is never appropriate. His actions may be disgraceful, but he is not a disgrace. Second, use of profanity around or directed at a student is never acceptable. It is offensive and unprofessional. The best way to make sure we don't use foul language at school is to completely eliminate it from our personal vocabulary.
Krizek v. *Cicero-Stickney Township High School* Illinois, 1989	Teacher was dismissed for showing an R-rated movie to her class as a modern-day parallel to *Our Town*. She apparently told her students they would be excused if their parents objected, but she did not communicate directly with parents. The court upheld dismissal saying the movie was a planned event, and not an inadvertent mistake, and that her methodology was problematic.	All schools require parental permission in writing for students to watch R-rated movies. This fact can't be ignored; doing so constitutes *neglect of duty*. If you ever have doubt about an activity, take that doubt as a sure sign that you should ask an administrator for advice.
Faulkner v. *New Bern-Craven County Board Of Education* North Carolina, 1984	Teacher was found to habitually and excessively use alcohol. He even consumed some form of alcoholic beverages at school, or, at least, had the odor of alcohol on his breath at school during instructional hours after warnings against doing so.	While drinking alcohol is legal for adults, doing so in excess in a community harms a teacher's reputation for using good judgment. Certainly consuming alcohol at school is absolutely wrong. All it takes is the odor of alcohol to cause an investigation. This is a case of *conduct unbecoming a teacher*, with personal behavior affecting perception of professional competence.
School District No. 1 v. *Cornish* Colorado, 2002	Teacher refused to teach the approved math curriculum she considered to not meet state standards. She also did not provide lesson plans per the principal's resulting directive.	Yes, teachers know what students need to learn and be able to do to meet standards. However, we are not in a position to dictate school or district curriculum by ourselves and refusal to teach the designated curriculum amounts to *insubordination*. We must teach the curriculum provided and, if we think it's lacking, supplement what we feel is necessary while making our opinion known to those in authority. There is a fine line between doing what we know is best for students and being insubordinate in the face of mandates. The surest stance for everyone's sake is to do what is mandated and try to change it with reasoning, not refusal. Remember, if we do not have a teaching position, we have no impact on kids.
Crosby v. *Holt* Tennessee, 2009	Teacher had an inappropriate relationship with a female student, sent inappropriate e-mails over the school's system to a married female teacher, and gave misleading information during investigation of the allegations.	This case has three elements that, alone, would be grounds for dismissal. An inappropriate relationship with a female student constitutes an *illegal activity*; using the school's e-mail system to send inappropriate e-mails to a married female teacher is *conduct unbecoming a teacher*; and giving misleading information is *insubordination*. Concerning the inappropriate relationship with a female student, sometimes all it takes is an accusation by a student who is, for some reason, unhappy with you to set legal wheels turning. Male teachers, in particular, must be very careful to never be alone with a student and should not make remarks that may be misconstrued as sexual harassment.

Sources: Schimmel, D., & Stellman, L., & Fischer, L. (2011). *Teachers and the law* (8th ed.). Upper Saddle River, NJ: Pearson. LaMorte, M. W. (2012). *School law: Cases and concepts* (10th ed.). Upper Saddle River, NJ: Pearson.

TABLE 10.3 Cases decided in favor of teachers retaining positions

Case	Explanation	Implications for Teachers
Pickering v. *Board of Education* Illinois, 1968	Teacher wrote a letter criticizing local school board actions. He was dismissed and the state supreme court upheld the decision. When Pickering took the case to the U.S. Supreme Court, the decision was overturned and he kept his job.	This is a good news case! As teachers we are entitled to our opinions, even when they are critical of our school. We may express opinions in the same ways as any other citizen and should do so. Everyone benefits when teachers are active citizens. However, keep in mind that for every action there is a reaction. When we have strong opinions it's tempting to blurt them out, sometimes in unprofessional ways. Expect not-so-pleasant repercussions. There is a time and a place to express ourselves…and always professionally. While you most likely won't be fired because of your opinions, hostility or poor judgment in terms of time or place can cause ill will and lasting rifts in relationships. Is it worth it? Will your goal be furthered? Think it through!
Lusk v. *Estes* Texas, 1973	Teacher testified in school board meeting that his principal and coworkers were "mentally and sociologically unqualified to deal with modern, complex, multiracial student bodies." The statement received widespread media coverage. The teacher was dismissed, but reinstated when the court said his opinions were relevant to the Dallas community.	Because of the *Pickering* ruling (case law), this case was decided in favor of the teacher. Did he have evidence that his statements were founded in fact? Maybe, maybe not. But he had a right to make the statements because his view was relevant to the well-being of his community. As with the *Pickering* implications, we generally get more mileage from our efforts if we act with respect. However, the time may come when you have tried other remedies without bringing about the change you think is needed and making generalizations may be your only recourse. The responsibilities of citizenship can be heavy.
Keefe v. *Geanakos* Massachusetts, 1969	Teacher assigned an article for his high school students to read and later discuss. The article contained some offensive language, some of which Keefe said out loud in class. He was dismissed, but a district court overturned the dismissal when it was discovered that the same language could be found in some school library books.	This case speaks to academic freedom. Yes, we may be free to speak offensive language in class if part of an academic lesson. The question is "should we?" The courts defend such language if used in a literary sense or part of a current events discussion, but offensive language when discussing the Pythagorean theory is probably unnecessary. Always consider your community and your students. It's a good idea to check with an administrator if you know the language you will use may be considered in poor taste.
Sterzing v. *Fort Bend Independent School District* Texas, 1972	Teacher used board-approved materials to teach a senior-level civics class. The nature of the class created questions that the teacher answered truthfully, many of which dealt with anti–Viet Nam War opinions. Parents complained and teacher was asked to stick to the prescribed curriculum. Teacher explained that it was impossible to teach the class and avoid discussion of controversial issues such as war and race. The teacher continued to talk with students about his opinions and was dismissed. The court found both the teacher and the district were at fault, but ordered the teacher reinstated.	A teacher's topics and methods have limits justifiably set by district and state curricular guidelines. When questioned about either what we teach or how we teach it, it's a good idea to apply the "Is this my hill to die on?" self-reflection question. If you feel strongly enough that you can't do your job without the freedom to continue when asked to not do so, then possibly this is your career "hill to die on." In this case, the teacher felt it was necessary to express his personal opinions to his class of high school seniors. If, however, once you have thought it through you decide that teaching is what's important, more so than a dispute you have the power to end, perhaps a better way to conduct the class would be to encourage students to express their opinions and guide them into critical thinking without the prompting of teacher opinions.
Scruggs v. *Keen* Virginia, 1995	Teacher supervised study hall and was asked by two female students her opinion of interracial dating. After parental complaints about her negative statements the teacher was dismissed because she was told her job was to teach math and her comments were potentially disruptive. A federal court ordered that she be reinstated because her job in study hall was to guide students as best she could and was not expected to stand mute when asked about an important social issue of the day.	This case involves the white sister of one of the girls asking questions, who was dating a black youth. Discussing topics considered controversial by some is best done with other adults. Perhaps a way around giving opinions you sense may not be aligned with the questioner is to turn the question around with "Well, what do you think?" We can act as sound boards for students without injecting our opinions. It's hard, but gets easier with practice.
Rothschild v. *Board of Education of Buffalo* New York, 1991	Teacher participated in a private, experimental videotape that included extensive vulgar language and was filmed in the school during nonschool hours, with permission of administrators. After being dismissed for the content of the film, a federal district court ordered her reinstatement because the film did not damage the functioning of the school.	We are citizens and cannot be dismissed for many of our actions outside the school day. However, good judgment and taste should guide our words and behavior. No, the teacher wasn't fired, but if the community became aware of her participation, her reputation—and that of the school, because she represents it—would likely be harmed.

Sources: Schimmel, D., Stellman, L., & Fischer, L. (2011). *Teachers and the law* (8th ed.). Upper Saddle River, NJ: Pearson. LaMorte, M. W. (2012). *School law: Cases and concepts* (10th ed.). Upper Saddle River, NJ: Pearson.

child as a single parent. The judge found in favor of the teacher and said that she had a due process right to conceive and raise her child, even out of wedlock, and without school board intrusion (Schimmel et al., 2011).

As with personal conduct, if a district wants to fire a teacher for health reasons (e.g., obesity, disabilities, or AIDS), it must show a direct link between the health problem and impaired classroom function.

There's so much to know about laws and their impact on our profession. A good way to immerse yourself in the cases and their implications is to create a wiki among your cohort of students interested in becoming teachers. A wiki allows you to build notes concerning the laws to further your understanding. This chapter's *SocialMEdia* feature is all about wikis for professional development, as well as how they can be used for teaching and learning in your classroom.

Misconduct with students. The most clear-cut decisions involving the firing of teachers on moral grounds involve misconduct with students. When a teacher's personal life or habits intersect a student's in illegal or morally questionable ways, it is relatively easy for a school district to dismiss a teacher for:

- sexual relations with students
- profane, abusive language directed at students
- allowing students to drink alcohol
- encouraging students to be dishonest

Of course there are many court rulings as a result of challenges brought by teachers against districts, and districts against teachers, that do not result in the threat of dismissal or any sort of action against the teacher. These cases decide certain issues and teachers continue to teach, abiding by the decisions. Both Tables 10.4 and 10.5 consist of cases involving teachers' personal lives, with their positions in jeopardy.

Points of Reflection 10.4

Do you think the role of teacher carries with it personal restraints? Would you be willing to alter your lifestyle somewhat to conform with what a particular community considers moral and professional behavior?

SocialMEdia

The word "wiki" means quick or fast in the Hawaiian language. A wiki can bring people together quickly in a simple, easy to use format. In the world of social media, a wiki is a shared space for collaboration on the Internet. Wikis are easily editable, encouraging members of the wiki group to comment on what others ask and write. Wiki tools are similar to regular word processing tools. Users can upload documents, create links to other sites, and embed video. This technology's interactive nature makes wikis ideal for both teacher professional development and for classroom teaching and learning.

A community of teacher-learners can share questions, experiences, and practices through a wiki. Through wikis teachers may

- Plan units of study together
- Share what works in the classroom
- Discuss problems with students; give and receive advice
- Learn new practices and discuss their value
- Share logistical information such as field trip requirements and trip planning progress
- Compose reports or letters to send to parents
- Create a storage place for ideas and instructional materials and strategies

Wikis can be valuable tools for teaching and learning. Through wikis students may

- Access class information posted by the teacher
- Organize projects with shared responsibility anytime and anywhere they have Internet access
- Create study guides using each other's knowledge
- Write a group report
- Share editing responsibilities for either group assignments or individual writing
- Keep an ongoing list of vocabulary words, along with real-world word usage and ways of remembering definitions
- Share what occurred in class with absent students
- Ask questions about something that's being studied and receive answers written by students, for students

Wikis may be developed for free by going through services such as TeachersFirst, a Wikispaces site dedicated to teachers and students. In fact, wouldn't it be a good idea for you and your cohort of future teachers to create a wiki dedicated to sharing your experiences in teacher education?

TABLE 10.4 Teachers' personal lives dismissal cases and implications

Case	Explanation	Implications for Teachers
Ware v. *Morgan County School District* Colorado, 1988	Teacher took a misbehaving student outside and used obscene language to tell him he was a disgrace to the band. The teacher was fired and the court sided with the school district.	Using obscene language is never appropriate in a school setting or with students.
Cooper v. *Eugene School District* Oregon, 1986	Teacher converted to the Sikh religion and explained to her students that she would now wear a white turban and, occasionally, all white clothing. Her administrator said she violated both state and district policy against teachers being demonstrative of a particular religion and dismissed the teacher. The court upheld the school's decision.	Public schools must, by law, remain religiously neutral. Teachers need to understand that although we are free to have different beliefs, we still represent the school system. We can practice whatever faith we wish, or none at all, but we can't appear to promote any particular belief system. This is difficult when we have strongly held beliefs, but it is part of separation of church and state that helps keep all of us free to worship, or not, as we desire.
Elvin v. *City of Waterville* Maine, 1990	A divorced female fourth grade teacher was fired for having sexual relations with a 15-year-old neighbor boy. Although he had never been her student, the court agreed with the school district's decision to fire her, saying she had proven herself unfit to teach. The judge added that public awareness of her conduct undermined her ability to deal with students and parents.	The teacher was indicted for sexual misconduct with a minor, but the charge was reduced to one count of assault. Even so, the school board dismissal was upheld. This teacher's behavior was despicable and showed a complete lack of judgment and disregard for the well-being of a public school student. Needless to say, never involve yourself in any type of sexual relationship with a minor.
Spanierman v. *Hughes* Connecticut, 2008	Teacher established a MySpace page, originally in an attempt to communicate with students about homework and other school issues. However, over time the page also contained objectionable material, including pictures of naked men, and the communications took on more of a social rather than academic nature. Following complaints from teachers who accessed the site, the teacher was dismissed. A U.S. District Court upheld the dismissal.	There have been very few cases so far involving teachers and social media, but more are sure to come. In this one the teacher's initial intentions appear to be legitimate. We must remember that what we do online is not private. There is danger in electronic communication; use it wisely. This means being careful with student and parent communication, as well as what you post on Facebook and other personal-oriented sites. Never post anything you wouldn't want your principal, parents, or students to see. They might!
Oleske v. *City School District Board of Education* Ohio, 2001	Teacher was dismissed for telling sexually-oriented jokes to 8th grade students. A state court upheld the dismissal, saying that teachers should recognize that this behavior detracts from their role model status.	Some new teachers have a tendency to want to be "friends" with students in ways that make them popular. This is very understandable, but, nonetheless, unacceptable. One way to make students our "friends" is to participate with them in conversation, sometimes inappropriately. The temptation is to allow topics and language that belong only in adult conversations to spill over into what we say when we are with adolescents. Be very careful, because you will be "the teacher."
Flaskamp v. *Dearborn Public Schools* Michigan, 2004	Teacher began a romantic and sexual relationship with a former student that was discovered about a year after graduation. She was dismissed. The court upheld her dismissal and stated that there must be at least two years between graduation and the beginning of a personal relationship between teacher and former students.	If you are 21 when you begin teaching, your students may be 17 or 18, creating a relatively small age difference. This court ruling is an important one to understand. Students must be at least 2 years past graduation before you may have any sort of romantic relationship. At this point in your life, the chronological age may be close, but you will be a college graduate with a career and adult responsibilities.
Katz v. *Ambach* New York, 1984	Teacher was dismissed after it was proven that he kissed 6th grade girls, patted them on the behind, and permitted obscene jokes and profanity in the classroom. The court upheld the dismissal.	This behavior is totally inappropriate! Male middle and high school teachers must be especially careful to not create any appearance of inappropriateness. The teacher in this case went well beyond the "appearance."
Board of Education v. *Wood* Kentucky, 1986	Teachers were fired for having a summer party with two 15-year-old students present. At the party the teenagers smoked marijuana. The two teachers were fired after arguing that school was not in session and their rights to privacy were breached. The court determined that smoking marijuana with students is immoral and criminal behavior and upheld the dismissal.	You are a teacher during the school year *and* in summer, or whenever school is not in session. If you go to the same pool or participate in the same activities as students during holidays, you don't shed your responsibility to be an adult role model.
Jefferson Union High School District v. *Jones* California, 1972	Teacher was fined for possession of marijuana while on vacation. The arrest and fine appeared in a Honolulu newspaper and someone in the teacher's hometown saw it. He was dismissed when it was discovered and the court upheld his firing.	Even on vacation we are subject to tougher standards than many of our peers. This reality is part of teaching. Be mindful that our behavior follows us, even when it may seem unlikely.

Sources: Schimmel, D., Stellman, L., & Fischer, L. (2011). *Teachers and the law* (8th ed.). Upper Saddle River, NJ: Pearson. LaMorte, M. W. (2012). *School law: Cases and concepts* (10th ed.). Upper Saddle River, NJ: Pearson. National Association of Secondary School Principals. (2006). Teachers' privacy rights. *A Legal Memorandum, 6*(3). Retrieved March 17, 2013, from http://www.nassp.org/portals/0/content/53842.pdf

TABLE 10.5 Cases involving personal lives decided in favor of teachers

Case	Explanation	Implications for Teachers
Morrison v. *State Board of Education* California, 1969	Teacher participated in a brief homosexual relationship with another teacher. He was dismissed but reinstated due to a court decision in his favor citing that the behavior does not directly affect job performance.	Remember that this case was relatively shocking in 1969. Today we assume personal rights when it comes to sexuality. Because we are role models, using discretion in our demonstration of romantic involvement, whether heterosexual or homosexual, is best for our communities.
Thompson v. *Southwest District* Missouri, 1980	Teacher dismissed because she lived with her boyfriend, not publicizing it, but also not making it a secret. When the school board dismissed her for immorality, they made a public display of it. The court found that living with her boyfriend did not diminish the teacher's classroom effectiveness and ordered her reinstated.	As with *Morrison*, this seems a bit frivolous now as most of us would not question a teacher's right to live with whomever he or she pleases. The court not only ruled in favor of the teacher, but also chastised the school district for making the teacher's personal choices public knowledge.
Eckmann v. *Board of Education* Illinois, 1986	Teacher was fired when she became pregnant while unmarried. The court ruled that she had a right to both raise her child and keep her teaching position.	There was a time not so long ago when even married women were asked to stop teaching when their condition became evident. Now schools more closely mirror the world outside the schoolhouse door.
Nichol v. *ARIN Intermediate Unit* Pennsylvania, 2003	Teacher wore a small cross to her elementary school and was dismissed based on a district/state policy. The policy prohibited school employees from wearing religious dress, emblems, or insignia (specifically crosses and Stars of David) while performing their duties in public schools. A federal court found the policy unconstitutional and the teacher was reinstated.	Given that teachers are not allowed to wear in-your-face symbols of their faith, small pieces of jewelry are exempt. States and districts cannot make policies that are unreasonably restrictive.
Keyishian v. *Board of Regents of New York* New York, 1967	Teacher affiliated with the Communist Party and was dismissed for doing so. The U.S. Supreme Court ruled that the teacher should be reinstated and that he had broken no laws and was not trying to convert students to his belief system.	The Supreme Court used the logic that the school's function was not impaired by the teacher's political leanings. In America, citizens are allowed to adopt whatever philosophy they choose and may participate in its functions as long as others are not harmed.
Randle v. *Indianola Municipal Separate School District* Mississippi, 1975	Teacher married a controversial civil rights advocate and was not rehired. A federal court of appeals declared that a school district cannot refuse to hire or rehire based on with whom a teacher decides to affiliate.	As with *Keyishian*, the court declared that teachers may marry or affiliate with anyone they wish. The limitation is whether the affiliation interferes with the person's function as a teacher.
Weaver v. *Nebo School District,* Utah, 1998	Teacher and volleyball coach was dismissed because of negative reaction to her sexual orientation. She had received letters from the school district instructing her to not make any comments to students, staff members, or parents about her homosexuality and rights under the First and Fourteenth Amendments. The court ruled there was no job-related basis for the dismissal and ordered that she be reinstated.	Think about how our freedoms have increased in less than two decades. We don't have to hide our affiliations, opinions on societal issues, or political beliefs. As representatives of schools, however, our first consideration should be our students and the messages we send them, both consciously and unconsciously. Make your choices, and always be mindful that how you demonstrate them will impact impressionable and developing students.

Sources: Schimmel, D., Stellman, L., & Fischer, L. (2011). *Teachers and the law* (8th ed.). Upper Saddle River, NJ: Pearson. LaMorte, M. W. (2012). *School law: Cases and concepts* (10th ed.). Upper Saddle River, NJ: Pearson. National Association of Secondary School Principals. (2006). Teachers' privacy rights. *A Legal Memorandum, 6*(3). Retrieved March 17, 2013, from http://www.nassp.org/portals/0/content/53842.pdf

Remember not to dismiss older cases; decisions are still relevant as case law. Take time to consider the implications of each case. In Table 10.4 we read about implications from cases involving teacher dismissal; Table 10.5 includes cases with teachers keeping their positions.

What Are the Legal Responsibilities of Teachers?

Teachers have many responsibilities, some dictated by laws and others by state, district, or school policies. Some responsibilities are governed by ethical and professional guidelines.

Focus teacher Chris Roberts believes in teaching through a variety of experiences. He is responsible for student safety when he takes his class on field trips.

LIABILITY

To be **liable** means to be responsible for. We generally hear the term in a negative sense, for instance, "He was found liable for the accident" or "That will raise my liability insurance premium." In a positive sense, though, liability is what teaching is all about—accepting responsibility for students while they are under our supervision. This is why we study such aspects as child development, subject matter, instructional and assessment strategies, guidelines for health and safety, and school law. However, being held liable when something goes wrong is far from positive. Depending on the severity of the issue, liability for a situation can end a career.

Teachers serve ***in loco parentis***, meaning "in place of parents." They are bound by law to care for and protect children in the school setting as a parent would and are held to a standard of reasonableness. Teachers, schools, and districts are frequently sued over issues related to liability. For a school employee to be considered liable for something, the following four components must be proven to be present:

1. The person has a legal duty to protect students.
2. The person fails to act within reason and provide the appropriate standard of care.
3. There is a causal connection between the person's conduct and the result of the injury.
4. Actual damage occurs to the injured person. (LaMorte, 2008)

In the case of *Mancha* v. *Field Museum of Natural History,* 1971, students ages 12 to 15 went on a field trip with teachers to the Chicago Natural History Museum. The students were allowed to tour the exhibits on their own. One student was beaten up by teenagers from another school. In this case, the teachers had a legal duty to protect students (1), and there was actual damage (4). The court had to decide if the teachers failed to act within reason and provide an appropriate standard of care (2) and if there was a causal connection between the teachers' conduct and the injury (3). The teachers were not held liable for the student's injuries because the court determined there was minimal risk at the museum, and the teachers could not reasonably have been expected to directly supervise them.

In a similar case the same year, an eighth grader sustained a severe eye injury when a student threw rocks during a baseball game. The teacher involved in *Sheehan* v. *St. Peter's Catholic School,* 1971, had accompanied the students outside but then returned to the building. The courts determined that the teacher left the area and therefore was not properly supervising the students. She was found liable for leaving students alone in a potentially dangerous setting.

Teachers can take some precautions that will lessen the causal connection between their actions and any harm that may come to students. Here are a few to consider:

- Be 100% present when with students. Limit personal distractions and remain focused.
- Think through situations and, if possible, avoid those that have unusual potential for danger.
- Establish routines and rules that make safety a habit among students.
- Remind students of appropriate behavior to help them remain safe.

Accidents happen—in the classroom, the hallway, the cafeteria, the science lab, the gym, on school grounds, and on field trips. Using good judgment in the *in loco parentis* role will be enough for most teachers. But occasionally students are injured and teacher liability may be questioned. Liability insurance is a good idea. Teacher organizations offer reasonably priced policies that are recommended even for student teachers. These

Points of Reflection 10.5

Have you considered the many ways things may go wrong for teachers and students? Were you ever involved in a situation where a teacher's liability was questioned? If so, what were the circumstances?

organizations often also provide legal assistance to members who find themselves involved in a school-related lawsuit.

In Table 10.6 we read about cases brought against teachers involving teacher liability. As with the other tables, take time to consider the implications after reading the brief facts of each case.

TABLE 10.6 Teacher liability cases and implications

Case	Explanation	Implications for Teachers
Kaufman v. *City of New York* New York, 1961	Teacher was supervising in the gym when two boys knocked heads while playing basketball and one was seriously injured. The court ruled that any amount of supervision could not have prevented the accident and that the school and teacher were not liable.	This teacher was where he was supposed to be when the accident occurred, releasing him from liability for it. Never do anything less than be where you are supposed to be at all times. Ducking around the corner to make a phone call or texting when you are supposed to be paying attention to students in your care is never wise.
Morris v. *Douglas County School District* California, 1965	Teacher took a class of first graders to the beach for an outing. The children were walking on the edge of the water when a large log rolled up with a wave and seriously injured a child. The court found that the teacher was liable because this kind of injury was not uncommon and the teacher was responsible for the safety of the young children in her care.	Use good judgment! Of course first graders will want to be as close as possible to the water, if not in it. Apparently large logs forcefully coming to shore on this particular coastline are a frequent occurrence. Do your research and anticipate dangers to help avoid student injury, a suit against you, and, if not a suit, the sense of guilt that accompanies a child being injured.
Mancha v. *Field Museum of Natural History* Illinois, 1971	Teachers allowed 12- to 15-year-old students to "self-guide" during a field trip to a museum. When not in their sight, a boy was beaten by other boys not part of the field trip. The parents sued, but the court determined that it was very unlikely that this sort of incident would happen, making it unforeseeable. The teacher was not held liable for the student's injuries.	The students are old enough on this common type of field trip to self-direct their exploration and most parents would allow them to do so as well. The key here is that the teachers did not take unreasonable risks in the museum and they were present. Always think through what you are planning to make sure you are showing good judgment.
Sheehan v. *St. Peter's Catholic School* Minnesota, 1991	Teacher accompanied 20 girls outside for recess, sitting them on benches on the third base line while 8th grade boys played baseball. She then returned to the building. In her absence some boys started throwing pebbles at the girls and one girl was hit in the eye and seriously injured. The court determined this sort of behavior could be foreseen and found the teacher liable for not properly supervising the students.	The only reason to leave children placed in your care is to go for help if an emergency occurs. Otherwise, no matter how important a call may be or the need to retrieve something you forgot or your need to run in for "just a minute" for any reason, don't do it.
Eisel v. *Board of Education of Montgomery County* Maryland, 1991	Two guidance counselors were informed by high school students that one girl had made a suicide pact with another. The counselors met with the girl, who denied any plan to commit suicide. She subsequently did kill herself and the parents sued the counselors. The court agreed that, in matters potentially dealing with life and death, the counselors were obligated to contact the parents. The counselors were held liable.	It is relatively common to hear from students about talk of suicide, especially among girls. Although teachers are not charged with being guidance counselors, we are, however, responsible for student well-being. The verdict in this case is not common, but the court decided that the counselors knew that the threat was more than a rumor and had the obligation to call the parents. As a teacher, this kind of parental contact should be handled by counselors and administrators. The best advice is to tell one or both of these individuals about your suspicions and let them contact parents.
Santiago v. *Cooper* Tennessee, 2006	Teacher conducted kindergarten recess indoors because of inclement weather. The students played with age-appropriate toys, with one boy hitting another in the eye with a plastic hammer. Although initially thought not to be serious and with no outward sign of damage, it was later revealed that the child had lost vision in the eye that was hit. After mounting medical bills, the teacher was sued. The court did not rule in favor of the family because the teacher was present and supervising.	Of course the teacher felt very bad about what happened, but because she was there and the toys were plastic, she was not found to be liable. Had she gone to the restroom or to get a cup of coffee and left the children, she would have likely been held liable. Never leave students alone while you are in charge of them.
Wilson v. *Vestal Central School District* New York, 2006	Teacher was aware that one student repeatedly picked on another student for several years. When a 9th grade girl pulled a chair out from under the targeted student in the cafeteria, the teacher on supervision duty was sued. The court agreed that the teacher and the school were liable because they had adequate knowledge of bullying of one student by another.	This decision is fairly rare. First, the incident happened among adolescents in a cafeteria with an adult present. Second, anticipating that one student would pull a chair out from beneath another seems unreasonable. But this case is included to show that courts may indeed perceive teacher responsibility in more stringent ways.

(continued)

TABLE 10.6 Teacher liability cases and implications (*continued*)

Case	Explanation	Implications for Teachers
Davis v. *Monroe County Board of Education* Georgia, 1999	Teachers were aware that a fifth grade girl was being physically and verbally harassed by a classmate, according to the court ruling. She and her parents repeatedly reported it to the school, but it continued. The family filed a lawsuit, and 6 years later the U.S. Supreme Court ruled the school failed to act appropriately to protect the girl.	This ruling determined that educators can be held liable if they do not respond to complaints of physical and verbal harassment. Teachers often concentrate on lessons and forget to use their peripheral vision to monitor student relations. Be conscious that for 8 hours a day you should watch and listen to take care of your students.
Spears v. *Jefferson Parish School Board* Louisiana, 1994	Teacher pretended that a kindergarten student, while in physical education, had hanged two of his friends. The sight of his "dead" friends caused severe and ongoing trauma for the young child, whose parents sued for the cost of psychotherapy for the child and won the case in court.	Fortunately, teacher liability for student emotional damage is rare. But this is a cautionary tale for all of us because children do not have adult senses of humor, nor do they understand sarcasm. They often don't understand when something is a "joke." Developmentally appropriate communication is an absolute necessity for the well-being of children.

Sources: Schimmel, D., Stellman, L., & Fischer, L. (2011). *Teachers and the law* (8th ed.). Upper Saddle River, NJ: Pearson. LaMorte, M. W. (2012). *School law: Cases and concepts* (10th ed.). Upper Saddle River, NJ: Pearson.

COPYRIGHT LAWS

Copyright laws provide guidelines for authorized use of someone else's intellectual property and are intended to protect the rights of creators of intellectual property by preventing others from copying or distributing it without permission. Intellectual property includes written material, original audio and visual work, and computer programs.

Copyrighted materials may be used under three conditions: the user has permission from the copyright owner, the work is in the public domain, or the use is considered "fair use." A work is in the **public domain** if it is more than 75 years old or is published by a government agency. **Fair use** allows the nonprofit reproduction of certain materials in the classroom without permission of the copyright owner (Schimmel et al., 2011). Generally, fair use stipulates that the material copied must be for educational purposes and that the amount copied must fall within certain guidelines, some of which are listed in Figure 10.4. Teachers may not, however, make copies of consumable products such as textbooks, workbooks, and standardized test materials. If copies could be freely made of these kinds of materials, then their creators and publishers would lose money because the need for them would diminish.

Because teachers often want students to create work using certain computer software, it is important to know that computer software is copyrighted and that fair use guidelines do not apply. Some software publishers allow one backup copy to be made,

Figure 10.4 Guidelines for classroom copying

1. A single copy may be made of any of the following for your own scholarly research or use in teaching:
   - a chapter from a book
   - an article from a periodical or newspaper
   - a short story, short essay, or short poem
   - a chart, graph, diagram, drawing, cartoon or picture from a book, periodical, or newspaper.
2. Multiple copies (no more than one per student) may be made for classroom use if each copy gives credit to the copyright holder and passes three tests.
   - The brevity test includes guidelines such as poems of fewer than 200 words and prose of fewer than 2,500 words.
   - The spontaneity test generally says that you are inspired to copy and use material for the sake of teaching effectiveness and there was not time to ask and receive permission.
   - The cumulative effect test generally restricts the length of time copied material is used and how many instances of copying take place in a period of time.
3. Teachers cannot copy individual works and put them together to serve as an anthology.
4. Students cannot be charged for the photocopying of copyrighted works.

Source: Underwood, J., & Webb, L. D. (2006). *School law for teachers: Concepts and applications.* Upper Saddle River, NJ: Merrill/Prentice Hall.

but more than this is illegal. Additionally, commercially produced videos may not be copied. Copies made of television programs can be kept for 45 days and then must be erased or destroyed.

With the Internet serving as a major research tool in classrooms today, teachers must be aware that what is on the Internet is not in the public domain. Because the Internet is international, laws governing its use are somewhat unclear. Following fair use guidelines is a safe way to use Web resources.

Whether using written works, audiovisual materials, computer software, or information from the Internet, teachers must take copyright laws seriously. School districts have policies based on fair use guidelines. A school's media specialist is often a helpful, knowledgeable source of information about what is lawful and what is not. Teachers should ask for advice if there is any question about how they plan to use any form of intellectual property.

REPORTING SUSPECTED CHILD ABUSE

A teacher who has a reasonable suspicion of child abuse or neglect has a legal obligation to report it to a school counselor or administrator, who in turn will report it to a social services agency or the police. Teachers don't have to be certain that they are correct. They are granted immunity and may not be sued for reporting their suspicions (Schimmel et al., 2011).

It is a good idea for teachers to keep lists of signs of abuse and neglect handy for easy reference. Teachers should never become too busy to be observant. Physical abuse may be visually evident and difficult to miss. However, sexual abuse may be more subtle in terms of symptoms, and emotional or mental abuse may be even more difficult to detect. Reviewing the signs periodically, watching for behavioral or emotional changes, and reporting suspicions of abuse or neglect to administrators or school counselors will help protect students. This is a teacher's legal and ethical responsibility—and simply the right thing to do.

Teacher responsibilities obviously include protecting their students however and whenever they can. Teacher responsibilities also include safeguarding students' rights.

> We discuss signs of abuse and neglect in Chapter 9, specifically Figure 9.2.

How Does the Law Impact the Relationship Between School and Religion?

The First Amendment makes it clear that the founders of the United States did not want government to have any say in how or whether citizens worship. Because public schools are government entities, they may neither establish religion nor interfere with the free exercise of it. As clearly stated as it is in the Constitution, the issue is anything but clear cut in practice. Few topics are as charged with emotion and passion, and hence with such potential to polarize people, as religion.

Let's establish some basic "do's and don'ts" for teachers and students with regard to religion and education. In 1998 President Clinton asked Secretary of Education Richard Riley to prepare guidelines based on law and court decisions to help educators determine the rights of students and staff regarding religion and public schools. For easy reference, these guidelines are adapted into a question and answer format in Figure 10.5.

RELIGION AND COMPULSORY EDUCATION

Compulsory education laws require students to attend school through a certain age. *Pierce* v. *Society of Sisters,* 1925, established that compulsory education laws could be met through attendance at private or parochial schools. In the 1970s, Amish families asked to be exempt from compulsory education beyond eighth grade on the grounds that attendance in upper grades would have a negative effect on their

Figure 10.5 Guidelines for religious expression in public schools from the U.S. Department of Education

Can students pray in school?
Yes. Students may pray individually or in a group as long as they are nondisruptive. For instance, students may pray before meals or tests to the same extent they may engage in comparable nondisruptive activities.

Can students read religious materials and discuss religion among themselves?
Yes. Students may read and talk about religion to the same extent as they may read and talk about anything else in school.

Can students meet to express their religious beliefs during the school day and on school grounds?
Yes. Students may meet for nondisruptive purposes during their lunch periods or other noninstructional time during the school day, as well as before and after the school day. This includes religion-related meetings.

Is it legal to have organized prayer at sporting events or other school functions?
No. Under current Supreme Court decisions, school officials may not mandate or organize prayer at any school-sponsored event or graduation.

Can teachers participate in religious meetings while at school?
No. Teachers and school administrators, when acting in those capacities, are representatives of the state and are prohibited from soliciting or encouraging religious activity, and from participating in such activity with students.

Can teachers teach about religion in schools?
Yes. Teachers may teach *about* religion, including the history of religion; comparative religion; the Bible (or other scripture) as literature; and the role of religion in the history of the United States and other countries. Teachers may also prompt students to consider religious influences on art, music, literature, and social studies.

Can teachers display religious-related holiday items or encourage the celebration of religious holidays in school?
No. Although public schools may teach *about* religious holidays, including their religious aspects, and may celebrate the secular aspects of holidays, schools may not observe holidays as religious events or encourage students to do so.

Is it acceptable for students to express religious beliefs in school assignments?
Yes. Students may express their beliefs about religion in the form of homework, artwork, and other written and oral assignments free of discrimination based on the religious content of their work. The assignments should be graded according to the standards the lesson is intended to address.

If a lesson may be considered offensive by a student and/or the student's family, can the student opt not to participate?
Yes. Schools can excuse individual students from lessons that are objectionable to the student or the students' parents on religious or other conscientious grounds.

Can students opt out of a particular dress code or uniform for religious reasons?
Legally, the answer is no. However, schools have discretion to interpret this in ways that make sense in their communities.

Can students wear religious messages or symbols on their clothes?
Yes. The restrictions are the same as for any other comparable messages. Schools cannot single out religion-related messages and symbols to prohibit.

Source: Adapted from Riley, R. W. (1998). *Secretary's statement on religious expression.* Retrieved November 12, 2006, from http://www2.ed.gov/policy/gen/guid/religionandschools/prayer_guidance.html

Private and parochial schools and homeschooling are discussed in Chapter 3.

traditions and way of life. The Supreme Court ruled in their favor in *Wisconsin* v. *Yoder,* 1972. This ruling is known as the "Amish exception." If non-Amish parents wish to isolate their children from public or private school beyond a particular grade (under age 16), they must show that school will somehow destroy their religion. Homeschooling is a legal option with very few requirements or constraints. Because families aren't required to supply a reason for homeschooling, it is unknown how many families use their right to homeschool their children as a way to avoid compulsory education laws.

PRAYER IN SCHOOL

Students may pray silently or quietly in small groups in school. But that's it. Legally there can be no school-sponsored public prayer, not even nondenominational prayer (Schimmel et al., 2011). This prohibition includes prayer at gatherings such as graduation ceremonies, football games, and assemblies. In *Santa Fe Independent School District* v. *Doe,* 2000, a Texas school district allowed students to vote on whether to have prayer and who would deliver it before football games. Groups of Mormon and Catholic students, alumni, and parents filed a suit claiming the district was violating the First Amendment. The U.S. Supreme Court ruled against the district, contending that the school would be endorsing a specific religion depending on who delivered the prayer.

Students may pray together on school grounds, as long as it is not disruptive to the education process.

Some communities choose to violate the First Amendment principle of separation of church and state by endorsing prayer in school-related settings. If challenged, they would likely lose in court. Some school boards even begin their meetings with prayer, often careful not to use language that would offend Christians or Jews. However, these prayers may offend Muslims, Buddhists, and other religious groups, as well as atheists. Regardless of who is present, prayer is not legal in public education meetings.

RELIGIOUS ORGANIZATIONS MEETING ON SCHOOL GROUNDS

If a school building is used before or after hours for organizations of any kind, it may also be used for organizations that are religious in nature. In *Good News Club* v. *Milford Central School,* 2001, the Supreme Court ruled that a private Christian organization for children ages 6 to 12 in New York could use a public school for weekly after-school meetings. Although some lower courts have ruled that teachers may be involved in student religious organizations on their own time, generally school employees may not sponsor the groups (Schimmel et al., 2011).

Religious holidays. Observing specific religious holidays in class is not allowed. This is a visible and controversial aspect of mixing school and religion. The longest traditional school breaks or vacations (other than summer) occur during Christian celebrations—December break at Christmas and spring break at Easter. What was once called Christmas break is now generally referred to as the winter holiday. The traditional holiday student presentation once called the Christmas Program is now the choral/band event that may be referred to as the Holiday or Winter Program. Students may sing Christmas songs with religious messages, such as "Silent Night," but these songs may not dominate the program.

Holiday displays that depict Christian or Christmas symbols may be used if they are balanced with other cultural symbols such as a Jewish menorah. The displays must be temporary and help show diversity. Parents and students may request to be exempt from activities focused on holidays.

Religion and curriculum. Must schools do away with all reference to religion to separate church and state? The answer is no. It is permissible to teach about religion but not with the purpose of convincing students that a particular belief should be followed. Use of the Bible, Talmud, Koran, and other religious books for teaching literature and history is permissible as long as one is not endorsed over another.

We discuss controversy and the curriculum in Chapter 4.

Points of Reflection 10.6

Did you or your family ever have religion-based views that conflicted with events at your school? Were your views conservative (i.e., opposition to dancing, nonacceptance of evolution theory, nonparticipation when certain movies were shown, etc.)? Were there restrictions imposed that you believed unnecessary?

Perhaps the greatest point of tension concerning religion and curriculum is the theory of evolution. In the so-called "Scopes Monkey Trial" in 1925, a high school teacher was convicted of violating a Tennessee regulation against teaching anything that contradicted the biblical Genesis account of the creation of humans. Although the conviction was overturned on a technicality, controversy over the teaching of evolution in schools has continued. In 1982 Louisiana passed the Balanced Treatment Act, which required the teaching of both creationism and evolution. The U.S. Supreme Court ruled the act illegal because it endorsed creationism, a Christian view, to the exclusion of other views. Some school districts, and even whole states, have attempted to give equal time both to what some Christians believe about creation as embodied in the literal translation of the Bible and to evolution. Some districts have attempted to outlaw the teaching of evolution or to require a disclaimer stating that it is only a theory, one of many that try to explain the origin of humans.

As you can see, the rights and responsibilities of teachers and students often intersect at the delicate point of separation of church and state. In some communities, and at some times of the year, preserving this separation is challenging.

What Are the Legal Rights of Students?

Students do not leave their constitutional rights at the schoolhouse door. You may notice that there isn't a section of this chapter devoted to students' legal responsibilities. If there were, the section would be short. Students have the responsibility to go to school as long as it is compulsory (usually to age 16, but to age 18 in some locations). That's about it in terms of legal responsibilities. Although we hope students take responsibility for their learning and behavior, unless their behavior is deemed illegal or extremely disruptive, there are no other laws binding them.

FREEDOM OF EXPRESSION

Before 1969, students were not recognized as having First Amendment rights to freedom of expression. The U.S. Supreme Court's decision in *Tinker* v. *Des Moines Independent Community School District,* 1969, provided a clear message that a student is entitled to freedom of expression. In this case, three students wore armbands to school to protest the war in Vietnam and were punished for doing so (LaMorte, 2012). The *Tinker* case reversed the school's stance and has been cited repeatedly since 1969. However, court challenges since *Tinker* have served to balance the rights of students to express themselves and the necessity of limiting personal freedom to ensure the safety and well-being of others. For students, understanding the need for this balance is a lesson in the principles of democracy.

Freedom of symbolic expression. The *Tinker* decision so influenced how students are viewed in relation to freedom of expression that it is known as the *Tinker doctrine*. This doctrine extends to symbolic freedom. Students are allowed to express their views symbolically through what they wear as long as it doesn't disrupt the educational process.

Dress codes. Since the 1960s, numerous lawsuits have been initiated over the restrictions imposed by dress codes, but the U.S. Supreme Court has not ruled on the issue. In 1972, Justice Black wrote that the U.S. Constitution doesn't require the courts to bear the burden of supervising clothing or hairstyles.

However, schools are concerned about immodest dress and unusual hairstyles because they could disrupt the educational atmosphere of the classroom as well as lead to more serious issues. For instance, violence generated by gangs and groups such as the "trench coat mafia" (the students associated with the 1999 Columbine school shootings) has prompted educators to identify and attempt to ban insignia clothing and hats associated with specific groups. LaMorte (2008) lists the following as school concerns:

- T-shirts depicting violence, drugs (e.g., marijuana leaves), racial epithets
- ripped, baggy, or saggy pants or jeans
- colored bandanas
- baseball or other hats
- words shaved into scalps
- brightly colored hair
- exposed underwear
- tattoos, . . . pierced noses
- decorative dental caps (p. 172)

These forms of symbolic expression are not protected by the First Amendment because they may contribute to school unrest. Most dress codes outlaw some or all of the items in LaMorte's list. However, because some of the items are associated with particular cultures, it is difficult for schools to designate them without appearing to be biased. Rules designating skirt length, requiring belts, and prohibiting exposed midriffs are more generic but still hard to enforce.

Uniforms. Dress codes are often ambiguous, leaving much room for interpretation. They can infringe on learning time if teachers are expected to watch for and report violations. Thus some schools and entire districts choose to impose a uniform policy, giving students several modest, relatively plain choices of clothing. Currently, more than half the states have schools with uniform policies. Some large cities, such as Long Beach, Chicago, and San Antonio, require at least elementary students to wear uniforms. In 2002 Memphis, Tennessee, became the nation's first large public school district to adopt a uniform policy in all of its 175 schools.

Public schools that impose uniform policies must provide an opt-out clause for parents who don't want their children to participate. For instance, some parents may not want their children to wear a uniform because it conflicts with the clothing traditions of their religion. Other parents may request to be exempt simply because their children don't want to wear the uniform and are persistently making that clear. Private schools do not receive government support and, unlike public schools, may impose a uniform policy on all students without allowing them to opt out.

Before we discuss student freedom of speech, consider focus teacher Brenda Beyal and a dilemma she faced that began with symbolic freedom in Figure 10.6. Reflect on the opportunities for Brenda and her students to learn about aspects of culture and a belief system with which they are not familiar, and then thoughtfully respond to the questions.

Freedom of speech. The freedom of speech implied in *Tinker* was challenged in 1986 when a student made a speech containing sexual innuendo in a high school assembly. He was reprimanded and subsequently sued the school, claiming that his freedom of speech was denied. The case, *Bethel School District No. 403* v. *Fraser,* 1986, went to the U.S. Supreme Court, where the adolescent lost. The court ruled that a school does not have to accept indecent or offensive speech.

Although students enjoy free speech, it does have limits. An individual student's freedom of speech, as well as freedom of the press, must be balanced against the school's ability to maintain a safe and civil atmosphere, where all students and teachers are shown respect.

Students often enjoy expressing personal taste in their choices of clothing and shoes.

Points of Reflection 10.7

Did your schools have dress codes or uniforms? What do you remember about them? Did you feel that your freedom of expression was restricted by what the schools said you could and couldn't wear?

As a future teacher, do you like the idea of dress codes or uniforms? Why or why not? Are they more important at particular levels of school?

Figure 10.6 Brenda Beyal's dilemma

As a teacher in a multiage classroom, Brenda Beyal enjoys the fact that her school, colleagues, and students are open minded and accepting of differences. She also enjoys the status of her school as an arts-focused elementary. The arrival of twin fifth grade girls in Benda's classroom 2 weeks after school began proved to be both a challenge and an opportunity.

Amira and Farah were the first children of traditional Muslim parents to attend Brenda's school. These 11-year-old twins walked into Brenda's classroom one Friday morning in September. They wore loose-fitting pants and long tunic tops, along with scarves on their heads that completely covered their hair. Amira and Farah smiled sweetly and took their seats at a table with three other children. Brenda welcomed them and invited the girls to introduce themselves to the class. Amira went first and explained that her name means *princess* in Islam. Then Farah followed suit by saying that her name means *happiness.*

Brenda had been told she would have two new students, but she had not been told that the girls were part of a very traditional Muslim family and that there would be some challenges because of their being the first students of the Islamic faith in the school. Here are some of the challenges Brenda faced:

- A school rule states that headgear may not be worn in the school building. The girls wore *hijab*, traditional Muslim headwear.
- Amira and Farah arrived in the middle of Ramadan, a Muslim month in which believers fast during daylight hours.
- Amira and Farah are required to pray five times a day, and two of the times fall within the school day.
- The parents of Amira and Farah talked with Principal Larsen and told him they are aware that his school is known for the arts. They have concerns because (in their tradition) dance serves no purpose, and needlessly causes girls and boys to come in contact; they find some music offensive; and Muslim children are not allowed to draw human figures.
- Although Islam is one of the fastest growing religious sects in the U.S. today, sentiment in the United States is often unfavorable toward people of the Muslim faith, especially following the events of 9/11. The uncle of one of Brenda's students was killed in the 2001 terrorist attack on the World Trade Center in New York City.

Think about Brenda's challenges and opportunities to help all her students learn about—and from—each other's similarities and differences. Respond to these items by writing one well-developed paragraph answering each of the following three questions:

1. Is it legal for Amira and Farah to pause twice each day for prayer and refuse to eat lunch during Ramadan? If not, why? If so, how might Brenda explain this to her students?
2. Should the school rules be relaxed to allow Amira and Farah to wear *hijab*? If not, how should Brenda handle the situation? If so, how might Brenda explain this rule variation to her students?
3. On September 11 of each school year, a tradition at Rees consists of students reading stories written by children about the heroes of the 2001 terrorist attack in New York City. Laura, the niece of a firefighter who lost his life in the World Trade Center bombing, brings a picture of her uncle each year as part of a memorial. When Amira and Farah arrive at Rees, the commemoration is only a few days away. Brenda anticipates there will be questions from students, perhaps expressed privately to her, about whether the new girls are part of the group responsible for the tragedy. What are three points Brenda should make to her students?

Freedom of the press. School publications have long been fertile ground for disputes about students' rights to express themselves. In attempts to make school newspapers relevant and truly student owned, students tend to write about what's on the minds of classmates, no matter how controversial. However, it is clear from court decisions such as *Hazelwood School District* v. *Kuhlmeier,* 1988, that teachers and administrators may exercise editorial control over school publications. The court upheld an educator's right to delete certain student writing from school-sponsored publications.

For all three forms of expression—symbolic, speech, and written—students' rights must be balanced with what is in the best interest of the school population. The adults in charge—school board members, district personnel, administrators, and teachers—must be vigilant and protect student rights while also protecting those who may be adversely affected by the exercise of those rights.

THE RIGHT TO BE PROTECTED

Freedom of expression refers to what students may do. The right to be protected is freedom from actions that may be imposed on students.

Search and seizure. The Fourth Amendment provides for citizens to be secure from unreasonable search and seizure. This right applies to students in schools—to a point. The courts have attempted to balance the student's right to privacy and the school's need to know. The key term is *reasonableness*. In *New Jersey* v. *T.L.O.*, 1985, two high school girls were accused of smoking in the bathroom. After finding drug paraphernalia in her purse, T.L.O. was turned over to juvenile court. Her family sued for invasion of privacy. The U.S. Supreme Court ruled against her and maintained that the search and seizure were reasonable.

In most cases the courts have ruled against schools that arbitrarily and routinely search lockers, use drug-sniffing dogs, and search through students' clothes. Privacy is upheld as a right unless a search is deemed reasonable. But school lockers are part of school property. If there are reasonable suspicions of contraband in lockers, they may be searched.

Drug testing as a form of search of students remains controversial among the general public. However, since about 2000 most court decisions have ruled that drug testing is permissible for all students who participate in extracurricular activities, making no distinction, for example, between basketball and debate teams.

If there is reasonable suspicion for a search, the search itself must be reasonably conducted. Age and gender need to be considered. Walking through a metal detector or putting a book bag through a detector is noninvasive and considered reasonable if there have been problems with weapons at the school. Searching lockers, either by hand or using dogs, is more invasive but reasonable if there is suspicion. Asking students to empty their pockets and take off coats may be called for and is reasonable. However, strip searches are very invasive and should only be done if there is probable cause (more stringent than reasonable suspicion) and by proper authorities, not by teachers. The courts have been split on the legality of strip searches. In elementary school strip searches are typically supported by the courts, whereas in middle and high school they are sometimes not supported by court decisions. This kind of intrusive search should not be done by teachers alone under any circumstances.

Sexual harassment. According to the American Association of University Women (AAUW) (2001), **sexual harassment** is behavior with sexual implications that is neither wanted nor welcome. It interferes with a person's life. Sexual harassment may include obvious looks with lewd intent, taunts with sexual innuendo, touching, kissing, groping, and any actions or behaviors that have sexual connotations. The AAUW conducted a survey of eighth and eleventh grade students in 1993, and again in 2001, to gauge the extent of sexual harassment in schools. The survey revealed that 80% of students in both grade levels experienced sexual harassment. The results served as a wake-up call for schools as sexual harassment came into the public eye. However, a positive change is that in 2001, 69% of respondents, as opposed to only a small percentage in 1993 reported knowing about school policies against sexual harassment and the consequences for harassing. Awareness has increased, but the problem persists.

When students report incidents that appear to be sexual harassment, teachers must take their complaints seriously. The ruling in *Davis* v. *Monroe County Board of Education,* 1999, determined that educators can be held liable if they do not respond to complaints of sexual harassment. A fifth grade girl in Georgia was groped and verbally harassed by a classmate. She and her parents repeatedly reported it to the school,

Points of Reflection 10.8

Did you ever sense that your freedom of speech or press was restricted in some way in high school? Were you on a newspaper staff? Did anyone censor or limit in any way how students could express themselves in the paper? If so, how? What was your reaction?

Points of Reflection 10.9

Did you ever experience any form of search as a student in K–12 schools? What experiences do you recall of teachers or administrators acting on their suspicions of contraband? Have you or has anyone you know been subjected to a locker or clothing search? If so, what were the circumstances, and how did you or the other person respond?

Do you think teachers and administrators should be able to conduct random searches?

but it continued. The family filed a lawsuit, and 6 years later the U.S. Supreme Court ruled in a 5-to-4 decision that the school failed to act appropriately to protect the girl.

Teachers must also be conscious of their own behavior with students to prevent it from being misconstrued as harassment. In the 2001 AAUW survey, 7% of the respondents said that teachers sexually harassed them. Teachers must be constantly aware of how students may perceive their actions.

When sexual harassment is detected, the school is likely to take disciplinary action. The range of possibilities, governed by both common sense and lawful procedures, is broad.

Disciplinary action. The U.S. court system has been clear that schools have the right to administer a variety of punishments based on policy. Relatively minor rule infractions call for relatively minor consequences or punishment that may be administered at the classroom or school level. Rule infractions that are more serious require more serious consequences.

Corporal punishment. Fewer than half of states allow corporal punishment. Individual districts may choose not to allow corporal punishment even if allowed by the state. People who are in favor of corporal punishment say it's necessary and educationally sound, while those who oppose it call it archaic, cruel, inhumane, and unjustifiable (LaMorte, 2012).

In *Ingraham* v. *Wright*, 1977, the Supreme Court found that corporal punishment does not violate the tenets of the Constitution and is legal in states that have not banned the practice. The most common restrictions in states that permit corporal punishment are that only an administrator can spank or paddle a student, and there must be an adult witness. Teachers can lose their jobs if they violate state laws or local policies related to corporal punishment (Schimmel et al., 2011).

Exclusionary punishment. Exclusionary discipline, or discipline that takes students out of school, such as suspension and expulsion, carries with it the need for student due process, or steps that protect student rights (Pauken, 2006). Excluding students from school through suspension or expulsion has been ruled a denial of property rights to an education. Suspension is time out of school that may range from 1 day to less than a semester but is usually 10 days or less. Expulsion is more permanent and is generally for a semester or for an indefinite period.

Exclusionary punishment carries possible long-term consequences that may exceed the seriousness of the original offense. Any time away from school can be harmful to students in many ways. For instance, if a brief suspension causes a student to miss an exam, grades will suffer. Being out of school more than 10 days makes it almost impossible for a student to catch up. An expulsion almost always means a grade must be repeated. For some students a lengthy suspension or expulsion may make admission to certain colleges difficult or impossible.

Students are entitled to due process when exclusionary punishment is imposed or when the rule infraction and resulting punishment will become part of a student's permanent record. In the case of *Goss* v. *Lopez*, 1975, several Ohio high school students were suspended for up to 10 days without receiving a hearing. The students maintained complete innocence and were never informed of what they were accused of doing. When a federal district court agreed with the boys in their suit against the school, administrators appealed to the U.S. Supreme Court, where the decision went in favor of the students again. The justices wrote that students have a property right in school and that they may not be withdrawn without due process that includes

- written notification of time and place of hearing, along with a description of the procedures to be followed

Points of Reflection 10.10

Have you ever experienced sexual harassment? What were the circumstances? Was it addressed by anyone, or did it go unnoticed by everyone but you? How did it make you feel? Have you ever been guilty of sexually harassing someone else?

Points of Reflection 10.11

Have you ever received corporal punishment in a school setting? If so, how did it make you feel? Have you ever been suspended or expelled? If so, did the exclusionary punishment take care of whatever behavior it was intended to curb?

Are corporal punishment, suspension, and expulsion ever justified? If not, why not? If so, under what circumstances?

- list of evidence to be presented and names of witnesses
- description of the substance of witnesses' testimonies
- taped or written record of the proceedings and findings
- notification of the right to appeal (Schimmel et al., 2011)

Student right of nonparticipation. Students have a right to refuse to participate in some activities. The following rights have been upheld in the courts:

- Students may refuse to recite the Pledge of Allegiance.
- Students may refuse to dance, even when it is part of the physical education curriculum.
- Students may have other literature substituted for the planned curriculum if they object for religious or other reasons.
- Students may opt out of certain courses (usually dealing with sex education) if they and their parents object to content.
- Parents may refuse to follow guidelines that require students to be immunized.

This list will no doubt grow as parents and students have their voices heard in the courts. Administrators and teachers need to be aware of students' rights to nonparticipation, or at least question the legitimacy of insisting on compliance with school policies and traditions.

Student Records: Access and Privacy. The **Family Educational Rights and Privacy Act (FERPA) of 1974**, commonly called the **Buckley Amendment,** allows parents and guardians access to their students' academic records and requires written parental permission for the records to be shared with anyone else. When students turn 18, they have control over who sees their records.

The Buckley Amendment establishes the minimum standards regarding privacy of records, with some states and districts going beyond to allow students access to their own records. Some items, however, are not subject to student or parent viewing. For instance, teachers' grade books, notes kept by teachers for their own use, and the private notes kept by school law enforcement teams typically remain inaccessible to others.

The extent to which student records must be kept private was tested when an Oklahoma parent challenged the long-standing practice of students grading one another's work in *Owasso Independent School District* v. *Falso,* 2002. The parent sued an Owasso school saying peer grading was embarrassing and often inaccurate. Because of conflicting court actions, the case ended up in the U.S. Supreme Court, which ruled unanimously that day-to-day grading is not covered by FERPA.

Right to nondiscrimination. Students may not legally be discriminated against by public schools. Discrimination cases that have been tested in U.S. courts have resulted in the following principles:

- Students of any race, religion, or disability may attend U.S. public schools.
- Students who are married, are parents, or are divorced may attend the same public schools as those who are not.
- Students with HIV/AIDS pose no significant risk to others and may attend public schools.

Not only are all students guaranteed the right to attend public schools, but the right has also been extended to extracurricular activities.

Table 10.7 includes sample court cases involving student rights. Teachers need to be as informed as possible about what the courts have decided.

TABLE 10.7 Cases involving student rights

Case	Explanation	Implications for Teachers
Tinker v. *Des Moines Independent Community School District* Iowa, 1969	This case involved three students who wore arm bands to protest the war in Vietnam. They were suspended and subsequently sued the district. In this monumentally important case, the U.S. Supreme Court ruled that teachers and students do not "shed their rights to freedom of speech or expression at the schoolhouse gate." The *Tinker* case has been cited repeatedly since 1969.	The rights of teachers and students differ inside the schoolhouse. When teachers express their views, they have a legally captive audience of people (their students) who have to listen to them. Therefore, their overt display of opinions is not allowed. However, students have the right to express their views in peaceful, nondisruptive ways.
Goss v. *Lopez* Ohio, 1975	Several high school students were suspended for up to 10 days without receiving a hearing. The students maintained complete innocence and were never informed of exactly what they were accused of doing. When a federal district court agreed with the students in their suit against the school, administrators appealed to the U.S. Supreme Court, where the decision went in favor of the students again. The justices wrote that students have a property right to school attendance.	Often teachers will be aware of, or even report, grave discipline infractions of students. Within a day or two the students are back in school, leaving teachers disgruntled with administrators. We need to realize that sometimes principals are not in control of when students are in or out of school.
Ingraham v. *Wright* Florida, 1977	In this case two boys were paddled, causing bruises that kept them out of school for a few days. The court commented that schools can be held liable for injuries, but that students are not entitled to due process before district- or state-sanctioned corporal punishment is administered.	Fewer and fewer states allow this antiquated practice. However, if you are in a state and district where corporal punishment is allowed, never administer it yourself. The best advice is to maintain a classroom environment that encourages respect. Handle relatively minor discipline issues when you can to avoid the use of corporal punishment on the students you serve.
New Jersey v. *T.L.O.* New Jersey, 1985	Two high school girls were accused of smoking in the bathroom. One admitted it, and one (T.L.O.) denied it. In the principal's office, T.L.O. was asked to empty her purse. In it were cigarettes, cigarette-rolling paper, marijuana, a pipe, a roll of money, and a list titled "People who owe me money." The student was turned over to juvenile court. She sued the school for invasion of privacy. The U.S. Supreme Court ruled against her and maintained that the search and seizure were reasonable.	It's very tempting at times, especially in middle and high school, to look the other way when we suspect students are engaging in the kinds of activities implied in this case. But try to resist the temptation. When you smell smoke, or detect alcohol or marijuana on students, or you see things happening in the halls or school grounds that appear to involve substance abuse or violence, tell an administrator. Their eyes can't be everywhere. They depend on aware teachers to help keep the school safe and healthy.
Bethel School District No. 403 v. *Fraser* Washington, 1986	The freedom of speech implied in *Tinker* was challenged in 1986 when a student made a speech containing sexual innuendo in a high school assembly. He was reprimanded and subsequently sued the school, claiming that his freedom of speech was denied. The court said that schools have the right to censor communication in schools to avoid disruption.	If language and innuendo are not tolerated in a school assembly, then they should never be tolerated in your classroom. This sort of problem is most prevalent with adolescents who, at times, seem very adult-like. It's tempting to allow conversations to include language and innuendo that would not be acceptable, because the students' vocabulary and knowledge are increasing. But never let this happen. Teachers cannot tolerate, and certainly cannot condone, offensive student language.
Morse v. *Frederick* Alaska, 2007	As the Olympic torch made its way down a street across from his school, a student displayed a banner reading "Bong Hits 4 Jesus." The principal took the banner and suspended the student for 10 days because she perceived the banner promoted the use of illegal drugs. The student sued the principal and won the suit in a federal court. The principal, in turn, sued the student and the case went to the U.S. Supreme Court, where the federal court decision was narrowly overturned in favor of the principal and the school district.	By some accounts, the students involved simply wanted to be televised. Some Supreme Court justices considered the whole incident silly, implying the old "kids will be kids" adage. As teachers, we can discourage our students from doing foolish things.
Hazelwood School District v. *Kuhlmeier* Missouri, 1988	In this case, two articles written by students for a high school newspaper were deleted by the principal. The main topics of the articles were teen pregnancy and divorce, and they contained references to sexuality that the principal thought inappropriate for younger students. In addition, even though their names were changed, the principal was concerned that students written about in the articles were identifiable. The Supreme Court ruled in favor of the district, stating that educators may exercise substantial control over school-sponsored publications and events.	Schools have the right to censor controversial articles in school publications. Of course this is important for those who sponsor publications, but it's also important for all teachers. Students will often push the limits and need to understand that educators can censor writing. If in doubt, always ask an administrator.

TABLE 10.7 Cases involving student rights (*continued*)

Case	Explanation	Implications for Teachers
Isaacs v. Board of Education of Howard County Maryland, 1999	A high school girl was not allowed in school because she wore a head wrap to celebrate her cultural heritage in violation of the "no hats" rule. A judge ruled in favor of the school and for the following reasons: 1. Hats increase horseplay and conflicts. 2. Hats block teachers' and students' views in classrooms. 3. Hats allow students to hide drugs and other contraband. 4. Hats foster a less respectful learning climate. The judge concluded that it was unrealistic to expect schools to make hat-by-hat decisions.	This is becoming more and more controversial as cultural and religious diversity increase. Had this case made it to the U.S. Supreme Court, the outcome may have been different. However, if there is a school-wide "no hats" rule, teachers must comply and report infractions, even if you think a student should be allowed to wear a head covering.

Sources: Dunklee, D. R., & Shoop, R. J. (2002). *The principal's quick-reference guide to school law: Reducing liability, litigation, and other potential legal tangles.* Thousand Oaks, CA: Corwin Press. LaMorte, M. W. (2012). *School law: Cases and concepts* (10th ed.). Upper Saddle River, NJ: Pearson. Schimmel, D., Stellman, L. R., & Fischer, L. (2011). *Teachers and the law* (8th ed.). Upper Saddle River, NJ: Pearson.

CONCLUDING THOUGHTS

Controversial issues—such as sex and AIDS education, Internet usage, school choice, high-stakes testing, school uniforms, protection for homosexual students, and funding for public education—continue to emerge and will no doubt prompt legal questions. The courts will interpret the Constitution or rely on case law to settle such disputes. Teachers need to stay current on how laws affect what takes place in classrooms and schools.

When you choose to teach, you make a commitment to a service profession. You take on the serious responsibility not only to abide by laws but also to continually promote what is ethical for students and for yourself, both in the big issues as well as in the seemingly minor issues that test you every day. You commit to thoughtful and deliberate decision making, to showing the courage to do what's right for students, and to having the good sense to ask for advice and guidance when needed.

We began this chapter by considering Derek Boucher and his classroom at Roosevelt High School in California. Now as the chapter comes to an end we join Derek as he addresses issues that have come about as he sponsors a newsletter written by students in his reading remediation class. Read through *Chapter in Review* to help refresh your memory of what we have discussed, and then interact with Derek as he confronts challenges in *Developing Professional Competence.*

Chapter in Review

What does it mean to be an ethical teacher?

- Laws tell us what we can and can't do. Ethics tell us what we should and shouldn't do.
- The National Education Association provides a professional code of ethics for educators.
- To be an ethical teacher means to be guided by a set of beliefs that leads to attitudes and actions focused on what's best for students.
- Six characteristics that help teachers make ethical decisions include appreciation for moral deliberation, empathy, knowledge, reasoning, courage, and interpersonal skills.

- Ethical attitudes, decisions, and actions involve both major and seemingly minor issues.
- It is important to have a vision of the characteristics we want to help cultivate in our students.

How do laws affect schools, teachers, and students?

- The laws that affect schools, teachers, and students are based on a balance of rights and responsibilities.
- Four basic sources of law directly impact the work of teachers: the U.S. Constitution, federal laws, state and local laws and policies, and case law.

What are the legal rights of teachers?

- The legalities of employment include contracts, tenure, and dismissal.
- Due process involves a set of guidelines that must be followed to ensure that individuals are protected from arbitrary or capricious treatment by those in authority.
- Teachers enjoy the same rights as other citizens, including freedom of expression—whether symbolic, written, or spoken—but with restraints based on the responsibilities of teaching.
- Academic freedom is a form of expression that allows teachers to use their judgment concerning what and how to teach.
- Teachers have some restrictions on their personal lives that other people do not have because of the nature of the teaching profession.

What are the legal responsibilities of teachers?

- Teachers serve *in loco parentis* and are responsible to care for and protect the students they supervise.
- Among other things, teachers have the legal responsibility to avoid liability, abide by copyright laws, and report suspected child abuse.

How does the law impact the relationship between school and religion?

- The First Amendment says that government (public schools) can neither establish religion nor interfere with the free exercise of it.
- Public prayer is illegal in public school. Religious organizations may meet and pray in school facilities outside regular school hours.
- It is permissible to teach about religion but not with the purpose of persuading students to believe in a particular religion.

What are the legal rights of students?

- Court decisions attempt to balance the rights of students to express themselves and the necessity of limiting personal freedom to ensure the safety and well-being of others.
- Students have freedom of symbolic expression, speech, and the press.
- Student privacy is protected from unreasonable search and seizure.
- Students have the right not to be sexually harassed.
- Students have due process rights when facing serious disciplinary action.
- Students and parents have rights concerning privacy and access to records.
- Students may not legally be discriminated against by public schools.

Developing Professional Competence

Thoughtfully reading this scenario and responding to the items that follow it will help you prepare for licensure exams.

Derek Boucher's mission to ensure literacy for all his students at Roosevelt High School often leads him to be quite innovative. Because most of the students in his sophomore reading remediation class speak Spanish as their primary language, one of his ideas led to the development of an English-language newsletter written for, and by, Latino students. The purpose of the newsletter is to encourage English-language learners to write articles that the students who are also learning to speak English would enjoy reading.

Derek followed the proper channels to get permission to initiate the newsletter and to use school supplies to publish it twice a month. Things went fine for 3 months, and Derek was quite pleased with how much his students were learning about writing and editing and, as an added bonus, about expressing themselves in English. Articles ranged from reporting of some school and local issues to movie reviews to opinion pieces. After school every other Thursday when the pieces were due, Derek would read them for content and mechanics, make notes, return them Friday at the beginning of class, and then spend all of the Friday class period helping with rewrites and putting the pieces together in the four-page format in which it would be published.

Although most of the content of the student-written articles proved to be noninflammatory, one Thursday Derek found in the stack of articles two pieces that implicated several students in marijuana possession and sales. No names were given as the authors of the two pieces spoke out against the illicit drug activity, but from what Derek knew about the kids at Roosevelt and what the authors implied, he was fairly certain he could identify the culprits. Although students knew Mr. Boucher had the ultimate responsibility to edit what they wrote, censorship had not yet been a topic of discussion. Now Derek faced a number of serious questions about how he would proceed.

Think through this scenario and answer the following multiple-choice questions:

1. The student newsletter is a good idea for all of these reasons except which one of the following?
   a. Students saw a purpose for writing.
   b. Students learned to communicate better in their native language.
   c. The newsletter helped give Latino students an identity on campus.
   d. Derek was able to build literacy skills in a way that engaged his students.

2. Derek had a right as a teacher to censor the content of the student-generated newsletter because of which of the following case law precedents?
   a. *Pickering* v. *Board of Education*
   b. *Brown* v. *Board of Education*
   c. *Tinker* v. *Des Moines Independent Community School District*
   d. *Hazelwood School District* v. *Kuhlmeier*

3. Derek knows that if he tells Ms. Romero or Mr. Lael, the principal and assistant principal at Roosevelt, they will have the right to search the lockers of students who are implicated in drug possession and sales. The case that grants school officials the right to search lockers of students if they have reasonable suspicion is
   a. *New Jersey* v. *T.L.O.*
   b. *Hazelwood School District* v. *Kuhlmeier*
   c. *Tinker* v. *Des Moines Independent Community School District*
   d. *Pickering* v. *Board of Education*

4. The most meaningful reason Derek demonstrates one of the six characteristics of teachers who make ethical judgments, *appreciation for moral deliberation*, is that
   a. Derek believes strongly that marijuana use is wrong.
   b. Derek believes that any lengths he may go to in order to encourage reading and writing are justified.
   c. Derek recognizes that this situation is complex and that the rights of everyone involved should be protected.
   d. Derek is concerned that the way he communicates his concerns to the administrators does not imply his students are involved.

Now it's time for you to respond to two short essay items involving the scenario. In your responses, be sure to address all the dilemmas and questions posed in each item. Your responses should each be between one half and one full double-spaced page.

5. Is Derek obligated to reveal what he knows to the administration? How is Derek's decision related to his personal code of ethics? If, from an administrator's viewpoint, the newspaper is somehow fueling problems at Roosevelt and Derek is asked to stop publishing it, how might Derek defend the newsletter as a valuable teaching tool?

6. Derek knows that he has to talk with the students in his reading remediation class. When should he approach the subject? What should he say about his right and responsibility to act as a censor of newsletter content? How could he encourage his students to continue to write about relevant issues now that they know he can block items if he sees the need?

Governing and Financing Public Schools

Dear Reader

As professionals, we need to understand where, when, and how decisions are made that affect our schools and classrooms, and, ultimately, our students, families, and communities. Perhaps in a perfect world, these decisions would be made by people who have first-hand experience with teaching and learning. These would be people who understand the complexity of the processes that lead to the development of engaged, curious, and productive citizens who never stop learning and whose actions reflect civility. However, in the U.S. we often find ourselves bogged down in bureaucracy, with levels of government imposing policies that not only are difficult to comprehend, but also may make us feel powerless to influence.

Public education costs a lot of money. People not directly involved with teaching and learning often say schools spend too much yet achieve minimal results. True, money doesn't buy learning, but it does provide the facilities, programs, and personnel that help make education accessible to all.

Developing an overview of governance and finance now will help you put in context what you read in the newspaper or see on TV about issues such as school board proceedings, hiring of administrators, legislative decisions, and test score reports. As we explore the complex array of individuals and groups that have governing and financial authority over public schools in the United States, we consider the following questions:

- How does the federal government influence public education in the United States?

- What is the state's role in public education?

- How do school districts function?

- What is the management structure of individual schools?

- What other entities impact the governance of public schools in the United States?

- How are public schools financed?

- How are funds for education spent?

Teaching in Focus

Chris Roberts, Brenda Beyal, and Tim Mendenhall teach in multiage classrooms of third, fourth, and fifth graders at Rees Elementary, Utah. They function beautifully as a team and enjoy working together as they shape their multiage program. Because multiage education is not the norm, teachers and administrators must have an interest in initiating the concept. Chris, as a former special education teacher, is very aware that students of different ages can actually learn at the same level and rate. Brenda and Tim, teachers who routinely find ways to individualize instruction, know that the learning capabilities of students the same age can vary widely. Experience has taught all three that 8- to 12-year-olds may be able to grasp some concepts at the same time from basically the same experiences, whereas other concepts may come easily or prove more difficult for individual students to grasp regardless of age. This knowledge prompted them to establish multiage classrooms.

As accomplished and respected teachers, Chris, Brenda, and Tim had workable plans to go with their idea. They learned a lot about district governance policies as they worked through the approval process, beginning with their principal; then the district director of elementary education; and, finally, the school board and superintendent. After hours of talking and preparing, district authorities approved the idea of multiage education. Although school board approval was almost certain once the district director of elementary education endorsed the plan, Chris, Brenda, and Tim still needed to present their ideas in a formal meeting of the board and superintendent. Watch **Chris' interview** and revisit **Tim's interview** and **Brenda's interview** to understand more about these three outstanding teachers' philosophies of education.

How are the geographic boundaries drawn that determine who attends your school? If the principal is your boss, who is the principal's boss, and what is the chain of command? Who decides whether your school building gets a new wing and how it is financed? Who decides what standardized tests your students take? Why do you have so many forms to fill out? Who pays for special programs for kids in low socioeconomic settings? These questions, and a myriad more, are all related to the governing and financing of public schools in the United States. Figure 11.1 shows the four basic governing levels of public schools, and this chapter will explain at what levels particular decisions are made. As we discuss the levels, Figure 11.1 will expand to display some of the positions and responsibilities of each level.

How Does the Federal Government Influence Public Education?

Because education is not addressed in the Constitution, it has historically been interpreted as a state's responsibility. However, the federal government's involvement in the functioning of schools through the institutions and agencies shown in Figure 11.2 has increased in recent decades.

PRESIDENTIAL INFLUENCE

Almost every presidential candidate in the 20th century included education in his or her campaign platform; most had boldly articulated plans and promises. From its establishment in 1857 until 1980, the U.S. Department of Education served in an advisory capacity with little impact on public schools. President Ronald Reagan (1980–1988) was the first

Figure 11.1 Overview of American public school governance

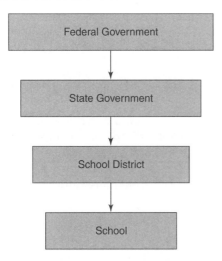

president to experience the department as a cabinet-level agency, resulting from action taken by President Jimmy Carter's administration in 1979. Since 1980 the influence of the U.S. Department of Education has steadily increased. President Bill Clinton (1992–2000) worked vigorously toward achieving the objectives of *Goals 2000,* an ambitious list of goals for students in U.S. public schools. President George W. Bush's legacy (2000–2008) regarding education is the No Child Left Behind Act of 2001, discussed throughout this text.

President Barack Obama declared his commitment to public education on Inauguration Day in 2009. On the official White House Web site (2010) we read,

> Providing a high-quality education for all children is critical to America's economic future. Our nation's economic competitiveness and the path to the American Dream depend on providing every child with an education that will enable them

Figure 11.2 Federal government role in American public school governance

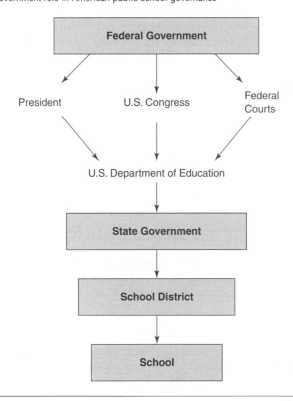

to succeed in a global economy that is predicated on knowledge and innovation. President Obama is committed to providing every child access to a complete and competitive education, from cradle through career.

The American Recovery and Reinvestment Act of 2009 invests heavily in education—both as a way to provide jobs now and to prepare for the future—with almost $100 billion pledged as additional support for public education, including emphasis on teacher effectiveness, early learning programs, programs for children with special needs, and greater achievement in low-performing schools. The Obama administration is working to ensure that teachers are supported as professionals and that they are held accountable for student learning. One means of accomplishing both aims is to provide competitive funding to states that develop innovative plans to deliver a 21st-century education that prepares all children for success in a global workplace, with teachers both qualified and responsible. This funding is delivered in the form of *Race to the Top* grants (White House, 2010).

CONGRESS AND THE COURTS

The U.S. Congress has passed many influential laws regarding education, and the federal court system has made numerous rulings impacting education. For example, the Bilingual Education Act of 1968 made provisions for English-language instruction. The Education for All Handicapped Children Act of 1975 was the first to guarantee a free public education for students with disabilities. The No Child Left Behind Act of 2001 has impacted K–12 schools, teachers, and students, although assessments of its success have been both mixed and impassioned.

Laws affecting education are discussed in Chapters 2 and 10.

U.S. DEPARTMENT OF EDUCATION

The U.S. Department of Education has had some influential secretaries over the years. The term *secretary* as used here indicates the head of a presidential cabinet–level department. The secretary of education is chosen and appointed by the president, making the position political. The incumbents' favor with citizens and educators rises and falls with the popularity of the president and the party in power. The secretary of education influences policies established by the U.S. Department of Education, which has a sizable budget and exercises its power through these policies and programs. The federal government sponsors programs that impact schools and students such as Head Start and the National School Lunch Program, both of which benefit children in low socioeconomic settings.

Funding provided to schools by the federal government is distributed in the form of assistance to implement approved programs and to conduct educational research. These funds are also used as leverage to help ensure that state departments of education both comply with specific federal mandates, such as guidelines and policies related to attempts to equalize educational opportunities for all children, and comply with the use of widespread testing programs. In some cases, states may choose whether to comply with U.S. Department of Education policies. However, the federal government withholds funds from states and their schools when they choose not to comply.

What Is the State's Role in Public Education?

Governors, legislators, and judges, as well as state boards of education, state departments of education, and state superintendents, have much influence on public schools. Figure 11.3 is an overview of the basic state structure that impacts schools in the United States.

BALANCE OF POWER AT THE STATE LEVEL

States govern under a balance of power with three major branches of government, similar to what exists at the federal level. Governors have executive authority; legislatures have lawmaking authority; and state courts uphold and interpret laws, as well as establish constitutional guidelines.

Figure 11.3 State government role in American public school governance

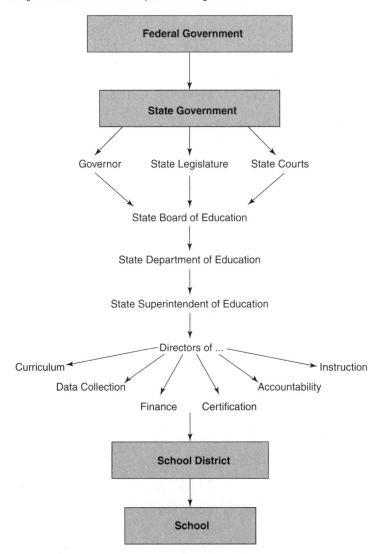

Governors. Governors, as leaders of state governments, potentially have tremendous impact on public schools. A governor's attitude toward education has far-reaching influence on policies and laws. In many states the governor appoints the state's superintendent of education, as well as members of the state board of education. In addition, governors make budgetary recommendations that impact schools.

The National Governors Association (NGA) was founded in 1908 and serves as the collective voice of the nation's governors. The NGA Center for Best Practices is an online clearinghouse that provides governors and the public with information about public education, including such topics as disparities in academic achievement, turning around low-performing schools, and quality of teaching. The organization describes policy options for states, identifies how states cope with dilemmas pertaining to education, helps governors establish and maintain quality education in their states, and counsels them on how to work effectively with state legislatures (National Governors Association [NGA], 2010). Recall that the NGA was one of two organizations originating and propelling the development of the Common Core State Standards.

The Common Core State Standards Initiative and the National Governors Association are discussed in Chapter 4.

State legislatures. Members of state legislatures have significant influence on public education. State legislators impact schools as they determine:

- state laws that affect every aspect of public education
- how state chief officers of education and state school board members are selected

- responsibilities of state-level school officials
- how taxes are used to support schools
- the general direction of the curriculum
- the length of the school day and year
- aspects of teacher employment, including issues involving tenure, retirement, and collective bargaining

There are no requirements in terms of educational background or experience for state legislators. Teachers and school administrators frequently question the wisdom of decisions made in the legislature. Having conversations, inviting legislators to visit schools, and writing letters are vehicles for influencing legislative viewpoints.

State courts. When state laws require interpretation, or when there is a conflict between state laws and federal regulations or the U.S. Constitution, state courts impact public education. State courts hear arguments and make decisions about school compliance with state laws that are often written in broad terms.

STATE BOARD OF EDUCATION

Almost every state has a **state board of education**, generally composed of seven to nine volunteers who are either elected or appointed by the governor. State legislatures give state boards oversight authority; in other words, state boards act in regulatory and advisory capacities. State boards of education make major decisions concerning the operation of public schools as they

- set goals and approve standards and assessments for schools
- establish the standards by which schools are accredited (allowed to function)
- advise the governor and the legislature on educational issues
- make many of the decisions about how state funds are used
- represent and report to the public on education issues
- serve as the governing body of the state department of education (National Association of State Boards of Education, 2005)

The state board of education is primarily a policy-making body with broad responsibilities. The many detailed responsibilities that deal with education on a statewide basis are overseen by the state's department of education.

STATE DEPARTMENT OF EDUCATION

A **state department of education** (also known as state office of education or department of public instruction) operates under the guidance of the governor, legislature, and state board of education. These state agencies are large, with a complex array of responsibilities and employees. Governors, state legislators, and state board members may not have expertise in education. However, most of those who hold nonclerical positions within a state department of education are professional educators. There is one notable exception. The chief state officer, or state superintendent of education, is likely to be either publicly elected or a political appointee and may not be a professional educator.

State superintendent of education. The one person with responsibility for managing the state department of education may be called the **state superintendent**, chief state education officer, or commissioner of education. This person may either be elected by the voters or appointed by the governor or state school board, depending on the state's policy. The state superintendent position is both public and political. The superintendent is in charge of the bureaucracy that is usually centralized in the state's capital city, and travels throughout the state as the acknowledged authority on how schools operate and are assessed for effectiveness.

State department of education responsibilities. The state superintendent of education generally has a large staff of individuals with varied expertise. The people who work as department directors are in charge of divisions within the state department that address, among other issues,

- teacher certification (or licensure)
- curriculum standards and accountability
- instruction (usually a director for each content area)
- special education
- school levels (high, middle, elementary, early childhood)
- technology
- charter schools
- teacher professional development
- state budget funds
- communication and public relations
- collection and reporting of school data

Although not a common occurrence, a state department of education may take over the operation of a school—or even an entire school district—that is deemed unsatisfactory.

How Do School Districts Function?

A **school district** is an organizational structure of local schools defined by geographic boundaries. Figure 11.4 provides an overview of the basic structure that exists in most school districts.

School districts have at least one **feeder system** of schools, i.e., early childhood/elementary schools that feed into middle schools that feed into a particular high school. There are over 15,000 school districts in the United States. In the early to mid-20th century, there were almost 10 times as many. The decrease occurred as people realized it was more efficient to combine small districts and share services and administration. Interestingly, the entire state of Hawaii is one school district, whereas the state of Texas has more than a thousand separate districts (National Education Association [NEA], 2009).

School districts vary greatly in size, from one building that houses all grade levels, as in Gilpin County School District in Colorado with about 300 students, to New York City public schools, with over 1 million students. Small and large districts both have distinct advantages as well as limitations. Small and medium districts have the advantage of accessibility. Teachers feel as though they can be heard in policy matters, and parents often sense a distinct connection to the schools and faculty. In very large districts, teachers may sense that they are far removed from where policy decisions are made. Large districts generally have the advantage of availability of numerous services and specialists who oversee the many aspects of life in schools and classrooms. In small and medium districts, individuals tend to have an array of duties, and fewer curricular and service options are offered. Regardless of size or complexity, each district has a school board and a superintendent who function as leaders of central administration.

Points of Reflection 11.1

Were your K–12 experiences in a small, medium, or large district? What advantages or limitations because of the size of your district were you aware of? Did you attend school from kindergarten through 12th grade in one feeder system, or did you move frequently?

DISTRICT SCHOOL BOARDS

District school boards are unique American institutions composed of elected citizens who volunteer their time. This form of governance originated in the locally controlled schools of the colonies and in the common schools movement. Through one reform effort after another, the basic structure of school boards has not changed. They represent democratization by linking the public to public schools. Many educators find school boards to be flawed in terms of how they govern, but most agree that they serve a worthwhile purpose (Hess, 2010). Because local schools are profoundly affected by district school board decisions, we spend more time discussing them than the other levels of governance.

Schools in colonial America are discussed in Chapter 7.

Figure 11.4 School district role in American public school governance

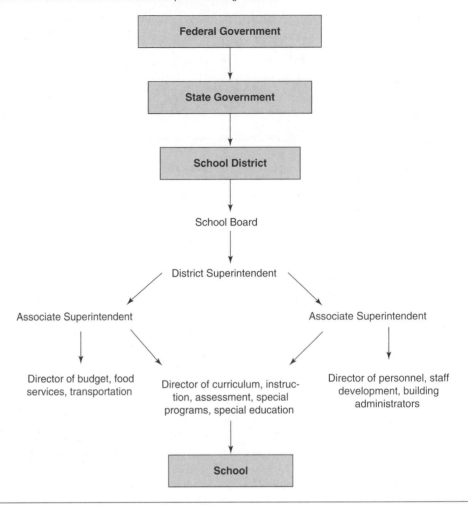

Most members of public district school boards are neither parents nor educators and receive little or no compensation. A 2010 study (National School Boards Association, 2011) involving board members from about two thousand districts yielded the information in Figure 11.5, as well as the following information about district school board members:

- Over 90% have or had children who live in the district in which they serve.
- About 25% have been teachers at some point.
- 96% say that their districts provide safe environments for teachers and students.
- 92% say that parents in their districts are not willing to serve on the school board.
- 88% have lived in their communities more than 5 years.
- 90% say they will continue to live in their districts indefinitely.

Board elections. It can be costly to campaign for a school board seat, especially in medium to large districts (at least 20,000 students). The two basic kinds of school board elections are at-large and single-member elections. In **at-large elections**, voters may choose any candidate regardless of the area in the district the candidate represents. If there are five distinct areas in a school district, each will have specific candidates who live in the areas, but *every* voter in the *entire* district may vote for their choices regardless of where they live.

Figure 11.5 Profile of school board members

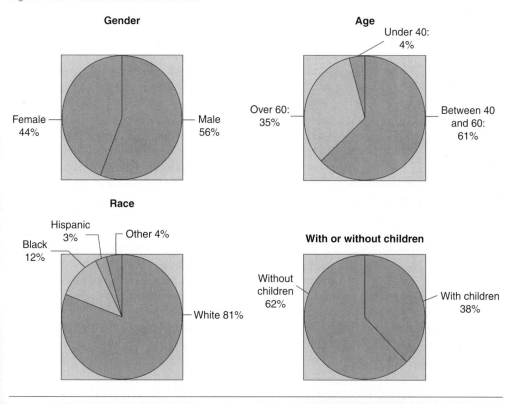

Gender

Female 44%
Male 56%

Age

Under 40: 4%
Over 60: 35%
Between 40 and 60: 61%

Race

Hispanic 3%
Other 4%
Black 12%
White 81%

With or without children

Without children 62%
With children 38%

Source: Based on National Association of School Boards (2011). *School Boards Circa 2010: Governance in the Accountability Era.* Retrieved September 8, 2013, from http://www.nsba.org/Board-Leadership/Surveys/School-Boards-Circa-2010/SBCirca10-Tables.pdf

In **single-member elections**, only those who live in a specific area can vote for the representatives in their area. The single-member process has the potential to elect more representative school board members because neighborhoods are more likely to have candidates and voters who share ethnicity and socioeconomic status. As you can see in Figure 11.5, over 80% of school board members are White, indicating that members are often not representative of many of the families in the United States.

Board responsibilities. District school board members are responsible for setting policies that affect the operation of schools. In a poll sponsored by the National School Boards Association, the five biggest concerns and responsibilities of school board members from small, medium, and large districts were funding, student achievement, teacher quality, improving technology, and special education (Hess, 2002). Dealing with these concerns and fulfilling other duties require numerous meetings and research. Among other responsibilities, school board members

- decide how much money will be spent on teacher salaries, facilities improvement, and instructional materials
- hire and fire personnel, both professional and classified (clerical, custodial, etc.)
- approve and evaluate programs that may affect some or all schools, teachers, and students within the district
- make curricular decisions within state guidelines
- determine organizational policy

Teachers, families, and community members voice their questions and opinions at public school board meetings.

School boards and the public. Controversy is never far from school boards. Members are easy targets for both oral and written chastisement by the community. It's a rare moment indeed when school board members are not perceived by some segment of the population as incompetent, downright stupid, or even evil. As trustees of public schools, their often unappreciated position requires them to make hard decisions. When one group feels slighted or excluded, the board hears its complaints, but must still make decisions that may not be satisfactory to those affected. When it makes fiscal (monetary) sense to close a school, parts of the community storm the board with emotionally charged, often valid, objections. The board listens and makes decisions. When community groups work diligently to help improve education for all students and present research and suggestions, the board listens and makes decisions. When teachers take positions on issues such as board choices to transfer administrators, or program alterations, they make their case to the school board. The board listens and makes decisions.

An ongoing challenge for school boards is to be both accountable and **transparent**, meaning that decisions are made with full disclosure of information and reasoning. With technology today, there is little justification for data not to be available to the public. Methods for making information gathered by school boards easily searchable are also possible. But this organizational structure, almost as old as the United States itself, will likely be slow in following any new guidelines calling for complete transparency. Snider (2010) tells us that organizations composed of elected citizens sometimes have a sense of "we know best." This attitude may appear to permeate local school boards and, even in the second decade of the 21st century, it may take some digging to find the logic behind school board decisions.

With all this responsibility, and frequent community wrath, why would any citizen want to be a school board member? Many do it as a service to the community. They have a genuine interest in doing what they can to benefit local schools and students. Others seek the position to gain power and visibility, to further political ambition, or to advocate for a particular cause (Mizell, 2010). Regardless of their motivations, school board members dedicate long hours to the governance of public schools, including the hiring of a district superintendent.

Points of Reflection 11.2

Have you observed the functioning of a district school board, either firsthand or through television news or newspapers? What impressions did you have?

DISTRICT SUPERINTENDENT AND STAFF

A **district superintendent** functions as the school district's chief executive officer. The superintendent is hired by the board and serves at its pleasure, which means the board can also dismiss the superintendent. The superintendent is expected to both advise the board and carry out board policies. As largely noneducators, board members often choose an educator as superintendent to keep schools running smoothly on a day-to-day basis. The relationship between the board and the superintendent can become awkward when school board members go beyond policy making into what is considered the authority of the superintendent. When board members get involved in day-to-day operations, it is often referred to as **micromanagement**. If tensions develop over policies or decisions, a school board may dismiss a superintendent. Generally, before things escalate to this point, the public is involved and meetings are held to discuss the situation. These can be trying times for communities. If a superintendent is dismissed, a very public search process is usually conducted to find a replacement. Generally, a community is invigorated at the prospect of new leadership and will rally around the person hired to lead the public schools. A "honeymoon" period is seen as a positive time, with the new superintendent greeted and embraced while getting to know schools and school personnel and all the community **stakeholders**, or those who will be ultimately affected by public school district governance. In a rather sarcastic—yet realistic—way, this chapter's **The Opinion Page** feature describes the Charlotte Mecklenburg School District's "honeymoon" with new Superintendent Dr. Heath Morrison, hired by the North Carolina district in 2012.

In small districts, superintendents may handle *all* the responsibilities listed in Figure 11.4. The larger the district, the more necessary it is for the superintendent to delegate. Medium-to-large districts have associate or assistant superintendents who handle specific duties such as supervision of the different levels—early childhood, elementary, middle, and high. They work with district curriculum and instruction directors to coordinate efforts. Larger districts also have associate superintendents in charge of areas such as personnel, facilities, and finance.

THE OPINION PAGE

This Opinion Editorial appeared in the Charlotte Observer, *North Carolina, on May 9, 2012.*

What Were You Thinking, Supt. Morrison?

by Mark Washburn

Mark Washburn writes television and radio commentary for the Charlotte Observer.

It is our pleasure to welcome you, Heath Morrison, to our wonderful community.

Now that your salary as new superintendent of schools has been negotiated, it is time to talk about your benefits package, which we think you will find is superior.

For the first nine to 12 months of your employment, everyone in town will be gracious and fawning. We will listen to your ideas with eyes a-sparkle and jaws a-droop. We will tell you again and again how thrilled we are to have a smart cookie like you. We will find magic money in the budget to carry out your clever initiatives. We will compare your leadership abilities to those of Gandhi. We will surprise you with ice cream on Fridays.

At the 13-month mark, we will recognize you're getting weary of vast adoration. We will then start a program we call "gracious wondering." For a time, not exceeding two years, we will wonder about the progress our school system is making. In the latter part of this phase, we will hold mock tribunals and invite you to testify about why things are the way they are. Our former superintendents have all found this to be a time of introspection and personal growth. This will be facilitated by our supportive and caring school board. You have met them by now and know what a wise and harmonious group they are.

At the four-year mark, you will become fully vested in the executive incentive package called "unrelenting demonization." Your annual performance review will be a glorious spectacle of pursed lips, sour faces and slowly shaken heads. Around town, your name will be synonymous with epic failure. Parents and teachers will be united in the notion that *Something Must Be Done*.

In year five, we will celebrate the nadir of your career. You will be considered personally responsible for unsatisfactory test scores (no matter what they are, they will be unsatisfactory), every breach of classroom discipline and whatever clunkers are drafted by the Bobcats.

At this juncture, you will be hired by another district and slink out of town. For both of us, the cycle will begin anew. It will, in short, be just like the reign of any school superintendent anywhere.

We cannot tell you how excited we are to have you aboard. We have felt an emotional void since our last superintendent mysteriously vanished. We look forward to you providing a service to our community that we think you'll find is absolutely critical.

This Opinion Page piece reveals a familiar reality through the use of sarcasm. Mr. Washburn has obviously observed the coming and going of a number of district superintendents. Write a well-developed paragraph in response to each of the following questions:

1. Mr. Washburn writes this piece to Dr. Morrison. He refers to his benefits package as the reception he will receive from the community. In his first year as superintendent, why do you think the community will be so welcoming? What need, or perceived need, must the community have?

2. Overall, what sort of community attitude is Mr. Washburn predicting for the middle of Dr. Morrison's time in Charlotte? What circumstances are community members likely ignoring when they appear to put exclusive blame on leadership?

3. "Nadir of your career" refers to the lowest point of Dr. Morrison's time as superintendent. Do the last three paragraphs say more about a leader and his or her ability or us as community members? Explain your opinion.

People in the community sometimes complain there are too many administrators and non-classroom teachers doing supervisory work rather than directly teaching children. Before making this judgment, citizens should recognize how complex it is to operate school districts and individual schools in ways that free teachers to teach and students to learn.

What Is the Management Structure of Individual Schools?

Now we consider individual schools, the places where teachers and students interact. Within the school building, the management structure often depends on both the size and the level of the school. Figure 11.6 lists some of the people who may contribute to the management of local schools, including the one constant person in almost all building-level management structures, the principal.

Figure 11.6 Local American public school governance

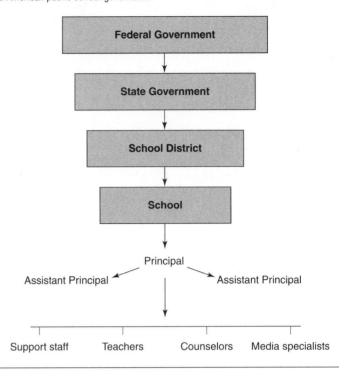

PRINCIPALS

The **principal** oversees every aspect of school life and is responsible to the district for all that occurs at the school. The principal's role involves oversight of administrative tasks such as facility maintenance, attendance, discipline, parent and community relationships and communication, transportation, and all manner of paperwork. Principals also have the role of instructional leader, with knowledge of, and experience with, the teaching and learning process. Instructional leaders have the ability to make positive suggestions and model practices that enhance student learning. A principal who is an instructional leader focuses teachers on improved learning for all students. Many principals who are confident in their administrative and instructional leadership skills believe in the benefits of sharing leadership with teachers and members of the community.

Site-based management. In *Leadership Capacity for Lasting School Improvement* by Linda Lambert (2003), we are told that the most effective principals build leadership capacity in teachers and others who are sincerely interested in student learning. **Site-based management** is a form of local school governance that puts much of the decision-making power regarding curriculum, textbooks, student behavior, staff development, budget, and hiring in the hands of teachers, family members, and the community. Principals who want to share leadership and management of schools employ some or all of the actions listed in Figure 11.7. Serving on a site-based management team gives teachers deeper insight into the role of the principal.

From the list in Figure 11.7, perhaps the most fundamental thing principals do to empower teachers to take responsibility for student learning is the third statement: *insist that student learning is at the center of*

Rees Elementary principal Mike Larsen takes a personal interest in students and their success.

Figure 11.7 Building leadership capacity

Principals who build leadership capacity in teachers and others

- Consider community values as they develop a shared vision
- Consistently keep the focus on teaching and learning
- Find ways to dismiss ineffective teachers by using district evaluation systems
- Make decisions using community input
- Tirelessly seek and secure resources and support for the school

Source: Based on Lambert, L. (2003). *Leadership capacity for lasting school improvement.* Alexandria, VA: Association for Supervision and Curriculum Development.

the conversation. In other words, students take precedence and empowered teachers do what's best for them. In **Teaching in Focus,** Tim Mendenhall advises teachers to experiment to find what works for their students in their own circumstances. As you consider the technology in the **SocialMEdia** features so far, and their potential impact on learning, you can be a leader in your school by finding technologies that excite and motivate your students and then sharing what works with other teachers. This chapter's **SocialMEdia** feature is a hit in most classrooms because of the face-to-face encounters they experience.

Understanding the role of the principal. As you begin your teaching career, your principal will have a major impact on you. Your memories of the principals you

SocialMEdia

Web conferencing is a way to connect students with people and places around the world. The technology may be accessed using the tools (computer, webcam, and microphone) already available in most classrooms. Enhancing the ability to use web conferencing with not only individual students, but also whole classes, requires tools such as tablet computers and interactive white boards.

Currently, the leading facilitator of web conferencing for education is Skype, a free online communication tool. **Skype in the Classroom** is a valuable resource, providing set-up guidelines, a help center for questions, ways to connect with teachers around the world who seek classroom connections, sample lesson plans for using web conferencing, and more. FaceTime is another vehicle for web conferencing. It's available on iPhones, iPads, and other Mac technology. In the near future other manufacturers will roll out the same type of technology.

The many possibilities for using web conferencing in the classroom include:

- Cultural exchanges that otherwise would probably never occur
- Elevating pen pals to a new, exciting level
- Proving language practice in authentic ways, including practicing English for ELLs
- Introducing students to people and places in the setting of a book they're reading or a geographic area they're studying
- Connecting with organizations such as NASA for tours and lessons in aeronautics

- Taking virtual field trips
- Communicating with authors and experts

Other benefits of using web conferencing include:

- Rural schools are using web conferencing to connect them with opportunities enjoyed by urban and suburban learners because of their proximity to museums, zoos, concerts, and more. On the flip side, urban and suburban students can virtually experience what rural life is like.
- Teachers can hold parent conferences with web technology and parents can view student performances.
- Teachers can connect with each other and with worldwide experts to learn new content, theory, and instructional practices. Web conferencing is an excellent professional development tool.

Many skills can be taught through Skype that span subject areas and provide authentic use of knowledge and skills. As students plan web conferences they learn to:

- set goals and formulate questions to be addressed
- communicate to arrange the session
- execute logistics of the session
- use appropriate etiquette and clear speech
- reflect on their experiences

Testimonials from teachers who have taken the time and energy required to use web conferencing in their classrooms say it's more than worth the effort. Exciting possibilities for your future classroom!

have experienced may factor into how you view your first principal when you become a teacher. He or she will select you and ask the school board to hire you, will determine the grade level or subject you teach, will likely assign a teacher mentor for you, will evaluate your teaching performance, and will make the decision whether to offer you a contract for the following year.

Principals have multiple responsibilities and answer to various constituencies, including superintendents, community members, families, and teachers. They are often privy to information that impacts their decisions, some of which they cannot share with their staffs. Too many teachers tend to pass judgment on a principal's decisions and sometimes hold grudges. As a new teacher you need to realize that you won't always understand why or how decisions are made. Your best path is to be supportive of your principal and helpful to the programs and people aligned with your school's mission.

Figure 11.8 illustrates gender, age, and racial characteristics of school principals at the elementary and secondary (high school/middle school) levels. You will notice that the overwhelming majority of these school leaders are white, and, overall, male and

Teacher characteristics and the importance of diversity are discussed in Chapter 1.

Figure 11.8 Characteristics of elementary and secondary school principals

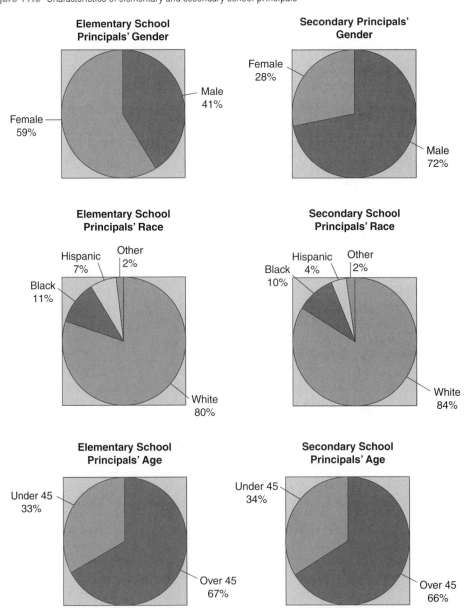

Source: Based on U.S. Department of Education. (2009). *Characteristics of public, private, and Bureau of Indian Education elementary and secondary school principals in the United States.* Washington, DC: Author.

Assistant principals may be perceived as stern in their roles of student disciplinarian and yet be approachable as supporters of teachers.

over the age of 45. Just as there is a need for a more diverse teaching force, there is also a need for principals who more closely mirror student gender, racial, and ethnic characteristics. Regardless of their gender or race, most principals in all but small schools (fewer than 400 or so students) generally receive help in fulfilling their administrative and instructional leadership roles from assistant principals.

ASSISTANT PRINCIPALS

The position of assistant principal entails a variety of duties. If there is only one in a school, then the responsibilities may be general and similar to the principal's, or as specific as the principal chooses to make them. When there are multiple assistants, they generally have designated areas of responsibility. For instance, a medium-size elementary school (400 to 700 students) may have a principal and one assistant who may do various aspects of the principal's job, depending on day-to-day needs. A large middle school (more than 1,000 students) may have a principal and three assistants, each responsible for a grade level. A principal of a large high school (more than 1,500 students) may have more than three assistants who specialize in areas such as student discipline, athletics and extracurricular activities, transportation, and materials. Teachers often work with assistant principals. A teacher in a large school may be more connected with the assistant principal(s) than with the principal.

TEACHER LEADERS

The phrase *teacher leader* has come to mean in many circles that a teacher has taken on additional responsibilities such as chairperson of a grade level of teachers or perhaps a subject-area specialist who works with other teachers to help them improve their knowledge and/or skills. But individuals can be leaders in their schools, as well as in their districts and states, simply by being dynamic, well-informed classroom teachers. They don't need official titles to impact other educators around them, their own students and other students in their buildings, and their communities.

A growing number of teachers with specialized training are relieved of some or all of their classroom teaching duties to lead a grade level or be an in-school subject area expert. For instance, a school may have an instructional coach, a teacher who works with individual teachers as they improve or add to their toolboxes of instructional strategies. Another school may have a math specialist who teaches math to all fourth and fifth graders, regardless of their homeroom. These specially designated teacher leaders may become part of the school management team along with the principal and assistant principal(s).

What Other Entities Impact the Governance of Public Schools in the United States?

The decisions about policies and laws by the individuals and groups discussed so far in this chapter are influenced by many constituencies. Among them are parents, businesses, universities, and special interest groups.

Points of Reflection 11.3

What do you remember about your schools' principals? Were they accessible or did they seem aloof? Did you view them as disciplinarians to be feared or as friendly adults who were helpful to teachers, parents, and students?

Instructional strategies are discussed in Chapter 6.

PARENTS

Parents, including stepparents, foster parents, and guardians, have the potential to be among the most influential players in the education of children. Parents, by virtue of their position, are influential in the lives of their own children and, if they are informed and involved in schools, can make a positive difference in the lives of many children in their local schools. One question is "How can they do this?" But perhaps even more important to ask is "Why don't they do it more often?"

One way for parents to be involved in the life of the school is through the **Parent Teacher Association** (PTA), a national organization with millions of members at thousands of schools across the country. School PTAs have varying degrees of impact and some are called PTOs (Parent Teacher Organizations). Some groups boast large numbers of members whose only involvement is the payment of small annual dues ($2 to $10). Other groups have very active members who volunteer to help out at school in a variety of ways. Although individual PTAs contribute to school life, rarely do they impact decision-making bodies.

Focus student Amanda Wiley and her two sisters are fortunate to have a mom who is very active at Rees Elementary School in Utah. She serves as PTA president. Watch an interview with Amanda's mom.

Points of Reflection 11.4

In what school activities do you recall parent volunteers participating? Were your parents members of a PTA or other organized school groups? What do you remember about their involvement?

Parents can volunteer to help in schools and classrooms and impact the quality of students' school-related experiences. They also have opportunities to serve on committees that address school issues. In some school districts, parents are encouraged to be part of site-based management groups sometimes called School Improvement Councils (SICs) or Local School Councils (LSCs). Being part of an SIC or LSC is a serious responsibility that far too few family members are willing to accept. Parents are usually busy providing for their families and often feel that their time is too limited to commit to membership in a site-based management group. Some parents may be intimidated by the process or may feel they are not qualified to represent families.

BUSINESSES

Businesses have a vested interest in education. Having competent employees is a major key to business success, and these employees are likely to be products of public education. Large businesses and their chief executive officers are increasingly becoming involved in **education summits,** or organized meetings to advocate for school improvement. This is a positive step because business leaders can potentially support schools and students in meaningful ways.

Business leaders can be influential in supporting educational initiatives. Some businesses offer scholarships to promising students. Other businesses, whether locally owned or national franchises, form partnerships with schools to sponsor events, such as science fairs, and contribute resources to enhance school activities. Additionally, some large businesses give employees paid time off to volunteer in schools and may match funds their employees donate to school organizations.

UNIVERSITIES

Schools of education and teacher educators have an important influence on schools because most classroom teachers are prepared on university campuses. Future teachers learn about the concepts in this text and more as they go through teacher preparation programs. The more teachers know, the better prepared they are to take active roles in influencing policies and working toward school improvement.

Teacher educators have the knowledge, and ideally the will, to exert influence by expressing their views to school administrators, school board members, and legislators. They can serve on School Improvement Councils, curriculum revision and textbook adoption committees, and, in general, be active in local, state, and national education associations. University faculties also have an impact on schools through research focused on classroom programs and practices and by facilitating staff development. These activities can form the foundation for recommending policy changes and promoting effective practices.

SPECIAL INTEREST GROUPS

When a group of people join together with a common mission and work to have an impact, they are often called a **special interest group**. An example would be a group composed of parents of children who have special needs. Informal groups of parents of children with autism or Down syndrome, for example, may band together to help ensure more effective services for their children.

Sometimes community members join forces to form local **watchdog groups,** meaning they keep an eye on school district accountability by examining policies and practices. One such group is the Charleston Education Network (CEN). This group of citizens meets regularly to review happenings in, and policies of, the Charleston County School District in South Carolina, where one of this text's four focus schools, Cario Middle, is located. Members of CEN often fund or conduct research on issues, articulate findings and viewpoints, and lobby school board members and state legislators to bring about change. Groups like CEN offer effective services by asking hard questions and being persistent in their search for answers.

Now that we have examined governance structures of public schools and those who influence these structures, let's explore how schools are financed and how the money is spent.

How Are Public Schools Financed?

Free public education—think about it. What a remarkable and noble concept. But is it really free? Hardly. It's true that students don't pay tuition. However, their parents often pay fees for specific items, such as science equipment, gym clothes, band instruments, and workbooks, as well as vague charges for grade-level fees. Parents are also asked to supply certain materials each school year. But these expenses barely make a dent in what it costs to provide K–12 education. So where does all the money come from?

SOURCES OF EDUCATION FUNDING

Most of the funding for public education comes from federal, state, and local governments in the proportions shown in Figure 11.9. It's interesting to note how these three major sources of funding have shifted over the years, from local funding as the primary source in the early part of the 20th century, to local and state sources currently sharing funding responsibilities at approximately the same levels today. The call for equitable funding, regardless of race, socioeconomic status, or geographic location, has led states to increase their portion of funding responsibility. Both states and local districts have come to recognize that the quality of public education has lifestyle and economic

---

Figure 11.9 Percentage of revenues received from federal, state, and local sources for public elementary and secondary schools

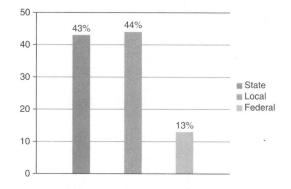

Source: Based on Federal Education Budget Project School Finance (2013). *Federal, State, and Local K–12 School Finance Overview.* Retrieved September 8, 2013, from http://febp.newamerica.net/background-analysis/school-finance

implications. As indicated in Figure 11.9, the federal government's contribution to public schools is relatively small.

Federal funding. The federal government budget is supported through income taxes, investments, and various charges for services and goods. Federal government contributions to public education account for only about 2% of the U.S. government budget.

The federal government supplies a little over 10% of the total education budget. Although this doesn't sound like a lot, federal contributions have a major impact on public schools because the money is allocated as **categorical grants**, or funds earmarked for specific purposes. Programs previously discussed such as Head Start, Title I, the Bilingual Education Act, and the Education for All Handicapped Children Act are examples of categorical grants. As a group, these and other grants are referred to as **entitlements**, meaning that certain segments of the population have specific needs and the federal government deems these individuals as entitled to extra assistance.

The Reagan administration attempted to diminish the influence of the federal government on schools while still funding their efforts. In the 1980s, some federal funding changed from categorical grants to **block grants**, which provide funding with few restrictions for its use. This type of funding allows states and school districts the freedom to use the money in ways that meet their specific needs.

The No Child Left Behind Act of 2001, as a reauthorization of the 1965 Elementary and Secondary Education Act, involved federal funds tied to school improvement as prescribed by the act's specific guidelines. Schools were required to meet the mandates of NCLB to receive the funds. In most cases, states attempted to protect federal funding by complying with the mandates.

State funding. About half of the funding for public education comes from state sources. State money for schools is basically raised through taxes, such as:

- state income tax based on personal earnings
- state corporate tax based on company earnings
- state sales tax added as a percentage of the cost of goods and services
- **excise tax**, or tax on luxury items such as boats and travel trailers
- **"sin" tax** on items some consider vices, such as alcohol and cigarettes

As of 2013, 43 states had lottery games with portions of the funds specifically earmarked for education (U.S. Government, 2013). Although lottery-based funding may sound appealing and, indeed, has been used productively in many instances, there are inherent problems. First, gambling through state-run lotteries appears to attract a disproportionate number of low-income people who often have little schooling. Many disagree with the concept of a lottery system for this reason. Second, although lottery funding is initially viewed as extra money to supplement other, more stable sources, over time having this easy source of funds often leads to the reduction of more stable funding. In other words, a state's attitude may be "We have all this lottery money so we don't need to give schools as much from the state budget." This is risky business, from both state and local standpoints, considering the uncertainty of a lottery's ability to provide money consistently for schools.

In tough economic times, difficult budgetary decisions must be made at all levels. This often proves especially difficult at the state level. When money is tight, some services and programs must be cut. Because education is such a large part of a state's overall budget, the decision to withdraw funding from schools is both public and painful. In 2010 most states faced shortfalls. We use California as an example, where some citizens have gone from passive disapproval to aggressive action. More than 60 individual students and their families, 9 school districts from throughout the state, the California School Boards Association, the California State PTA, and the Association of California School Administrators filed a lawsuit against the state based on their view that the current educational finance system is unconstitutional. Through *Robles-Wong* v. *State of California*, filed in 2010, the plaintiffs are asking that California's finance

Figure 11.10 Sample community responses to property taxes and their use to fund schools

We moved into this home in 1968 .We made the last of our monthly mortgage payments the same year we both retired. Our pensions were supposed to give us enough income to stay right here for as long as our health allows. But year after year the value of the house goes up, with all the new stores and shopping centers popping up in the area. Our property taxes have doubled. If they go much higher, we may have to move. We raised our kids, and now they're raising their own. I'm all for good schools, but not if we lose our home.

I have a good job that allows my wife, who used to be a third grade teacher, to homeschool our two kids. We live in an upscale neighborhood and are very happy with our lives. But what we're not happy about is the way our property taxes are skyrocketing. I believe in public education, but we can afford to homeschool while the kids are young, and then they'll go to our church's private 6–12 school. Why should I have to pay exorbitant property taxes for schools I'll never use?

I don't have kids and never plan to. I like my life as it is, with good friends and a job that calls for me to travel to interesting places. I bought a great downtown loft apartment with payments I can afford. However, now that this area of downtown is being revitalized, the value of my place is on the rise, along with escalating property taxes. I understand that most of this money goes for public schools. Well, the school a few blocks away sure doesn't look like much of my money, or anyone else's, is being spent there. If that school represents how this school district is spending my money, I'll vote for any decrease of the spending cap.

system, specifically its funding policies for education, be changed. They are asking that the state determine the cost to adequately fund public education to meet both the state's own program requirements and the needs of the students. The state would then have to develop and implement a new finance system consistent with California constitutional requirements.

The source of local funding for schools is primarily **property taxes**. Values of property are determined, and a small percentage of the assessed amount (usually less than 1%) is collected annually and used for local services. Most goes to schools. On the surface, using property taxes to finance education seems reasonable. After all, everyone benefits from an educated citizenry. However, as illustrated in Figure 11.10, many people believe an alternative method of funding public education should be imposed. In 1978, California was the first state to put a limit on how high property taxes could go. California's Proposition 13 was a model for other states. Now almost all states impose what is called a **tax cap** on local property taxes, or an upper limit to taxation.

Impact of reliance on property taxes. Let's consider what reliance on property taxes for almost half of public school funding might mean for different communities. A district composed of middle-to-upper socioeconomic suburban neighborhoods with prospering retail stores and a couple of thriving industries will likely generate a healthy amount of money with a relatively low percentage of the assessed property value. In this case people who own homes and businesses pay what might be considered reasonable taxes on their property and appear to have adequate funding for schools. Now think about a district in a very rural area, with a lot of land, but few homes, with families who drive out of the area for jobs or who work in the few businesses located in the district. In this case, home and business owners may have to pay a much larger percentage of the assessed value of their property to support schools. There may simply not be enough property value to generate adequate funding. Finally, consider a densely populated urban area, with many people who are renters in high-rise buildings and often living on government subsidies such as welfare. An area such as this may have large numbers of children, but very few home or property owners. In some urban areas, business and industry provide an adequate tax base, but in others the base is very low, resulting in inadequate school funding.

Figure 11.11 The funding gap

"Closing the achievement gap is a familiar theme these days. But lurking behind the achievement gap is another contentious issue: funding. Excellence in education doesn't come without a price tag. "This statement by Amy Azzam, associate editor of *Educational Leadership*, begins her 2005 special report on *The Funding Gap 2004*, a study conducted by the Education Trust.

The study used the financial data from the U.S. Census from each of the more than 14,000 school districts. The focus of the study was on funding disparities by state between high-poverty and low-poverty districts, as well as between high-minority and low-minority districts. The results revealed that more than half the states provide less money to high-poverty districts than to low-poverty districts. This translates into less money for high-minority areas since there tends to be a higher concentration of minorities in high-poverty areas.

The disparities become even more glaring when we consider the fact that it costs more for high-poverty districts to meet the same standards as low-poverty districts, by some estimates as much as 40% more. Education Trust found that with this cost adjustment, 36 states provide an average of $1,348 per student less for high-poverty versus low-poverty districts. Some states have disparities as high as $2,500 per student.

Given the study results, Education Trust recommends that states:

- reduce reliance on local property taxes
- spend extra money to help low-income children
- do away with funding gaps among individual schools within districts

Azzam closes her report by stating "Closing the achievement gap starts with closing the funding gap. Only by providing the necessary resources can states help ensure quality education for all students.""

Source: Azzam, A. M. (2005). The funding gap. *Educational Leadership, 62*(5), 93.

Relying on property taxes to provide a substantial portion of support for public education can create a funding gap that further exacerbates socioeconomic differences. And, as we have discussed, where there are socioeconomic gaps, there are almost certainly achievement gaps. In states with tax caps, it may not be possible for communities to raise the percentage of the tax on assessed property value, even when most people believe it should be done to support their schools. They are stuck with the limit, despite what may be unfair and nonproductive funding. If you hear or see an expression such as "Drop the cap, end the gap," you'll better understand the meaning of this slogan. Read more about the funding gap in Figure 11.11. With all the problems inherent in using property taxes as the primary source of local funding, alternatives are often sought.

Local funding alternatives. Some communities are attempting to support public education through an increase in sales taxes. For instance, when the sales tax is raised from 6% to 7%, an extra penny is collected for every dollar spent on taxable goods. This translates into a sizable amount of money. For a school district, such an increase could mean less dependency on property taxes as the source of local funding.

Another way school districts acquire funds is to borrow money through what is called a bond issue, the sale of bonds to raise an amount of money stipulated for specific projects. When using a **bond referendum**, the school board asks voters in their district to approve the borrowing of the money (the bond) that will be repaid over a period of time. Bond offerings can be for hundreds of millions of dollars. In some states, boards are not required to ask voters for permission to borrow money for schools. The request may need only city or county council approval.

Private donations. In addition to federal, state, and local funding, many districts and individual schools receive private gifts of either money or goods. These gifts rarely account for more than 3% of the total amount of school funding. Individuals and foundations may contribute to a particular program or project and have a significant impact on that particular segment of school life. However, states, districts, and schools should be cautious about considering private gifts when planning budgets. These sources are often one-time donations or may prove to be unstable.

How Are Funds for Education Spent?

Just as the ability to generate money varies greatly from state to state and district to district, the amount each state spends on public education varies as well. Rather than totals per state, the number that is most meaningful is the amount of money spent per pupil.

EXPENDITURE PER PUPIL

The average amount of money spent from federal, state, and local sources on an individual student is called the **expenditure per pupil**. A comparison of expenditures per pupil by state is found in Figure 11.12. Keep in mind as you look at this figure that the cost of living, and consequently the cost of education, varies from state to state

Figure 11.12 Average expenditures per pupil by state, 2011

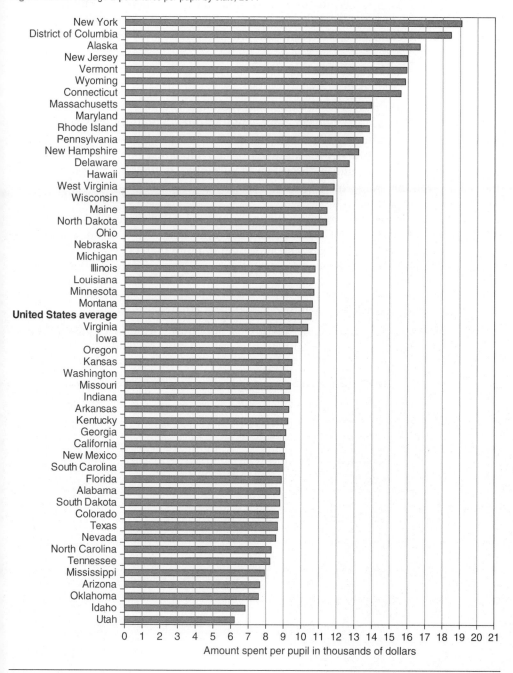

Source: Based on *Public Education Finances: 2011* (2013) by M. Dixon. Retrieved September 8, 2013, from http://www2.census.gov/govs/school/11f33pub.pdf

and region to region. Does almost three times the learning occur in New York, where expenditures per pupil are over $19,000, as in Utah, where per pupil spending is about $6,300? The answer, of course, is *no*. Look back at Figure 11.11, which points out that children living in poverty require 40% more spending. Spending more to educate students who need extra services to succeed in school is being responsive to differences that often relate to race, socioeconomic status, and levels of disabilities. There are so many variables to consider, including issues such as the percentage of teachers who are experts in their teaching fields, state-of-the-art instead of dilapidated facilities, and whether class sizes are small instead of large. These all cost money.

The national average expenditure per pupil has continually increased. As with any large enterprise, everything required to fund education becomes more expensive. When gas prices rise, so does the cost of transportation. When construction costs rise, so does the cost of building new schools. The more diversified student populations become, the more expensive it is to hire personnel to meet their needs. It is understandable that public education is criticized for increased spending when there appears to be little progress in terms of test scores. But it is a complicated issue as schools continue to struggle with the connection between spending and levels of learning.

Points of Reflection 11.5

What is your view of the connection between spending on education and student achievement? On what do you base your opinions?

ALLOCATION OF EDUCATION FUNDING

With any large endeavor there are administrative and other costs that affect, either directly or indirectly, the cause or people served. So it is with education. It would be wonderful if 90% of an education budget could go directly into the classroom to pay teachers, buy books and supplies, and provide the latest technology. But as you saw earlier in this chapter, support for the work of individual teachers in their classrooms requires (at least as the education system is currently configured) people in district and state positions. Some of the current programs with the greatest impact require national-level support as well.

Figure 11.13 shows the average expenses of a school district. Considering there are more than 15,000 school districts, labeling only about 10% of the spending as "Other support services" isn't bad. The allocation of more than 60% directly to instruction is impressive, with most spent on teacher salaries. The rest buys books, classroom supplies, technology, and so on.

- *General administration* includes district-level administrators.
- *Student transportation* mainly involves school buses. The buses must be purchased, maintained, and filled with gas. Drivers must be paid.

Figure 11.13 How funds are spent at the district level

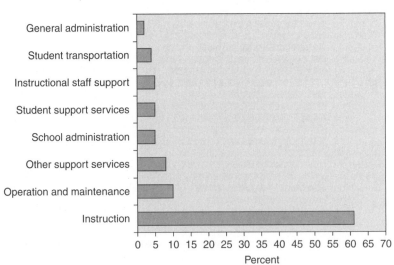

Source: U.S. Census Bureau. (2009). *Public education finances*. Washington, DC: Author.

- *Instructional staff support* includes curriculum and instruction specialists, teacher training, and teacher assistants.
- *Student support services* include school psychologists, nurses, behavior specialists, home liaisons, and others who work with students with needs, special and otherwise (not including special education teachers).
- *School administration* refers to principals and assistant principals and funds needed to support their positions. Notice that over twice as much is spent at the school level versus the district level.
- *Operation and maintenance* includes anything related to facilities—building repair, custodial staff, lights, water, heat, air-conditioning, and grounds.

CONCLUDING THOUGHTS

The only way teachers can hope to understand and possibly influence the more political aspects of education in the United States—basically what happens outside the individual classroom—is, first of all, to be informed. It's actually very interesting to learn about the support systems that help us do what we do in the classroom. You can be engaged by keeping up with education-related current events at all levels and informed by reading education journals and books. The second step to affecting the bigger picture of education is to have the will to be involved—to step outside the classroom doors and advocate for children in the larger arena of the community, the district, the state, and the nation.

Chapter in Review

How does the federal government influence public education in the United States?

- The president, the U.S. Congress, and the federal court system endorse specific programs and make and enforce laws that impact schools.
- The U.S. Department of Education initiates programs and mandates the compliance of states using federal money as leverage.

What is the state's role in public education?

- Each state has its own unique governance system.
- State governors, legislatures, and court systems all impact the functioning of education within the state.
- A state board of education is a volunteer policy-making body that has oversight responsibilities.
- A state department of education functions under the leadership of a state superintendent and many administrators who work to support schools and teachers.

How do school districts function?

- A school district is made up of schools defined by geographic boundaries.
- District school boards set policies that affect the operation of schools.
- A district superintendent is the chief executive officer of a school district and may have a staff with specified duties.

What is the management structure of individual schools?

- The principal oversees every aspect of a school and answers to the district for all that occurs.
- Assistant principals and teacher leaders play important roles in school management.

What other entities impact the governance of public schools in the United States?

- Parents and families have the potential to positively impact student success in school.
- Businesses have a vested interest in effective schools that prepare their employees and consumers. Business–school partnerships benefit both parties.
- Universities and teacher education faculty prepare teachers and impact education.
- Special interest groups are composed of concerned citizens who work for the benefit of specific causes within schools.

How are public schools financed?

- On average, state and local funding share about 92% of the funding burden equally, with federal funds accounting for most of the rest.
- Federal funds are either earmarked for specific purposes in the form of categorical grants or given for states to use at their discretion in the form of block grants.
- State funds are generated primarily through sales taxes and income taxes.
- Most local funds usually come from property taxes, a controversial source.
- Private donations provide boosts to specific programs and efforts but account for a very small percentage of total school funding.

How are funds for education spent?

- The amount spent on each student, the expenditure per pupil, varies greatly from state to state.
- Over half of the money spent on public education goes for expenses related to classroom instruction. The rest is spent on support services, including administration, facilities, and transportation.

Developing Professional Competence

Thoughtfully reading this scenario and responding to the items that follow it will help you prepare for licensure exams.

The arts emphasis at Rees Elementary School is more extensive than in most elementary schools. Both fine arts and performance arts are part of the everyday world of Rees students. They learn about art and "do" art during the school day, with evidence of this on display throughout the school. But as the student population begins to shift, the teachers become aware of more and more of their students going home to empty houses and remaining there for several hours before their parents get home from long days at work. Chris, Brenda, and Tim decide it's time to take art beyond the 3 P.M. afternoon dismissal bell. To do this will take time and money.

Chris Roberts has a good idea about what's involved in working through the public school governance system, thanks to his experiences with the initiation of multiage classrooms. He has volunteered to take on the task of finding support for the idea of "Afternoon Arts" and finding funding to make it happen. He understands the meaning and value of these two pertinent standards:

InTASC Standard 10

The teacher seeks appropriate leadership roles and opportunities to take responsibility for student learning, to collaborate with learners, families, colleagues, other school professionals, and community members to ensure learner growth, and to advance the profession.

NBPTS

Accomplished teachers can evaluate school progress and the allocation of school resources in light of their understanding of state and local educational objectives.

Think through this scenario and answer the following multiple-choice questions:

1. What challenges do you anticipate that may stem from the fact that Rees Elementary is in Utah?
   a. Utah is a rural state and incorporating the arts may be difficult.
   b. Utah's per pupil expenditure is comparatively quite low.

c. There may be resistance among the new families in the Rees attendance zone.

d. There are few models of arts programs.

2. In what order would Chris want to present the Afternoon Arts program to individuals and groups to gain approval and possible funding?

a. principal, district arts director, community businesses, families.

b. families, principal, district arts director, state curriculum director.

c. principal, community businesses, families, district arts director.

d. principal, district arts director, state curriculum director, families.

3. Rees has a state arts grant, but this funding will be withdrawn next year, given the tough economic times. Which of the following would *not* be a possible source of funding for Afternoon Arts?

a. community businesses contributing to the program

b. district funding designated for at-risk students

c. federal categorical grant

d. federal block grant

Now it's time for you to respond to two short essay items involving the scenario. In your responses, be sure to address all the dilemmas and questions posed in each item. Your responses should each be between one half and one full double-spaced page.

4. Refer to question 2. In one well-developed sentence for each, describe the kind of support Chris might expect from the people/groups in the response choices.

5. The teachers who believe in the potential of Afternoon Arts will likely want to be part of the program. Should they be paid for the 3 hours a day required, or should the intrinsic value of the program and what it may mean to kids who need it be enough reward for their efforts? Justify your response.

Professionalism in Relationships, Reality, and Reform

 Dear Reader

Teaching is a lifestyle, a career that occupies both your head and your heart. It takes both content knowledge and skills to teach children and adolescents. It takes a level of care and concern beyond that of most other professions to apply knowledge and skills in ways that engage and inspire. As teachers, we must develop a level of professionalism to guide our interactions with students, families, the community, school personnel, and each other. These interactions may surround content, logistics of the school, public relations, and more.

As long as we have public education we will have efforts to improve it. Most widespread initiatives are not started by teachers, but the responsibility to implement the reform *du jour* is usually ours. This is a reality. Sometimes realities are negative and encumbering, leaving teachers to swim upstream to do what's best for students. But swim we will, because the teaching profession is what holds our nation together and gives it hope for the future.

Here are the questions addressed in this chapter:

- How can I develop as a professional?
- How do I develop and maintain professional relationships?
- What are some realities of teaching?
- What is my role as a professional in education reform?

Teaching in Focus

As the English-language arts and social studies teacher for Cario Middle School's CARE (Cario Academic Recovery and Enrichment) program, Deirdre Huger-McGrew has some unique challenges. Her students have experienced little academic success so far in school. Deirdre's responsibility is to provide learning opportunities for her students, along with the assistance necessary for them to progress to their appropriate grade levels in both knowledge and skills. Deirdre believes that computer skills are essential for her students and she uses computer technology as an integral part of instruction. Deirdre is fulfilling her professional responsibilities by exploring, and then choosing and using, approaches that match the learning needs of her CARE students.

The Scholastic READ 180 program Deirdre chose for her students is designed to teach older students to read with fluency and comprehension. Reading intervention is accomplished through individualized instruction based on both ability level and specific need. READ 180 follows a comprehensive cycle of instruction that includes:

1. a brief anchor video that provides background information to help the student understand what will be read
2. text about the video written at the student's predetermined reading level
3. prompts that allow the student to access help in decoding words, phrases, or whole passages
4. comprehension questions
5. a summary of how many words and phrases are correctly read and how many questions are correctly answered
6. opportunities to reread the passage with varying levels of support to build speed and accuracy (Hasselbring & Bausch, 2006)

The students in Deirdre's class have access to a library of books specifically related to the topics presented in the computerized videos and reading passages, as well as audiotapes of most of the books, allowing them to follow along as they listen. Focus student David McBeath's mom has encouraged him for years to listen to tapes and follow along in books to help increase his reading proficiency. So the instructional strategies used in Deirdre's classroom are reinforced at home. Watch **Deirdre's lesson and interview** to get to know her better.

Professionalism is called for in all that teachers do. There is no on-off switch for professionalism based on circumstances. We never stop growing as professionals; opportunities are everywhere to hone the science, art, and service of teaching. When faced with realities that are negative in nature, we respond in professional ways to make a positive difference. When inevitable reform initiatives come our way, we are professional in our participation, reflection, and assessment of potential for benefits and actual results.

How Can I Develop as a Professional?

Professionalism entails meeting responsibilities head on, as well as taking full advantage of opportunities involving teaching and learning. Responsibility and opportunity have a symbiotic relationship. You may recall from biology that when organisms are symbiotic, they have a mutually close relationship that is advantageous to both. Responsibilities and opportunities are so close that they flow into one another. When responsibilities are fulfilled, opportunities are created; when opportunities are recognized and acted upon, they often incur responsibilities.

The close and mutually advantageous relationship between responsibility and opportunity is illustrated in Figure 12.1. Like the sand flowing from one chamber into the other in an hourglass, when responsibility is on top and is being fulfilled, it flows into opportunity. Similarly, when we make the most of opportunities, we are turning the hourglass over and watching each grain of our efforts create new responsibilities. This concept applies to each section of this chapter. Think of it often as you read.

Figure 12.1 The relationship between responsibility and opportunity

PROFESSIONALISM DURING TEACHER PREPARATION

It's not too early to approach every aspect of becoming a teacher with ever-developing professional attitudes and actions.

Professional approaches to coursework. Preparing to be a teacher in a university-based program entails both general, or core, courses as well as courses that specifically address your future career as a classroom teacher.

General education courses. Most of your classes so far have likely been core courses required for most of the students who attend your college. They should not be viewed as fillers or as experiences that must be endured until you can enroll in classes specifically designed for teacher preparation. Because teachers need to be informed, interested, and interesting, core courses enhance teacher preparation by providing a wide spectrum of information and skills that are foundational for teachers and contribute to your status as a well-rounded adult. What you learn will help you put much of what you teach into context.

Some core courses provide opportunities for you to develop dispositions, or the attitudes and values you carry with you for life. Others lay the groundwork for a content area major required of most high school teachers, many middle-level teachers, and a growing number of elementary and early childhood teachers, depending on state licensure requirements and individual university programs.

Teacher education courses. What you learn in your education classes lays the groundwork for your professional life. This realization should inspire you to pay attention, complete all readings, participate in class group work (with enthusiasm!), and keep up with assignments. You should do what is necessary to *own* the knowledge and skills, not simply *borrow* them until the end of the semester. This means internalizing and reflecting on what you learn through reading, lecture, class discussion, and experiences in real schools. Put more into your course assignments than required. Apply the content and skills to everything you know and are learning about schools, students, and teaching.

Points of Reflection 12.1

Which core courses do you enjoy or find exceptionally interesting? Which do you credit more for your affinity for these classes: the subject matter or the instructors' strategies? Why?

Figure 12.2 Survey results of perceived new teacher preparedness

New teachers feel most prepared to . . .

- create collaborative classroom environments
- teach all students
- develop curriculum that builds on student interests and needs
- understand how student development influences learning
- relate classroom experience to the real world

New teachers feel least prepared to . . .

- address learning needs of English-language learners
- work with families
- develop interdisciplinary curriculum
- address special learning needs
- assume leadership

Source: Public Education Network (2003). *The voice of the new teacher.* Washington, DC: Author.

The Public Education Network surveyed new teachers about what they felt prepared and unprepared to do as a result of teacher preparation. Consider the results, shown in Figure 12.2. These areas of professionalism should be points of emphasis for you to help you enter the profession with a sense of preparedness that perhaps the surveyed teachers did not have.

Professional approaches to field experiences. One of the most valuable aspects of a teacher preparation program is the opportunity to spend time in schools. **Field experiences**, or **practicum experiences**, involve observing and/or participating in actual classrooms. You may have the opportunity for field experiences in early childhood, elementary, middle, and high school classrooms before you are required to declare your chosen level of certification. You may also have a chance to observe in related arts and special education classes. Ideally, you will have the opportunity to visit rural, suburban, and urban schools. All of these experiences will help you decide who, what, and where you may want to teach.

Here are some general guidelines for approaching field experiences in a professional manner. Following these guidelines with enthusiasm will make your field experiences, in schools with real teachers and real students, much more meaningful.

Points of Reflection 12.2

Are you excited about field experiences? What aspects do you think you will enjoy most? What aspects do you think will cause some level of anxiety for you? Why?

1. Know your instructor's expectations.
2. Dress and behave with respect.
3. Remember that you are a guest in the school.
4. Keep a detailed log of your experiences, even if it is not required.
5. Spend time after each field experience reflecting on your time in schools. Write questions about what you observed.

Early field experiences will likely be devoted to **structured observations**. This means you will be looking for specific things and responding to prompts that purposefully call attention to certain aspects of the classroom. Field experiences that are associated with, or embedded in, **methods courses** will likely incorporate your first teaching experiences. Methods courses are those that emphasize particular strategies for specific subjects and will probably incorporate opportunities to actually apply what you are learning.

Student teaching, or clinical practice, is the capstone internship experience of your teacher preparation program. This one- or two-semester experience will allow you to use what you have learned in your courses and practiced in your other field experiences. You will get to know a group of students well as you gradually take over full teaching duties. Your student teaching experience will probably require the hardest work you've ever done. George Posner (2005), a recognized expert on field experience, gives us six simple, practical goals for student teaching. He tells us that student teaching will allow you to:

1. find out what teaching is really like
2. see if you really like teaching
3. see if you really can do it
4. learn some skills and modify certain habits and characteristics
5. begin to develop your own approach or style
6. apply what you've learned in college to real students and to real classrooms (p. 16)

Your college supervisor during student teaching can be a valuable resource and confidant.

As with other field experiences, there are commonsense things you can do to make the most of student teaching. Here are some professional attitudes and actions that will be valuable to you:

1. *Keep a journal.* You will probably be asked to do this by your supervising instructor. Keeping a journal will help you reflect and learn more from your experiences.
2. *Keep up.* You will be very busy, with more responsibility and pressure than you've ever experienced. There will be lesson plans to write, materials to gather, and paperwork to complete—all this while you are learning your craft, your profession. Don't let any aspect slide, and don't get behind.
3. *Be positive.* We choose our attitudes. Being positive is a choice. It doesn't mean glossing over difficulties, but rather approaching each day with possibilities in focus.
4. *Be realistic.* Being realistic is not in conflict with being positive. It is acceptance that some of your lessons will not go as planned, nor are you going to solve all the problems of the students in your classroom. You are learning to be a teacher.
5. *Confide in someone you trust.* You will find that no one understands what you are experiencing as completely as another clinical intern. You should also confide in your supervisor.
6. *Be respectful.* Dress and speak respectfully; be respectful of the adults and students in your school. Earn their respect.

You will probably be required to develop a cohesive package of your representative products, commonly referred to as a **teacher preparation portfolio**. This portfolio may either document growth or display best work, depending on its purpose. A teacher preparation portfolio may be composed of items such as lesson plans, student artifacts, sample assessments, journal entries, sample letters to parents, and your resume. A portfolio that documents growth will help you see areas of progress and detect areas of either weakness or lack of experience. A portfolio that displays your best work can be used to document accomplishments and may be an excellent tool when you begin looking for a teaching position.

PROFESSIONALISM AS A TEACHER

Professional growth is an absolute necessity for teacher effectiveness. There is a documented relationship between professional self-growth leading to improved teaching quality and student achievement (Darling-Hammond & Youngs, 2002). In addition to professional opportunities to grow with help from your colleagues and participation in professional organizations, a wealth of literature addresses the many aspects of teaching and learning. Reading articles and books pertinent to content and students, and then using the ideas and advice, is another way for teachers to continue to grow professionally. Collegial conversations allow for sharing both questions and solutions.

Professional development. *Professional development* is a phrase used to describe efforts to help teachers improve their knowledge and skills. Some districts refer to professional development as in-service training, staff development workshops, or teacher retreats. Many opportunities for professional growth will be presented to you. Some are required and others are optional.

You will likely hear more than a few teachers complain that a professional development workshop or staff retreat is sure to be a waste of time. They may have become jaded by ineffective sessions, or they may not be open to exploring new ideas. But remember this: there is always something to be learned when teachers get together, regardless of the perceived quality or relevance of what is formally presented.

Teachers don't have to actually go somewhere or be in a particular place to learn more about their craft. Twenty-first century technology allows teachers to access knowledge in a variety of ways, presenting options for ongoing and specifically tailored professional development.

Some schools and districts are using the *Moodle* format for e-learning. Moodle stands for Modular Object-Oriented Dynamic Learning Environment and is a course management system that allows teachers to share information and plans. Other e-learning vehicles include wikis, blogs, and Ning. Although face-to-face professional development will always have a place in teachers' careers, online learning has the capacity to reach more teachers in convenient, immediate ways (Huber, 2010).

Advanced degrees. Teachers can continue their professional education by seeking advanced degrees. Combinations of on-site and distance learning often allow coursework to fit more easily into a teacher's schedule. Master of education degrees are offered at numerous universities. Secondary teachers often seek advanced degrees in the subject area they teach; elementary teachers may seek advanced degrees in a more generic area such as curriculum and instruction. Not only does more in-depth study of content, curriculum, and instruction enrich teaching, but it also opens leadership doors.

National Board for Professional Teaching Standards certification. One of the most recognized, state-endorsed opportunities for professional growth is certification through the **National Board for Professional Teaching Standards (NBPTS)**. The organization was created in 1987 to emphasize what teachers should know and do to positively affect student learning. The philosophical foundation of NBPTS (2013) is composed of five core propositions:

- Teachers are committed to students and learning.
- Teachers know the subjects they teach and how to teach those subjects to students.
- Teachers are responsible for managing and monitoring student learning.
- Teachers think systematically about their practice and learn from experience.
- Teachers are members of learning communities.

In addition to the five core propositions, NBPTS has specific standards that must be met in each of the categories of certification. There are 25 certification areas that align with content and the levels of school, including early childhood, middle childhood (elementary), early adolescence (middle school), and adolescence and young adulthood (high school). As of 2013, over 100,000 teachers were certified through NBPTS (NBPTS, 2013).

Teacher evaluation as opportunity for professional growth. It is perfectly normal to be apprehensive about being evaluated, especially in your first few years in the classroom. Evaluations should be viewed as opportunities for professional growth. There is always more to know and new skills to develop, even for experienced teachers.

The methods school districts use to evaluate teachers vary. Most involve elements such as observation of teachers with students, opinions of administrators concerning planning for instruction, evidence of collaboration with colleagues, attendance at professional development sessions, and classroom management skills. New teachers are usually assigned a mentor teacher who will informally observe and do formative assessments, ongoing looks at how new teachers function with no formal affirmation or unfavorable consequences. Formative assessments are used to promote growth.

Teachers usually receive an annual summative evaluation, one that will be accompanied by a written report of performance (as measured using whatever criteria the state and district choose) and used as the basis for continuing employment decisions. This summative evaluation will be conducted by a building-level administrator who may use a detailed form on which a kind of "score" is kept of both if, and to what extent, a teacher does certain things associated with effective instruction. Some evaluations are much less prescriptive, with the evaluator taking detailed notes about what's observed and then writing a description from the notes. Either method will be the basis for follow-up conferences. Teacher evaluation will be discussed in more depth later in the chapter.

CONTRIBUTING TO THE TEACHING PROFESSION

The teaching profession is bolstered every time an engaging lesson is taught or learning is facilitated in whatever way is appropriate for students. In this respect, effective teachers routinely contribute to the profession. In addition, there are specific activities that reach beyond the classroom to have a positive impact on the teaching profession.

Teacher involvement in professional organizations. The effectiveness of any organization depends in large measure on its membership. Teachers are responsible for the effectiveness of professional teacher organizations, whether large and politically aggressive, like the National Education Association (NEA) and the American Federation of Teachers (AFT), or small, like a district social studies council organized to provide resources and information for area social studies teachers. In most cases, membership in professional organizations is voluntary, although there are instances when teachers may feel pressured into joining specific groups.

Subject-area organizations, such as the National Council of Teachers of English (NCTE) and the National Council of Teachers of Mathematics (NCTM), provide valuable information and resources. Being a member helps teachers do what they do more effectively; every teacher who belongs makes the subject-area organization stronger. Most states have their own subject-area organizations that are affiliates of the national subject-area groups. State membership fees are generally less and conferences are more accessible because they are held within that individual state. Membership in state organizations is a good place to begin.

It is important for teachers to take advantage of the opportunities professional organizations provide. In turn, teachers should feel a responsibility to join professional organizations to help build the teaching profession.

Professional organizations are discussed in Chapters 1 and 4, with a list and contact information in Chapter 1.

Systemic involvement. Extending teacher influence at the local and district levels is what **systemic involvement** is all about. It is possible and desirable—although it consumes time and energy—for teachers to have an impact on both adults and students well beyond the classroom door. You can grow into many of these responsibilities and opportunities with time and experience.

Teacher involvement in the school. Being an active participant in the collegiality of a school is a positive way to be involved. For new teachers this may mean benefiting from a strong mentor relationship with experienced teachers and maintaining a helpful, open spirit. When you become more confident in your new role, you will have opportunities to be part of committees and task forces with specific decision-making and action responsibilities.

Renee Ayers is involved in her school in many ways, including serving as a mentor to new teachers. Read what she has to say in *Teaching in Focus.*

Teaching in Focus

Renee Ayers, Grade 2, Summit Primary School, Ohio. *In her own words....*

Many wonderful people supported and helped me during my first years of teaching: the clever curriculum director who told me about the "question chair" to stop interruptions during reading groups; the kind principal who cheered me on even when I was in tears in his office; the caring special education teacher who would come to my classroom during her planning period to tutor a student with special needs; the 30-year-veteran teacher next door who taught me all of his "sing to learn" songs; and the school counselor who assisted me in doing hands-on science experiments with 27 second graders. I look back with such fondness as I consider the people who nurtured me.

As I grew in my career I decided I had a responsibility to pass this support on to other new teachers. In my sixth year of teaching I became a Praxis mentor with every intention of going into my protégés' classes and dishing out all my experience and advice. What I found from this experience was that by observing and supporting first-year teachers, I had created an opportunity for myself to learn. Every protégé has become a resource and friend to me. Their enthusiasm is contagious, their teaching practices are fresh, and their ability to persevere through the extreme pressure and demands of a first classroom never ceases to amaze me.

Teacher involvement in the district. Every district functions within state guidelines and with the use of state funds. Being informed about how your district functions begins with paying attention to who is in leadership roles and how the chain of influence works. After teaching for a few years you may have opportunities to participate in district-level committees that may make decisions and take actions such as

- textbook selection (within state guidelines, if applicable)
- curricular planning to incorporate state standards
- recommendations for creating activities to involve parents

Derek Boucher, one of our focus teachers at Roosevelt High School in California, chooses to contribute to the teaching profession by expressing his opinions in public ways. Read about his contributions in *Teaching in Focus.*

Contributions to the professional knowledge base. When a teacher tries an instructional strategy that works well with a particular topic, or with a specific group of students, sharing the experience will help other teachers. This sharing can happen

Teaching in Focus

Derek Boucher, High School History and Reading, Roosevelt High School, California. *In his own words....*

In 2002 I read *Resisting Reading Mandates* by Dr. Elaine Garan. Her book exposed many of the biases and conflicts of interest that exist among those who make national policy decisions regarding K–12 reading instruction.

I was so inspired by her revealing work that I wrote an opinion editorial that was published in our local newspaper. What happened next shocked me. Attorneys from a large educational publishing company that was implicated in Dr. Garan's book contacted me. This company stood to benefit financially from the new reading policy.

They wanted to stop me from expressing my opinion and the newspaper from publishing opinions that disagreed with their position. At that moment, I realized the power and responsibility teachers have to express their opinions about what works in the classroom.

Since that time, I have submitted opinion pieces to educational journals, as well as over a dozen letters to the editor of our local newspaper. Many outside the classroom feel they know what is best for our children and classrooms. It is our responsibility as professionals on the front line, who work with children on a daily basis, to share our experience and perspective.

in a team or grade-level meeting, through a Moodle or other online vehicle, at a meeting of a professional organization, or in an article written for an education journal. Teachers who try a new strategy, develop a way to gather evidence concerning its effects, interpret the evidence, and make inferences from it are conducting a kind of research referred to as **action research**. Reporting findings and continuing inquiry adds to the professional knowledge base.

How Do I Develop and Maintain Professional Relationships?

As a service, or "helping," profession, teaching involves relationships to a larger extent than almost any other profession. From students, to families, to the community, relationships are key to success. Within the profession, other adults in our schools and in the district present opportunities for mutually advantageous relationships. When we fulfill our responsibilities and take advantage of our opportunities involving relationships, we are doing so for the children and adolescents we teach. Building and maintaining strong relationships helps us ask and answer the recurring questions, "And how are the children? Are they all well?" in resoundingly positive ways.

RELATIONSHIPS WITH STUDENTS

For teachers, students are absolutely at the top of the list of professional responsibilities and the primary focus of opportunities.

Taking responsibility for student learning. The common link among teachers who consistently reach students whom others might consider unreachable is that they take responsibility for student learning. These teachers assert, "All students can learn," not, "All students can learn, but . . . " (Corbett, Wilson, & Williams, 2005, p. 8). We may not be able to change conditions outside school that impinge on student achievement, but we can absolutely change what happens in our classrooms to increase learning.

Teachers who take responsibility for student learning take no excuses—from students, parents, or themselves. They find ways to engage students in learning. They use instructional strategies appropriate for both the content and the learners, and they model respect and enthusiasm. To them, "effective teaching means giving students no other choice but success" (Corbett et al., 2005, p. 12).

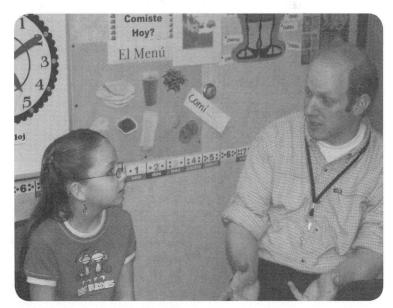

High expectations. When we take responsibility for teaching all students unconditionally, regardless of the circumstances, we necessarily have high expectations for them (Gehrke, 2005). In his article "They Can Because They Think They Can," Richard Vacca (2006), noted expert in the field of reading instruction, states that providing learning experiences that allow students to be successful will increase their sense of **self-efficacy**. Vacca tells us, "Self-efficacy is an 'I can' belief in oneself that leads to a sense of competence" (p. 56). High expectations can foster this sense of competency. Unlike sometimes empty techniques that focus on building self-efficacy with words but are devoid of actual accomplishments, Vacca's concept of self-efficacy is solidly grounded in the accomplishment of a continuum of increasingly difficult challenges. As students master a concept or skill, they are encouraged to attempt even more difficult tasks. In this way, our high expectations for students lead to their own high expectations for themselves.

Focus teacher Tim Mendenhall maintains high expectations for his students while creating an inviting environment.

RELATIONSHIPS WITH FAMILIES

Involving families in the life of the school benefits the educational process in many ways. Parents are a child's first teachers. During the critically important years between birth and age 5, parents (and their choice of child-care providers) have great impact on children. In addition, for the rest of childhood and adolescence, parental modeling and attitudes influence students' success in school. "The way schools care about children is reflected in the way schools care about the children's families" (Epstein et al., 2002, p. 7). Throughout this section, the words *parents* and *families* are used interchangeably to acknowledge the multiple ways people come together in a home.

Marzano (2003) tells us that parental and family involvement increases academic achievement and attendance rates and leads to more positive attitudes and behavior of students in the classroom. That's a formula for success! Although all students benefit from parental involvement, low-income and culturally diverse students are particularly more likely to succeed when family members communicate with, and are active in, the life of the school (Epstein et al., 2002).

Involving families. Family involvement can take many forms, from consistently encouraging students to complete homework, to attending parent-teacher conferences, to volunteering regularly in the school or classroom, or even to serving on a district school board. James Comer (2005), a professor at the Yale University School of Medicine's Child Study Center since 1968, endorses the development of "a yearlong, school-wide schedule of activities designed to support instruction and to create positive relationships in the school" (p. 40). This schedule may include:

- parent volunteer opportunities that include materials preparation and working with students who may need extra help
- parent-student-teacher events, such as family math night and career exploration workshops
- student performances, such as chorus and band concerts, sports events, and club activities

Through participation, parents show support for both students and teachers. In turn, they gain a sense of connection with the education of their children.

Family communication. Events such as Back-to-School Night, Open House, and parent conferences provide opportunities for teachers to talk about their curriculum, classrooms, and students. New teachers should ask experienced teachers about the format and general procedures for these events.

In addition to school-wide and regularly-scheduled forms of communication, there are many other ways teachers can invite families to participate in their students' education, including:

1. *Welcome letter.* Sending a letter to families at the beginning of the school year is a good way for you to introduce yourself, inform parents about policies and procedures that are specific to your class, tell parents about volunteer opportunities, and let parents know how and when to reach you.

2. *Classroom newsletter.* Weekly or monthly newsletters sent home with students can keep parents informed and give them ideas for how to encourage students to complete school assignments and homework. Make sure the written communication you send home is error free.

3. *Phone calls.* Not all phone calls home signal trouble at school. Using the telephone to communicate good news is powerful. Imagine a parent hearing, "Good afternoon, Mrs. Lawson. This is Annie Morgan, Brandon's math teacher. I just wanted to tell you that Brandon took the lead today in his group's problem-solving activity. I was so proud of how he worked with the other students to come up with a unique solution!" Now imagine the smile that spreads across Mrs. Lawson's face, especially if Brandon is often the object of not-so-positive school communication. The teacher has taken an important step toward gaining Mrs. Lawson as a partner in Brandon's education and support should she need

assistance in the future to help correct an undesirable trait Brandon might demonstrate. She has also encouraged Brandon to continue his positive behavior.

Some phone calls home may be for reasons that include a negative change in a student's achievement or attitude, unacceptable behavior, and incomplete or missing work. These calls need to be handled professionally. If possible, it's best to have negative discussions in person so there can be face-to-face dialogue, but the initial call may be an invitation for such a meeting. Always prepare for phone calls, positive or negative, beforehand.

4. *Electronic communication.* Parent and teacher communication via e-mail has become the norm. It can be done day or night, without disturbing the receiving party. When using e-mail, don't be sloppy. Use a salutation, as well as uppercase and lowercase letters. Do not use faddish abbreviations. The guidelines for both written and telephone communication apply to e-mail communication as well.

5. *Classroom web page.* Most schools provide space for individual teacher or classroom web pages. These are often used for assignments and reminders. Be creative, but most of all, be up-to-date. When web pages contain beginning-of-the-year greetings in November, it gives parents and others a very negative impression.

Parent-student-teacher conferences. For many beginning teachers, as well as a fair share of experienced ones, conference time is anticipated with dread. Rather than viewing conferences as responsibilities to be endured, approach them as opportunities to cultivate a partnership with parents for the sake of the students.

One of the most helpful ways for new teachers to become comfortable with parent-student-teacher conferences is to sit in when experienced teachers are talking with parents and students. Ask teachers you admire if it would be possible for you to be a silent observer. You will pick up phrases, mannerisms, and strategies that will help guide your own conferences.

Some conferences include only adults, while others include students. Many teachers are finding great benefits in student-led conferences, with students talking directly to family members and teachers merely onlookers.

Parental barriers to family involvement.
Some barriers to parental involvement result from the attitudes and actions of parents, and some from the attitudes and actions of teachers. James Comer (2005), speaking of what he and his team of researchers experienced, tells us, "From the beginning of our work in schools, we were struck by this mixture of parents' hesitancy to get involved and educators' subtle and even unintentional resistance to parental involvement" (p. 39).

Socioeconomic barriers. Regardless of socioeconomic status, culture, language, or educational background, there are many legitimate barriers to parental involvement, including:

Parental involvement can positively affect not only their own children but also whole classes and schools.

- Families in low-income settings may be more mobile than other families. Communication sent through the mail may not reach these families. Families may have a phone one week but not the next. Many low-income homes do not have access to the Internet, so e-mail communication is not an option.

- Transportation may present a challenge for low-income families. Some families depend entirely on public transportation, making getting to and from their students' schools very difficult.

The relationship of socioeconomic status and school success is discussed in Chapters 2 and 9.

- Finding or paying for child care can be difficult as well, and younger siblings may need to accompany parents to school functions.
- Work can be a barrier to parental involvement at any socioeconomic level. Often in low-SES families, both parents may work two or three jobs, and their time is extremely limited. At the other end of the socioeconomic spectrum, parents who are highly paid professionals may also have severe limitations on their time. In both cases, showing up at school between 8:00 A.M. and 4:00 P.M. may be virtually impossible.

Cultural and language barriers. Children do not choose the culture in which they are born. Their families may value education, or they may consider formal education unnecessary beyond the stage of being able to read and write at survival levels.

The language of a student's family may be a major barrier to parental involvement. The families of three of our focus students speak little English in their homes. Hector, our fourth grade student at Rees Elementary, is the only one in his family who speaks fluent English. He is the link between his family and the school. Hugo, our focus student at Roosevelt High School, speaks very little English himself, and his parents speak even less. Khammany, also at Roosevelt High School, is fluent in English, but her mother speaks no English at all. Engaging these parents in the life of the school is difficult. Watch Khammany's mom's interview.

Educational background barriers. If parents were not successful in school, they are unlikely to be enthusiastic about stepping through the doors of their children's schools. If they quit school in sixth grade, or eighth grade, or if they never graduated from high school, they may be intimidated and hesitant to talk with teachers, believing that they themselves are incapable of helping students with anything academic.

Table 12.1 consists of strategies for teachers and schools as they work toward increasing parental involvement.

TABLE 12.1 Strategies to overcome barriers to parental involvement

Barrier	Strategy
Frequent address changes	Organize student families into small groups, being careful to include a family that is rooted in the community. Devise ways to help these small groups stay in touch, with the more settled family taking the lead in communicating with the teacher when families move.
Disconnected phones	Using the group idea just described, establish a phone tree as a source of class information. In this way teachers learn about phone problems, perhaps before there is a need to call the family on a more urgent matter.
Lack of transportation	Make school events compatible with public transportation schedules. Have a teacher ride along on a route where many of the students live to serve as a welcoming guide to and from the event.
Time barriers	Schedule parent-student-teacher conferences at times that accommodate more parents. Split sessions could be 3:00–5:00 P.M. and 7:00–9:00 P.M. Provide ways for working parents to volunteer time, perhaps with weekend and evening projects that also involve students.
Child-care dilemmas	Provide child care onsite during school events and planned conference times. High school classes and organizations can be responsible for taking care of children while parents involve themselves in the life of the school.
Cultural differences	Acknowledge different perspectives and incorporate activities, artwork, and celebrations that draw families into the life of the school.
Language barriers	Find people who will serve as interpreters at events and conferences. Advertise the presence of interpreters to let parents know they will be able to communicate with teachers. Translate newsletters and forms into the languages spoken and read at home.
Limited education	Warm, friendly teachers who use jargon-free language in their communications help encourage parental involvement. Providing after-school homework help can ease parental guilt over not knowing how to help their children with assignments.

Teacher barriers to parental involvement. Teacher-generated barriers to parental involvement are less legitimate than parent-generated barriers. A teacher's failure to invite parental involvement may stem from timidity, lack of conviction that parental involvement matters, or lack of effort.

Timidity. Some teachers become nervous when they anticipate speaking to, or with, parents. You may hear them say, "I can be up in front of my sophomores all day long, but bring in their parents, and I freeze." A skilled communicator with students can become a skilled communicator with adults. Experience makes it easier.

Some teachers are uncomfortable having other adults watching and listening to them. They may worry about facing questions and possible criticism. They may find the presence of parents in their classrooms inhibiting and intimidating. This form of timidity can be overcome by planning excellent learning experiences for the classroom and being at your best every day with the attitude that parents are your partners. The more hands and minds the better when it comes to increasing student learning.

Not believing that parents matter. Some teachers appear to be unconvinced that parental involvement matters. They do not actively reach out to the parents of their students to seek their involvement. Traci Peters is not one of them. She believes strongly in the value of parental involvement, as expressed in *Teaching in Focus.*

Lack of effort. The most frustrating teacher barrier to parental involvement in schools and classrooms is lack of effort. There is no legitimate reason not to make that call, write that note, or invite parents into the classroom. If you are convinced that parental involvement matters and that parents are your allies in the education of students, you will draw parents into—rather than excluding or even alienating them from—the educational process. Not only is this good for children and adolescents, it's also very rewarding, according to Brenda Beyal in *Teaching in Focus.*

Whatever the barriers to parental involvement, teachers need to break down barriers and cultivate an invitational attitude. Parents are part of the larger community. When teachers engage parents as active participants in the life of the school, we are reaching out into the community.

RELATIONSHIPS WITH THE COMMUNITY

Education is a public enterprise. Pick up a newspaper and you will find something in it that features or refers to schools and teachers. The community reads and hears about schools, forming impressions along the way. Teachers, and those who work in and

Points of Reflection 12.3

Do you believe that what a teacher does in the classroom can overcome obstacles to learning that students face outside the classroom, such as poverty, lack of family involvement, and a background deficient in content and skills? Why or why not?

Points of Reflection 12.4

How might you overcome any reluctance you have to making parents your partners? How do you envision drawing parents into the process of educating their children? How would you overcome barriers to parental involvement?

Teaching in Focus

Traci Peters, Grade 7 Math, Cario Middle School, South Carolina. *In her own words. . . .*

When parents send you their children, they are sending you the best ones they have. They're not keeping their brighter, better behaved children at home. They are sending you their "babies," even in middle school. In an instant, teachers become the ones who spend more time each day with these children than the parents. Most parents want to be informed and involved, and they want what is best for their child. Parents and teachers are on the same side—the student's side. As teachers we need to reach out. There are many benefits to parental involvement for students, teachers, and the parents themselves.

There are many ways to involve parents, from simple occasional e-mail communication and a classroom newsletter, to more complex strategies such as home visits and family math nights. What matters is that we establish positive connections between the classroom and the homes of students. If you think of it as a give-and-take relationship, you may find very practical benefits to parental involvement. They can simplify some of your tasks by doing things such as copying and preparing materials, shopping for "fun with food" day, and displaying student work in the classroom or in the halls. They will enjoy their involvement and support your efforts in the classroom!

Teaching in Focus

Brenda Beyal, Grades 3–5 Multiage Classroom, Rees Elementary School, Utah. *In her own words. . . .*

Tucked away in a drawer I have a note that was given to me by a parent over 10 years ago. I take it out on occasion when I am having a particularly hard time with a school situation, or when I'm feeling ineffective. I read the salutation, "Dear Respected Madam." This is one of the most gracious openings to a note that I have ever received. The note is from parents who had just emigrated from India. They had asked for help with a small matter, and I was able to help solve a dilemma for them.

The words still send a surge of renewal and recommitment within me for my chosen profession—teaching. Families and parents can make emotional deposits into our teaching lives, and then some can make deep withdrawals. As a teacher, I hold on to the unintentional deposits that parents make, and, with their help, I let the withdrawals slip away from my teaching so they will not keep me from making powerful teaching and learning connections.

with schools, are acutely aware of how public their endeavors are. For most people in a community, the sum total of their knowledge about schools is what they know from the media and what they hear from their personal acquaintances about teachers, students, and classrooms. For this reason, teachers have the responsibility to be public relations agents for schools. We must put our best professional selves forward to represent education—in community groups, in places of worship, in social gatherings, in the grocery store—everywhere we go.

The community can provide support, resources, and services that are valuable lifelines for students and their families. Individuals can volunteer their time, give money and materials, and share their expertise as student mentors and guest speakers. Corporations can fund programs and events, offer employees release time to volunteer in schools, and provide political support for needed policy changes. Teachers should know what is available and, along with administrators and counselors, make sure families are aware of how to access community services such as health clinics, family counseling, and tutoring. When school, families, and the community work together, students receive optimum benefits, as illustrated in Figure 12.3.

PROFESSIONAL RELATIONSHIPS WITH COLLEAGUES

"One incontrovertible finding emerges from my career spent working in and around schools: The nature of relationships among the adults within a school has a greater influence on the character and quality of that school and on student accomplishment than anything else" (Barth, 2006, p. 9). This bold statement was made by Roland Barth, highly respected former teacher and principal and founding director of the Principals' Center at Harvard University. He continues by saying, "In short, the relationships among the educators in a school define all relationships within the school's culture" (p. 9). Is it possible that as a teacher, your relationship with another teacher down the hall affects these other relationships? Yes, according to Barth, who tells us we must find a way to confront this "elephant in the room": the relationships that loom so large within the school but are seldom addressed.

Basic relationships among teachers. The four basic relationships among teachers as defined by Barth (2006) are parallel play, adversarial relationships, congenial relationships, and collegial relationships.

Parallel play. When children sit on the floor just inches from one another, so absorbed in their own toys that they never acknowledge each other's presence or

Points of Reflection 12.5

How do you envision being a community ambassador for schools? Do you think it's important to know what services are available for your students and their families? Should this be part of the professional responsibilities of teaching? Why or why not?

Figure 12.3 Optimum benefits for students

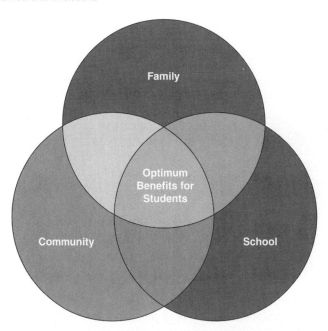

offer to share or play together in any way, we say they are engaged in parallel play. This behavior is considered normal development for 1- and 2-year-olds. Sadly, a sort of *teacher* parallel play is the norm in many schools. Too often teachers close their doors, hoard their lessons and materials, and infrequently share their tools of the trade—their knowledge of curricula and repertoire of instructional strategies. This isolating approach robs teachers of potential individual and collective growth.

Adversarial relationships. Barth tells us that one reason so many teachers engage in a sort of parallel play is that they are attempting to avoid adversarial relationships, or those relationships characterized by blatant criticism, talking behind the backs of others, and unwarranted and destructive competition. This amounts to unprofessional behavior.

Congenial relationships. You will no doubt develop congenial relationships with many of your colleagues. You will enjoy one another's company. People of different ages, personality types, interests, cultures, and races are teachers. You will find some with whom you have much in common and others very different from yourself. Developing congenial relationships makes school more fun. Students can sense when their teachers enjoy the people around them. That's being a role model in one of the most practical ways.

Collegial relationships. Relationships with other teachers that promote growth through sharing of professional expertise are **collegial**. Barth (2006) quotes famous baseball manager Casey Stengel: "Getting good players is easy. Getting 'em to play together is the hard part" (p. 11). There are lots of "good players," or competent teachers, in schools. Developing collegiality means getting teachers to "play" together. When Barth visits schools and looks for signs of collegial relationships, he looks for three components:

- Educators talking with one another about practice and sharing craft knowledge
- Educators observing one another while they are engaged in practice
- Educators rooting for one another's success

Points of Reflection 12.6

Do you recall teachers in your K–12 experience who genuinely appeared to enjoy one another's company? How could you tell?

Teachers who share a congenial relationship are more likely to collaborate in collegial ways to engage learners.

Teacher professional relationships with principals and assistant principals are discussed in Chapter 11.

PROFESSIONAL RELATIONSHIPS WITH OTHER ADULTS IN THE SCHOOL

It's a good idea to get to know each adult who contributes to the daily work in schools, including administrators, administrative assistants, cafeteria and custodial workers, counselors, social workers, nurses, media specialists, and teacher assistants. They all have the interests of students as priorities and can be our partners in teaching and learning.

Paraprofessionals are also known as teacher aides or teacher assistants. The people who hold these positions are typically not certified teachers. Paraprofessionals are most commonly employed in early childhood and elementary settings. They may be in one classroom full time or may rotate among teachers. For instance, a paraprofessional may be assigned to second grade in a school with five second grade teachers. These teachers may decide that the best use of another adult is to have the paraprofessional join the classes during the times when the children are in reading circles. Or the teachers may want extra help in their classrooms when students are working on projects that require the use of multiple materials.

Some schools are fortunate to have paraprofessionals who have worked for 20 or 30 years in schools. They may know the community well and be valuable assets. If you are fortunate enough to have a teacher assistant in your classroom, treat him or her with respect. You have professional knowledge that may exceed that of a paraprofessional in some ways, but chances are your assistant has a lot of experience with students and families. Learn from them even as you direct their participation with the students in your classroom.

What Are Some Realities of Teaching?

Teaching is complex. As with any endeavor that's multifaceted, being a teacher has its wonderful aspects and rewards layered on top of, and in between, the hard realities that make the profession challenging. But the benefits and satisfaction of effective teaching are more than just layers—more importantly, they are *foundational* when we understand that what we do day-to-day makes our country stronger and our way of life richer, and gives opportunities to children and adolescents that only education can provide. Remember this as you read about challenges that will likely be part of your reality as a teacher.

Bureaucratic overload. It takes administrators and district personnel to make schools function. These individuals can't be out-of-sight, out-of-mind. We need them to do all the things they do to keep schools open and functioning and to keep us in our classrooms, teaching. However, the paperwork and recording responsibilities in response to administrative demands can seem overwhelming at times. Teachers must keep up with periodic school/district/state testing and all it involves, including test preparation and monitoring as well as interpreting and using results. Increasing numbers of students with special needs require not only additional planning, but also documentation.

Wise administrators will keep meetings to a minimum and make the ones that are unavoidable, meaningful and useful. However, with each new initiative comes the need for explanations and training, follow-up, and record keeping. Meeting fatigue is a common teacher ailment and the cure seems to elude us. Be patient and remember that when teachers gather, there's always something to learn from each other.

When teacher preparation doesn't match reality. It's very likely that you will see and hear things in schools that are contrary to what you are learning in teacher preparation. In real classrooms, the variables are many and teachers, as human beings, do not always approach responsibilities and opportunities in the best possible ways, or even in ways that seem acceptable. One of the purposes of field experiences is to let you observe reality, reflect on what you see, and formulate possible solutions to the dilemmas that you witness.

You may see what you consider poor instruction. You will probably hear a teacher or two scream at children or humiliate a child in front of the class. It is difficult to watch this type of behavior and yet say nothing. Remember: You are the guest. It is not your place to correct a teacher or act indignant in the face of teacher behavior you view as inappropriate. Also realize that you do not know the whole picture. You are seeing a snapshot. The time to express your dismay, or even outrage, is in your college class or student teaching seminar with an instructor and classmates. We learn a great deal from observing incorrect methods and behavior. Learning what *not* to do as a result of seeing its actual or potential damage is powerful.

Many new teachers enter the classroom full of ideas and enthusiasm for all they have learned in teacher preparation. The problems begin when new teachers find it difficult to use the strategies they know are research-based and, in theory, beneficial to teaching and learning. The reasons for this dilemma are complicated and include occasional low levels of administrative support, class size that limits the kind of engagement necessary, lack of resources and materials, and extreme emphasis on test preparation. Professional teachers work toward balance between doing the things they have to do and using the strategies that are more easily implemented while still finding ways to meet their students' needs in ways that optimize learning.

Classroom management. It is valuable to understand the theories of structuring and maintaining a classroom that result in optimal student behavior. Much has been written on the topic. However, when new teachers are asked about the most trying aspects of teaching, classroom management inevitably surfaces on the list.

Most teachers agree that the only way to become comfortable with what theories tell us, or experienced teachers advise, is to actually be in the classroom . . . on-the-job learning. This means your first couple of years may be frustrating as you get your classroom "sea legs." The majority of students will behave reasonably and respond to reminders of the correct things to do. However, you will likely encounter students who don't behave appropriately, who try your patience and push you to *react* to them rather than calmly responding. You aren't alone. This happens at times to every teacher. The better we know our students, the more prepared we can be to respond to discipline issues. Stay cool, stay focused, and stay consistent. Ask for advice and help.

> The learning environment and issues involving classroom management are discussed in Chapter 6.

Changing demographics. In numerous places in this text we've explored the changing demographics of the United States. Even though multicultural opportunities make us stronger and enrich our classrooms, the challenges are undeniable. This is reality.

Although children and adolescents from many ethnicities and cultures are coming to the United States, the predominant minority—and foreseeable majority—ethnicity is Hispanic, particularly those coming here from Mexico. Between 2000 and 2010, the U.S. population of people of Hispanic origin grew from 35 million to 51 million, making the Hispanic population 16.4% of the total U.S. population, growing from 12.5% in 2000. Many of these new U.S. residents are living in states that previously had very little Hispanic presence such as Georgia, South Dakota, Mississippi, Wisconsin, Pennsylvania, Tennessee, Virginia, and North Carolina. More Hispanic immigrants are also moving to rural areas and small towns (Wortham, Clonan-Roy, Link, & Martinez, 2013).

Large cities and suburban areas are making progress, although in some places the strides are minimal, to help Hispanic children and adolescents achieve academic goals by providing English-language learning opportunities through bilingual classes, English as a Second Language programs, and Structured English Immersion. In many

Programs for
English-language learners
are discussed in
Chapters 2 and 3.

rural areas and small towns, these programs are problematic due to limited teaching staffs and funding. Communication with families becomes particularly difficult when there are few bilingual teachers and translators.

Involving families in the education of their children is an important teacher responsibility. Hispanic parents are valuable resources for teaching and learning. "The Hispanic family structure epitomizes the values normally associated with high academic performance . . . clear boundaries and rules, and the sort of open communication that allows parents to inquire about school" (Cattanach, 2013, p.23). Often, however, the level of engagement with which Hispanic parents are comfortable consists of making sure students are in school, with homework at least attempted. Families need encouragement to increase engagement with the school and the classroom to help their children fulfill their academic potential. As schools adjust to the demographic shift that's frequently accompanied by low socioeconomic status, they are faced with not only teaching the students, but the families as well.

Approximately 65,000 undocumented students graduate from high school each year in the United States. Currently fewer than 10% of these students pursue any form of higher education. This will likely dramatically change in the future. In 2012, Homeland Security announced that children brought to the U.S. can stay in our country for two years following high school graduation without fear of deportation. They may apply for work authorization and attend college. Many states have recently declared that these same adolescents may attend public colleges at in-state tuition rates. Only five states have passed laws stating that undocumented adolescents may not receive in-state tuition—Arizona, Colorado, Georgia, South Carolina, and Indiana (National Conference of State Legislatures, 2012).

A generation of teachers in U.S. classrooms never faced substantial language and culture differences. They are now trying to adjust. Your classroom will likely be very diverse and your career will begin with challenges inherent in multilanguage, multicultural students.

Budget issues. Rarely is there enough money to fund what needs to be done to facilitate the learning results we want to see. In particular, states and school districts have struggled with budget issues since the economic downturn of 2008. Some districts have announced each April that teachers and teacher assistants will be laid off, often only to hire them back in August when funds somehow appear. The threat of losing a job is stressful and when it happens year after year, it's definitely counterproductive. The actual reductions in force are devastating not only to the individuals who lose their jobs, but also to those who remain and are forced to do more with larger numbers of children for the same or less compensation. Classes get bigger, resources become scarce, and morale plummets. This is a sad reality.

Furloughing is a way some states and districts are choosing to deal with the budget crisis. When teachers or assistants are asked to not work for a certain number of days, they lose their salary for those days, and it's referred to as furloughing. Not giving step raises is another way districts save money. There are teachers who have not received a raise in four or more years. Some districts are closing schools or consolidating smaller schools to save operating budget funds. Many districts have dismissed teacher assistants and other support personnel who help teachers do their job of teaching students. This is devastating news for early childhood teachers.

Drop in teacher satisfaction. According to the MetLife Survey of the American Teacher (2012), teacher satisfaction, as judged by the results of 1000 public school teachers, is at its lowest level in 25 years. Budget problems, excessive emphasis on testing, the influence politicians and others outside of education have on the profession, the new models of teacher evaluation based on student test scores, performance pay initiatives, and more are impacting teacher satisfaction. The hope of many people within education is that as the U.S. economy improves, so will teaching conditions and teacher satisfaction.

The irreplaceables. The New Teacher Project (TNTP) is an organization focused on providing quality education for low income and minority students. The results of a widespread study of four large urban school districts including 90,000 teachers, 2,100 schools, and 1.4 million students determined that the real teacher retention problem is not just about teachers leaving the profession, but rather about the *best* teachers leaving (TNTP, 2012).

The study used multiple measures to designate the top 20% of teachers in the districts. According to the study, these top 20% are, as in the title of the study indicates, *The Irreplaceables*. TNTP tells us:

- These teachers advance student learning to such an extent that they are almost impossible to replace.
- When one of them leaves a low-achieving school, it can take 11 hires to find just one teacher of comparable quality.
- Teachers of this caliber provide more engaging learning experiences for students and help them achieve five to six more months of learning each year than students of low-performing teachers—academic results that can be life-changing.

The study recommends two strategies for retaining the top teachers: make retention of the best teachers a priority and strengthen the teaching profession through higher expectations.

The reality is that *you* can be an irreplaceable teacher! Even on the most discouraging days, children and adolescents need the best teachers to believe in them and help them learn. Perhaps this is the most meaningful reason to teach.

What Is My Role as a Professional in Education Reform?

To reform is to change, to make different, or to improve. The word **reform** in education usually involves funding allocations; school choice; new instructional programs; and, basically, the promotion of one ideology or another. People who propose reform in K–12 education do so with the goal of improving student learning. To be sure, reform initiatives can change the way some aspects of schools operate, either permanently or for a period of time until the particular ideology falls out of favor. There have been many reform efforts in the last few decades; there will be many more in the future, some that will advance student learning and others that will not. Fragmented efforts that do not view the big picture of teaching and learning will fail.

So how do professional teachers respond to calls for reform? Public schools continue to be works in progress. Reform of one sort or another will always be with us. Professional teachers know this. They also care deeply about students and the teaching profession and support ideas and efforts intended to increase learning. They do so with common sense. If a particular reform doesn't appear to make sense for the students they know well, they speak up concerning their objections, they work cooperatively with others even as they try to influence the course of events, and they continually keep the question "And how are the children?" at the forefront of all discussions. Being an informed professional is a position from which to impact reform.

The following reform efforts are briefly and simply described. This is just a sampling. Each is actually quite complex and teacher professionalism propels us to learn more about the issues.

REFORM OF TEACHER EVALUATION

There is growing sentiment that teacher evaluation is not working. U.S. Secretary of Education Arne Duncan wrote in 2010,

> No area of the teaching profession is more plainly broken today than that of teacher evaluation. . . . In district after district, more than 95 percent of teachers are rated as good or superior, even in schools that are chronically underperforming

year after year. Worse yet, evaluations typically fail to take any account of a teacher's impact on student learning. . . . As a result, great teachers don't get recognized, don't get rewarded, and don't help their peers grow. (Duncan, 2010)

An unprecedented incentive for improvement of teacher evaluation is part of President Obama's plan to reauthorize the Elementary and Secondary Education Act (known as No Child Left Behind from 2001 to 2010). In 2010 the federal government offered states $4.3 billion in *Race to the Top* grants for making changes in school systems, including planning new ways to evaluate teachers. Most states are in the process of redesigning teacher evaluation.

Purposes of teacher evaluation. There are two distinct purposes of teacher evaluation. Although some models attempt to do both, their attempts either are, or are perceived to be, one-sided in purpose.

Measuring teachers and *developing* teachers are two very different purposes of teacher evaluation. Strictly measuring teacher effectiveness allows for decisions concerning rehiring or dismissing and decisions about whether to promote. The use of teacher evaluation to differentiate teacher pay will be discussed in the next section. One model designed to measure teacher effectiveness considers 10 categories of teacher behavior listed in Figure 12.4. Studies indicate that this model, **Rapid Assessment of Teacher Effectiveness** (RATE) more accurately differentiates between effective teachers and ineffective teachers than many other models (Strong, 2011).

Because the 10 behaviors in Figure 12.4 are indicative of effective teaching, teachers can discover which behaviors they have mastered and which ones are still challenges, and then use that knowledge to find ways to improve. If a school decides to use RATE in this way, then RATE can be utilized for the purpose of teacher evaluation that focuses on *development*, rather than just on *measurement*. An old adage says, "You can't fatten a pig by weighing it." By the same token, you can't develop more effective teachers simply by measuring them. According to many experts, current models of teacher evaluation don't accomplish either purpose adequately. Robert Marzano, one of the most highly respected educators and a prolific writer, says, "Teacher evaluation systems have not accurately measured teacher quality and have not aided in developing a highly skilled teacher workforce" (2012, p.15).

Value-added teacher evaluation. When student test scores are used to evaluate teacher effectiveness, it is referred to as **value-added teacher evaluation**. This simply means that teachers either have helped students learn more as measured by test scores (value added), or they haven't. Isn't this what effective teaching is all about? Of course!

So why is this premise—that students of effective teachers will improve their standardized test scores—controversial? Let's explore some "big picture" issues associated with value-added teacher evaluation.

Figure 12.4 Ten categories of Rapid Assessment of Teacher Effectiveness

Providing clear lesson objectives.
Understanding students' background and comfort with the material.
Using more than one delivery mechanism.
Providing multiple examples.
Providing appropriate nonexamples (illustrations of the wrong way to do something).
Maintaining an effective pace.
Providing students with feedback about their learning.
Engaging in timely use of guided practice.
Explaining important concepts clearly.
Keeping students actively engaged throughout a lesson.

Source: Marzano, R. J. (2012). The two purposes of teacher evaluation. *Educational Leadership, 70*(3), p.16.

Many educators who seriously consider the value-added concept of teacher effectiveness seem to agree on at least four flaws:

1. Experience indicates that a teacher's success from year to year as measured by standardized test scores varies, often by quite a bit.

2. Test scores vary by students assigned to teachers. For instance, teachers with large numbers of English-language learners and students with special needs typically have slower test score gains than teachers with other students. Attempts to control for these differences are inadequate.

3. The impact of an individual teacher is tempered by forces outside the teacher's control. Neighborhoods, homes, societal pressures, and other factors influence learning.

4. Not all teachers have students subjected to standardized testing. This includes most primary grade teachers and related arts teachers whose subjects are not tested.

Balance. Most teacher evaluation models attempt to incorporate balance by making the value-added concept half or so of the final teacher score. The *Measures of Effective Teaching Project* (MET), funded by the Gates Foundation, concludes that teachers should be evaluated based on three factors:

- Classroom observations
- Student achievement gains
- Feedback from students (Marshall, 2012)

The credibility of observations of teachers as they work depends on many factors, including the perspective and training of the observer, the frequency and timing of the observations, the preconceived notions of the observer concerning the teacher, and more. As we've discussed, there are complex problems involved in using student test scores to sort teachers into categories of either effective or ineffective. Feedback from students is problematic and a relatively new measure of teacher quality. MET suggests the items students consider include:

- Our class stays busy and does not waste time.
- I understand what I'm supposed to be learning in this class.
- If I don't understand something, my teacher explains it another way.
- My teacher pushes everyone to work hard.
- My teacher takes the time to summarize what we learn each day. (Marshall, 2012)

This is a great list of things to remember when teaching! However, students sometimes don't appreciate what they learn, or how they learn it, until months or years later. They are likely to respond negatively, or positively, for reasons other than the ones targeted. This fact causes some teachers to disagree with the use of students' opinions.

Obviously much work is needed to create teacher evaluation models that accomplish both purposes of evaluation, measurement and development, and result in stronger, more effective teachers. "Becoming an expert teacher is not a gift bestowed on a chosen few, but a journey through a challenging, thorny pathway that requires constant pruning" (Mielke & Frontier, 2012, p. 11).

PERFORMANCE-BASED PAY

This hot topic in education involves paying teachers more when they produce whatever results are designated as desirable. In the first decade of this century, one estimate puts the number of news stories on the topic of performance-based pay at almost 50,000 (Springer & Gardner, 2010). That's a lot of opinions from a lot of people—but, by most accounts, we aren't much closer today to figuring out how to judge teacher performance

Points of Reflection 12.7

Do you want your teaching evaluation to include student test scores? Why or why not?

accurately and fairly, and how to reward it, than we were in 2000. Is it what we observe teachers doing that counts? Are extra duties worth extra pay? Should teachers in hard-to-staff schools be paid more? Do high school science and math teachers deserve more money than fifth grade teachers? Or is the bottom line how teachers affect student test scores?

Performance-based pay for teachers is not a new concept. Every 20 years or so the idea surfaces, some districts and states try it, flaws in the system emerge—and the idea is abandoned, again. But performance-based pay makes sense, doesn't it? Simply put, the teachers who do the best jobs should be paid the most. From a business-model perspective, where production may be relatively easy to measure, performance-based pay may be incentive enough to see sustained positive results. In education, if performance-based pay increases were given for longer working hours or more graduate degrees, measurement would be easy. However, if sustained positive results are increased student learning, the questions remain: "How do we quantify student learning?" and "Which parts of student learning, by whatever measure we use to judge it, are directly attributable to the teacher who has had the students in class for 9 months?" For instance,

- If a teacher's fourth grade students show marked improvement in math, who's to say that the foundation for the increased learning wasn't built in third grade and simply all came together in fourth grade?

- If tenth graders demonstrate improved writing skills, is it due at least in part to the ninth grade teacher's concentration on mechanics that the tenth grade teacher used in the process of teaching about idea development? Should the tenth grade teacher be rewarded but not the ninth grade teacher?

Can you see how complex the issue of performance-based pay becomes?

Common salary model. The most widely used way to pay teachers is on an established scale that uses years of services and education level as the only variables. Teachers qualify for steps that determine salary. For instance, if you begin teaching with a bachelor's degree, you will be on the bottom of the scale. Each year you will receive a step raise based on years of service. If you receive a graduate degree, you will receive a raise and be on a different path than those with bachelor degrees. You will continue to receive longevity raises, but your pay will be higher than teachers without graduate degrees.

Some teacher salaries are enhanced because of extra duties assumed such as coaching, sponsoring a student organization, working on a school-based project, or mentoring new teachers. For some teachers, the only feasible way of making more money is to become an administrator. This is very unfortunate, because we lose excellent classroom teachers to positions not directly involved in classroom and student interactions. But it's a fact of life in K–12 education.

Controversy over performance pay. Performance pay will continue to be debated and attempted as part of ongoing efforts of educational reform. Some states are developing aggressive plans for performance pay, including Colorado, where Senate Bill 191 not only ties 50% of an evaluation for principals and teachers to student academic growth but also changes the way teachers get and keep tenure. Bills such as this remain controversial. Note that many initiatives, such as this one in Colorado, are put in place not by educators, but rather by legislators. Table 12.2 lists some of the beliefs of advocates and critics of performance pay.

Teacher professionalism and performance-based pay. Because pay based on performance has been attempted a number of times over the past four or five decades, almost always unsuccessfully, there may be considerable pessimism among veteran teachers who have seen plans come and go. Still, professionals remain optimistic that ways will be found to judge their competency, at least in part, on the degree of learning experienced by their students. They know, however, that the current method

TABLE 12.2 Advocates and critics of performance pay based on student learning

Advocates Believe That Performance-Based Pay:	Critics Believe That Performance-Based Pay:
Can be a catalyst for change	Amounts to tweaking, rather than fixing, the problem of uneven or lagging achievement
Increases student learning	Penalizes teachers who do not directly teach the tested subjects
Motivates teachers who aren't trying hard enough	Encourages teaching to the test, thereby narrowing the curriculum
Makes teaching more competitive and increases effectiveness	Fails to instill systemic responsibility for increasing student learning
Is a fair way to differentiate among varying levels of teacher effectiveness	Perpetuates measuring success by test scores alone

of measuring student learning solely by standardized test scores does not present the whole picture of their teaching effectiveness. Even so, professionals encourage exploration in education that may positively impact teaching and learning.

STATEWIDE REFORM EFFORTS

Whole states may be involved in sweeping changes, all with the purpose of reforming schools to increase student learning. The 2012 Louisiana reform initiative propelled by Governor Bobby Jindal is an example. One of the most notable changes involved is making vouchers available to all students in the state, thus encouraging parents to exercise choice in their students' schools. Another voucher bill allows individuals or corporations to fund private-school tuition grants, with the donors then recouping most of the money through a rebate from the state general fund. Governor Jindal's education agenda also includes establishing statewide oversight of early childhood education programs that receive public money. These ideas and actions are pro–school choice and pro–charter/private schools.

As you can imagine, many teachers and administrators in public schools are not fans of Governor Jindal's reform efforts. Included in his plan is a partial abolishment of teacher tenure, something that's also happening in other states. His plan links teacher compensation partially to student performance assessed through state tests. Some aspects of the plan are being tested in courts, as well as tried in the court of public opinion. The unrest reported by some in Louisiana is perhaps a lesson in what may result from too much change too fast, and change without educator buy-in. It's too early to know if learning will increase because of the governor's reform agenda.

DISTRICT REFORM EFFORTS

Almost all school districts initiate reforms and make changes that will hopefully increase student learning. One that comes along every decade or so is the effort to change the school calendar. After all, we are no longer an agrarian-based society with all hands needed to plant and harvest crops. Most current calendars are still based on this paradigm of 9 months on and 3 months off to work in the fields. Many new calendar paradigms make sense for increasing student learning. For instance, the schedule that would have students in school for 9 weeks and then off for 3 weeks would eliminate what many term the "summer slide." Three months of no formal learning is especially detrimental to economically disadvantaged students (Huebner, 2010). In the 9 week–3 week model, and others with similar patterns, the breaks are frequent, but not long enough to adversely affect knowledge and skill retention. The shorter breaks would provide opportunities for enrichment and remediation as needed.

The district level is often where reform initiatives blossom because of local involvement and investment in successful schools. One example of a community joining forces to increase student learning and well-being is happening in La Crosse, Wisconsin.

The district consists of 12 elementary schools, 6 middle, and 3 high schools. Of these 21 schools, 10 are charter or choice schools, including an elementary school and a middle-level Montessori school, an early childhood center, and two vocational and arts schools. The district serves about 7,000 students with about 600 teachers. The students are 79% white, 10% Asian, 7% black, and 3.5% Hispanic.

The La Crosse reform effort is a collaborative process based on the framework in Adelman and Taylor's 2008 book, *Rebuilding for Learning: Addressing Barriers to Learning and Teaching, and Re-engaging Students*. The collaborative group composed of over 150 community participants and 30 unique agencies and cultural/ethnic groups has conducted three La Crosse Community Summits. The goals of the summit participants include:

- Identify and address, in a systematic way, gaps in support systems for families
- Identify the barriers to learning in our community.
- Create a deeper level of trust and communication that will enhance the academic growth of their children in our schools.
- Create a comprehensive web of organized learning supports designed to remove barriers to learning.

Six subcommittees are actively bringing a greater focus to the accomplishment of Summit goals. The Home/Family Involvement in Schooling Committee works with African American, Hmong, and Ho-Chunk/Native American liaisons—with community groups and cultural centers as part of the loop—in an effort to reach as many individuals as possible to gather ideas and solutions. The University of Wisconsin–La Crosse is assisting with information gathering and analysis. This is an example of a very admirable collaboration that will have a positive impact on teaching and learning!

Teacher professionalism in state and district reform. Professionalism, when faced with state and district reform efforts, leads teachers to find out as much as possible about initiatives and to explore how they can be part of positive results. After teaching for 10 or more years, many teachers are tempted to respond, "Been there, done that." And, indeed, they may have. Ideas for reform tend to be cyclical. Many are tried with few or no results, only to be repackaged years later and tried again. This is the case with performance pay. However, professional teachers look very carefully at proposals for elements that may be right for current circumstances in education or improved to the point of being valid this time around. Professional teachers choose to be involved as much as possible in decision making. They reflect on efforts and do what they can to improve teaching and learning, while avoiding negativity.

ASSESSING THE COMMON CORE STATE STANDARDS

Now that almost every state has officially adopted the Common Core State Standards and we have looked at how both advocates and critics view the standards, the part of the reform that's still unknown is whether the standards will result in increased student learning. Although many applaud the rigor of the standards, they fear that the tests that will assess the standards may be too difficult, too soon. All grade levels will begin testing at the same time, rather than beginning the tests with only the primary grades and then working up a grade level each year so prior learning based on the standards will impact learning in subsequent grades. Preliminary results from a couple of states show sharp decreases in the number of students scoring at the proficient level. Those directly involved with teaching and learning understand the dilemmas that may accompany curricular changes, but all the general public will see and read is that students are not achieving. It will likely be a difficult period until students and teachers are very familiar with the standards and accompanying assessments.

Teacher professionalism and Common Core assessments. States and districts can use the knowledge and skills specified in the standards as goals on which to build their grade-by-grade and subject-by-subject curricula. The common standards do not propose to tell teachers how to teach. Instructional strategies based on the standards can be chosen or developed by individual teachers or groups of teachers to best promote teaching and learning.

Although choices in instruction are still the teacher's to make, the choice whether to give or not give standardized assessments is not. Professionalism with regard to standards involves making the standards come alive for our students. We do this by knowing their interests and needs, by developing lessons and experiences that are standards-based and developmentally appropriate, and by then engaging learners in knowledge and skills that build on prior learning. Professionalism related to standardized assessment leads teachers to face the testing in positive ways and to emphasize to students that the exams provide ways for them to show what they know and can do.

> Common Core State Standards are discussed in Chapter 4.

INSTRUCTIONAL REFORMS

At any given time in American schools, dozens of reforms involving instruction are evident. Some may tweak methodology but be touted as revolutionary, and others may truly amount to a paradigm shift. Often the new strategies are abandoned before having a real opportunity to make a difference; others continue to be practiced long after being shown to not have a positive impact on learning.

The *flipped classroom* is an example of a paradigm shift. In a flipped classroom, students watch a video teacher lecture or demonstration after school as homework and then come to class ready to interact with the knowledge and skills. The traditional classroom/homework model is turned upside down, or *flipped*. This instructional hot topic has been around for several years and is gaining momentum. The popularity of the model is based on the opportunity to use class time for discussion, activities, collaborative projects, application of knowledge, and practice of skills. Teachers who have committed to flipping their classrooms have generally become outspoken advocates of the model.

Some critics of the flipped classroom say it relies too heavily on lecture—rather than students sitting in class, they instead sit in front of a computer screen. Teachers who like flipping counter this criticism with the benefits of using their time with students to actively engage them in their own learning. Another criticism is that some students don't have reliable access to computer technology apart from school. **Jon Bergmann, flipped classroom advocate** and technology director in Kenilworth, Illinois, reports beginning flipped classrooms in his school in 2007 and burning DVDs for students without Internet access. Another solution may be to make computers available to students before and after school. Critics ask, "If students won't do traditional homework, what makes us think they will sit in front of a screen and listen to a lecture?" An additional negative is that if every teacher "flips," students may watch lectures for a couple of hours a night. Countering this is advocates' claim that flipping individualizes learning because students can watch the lecture or demonstration as many times as necessary to "get it."

An extreme example of classroom flipping is Clintondale High School in Michigan, where every teacher flips their classroom. The school's principal reports that state test scores improved in every subject and the graduation rate has increased from 80% to 90%. In addition, disciplinary incidents decreased from 736 in 2009–2010 to 187 in 2011–2012 (Ullman, 2013). These are incredible results. The question remains if similar results can be replicated.

This chapter's **SocialMEdia** feature presents more information about flipping your classroom and some of the tools available to help you get started.

Teacher professionalism and instructional reforms. Not all instructional strategies will be appropriate for your classroom. We've discussed many variables that make you and your students, in your school circumstances, unique. These variables must be considered when deciding if and when to use instructional strategies. Occasionally a school district will adopt a particular package of strategies and dictate that all teachers use them. In some cases you won't have a choice. The professional teacher will remain open minded and present evidence that particular strategies either are working, or are counter-productive. If the initiative continues, you will know your students well enough to tweak or supplement to keep learning moving forward.

SocialMEdia

Flipping your classroom doesn't have to be an everyday or long-term commitment. The tech tools already available to you allow you to do a trial run, thanks to social media and technology for teaching and learning. You can start small by using your smartphone to make a brief video of you explaining a concept, demonstrating a math procedure, creating a mini-lecture about a character in a novel or historical setting, and more. Then post the video on the class website or class wiki. Ask students to view the video before class. During class, engage students in exploration of the topic with which they are already familiar because of what they watched before class.

Flipping your classroom doesn't require expensive equipment. *Jing* allows you to *capture* anything you find on your computer including both still shots and video. You can annotate what you've captured with the software tools provided to point out particular aspects of the photo or video. Videos are limited to 5 minutes. To create a longer video, *Snagit* will come in handy. Once you have captured what you want students to see and hear, the piece can be saved to your computer. The next step is to share what you've created. With a free Jing account you receive a *Screencast* account that turns what you've created into a link. This link can be shared in any way you want. Jing incorporates a history function that saves all your episodes so you can easily help students review lessons they may have missed or need for remediation purposes. User-friendly videos and texts help you get started using **Jing and Screencast** to add to your instructional toolbox for a number of purposes or to use to flip your classroom.

REAUTHORIZATION OF THE ELEMENTARY AND SECONDARY EDUCATION ACT

Perhaps the most significant overarching reform elements that will affect your first years of teaching are part of ***A Blueprint for Reform***, the reauthorization of the Elementary and Secondary Education Act (2010). Recall that the last reauthorization was the No Child Left Behind Act of 2001.

These are the key priorities of the reauthorization of the Elementary and Secondary Education Act:

- Promote college- and career-ready students
- Provide great teachers and leaders in every school
- Ensure equity and opportunities for all students
- Raise the bar and reward excellence
- Promote innovation and continuous improvement

(U.S. Department of Education, 2010)

To accomplish these priorities, a variety of reform efforts are being put in place. One proposal in the ESEA reauthorization intended to turn around low-performing schools involves intervention models designed to bring about significant changes in the operation, governance, staffing, and instructional programs of schools deemed unsuccessful in educating students. Figure 12.5 briefly explains four intervention models that may be applied to schools as part of the ESEA reauthorization.

Figure 12.5 Intervention models

- *Transformation model:* Replace the principal, strengthen staffing, implement a research-based instructional program, provide extended learning time, and implement new governance and flexibility.
- *Turnaround model:* Replace the principal and rehire no more than 50 percent of the school staff, implement a research-based instructional program, provide extended learning time, and implement new governance structure.
- *Restart model:* Convert or close and reopen the school under the management of an effective charter operator, charter management organization, or education management organization.
- *School closure model:* Close the school and enroll students who attended it in other, higher-performing schools in the district.

Source: U.S. Department of Education (2010).

Teacher professionalism and *A Blueprint for Reform*. If you are teaching in a school that is placed on an intervention plan, you will no doubt experience upheaval in your professional life. This likelihood is slim, but possible, if the guidelines attached to the reauthorization of ESEA, *A Blueprint for Reform,* are enforced.

The five priorities of the reauthorization are sound principles of effective education. Teacher professionalism pushes us to be great teachers and leaders, to promote innovation and continuous improvement, and to help our students become ready for college and careers. *A Blueprint for Reform* calls for us to create equitable opportunities for all students.

In this chapter's **The Opinion Page** feature, Dr. Tom Watkins, former Michigan state superintendent of schools, urges us to make all decisions about school reform based on how teaching and learning are affected. Carefully read what he has to say.

REFORM IN PERSPECTIVE

"Educators are drowning under the weight of initiative fatigue—attempting to use the same amount of time, money, and emotional energy to accomplish more and more objectives" (Reeves, 2006, p. 89). Veteran teachers will tell you about initiatives and reform efforts that lasted maybe a year, maybe two, with lots of buildup and preparation—some with a flurry of activity, but few with lasting positive effects. This doesn't mean we shouldn't keep trying, but it does mean we need to be steady, professional educators who care deeply about all children and their learning, even as initiatives and reform efforts come and go.

In his book, *So Much Reform, So Little Change,* Charles Payne (2008) laments the fact that so many reform efforts end in disappointment. Educators and, unfortunately, elected officials come up with, or push, ideas and programs that look good on paper, and may make sense from a business perspective, but fail to view schools and school systems from the human perspective. Payne tells us that relationships and trust-building are foundational, rather than side issues. They matter to the success of any reform.

As part of his *School Reformers' Pledge of Good Conduct,* Payne urges us to approach any effort to improve schools without a hint of doing anything behind the principal's back or showing disrespect for school leaders. We should also not expect change overnight. In other words, to contribute to the success of efforts aimed at school improvement, we need to be professionals.

Often the most effective reform is accomplished day by day through the attitudes and actions of teachers who live and teach in ways that are guided by professionalism. Such is the case with Traci Peters, one of our focus teachers at Cario Middle School, South Carolina. In **Teaching in Focus** Traci writes directly to you, giving advice based on her years as an effective, happy teacher.

As this book comes to an end, let's revisit reasons for teaching. In conversations with teachers they often talk about why they teach. They share anecdotes and reflections about their students and classrooms. This is a compilation of some thoughts recently gathered.

I teach because . . .

- children are our most precious resources for the future.
- the quality of education determines the character of our community and our society.
- I get to be with other teachers who are creative, hopeful, patient, and collaborative.
- when a student understands something after struggling with a concept, that's the best feeling of all.
- my students have the potential to impact our world in positive ways.
- I learn my subject better every day by digging deeper to make science come alive for my students.
- I laugh multiple times every day when either I make a silly joke or a student makes a funny comment that gets us all laughing.

This Opinion Editorial appeared in the Kalamazoo Gazette, *Michigan, on December 30, 2012.*

Future of State, Nation Inextricably Linked to Quality of Our Teachers

by Tom Watkins

Tom Watkins served as Michigan's state superintendent of schools from 2001 to 2005. He is an advocate for public education and sensible school reforms, and a 2010 Upton Sinclair Award winner from Ednews.org. He is a U.S./China business and educational consultant.

Business owners know you must engage your employees in the change process. Training our adults to be competitive on the world stage and educating more of our children to be able to collaborate and compete globally is the key to the country's future prosperity.

Education holds the key to our collective futures. The city, state, and nation that creates an effective system of learning will thrive. Our goal should be to make Michigan and America the brain bank of the world where everyone wants to come for deposits and withdrawals.

Yet, rather than seeking ways to develop a shared vision and common agenda to make this happen, political and ideological battles sharpen and continue to beat down the very people we need to build up—our teachers.

Teachers are key.

The voice of the classroom teacher must be heard, especially around issues of classroom discipline, instructional design, and delivery above the reform chatter. Our public schools are the true Statue of Liberty in this great country of ours—taking the tired, hungry, poor, kids who speak English as a second language, and children with disabilities to give them hope and opportunity. Our great teachers are the torches lighting the way for us all.

Rhetoric from the state and our nation's capital have never educated a single child. It is our teachers who know their subject matter, who have a passion for teaching and learning, and who are provided the support and tools from administration, that we must invest our resources and energy moving forward. As Michigan's state superintendent of schools from 2001 to 2005, I had a simple measuring stick against which ALL decisions made by the Department of Education and state Board of Education were judged: "Show me how this helps our teachers teach and our children learn."

We need to engage teachers in the process of reform to attract and retain the very best in the classroom. The state Board of Education, in an overt effort to engage teachers, invited the annually selected Michigan Teacher of the Year to have a seat, but more importantly; a voice at the state board table. The teachers' voice is always the last heard prior to policy being enacted.

So as the New Year rings in, rather than hammering our teachers down, let's snap that symbolic hammer in half and turn it instead into a ladder that helps lift up our schools, teachers, and most importantly, our children. Do our schools and teachers need to constantly evolve, embrace change and adapt to a disruptive world where ideas and jobs can and do move around the globe effortlessly? Of course. Yet, without the ability to tap the energy, talents, skills, and passions of these great educators that are touching our collective futures every day, we are missing a major ingredient necessary to soar in the 21st century knowledge economy.

Research and common sense reinforce that quality teachers matter. In the education enterprise we must always remember that teachers have the lead role (along with parents and students). The teacher is Diana Ross and the rest within the school building are singing "doo-opp." We need to actively seek ways to engage teachers and make them a key member of any education reform effort.

If you can read this, thank a teacher!

But if you are a policy-maker (governor, legislator, school board member, superintendent, principal), consider re-evaluating how you can harness the talents of the master-link in the learning process—our great teachers.

The future of our state and nation is inextricably linked to the quality of our teachers.

This Opinion Page piece is a thoughtfully and professionally written case for the value of teachers in our schools, states, and nation. Dr. Tom Watkins, a veteran educator, speaks from a foundation of experience and expertise. Write a well-developed paragraph in response to each of the following questions and prompts:

1. Dr. Watkins writes " . . . political and ideological battles sharpen and continue to beat down the very people we need to build up—our teachers." Summarize what you have read so far in this chapter that supports his view of the political and ideological battles that affect teaching and learning.

2. We are told that all decisions should be measured by "Show me how this helps our teachers teach and our children learn." Choose one reform initiative discussed in this chapter that you think has the potential to measure up and explain why. Then choose one reform initiative that you predict will not measure up and explain your reasons for choosing it.

3. There are so many analogies and metaphors in this Opinion Page that convey meaning. Choose one that particularly speaks to you and discuss why.

Teaching in Focus

Traci Peters, seventh grade math, Cario Middle School, South Carolina. *In her own words. . . .*

Dear Teacher Candidate,

What an exciting career you have chosen. I can assure you that your years as a teacher will be filled with memories that last a lifetime! Many things change each year as a new group of students enter your life. Yet many things must stay the same. Here are just a few things on my "have to do each year" list:

- Love your students as if they were your own children, even the ones that know just what buttons to push. In order to love them, you have to get to know them. So talk to them about things other than the textbook!
- Laugh with your students. If you don't enjoy teaching, then why do it? Middle school kids are especially funny and definitely want all the attention they can get.
- Follow a routine every day. This doesn't mean that you have to do the same thing every day, but it does mean that kids like structure.
- Stay organized—it saves lots of time and frustration!
- Plan with your colleagues. It'll make for more exciting lessons and give you some much needed "adult time." Don't forget to ask for help when you need it!
- Respect your students and their parents, and, in turn, they will respect you. Most importantly, respect yourself. A happy teacher makes a happy class!
- Be consistent with your discipline, from day to day and from student to student. Be sure you don't overuse the word "no" when "yes" is sometimes more appropriate. Remember to reward good behavior, and be sure the consequence fits the not-so-good behavior.

Good luck to you in your first year of teaching. Be confident that you will make a difference in your students' lives and that all of your hard work does pay off!

Sincerely,
Traci

- being around kids everyday helps me stay young and keep up with current trends and ideas.
- I enjoy a measure of autonomy when it's just my students and me; I feel like an artist working on an immensely valuable canvas.
- the school schedule fits perfectly with my family life, allowing me to do something very important as a profession and as a wife and mom.
- it's a way to make a difference, hopefully over and over.
- teaching is more than a job, it's a meaningful career.
- I have always loved math and I want to engage my students in actually doing math, not just learning procedures.
- there's never a dull moment!
- I like to learn!
- I want to pass along my passion for literature.
- it's my way of serving my community and my country.

CONCLUDING THOUGHTS

It's possible to spend an entire career in the position of teacher and never accept the inherent professional responsibilities that accompany the position. How unfortunate and sad for the individual who chooses to go through the motions but never invests the commitment and care necessary to be a true professional.

On the positive side, it is possible to spend an entire career accepting responsibilities to students, families, community, colleagues, the educational system, the profession, and self-growth. Fulfilling each responsibility brings opportunities to affect students' lives and to enjoy a career filled with challenge and satisfaction.

Congratulations on completing this text and the course that made it required reading! For those of you who are sure that teaching is in your future, or who are still seriously considering the profession, you have quite an adventure ahead of you. If this is your first course in teacher preparation, you now probably have a sense of what's ahead in your college program. With each step in teacher preparation, your passion for education will likely grow.

If, however, you have decided that teaching is not for you, thank you for opening your mind to what education in the United States is like and to the needs of the more than 50 million students who attend PreK–12 schools. You are more informed than most of the American public. Expressing your opinions will be easier (and hopefully more valid) now that you have a greater understanding of the challenges and opportunities that lie within U.S. schools. Be an advocate for children and their futures—and thus for the future of us all. Please frequently ask, "And how are the children? Are they all well?"

Each page in this book is written by the hands, and from the heart, of a teacher. To be a teacher is to live in a world of possibility—to know that what we do matters. Join us.

After reading the ***Chapter in Review,*** read about Deirdre's plan to recruit minority teachers for Cario Middle School and respond to items in this chapter's ***Developing Professional Competence.***

Chapter in Review

How can I develop as a professional?

- When professional responsibilities are fulfilled, opportunities are created; when opportunities are recognized and acted upon, their benefits incur responsibilities.
- As a student, all coursework is valuable, along with field experiences.
- Clinical practice, or student teaching, is the capstone internship experience of your teacher preparation program.
- It is important for teachers to balance their professional and personal lives by developing interests and friendships that promote healthy lifestyles.
- The teaching profession is bolstered every time an engaging lesson is taught or learning is facilitated in whatever way is appropriate for students.
- Teachers have a responsibility to extend their influence beyond the classroom and into the school arena and, perhaps, the district, state, and even national arenas.
- Teachers have many opportunities to add to the teaching knowledge base through research, writing, and participation.

How do I develop and maintain professional relationships?

- Teachers should develop and maintain a sense of responsibility for student learning.
- Parental involvement increases academic achievement and attendance rates and leads to more positive attitudes and behavior.
- The community provides valuable support and services for children and their families.
- To be collegial requires overt efforts to create and maintain mutually beneficial relationships.

What are some realities of teaching?

- The paperwork and recording responsibilities in response to administrators can seem overwhelming at times.
- It's very likely that you will see and hear things in schools that are contrary to what you are learning in teacher preparation. In real classrooms, the variables are

many and teachers, as human beings, do not always approach responsibilities and opportunities in the best possible ways, or even in ways that seem acceptable.

- Most teachers agree that the only way to become comfortable with what theories tell us, or experienced teachers advise, is to actually be in the classroom . . . on-the-job learning.
- Even though multicultural opportunities make us stronger and enrich our classrooms, the challenges are undeniable.
- Your classroom will likely be very diverse and your career will begin with challenges inherent in multilanguage, multicultural students.
- Rarely is there enough money to fund what needs to be done to facilitate the learning results we want to see.
- Teacher satisfaction, as judged by the results of 1,000 public school teachers, is at its lowest level in 25 years.
- Two strategies for retaining the top teachers are making retention of the best teachers a priority and strengthening the teaching profession through higher expectations.

What is my role as a professional in education reform?

- Professional teachers support ideas and efforts intended to increase learning.
- Being an informed professional is a position from which to impact reform.
- Professionals remain optimistic that ways will be found to judge their competency accurately and fairly.
- Professionals encourage exploration in education that may positively impact teaching and learning.
- Teacher professionalism pushes us to be great teachers and leaders, to promote innovation and continuous improvement, and to help our students become ready for college and careers.

Developing Professional Competence

Thoughtfully reading this scenario and responding to the items that follow it will help you prepare for licensure exams.

Cario Middle School is considered a suburban school. The population is about 75% White students and 20% Black students, with the rest a mix of students of Asian and Hispanic ethnicities. Of the 67 teachers at Cario, only 2 are African American. This has always bothered Deirdre a little, but now that she teaches the CARE students, most of whom are Black, she has become even more aware of the lack of diversity of the teachers with whom she works.

Deirdre received a master's degree from the College of Charleston (C of C), located about 15 miles from Cario. The college has a large teacher preparation program, with teacher candidates recruited by local schools because of their proven ability. Deirdre has decided she wants to do some recruiting herself, primarily among the nonwhite teacher candidates. Now she has some decisions to make.

Think through this scenario and answer the following multiple-choice questions:

1. Before Deirdre begins planning recruitment she should
   a. talk with several instructors at the C of C to gauge whether they will be open to her efforts
   b. discuss her desires with Cario principal Carol Bartlett
   c. determine the percentage of nonwhite teacher candidates at C of C
   d. contact the NAACP to ask if there are established procedures

2. From whom will Deirdre need to seek support for her recruiting activities?
   a. the dean of the C of C School of Education, Carol Bartlett, the NAACP, the state department of education
   b. Carol Bartlett, the NAACP, the state department of education

c. the dean of the C of C School of Education, Carol Bartlett
d. the dean of the C of C School of Education, Carol Bartlett, the NAACP

3. Which reason for applying to teach at Cario will probably have the least impact on C of C teacher candidates?
   a. Cario's administration supports teacher professional development.
   b. This is an opportunity to further integrate the teaching faculty of a school.
   c. Cario is known for quality relationships among teachers.
   d. They will have a chance to work with a majority of white teachers.

Now it's time for you to respond to two short essay items involving the scenario. In your responses, be sure to address all the dilemmas and questions posed in each item. Your responses should each be between one half and one full double-spaced page. Consider the following teacher standards as you respond.

InTASC Standard 9, Professional Learning and Ethical Practice

The teacher engages in ongoing professional learning and uses evidence to continually evaluate his/her practice, particularly the effects of his/her choices and actions on others (learners, families, other professionals, and the community), and adapts practice to meet the needs of each learner.

AMLE Standard 5: Middle Level Professional Roles

Middle level teacher candidates understand the complexity of teaching young adolescents, and they engage in practices and behaviors that develop their competence as professionals.

InTASC Standard 10, Leadership and Collaboration

The teacher seeks appropriate leadership roles and opportunities to take responsibility for student learning, to collaborate with learners, families, colleagues, other school professionals, and community members to ensure learner growth, and to advance the profession.

4. Deirdre is not sure her desire for more nonwhite teachers at Cario will be met with enthusiasm from her colleagues. She knows they won't object, but they likely won't share her passion. How might she approach them? What information could she present that would make her case in a professional way? Why is it important for the teachers at Cario to know about Deirdre's recruitment? How does InTASC Standard 9 apply?

5. Deirdre thinks that some teacher candidates may be swayed toward Cario if they meet some of the parents of students who are in the racial minority. How should Deirdre go about arranging a meeting? Who would need to be involved? How does InTASC Standard 10 apply?

Glossary

Academic freedom A form of expression that allows teachers to use their judgment in making decisions about what to discuss, what to assign as readings, what teaching strategies to use, etc.

Academic rigor The content of what we teach is meaningful, and our expectations of the learning of that content are demanding.

Academies Early secondary schools designed to teach content intended to prepare students to participate in business and trade.

Accountability Holding a person or program responsible for an outcome.

Achievement gap Disparity among students, with some excelling while others languish with respect to learning and academic success.

Action research Research conducted by teachers in their classrooms around a concept or question that captures their interest; results of research may be added to the teaching knowledge base.

Active engagement Involving students in meaningful experiences that promote learning; providing an environment for creativity and collaboration, all with increased learning as the goal.

Adequate Yearly Progress School report that consists of a number of elements determined by each individual state with guidance from No Child Left Behind requirements. AYP data are kept by race, socioeconomic status, and gender. Typical components of the AYP report include graduation rate, attendance, math scores, reading/language arts achievement data, and other indicators of student progress.

Adversarial relationships Characterized by blatant criticism, talking behind the backs of others, and unwarranted and destructive competition.

Advocate for students Support and defend students, always putting their needs first.

Alternative assessment Generally any assessment other than traditional paper and pencil and/or forced choice assessment.

Alternative school School designed for students who are not successful in a traditional school setting.

American Federation of Teachers (AFT) America's second largest professional association for teachers.

Amish exception Amish children may ask to be exempt from compulsory education beyond eighth grade on the grounds that attendance in upper grades would have a negative effect on their traditions and way of life.

Analytic rubric Specifies separate parts of an assessment task, product, or performance and the characteristics of various levels of success for each.

A Nation at Risk: The Imperative for Educational Reform Report commissioned by President Reagan in 1983 that referred to U.S. public education as a "rising tide of mediocrity." In response, various proposals for reform and improvement surfaced.

Art of teaching Knowing how and when to use particular strategies to teach the curriculum; the ability to logically, and in a variety of ways, divide content and skills into manageable components and create experiences that lead to student learning.

ASCD Learn Teach Lead Professional organization dedicated to promote all aspects of teaching and learning.

Assessment Gathering evidence of student learning.

Assimilation Process of bringing persons of all races and ethnicities into the mainstream by having them behave in ways that align with the dominant culture.

Assistive technology Devices and services that benefit students with disabilities by helping them communicate, increasing their mobility, and aiding in multiple ways that enhance their capacity to learn.

Association for Childhood Education International (ACEI) Professional organization that focuses on global education issues.

Association for Middle Level Education (AMLE) Organization that provides standards for the preparation of teachers for grades 5–9, and advocates for the needs and education of young adolescents; formerly National Middle School Association (NMSA).

Associative play Children begin to share toys and verbally communicate.

At-large election Voters may vote for any candidate regardless of the area in the district the candidate represents.

At-risk students Those who are in serious danger of not completing school and/or who may be heading toward nonproductive or counterproductive lifestyles.

Attention deficit/hyperactivity disorder (AD/HD)
A learning disability in which students demonstrate three defining characteristics—inattention, hyperactivity, and impulsivity—in persistent patterns that are more severe than in others of the same age.

Authentic assessment Students show what they know and can do in a real-life setting or situation.

B

Backward design An approach to planning for teaching and learning that starts with deciding on the desired learning results (curriculum), then identifies how to collect the evidence necessary to know if the results have been achieved (assessment), and then proceeds to choosing how to help students acquire the desired knowledge and skills (instruction).

Benchmarks Statements of what students should know and be able to do at specific developmental stages.

Bilingual education The delivery of instruction in two languages.

Bilingual Education Act of 1968 Provided funds to assist non-English-speaking students (mostly Hispanic) who were dropping out of high school at a rate of about 70%.

Black Codes or Laws Prior to the Civil War, Black Codes or Laws were enacted, predominantly in the South, that prohibited the education of slaves.

Block grants Grants that provide funding with few restrictions for its use, allowing states and school districts the freedom to use the money in ways that meet their specific needs.

Block schedule A schedule allowing for longer class periods; a block schedule may be comprised of a wide variety of schedule options.

Bloom's taxonomy A classification system of thinking and processing skills that range from simple to complex; used to classify various levels of learning objectives and experiences.

Blueprint for Reform Part of the 2010 proposal to reauthorize the Elementary and Secondary Education Act.

Bond referendum Allows school districts to borrow money stipulated for specific projects. The school board asks voters in the district to approve the borrowing of the money (the bond) that will be repaid over a period of time.

Breach of contract Contracts are binding on both parties. If a person signs one and then backs out or takes a different job, or if the district backs out, the person or the district may be sued for damages.

Brown v. Board of Education In 1954 Chief Justice Earl Warren declared that segregating children based solely on race was wrong and illegal. Some schools integrated peacefully, while others did not.

Buckley Amendment Also known as the Family Educational Rights and Privacy Act (FERPA) of 1974. Allows parents and guardians access to their students' academic records and requires written parental permission for the records to be shared with anyone else. When students turn 18, they have control over who sees their records.

Bullied The person who is the target of bullying.

Bullying Relationally aggressive behavior; a type of emotional or physical violence where individuals use relationships to harm others.

Bystander Anyone who witnesses bullying. A bystander has choices to make: simply watch, walk away, join in, or intervene.

C

Case law Based on the doctrine of *stare decisis*, a Latin phrase meaning "let the decision stand;" once a decision is made in a court of law, the decision sets a precedent for future cases of a similar nature until challenged or overturned.

Categorical grants Money that is allocated or funds that are earmarked for specific purposes.

Charter school A public school that is freed in specific ways from typical regulations required of other public schools.

Child abuse Any act that results in death, serious harm, or exploitation of children.

Child neglect A form of abuse resulting from the failure to act in the best interest of children.

Civil Rights Act of 1964 Stipulates that if schools discriminate based on race, color, or national origin, they are not eligible for federal funding.

Civility Treating others the way we want to be treated.

Classroom assessment Encompasses every deliberate method of gathering information about the quantity and quality of learning.

Classroom climate The everyday environment of teachers and students working together.

Classroom community A classroom where students and teacher tend to be like-minded and have common beliefs, understandings, and aims.

Classroom management The establishment and enforcement of rules and disciplinary actions; teacher strategies to ensure an orderly classroom environment.

Clinical internship Also known as student teaching or clinical practice; involves extended fieldwork in which teacher candidates teach lessons and, for a designated period of time, take over all classroom duties.

Cognitive development One of the five basic categories of development; intellectual development and the primary focus of school.

Coleman Report Report written in 1966 that concluded that family and community factors such as poverty and parental levels of education prevented some children from learning, that no matter what schools did, some children would not be successful in school.

Collective bargaining Act of negotiating with employers and/or states to gain additional benefits for members of the bargaining group; a right practiced in most states by teacher associations and unions. States often allow unions to negotiate with school boards concerning elements of teacher contracts and working conditions.

Collegial relationships Relationships with other teachers that promote growth through sharing of professional expertise.

Common Core State Standards Initiative Efforts to develop and promote common national standards by the National Governors Association (NGA) and the Council of Chief State School Officers (CCSSO).

Common schools Community-supported elementary schools for all children established in response to many economic, social, and political factors.

Community The neighborhood, town, city, and/or county in which a person lives.

Compulsory education law Requires children to attend school until a specified age.

Congenial relationships Relationships characterized by pleasant encounters and friendliness.

Consequences Implies more natural ramifications for wrongdoing than the word *punishment*, which can be arbitrary.

Constructive correcting Assigning consequences in ways that serve as student learning experiences.

Constructivism A way of approaching instruction that builds on progressivism as students are challenged to construct, or discover, knowledge about their environments. Process is valued in progressivism, often more than product. The theory is that students who learn through the processes of construction, discovery, and problem solving will be better able to adapt to a changing world.

Content standards Specific knowledge students should have and skills they should be able to do.

Contract An agreement between parties that includes the rights and responsibilities of each. When teachers begin jobs in schools they sign initial contracts.

Cooperating teacher A classroom teacher who serves as the host and mentor during clinical practice.

Cooperative learning Loosely defined, any instance of students working together in small groups.

Cooperative play Children actively coordinate ways to keep interaction going.

Copyright laws Federal laws that protect the rights of a creator or author to own intellectual property and to prevent others from copying or distributing it without permission. Intellectual property includes written material, original audio and visual work, and computer programs. Copyright laws also provide guidelines for authorized use of someone else's intellectual property.

Core subjects Generally considered language arts, math, science, and social studies.

Corporal punishment Physical punishment practiced in some school settings.

Council for the Accreditation of Educator Preparation (CAEP) Agency that scrutinizes university teacher education programs, the result of the merger of the National Council for the Accreditation of Teacher Education (NCATE) and the Teacher Education Accreditation Council (TEAC).

Council of Chief State School Officers An organization composed of school superintendents and other school leaders.

Council for Exceptional Children (CEC) National organization that represents the needs of students with exceptionalities and fosters appropriate education for them.

Criterion-referenced Student scores indicate levels of mastery of a subject and are not dependent on how other students perform.

Critical thinking Higher order thinking involving observing, comparing and contrasting, interpreting, analyzing, seeing issues from a variety of perspectives, weighing variables, and then making decisions and solving problems.

Cultural identity Results from the interactions of many factors, including language, religion, gender, income level, age, values, beliefs, race, and ethnicity.

Cultural pluralism Involves the recognition that our nation is populated by a rich variety of people of varying races and ethnicities, and thus cultures, all with potential to positively contribute to our common goal of a productive, free society.

Culturally responsive Purposefully including contributions and viewpoints from the perspectives of different cultures, ethnicities, races, genders, socioeconomic levels, and so on.

Culture A composite of social values, cognitive codes, behavioral standards, worldviews, and beliefs that characterize a group of people.

Curriculum The educational term for what students experience in schools.

Cyberbullying Using technology to bully.

Cybercitizenship Responsibly using technology in ways that do not harm others.

D

Dame schools In colonial days, dames were respected women who, usually without formal schooling, had learned to read and write and who turned their homes into schools where parents paid to have their children educated.

Democratic classroom A classroom setting that promotes choice, community, authentic learning, and a relevant, creative curriculum; students participate in the establishment of behavioral expectations.

Departmentalized School organizational pattern in which teachers teach their own subjects and meet occasionally with other teachers who teach the same subject.

Depression Mental illness characterized by a deep sense of sadness and a loss of interest or pleasure in activities.

Developmental appropriateness Teaching and learning that matches students' physical, cognitive, social, emotional, and character development.

Diagnostic assessment Assesses student knowledge and skill levels before beginning a unit of study; commonly referred to as pretesting.

Dialects Deviations from standard language rules used by identifiable groups of people.

Differentiation of instruction Varying instruction based on the needs of students.

Discrimination Showing bias against another by race in American public schools.

Dispositions Attitudes and beliefs that guide and determine behavior.

Distance learning Involves the acquisition of knowledge and skills through instruction delivered using technology.

District school board Governing body composed of elected citizens responsible for setting policies that affect the operation of schools.

District superintendent Functions as the school district's chief executive officer; hired by the board and serves at its pleasure.

Dropout Students who do not complete high school in 4 years.

Due process The steps a district must take to pursue the charges when a tenured teacher is threatened with dismissal; important principle that requires guidelines to be followed to ensure that individuals are protected from arbitrary or capricious treatment by those in authority.

E

Early childhood education The care and education of the youngest students in the United States, typically considered birth through age 8.

Ebonics Black English, one of the best-known and most controversial dialects in the United States.

Education The lifelong process of learning.

Education for All Handicapped Children Act (Public Law 94-142) Federal law passed in 1975 that guaranteed a free and appropriate education to all children with disabilities in the least restrictive environment; renamed Individual with Disabilities Education Act in 1990.

Education Maintenance Organization (EMO) An organization contracted to take over the management of a public school for profit.

Education summit Organized meeting to advocate for school improvement.

Educational technology Any technology that assists teachers in teaching and students in learning.

Effective schools Schools that meet the learning needs of the students who attend them.

Effective Schools Movement Originated in the 1970s to develop research pertaining to the assertion that all children can learn; purpose was to find schools deemed effective for all children and identify common characteristics.

Elementary Level of school that usually includes grades K through 5.

Elementary and Secondary Education Act Enacted during the presidency of Lyndon B. Johnson to provide extra funding, called Title I funding, for schools with high numbers of children from low-income homes.

Emotional intelligence quotient (EQ) A set of skills that accompany the expression, evaluation, and regulation of emotions. A high-level EQ indicates a person's ability to understand others' as well as his or her own feelings, respond appropriately to them, and, in general, get along.

Encore courses Also known as related arts or exploratory courses; all courses other than what are considered the core courses of math, English language arts, social studies, and science.

English as a second language (ESL) Students receive individualized assistance; unlike bilingual education, ESL services are delivered only in English; little or no emphasis is placed on preserving native language or culture; and ESL teachers do not need to speak another language.

English language learners (ELL) Non-English speakers and students with limited English proficiency.

Entitlements Grants given to certain segments of the population that have specific needs; the federal government deems these individuals entitled to extra assistance.

Era of standards A time when content standards determined curricular learning goals; generally considered 1990 through the present.

Essentialism A philosophy of education based on the belief that there is a core curriculum that everyone in the United States should learn. This core can shift in response to societal changes, but should always be basic, organized, and rigorous.

Ethics Standards of conduct based on moral judgments; the determination of what's right and what's wrong.

Ethnicity An individual's country of origin and ancestry.

Eurocentric Contributions and traditions centered on European values.

Evaluation Judgments about, and the assigning of values to, the *results* of assessments.

Excise tax Tax on luxury items such as boats and travel trailers.

Exemplars Samples of work that fit various criteria for scoring so that students actually see what a product looks like that earns a particular number.

Existentialism Primary emphasis is on the individual. As a philosophy of education, existentialism contends that teachers teach the whole person, not just math, reading, science, or any other particular subject. Each student searches for personal meaning and personal understanding. If learning about a subject area increases a student's sense of self, then it's worthwhile.

Expectations A word with positive connotations that may be used in place of *rules,* a word with negative connotations.

Expenditure per pupil The average amount of money spent from federal, state, and local sources on an individual student.

Explicit curriculum What teachers are expected to teach, what students are expected to learn, and what society expects of schools; also referred to as the formal curriculum.

Exploratory courses Also known as related arts or encore courses, all courses other than math, English language arts, social studies, and science; may include art, music, physical education, industrial arts, languages, drama, computer education, and others.

Expulsion Semipermanent or permanent dismissal from school for a semester or for an indefinite period.

Extracurriculum Includes the organized experiences students have that are beyond the formal curriculum.

Extrinsic incentives Incentives that are imposed, or originate outside the individual.

F

Fair use Specific limitations on the use of copyrighted materials.

Family Educational Rights and Privacy Act (FERPA) of 1974 Commonly called the Buckley Amendment, allows parents and guardians access to their students' academic records and requires written parental permission for the records to be shared with anyone else. When students turn 18, they have control over who sees their records.

Feeder system Configuration of schools in a district; typically in one feeder system of schools early childhood/elementary schools feed into middle schools that feed into a particular high school.

5-E lesson plan A way for teachers to guide students through a cycle of inquiry learning; most commonly used for science exploration.

Field experience Observing and/or participating in actual classrooms; also referred to as practicum experiences.

Flipped classroom Students watch a video teacher lecture or demonstration after school as homework and then come to class ready to interact with the knowledge and skills.

Formal curriculum Encompasses what is intentionally taught, what is stated as the goals of student learning.

Formative assessment A series of assessments in a variety of formats that help monitor student progress.

For-profit schools Schools that are operated by private companies for profit.

Full-service school A public school that provides a comprehensive program of education and includes student and community services such as after-school and family education programs.

Functional behavioral assessment (FBA) A management plan through a team of educators utilizing a process that looks for events and actions that may lead to misbehavior and devises strategies to help students abide by classroom expectations.

Furloughing Teachers or assistants asked to not work for a certain number of days, losing the salary for those days.

G

Gender The sense of being male or female, as opposed to sex, which refers to anatomical differences.

Gender bias The favoring of one gender over the other in specific circumstances.

Gender equity The fair and balanced treatment of males and females.

Gender stereotyping Occurs when perceived gender differences are assumed for all people.

Gifted and talented Exceptional learners who demonstrate high levels of intelligence, creativity, and achievement.

Global awareness Involves understanding environmental, societal, cultural, political, and economical concepts and issues that impact our world.

Graduation rate Percentage of students who graduate from high school with a regular diploma in the standard number of years.

Grade Judgment of assessment quality (evaluation) with a number attached to it.

Great Books The writings of those considered to be the great thinkers throughout the history of Western civilization, such as Homer, Shakespeare, Melville, Einstein, and many others.

Grievance A formal complaint filed by an individual teacher or group of teachers against a district.

Guided practice Opportunities for students to work independently on applying knowledge in a nonthreatening setting that includes teacher feedback.

H

Head Start The largest provider of government-funded preschool education, employing one of every five U.S. preschool teachers.

Hidden curriculum Curriculum that is not explicit or openly expressed; similar to the informal curriculum, but with negative connotations.

Hierarchy of needs Maslow's (1908–1970) theory that all human beings experience the same needs.

High schools Schools that most often encompass grades 9–12.

High/Scope An approach to early childhood education built on consistency and few transitions during the day.

High-stakes tests Standardized tests that have far-reaching consequences.

Highly qualified Those who meet government guidelines for teacher quality in public schools.

Holistic rubric A grading instrument that uses one scale for an entire project.

Homeschooled Refers to students who receive most of their academic instruction in their homes.

Homework Independent practice outside the classroom.

Homosexuality The romantic or erotic attraction of a person to another of the same sex.

I

Idealism A philosophy based on the belief that ideas are the only reliable form of reality. Idealists believe that the physical world changes continually, and ideas are what should be taught.

Implicit curriculum Curriculum that is implied and subtle; the informal curriculum.

Incentives A word that may be used in place of the overused and value-laden word *rewards*.

Inclusion Students attend their home school with their age- and grade-appropriate peers, participate in extracurricular activities, and receive special education and support services to the maximum extent possible in the general education classroom.

Individualized educational program (IEP) A plan developed for a student by educators, the family, and others as appropriate, involving details of how to reach specific goals. A student's IEP must be revisited annually and student progress evaluated.

Individuals with Disabilities Education Act (IDEA) Also referred to as PL94-142 (and the revised version of the Education for All Handicapped Children Act of 1975), this act made special education services a right, not a privilege, because it required schools to place students in least-restrictive environments within public schools.

Individuals with Disabilities Education Improvement Act Reauthorization of IDEA in 2004 that compiled all U.S. laws that affect children with disabilities into one statute.

Informal curriculum What students learn that isn't written in a lesson plan or necessarily intentionally transmitted to students.

Information literacy Involves recognition of when information is needed, knowing how to access information, and judging information credibility.

In loco parentis Serving in place of parents.

Inquiry learning When students pursue answers to questions posed by others or developed on their own, they are involved in inquiry learning. Observation, questioning, hypothesizing, and predicting are all part of inquiry-based learning.

Instruction Encompasses the strategies used to convey the curriculum with the desired end result of student learning.

Instructional time Time available for teaching and learning.

Instrumental aggression Aggression based on attempting to meet a specific goal, such as grabbing a particular toy or establishing dominance in an activity; most common among boys.

Integrated curriculum Involves making connections among subject areas through the use of a unifying topic or theme.

Intelligence The capacity for knowing and learning.

Intelligence quotient (IQ) The results of a test that affixes a number to intelligence.

Intelligent design Includes a belief that certain features of the universe and of living things are best explained by an intelligent being (God), not by the process of natural selection espoused by evolution.

Interdisciplinary Term often used to describe curricular links or connections among subjects.

Interdisciplinary team The preferred organizational structure for middle level education, involving a team of teachers (2–5) working with a distinct group of students for an entire year.

Interstate Teacher Assessment and Support Consortium (InTASC) Organization that sets standards for what teachers should know and be able to do.

Intrinsic incentives Incentives that come from within and result from students' natural drives.

Irreplaceables Study showing exceptionally effective teachers are vital to success and are leaving the profession unnecessarily.

J

Jigsaw Strategy involving students becoming experts on particular topics and then teaching those topics to the other students.

Junior high Schools developed in 1909 to be a bridge between elementary and high school; typically grades 7–9.

K

Kalamazoo Case Established that the legislature could tax for support of both common and secondary schools, propelling public high schools into school systems in every state.

Kappa Delta Pi International honor society for preservice and inservice teachers.

Kindergarten German for "children's garden," the school year that precedes first grade.

Knowledge is Power Program (KIPP) Charter school system designed especially for at-risk student populations.

L

Language Primary means of communication; transmits knowledge and passes on culture.

Language minority students Students whose native language is other than English, regardless of their current level of English proficiency.

Latin grammar school First established in 1635 in Boston for boys whose families could afford to send them on for more education beyond the dame school; considered the forerunner of modern high schools and specifically prepared boys to attend Harvard University, established in 1636.

Learning disabled (LD) A general category of students with disorders involving problems understanding or using language that results in significant differences between learning potential and achievement.

Learning modalities Auditory (hearing), visual (seeing), tactile (touch), and kinesthetic (movement); all four are used in the process of learning, but individuals tend to favor one or two over the others.

Learning styles Ways in which individuals learn most effectively and efficiently.

Least restrictive environment (LRE) The setting within which students with disabilities can function at capacity; generally the setting with students who do not have disabilities that also meets the educational needs of the students with disabilities.

Lesson plan Devising experiences for students as part of the formal curriculum.

Liable To be responsible for; liability is what teaching is all about—accepting responsibility for students while they are under our supervision.

Limited English proficiency (LEP) Students with LEP may speak and understand some English, but not enough to be successful in classes taught in English without additional assistance.

Literacy Involves ability to analyze and apply knowledge and skills necessary to solve problems within a discipline.

Long-range plans Lesson plans that may encompass a nine-week timeframe, a semester, or a year.

Looping School practice that keeps a teacher with a particular group of students for more than 1 year.

M

Magnet school A public school with a specific emphasis or theme and curriculum and instructional programs tailored with unique opportunities that attract certain students.

Manipulatives Hands-on objects that enhance and illustrate concepts and skills.

Massachusetts Act of 1642 First compulsory education law in the New World; required all White children to attend school.

McKinney-Vento Act of 1987 Federal government's response to homelessness; act addresses the problems homeless children and youth face in enrolling, attending, and succeeding in school.

Methods courses Courses that emphasize particular strategies for specific subjects and will probably incorporate opportunities to actually apply what you are learning.

Micromanagement Managing to a level of detail that is inappropriate for a particular position. For instance, when school board members go beyond policy making into what is considered day-to-day operations, they may be seen as micromanaging.

Middle level schools Schools for young adolescents with a distinct philosophy that embraces both academic rigor and developmental appropriateness; may include any combination of grades 5–9.

Mini-lecture Shortened, focused versions of the lecture.

Montessori An approach to early childhood education with mixed-age grouping and self-pacing.

Morrill Act In 1862 the government granted states 30,000 acres of land for every senator and representative in Congress in 1860. The income the state generated from this land was to be used to support at least one college.

Multiage classroom Classroom where children in two, three, or more grade levels learn together.

Multicultural curriculum Curriculum that purposefully includes contributions and viewpoints from the perspectives of different cultures, ethnicities, races, genders, and socioeconomic levels.

Multicultural education An instructional approach that celebrates diversity and promotes equal educational opportunities.

Multiple intelligences theory (MI) A theory developed by Howard Gardner that intelligence is multidimensional, that individual brains work in ways that give each of us our own personal intelligences; includes eight intelligences.

N

National Assessment of Educational Progress (NAEP) Only standardized test systematically administered to a sampling of students across the United States. The NAEP is administered to fourth, eighth, and twelfth graders in math, reading, writing, science, history, economics, geography, civics, foreign language, and a variety of the arts; often called the nation's report card.

National Association for the Education of Young Children (NAEYC) Professional organization promoting the education and welfare of children birth through age 8.

National Board for Professional Teaching Standards (NBPTS) Board that sets standards, establishes policies, and issues certificates designating teachers with skills to perform effectively.

National Defense Education Act of 1958 Called for strengthening of science, math, and foreign language programs; teachers were given training in the use of new methods and materials in hopes of bringing American student learning up to, and beyond, the levels of learning in other countries.

National Education Association (NEA) The largest professional education association in the United States, with a total of over 5 million members including teachers, administrators, professors, counselors, and other educators.

National Governors Association Organization of governors enabling them to share expertise and tackle dilemmas collectively.

National Service-Learning Clearinghouse A major resource for information about service learning projects.

Nature Refers to the genetically inherited influences on who we are.

Neighborhood school Students in a geographical area attend school close to their home.

New England Primer First published in 1690 for children in upper elementary and secondary levels. Published for over 150 years with few substantial changes over its lifetime, the *New England Primer* included a spelling guide based on the alphabet denoted in brief rhymes and pictures, the Lord's Prayer, the Apostles' Creed, the Ten Commandments, a list of the books of the Bible, the Puritan catechism, and numbers 1–100.

No Child Left Behind Act of 2001 (NCLB) Federal law that holds schools accountable for student learning, regardless of student diversity. States are required to test all students in grades 3–8 annually to determine progress.

Norm referenced Tests used to compare students; administered to a group of students selected because they represent a cross section of U.S. students (norm group).

Normal schools Publicly funded secondary schools specifically designed to prepare teachers for the classroom.

Northwest Land Ordinance of 1787 Divided federally owned land in the wilderness into townships and required that schools be built.

Null curriculum What is not taught in school.

Nurture Refers to the influence of the environment, including everything that happens except for what can be accounted for genetically.

O

Obesity Extreme overweight as indicated by body mass index (BMI), a measure of how much a person weighs relative to height.

Objective Concise statement about what students are expected to learn and be able to do as a result of the lesson.

Old Deluder Satan Act Because education was considered the best way to fight the devil, the act (also known as the Massachusetts Act of 1647) established that every town of 50 or more households must provide a school.

Open enrollment A plan that allows students to choose from among virtually all the schools in a school district.

Overlapping A teacher's ability to multitask, to take care of several things at once.

P

Pacing guide A document that dictates the timing of content coverage; helps assure that all grade level standards are part of the curriculum.

Parallel play Children agreeably sharing the same space, but not communicating; in teachers, not sharing knowledge and skills with other teachers.

Paraprofessional A teacher aide or assistant teacher; typically not a certified teacher.

Parent Teacher Association (PTA) National organization of parents and others interested in the welfare of students; some PTAs are called PTOs (Parent Teacher Organization).

Parochial schools Schools affiliated with religious organizations.

Partnership for 21st Century Skills Leading advocacy organization focused on infusing 21st century skills into education.

Perennialism A philosophy of education based on a core curriculum with themes and questions that endure, that are everlasting; as life changes and times change, the real substance and truths of life remain the same.

Performance assessment May be a project, a demonstration, a creation, or anything that requires the application of knowledge and skills.

Performance-based pay Involves paying teachers more when they produce whatever results are designated as desirable.

Performance standards Designated levels of the knowledge or skills that are considered acceptable at a particular grade level.

Philosophy *Philo* means "love," and *sophos* means "wisdom." Philosophy, then, means "love of wisdom." This love of wisdom, or philosophy, becomes a means of answering fundamental questions.

Philosophy of education The *love of wisdom* regarding teaching that expresses itself in attitudes and actions every day in the classroom.

Portfolio Assessment tool for which either students or teachers assemble a cohesive package of representative evidence of student learning.

Postmodernism Grew out of a sense that those in power control those who don't have power. This control, postmodernists believe, is manifested through major institutions like schools.

Practicum experiences Involve observing and/or participating in actual classrooms; also referred to as field experiences.

Praise Complimenting others for real or perceived positive actions or attributes.

Praxis Series Battery of tests published by the Educational Testing Service (ETS) that may be used to determine the qualifications of individuals to be licensed or certified to teach in a variety of disciplines and grade levels.

Preschool A semistructured environment for 3- and 4-year-olds housed in a school setting; care is enhanced by exposure to basic educational concepts.

Pretesting Assessing student knowledge and skill levels before beginning a unit of study; also called diagnostic assessment.

Primary classrooms Typically grades 1–3. Kindergarten is a stand-alone category.

Principal Oversees every aspect of school life and answers to the district for all that occurs at the school. The principal's role involves administrative tasks such as facility maintenance, attendance, discipline, parent/community relationships and communication, transportation, and all manner of paperwork. Principals are also instructional leaders with knowledge of, and experience with, the teaching and learning process.

Private schools The two elements that make schools public—public funding and public accountability—are both absent in private schools.

Privilege gap Gap between the haves and the have-nots.

Problem solving Process involved in finding a solution to a problem.

Process standards Processes that support content learning by explaining how the content might be best learned and how to use the content once it is acquired.

Processing Sending a student out of the classroom with the purpose of reflection and planning for better choices.

Profession An occupation that meets certain criteria, including (1) extensive training to enter, (2) inclusion of a code of ethics, and (3) service as the primary product.

Professional development Efforts to help teachers improve their knowledge and skills.

Professional learning community (PLC) School-based group of teachers and administrators who work collaboratively to share practices and data analysis of student progress to improve teaching and learning.

Professionalism A way of being involving attitudes and actions that convey respect, uphold high standards, and demonstrate commitment to those served.

Progress In International Reading Literacy Study (PIRLS) The only international test of reading proficiency that compares students worldwide.

Progressive education In 1896 John Dewey established a method of involving students in their own learning through cooperative groups, which grew into a major movement with far-reaching implications; interests guide what is learned about traditional subjects.

Progressivism A student-centered philosophy of education that focuses on curriculum that is of interest to students. Progressivists view education as more than preparation for the future; it is life itself. The progressive philosophy of education endorses experiential learning full of opportunities for student discovery and opportunities to solve problems.

Property taxes Values of property are determined, and a small percentage of the assessed amount (usually less than 1%) is collected annually and used for local services.

Proximity The accessibility of teacher to students.

Public domain A work is in the public domain if it is more than 75 years old or is published by a government agency; work in the public domain is not protected by copyright.

Public Law 94-142 (PL94-142) Common way of referring to the Individuals with Disabilities Education Act (IDEA), an act that made special education services a right, rather than a privilege.

Public schools Public schools are funded through some form of taxation and are accountable to the community through elected or governmental officials who have policy and oversight responsibilities.

R

Race Term used to classify people according to their physical characteristics that are nature given. Race classifies people at birth.

Race to the Top A federal initiative challenging states to make bold efforts to improve teaching and learning; over 4 billion dollars in federal money awarded to states on a competitive basis.

Racism A form of prejudice that may be perpetuated by individuals or governments stemming from a belief that one race is superior to another.

Rapid Assessment of Teacher Effectiveness (RATE) Teacher evaluation strategy that accurately differentiates between effective teachers and ineffective teachers than many other models.

Reading across the curriculum Infusing the curriculum with reading, regardless of content area.

Reduction in force Occurs in schools when there are fewer students, budget cuts, or the cancellation of a program. Reduction in force (rif) may also apply to tenured teachers. The general rule of "riffing" is that the last hired are the first to go if it becomes necessary.

Reflection Thinking about what is done, how it's done, and the consequences of actions or inactions, all with the goal of being a better teacher.

Reflective practitioner A teacher who thinks critically about teaching and the consequences of actions or inactions, all with the goal of being more effective with students.

Reform To change, to make different, or to improve.

Reggio Emilia An approach to early childhood education for ages 3 months to 6 years based on relationships among children, families, and teachers.

Related arts courses Also known as exploratory courses or encore courses; all courses other than math, English language arts, social studies, and science; may include art, music, physical education, industrial arts, languages, drama, computer education, etc.

Relational aggression Subtle actions that may hurt emotionally rather than physically; may include name-calling, gossiping, or saying mean things just to be hurtful; most common among girls.

Reliability The degree to which an assessment yields a pattern of results that is repeatable and consistent over time.

Resilience The ability to bounce back and meet life's challenges.

Resource teacher A special education teacher who helps students develop strategies for school success.

Ripple effect An effect that occurs when one action directly affects another.

Romanticism A philosophy of education that contends that the needs of the individual are more important than the needs of society; also known as naturalism.

Routine An expected action that occurs in a given circumstance to accomplish a task efficiently.

Rubric Assessment tool that makes explicit what is being assessed, lists characteristics of degrees of quality, and provides a rating scale to differentiate among these degrees.

Rural schools Schools in areas with fewer than 2,500 people and a minimum of retail stores and services.

S

Scaffolding The support given to children to help them move through progressive levels of learning.

School choice Method of letting parents decide which schools their students attend.

School connectedness Student bonding and engagement in the school experience.

School culture The prevailing atmosphere of a school that provides the context of learning experiences; as places where people work together and learn together, schools function according to their cultures.

School district An organizational structure of local schools defined by geographic boundaries.

Schooling Formalized delivery system of teaching and learning.

School-to-Work Federal government program initiated to bring real-world, work-related skills and understanding to students through courses and experiences that introduce them to career possibilities.

School venues The variety of ways Americans "do school" in the over 120,000 schools in the United States. The most prominent venues are public schools and private schools.

Science of teaching Curriculum, assessment, and instruction.

Secondary schools Schools for grades 7-12.

SEED Public Charter Schools The only public boarding schools in the country.

Self-contained classroom An organizational structure involving one teacher and a group of students for whom the teacher is accountable much of the school day.

Self-efficacy An "I can" belief in oneself that leads to a sense of competence; the concept of self-efficacy is solidly grounded in the accomplishment of a continuum of increasingly difficult challenges.

Service dimension of teaching An attitude that approaches students as complete human beings, with cognitive, physical, emotional, social, and moral components; an approach to teaching from a service point of view is all-inclusive rather than focused only on academic and cognitive progress.

Service-learning When student experiences combine service with a purposeful learning component.

Settlement houses Established by early American reformers to confront the problem of urban poverty; community service centers that provided educational opportunities, skills training, and cultural events.

Sexual harassment Behavior with sexual implications that is neither wanted nor welcome; may include obvious looks with lewd intent, taunts with sexual innuendo, touching, kissing, groping, and any behavior that has sexual connotations.

Sexual orientation The sex to which a person is romantically or socially attracted is considered a person's sexual orientation.

Single gender All male or all female.

Single-member elections Only those who live in a specific area can vote for the representatives in their area.

Sin tax Tax on items some consider vices, such as alcohol and cigarettes.

Site-based management Public school management structure in which governance is in the hands of those closest to it, generally teachers, administrators, and parents.

Social cognition Process of relating to others and thinking about them and oneself.

Social media Communication using technology such as Smartphones, Instant Messaging, etc.

Social reconstructionism A philosophy of education that looks to education to change society, rather than just teach about it. Social reconstructionism as an education philosophy calls on schools to educate students in ways that will help society move beyond all forms of discrimination to the benefit of everyone worldwide.

Socialization Occurs through a variety of influences including home, family, church, print and electronic media, peers, and school.

Socioeconomic status (SES) Status based on economic level and other sources of power.

Special education services Services provided by schools to help students with disabilities function and learn in ways optimal to each.

Special interest group Group of people with a common mission who work to have an impact.

Stages of cognitive development Jean Piaget (1896–1980) recognized distinct differences in children's and adolescents' responses to questions that directly correlated to their chronological ages and categorized these differences into stages.

Stages of moral reasoning Noted developmental psychologist Lawrence Kohlberg contends that people pass through distinct stages as they develop morally.

Stakeholders Those who have legitimate involvement and stand to gain or lose from the situation

Standard English A composite of the language spoken by educated, middle-class people in the United States.

Standards-based reform movement Efforts to improve teaching and learning through content standards; another way of expressing the era of standards.

Standardized test Test given to multiple groups of students, designed for specific grade levels, and typically repeated annually. These tests are administered and scored under controlled conditions, and their exact content is unknown to everyone except the test makers before they are administered.

Standards Expectations for what individuals should know and be able to do.

Standards-based test Test written using the content of a specific set of standards.

Stare decisis Latin phrase meaning "let the decision stand;" the basis for case law.

State board of education Volunteers who are either elected or appointed by the governor; state legislatures give state boards oversight authority; boards act in regulatory and advisory capacities.

State department of education Operates under the guidance of the governor, legislature, and state board of education; also known as state office of education or perhaps department of public instruction.

State superintendent The one person given responsibility for managing the state department of education; also known as chief state education officer or commissioner of education.

STRIVE Preparatory Schools A successful charter system in Denver, Colorado, serving primarily at-risk, disadvantaged students.

Structured English immersion Approach includes significant amounts of the school day dedicated to the explicit teaching of the English language, with other content supporting instruction, but not as the primary focus.

Structured observation Early field experiences involving looking for specific things and responding to prompts that purposefully call attention to certain aspects of the classroom.

Student self-monitoring Students assume control of their own behavior as they develop a sense of ownership for that behavior.

Student teaching Also known as clinical internship or clinical practice; involves extended fieldwork in which teacher candidates teach lessons and, for a designated period of time, take over all classroom duties.

Student voice Giving students choices, asking for their opinions, teaching them to reflect on their own learning, and giving meaningful writing assignments help develop student voice.

Students with exceptionalities Learners with abilities or disabilities that set them apart from other learners.

Substance abuse A pattern of alcohol or drug use that can lead to detrimental and habitual consumption, impaired functioning at school and work, and legal difficulties.

Suburban schools Schools in neighborhoods and small-to-medium-size towns that are located on the fringe of cities or are their own distinct locations.

Summative assessment A formal assessment involving judgments about the success of a process or product; most often occurs at the end of a unit of study.

Superintendent A school district's chief executive officer; hired by the district school board; advises the board and carries out board policies.

Suspension Time out of school that may range from 1 day to less than a semester, but is usually for 10 days or less.

Systemic involvement Extending teacher influence at the local and district levels.

T

Tax cap An upper limit to taxation.

Teach for America Most widely known of all alternative licensing programs; TFA recruits individuals who are college seniors or recent graduates who agree to teach in high-needs rural or urban schools for at least 2 years.

Teacher leader A teacher with additional responsibilities such as chairperson of a grade level of teachers or perhaps a subject area specialist who works with other teachers to help them improve their knowledge and/or skills; more generally, teachers who prove to be leaders in their schools, as well as in their districts and states, simply by being dynamic, well-informed classroom teachers.

Teacher preparation portfolio Cohesive package of representative products; may either document growth or display best work, depending on its purpose.

Teaching in 3D Teaching that incorporates service along with curriculum, instruction, and assessment.

Tenure Continuing contract status; a teacher with tenure is entitled to a contract each year unless the district has reason to not renew it or the teacher decides to go elsewhere. In most states tenure doesn't guarantee a particular position in a particular school, but it does guarantee employment in the district.

Thinking skills Skills that aid in processing information.

Time-on-task Productive learning time.

Tinker Doctrine Extends symbolic freedom; students are allowed to express their views symbolically through what they wear as long as it doesn't disrupt the educational process.

Title I funding Federal compensatory funds provided through the Elementary and Secondary Education Act given to public schools where more than 50% of the students qualify for free or reduced-price meals; used to supplement regular school funding in schools with high numbers of students from low-income settings.

Title IX of the Education Amendments Act Prohibits government money from being used for anything that discriminates on the basis of gender.

Token economy A system of giving symbolic rewards for appropriate behavior and withholding or taking away rewards for inappropriate behavior.

Town schools Early American schools established for whole communities; while some schools still limited curriculum to reading, writing, and the classics, specialized schools in the form of academies became popular.

Traditional public schools Schools that have no admission criteria, other than perhaps residency in a particular attendance zone.

Transition When students change activities or locations, they are in transition; generally a time when most classroom disruptions happen.

Transparent Decisions are made with full disclosure of information and reasoning.

Trends in International Mathematics and Science Study (TIMSS) International tests that compare students worldwide; administered every 4 years since 1995.

Truancy Nonattendance during compulsory education, not including excused absences generally granted for health reasons.

Tyler Rationale Ralph Tyler developed four questions that should be asked throughout the stages of curriculum development.

U

Unconditional teaching Accepting students for who they are, not for what they do.

Unfunded mandate A legally enforceable law without monetary support provided.

Unit of study Organizes curriculum, instruction, and assessment around a major theme or distinct body of content; provides planned cohesion.

Unobtrusive intervention Consequences that do not disrupt instruction.

Urban schools Schools in cities with large downtowns and dense populations.

V

Validity The degree to which an assessment measures what it is supposed to measure.

Value-added teacher evaluation When student test scores are used to evaluate teacher effectiveness.

Vocational Education Act of 1963 Quadrupled the amount of money allocated for vocational education.

Volunteerism Choosing to give time or effort to serve or support a cause without the expectation of receiving anything in return.

Voucher Government-issued piece of paper that represents part of a state's financial contribution for the education of a student; parents choose a school and present the voucher, and the government allocates funding to the school accordingly.

W

Watchdog group Community members who join forces to keep an eye on school district accountability by examining policies and practices.

Wayside teaching Teaching that occurs inside and outside the classroom through attitudes, values, habits, interests, and classroom climate.

Webinar A web-based seminar with give-and-take participation through online means, video cams, and/or voice.

Whole child Attending to student developmental stages and needs, along with teaching them grade-level and subject-area content.

Withitness Refers to a teacher's awareness of what's going on in the whole classroom, enabling the teacher to step in when needed to keep the environment positive; originated with Jacob Kounin.

Writing across the curriculum Infusing the curriculum with writing, regardless of content area.

Y

Young adolescents Students between ages 10 and 15.

Z

Zone of proximal development The level at which a child can almost, but not completely, grasp a concept or perform a task successfully; theory proposed by Lev Vygotsky.

References

Chapter 1

Berliner, D. C. (2000). A personal response to those who bash teacher education. *Journal of Teacher Education, 51*(5), 358–371.

Bushaw, W. J., & Lopez, S. J. (2012). Public education in the United States: A nation divided. *Phi Delta Kappan, 94*(1), 9–25.

Bushaw, W. J., & McNee, J. A. (2009). The 41st annual Phi Delta Kappa/Gallup poll of the public's attitudes toward the public schools. *Phi Delta Kappan, 91*(1), 8–23.

Codell, E. R. (1999). *Educating Esme: Diary of a teacher's first year.* Chapel Hill, NC: Algonquin Books of Chapel Hill.

Corbett, D., & Wilson, B. (2002). What urban students say about good teaching. *Educational Leadership, 60*(1), 18–22.

Council of Chief State School Officers. (2011, April). Interstate Teacher Assessment and Support Consortium (InTASC) Model Core Teaching Standards: A Resource for State Dialogue. Washington, DC: Author. Retrieved January 12, 2013, from http://www.ccsso.org/Documents/2011/InTASC_Model_Core_Teaching_Standards_2011.pdf

Darling-Hammond, L. (2003). Keeping good teachers: Why it matters, what leaders can do. *Educational Leadership, 60*(8), 7–13.

Dewey, J. (1933). *How we think: A restatement of the relation of reflective thinking to the educative process.* Boston: D.C. Heath.

Duncan, A. (2009/2010, Winter). Evaluating the teaching profession. *American Educator, 33*(4), 1–5. Retrieved January 31, 2010, from http://www.aft.org/pdfs/americaneducator/ae_winter09.pdf

Feistritzer, C. E. (2009). Alternative teacher certification: A state-by-state analysis 2009. Retrieved January 24, 2010, from www.teach-now.org/overview.cfm

Fessenden, F., & Barbanel, J. (2005). The rise of the six-figure teacher. *The New York Times.* Retrieved May 20, 2005, from http://query.nytimes.com/gst/fullpage.html?res=9C04EED61330F936A25756C0A9639C8B63

Ginott, H. G. (1993). *Teacher and child.* New York: Collier Books/Macmillan.

Haycock, K. (2003). Toward a fair distribution of teacher talent. *Educational Leadership, 60*(4), 11–15.

Interstate Teacher Assessment and Support Consortium. (2011). InTASC Model Core Teaching Standards. Retrieved March 30, 2013, from http://www.ccsso.org/Documents/2011/InTASC_Model_Core_Teaching_Standards_2011.pdf

Johnson, S. M., & Kardos, S. M. (2005). Bridging the generation gap. *Educational Leadership, 62*(8), 8–14.

National Center for Education Statistics. (2012). The condition of education 2012. Retrieved January 8, 2013, from http://nces.ed.gov/pubsearch/pubsinfo.asp?pubid=2012045

National Education Association. (2010). Status of the American public school teacher 2005–2006. Retrieved January 8, 2013, from http://www.breakthroughcollaborative.org/sites/default/files/NEA%20-2005-06-Statusof%20Public%20School%20Teachers.pdf

Nieto, S. (2009). From surviving to thriving. *Educational Leadership, 66*(5), 8–13.

Partnership for 21st Century Skills. (2011). Overview. Retrieved January 10, 2013, from http://www.p21.org/overview/p21-faq

Phelps, P. H. (2003). Teacher professionalism. *Kappa Delta Pi Record, 40*(1), 10–11.

Public Agenda. (2003). Attitudes about teaching. New York: Author.

Ripley, A. (2010, January/February). What makes a great teacher? *The Atlantic.* Retrieved January 29, 2010, from http://www.theatlantic.com/doc/201001/good-teaching

Stronge, J. H. (2002). *Qualities of effective teachers.* Alexandria, VA: Association for Supervision and Curriculum Development.

Teach for America. (2013). *Our organization.* Retrieved January 24, 2013, from http://www.teachforamerica.org/our-organization

Teacher Portal. (2013). *Teacher salaries by state.* Retrieved March 18, 2013, from www.teacherportal.com/salary

Tell, C. (2001). Who's in our classrooms: Teachers speak for themselves. *Educational Leadership, 58*(8), 18–23.

Webb, L. D., Metha, A., & Jordan, K. F. (2013). *Foundations of American education* (7th ed.). Upper Saddle River, NJ: Pearson.

Chapter 2

American Psychological Association. (2000). *Diagnostic and statistical manual of mental disorders* (4th ed., rev.). Washington, DC: Author.

American Academy of Pediatrics. (2013). Talking to kids and teens about social media and sexting. Retrieved August 18, 2013, from http://www.aap.org/en-us/about-the-aap/aap-press-room/news-features-and-safety-tips/Pages/Talking-to-Kids-and-Teens-About-Social-Media-and-Sexting.aspx

Banks, J. A. (Ed.). (2004). *The handbook of research on multicultural education.* San Francisco: Jossey-Bass.

Campbell, A., Shirley, L., & Candy, J. (2004). A longitudinal study of gender-related cognition and behavior. *Developmental Science, 7,* 1–9.

Clark, K. (2009). The case for structured English immersion. *Educational Leadership, 66*(7), 42–46.

Delgado-Gaitan, C., & Trueba, H. (1991). *Crossing cultural borders: Education for immigrant families in America.* New York: Falmer.

Diversity Data. (2000). *Principal Magazine, 79*(5), 18.

Feldman, R. S. (2011). *Development across the life span* (6th ed.). Upper Saddle River, NJ: Prentice Hall.

Gallahue, D. L., & Ozmun, J. C. (2012). *Understanding motor development: Infants, children, adolescents, adults.* 7e. Boston: McGraw-Hill.

Gardner, H. (1999). *The disciplined mind: What all students should understand.* New York: Simon & Schuster.

Gay, G. (2000). *Culturally responsive teaching.* New York: Teachers College Press.

Gilligan, C. (1993). *In a different voice: Psychological theory and women's development.* Boston, MA: Harvard University Press.

Glazer, S. (2005). Gender and learning. *Congressional Quarterly Researcher, 15*(19), 445–468.

Goleman, D. (1995). *Emotional intelligence.* New York: Bantam Books.

Gollnick, D. M., & Chinn, P. C. (2013). *Multicultural education in a pluralistic society* (9th ed.). Upper Saddle River, NJ: Merrill/Prentice Hall.

Hernandez, D. J. (2011). Double jeopardy: How third-grade reading skills and poverty influence high school graduation. Retrieved January 19, 2013, from http://fcd-us.org/sites/default/files/DoubleJeopardyReport.pdf

Heward, W. L. (2013). *Exceptional children: An introduction to special education* (10th ed.). Upper Saddle River, NJ: Merrill/Prentice Hall.

Kohlberg, L. (1984). *The psychology of moral development: Essays on moral development* (Vol. 2). San Francisco: Harper & Row.

Levine, M. (2003). Celebrating diverse minds. *Educational Leadership, 61*(2), 12–18.

Maslow, A. H. (1999). *Toward a psychology of being* (3rd ed.). New York: Wiley.

McDevitt, T. M., & Ormrod, J. E. (2012). *Child development and education* (5th ed.). Upper Saddle River, NJ: Merrill/Prentice Hall/Pearson.

Migration Policy Institute. (2010). Top languages spoken by English language learners nationally and by state. Retrieved January 18, 2013, from http://www.migrationinformation.org/ellinfo/FactSheet_ELL3.pdf

Mukhopadhyay, C., & Henze, R. C. (2003). How real is race? Using anthropology to make sense of human diversity. *Phi Delta Kappan, 84*(9), 669–678.

National Association for Single-Sex Public Education [NASSPE]. (2013). Single-sex schools/schools with single-sex classrooms/what's the difference? Retrieved January 16, 2013, from http://www.singlesexschools.org/schools-schools.htm

National Center for Education Statistics. (2011). *The condition of education 2011* (NCES 2011-045), INDICATOR 6. Retrieved January 18, 2013, from http://nces.ed.gov/pubsearch/pubsinfo.asp?pubid=2011033

National Center for Education Statistics. (n.d.). Common Core of Data (CCD), "State Nonfiscal Survey of Public Elementary/Secondary Education," 1999–2000 and 2009–10. Retrieved January 17, 2013, from http://nces.ed.gov/programs/digest/d11/tables/dt11_044.asp

National Kids Count Program. (2013). *Children in single-parent families (Percent)—2011*. Retrieved January 17, 2013, from http://datacenter.kidscount.org/data/acrossstates/Rankings.aspx?ind=106

National Poverty Center. (2013). How many people were poor in 2010? Retrieved January 17, 2013, from http://www.npc.umich.edu/poverty/#2.

New American Foundation. (2013). Federal School Nutrition Programs. Retrieved January 17, 2013, from http://febp.newamerica.net/background-analysis/federal-school-nutrition-programs

Nieto, S. M. (2003). Profoundly multicultural questions. *Educational Leadership, 60*(4), 6–10.

Partnership for 21st Century Skills. (2011). Global awareness. Retrieved August 1, 2010, from http://www.p21.org/index.php?option=com_content&task=view&id=256&Itemid=120

Payne, R. (2008). Nine powerful practices. *Educational Leadership, 65*(7), 48–52.

Pew Forum. (2010). *U.S. religious landscape survey*. Retrieved August 1, 2010, from http://religions.pewforum.org/reports/

Powell, S. D. (2011). *Introduction to middle school* (2nd ed.). Boston: Allyn & Bacon.

Rance-Roney, J. (2009). Best practices for adolescent ELLs. *Educational Leadership, 66*(7), 32–37.

Richardson, R. C., & Norman, K. I. (2000). Intrinsic goodness: Facilitating character development. *Kappa Delta Pi Record, 36*(4), 168–172.

Rosenberg, M. S., O'Shea, L. J., & O'Shea, D. J. (2006). *Student teacher to master teacher: A practical guide for educating students with special needs*. Upper Saddle River, NJ: Merrill/Prentice Hall.

Short, D. J., & Fitzsimmons, S. (2007). *Double the work: Challenges and solutions to acquiring language and academic literacy for adolescent English language learners—A report to the Carnegie Corporation of New York*. Washington, DC: Alliance for Excellent Education.

Silver, H. F., Strong, R. W., & Perini, M. J. (2000). *So each may learn: Integrating learning styles and multiple intelligences*. Alexandria, VA: Association for Supervision and Curriculum Development.

Sternberg R. J. (2007). Who are the bright children? The cultural context of being and acting intelligent. *Educational Researcher, 36*(3), 148–155.

Turnbull, R., Turnbull, A., Wehmeyer, M., & Shogren, K. A. (2013). *Exceptional lives: Special education in today's schools* (7th ed.). Upper Saddle River, NJ: Merrill/Prentice Hall.

U.S. Census Bureau. (2011). Child poverty in the United States 2009 and 2010: Selected race groups and Hispanic origin. Retrieved January 17, 2013, from http://www.census.gov/prod/2011pubs/acsbr10-05.pdf

U.S. Census Bureau. (2012). U.S. population projections. Retrieved April 8, 2013, from http://www.census.gov/population/projections/data/national/2012.html

U.S. Census Bureau. (n.d.). Poverty thresholds for 2011 by size of family and number of related children under 18 years. Retrieved January 17, 2013, from http://www.census.gov/hhes/www/poverty/about/overview/measure.html

U.S. Department of Education. (2011). Improving basic programs operated by local educational agencies. Retrieved January 17, 2013, from http://www2.ed.gov/programs/titleiparta/index.html

U.S. Department of Education. (2011). Individuals with Disabilities Education Act (IDEA) data (Table 1.3). Washington, DC: Author.

Vermeer, H. J., Boekaerts, M., & Seegers, G. (2000). Motivational and gender differences: Sixth-grade students' mathematical problem-solving behavior. *Journal of Educational Psychology, 92*, 308–315.

Chapter 3

Barth, R. S. (2001). *Learning by heart*. San Francisco: Jossey-Bass.

Carter, G. R. (2003). *NCLB and the diverse needs of rural schools*. Retrieved September 26, 2004, from www.ascd.org/cms/index.cfm

Children's Defense Fund. (2012). *Policy priorities: Full-day kindergarten*. Washington, DC: Author. Retrieved January 16, 2013, from http://www.childrensdefense.org/policy-priorities/early-childhood-education-care/full-day-kindergarten.html

Eisner, E. W. (2004). Preparing for today and tomorrow. *Educational Leadership, 64*(6), 6.

Goodlad, J. I. (1984). *A place called school*. New York: McGraw-Hill.

Haycock, K. (2003). Toward a fair distribution of teacher talent. *Educational Leadership, 60*(4), 11–15.

Knowledge is Power Program. (2013). About KIPP. Retrieved January 16, 2013, from http://www.kipp.org/about-kipp

Kostelnik, M. J., Soderman, A. K., & Whiren, A. P. (2004). *Developmentally appropriate curriculum: Best practices in early childhood education* (3rd ed.). Upper Saddle River, NJ: Merrill/Prentice Hall.

Kozol, J. (1991). *Savage inequalities: Children in America's schools*. New York: Crown.

Merrow, J. (2004). Meeting superman. *Phi Delta Kappan, 85*(6), 455–460.

Morrison, G. S. (2008). *Fundamentals of early childhood education* (5th ed.). Upper Saddle River, NJ: Merrill.

National Center for Education Statistics [NCES]. (2010). *Digest of education statistics, 2009*. Washington, DC: U.S. Department of Education.

National Center for Education Statistics [NCES]. (2012). *The condition of education 2012*. Retrieved January 15, 2013, from http://nces.ed.gov/pubsearch/pubsinfo.asp?pubid=2012045

National Center for Education Statistics [NCES]. (n.d.-a). *Public Elementary/Secondary School Universe Survey, 2009–10 (version 1b); and Private School Survey (PSS), 2009–10*. Retrieved January 16, 2013, from http://nces.ed.gov/pubsearch/pubsinfo.asp?pubid=2011347

National Center for Education Statistics [NCES]. (n.d.-b). *Public Elementary/Secondary School Locale Code File," 2003–04, and "Public Elementary/Secondary School Universe Survey," 2003–04*. Retrieved January 15, 2013, from http://nces.ed.gov/ccd/TableDisplay.asp?TablePath=tables/table_03.asp

National Middle School Association. (2010). *This we believe: Keys to educating young adolescents*. Westerville, OH: Author.

Ray, B. D. (2011). 2.04 million homeschool students in the United States in 2010. Salem, Oregon: National Home Education Research Center. Retrieved January 15, 2013, from http://www.nheri.org/research/nheri-news/homeschool-population-report-2010.html

Roberts, P. L., Kellough, R. D., & Moore, K. (2006). *A resource guide for elementary school teachers* (6th ed.). Upper Saddle River, NJ: Merrill/Prentice Hall.

Routman, R. (2012). Mapping a pathway to schoolwide highly effective teaching. *Phi Delta Kappan, 93*(5), 56–61.

Scherer, M. (2005). Our cities, ourselves. *Educational Leadership, 62*(6), 7.

Shannon, G. S., & Bylsma, P. (2007). *The nine characteristics of high-performing schools: A research-based resource for schools and districts to assist with improving student learning*. (2nd ed.). Olympia, WA: OSPI.

Snyder, T. D., Dillow, S. A., & Hoffman, C. M. (2009). *Digest of education statistics, 2008* (NCES 2009-020). National Center for Education Statistics, Institute of Education Sciences. Washington, DC: U.S. Department of Education.

STRIVE Preparatory Schools. (2013). *About us*. Retrieved January 16, 2013, from http://www.striveprep.org/about-us/

U.S. Department of Education. (2010). Elementary and Secondary Education Act (ESEA). Retrieved July 31, 2010, from www2.ed.gov/policy/elsec/leg/esea02/beginning.html

U.S. Department of Education. (2012). ESEA flexibility requests and related documents. Retrieved January 15, 2013, from http://www2.ed.gov/policy/elsec/guid/esea-flexibility/index.html

U.S. Department of Health and Human Services. (2012). Head Start services. Retrieved January 15, 2013, from http://www.acf.hhs.gov/programs/ohs/about/head-start

Chapter 4

American Council for the Teaching of Foreign Languages. (2005). *Standards for foreign language learning*. Retrieved July 1, 2005, from http://www.actfl.org

Banks, J. A. (2003). *Teaching strategies for ethnic studies* (7th ed.). Boston: Allyn & Bacon.

Cornett, C. E. (2003). *Creating meaning through literature and the arts: An integration resource for classroom teachers* (2nd ed.). Upper Saddle River, NJ: Merrill/Prentice Hall.

Dewey, J. (1900). *The school and society*. Chicago: University of Chicago Press.

Dewey, J. (1902). *The child and the curriculum*. Chicago: University of Chicago Press.

Dewey, J. (1938). *Experience and education*. New York: Macmillan/Collier.

Eisner, E. (2002). *The educational imagination: On the design and evaluation of school programs* (3rd ed.). New York: Macmillan College.

Estes, T. H., Mintz, S. L., & Gunter, M. A. (2011). *Instruction: A Models Approach* (6th ed.). Boston: Allyn & Bacon.

Gregoire, M. A., & Lupinetti, J. (2005). Supporting diversity through the arts. *Kappa Delta Pi Record, 41*(4), 159–163.

Holloway, J. H. (2000). Extracurricular activities: The path to academic success? *Educational Leadership, 57*(4), 87–88.

International Association for the Evaluation of Educational Achievement. (2012a). IEA Studies. Amsterdam, The Netherlands: Author. Retrieved March 14, 2013, from http://www.iea.nl/

International Association for the Evaluation of Educational Achievement. (2012b). *TIMSS 2011 Assessment*. TIMSS & PIRLS International Study Center, Lynch School of Education, Boston College, Chestnut Hill, MA and International Association for the Evaluation of Educational Achievement (IEA), IEA Secretariat, Amsterdam, the Netherlands. Retrieved January 4, 2012 from http://timssandpirls.bc.edu/pirls2011/downloads/P11_IR_AppendixE.pdf

International Association for the Evaluation of Educational Achievement. (2012c). *PIRLS 2011 Assessment*. TIMSS & PIRLS International Study Center, Lynch School of Education, Boston College, Chestnut Hill, MA and International Association for the Evaluation of Educational Achievement (IEA), IEA Secretariat, Amsterdam, the Netherlands. Retrieved January 4, 2012, from http://timssandpirls.bc.edu/pirls2011/downloads/P11_IR_AppendixE.pdf

International Society for Technology in Education. (2005). *Mission statement*. Retrieved July 1, 2005, from http://www.iste.org

Johnson, J., & Duffett, A. (2003). *Where we are now: 12 things you need to know about public opinion and public schools*. New York: Public Agenda. Retrieved April 11, 2007, from http://www.policyarchive.org/handle/10207/5620

Jones, R. (2000, December). Textbook troubles. *American School Board Journal*, pp. 18–21.

Little, C. (2001). What matters to students. *Educational Leadership, 59*(2), 61–64.

Lounsbury, J. H. (1991). *As I see it*. Columbus, OH: National Middle School Association.

Marzano, R. J. (2000). *Transforming classroom grading*. Alexandria, VA: Association for Supervision and Curriculum Development.

National Center for Education Statistics [NCES]. (2006). *The nation's report card*. Retrieved April 10, 2007, from http://nces.ed.gov/nationsreportcard/

National Council for the Social Studies. (2005). *Curriculum standards for social studies: Executive summary*. Retrieved July 1, 2005, from http://www.socialstudies.org/standards/execsummary/

National Council of Teachers of Mathematics. (2000). *Principles and Standards for School Mathematics*. Reston, VA: Author.

National Governors Association Center for Best Practices, Council of Chief State School Officers. (2010). *Common Core State Standards*. Author. Retrieved January 1, 2013, from http://www.corestandards.org/

National Science Teachers Association. (2005). *National Science Education Standards*. Retrieved July 1, 2005, from http://books.nap.edu/html/nses/6a.html

O'Connor, K. (2002). *How to grade for learning*. Arlington Heights, IL: Skylight Professional Development, Pearson Education.

Partnership for 21st Century Skills. (2012). *21st century assessment*. Retrieved March 16, 2013, from http://www.p21.org/overview/skills-framework/27

Powell, S. D. (2011). *Introduction to middle school* (2nd ed.). Boston: Allyn & Bacon.

Reeves, D. B. (2004). *Accountability for learning: How teachers and school leaders can take charge*. Alexandria, VA: Association for Supervision and Curriculum Development.

Renzulli, J. S., Gentry, M., & Reis, S. M. (2004). A time and place for authentic learning. *Educational Leadership, 62*(1), 73–77.

Stiggins, R. (2008). Assessment for learning, the achievement gap, and truly effective schools. Portland, OR: ETS Assessment Training Institute. Retrieved March 19, 2013, from http://www.murrieta.k12.ca.us/cms/lib5/CA01000508/Centricity/Domain/2241/Assessment%20for%20the%20learning%20gap%20in%20effective%20schools.pdf

Tyler, R. (1949). *Basic principles of curriculum and instruction*. Chicago: University of Chicago Press.

Wolk, S. (2007). Why go to school? *Phi Delta Kappan, 88*(9), 648–658.

Chapter 5

Anderson, L. W., & Krathwohl, D. R. (Ed.). (2001). A taxonomy for learning, teaching, and assessing. New York: Longman.

Ball, D. L., & Forzani, F. M. (2011). Teaching skillful teaching. *Educational Leadership, 68*(4), 40–45.

Barth, R. S. (2006). Improving Relationships within the schoolhouse. *Educational Leadership, 63*(6), 8–13.

Coley, R. J., & Sum, A. (2012). *Fault lines in our democracy*. Princeton, NJ: Educational Testing Service.

Damon, W. (2012). Failing liberty 101. *Educational Leadership, 69*(7), 22–26.

Fried, R. L. (2001). *The passionate teacher*. Boston: Beacon Press.

Goodlad, J. I. (1984). *A place called school*. New York: McGraw-Hill.

Jensen, E. (2005). *Teaching with the brain in mind* (2nd ed.). Alexandria, VA: Association for Supervision and Curriculum Development.

Johnson, D. W., & Johnson, R. T. (1999). *Learning together and alone: Cooperative, competitive, and individualistic learning*. Boston: Allyn & Bacon.

Johnson, L. (2005). *Teaching outside the box: How to grab your students by their brains*. San Francisco: Jossey-Bass.

Krashen, S. (2002). Whole language and the great plummet of 1987–1992. *Phi Delta Kappan, 83*(10), 748–753.

Marzano, R. J. (2007). *The art and science of teaching*. Alexandria, VA: Association for Supervision and Curriculum Development.

Marzano, R. J. (2011). Art & science of teaching/ What teachers gain from deliberate practice. *Educational Leadership, 68*(4), 82–85.

McHugh, J. (2005). Synching up with the kids. *Edutopia, 1*(7), 32–35.

Moats, L. C. (2001). When older students can't read. *Educational Leadership, 58*(6), 36–40.

National Center for Education Statistics. (2011). Civics 2010. Retrieved September 15, 2013, from http://nationsreportcard.gov/civics_2010/civics_2010_report/

National Service-Learning Clearinghouse. (2012). Theory and practice. Retrieved April 23, 2013, from http://www.servicelearning.org/topic/theory-practice

National Youth Leadership Council (2008). K–12 Service-Learning Standards for Quality Practice. Retrieved from http://www.nylc.org/sites/nylc.org/files/files/Standards_Oct2009-web.pdf

Noddings, N. (1992). *The challenge to care in schools: An alternative approach to education*. New York: Teachers College Press.

Osterman, K. (2002). Schools as communities for students. In G. Furman (Ed.), *School as community: From promise to practice*. New York: State University of New York Press.

Pianta, R. C. (1999). *Enhancing relationships between children and teachers*. Washington, DC: American Psychological Association.

Powell, S. D. (2010). *Introduction to middle school* (2nd ed.). Boston: Allyn & Bacon.

Renard, L. (2005). Teaching the DIG generation. *Educational Leadership, 62*(7), 44–47.

Renzulli, J. S., Gentry, M., & Reis, S. M. (2004). A time and place for authentic learning. *Educational Leadership, 62*(1), 73–77.

Roblyer, M. D. (2013). *Integrating educational technology into teaching*. Upper Saddle River, NJ: Merrill/Prentice Hall.

Smith, R., & Lambert, M. (2008). Assuming the best. *Educational Leadership, 66*(1), 16–21.

Stipek, D. (2006). Relationships matter. *Educational Leadership, 64*(1), 46–49.

Tomlinson, C. A. (1999). *The differentiated classroom. Responding to the needs of all learners*. Alexandria, VA: Association for Supervision and Curriculum Development.

Tomlinson, C. A. (2010). *Leading and managing a differentiated classroom*. Alexandria, VA: Association for Supervision and Curriculum Development.

Tomlinson, C. A. (2012). One to grow on/Watching us work. *Educational Leadership, 69*(7), 46–49.

Tomlinson, C. A., & McTighe, J. (2006). *Integrating differentiated instruction + understanding by design*. Alexandria, VA: Association for Supervision and Curriculum Development.

Vacca, R. T. (2002). From efficient decoders to strategic readers. *Educational Leadership, 60*(3), 7–11.

Wiggins, G. P., & McTighe, J. (2005). *Understanding by design* (2nd ed.). Alexandria, VA: Association for Supervision and Curriculum Development.

Chapter 6

Boynton, M., & Boynton, C. (2005). *The educator's guide to preventing and solving discipline problems*. Alexandria, VA: Association for Supervision and Curriculum Development.

Dewey, J. (1944). *Democracy and education*. New York: Free Press.

Dunklee, D. R., & Shoop, R. J. (2002). *The principal's quick reference guide to school law: Reducing liability, litigation, and other potential legal tangles*. Thousand Oaks, CA: Corwin Press.

Erwin, J. C. (2003). Giving students what they need. *Educational Leadership, 61*(1), 19–23.

Farrell, C. (2010). *Corporal punishment in the United States*. Retrieved August 7, 2010, from http://corpun.com/counuss.htm

Glasser, W. (1998). *Choice theory*. New York: Harper Collins.

Jones, V. (2011). *Practical classroom management*. Boston: Pearson Education, Inc.

Kohn, A. (2005). Unconditional teaching. *Educational Leadership, 63*(1), 20–24.

Kounin, J. S. (1970). *Discipline and group management in classrooms*. New York: Holt, Rinehart and Winston.

Lemlech, J. K. (2010). *Curriculum and Instructional Methods for Elementary and Middle School* (7th ed.). Upper Saddle River, NJ: Merrill/Prentice Hall.

Loeper, J. L. (1973). *Going to School in 1776*. New York: Macmillan.

Lumpkin, A. (2007). Caring teachers: The key to student learning. *Kappa Delta Pi Record, 43*(4), 158–160.

Manning, L., & Bucher, K. T. (2013). *Classroom management: Models, applications, and cases* (3rd ed.). Boston: Pearson Education, Inc.

Marzano, R. J. (2003a). *Classroom management that works: Research-based strategies for every teacher*. Alexandria, VA: Association for Supervision and Curriculum Development.

Marzano, R. J. (2003b). *What works in schools: Translating research into action*. Alexandria, VA: Association for Supervision and Curriculum Development.

McCloud, S. (2005). From chaos to consistency. *Educational Leadership, 62*(5), 46–49.

Noddings, N. (1992). *The challenge to care in schools: An alternative approach to education*. New York: Teachers College Press.

Prensky, M. (2010). Shaping tech for the Classroom: 21st-century schools need 21st-century technology. Retrieved April 9, 2010, from http://www.edutopia.org/adopt-and-adapt

Ray, B. (2010). Guest Blog: Making the Case for Social Media. Retrieved April 9, 2010, from http://www.edutopia.org/social-media-case-education-edchat-steve-johnson

Stevenson, C. (2002). *Teaching ten to fourteen year olds* (3rd ed.). New York: Longman.

Weinstein, C. S., Romano, M., & Mignano, A. (2011). *Elementary classroom management: Lessons from research and practice* (5th ed.). New York: McGraw-Hill.

Chapter 7

Adler, M. (1982). *The Paideia proposal: An educational manifesto*. New York: Simon & Schuster.

Banks, J. A., & Banks, C. A. M. (Eds.). (2010). *Multicultural education: Issues and perspectives* (7th ed.). New York: Wiley.

Bloom, B. S. (1956). *Taxonomy of educational objectives: Handbook I. Cognitive domain*. New York: Longman, Green.

Boyer, P., & Stuckey, S. (2005). *American nation in the modern era*. Austin, TX: Holt, Rinehart and Winston.

Button, W. H., & Provenzo, E. F., Jr. (1989). *History of education and culture in America*. Upper Saddle River, NJ: Prentice Hall.

Carnegie Corporation. (1989). *Turning points: Preparing American youth for the 21st century*. New York: Author.

Chartock, R. K. (2004). *Educational foundations: An anthology* (2nd ed.). Upper Saddle River, NJ: Merrill/Prentice Hall.

Cohen, S. S. (1974). *A history of colonial education, 1607–1776*. New York: Wiley.

Cubberly, E. (1934). *Public education in the United States*. Boston: Houghton Mifflin.

Dewey, J. (1956). *The child and the curriculum, and the school and society*. Chicago: University of Chicago Press.

Eisner, E. W. (2000). *Prospects: The quality review of comparative education*. Paris: UNESCO Publication, 30(3).

Franklin, B. (1931). Proposals relating to education of youth in Pennsylvania. In T. Woody (Ed.), *Educational views of Ben Franklin*. New York: McGraw-Hill.

Good, H. G. (1964). *A history of American education*. New York: Macmillan.

Gutek, G. L. (2005). *Historical and philosophical foundations of education* (4th ed.). Upper Saddle River, NJ: Merrill/Prentice Hall.

Holmes, M., & Weiss, B. J. (1995). *Lives of women public school teachers: Scenes from American educational history*. New York: Garland.

Johnson, J. A., Musial, D., Hall, G. E., Golnick, D. M., & Dupuis, V. L. (2011). *Introduction to the foundations of American education* (15th ed.). Boston: Allyn & Bacon.

Kaplan, L. S., & Owings, W. A. (2011). *American education: Building a common foundation*. Belmont, CA: Wadsworth, Cengage Learning.

Kneller, G. F. (1971). *Introduction to the philosophy of education*. New York: Wiley.

Loeper, J. L. (1973). *Going to School in 1776*. New York: Macmillan.

McNeil, J. D. (1995). *Curriculum: The teacher's initiative*. Upper Saddle River, NJ: Prentice Hall.

McNergney, R. F., & McNergney, J. M. (2009). *Education: The practice and profession of teaching*. Boston: Allyn & Bacon.

Montessori, M. (1967). *The discovery of the child*. Notre Dame, IN: Fides.

Orfield, G. (2009). *Reviving the goal of an integrated society: A 21st century challenge*. Los Angeles: The Civil Rights Project/Proyecto Derechos Civiles at UCLA.

Ornstein, A. C., & Levine, D. U. (2006). *Foundations of education* (9th ed.). Boston: Houghton Mifflin.

Pulliam, J., & Van Patten, J. (2013). *History of education in America* (10th ed.). Upper Saddle River, NJ: Merrill/Prentice Hall.

Rippa, S. A. (1997). *Education in a free society: An American history* (8th ed.). New York: Longman.

Stanford News Service. (1994). *Ralph Tyler, one of the century's foremost educators, dies at 91*. Retrieved March 1, 2006, from Stanford University News Service Web site: http://www.stanford.edu/dept/news/pr/94/940228Arc4425.html

Takaki, R. (1993). *A different mirror: A history of multicultural America*. New York: Little, Brown.

Tehie, J. B. (2007). *Historical foundations of education*. Upper Saddle River, NJ: Merrill/Prentice Hall.

Tyler, R. (1949). *Basic principles of curriculum and instruction*. Chicago: University of Chicago Press.

U.S. Census Bureau. (2008). *American Factfinder: BO3001. Hispanic or Latino origin by specific origin*. Retrieved May 22, 2010, from http://www.census.gov/prod/cen2010/briefs/c2010br-02.pdf

U.S. Census Bureau. (2009). *Facts for features: Asian/Pacific American heritage month 2009*. Retrieved May 24, 2010, from http://www.census.gov/Press-Release/www/releases/archives/facts_for_features_special_editions/013385.html

Webb, L., Metha, A., & Jordan, K. F. (2012). *Foundations of American education* (7th ed.). Upper Saddle River, NJ: Pearson Education, Inc.

Chapter 8

Adler, M. (1982). *The Paideia proposal: An educational manifesto*. New York: Simon & Schuster.

Brameld, T. (1956). *Toward a reconstructed philosophy of education*. New York: Holt, Rinehart, and Winston.

Chartock, R. K. (2004). *Educational foundations: An anthology* (2nd ed.). Upper Saddle River, NJ: Merrill/Prentice Hall.

Counts, G. (1932). *Dare the school build a new social order?* New York: John Dey.

Friere, P. (1970). *Pedagogy of the oppressed*. New York: Herder and Herder.

Greene, M. (1978). *Landscape of learning*. New York: Teachers College Press.

Greene, M. (1995). What counts as philosophy of education? In W. Kohli (Ed.), *Critical conversations in philosophy of education*. New York: Routledge.

Gutek, G. L. (2005). *Historical and philosophical foundations of education* (4th ed.). Upper Saddle River, NJ: Merrill/Prentice Hall.

Hirsch, E. D. (1987). *Cultural literacy: What every American needs to know*. Boston: Houghton Mifflin.

Illich, I. (1971). *Deschooling society*. New York: Harper & Row.

Jacobsen, D. A. (2003). *Philosophy in classroom teaching: Bridging the gap* (2nd ed.). Upper Saddle River, NJ: Merrill/Prentice Hall.

Neill, A. S. (1960). *Summerhill: A radical approach to child rearing*. New York: Hart.

Ornstein, A. C. (2003). *Pushing the envelope: Critical issues in education*. Upper Saddle River, NJ: Merrill/Prentice Hall.

Ozmon, H., & Craver, S. (2008). *Philosophical foundations of education* (8th ed.). Upper Saddle River, NJ: Merrill/Prentice Hall.

Perrone, V. (1991). *A letter to teachers: Reflections on schooling and the art of teaching*. San Francisco: Jossey-Bass.

Pulliam, J., & Van Patten, J. (2013). *History of education in America* (10th ed.). Upper Saddle River, NJ: Merrill/Prentice Hall.

Ravitch, D. (2000). *Left back: A century of failed school reforms*. New York: Simon & Schuster.

Sizer, T. R. (1985). *Horace's compromise*. Boston: Houghton Mifflin.

Webb, L., Metha, A., & Jordan, K. F. (2012). *Foundations of American education* (7th ed.). Upper Saddle River, NJ: Merrill/Prentice Hall.

Chapter 9

Alcoholism Information and Resources. (2010). Learn-about-alcoholism. Retrieved June 5, 2010, from http://www.learn-about-alcoholism.com/index.html

Alliance for Excellent Education. (2009). *High school dropouts in America*. Retrieved June 7, 2010, from http://all4ed.org/files/Graduation_Rates_FactSheet.pdf

American Academy of Child and Adolescent Psychiatry. (2009). *Facts for families: Teen suicide*. Retrieved June 3, 2010, from http://www.aacap.org/cs/root/facts_for_families/teen_suicide

American Association of Suicidology. (2013). *Youth suicidal behavior fact sheet based on 2010 data*. Retrieved March 11, 2013, from http://www.suicidology.org/c/document_library/get_file?folderId=262&name=DLFE-627.pdf

American Psychiatric Association. (2005a). *Let's talk facts about depression*. Retrieved April 6, 2006, from http://www.fcphp.usf.edu/courses/content/rfast/Resources/depression.pdf

American Psychiatric Association. (2005b). *Let's talk facts about teen suicide*. Retrieved April 6, 2006, from http://www.depressioncenter.org/education-outreach/programs/schools/resources/pdf/teen-suicide-apa.pdf

Annie E. Casey Foundation. (2013). *The Annie E. Casey Foundation 2012 Kids Count Data Book.* Baltimore, MD: Author.

Ariza, E. N. (2002). Cultural considerations: Immigrant parents involvement. *Kappa Delta Pi Record, 38*(3), 134–137.

Bridgeland, J. M., Dilulio, J. J., & Morison, K. B. (2006). *The silent epidemic: Perspectives of high school dropouts.* Retrieved April 8, 2006, from http://www.ignitelearning.com/pdf/TheSilentEpidemic3-06FINAL.pdf

Centers for Disease Control. (2010). *Teen birth rates drop in 2008 following a two-year increase.* Atlanta, GA: Author.

Centers for Disease Control and Prevention. (2012a). *Youth risk behavior survey fact sheets.* Atlanta, GA: Author. Retrieved March 10, 2013, from http://apps.nccd.cdc.gov/youthonline/App/QuestionsOrLocations.aspx?CategoryID=3

Centers for Disease Control and Prevention. (2012b). *Trends in the Prevalence of Sexual Behaviors and HIV Testing National YRBS: 1991–2011.* Atlanta, GA: Author. Retrieved March 10, 2013, from http://www.cdc.gov/healthyyouth/yrbs/pdf/us_sexual_trend_yrbs.pdf

Centers for Disease Control and Prevention. (2012c). *Sexual Risk Behavior Data & Statistics.* Atlanta, GA: Author. Retrieved March 10, 2013, from http://www.cdc.gov/healthyyouth/sexualbehaviors/data.htm

Centers for Disease Control and Prevention. (2012d). *Birth rates for U.S. teenagers reach historic lows for all age and ethnic groups.* Atlanta, GA: Author. Retrieved January 27, 2013, from http://www.cdc.gov/nchs/data/databriefs/db89.htm#babies

Centers for Disease Control and Prevention. (2013). *Health effects of childhood obesity.* Atlanta, GA: Author. Retrieved January 27, 2013, from http://www.cdc.gov/healthyyouth/obesity/facts.htm

Child Welfare Information Gateway. (2006). *Recognizing child abuse and neglect: Signs and symptoms.* Retrieved April 22, 2007, from http://www.bvsd.org/neo/Documents/Child%20Abuse%20Signs.pdf

ChildHelp (2013). *National child abuse statistics.* Retrieved January 27, 2013 from http://www.childhelp.org/pages/statistics?gclid=CNPFutywibUCFQGvnQod2R4AAQ

Coloroso, B. (2008). *The bully, the bullied, and the bystander.* New York: Harper Resources.

Craig, G. J., & Dunn. W. L. (2007). *Understanding human development.* Upper Saddle River, NJ: Prentice Hall.

Dinkes, R., Kemp, J., & Baum, K. (2009). *Indicators of school crime and safety: 2009* (NCES 2010–012/NCJ 228478). Washington, DC: National Center for Education Statistics, Institute of Education Sciences, U.S. Department of Education, and Bureau of Justice Statistics, Office of Justice Programs, U.S. Department of Justice.

Dynarski, M., Clarke, L., Cobb, B., Finn, J., & Rumberger, R. (2008). *Dropout prevention.* Retrieved June 8, 2010, from http://ies.ed.gov/ncee/wwc/pdf/practiceguides/dp_pg_090308.pdf

Education Vital Signs. (2006). *As educators face a childhood obesity "epidemic," other indicators of well-being improve.* Retrieved March 30, 2006, from http://connection.ebscohost.com/c/articles/20553095/as-educators-face-childhood-obesity-epidemic-other-indicators-well-being-improve

First Amendment Center. (2006). *Public schools and sexual orientation: A First Amendment framework for finding common ground.* Retrieved April 2, 2006, from www.firstamendmentcenter.org/pdf/sexual.orientation.guidelines.pdf

Focus Adolescent Services. (2006). *Youth who drop out.* Retrieved April 20, 2006, from http://www.focusas.com/Dropouts.html

Gollnick, D. M., & Chinn, P. C. (2013). *Multicultural education in a pluralistic society* (9th ed.). Upper Saddle River, NJ: Pearson.

Hamilton, B. E., Martin, J. A., & Ventura, S. J. (2012). Births: Preliminary data for 2011. *National Vital Statistics Reports, 61*(5). Hyattsville, MD: National Center for Health Statistics. Retrieved January 27, 2013 from http://www.cdc.gov/nchs/data/nvsr/nvsr61/nvsr61_05.pdf

Hamilton, B. E., & Ventura, S. J. (2012). Birth rates for U.S. teenagers reach historic lows for all age and ethnic groups. *NCHS Data Brief, 89.* Hyattsville, MD: National Center for Health Statistics.

Haynes, C. C. (2006, March). A moral battleground, a civil discourse. *USA Today.* Retrieved March 23, 2006, from http://www.usatoday.com/news/opinion/editorials/2006-03-19-faith-edit_x.htm

Healthcommunities.com. (2010). *Overview, consequences of teenage pregnancy.* Retrieved June 4, 2010, from http://www.healthcommunities.com/teen-pregnancy/children/overview-of-teen-pregnancy.shtml

Infoplease. (2009). *Teen birth rates in the U.S., 1980–2006.* Retrieved June 2, 2010, from http://www.infoplease.com/ipa/A0193727.html

Jensen, E. (2009). *Teaching with poverty in mind: What being poor does to kids' brains and what school can do about it.* Alexandria, VA: Association for Supervision and Curriculum Development.

Johnston, L. D., O'Malley, P. M., Bachman, J. G., & Schulenberg, J. E. (2012). *Monitoring the future: National results on adolescent drug use.* Bethesda, MD: U.S. Department of Health and Human Services. Retrieved April 15, 2013, from http://www.monitoringthefuture.org/pubs/monographs/mtf-overview2011.pdf

Kids Count. (2013). *Data across states.* Retrieved January 27, 2013, from http://datacenter.kidscount.org/data/acrossstates/Rankings.aspx?loct=2&by=v&order=a&ind=43&dtm=322&tf=867

Landsman, J. (2006). Bearers of hope. *Educational Leadership, 63*(5), 26–32.

Lewis-Charp, H. (2003). Breaking the silence: White students' perspectives on race in multiracial schools. *Phi Delta Kappan, 85*(4), 279–285.

MacDonald, G. J. (2004, October 19). Schools lay tender trap for truants. *Christian Science Monitor.* Retrieved April 6, 2006, from http://www.csmonitor.com/2004/1019/p11s02-legn.html

McCarthy, D. M., & Brown, S. A. (2004). Changes in alcohol involvement, cognitions and drinking and driving behavior for youth after they obtain a driver's license. *Journal of Studies on Alcohol and Drugs, 65*(3). Retrieved June 6, 2010, from http://www.jsad.com/jsad/article/Changes_in_Alcohol_Involvement_Cognitions_and_Drinking_and_Driving_Behavio/1062.html

Mukhopadhyay, C., & Henze, R. C. (2003). How real is race? Using anthropology to make sense of human diversity. *Phi Delta Kappan, 84*(9), 669–678.

National Center on Addiction and Substance Abuse. (2007, October). *Tobacco: The smoking gun.* Retrieved June 9, 2010, from http://www.casacolumbia.org/templates/PressReleases.aspx?articleid=508&zoneid=65

National Center for Education Statistics. (2011). *Indicators of school crime and safety: 2011.* Washington, DC: Author. Retrieved March 12, 2013, from http://nces.ed.gov/programs/crimeindicators/crimeindicators2011/ind_13.asp

National Center for Homeless Education. (2012). *Education for Homeless Children and Youths Program.* Retrieved January 28, 2013, from http://center.serve.org/nche/pr/data_comp.php

National Coalition for the Homeless. (2009a). *Education of homeless children and youth.* Retrieved May 11, 2013, from http://www.nationalhomeless.org/factsheets/education.pdf

National Coalition for the Homeless. (2009b). *Homeless families with children.* Retrieved June 7, 2010, from http://www.nationalhomeless.org/factsheets/families.pdf

Obama, M. (2010). *Learn the facts.* Retrieved march 10, 2013, from http://www.letsmove.gov/blog/2013/03/08/watch-travels-first-lady-lets-move-anniversary-tour

Ophelia Project. (2005). *Bullies, broken hearts . . . and the harsh reality of relational aggression.* Retrieved April 9, 2006, from www.opheliaproject.org

Paxson, C., Donahue, E., Orleans, C. T., & Grisso, J. A.(2006). Introducing the issue. *The Future of Children, 16*(1), 3–15.

Polite, L., & Saenger, E. B. (2003). A pernicious silence: Confronting race in the elementary classroom. *Phi Delta Kappan, 85*(4), 274–278.

Rank, M. R., & Hirschl, T. A. (2009). Estimating the risk of food stamp use and impoverishment during childhood. *Journal of the American Medical Association: Archives of Pediatrics & Adolescent Medicine, 163*(11), 994–999. Retrieved June 1, 2010, from http://archpedi.ama-assn.org/content/vol163/issue11/index.dtl

Rothstein, R. (2008). Whose problem is poverty? *Educational Leadership, 65*(7), 8–13.

Shine Global. (2012). *Homelessness for Children in the US.* Retrieved January 28, 2013, from http://www.shineglobal.org/index.php/hero-of-the-week/inocente/homelessness-for-children-in-the-us-some-startling-statistics/

Simmons, R. (2002). *Odd girl out: The hidden culture of aggression in girls.* Orlando, FL: Harcourt.

Story, M., Kaphingst, K. M., & French, S. (2006). The role of schools in obesity prevention. *The Future of Children, 16*(1), 109–131.

Thompson, M., & Grace, C. O. (2001). *Best friends, worst enemies: Understanding the social lives of children.* New York: Ballantine.

Thornburgh, N. (2006, April 17). Dropout nation. *Time,* pp. 30–40.

U.S. Census Bureau. (2008). *National population projections, released 2008.* Retrieved June 1, 2010, from http://www.census.gov/population/www/projections/summarytables.html

U.S. Department of Education. (2012). *Regulatory adjusted cohort graduation rate, all students: 2010–11.* Retrieved March 11, 2013, from http://eddataexpress.ed.gov/data-element-explorer.cfm/tab/data/deid/127/

U.S. Department of Health and Human Services [DHHS]. (2011). *Child maltreatment 2011.* Retrieved January 27, 2013, from http://www.acf.hhs.gov/sites/default/files/cb/cm11.pdf#page=69

U.S. Department of Health and Human Services [DHHS]. (2012). *Youth risk behavior surveillance – United States 2011, 61*(4). Retrieved January 29, 2013, from http://www.cdc.gov/mmwr/pdf/ss/ss6104.pdf

U.S. Department of Health and Human Services [DHHS]. (2013). *Lesbian, Gay, Bisexual, Transgender, Questioning (LGBTQ) Youth.* Retrieved March 11, 2013, from http://www.hhs.gov/ash/oah/resources-and-publications/info/parents/just-facts/lgbtq-youth.html

U.S. Department of Justice. (2011). *School Crime Supplement (SCS) to the National Crime Victimization Survey, various years, 1995–2009.* Retrieved March 10, 2013, from http://nces.ed.gov/programs/crimeindicators/crimeindicators2011/figures/figure_03_1.asp

United Health Foundation. (2012). *United States high school graduation rates: 1990–2012.* Retrieved March 11, 2013, from http://www.americashealthrankings.org/all/graduation

Ventura, S. J., Mathews, T. J., & Hamilton, B. E. (2001). Births to Teenagers in the United States, 1940–2000. *National Vital Statistics Reports, 49*(10). Retrieved January 27, 2013, from http://www.thenationalcampaign.org/resources/pdf/TBR_1940-2006.pdf

White, J. L., & Cones, J. H. (1999). *Black men emerging: Facing the past and seizing a future in America.* New York: Freeman.

White-Hood, M. (2006). Targeting the school bully. *Middle Ground, 9*(4), 30–32.

Chapter 10

American Association of University Women. (2001). *Hostile hallways: Bullying, teasing, and sexual harassment in school.* New York: Harris Interactive.

Dunklee, D. R., & Shoop, R. J. (2002). *The principal's quick reference guide to school law: Reducing liability, litigation, and other potential legal tangles.* Thousand Oaks, CA: Corwin.

Howe, K. R. (1986). A conceptual basis for ethics in teacher education. *Journal of Teacher Education, 37,* 6.

LaMorte, M. W. (2008). *School law: Cases and concepts* (8th ed.). Boston: Allyn & Bacon.

LaMorte, M. W. (2012). *School law: Cases and concepts* (10th ed.). Upper Saddle River, NJ: Pearson.

National Association of Secondary School Principals. (2006). Teachers' privacy rights. *A Legal Memorandum, 6*(3). Retrieved March 17, 2013, from http://www.nassp.org/portals/0/content/53842.pdf

National Education Association. (2005). *Code of Ethics.* Retrieved May 27, 2005, from http://www.nea.org/home/30442.htm

Pauken, P. D. (2006). Student rights. In C. Russo (Ed.), *Key legal issues for schools: The ultimate resource for school business officials.* Lanham, MD: Rowman & Littlefield Education.

Riley, R. W. (1998). *Secretary's statement on religious expression.* Retrieved November 12, 2006, from http://www2.ed.gov/policy/gen/guid/religionandschools/index.html

San Antonio, D. M. (2006). Broadening the world of early adolescents. *Educational Leadership, 63*(7), 8–13.

Schimmel, D., Stellman, L., & Fischer, L. (2011). *Teachers and the law* (8th ed.). Upper Saddle River, NJ: Pearson.

Underwood, J., & Webb, L. D. (2006). *School law for teachers: Concepts and applications.* Upper Saddle River, NJ: Merrill/Prentice Hall.

Chapter 11

Azzam, A. M. (2005). The funding gap. *Educational Leadership, 62*(5), 93.

Hess, F. M. (2002). *School boards at the dawn of the 21st century: Conditions and challenges of district governance.* Arlington, VA: National School Boards Association. Retrieved June 10, 2007, from http://www.nsba.org/Board-Leadership/Surveys/SchoolBoardsattheDawnofthe21stCentury.pdf

Hess, F. M. (2010). Weighing the case for school boards. *Phi Delta Kappan, 91*(6), 15–19.

Lambert, L. (2003). *Leadership capacity for lasting school improvement.* Alexandria, VA: Association for Supervision and Curriculum Development.

Mizell, H. (2010). School boards should focus on learning for all. *Phi Delta Kappan, 91*(6), 20–23.

National Association of State Boards of Education. (2005). *State education governance at-a-glance.* Retrieved June 20, 2006, from http://www.nasbe.org/Educational_Issues/Governance/Governance_chart.pdf

National Education Association [NEA]. (2009). *Rankings of the states 2008 and estimates of school statistics 2009.* Retrieved June 18, 2010, from http://www.nea.org/assets/docs/HE/09rankings.pdf

National Governors Association [NGA]. (2010). NGA center for best practices. Retrieved June 20, 2010, from http://www.nga.org/files/live/sites/NGA/files/pdf/CBPBROCHURE.pdf

Nylander, A. (2007). National school board survey. Retrieved June 23, 2010, from http://www.oldham.kyschools.us/files/reports/National_Surveys/National%20School%20Board%20Survey%202007%20Final%20Results_pdf.pdf

Snider, J. H. (June 2010). It's the public's data: Democratizing school board records. *Education Week.* Retrieved from http://www.edweek.org/ew/articles/2010/06/16/35snider.h29.html

U.S. Census Bureau. (2009). *Public education finances 2007.* Retrieved June 17, 2010, from http://www2.census.gov/govs/school/07f33pub.pdf

U.S. Department of Education. (2001). *Statistics of state school systems: Revenues and expenditures for public elementary and secondary education.* Washington, DC: U.S. Department of Education, National Center for Education Statistics. Retrieved August 2, 2006, from http://www.nces.ed.gov.

U.S. Department of Education. (2009). *Characteristics of public, private, and Bureau of Indian Education elementary and secondary school principals in the United States.* Retrieved June 18, 2010, from http://nces.ed.gov/pubs2009/2009323/tables.asp

U.S. Government. (2013). *Lottery results.* Retrieved April 8, 2013, from http://www.usa.gov/Topics/Lottery-Results.shtml.

White House. (2010). *Education.* Retrieved June 17, 2010, from http://www.whitehouse.gov/issues/education

Chapter 12

Barth, R. S. (2006). Improving relationships within the schoolhouse. *Educational Leadership, 63*(6), 9–13.

Cattanach, J. (2013). Support parents to improve student learning. *Phi Delta Kappan, 94*(6), 20–25.

Comer, J. P. (2005). The rewards of parent participation. *Educational Leadership, 62*(6), 38–42.

Corbett, D., Wilson, B., & Williams, B. (2005). No choice but success. *Educational Leadership, 62*(6), 8–12.

Darling-Hammond, L., & Youngs, P. (2002). Defining "highly qualified teachers": What does "scientifically-based research" tell us? *Education Researcher, 31*(9), 13–25.

Duncan, A. (2010). *Elevating the teaching profession.* Retrieved July 16, 2010, from http://www.aft.org/pdfs/americaneducator/winter2009/duncan.pdf

Epstein, J. L., Sanders, M. G., Simon, B. S., Salinas, K. C., Jansorn, N. R., & VanVoorhis, F. L. (2002). *School, family, and community partnerships: Your handbook for action.* Thousand Oaks, CA: Corwin.

Gehrke, R. S. (2005). Poor schools, poor students, successful teachers. *Kappa Delta Pi Record, 42*(1), 14–17.

Hasselbring, T. S., & Bausch, M. E. (2006). Assistive technologies for reading. *Educational Leadership, 63*(4), 72–75.

Huber, C. (2010). Professional learning 2.0. *Educational Leadership, 67*(8), 41–46.

Huebner, T. A. (2010). What research says about year-round schooling. *Educational Leadership, 67*(7), 83-84.

Marshall, K. (2012). Fine-tuning teacher evaluation. *Educational Leadership, 70*(3), 50–53.

Marzano, R. J. (2003). *What works in schools: Translating research into action.* Alexandria, VA: Association for Supervision and Curriculum Development.

Marzano, R. J. (2012). The two purposes of teacher evaluation. *Educational Leadership, 70*(3), 14–19.

MetLife. (2012). *The MetLife survey of the American teacher: Teachers, parents, and the economy.* Author.

Mielke, P., & Frontier, T. (2012). Keeping improvement in mind. *Educational Leadership, 70*(3), 10–13.

National Board for Professional Teaching Standards [NBPTS]. (2013). *The five core propositions.* Retrieved April 30, 2013, from http://www.nbpts.org/five-core-propositions

National Board for Professional Teaching Standards. [NBPTS]. (2013). *State and local information.* Retrieved April 30, 2013, from http://www.nbpts.org/nbpts-2013-01-08-nbct-student-achievement

National Conference of State Legislatures. (2012). In-state tuition and unauthorized immigrant students. Retrieved April 23, 2013, from www.ncsl.org?issues-research/immig/in-state-tuition-and-unauthorized-immigrant.aspx

Payne, C. (2008). *So much reform, so little change: The persistence of failure in urban schools.* Boston: Harvard Education Press.

Posner, G. J. (2005). *Field experience: A guide to reflective teaching.* Boston: Allyn & Bacon.

Public Education Network. (2003). *The voice of the new teacher.* Washington, DC: Author.

Reeves, D. B. (2006). Pull the weeds before you plant the flowers. *Educational Leadership, 64*(1), 89–90.

Springer, M. G., & Gardner, C. D. (2010). Teacher pay for performance. *Phi Delta Kappan, 91*(8), 8–15.

Strong, M. (2011). *The highly qualified teacher: What is quality and how do you measure it?* New York: Teachers College Press.

The New Teacher Project. (2012). *The irreplaceables.* Retrieved April 22, 2013, from http://tntp.org/irreplaceables

Ullman, E. (2013). Tips to help you flip your classroom. *Education Update, 55*(2). Alexandria, VA: ASCD.

U.S. Department of Education. (2009). *Race to the Top application for initial funding, CFDA Number 84.395A.* Washington, DC: Author.

U.S. Department of Education. (2010). *A blueprint for reform: The reauthorization of the Elementary and Secondary Education Act.* Retrieved July 14, 2010, from http://www.ed.gov/policy/elsec/leg/blueprint/blueprint.pdf

Vacca, R. T. (2006). They can because they think they can. *Educational Leadership, 63*(5), 56–59.

Wortham, S., Clonan-Roy, K., Link, H., & Martinez, C. (2013). The new Latino diaspora. *Phi Delta Kappan, 94*(6), 14–19.

Name Index

Subject Index

Photo Credits

COV, Mitch Diamond/Stockbyte/Getty Images; COV, Quavondo/Vetta/Getty Images; COV, Monkey Business/Fotolia; Design Icon, Bröc/Fotolia; Design Icon, Zoe/Fotolia; Design Icon, Konstantin L/Shutterstock; Design Icon, Poznyakov/Shutterstock; Sara Davis Powell, pp. 5, 6, 7, 11, 12, 14 (top, middle, bottom), 15 (top, bottom), 16 (top, bottom), 17 (middle), 20, 22, 27, 28, 31, 32, 33, 41, 42, 51, 61, 65, 66, 71, 72, 75, 78, 86, 87, 89, 90, 93 (middle left, middle right, bottom left, bottom right), 96, 103, 104, 111, 114, 117 (bottom left, bottom middle, bottom right), 118, 120, 122, 132, 135, 136 (top), 140, 145 (top, bottom), 146 (top, bottom), 161, 162, 163, 166, 170, 172, 176, 187, 193, 194, 218, 220, 223, 224, 225, 233, 236, 238, 245, 246, 250, 267, 277, 281, 282, 299, 306, 307, 312, 315, 316 (left, middle, right), 326, 329 (left, right), 337, 341, 342, 345, 348 (top), 349, 351, 353, 354, 369 (top, bottom); Jessica O'Rourke, pp. 17 (top, middle), 348 (bottom); Provided by the Francis Family, p. 34 (bottom left, bottom middle, bottom right); Provided by the Todd Family, p. 34 (middle, middle right); Provided by the Mancia Family, p. 35 bottom left, bottom middle, bottom right); Provided by the Wiley Family, p. 35 (top left, top middle, top right); Provided by the McBeath Family, p. 36 (bottom left, bottom middle, bottom right); Provided by the Ford Family, p. 36 (top left, top middle, top right); Provided by the Kutcher Family, pp. 37 (bottom left, bottom middle, bottom right), 64; Provided by the Sutton Family, p. 37 (top left, top middle, top right); Provided by the Toscano Family, p. 38 (bottom left, bottom middle, bottom right); Provided by the Reyes Family, p. 38 (top left, top middle, top right); Provided by the Douangsavanh Family, p. 39 (bottom left, bottom middle, bottom right); Provided by the Martinez Family, p. 39 (top left, top right); Cody White, p. 84; Nyul/Fotolia, p. 136 (bottom); Christine Ceraolo, p. 157; Barbara Hairfield, pp. 181, 356; School's 'The New England Primer' from 1727 (litho), American School/Private Collection/Peter Newark American Pictures/The Bridgeman Art Library, p. 199; B. Christopher/Alamy, p. 201, 203; Stocktrek Images, Inc./Alamy, p. 202; Mary Evans Picture Library/The Image Works, p. 205 (bottom); Everett Collection Historical/Alamy, p. 205 (top); Everett Collection Inc./Alamy, p. 206 (middle); Corbis, p. 206 (bottom); C.W. Bardeen/Library of Congress Prints and Photographs Division [LC-DIG-pga-00127], p. 206 (top); L.W. Hine/Library of Congress Prints and Photographs Division [LC-DIG-nclc-04341], p. 207 (bottom); North Wind Picture Archives/The Image Works, p. 207 (top); Frances Benjamin Johnston/ Library of Congress Prints and Photographs Division [LC-J694-255], p. 208; Hulton Archive/Getty Images, p. 209; Library of Congress Prints and Photographs Division [LC-USZ62-51525], p. 210; Library of Congress, Prints & Photographs Division, Carl Van Vechten Collection, [LC-USZ62-42476], p. 213 (top); Cornelius M. Battey/Library of Congress Prints and Photographs Division [LC-USZ62-16767], p. 211 (middle); Interfoto/Alamy, p. 211 (top); The Ohio State University Archives, p. 213 (bottom); Special Collections Research Center, University of Chicago Library, p. 214; Rebecca Dunbar, p. 229; Varina and Jay Patel/Shutterstock, p. 251; Rich Legg/E+/Getty Images, p. 257; Annedde/E+/Getty Images, p. 263; David Graham/Pearson Education, Inc., p. 271; Jim Corwin/Alamy, p. 292; Christopher Futcher/iStockphoto/Thinkstock, p. 304; Kristian Sekulic/E+/Getty Images, p. 322; Imtmphoto/Fotolia, p. 333 (middle left); Patrick Watson/Pearson Education, Inc., p. 333 (top left); Patricia Marks/Shutterstock, p. 333 (top right).